SCHOOL-BASED LEADERSHIP:
Challenges and Opportunities

third edition

Richard A. Gorton
San Diego State University
Gail Thierbach-Schneider
University of Wisconsin–Milwaukee

 Wm. C. Brown Publishers

Book Team

Editor *Paul L. Tavenner*
Developmental Editor *Ann Shaffer*
Production Coordinator *Kay Driscoll*

WCB Wm. C. Brown Publishers

President *G. Franklin Lewis*
Vice President, Publisher *George Wm. Bergquist*
Vice President, Publisher *Thomas E. Doran*
Vice President, Operations and Production *Beverly Kolz*
National Sales Manager *Virginia S. Moffat*
Senior Marketing Manager *Kathy Law Laube*
Executive Editor *Edgar J. Laube*
Managing Editor, Production *Colleen A. Yonda*
Production Editorial Manager *Julie A. Kennedy*
Production Editorial Manager *Ann Fuerste*
Publishing Services Manager *Karen J. Slaght*
Manager of Visuals and Design *Faye M. Schilling*

Cover design by Kay Dolby Fulton

Cover photos by James L. Shaffer

Library of Congress Catalog Card Number: 90–81255

ISBN 0–697–10404–4

Printed in the United States of America by Wm. C. Brown Publishers,
2460 Kerper Boulevard, Dubuque, IA 52001

10 9 8 7 6 5 4 3 2 1

Contents

Preface

Users of the second edition of this text expressed positive views about the substance and style of the book. However, changing developments in school administration and supervision, specifically, and education in general pointed to the need for revision. Therefore, the coauthors have addressed these new developments in the third edition, while at the same time keeping concepts and recommendations from the second edition that would be useful for those interested in improving school administration and supervision in the 1990s.

The third edition of this book continues to be directed to those individuals interested in developing a deeper understanding of the challenges and opportunities for leadership in school administration and supervision. The focus of the text is on principles and theories of administering and improving a school; however, many of the chapters are also relevant for other administrative levels. The intended readership includes prospective as well as experienced principals, assistant principals, district administrators, and persons responsible for preparing or working with school administrators.

In the process of revising the book, the literature on educational administration, supervision, and leadership was extensively and thoroughly reviewed. The review included relevant literature identified in *Education Index, Reader's Guide to Periodical Literature, Dissertation Abstracts, Books in Print,* professional association reference materials, and in Educational Resource Information Center, or, as it is commonly known, ERIC. (ERIC reports are identified by an ERIC number; such reports are available in most university libraries and can be ordered directly from ERIC Clearinghouse, 1787 Agate Street, Eugene, Oregon 97404–5207). Efforts have been made to utilize important ideas from the past (since much that has been recommended, though not implemented in many schools, is still sound) as well as current concepts and data.

As a result of the revision process, obsolete and less functional content has been omitted; a number of chapters have been reorganized to provide a more logical presentation of ideas; and the suggested review activities at the end of each chapter have been strengthened. In addition to a general updating of trends and programs, new topics and emphases have been added. These include school reform efforts, administrative team concepts, shared leadership and governance, teacher professionalism, collegial coaching, and special personnel problems such as employee drug and alcohol abuse and sexual harassment. Emphasis continues on the role of the administrator in program development and evaluation and in instructional leadership.

At this point it might be well to emphasize again that this is not a book which extols present administrative and supervisory practices in the schools, but rather one which offers recommendations and suggestions for improving current practices. Realistically speaking, school administration and supervision are neither as bad as some of their critics have claimed nor as good as many of their defenders would have us believe. However, most people would probably agree that there is room for improvement in school administration and supervision; it is toward meeting that need that this text is addressed.

Finally, the major thrust of the book continues to stress leadership responsibilities and opportunities of school administrators and supervisors. Although, as the text indicates, administration and supervision should be a team effort and there are others associated with the school who make an important contribution, the proposition is advanced that few problems can be resolved or school improvements initiated unless school administrators and supervisors exercise leadership. Given proper administrative and supervisory leadership, a school can do much to ameliorate its problems and improve educational services; in the absence of appropriate administrative and supervisory leadership, these goals are seldom achieved.

It is the authors' strong conviction that the way to begin improving education is by improving the administrative and supervisory leadership of the school. Hopefully, this book will make a positive contribution to that end.

Richard A. Gorton

Gail Thierbach Schneider

Acknowledgments

Although the authors are grateful to many people, such as the scholars who stimulated our thinking and the students and professors who provided useful reactions to the previous editions of this text, we are particularly indebted to several individuals:

First, we recognize Toni Gradisnek and Ellen Marie Rice, our graduate assistants, for their assistance during the library research phase of this project. Their contributions helped greatly to improve the documentation supporting the ideas presented in the text, and their upbeat personalities made working on the revision an enjoyable experience. In addition, the word processing contribution of Cathy Mae Nelson was greatly appreciated.

Second, we thank the anonymous reviewers who evaluated the manuscript before it became a text, the staff at Wm. C. Brown Company Publishers (especially Paul Travenner and Ann Schaffer), and Clare Walker for their valuable assistance.

Finally, we are most grateful to our spouses for their patience and support because without their understanding and encouragement this revision would not have been possible.

Meet the Authors

Richard A. Gorton received his doctorate from Stanford University, majoring in school administration. His master's degree in counseling and guidance and his bachelor's degree in political science were conferred by the University of Iowa. Dr. Gorton's school experience includes teaching, counseling and guidance, and administration. He was department chairperson and professor of administrative leadership and supervision at the University of Wisconsin at Milwaukee. He is currently senior professor of Administration, Rehabilitation Counseling, and Postsecondary Education at San Diego State University. A leader in state and national administrator organizations, he has collaborated on a national study of "the effective principal." Because of his expertise and practical experience, he is frequently called on as a consultant and workshop leader in the areas of teacher and administrator evaluation and inservice education, program evaluation, instructional supervision, student disciplinary problems, school-community relations, problem solving and conflict resolution. Dr. Gorton has published two textbooks, two monographs, and nearly 100 articles, book reviews, and abstracts on a variety of topics related to educational administration and supervision, as well as education in general. His other book, *School Leadership and Administration: Important Concepts, Case Studies, and Simulations,* published by Wm. C. Brown Company, is used in numerous university courses devoted to administrator preparation and by school districts for administrator inservice education. He also served as senior editor for the *Encyclopedia of School Administration and Supervision.*

Gail Thierbach Schneider received her doctorate and master's degree from the University of Wisconsin–Madison where she majored in educational administration and minored in curriculum and instruction. Dr. Schneider is presently an associate dean of the School of Education and associate professor of educational administration at the University of Wisconsin–Milwaukee. Her research and writing interests have focused on the areas of school organization, instructional leadership, site-based management, and teacher professionalism. She remains active within school settings by providing professional development workshops on topics such as school effectiveness planning, school restructuring, site-based management, instructional supervision, and teacher involvement in decision making; and, she is frequently engaged as a consultant on matters pertaining to strategic planning and conflict resolution. Dr. Schneider is active in a number of professional organizations and is a regular presenter at national, regional, and state conferences on issues pertaining to school leadership. In addition, she is currently president of the University Council for Educational Administration. Dr. Schneider is the author of numerous articles related to the improvement of school practices and she also served as editor of the *Encyclopedia of School Administration and Supervision.*

1

. . . . . .

Purpose/Direction/Accountability

1

· · · · ·

Role of the School in a Changing Society

Cheshire Puss . . . would you tell me please,
which way I ought to go from here? That
depends a good deal on where you want to get
to. . . .

Lewis Carroll
Through the Looking Glass

● ● ● ● ●

School administrators should not look on administration as an end in itself, but as a means to an end. That end should be represented by the goals and objectives which their schools are trying to achieve. Those goals and objectives give direction and purpose to the people associated with schools and help to identify the various tasks and activities that need to be accomplished if schools are to be successful in achieving their aims.

Without clear goals and objectives, administrators of schools or school districts are like captains of ships without rudders. Although their ships may not sink, the progress they make toward their destination is, at best, uncertain. Therefore, every administrator must not only become knowledgeable about various goals and objectives proposed for the schools but must also develop some vision and convictions about the direction that education should take in the future. A logical way to initiate this process is through the study of various goals and objectives proposed for the schools. Too often educators who have ignored the wisdom of the past have wasted time and energy reinventing the educational wheel. Our study begins, therefore, by considering early concepts of the role of the school and its objectives. Then we turn our attention to a number of more recent proposals for changing the nature of schooling.

EARLY CONCEPTS OF THE SCHOOL'S ROLE

INITIAL FOCUS

The American school was conceived as an institution whose main purpose was to teach students to read, write, and "cipher," often with a view toward attending college in preparation for the ministry or one of the other professions.[1]

Because the primary function of many schools at that time was to prepare students for college, they generally received an education predominantly classical in nature, with a strong emphasis on Latin. "Dame School" was the name commonly applied to the elementary school of that day, while the secondary school was frequently titled "Latin Grammar School." Although other types of schools existed, Dame Schools and Latin Grammar Schools were most prevalent during the period, 1647–1750.[2]

In 1751 a new secondary school with a different purpose and title was introduced. Called the academy, it was first chartered in Philadelphia by Benjamin Franklin.[3] The academy's primary objective, as contrasted with the purpose of the Latin Grammar School, was to provide students with an education that would be practical as well as college preparatory. In the words of Franklin, "As to their studies, it would be well if they could be taught *everything* that is useful and *everything* that is ornamental; But Art is long and their Time is short. It is therefore propos'd that they learn those Things that are likely to be most useful and most ornamental."[4]

Subsequently, additional academies sprang up in other states. In general, their goals also stressed the practical outcomes of education. Perhaps best typifying this priority was a 1781 statement by the donors of the Philips Academy in Andover, Massachusetts, indicating that the school's objective was to "lay the foundations of a public free School or Academy for the purpose of instructing Youth not only in English and Latin Grammar, Writing, Arithmetic and those Sciences wherein they are commonly taught; but more especially to learn them the Great End and Real Business of Living."[5] The concept of the academy, with its emphasis on a more comprehensive and practical education, later formed the basis for the early high schools, the first of which was instituted in Boston in 1821.

As the purpose of education gradually changed at the secondary school level after 1750, so changes also occurred at the elementary level. Education was more utilitarian; less emphasis was given to religion. Certainly, after 1750 emphasis shifted to reflect a greater concern with the educating of all the children and with providing a broader curriculum than previously. Even so, the curriculum of many of these elementary schools, frequently referred to as common schools, was still largely college preparatory in nature.[6]

A BREAK WITH THE PAST

Although the academy, the early high schools, and the common schools represented attempts to broaden the function of education, until the early 1900s the goals and purposes of many schools continued to emphasize students' preparation for college.[7] In 1913, however, the National Education Association appointed a Commission on the Re-organization of Secondary Education that ultimately issued a series of reports clearly indicating a break with the past, insofar as the goals of the secondary school were concerned. Their main report,

Cardinal Principles of Secondary Education, stressed the importance of preparing students to function in a democracy, rather than in college, as the central focus for secondary education.[8] Thus, to decide which goals were appropriate for secondary education, the commission analyzed the activities of individuals and found seven areas crucial to their existence. These, they decided, should constitute the basic objectives of education; namely, (1) health, (2) command of fundamental processes, (3) worthy home membership, (4) vocation, (5) citizenship, (6) worthy use of leisure, and (7) ethical character.[9]

Promulgation of the *Cardinal Principles of Secondary Education* was a landmark event in American education. Although written with secondary education in mind, the report affected thinking about the goals of elementary education as well. In 1932 a special Committee for Elementary Education appointed by the New York State Department of Education adapted the Cardinal Principles for the elementary school. They proposed that the primary functions of the elementary school were to help every child (1) understand and practice desirable social relationships, (2) discover and develop desirable individual aptitudes, (3) cultivate the habits of critical thinking, (4) appreciate and desire worthwhile activities, (5) gain command of common integrated knowledge and skills, and (6) develop a sound body and normal mental attitudes.[10]

Although implementation of the principles in the different classrooms across the country has been uneven and less than complete, it is nevertheless clear that their publication established a new direction for American education.

And, even though certain of the Cardinal Principles, such as the definition of "worthy home membership," now need to be updated to take into consideration changing social mores and expectations, the basic concepts continue to be relevant.

LATER EFFORTS TO DEVELOP SCHOOL GOALS

Since the publication of the *Cardinal Principles of Secondary Education,* numerous attempts have been made to define the goals of American education. These efforts indicate the continuing concern of educators and other Americans about the outcomes of education. This concern seems to reflect the periodic need to establish or, perhaps more accurately, to reaffirm the aims of education, and thus to provide direction and focus in times of turmoil or uncertainty in the larger society. Because one of the purposes of this book is to help administrators formulate ideas and convictions about the objectives the schools should adopt, three important proposals for goals in education are presented for consideration. Even though these proposals are in a sense historical documents, they deserve the thoughtful consideration of any administrators who hope to benefit from the wisdom of the past in their efforts to develop school objectives.

Figure 1.1 Cardinal Principles of Secondary Education.

HEALTH

In the area of health, the Commission felt that if the individual was to carry out his other responsibilities—family, vocation, citizenship—he needed to be healthy. Health education, to the Commission, included inculcating health habits in the students, organizing an effective program of physical activities, and cooperating with the home and the community in safeguarding and promoting health.

WORTHY HOME MEMBERSHIP

In regard to worthy home membership, the Commission felt that the school should be trying to develop those qualities that would make it possible for the individual to contribute to and derive benefit from membership in a family. These qualities included, for girls, interest and ability in the proper management and conduct of a home, and for boys, appreciation and skill in budgeting for and maintaining a home. Developing wholesome attitudes and relationships between boys and girls, and developing proper attitudes on the part of students toward their present home responsibilities were also considered important aspects of the objective of worthy home membership.

VOCATION

In the area of vocational education, the Commission took the position that the school should help the student to secure those understandings, attitudes, and skills which would make it possible for him to secure a livelihood for himself and those dependent upon him, and to serve society. It specifically stated that vocational education should help the student to find in his future vocation his own best development.

CITIZENSHIP

To achieve the citizenship goal, the Commission felt that the school should develop in the individual those qualities which he would need to function properly as a member of a neighborhood, town, city, state, or nation. The particular qualities which the Commission believed were essential were: "A many-sided interest in the welfare of the communities to which one belongs; loyalty to ideals of civic righteousness; practical knowledge of social agencies and institutions; good judgment as to means and methods that will promote one social end without defeating others; and, as putting all of these into effect, habits of cordial cooperation in social undertakings."

(continued)

Figure 1.1 Continued

WORTHY USE OF LEISURE

In regard to worthy use of leisure, the Commission believed that education should see to it that an adequate recreation program is provided both by the school and by other appropriate agencies in the community so that the individual could recreate his body, mind, and spirit, and enrich and enhance his personality. The Commission also asserted that education should attempt to foster in each individual one or more special avocational interests which could be used during leisure moments.

COMMAND OF FUNDAMENTAL PROCESSES

This principle included the development of adequate skills in reading, writing, arithmetic, and oral and written expression. This Commission did not look upon the development of these skills as an end in itself, but as an indispensable objective if the individual was to function satisfactorily in school and in later life.

ETHICAL CHARACTER

The final objective the Commission recommended was that of building ethical character. The Commission indicated that education for ethical character should include developing on the part of the student a "sense of personal responsibility and initiative and, above all, the spirit of service and the principles of true democracy which should permeate the entire school. . ." The Commission felt that no other objective was as important as the development of ethical character for, in a real sense, achieving all of the other objectives was dependent on the student's possessing ethical character.

THE PURPOSES OF EDUCATION IN AMERICAN DEMOCRACY

Following the issuance of the *Cardinal Principles of Secondary Education,* the first major proposal for school goals was entitled *The Purposes of Education in American Democracy.* This proposal, prepared by the Educational Policies Commission in 1938, advanced four basic objectives for American education: (1) self-realization, (2) human relationship, (3) economic efficiency; and (4) civic responsibility.[11] The commission divided each of these general objectives into subobjectives, examples of which are presented in figure 1.1.

The *Purposes of Education in American Democracy* builds and elaborates on the *Cardinal Principles of Secondary Education.* The document's value derives largely from its specification in greater detail and depth of the seven school objectives initially formulated in the Cardinal Principles. Its major limitation, similar to the Cardinal Principles, is that the terms used in stating the purposes frequently fail to lend themselves to precise interpretation; they are stated in such a manner as to make evaluation of the achievement of the purposes difficult. Still, the 1938 statement by the Educational Policies Commission deserves the consideration of administrators even today. Certainly the statement can be used as a basis for the development or revision of a school's educational objectives. For such use, however, efforts should be made to define terms more precisely so that meanings are clearer and evaluation of achievement more attainable.

THE IMPERATIVE NEEDS OF YOUTH

Probably one of the most influential documents dealing with the goals of secondary education, *The Imperative Needs of Youth of Secondary School Age* was published in 1944 by the National Association of Secondary School Principals.[12] The proposed objectives in the document were based on several assumptions:

- Education should be planned for all youth.
- Education should be free.
- All youth have certain educational needs in common, and education should be adapted to personal and social needs.
- Education should be continuous.[13]

Based on these assumptions, the association set forth the following ten important needs of youth to which education should address itself:

The Imperative Needs of Youth of Secondary School Age

1. All youth need to develop salable skills and those understandings and attitudes that make the worker an intelligent and productive participant in economic life. To this end, most youth need supervised work experience as well as education in the skills and knowledge of their occupations.
2. All youth need to develop and maintain good health and physical fitness and mental health.
3. All youth need to understand the rights and duties of citizens of a democratic society, and to be diligent and competent in the performance of their obligations as members of the community and citizens of the state nation, and to have an understanding of the nations and peoples of the world.
4. All youth need to understand the significance of the family for the individual and society and the conditions conducive to successful family life.

5. All youth need to know how to purchase and use goods and services intelligently, understanding both the values received by the consumer and the economic consequences of their acts.
6. All youth need to understand the methods of science, the influence of science on human life, and the main scientific facts concerning the nature of the world and humanity.
7. All youth need opportunities to develop their capacities to appreciate beauty in literature, art, music, and nature.
8. All youth need to be able to use their leisure time well and to budget it wisely, balancing activities that yield satisfactions to the individual with those that are socially useful.
9. All youth need to develop respect for other persons, to grow in their insight into ethical values and principles, to be able to live and work cooperatively with others, and to grow in the moral and spiritual values of life.
10. All youth need to grow in their ability to think rationally, to express their thoughts clearly, and to read and listen with understanding.[14]

Publication of *The Imperative Needs of Youth of Secondary School Age* was an important contribution that sharpened the focus of secondary school education at the end of World War II; undoubtedly it was useful to many administrators and school groups seeking direction at that time. The educational objectives implied in this statement of the needs of youth were comprehensive, covering many facets of student development. The statement also was visionary in its recommenation that education and the educational objectives set forth should be planned for all youth. Unfortunately, like many statements of proposed goals, implementation has been uneven or lacking in important respects.

A similar document was published for the elementary school, *Education for All American Children,* by the Educational Policies Commission in 1948. The document proposed that elementary schools attempt to develop fully the capabilities of each child by helping students to acquire a basic health education; a high degree of skill in reading, writing, and arithmetic; habits of good workmanship; skills of critical thinking, constructive discussion, and social responsibility; and cooperative skills.

FEDERAL INVOLVEMENT IN DEFINING SCHOOL GOALS

Schools experienced a period of growth and prosperity during the 1950s and 60s. The euphoria of this period was due in part to general agreement with the previously determined school goals and the resultant consensus that American education was thriving. School enrollments were soaring as post-World War II baby boom children entered school. The family structure was relatively stable and schools enjoyed a period of parental and community support.

The calm of this period was tested in 1957 when the Union of Soviet Socialist Republics launched *Sputnik I* causing educators to question whether or not U.S. schools were preparing students adequately in mathematics and science. The American public was concerned not only about our national security but also about our power as a world nation. As a result of this concern, where earlier goals for education were broad in nature, emergent national goals became more specific and targeted toward enhancing students' knowledge bases in mathematics and science.

NATIONAL DEFENSE EDUCATION ACT

The federal government intervened in public education at a significant level for the first time and enacted the *National Defense Education Act* (NDEA) which targeted specific funds for improving mathematics and science education. Prior to this time, federal policymakers had pursued a hands-off approach to most educational issues.[15]

Thus, during the 1960s, schools once again flourished as a result of the national attention on education. Educators designed programs to provide students with challenging courses of study in mathematics and science; they made efforts to identify and assist those students most likely to excel. Therefore, schools attempted to identify gifted and talented students and to provide unique programs of study for them. This effort frequently resulted in accelerated instructional groups, academic tracking, and individualization of instruction.

ELEMENTARY AND SECONDARY EDUCATION ACT

By the mid-60s, the passage of the *Civil Rights Act* placed attention on the elitist, segregationist nature of schools; therefore, the primary goal of educating all children was revisited. Once again, the federal government became involved in determining the direction of public education when Congress approved the *Elementary and Secondary Education Act* (ESEA). Through this act, the federal government provided categorical funds for special programs designed to meet the needs of disadvantaged students. Thus, schools implemented a plethora of compensatory and remedial programs.

These new programs, and those initiated through the NDEA, continued with varying levels of support through the 1970s; however, during the 1980s there was a marked reduction of federal financial support for education as states were encouraged to continue federally sponsored programs with state and local district funds. Although financial support declined, the national interest in quality education did not diminish. A number of studies and reports attempted to redefine the nature of schooling and the goals of education.

CONTEMPORARY VIEWS REGARDING THE ROLE OF THE SCHOOL

There has seldom been a shortage of proposals from educational leaders, or others outside the field of education, on what the aims of the school should be. Frequently these statements have just reaffirmed positions taken by earlier national groups, but in a number of instances new ground has been broken.

In the 1980s, educational reform was the watchword. In part due to a general sense of discontent with the quality of education and the schools' ability to meet the needs of an increasingly diverse student population, a number of educational experts began to explore the nature of schools and the processes of teaching and learning. Two studies, one conducted for the Carnegie Foundation by Ernest Boyer and the other by John Goodlad, received particular attention due to their thorough investigation of what schools are and what schools should be.[16] An overview of these studies should assist administrators in reaffirming the importance of educational goals.

CARNEGIE FOUNDATION FOR THE ADVANCEMENT OF TEACHING

The Carnegie Foundation for the Advancement of Teaching has conducted a major study of the American high school. The intent of the study, in addition to assessing the current status of high school education, was to determine directions for reinstating the goals and values of public education in the future. In the resultant report, lead researcher Ernest Boyer noted that "high schools to be effective must have a sense of purpose, with teachers, students, administrators, and parents sharing a vision of what they are trying to accomplish."[17]

Unfortunately, Boyer and his colleagues found that an understanding of goals and a sense of vision are frequently missing in schools. Principals and teachers are often hesitant to engage in structured processes designed to determine, clarify, or renew school goals. Boyer reported that when teachers, principals, and students were asked about school goals, "their response was one of uncertainty, amusement, or surprise. 'What do you mean?' 'Goals for what?' Some teachers just smiled. Others apologized for not knowing. Some referred to the teachers' manual. One faculty member thought goals and objectives were something 'to be learned in teacher education courses and then forgotten'."[18] And another noted, "How in the world are you going to know where you're going or if what you are doing is right if you don't have a plan? Things just sort of happen around here. There's no real organization; it's just random happenings."[19]

To assist schools in determining their direction and correcting the apparent lack of mission in schools, the Carnegie commission recommended four essential goals:

1. The high school should help all students develop the capacity to think critically and communicate effectively through a mastery of language.
2. The high school should help all students learn about themselves, the human heritage, and the interdependent world in which they live through a core curriculum based on consequential human experiences common to all people.
3. The high school should prepare all students for work and further education through a program of electives that develop individual aptitudes and interests.
4. The high school should help all students fulfill their social and civic obligations through school and community service.[20]

To meet these goals, the Carnegie commission indicated that each school should be considered a special place; hold high expectations for students; create a caring environment; have a cooperative faculty to monitor students' performance and behavior across courses; offer focused and challenging classes, and possess a shared sense of mission.

A STUDY OF SCHOOLING

John Goodlad, in his highly acclaimed *Study of Schooling,* indicated that the data he collected regarding general educational goals supported his belief that "the trends of the 1970s, many of them continuing in the 1980s, did not signal an abrupt turning away from the comprehensive expectations for education that have characterized this country historically."[21] This conclusion was reached after Goodlad and his colleagues examined a vast array of documents focusing on the ongoing effort to define education. Based on their analysis of these documents, Goodlad indicated that there were four broad areas of goals:

1. Academic—embracing all intellectual skills and domains of knowledge.
2. Vocational—developing readiness for productive work and economic responsibility.
3. Social and civic—preparing for socialization into a complex society.
4. Personal—emphasizing the development of individual responsibility, talent, and free expression.[22]

Although this list was consistent with many of the historical records of educational goals, Goodlad indicated that it would be a serious mistake to assume that schools in the future would operate as they had in the past. He argued that the educational processes and organizational systems used to accomplish educational goals would need to adapt to the changing and evolving needs of students and society. To this end, Goodlad proposed that if educators were to fulfill the educational goals, these two prerequisites would need to be met:

> First, the central charge to them [educators] must be clearly understood at all levels of the system and by those persons schools serve. Second, a new coalition comparable to the one that developed and sustained the present system of schooling must emerge. But this coalition must support more than schools. It must embrace new configurations for education in the community that include not only home, school, and church but also business, industry, television, our new means of information processing and all the rest of the emerging new technology of communications, and those cultural resources not yet drawn on for their educational potential. Education is too important and too all encompassing to be left only to schools.[23]

THE NATIONAL REPORTS

Also during the 1980s, a rash of reports was commissioned to investigate the status of American education and make recommendations for its improvement. Well over a dozen reports were issued. The most well known, in addition to Goodlad's *Study of Schooling* and the Carnegie Foundation's *High School* study, was *A Nation at Risk* prepared by the National Commission on Excellence in Education.[24] This report gained attention when its authors stated:

> Our nation is at risk. Our once unchallenged preeminence in commerce, industry, science, and technological innovation is being taken over by competitors throughout the world. . . . We report to the American people that while we can take justifiable pride in what our schools and colleges have historically accomplished and contributed to the United States and the well-being of its people, the educational foundations of our society are presently being eroded by a rising tide of mediocrity that threatens our very future as a nation and a people. What was unimaginable a generation ago has begun to occur—others are matching and surpassing our educational attainments.[25]

The report goes on, with conclusions even more graphic.

If an unfriendly foreign power had attempted to impose on America the mediocre educational performance that exists today, we might well have viewed it as an act of war. As it stands, we have allowed this to happen to ourselves. We have even squandered the gains in student achievement made in the wake of the _Sputnik_ challenge. . . . We have, in effect, been committing an act of unthinking, unilateral educational disarmament.[26]

The list of other notable reports included The _Paideia Proposal_ by Mortimer Adler, _Action for Excellence_ prepared by the Education Commission of the States, _Horace's Compromise_ by Theodore Sizer, and _Making the Grade_ prepared by the Twentieth Century Fund Task Force on Federal Elementary and Secondary Education Policy.[27] These reports and those previously mentioned created an atmosphere for change that forced educators to evaluate current practices and examine alternative proposals. Education was once again a national priority. Administrators interested in reading a concise summary of the various reports might find Marilyn Clayton Felt's book, _Improving Our Schools: Thirty-three Studies that Inform Local Action,_ useful.[28]

The strength of these reports rests in their overall agreement regarding the major recommendations for improving the quality of education. These general recommendations are summarized in figure 1.2. The recommendations for which there appeared to be general consensus among the reports were (1) revising the curriculum and strengthening subject area requirements, (2) revising vocational courses, (3) offering special help for gifted and talented students and for slow learners, (4) emphasizing reasoning and thinking skills, and (5) setting high expectations for students. Other recommendations which appeared in one or more of the reports focused on educational vouchers, tax credits, merit pay, and competency testing for teachers and students. These recommendations, unlike the general ones, were quite controversial and engendered lively public discussions because they challenged the traditional public school system and the means of assessing teacher and student performance.

In many respects the reports themselves were controversial, and rousing debates ensued following their issuance. Critics of the reports frequently noted that the authors exaggerated educational problems, stated only broad general goals, failed to specify the means by which these goals could be achieved, focused too heavily on secondary education, and ignored the complexity of the educational system.[29] Paul Peterson, of the Brookings Institute, summarized the sentiments of many critics when he noted that "the reports themselves, upon close examination, prove to be disappointing. If we judge them by the standards ordinarily used to evaluate a policy analysis—focused statement of the problem to be analyzed, methodological evaluation of existing research, reasoned consideration of options, and presentation of supporting evidence and argumentation for well-specified proposals—they simply do not measure up."[30]

Figure 1.2 Major Recommendations of Education Reform Reports.

Meeting the Need for Quality: Action in the South	An Open Letter to America	High Schools and the Changing Workplace	The Paideia Proposal	Education for Tomorrow's Jobs	America's Competitive Challenge	Educating Americans for the 21st Century	Horace's Compromise	High School	A Place Called School	Academic Preparation for College	Making the Grade	Action for Excellence	A Nation at Risk	CURRICULUM STANDARDS
	●	●				●	●	●		●		●	●	Revise Curriculum
		●	●			●	●	●		●	●	●	●	Strengthen Requirements – English
●		●	●			●		●	●	●	●	●	●	– Math
●		●	●			●		●	●	●	●	●	●	– Science
		●	●			●		●	●	●	●	●	●	– Social Studies
		●				●		●	●	●	●	●	●	– Technology/Computer Science
								●		●	●		●	– Foreign Languages
			●					●	●	●			●	– Art, Music
			●					●	●					– Physical Education
●		●	●	●			●	●	●				●	Revise Vocational/Work Courses
	●		●							●				Begin Education Earlier
●						●		●	●			●	●	Offer Special Help for Gifted and Talented
●		●				●		●	●		●	●	●	Offer Special Help for Slow Learners
	●						●	●	●			●	●	Set Core Curriculum
						●		●						Incorporate Outside Learning Opportunities
●	●	●				●	●		●	●		●	●	Emphasize Reasoning Skills
						●						●	●	Upgrade/Improve Textbooks
		●					●	●	●			●	●	Eliminate Tracking/Group by Mastery
					●	●		●				●	●	Raise College Admissions Standards
	●	●	●			●	●	●	●			●		Expect More of Students
	●	●				●				●	●	●	●	Test for Promotion/Graduation
	●	●	●			●						●	●	Increase Discipline
						●						●	●	Assign More Homework

Prepared by the editors of Education USA, National School Public Relations Assn., 1984. Reprinted by permission.

Figure 1.2 Continued

Meeting the Need for Quality: Action in the South	An Open Letter to America	High Schools and the Changing Workplace	The Paideia Proposal	Education for Tomorrow's Jobs	America's Competitive Challenge	Educating Americans for the 21st Century	Horace's Compromise	High School	A Place Called School	Academic Preparation for College	Making the Grade	Action for Excellence	A Nation at Risk	
														TEACHING
	•		•			•	•	•			•	•	•	Raise Salaries
						•		•	•		•	•	•	Set Career Incentives
•	•		•			•		•	•			•	•	Strengthen Teacher Education
•			•			•		•			•	•		Offer Incentives to Attract
•			•			•		•			•	•	•	Recognize Outstanding Teachers
•	•					•		•				•	•	Strengthen Evaluation Testing
	•		•			•	•	•	•			•	•	Provide More Control/Fewer Administrative Burdens
				•		•		•			•	•	•	Improve Math/Science Training Teaching
														ORGANIZATION
	•					•		•	•					Improve School Environment/ Working Conditions
•	•		•			•		•	•			•	•	Improve School Leadership/ Management
						•						•	•	Lengthen School Day/Year
						•		•	•			•	•	Use Existing School Time Better
	•					•		•	•			•		Reduce Class/School Size
		•				•							•	Increase Parent Involvement
	•	•		•	•	•		•				•	•	Increase Business/ Community Involvement
•					•	•		•		•			•	Form School/College Links
						•					•	•	•	Governance/Funding Responsibility – Local
						•		•			•	•	•	– State
	•					•		•			•	•	•	Main Federal Role Cited As: – Research
	•					•					•	•	•	– Equity/Civil Rights
	•			•	•	•		•			•	•	•	– Funding Specific Projects
	•					•					•	•	•	– Information/ Data Collection
		•				•					•	•	•	– Identification of National Initiatives
		•				•		•			•		•	– Teacher Training/Support

Prepared by the editors of Education USA, National School Public Relations Assn., 1984.

In spite of these criticisms, it is widely acknowledged that the reports were successful in focusing public attention once again on education. And, although many critics felt that the reports had limited value, others felt that through the widespread publicity and the legislative activity spawned by the reports, they might have a major impact on the standards and structure of American education in the years to come. As Albert Shanker, president of the American Federation of Teachers, noted in observing teachers' reactions to the reports, "That the initial cynicism gave way not to anger and despair but to great hope for genuine improvement in the climate, conditions, and outcome of education is a tribute—first, to the nation's two million teachers. It is a tribute to their almost unreasonable faith—given long-standing negative public attitudes—in the value of what they do and to their basic receptiveness to change."[31]

Because the authors of the various reports had no authority and, thus, no responsibility for implementing and fulfilling the goals they specified, the burden rests with local educational officials, administrators, and teachers not to disappoint the general public in its hope for a better future. Evidence suggests that state legislatures are taking action on the recommendations (see figure 1.3); however, the implementation of these reform initiatives is the responsibility of professional staff members at the local district and building levels.[32]

EQUITY AND EXCELLENCE

Many of the national reports advocated the development of a core curriculum to be required of all students and focused on recommendations aimed at improving academic achievement. In so doing, the authors of the reports attempted to promote the concept of excellence which was frequently "viewed by the American media and, therefore, the public, as a matter of test scores."[33] Thus, "movements for accountability, competency-based teacher education and testing, systems management, mandated 'basics,' academic standards, and so on were clear and growing in the many official and semi-official reports recently published."[34] This emphasis on excellence was often perceived to be at the expense of equity which was frequently defined as equal access and representation of all individuals regardless of race or gender. For example, as Nathan Glazer noted,

> If one is a politician, or a moralist, one can assert there is not conflict between equity and excellence—everyone can be excellent. And if everyone can be excellent, everyone can be treated alike, and there is no problem of equity. But that describes a utopia which is very far from ordinary experience. There, we regularly find conflicts between "excellence"—or encouraging and rewarding the highest achievement—and "equity," taken as equal treatment.[35]

Figure 1.3 A Summary of State Programs to Improve Education.

	A.	B.	C.	D.	E.	F.
Alabama	■	■	■			
Alaska	■	□	■			
Arizona	■	■	□		□	□
Arkansas	■	■	■	■	■	
California	■	■	■		■	■
Colorado	□	□	□		□	□
Conn.		□	□			□
Delaware	□	■		□		□
D.C.	■	■	■	■		□
Florida	□	■	■	■	■	■
Georgia		■	■	□	□	
Hawaii	□		□	□	□	
Idaho	□	■	■	■		■
Illinois	□	■		□		■
Indiana	■	■	■			
Iowa	■					
Kansas	□	■	■			□
Kentucky	■	■	■			□
Louisiana	■	■	■	■		
Maine		□	□			□
Maryland	□	□	■			□
Mass.	□		□		□	□
Michigan	■	■	■	■	■	
Minnesota	□	□	□			
Miss.	□	□	■	□	□	□
Missouri		■	■	□		

	A.	B.	C.	D.	E.	F.
Montana	■	■	□			
Nebraska	□	□		■	■	
Nevada	□	■	■		□	
N.H.	□	□	□			
N.J.	□	■	■			□
N. Mexico	■	■				□
New York	■	■	■		■	□
N. Carolina	□	■		■	■	□
N. Dakota	■	■			■	
Ohio	□	■	■	□	□	□
Oklahoma	■	□				
Oregon	□	■	□	□	□	□
Penn.	■	■	□			□
R.I.	□	□	■			
S. Carolina	□	□	□	□	□	
S. Dakota	□	■	■			
Tenn.	■	■	■		■	■
Texas	■	■	■		□	□
Utah	□	■		□		■
Vermont	■	■	■	□	□	□
Virginia	■	■	■			□
Wash.	■	■	■			□
W. Virginia	■	□	■			□
Wisconsin	■	■	■	□	□	□
Wyoming	□	□				

Source: U.S. Education Department

Here are some of the steps states are taking to improve education standards. Categories in the chart correspond to the letters for the reforms listed here. An empty box means a reform has been proposed, a blacked-in box means a reform has been enacted.

A. Curriculum reform: Toughening the number or type of courses offered at all grade levels.

B. Graduation requirements: Strengthening the number or type of classes required for high school graduation.

C. Student evaluation: Systemwide student testing for promotion or graduation or to assess strengths and weaknesses within a district.

D. Longer school day: Increase in the number of hours a student must be in class.

E. Longer school year: Increasing the number of days in the school year. Michigan did so by requiring that schools make up any days missed as a result of snow or other conditions.

F. Master teachers/ career ladders: Providing promotions and extra pay for teachers who stand out as a result of experience, talent or expertise.

The pressure for increased graduation requirements and the focus on test scores may push schools more and more into a class structure of achievers and nonachievers—the academic parallel of society's rich and poor. Carol Yeakey and Gladys Johnston predict that increasing standards without attending to instructional effectiveness may lead to more failure of students from the nation's enlarging population of educationally and economically disadvantaged citizens.[36] The result may be an increase in dropout rates and a return to an elitist educational structure.

In addressing the conflict between equity and excellence, Mario Fantini has proposed an expanded definition of excellence embracing the concept of equity. His formula for excellence contains five key ingredients:

Excellence = Quality + Equality + Effectiveness
+ Efficiency + Participation.[37]

To explain his formula, Fantini has defined his terms in the following manner: (1) quality—optimal standards; (2) equality—access for all; (3) effectiveness—productivity; (4) efficiency—economical educational systems; and (5) participation—involvement of community and parents. His formula and definitions, although not perfect, may assist in resolving the conflict regarding the issues of equity and excellence. Nonetheless, it is clear that as administrators address the reform issues contained within the national reports, they need to strive for excellence while maintaining equity.

THE QUESTION OF VALUES

In the proposals on educational aims presented to this point, reference has been made to developing ethical or moral values. The *Cardinal Principles of Secondary Education* referred to education for ethical character. The *Purposes of Education in American Democracy* mentioned "character" and "respect for humanity." The *Imperative Needs of Youth* stated that all youth need to develop insight into ethical, moral, and spiritual values. Similarly, Ernest Boyer stated

> We must not and cannot have a value-neutral education.
> Communicating values is at the heart of everything we do. But how are these values to be defined? What are the larger purposes of education we should seek to accomplish? The social and moral imperative of education is best fulfilled as students gain perspective, as we help them see the connectedness of things, an insight that touches the very foundation of morality, whether it be personal, social, or religious.[38]

One problem that confronts schools in their attempt to include the development of student values in their aims or objectives is that everyone does not subscribe to the same set of values. Many people continue to hold what

Figure 1.4 Traditional versus Emergent Values.

Traditional Values	Emergent Values
Self-Denial ——————> <——————	Enjoyment
Tradition ——————> <——————	Change
Authority ——————> <——————	Participation
Self-Control ——————> <——————	Expressiveness
Achievement ——————> <——————	Self-Realization

might be referred to as traditional values, while a number of other people espouse what social scientists term *emergent values.* Figure 1.4 provides examples of the potential conflicts between these value perspectives.[39] The previous discussion on equity and excellence may be viewed as an example of conflict between these two sets of values. Unfortunately, this conflict and others between traditional and emergent values cannot be easily avoided by schools.

PUBLIC EXPECTATIONS OF EDUCATION

As school administrators and their staff members consider the question of what the role of the school should be, they should also be aware of public expectations. Periodic polls of public attitudes toward education have been helpful in revealing preferences by the public as to the primary goals of education. For example, in a Gallup poll commissioned by the National Association of Elementary School Principals and the National Association of Secondary School Principals, a representative sample of citizens was asked what they wanted their children to gain from education.[40] The ten most important outcomes, from the perspective of parents, are identified and ranked in figure 1.5.

An examination of figure 1.5 indicates that school parents expect schools to give a high priority to career education and training, whereas personal development and interpersonal relations seem to receive a much lower priority. Somewhat distressing is the rather low priority assigned to intellectual development. However, whether or not educators agree with public expectations, these expectations need to be seriously considered. To paraphrase an important observation made in another context, the question of what should be the primary function or goals of education is too important to be left solely to educational authorities. School administrators need to become more aware of the public's point of view and to utilize data from national polls and local surveys of community attitudes in establishing or revising the goals of education in the school. Because the Gallup Poll is a national survey, school administrators should conduct their own studies of their local communities if they question the national findings.

Figure 1.5 Parents' School Outcome Expectations for their Children.

Desired Outcomes of Education	National Percentiles
To improve job opportunities / better job.	33%
To prepare for life / better life.	25
To obtain financial security / economic stability.	15
To obtain more knowledge.	9
To get a better paying job.	8
To become self sufficient (independent).	7
To enhance personal development / self realization.	7
To think / learn / understand.	6
Education is a necessity of life.	5
To become better citizens.	5
To have a sucessful life.	5

EDUCATION AND THE FUTURE

Goal proposals and public expectations are two useful sources of ideas for determining the role of a school. However, administrators need to recognize that when students now attending school become adults, they will in all probability be confronted by circumstances and problems very different from those faced by adults today. Certainly, if the amount of change in the past four decades is any indication, the type of society in which we will be living in the twenty-first century will be much different from that of the twentieth century. Therefore, if one of the functions of the school is to prepare students for the kind of world in which they will be living as adults, school administrators need to become more aware of projections and predictions of society in the future.

Although people have always tried to predict the future, not until recently have social scientists—particularly those in education—begun a systematic effort to project future trends and possibilities and their implications for education. As one might suspect, this has not been an easy task, for as Warren Ziegler has pointed out, "We have no way of validating our predictions until the future becomes present."[41] For this reason and because the field of predicting the future is so new, the predictions advanced by any group or individual are usually very tentative and their implications for education are frequently not specific.* Based on the authors' continuing review of the literature on the subject of the future and its implications for education, however, schools need to prepare students for a future in which the following abilities will be important:

- Directing and coping successfully with change in an ever-changing society.
- Conserving the environment and managing resources wisely in a society with increasingly scarce resources and a growing technology capable of destroying larger segments of the environment.
- Pursuing learning continuously in a society in which new knowledge will be coming to the fore constantly and much previously acquired knowledge will become obsolete.
- Developing computer skills for obtaining access to new approaches to learning and to sources of print and nonprint information.
- Utilizing increased amounts of leisure time wisely.
- Developing and maintaining rewarding human relationships in a society becoming increasingly impersonal.
- Developing and maintaining a set of ethical values and philosophy which will provide an individual with purpose, direction, and a basis for decision making in an increasingly pluralistic and valueless society.
- Perceiving the increasing interdependency of the various parts of the world, and supporting attempts to develop cooperative and peaceful solutions to increasingly difficult world problems.[42]

Many of the abilities predicted as necessary in the future are currently needed; several of them have been recommended for some time. If various predictions of the future are correct, however, these abilities will be not only desirable but also essential for successful adult lives.

Historically, schools have frequently been slow to respond to changes in society and have seldom anticipated change. Generally, schools have tended to react to change after it occurred in the larger society rather than trying to anticipate, plan for, and direct change. As a result, while one could argue that schools have done a good job, graduates have not been as well prepared as they might have been, had the future and its implications for education been taken into greater consideration.

Schools must prepare students for current circumstances and challenges as well as for their adult lives. School administrators can play a leadership

---

*For a discussion of an excellent approach that educators might utilize in gaining insight into what the future may hold, see Brother Eagan Hunter, "Educators' Quest to Confront the World of the Twenty-First Century," *NASSP Bulletin* (February 1989): 1–7.

role in achieving that goal by not only considering goals, proposals, and public expectations for the role of the school but also predictions, projections, and ideas about the future.*

Review and Learning Activities

1. Why should administrators be concerned about their schools' goals and objectives?
2. In which ways did the purpose and program of American schools change between inception and the twentieth century?
3. Discuss the main focus of the following goal proposals and their implications for the schools:
   a. *Cardinal Principals of Secondary Education,* or *Cardinal Objectives in Elementary Education*
   b. *The Purposes of Education in American Democracy*
   c. *The Imperative Needs of Youth of Secondary School Age,* or *Education for All American Children.*
4. What are the major implications of the national reports on educational reform for school administrators?
5. In deciding the goals and objectives, to what extent should the school consider the expectations of the community?
6. Why is it important for administrators to become aware of projected future school and societal trends?

Notes

1. Ellwood P. Cubberly, *Public Education in the United States* (Boston: Houghton Mifflin, 1934), 12–15.
2. Ibid., 27–33 for further detail about these schools.
3. H. G. Good, *A History of American Education* (New York: Macmillan, 1956), 72–77.
4. Quoted in Edgar W. Knight and Clifton L. Hall, *Readings in American Educational History* (New York: Appleton-Century-Crofts, 1951), 76.
5. Quoted in Elmer E. Brown, *The Making of Our Middle Schools* (New York: Longmans, Green & Co., 1903), 195.
6. Cubberly, *Public Education,* 330.
7. Ibid., 542–44.
8. *Cardinal Principles of Secondary Education,* Bureau of Education, Bulletin No. 35 (Washington, D.C.: Government Printing Office, 1918).

*Administrators interested in a magazine reporting predictions about the future should see *The Futurist,* a bimonthly publication of the World Future Society, 4916 St. Elmo Avenue, Washington D.C. 20014. And, for general discussions on preparing today's students for tomorrow's world, see *Educational Leadership* (September 1989); the entire issue was focused on the future needs of students.

9. Ibid., 5–10.

10. Committee for Elementary Education, *Cardinal Objectives in Elementary Education—A Third Report* (Albany: University of State of New York Press, 1932): 9–16.

11. Educational Policies Commission, *The Purposes of Education in American Democracy* (Washington, D.C.: National Education Association, 1938), 50, 72, 90, 108.

12. National Association of Secondary School Principals, *The Imperative Needs of Youth of Secondary School Age,* Bulletin No. 145 (Washington D.C.: National Education Association, 1947).

13. Ibid., 4.

14. Ibid., 43.

15. Thomas J. Sergiovanni, Martin Burlingame, Fred D. Coombs, and Paul W. Thurston, *Educational Governance and Administration* (Englewood Cliffs, N.J.: Prentice-Hall, 1987).

16. Ernest L. Boyer, The Carnegie Foundation for the Advancement of Teaching, *High School: A Report on Secondary Education in America* (New York: Harper & Row, 1983); and John W. Goodlad, *A Place Called School: Prospects for the Future* (New York: McGraw-Hill, 1984).

17. Boyer, *High School,* 66.

18. Ibid., 61.

19. Ibid., 43.

20. Ibid., 66–67.

21. Goodlad, *A Place Called School,* 34.

22. Ibid., 37.

23. Ibid., 46.

24. National Commission on Excellence in Education, *A Nation at Risk: The Imperative for Educational Reform* (Washington, D.C.: U.S. Government Printing Office, 1983).

25. Ibid., 12.

26. Ibid.

27. Mortimer J. Adler, *The Paideia Proposal: An Educational Manifesto* (New York: Macmillan, 1982); Education Commission of the States, *Action for Excellence: A Comprehensive Plan to Improve our Nation's Schools* (Denver: Education Commission of the States, 1983); Theodore Sizer, *Horace's Compromise: The Dilemma of the American High School* (Boston: Houghton Mifflin, 1984); and Twentieth Century Fund Task Force on Federal Elementary and Secondary Education Policy, *Making the Grade* (New York: The Twentieth Century Fund, 1983).

28. Marilyn Clayton Felt, *Improving Our Schools: Thirty-Three Studies that Inform Local Action* (Newton, Mass.: Education Development Center, 1986). See also David Hill, "Reform in the 80s: Fixing the System from the Top Down," *Teacher Magazine* (September/October 1989): 50–55.

29. The following articles provide interesting analyses of the national reports: Mary Hatwood Futrell, "Mission Not Accomplished: Education Reform in Retrospect," *Kappan* (September 1989); 9–14; and Thomas R. McDaniel, "Demilitarizing Public Education: School Reform in the Era of George Bush," *Kappan* (September 1989): 15–18; Michael Apple, "Producing Ideology and Economy in the National Reports on Education," *Educational Studies* (Summer 1987): 195–220; and these articles in *Education and Urban Society* (February 1985): Paul E. Peterson, "Did the Education Commissions Say Anything?"; Terrence E. Deal, "National Commissions: Blueprints for Remodeling or Ceremonies for Revitalizing Public Schools"; Carol Camp Yeakey and Gladys Styles Johnston, "High School Reform: A Critique and a Broader Construct of Social Reality"; and Robert K. Wimpelberg and Rick Ginsberg, "Are School Districts Responding to *A Nation at Risk?*"

30. Peterson, "Did the Education Commissions," 126.

31. Albert Shanker, "The Reform Reports: Reaction from the Front Lines," *Education and Urban Society* (February 1985): 216.

32. For an interesting discussion of the issues regarding implementation of the proposals for educational reform, see Ralph Tyler, "Educational Reforms," *Kappan* (December 1987): 277–80.

33. Harold Howe II, "Remarks on Equity and Excellence in Education," *Harvard Educational Review* (May 1987): 200.

34. Apple, "Producing Ideology," 201.

35. Nathan Glazer, "Equity and Excellence in Education: A Comment," *Harvard Educational Review* (May 1987): 196.

36. Yeakey and Johnston, "High School Reform," 160.

37. Mario D. Fantini, *Regaining Excellence in Education* (Columbus, Ohio: Merrill Publishing, 1986): 44.

38. Ernest L. Boyer, "Social and Moral Imperatives for the Future of Our Schools," *Education Digest* (April 1985): 14.

39. Figure 1.4 was developed from an analysis of the ideas expressed in the following sources: Paul Nash, "Student Protest: A Crisis of Values," *Boston University Journal* (Winter 1970): 23–31; Daniel Yankelovich, "New Rules in American Life," *Psychology Today* (April 1981): 35–91. The original source for a discussion of traditional versus emergent values was George Spindler, *Education and Culture* (New York: Holt, Rinehart and Winston, 1967): 132–46.

40. Stanley M. Elam and Alec M. Gallup, "The 21st Annual Gallup Poll of the Public's Attitude toward the Public Schools," *Kappan* (September 1989).

41. Warren L. Ziegler, *An Approach to the Future—Perspective in American Education.* (Syracuse, N.Y.: Educational Policy Research Center, Syracuse University Research Corporation, 1970), 12.

42. Rather than listing all the sources consulted, we list those books and articles most helpful in predicting the future and in provoking consideration about the implications for education:

Michael W. Apple, "Curricululm in the Year 2000: Tensions and Possibilities," *Kappan* (January 1983): 321–26.

Linda L. Bain, "Beginning the Journey: Agenda for 2001," *Quest* (August 1988): 96–106.

Marvin J. Cetron, "Class of 2000: The Good News and the Bad News," *The Futurist* (November–December 1988): 9–15.

Don Glines, "Can the School of Today Survive Very Far into the 21st Century?" *NASSP Bulletin* (February 1989): 49–56.

Thomas E. Jones, *Options for the Future* (New York: Praeger, 1980).

Allan C. Ornstein, "Emerging Curriculum Trends: An Agenda for the Future," *NASSP Bulletin* (February 1989): 36–48.

John Naisbitt and Patricia Aburdene, *Megatrends 2000* (New York: Morrow, 1990).

Diane Ravitch, "On Thinking About the Future," *Kappan* (January 1983): 317–20.

Alvin Toffler, *The Third Wave* (New York: Bantam Books, 1981).

2

· · · · ·

Development of School Mission
and Objectives

■

The ideas presented in chapter 1 should be viewed and utilized as conceptual tools for the development of a school's educational mission and objectives. Certainly one of the most significant leadership responsibilities that administrators and relevant others can perform today is to develop a school's mission statement and objectives, including not only the evaluation and revision of the current mission and objectives but also the generation of new ones. Although all of the administrative and leadership activities discussed in this book are important, they do not result in positive contributions to the school if the educational mission and supporting objectives to which they should be related are vague or nonexistent.

In generating a school mission and objectives, administrators and the people with whom they are working need to understand the context in which, and the process through which, these tasks are developed and approved. They must be prepared to deal with the major issues and problems arising during the process. The following sections take up each of these essential aspects.

MAJOR CONSIDERATIONS AND PROCEDURES

IMPORTANCE OF SCHOOL EFFECTIVENESS AND EDUCATIONAL PLANNING

The national reform efforts and the resulting educational goals described in chapter 1 were derived, in part, from the school effectiveness research conducted during the 1970s and 1980s. Within this time period, a number of studies examined school processes and their relationship to student outcomes.[1] The most frequently cited of these studies are Weber, Brookover et al., Rutter et al., Edmonds, and Purkey and Smith.[2] Although these studies were conducted within a rather compressed time frame, their findings were remarkably consistent. Each implied that effective schools demonstrated a commitment to a shared mission and common goals.

For example, Joseph Murphy, Philip Hallinger, and Richard Mesa indicated that effective schools are capable of interpreting district goals at the building level.[3] Using the district-level goals as a baseline, administrators and staff members formulate a school's mission or philosophy defining important activities and forming the basis for organizational expectations and standards. In addition, the building-level philosophy defines the academic agenda for the school; with this agenda in place, educators are able to measure products, ascertain accountability, and make decisions regarding future activities.

A school's mission should reflect the values guiding and controlling the behavior of the people within and associated with the school—administrators, teachers, professional support personnel, noncertified personnel, parents, and students. According to J. Howard Johnson these values are "not concrete-like policies, rules, budgets, or curriculum guides. Often, they are not even written down. But they are manifested in everything the school does because they guide the choices we make . . . choices about content and method of teaching, choices about how we spend our (and our students') time, choices about whom we reward and what we reward them for."[4] Thus, successful schools have (1) clear and articulate missions, (2) leaders who devote a lot of attention to the shaping and dissemination of the mission, and (3) mission statements mutually agreed on and shared by everyone within the school.

Mission statements have several attributes worthy of mention. First, they tend to be written in qualitative rather than quantitative terms. For example, a school's mission might include statements such as, "We believe that student achievement is our most important product," instead of a more narrowly defined notion, such as, "We want everyone to raise their achievement scores by one whole grade level."[5] Second, because a mission statement should inspire all individuals within the school, the statement should be written in such a fashion that anyone involved in the school who reads it can embrace its content and its intent. Finally, the statement should give guidance to virtually every decision made within a building. As decisions are made, then educators need to review their mission or philosophy and ask, "Does this make sense in terms of our mission?" Figure 2.1 provides an example of a middle school mission statement illustrating the broad, yet guiding, nature of such statements.

Regardless of how comprehensive the school's mission statement is, it is useless unless widely shared and believed by everyone in the school. Therefore,

Figure 2.1 Middle School Mission Statement.

Middle School Mission Statement

The middle school is designed to assist pupils in making the transition from childhood to adolescence, from elementary school to high school. The middle school recognizes that the children it serves are unique physically, socially, emotionally, and intellectually. Therefore, the middle school addresses the needs of this age group through an environment which is stimulating, diverse, secure, and stable. The middle school recognizes individuality, promotes exploration, encourages feelings of self-worth, and develops self-direction and respect from others. The success of the middle school is based on the active participation of children, parents, teachers, administrators, and community members.

Source: Wauwatosa Public Schools, Wauwatosa, Wisconsin

as administrators attempt to formulate their schools' missions, they must take time and care to involve as many people as is reasonable in the process of determining the mission.

Once school staff members have determined and agreed on their mission, they are ready to determine how their philosophy can be operationalized. In many instances, this is accomplished by engaging in a planning process which often results in the development of a school effectiveness plan. Generally, this planning process begins with a determination of building-based goals and then focuses on specifying a course of action for accomplishing the goals set forth. Goals included in a school's effectiveness plan should be compatible with district-level goals and may frequently be drawn from the national reports and recommendations stipulated in the research on school effectiveness.

The strongest plans are developed locally and involve a broad base of teachers and other staff members. Frequently, discussions focus on whether the planning process should embody either a bureaucratic model in which strategic planning at the central office level sets the goals and framework for planning at lower levels within the system, or a social system model advocating participative sharing throughout the loosely coupled levels and subunits of the system.[6] William McInerney noted that

While decisions and plans may be mandated from distant, centralized locations, they will inevitably be implemented at the building level. In a decentralized, participatory planning and decision-making setting, constructive adaptations to otherwise uniform centralized policy are possible. Moreover, the accommodations occurring between strategic planning extending downward through the organization and operational planning extending upwards should result in a checks and balances system which promotes the greatest organizational efficiency.[7]

In most school systems, the development of effectiveness plans follows a prescribed process of individualization at the building level while attending to district-level goals and needs. Thomas Good and Jere Brophy indicated that "Unfortunately, some districts have simply taken plans developed in other districts and applied them with few, if any, modifications. However, persons who have studied the literature rightfully advocate that schools or school districts need to develop plans that are relevant to their unique needs and populations."[8]

Exemplary school improvement plans provide for each of the school's objectives, supporting implementation strategies, staff development activities, and evaluation criteria. Thus, the planning process by which effectiveness plans are determined generally includes the following steps:

1. Determining building-level goals compatible with district-level goals.
2. Identifying operational school objectives indicating which activities are undertaken to accomplish the specified goals.
3. Specifying implementation strategies, including staff development activities, and a timeline for the completion of the plan's activities.
4. Identifying the resources necessary to engage in the activities and developing an appropriate building-level budget for the plan.
5. Determining appropriate criteria for evaluating whether each goal has been achieved.

The intent of school effectiveness plans is to increase the likelihood that the formal, espoused mission and goals of an organization are addressed, implemented, and evaluated in a logical, consistent manner. The remainder of this chapter discusses issues and processes which should be addressed and employed to tighten the coupling between educational goals, operational objectives, and organizational outcomes.

APPROACHES TO THE DEVELOPMENT OF SCHOOL OBJECTIVES

The traditional approach to developing school objectives is to establish a committee which examines various materials and, after considerable discussion and usually some compromise, arrives at a statement of proposed objectives. The main limitations of this approach are that committee discussions frequently generate more heat than light; the more influential members of the group tend to dominate the discussion and the decision making.

A proposed alternative or adjunct to the traditional approach of developing school objectives is the Delphi Method. The Delphi Method, which grew out of the work of Olaf Helmer and Norman Dalkey, was originally intended as a tool for the scientific and technological forecasting of the future.[9] It has, however, been adapted for use in generating objectives and in establishing priorities among those objectives.[10] The major steps involved in the method are the following:

1. Identifying those individuals and/or groups whose opinions, judgments, or expert knowledge would be valuable to obtain in the development of school objectives.
2. Soliciting anonymous recommendations for proposed objectives from those individuals and groups.
3. Compiling a list of the proposed objectives recommended by individuals and groups, and distributing this list to those who participated in step 2.
4. Requesting participants to indicate the importance or priority of each proposed objective on the list; for example, very important, important, somewhat important, unimportant, no opinion.
5. Summarizing the results of step 4 and distributing data to participants; requesting participants to review the results and indicate any change in their assessment of the importance of certain objectives. The activities of this step are repeated until there is a reasonable consensus on the objectives a school or school district should try to achieve.

Information regarding proposed school objectives and their importance is gathered and communicated by mailing questionnaires and reports of the data obtained. Generally, participants in Delphi groups never assemble nor do they know the identity of the other members of the group.[11] An important prerequisite or aspect of the Delphi Method is maintaining—in the initial stages particularly—the anonymity of any individual or group proposing a school objective or indicating its priority. The basic assumption is that an individual or group whose identity is not made known to the other participants is likely to be more candid in proposing school objectives and more flexible in considering and reconsidering their importance.

Another method for managing the involvement of group members in determining school objectives is the Nominal Group Technique.[12] In this process, participants engage in the following procedures:

1. Individual participants prepare a listing of their ideas. Participants list desired objectives and submit them either orally in a round-robin fashion or anonymously on cards.
2. The group leader lists the objectives offered by the participants without commenting on them or altering the language offered.

3. After all possible objectives have been listed, items are clarified and condensed during an open discussion.
4. Following the discussion, participants rank order the objectives by either assigning a value (i.e., 10 to 100) to each objective or by listing a specified number of top-ranked items.
5. The group leader compiles the results and indicates which objectives emerged as having top priority.

The Nominal Group Technique may be used with one large group or with multiple small groups which later convene as a whole group. As with the Delphi Method, this procedure allows for high levels of participation, encourages and promotes individual contributions, and protects group members from those who might dominate during group sessions. Another benefit is that the group leader is able to structure the activity in such a manner that participants can see an outcome (i.e., a list of desired objectives) within a specified period of time.

The Delphi Method and the Nominal Group Technique are excellent approaches for involving a large number of people in the development of school objectives and for minimizing the importance of status factors in deciding which objectives are most important. However, there are potential weaknesses and questions associated with the approaches which administrators and staff members may need to resolve.[13] In both processes, time must be carefully monitored. When mailed questionnaires are used in the Delphi Method, difficulty may be encountered in securing an adequate number of responses without too much delay. In the Nominal Group Technique, the group leader needs to pace the group session to ensure that no step is short-changed and that the session reaches closure without jeopardizing or stifling involvement. Also, there is the question of whether the responses should be the sole basis for determining school objectives or whether they should constitute only one of several bases for making decisions about school goals. And finally, there is the question of who should organize the process of generating objectives and attend to their implementation.

To resolve these problems and questions, administrators and their staffs may need to establish committees on school objectives to plan and implement the foregoing process and to prepare a report to the school board about the proposed objectives their schools would like to adopt. These committees—composed of representatives of various groups involved and interested in the school—could also be helpful in generating support by providing materials and data for the consideration of participants and by helping them to resolve problems. In working with these committees, as well as with the other participants, administrators should utilize their leadership skills to make the entire process more productive.

Other approaches to the development of school objectives also deserve administrators' consideration and merit further investigation. For example, Phi Delta Kappa's Commission on Education Planning distributes a manual and materials for developing and stating priorities among school goals and objectives which deserve further consideration by administrators. (The manual and materials can be ordered from Phi Delta Kappa, P.O. Box 789, Bloomington, Indiana 47401.) Regardless of the method employed, however, administrators and all other participants should adhere to the following principles proposed by the Joint Committee on Educational Goals and Evaluation.

1. The goal-setting process should be kept open to all points of view without domination or intimidation by any special interest group.
2. The purpose of bringing people together is not to dwell on past deficiencies or lay blame, but to evolve a mission; identify needs; determine goals, goal indicators, or subgoals and program objectives; and to establish priorities.
3. Participants should not expect to have everything their way; they should come seeking a better understanding of the community, its people, and problems.
4. A spirit of cooperation and trust should be established among individuals and groups involved in the process.
5. Roles of leadership in school community planning should be earned rather than based on authority.
6. Individuals and groups instrumental to the goal setting process should provide for the open flow of information.
7. The individual school should be the base of operation for bringing people together.
8. In the process of determining missions, goals, and objectives, opinions must be balanced with facts.
9. The interaction process must begin with those concerns having high priority for the people involved.
10. The governing board should commit the resources necessary to see the goal-setting process through to a satisfactory conclusion; board members should be encouraged to participate in the interaction process, not as board members, but as private citizens.
11. Teachers, administrators, and classified employees should honor their responsibility to the community by taking an active part in the goal-setting process.
12. A variety of meetings should be held as a part of the goal-setting process; mixed groups assist consensus building.

Figure 2.2 Organizational Framework for School Objectives.

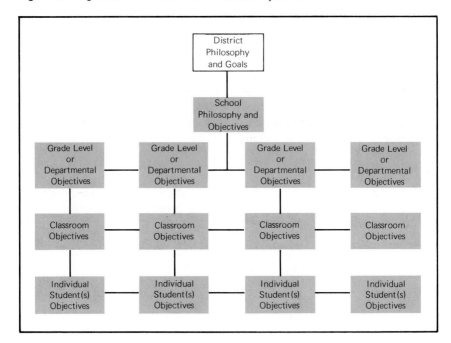

13. Inasmuch as the learning process is recognized as being dynamic and individualistic, any established objectives of education should not be so specific or restrictive as to preprogram the learning process for any student.
14. To ensure that the missions, goals, and objectives of public education continue to be relevant, a recycling process should be designed.
15. The goal-setting and planning process should result in observable action.[14]

ORGANIZATIONAL RELATIONSHIPS

The development of school objectives does not occur in a vacuum. School administrators need to take into consideration certain organizational relationships as they work with others on this important task.

Organizationally, a school is composed of several subunits and is itself a member of a large unit, the school district.[15] The relationship between the goals and objectives of these organizational units is depicted in figure 2.2.

The most important organizational fact which an administrator should understand from an examination of figure 2.2 is that a school is not a separate entity but a member of a school district with a mission and set of goals to which it must adhere. Consequently, administrators and the professional staff of a school are not free to act unilaterally in developing school objectives, but must work within the philosophical and goal framework set by the school district. Usually the district's philosophy and goals are stated in general enough terms to allow individual schools considerable latitude in developing their own objectives. Regardless of the degree of flexibility in a district's framework, the objectives of an individual school must be compatible with the district's goals.

Second, in the development of school objectives, the administrator and staff need to be aware of the organizational units within the school and their interrelationships. Most schools are organized according to grade level, and in secondary schools, by department also; within these organizational units are individual classrooms. Although the emphasis in this chapter and the previous one is on the development of schoolwide objectives, there should also be objectives for each grade level, department, classroom, and student—all related to the overall school objectives. Therefore, when school administrators and their staffs are working on the development of schoolwide objectives, they need to consider how these might be implemented at the grade, department, classroom, and student levels. It makes little sense to develop what may appear to be desirable schoolwide objectives if, for some reason, they cannot be implemented at more specific levels within a school.

SOCIAL FACTORS

In addition to organizational relationships, administrators and their staffs must examine major social factors in developing school objectives. These factors identified in figure 2.3 can affect the development of school objectives; therefore, they need to be taken into consideration by the school administrators and staff members.

MAJOR ISSUES AND PROBLEMS

ARE SCHOOL GOALS AND OBJECTIVES REALLY FUNCTIONAL?

There is no lack of ideas or methods for developing or revising school goals and objectives. In addition, a strong professional norm encourages, if not pressures, people into goal development. Therefore, underlying each traditional planning model is "an integrated view of educational organizations as goal-driven, rational systems in which operations can and should be programmed,

Figure 2.3 Major Social Factors Affecting the Development of Goals and Objectives.

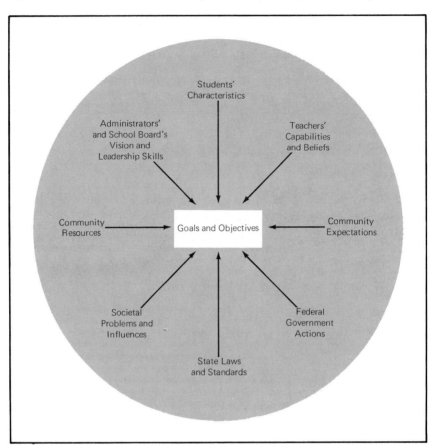

sequenced, monitored, and evaluated in short- and long-range planning cycles."[16] Thus, planning systems rely on the following requisites:

- Goals play a central role in the planning process.
- The planning process is sequential and rational.
- Communication must exist across hierarchical levels in the organization and adequate coupling must exist among the planning process steps to (*a*) facilitate consensus among goals, (*b*) allow cumulative goal building across organizational levels, and (*c*) provide for understanding of intentions.

- A comprehensive data base which includes internal and external impact factors should be available.
- There needs to be reasonable confidence in the predictability of events.
- There needs to be effective evaluation of the extent to which the plan is achieving the organization's goals.[17]

A major problem, however, is that most schools' educational goals or objectives do not seem to provide much direction and a basis for decision making by those associated with the school. Linda Lotto and David Clark noted that

organizational theorists have been challenging the appropriateness of goal-based, rational, sequential planning on the basis of its assumptions, to wit:

1. Not only is it unnecessary to insist that goals are on a priori condition for organizational planning, it is unreasonable to assume high levels of consensus about goals within organizations. In fact, it may not even be useful to retain the goal-based paradigm as a conception of organizations.
2. The image of educational institutions as rational bureaucracies might be inaccurate and unrealistic.
3. The linkage and responsiveness assumed by traditional planning is seldom found in educational organizations. They are almost always loosely coupled systems.

If one or more of these challenges were accurate, it would mean that the failure of goal-based, rational planning systems is grounded not in technical details of the systems but in the discrepancy between the assumptions underlying them and the reality of what actually occurs in educational organizations.[18]

Goal objectives are almost an entity in themselves, existing outside of the reality of what really occurs in a school. Their place seems to be in a handbook or curriculum guide, and their main value seems to be as a showpiece during an accreditation evaluation or a visitors' tour. Unfortunately, school goals and objectives also do not appear to be used very often as a basis for resource allocations or for evaluating school programs.[19] Whether or not their lack of value is an inherent characteristic is debatable, but there seems to be little doubt that, for the most part, they fail to exert a major impact on what goes on in a school.[20]

One important study which shed some light on the question of why many useful educational objectives and goals are not developed was conducted by Robert Larson. Essentially, he found four reasons why efforts to set functional school goals and objectives have frequently failed.

1. Goal setting was seen by most teachers as an isolated effort, just another one-shot activity on the long list of educational fads. The predominant attitude [by teachers] was that goal setting was just another fruitless experience.
2. When professional staff did discuss goals seriously, it was with decidedly "here and now" rather than with a future-oriented attitude. Purposes of education were rarely grappled with, an observation substantiated by the fact that in no school were any additions made to the original list of educational goals.
3. Educational personnel were reluctant to rank goals, despite pressures on schools to sort out priorities. Educators felt strongly that all goals were important if schools were to fulfill the societal mission.
4. Rating the performance of current programs relative to goals was avoided.[21]

The typical end result of this kind of goal setting is the development of ambiguous educational goals or objectives, thereby providing little direction to and generating little commitment by the people who work in the school organization. Even though it might seem that the remedy to this situation might be greater concentration on making the goals and objectives more definitive (and we address this aspect later), James March and his colleagues pointed out that goal ambiguity may be an intentional condition which is sought, or at least permitted, to provide greater freedom of choice to those people who work in the organization and to make evaluation of the achievement of educational goals and objectives more difficult.[22] If this is true, such goals become dysfunctional in terms of the original organizational purpose in generating them, but they may become very functional in meeting the needs of certain people in the organization. In this kind of a situation, goal substitution and goal displacement generally occur.[23]

If school goals or objectives are to become more functional in improving the educational program, clearly school administrators need to devote greater efforts to not only involving the professional staff and relevant others in meaningful decision making about school goals but also providing better inservice education to help the staff acquire the necessary skills for implementing the goals. (For additional guidelines on how to accomplish this, see Gorton.[24]) The primary purpose of this effort is to develop staff commitment to the goals or objectives. Without commitment, the staff is likely to be satisfied with or even desire goal ambiguity and is unlikely to try to utilize the goals or objectives in planning and evaluating school programs.

WHICH OBJECTIVES SHOULD BE INCLUDED?

Herbert Spencer alluded to the question of which educational objectives should be included in the school's program when he asked in 1880, "What knowledge is of the most worth?"[25] Since that time, and undoubtedly even before then, educators and others have debated the question. Over the years, general agreement has developed that schools should teach the basic skills of reading, writing, and arithmetic, as well as the ideas contained in certain subject matter disciplines, such as history and science; but there appears to be little consensus on what else is basic, and how much emphasis and time should be given to the achievement of various objectives.[26] Therefore, the debate continues, ebbing and flowing with the latest social pressures and needs.

A major issue administrators face in responding to the question of, "Which knowledge is of the most worth?" is whether a school's objectives should be limited to developing students' skills and knowledge, or whether the school should try to enlarge its mission to include the teaching of attitudes and values. Looking at the various proposed goals and roles of the school presented in the previous chapter, in most instances a broad and comprehensive role and set of objectives are recommended for the school. And yet, administrators will probably meet resistance and opposition from particular individuals and groups if they attempt to move their schools in the direction of teaching attitudes and values, particularly in a period of concern about student achievement. Despite such resistance, administrators should nevertheless recognize the considerable consensus that parents do want some type of education for their children in this area. In a Gallup Poll, 56 percent of the parents surveyed favored instruction in the schools on character education to help students develop personal values and ethical behavior; 62 percent indicated that it would be possible to develop subject matter for a course that would be acceptable to most of the people in a community.[27]

In spite of the recent emphasis placed on values, however, questions are being raised regarding the extent to which moral or values education should be included in school programs.[28] For example, some people may question whether schools should teach values and attitudes to students. Frequently, this inquiry is raised in the context of doubt as to whether there is a consensus on the values and attitudes to be taught; concern may also be expressed about whether the school knows how to teach attitudes and values, such as compassion or integrity.[29] This is a particularly relevant concern because many teachers themselves have difficulty in thinking and reasoning about values and morals.[30] These questions raise legitimate issues requiring discussion and analysis. However, what needs to be recognized is that the school already teaches values and attitudes, whether or not it intentionally sets out to do so. As Charles Silberman notes in his classic assessment of the classroom:

And children are taught a lot of lessons about values, ethics, morality, character, and conduct every day of the week, less by the content of the curriculum than by the way schools are organized, the way teachers and parents behave, the way they talk to children and to each other, the kinds of behavior they approve or reward, and the kinds they disapprove or punish. These lessons are far more powerful than the verbalizations that accompany them and that they frequently controvert.[31]

Silberman's observations suggest that the school does teach attitudes and values to students, regardless of whether or not explicit objectives and an organized program exist. Even though legitimate concerns may remain on the part of educators about how one can teach attitudes and values, there is really no lack of materials and approaches for developing these student characteristics.*

A more serious objection to the school's teaching of attitudes and values is the disagreement over which attitudes and values the school should emphasize. For instance, William Proefriedt noted that

the cry is raised that it is necessary for the public schools to contribute to the moral cohesion of the nation by fostering a set of traditional and commonly held values. Honesty, kindness, and courage lead a list difficult to challenge, and so long as the list is confined to such personal attributes and kept free of any social context, few of us quarrel with it. But if the list of personal virtues is looked at in terms of its application to such issues as abortion, race, the environment, housing, corporations, foreign policy, or changing life-styles, we run again into the difficulty of developing a moral education appropriate to a pluralistic society.[32]

Complicating the problem of achieving agreement on which specific attitudes and values schools should teach is the diversity of cultures and life-styles found in any particular community. Differences in ethnic and racial backgrounds, social class, and other personal and social factors all compound the school administrator's difficulty in trying to secure consensus on the attitudes and values that the school should teach to students.[33]

In attempting to resolve these problems, administrators and their staffs have available at least four main alternatives: They may chose to (1) resolve the problems and issues by focusing on dominant values in the local community, ignoring the possibility that a number of students may not stay in the local community (approaches for accomplishing this are described by a number

---

*For example, see Vincent Presno, *The Value Realms: Activities for Helping Children Develop Values* (New York City: Teachers College Press, 1980). Also see John Church, *Values Programs,* 440 Bret Harte Road, Sacramento, Calif. 95864.

of authors);[34] (2) focus on more generalized values transcending the local community; (3) involve students in an analysis of a variety of values for the purpose of helping students to select those values best for them; or (4) do nothing.[35] Clearly, staff and community involvement and inservice training are essential if the first three alternatives are to succeed.

Although each of these alternatives needs to be examined carefully for its consequences and implications, administrators cannot avoid a decision in this matter. Even deciding to choose alternative four is a decision to maintain the status quo. This probably means that, even a school not focusing in any explicit way on attitudinal or value objectives, will continue to teach attitudes and values in the ways Silberman noted. Whichever decision is made, the question of whether or not a school should concern itself with values and attitudes cannot readily be avoided.

HOW SHOULD SCHOOL OBJECTIVES BE STATED?

In recent years, the question of how school objectives should be stated has become an issue in American education. Ideally, they should be stated clearly so that they communicate in terms facilitating the evaluation of progress or achievement. This suggests that school objectives should be operationalized and defined in behavioral terms as recommended by Robert Mager.[36] And yet, administrators need to be aware of the continuing debate about the issue of behaviorally stated objectives. For example, W. James Popham noted that

> Proponents of behavioral objectives argued that such objectives embodied a rational approach to evaluation because they enhanced clarity regarding the nature of one's instructional aspirations. Critics countered that because the most important goals of education did not lend themselves readily to a behavioral formulation, the preoccupation with behavioral objectives would lead to instructional reductionism wherein the trivial was sought merely because it was measurable.[37]

While it is conceded that the critics raise important concerns, further analysis indicates flaws in the arguments used by those opposed to behaviorally stated objectives.[38] For example, despite some exceptions, the vast majority of objectives in education can be stated behaviorally, and progress or accomplishment can be measured in some reasonable manner.* On the other hand, although most objectives are measurable, administrators need to avoid the tendency to frame behavioral objectives in increasingly smaller and smaller units of analysis.[39] If this pitfall is not avoided, decision makers may well find themselves with an abundance of trivial objectives masking the broader, overriding objectives.

*For help in this area see *Program Evaluation Kit,* 2d ed. (Newbury Park, Calif.: Sage Publications, 1987).

Possibly the strongest argument against the use of behavioral objectives is the potential problem resulting from lack of student involvement. Although there is no reason why behavioral objectives could not be developed with the involvement of the learner, this has generally not been the case. Most behaviorally stated objectives are developed by educators with little or no involvement of the learners expected to achieve the objectives. This characteristic is not unique to behaviorally stated objectives; it is true of most school goals and objectives. Whether students should be involved in the development of school goals and objectives is a separate issue. However, nothing inherent in the behavioral objectives approach precludes student input in their development.

Finally, in developing a behaviorally stated objective with measurable achievement, there may be a tendency to overlook or ignore important outcomes arising spontaneously from a learning situation lacking previously stated goals. Also, operationalizing of objectives may focus efforts on the more measurable aspects of learning to the neglect of education's more humanistic elements. These are not inevitable or predictable consequences of behaviorally stated objectives, but they are potentialities administrators and staffs must consider. The resolution of these problems, however, does not lie in the rejection of behaviorally stated objectives and reliance on objectives which cannot be measured or arise spontaneously out of a classroom situation, because they may *not* arise spontaneously. Instead, administrators and staffs should be aware of potential limitations in the use of behavioral objectives and flexible enough to permit the adjustment of objectives when problems occur.

The basic case for behaviorally stated objectives is that, in contrast to nonbehaviorally stated objectives, the accomplishment of the former can be more easily evaluated while the latter frequently cannot be evaluated at all, or only with great difficulty. Therefore, rather than engaging in nonproductive arguments about whether objectives should or can be stated in behavioral terms, the essential task for administrators and others is to address themselves to the process of trying to operationalize school objectives. In pursuing this essential task, administrators should work closely with the professional staff, who may be ambivalent about the need to develop behaviorally stated objectives. Still, school administrators should utilize whatever resources are available to develop effective ways of working with the staff on this matter.[40]

WHO SHOULD BE HELD ACCOUNTABLE FOR ACHIEVING EDUCATIONAL OBJECTIVES?

Accountability has been and continues to be the most controversial and potentially explosive issue concerning school objectives. Simply defined in the context of school objectives, accountability means that somebody accepts the responsibility not only for developing and trying to achieve certain educational objectives but also for the negative or positive consequences of failing or succeeding in the achievement of those objectives.[41] For example, under the concept of accountability, it would not be sufficient for school administrators and staffs to *develop* school objectives; both would also be responsible in large part for *achieving* them and incurring the consequences of the extent of their attainment. An earlier but still relevant illustration of the concept of accountability is presented in figure 2.4.

The movement for school accountability developed in the late 1960s from dissatisfaction on the part of increasing numbers of people in regard to the kind of product (i.e., the students) emerging from schools.[42] Until the latter 1970s the primary thrust in the accountability movement was directed at getting school educators—teachers and administrators—to accept greater responsibility for improving the education of students. Educators responded to pressures for greater accountability in a variety of ways, ranging from rejection of the notion that the schools are responsible for any more than providing an opportunity for students to learn, to specification of their responsibilities for the achievement of school objectives.[43]

Recently the emphasis in the accountability issue has broadened to include a greater stress on students' and parents' accountability for the achievement of educational objectives.[44] In the case of parents, this has taken the form of greater efforts by the school to have them accept more responsibility for monitoring their children's learning and providing better home* study conditions. To promote greater accountability by students, a large number of schools and states have developed competency-based educational programs and minimum competency testing programs which students must pass to advance to the next grade.[45] These programs that tend to emphasize, although are not limited to, the development of basic skills have been attacked on several fronts.[46] As Edward McDill, Gary Natriello, and Aaron Pallas asserted, "If academic standards are raised and students are not provided substantial additional help to attain them, we predict that socially and academically disadvantaged students will be more likely to experience frustration and failure, resulting in notable increases in absenteeism, truancy, school-related behavior problems, and dropping out."[47]

Minimum competency testing has also come under attack; critics charge that the tests are biased; that the school's educational program is not preparing students adequately to pass the tests; and perhaps of greatest importance, that minimum competency testing tends to shift the responsibility and accountability for student failure from schools to students.[48] However, both

---

*A good example is a contract plan developed in Oakland, California, involving parents, school officials, and students—all of whom agree to perform certain responsibilities in regard to the achievement of educational objectives.

Figure 2.4 Recalled for Revision.

RECALLED FOR REVISION

By William C. Miller

Many of us who own recent model automobiles have received a communication from the factory, asking us to return the vehicle to the dealer so that defects can be corrected. Although I have gotten used to call-backs initiated by car manufacturers, I must admit I was startled to receive the following letter from my son's high school:

EDSEL MEMORIAL HIGH SCHOOL

. . . . .Anywhere, U.S.A.

August 1, 19

Dear Parents of our Graduates:

As you are aware, one of your offspring was graduated from our high school this June. Since that time it has been brought to our attention that certain insufficiencies are present in our graduates, so we are recalling all students for further education.

We have learned that in the process of the instruction we provided we forgot to install one or more of the following:

. . . at least one salable skill;
. . . a comprehensive and utilitarian set of values;
. . . a readiness for and understanding of the responsibilities of citizenship.

A recent consumer study consisting of a follow-up of our graduates has revealed that many of them have been released with defective parts. Racism and materialism are serious flaws and we have discovered they are a part of the makeup of almost all our products. These defects have been determined to be of such magnitude that the model produced in June is considered highly dangerous and should be removed from circulation as a hazard to the nation.

Some of the equipment which was in the past classified as optional has been reclassified as standard and should be a part of every product of our school. Therefore, we plan to equip each graduate with:

. . . a desire to continue to learn;
. . . a dedication to solving problems of local, national, and international concern;
. . . several productive ways to use leisure time;
. . . a commitment to the democratic way of life;
. . . extensive contact with the world outside the school;
. . . experience in making decisions.

Figure 2.4 Continued

> In addition, we found we had inadvertently removed from your child his interest, enthusiasm, motivation, trust, and joy. We are sorry to report that these items have been mislaid and have not been turned in at the school Lost and Found Department. If you will inform us as to the value you place on these qualities, we will reimburse you promptly by check or cash.
>
> As you can see, it is to your interest, and vitally necessary for your safety and the welfare of all, that graduates be returned so that these errors and oversights can be corrected. We admit that it would have been more effective and less costly in time and money to have produced the product correctly in the first place, but we hope you will forgive our error and continue to respect and support your public schools.
> Sincerely,
> P. Dantic, Principal

Reprinted by permission of Phi Delta Kappa Inc., December 1971.

opponents and proponents of minimum competency testing agree on several basic points: (1) The practice of social promotion of students is not desirable; (2) testing of students could be useful; (3) a test should not be the only criterion for awarding or denying a high school diploma; (4) the use of competency testing should be phased in over several years; and (5) students who fail the test should be given remedial help and have several opportunities to pass the test.[49]

As the accountability movement has taken different turns and directions, the basic issue remains the same and can be stated in three brief questions. Who is accountable? For what? And to whom? While several answers might be given to the first question, the authors' position is that accountability for the achievement of educational objectives is—or should be—a shared responsibility among educators, students, parents, governmental agencies, and the general public. A problem experienced frequently in education, however, is that most individuals and groups stress the accountability of the other parties while underplaying their own accountability. It would seem that if the concept of accountability is ever going to result in major positive changes in education, each group needs to put forth greater efforts to understand and accept its own accountability for the achievement of schools' objectives, while placing less emphasis on trying to make other groups more accountable.

At this point readers may ask, "But what is the basis of the school administrators' accountability?" In the American system of education, local schools are creations of the states, which have delegated certain broad responsibilities and authority to local school boards elected by the communities. To accomplish the objectives of the school districts, the school boards delegate certain responsibilities to administrators of the districts. Therefore, in a real sense, school administrators can and should be held accountable to the members of the school board, who in turn can and should be held accountable to their constituents and to the states that gave them a charter and form of organization.

The question of what schools (or more specifically, administrators and their staffs) are accountable for is less easily answered. Staff members and administrators could be held accountable for achieving the educational objectives their schools have set forth. However, this position has been challenged on two grounds: (1) that the staff and administrator have little or no control over many variables; for example, a student's home environment which may affect the achievement of the school's educational goals; and (2) that the accomplishment of many of the school's objectives is a shared responsibility with other agencies or institutions in society, such as the family, and that the staff and administrator should not be held totally accountable for the achievement of school goals.[50]

Although both of these arguments are valid to a point, they leave unresolved the basic issue of the degree to which administrators and staff members should be held accountable. If, in fact, the achievement of school objectives depends on many variables over which they have little or no control, does this mean that neither should be held accountable at all for the achievement of school objectives? Obviously not, but researchers, educational theorists, and other educators have not been very helpful in identifying the extent to which administrators and staffs should be held accountable.

If the achievement of many educational objectives is a shared responsibility, what specifically is the staff's and school administrators' share, as compared to that of other agencies of society? All too frequently when the argument of shared responsibility is advanced, the end result is that no one takes responsibility or accepts accountability for achieving a particular objective. The concept of shared responsibility has merit if it leads to efforts to coordinate resources and activities. Too often, when proposed, it fails to affix a specific degree of accountability to the parties responsible for achieving the objective.

Educators in a school must think through their own positions on the issue of accountability. In general, if administrators and their staffs are going to establish certain educational objectives, they should be held accountable for their achievement. If particular conditions affect the degree to which those objectives can be achieved, staff members and administrators have the responsibility of taking this into consideration in stating the objectives.

In regard to school administrators' own accountability, in addition to being responsible for carrying out the typical duties assigned, they should also be held accountable for:

- Identifying and clearly defining, with the help of others, the educational objectives of the school.
- Specifying which teaching, supervisory, or administrative procedures and resources are needed to achieve those objectives.
- Developing and implementing a plan for evaluating the extent of progress or achievement of the school's objectives.
- Informing the school board and the community periodically about the degree to which objectives have been achieved, and the reasons for problems, if they occur.

The entire issue of accountability is emotionally charged. Undoubtedly, several significant factors should be considered in limiting the degree of the staff's and the school administrator's accountability. However, these factors should not be weighed so heavily that they become an argument for avoiding accountability completely or for avoiding the responsibility of making explicit the extent to which the staff or the school administrator should be accountable. In a true sense, the extent to which an administrator is willing to be held accountable for achieving objectives is a valid indicator of real commitment to achieving those objectives, as opposed to merely giving lip service to their importance.

EVALUATING EFFORTS TO ESTABLISH AND IMPLEMENT SCHOOL OBJECTIVES

The end product that should result from consideration and resolution of the various issues and problems discussed in this chapter is the establishment of a set of educational objectives or aims to which the school is committed and which it is prepared to implement. The following specific criteria can aid administrators in evaluating the strengths and weaknesses of their schools' educational objectives and plans for implementation:

Criteria Questions for Assessing the School's Efforts in Establishing, Implementing, and Evaluating School Objectives

1. Do the school's objectives reflect and maintain an appropriate balance between the needs of the individual and those of society?

2. Are the school's objectives comprehensive, rather than restricted to knowledge and skill outcomes? Is the development of student interests, attitudes, and values also included in the objectives of the school?
3. Does the school make clear which objectives are its sole or primary responsibility and which objectives it shares with other institutions? If the school shares a responsibility with other institutions, does it make explicit the extent to which it is responsible?
4. Do the school's objectives focus on student outcomes rather than school functions, activities, or processes?
5. Are the school's objectives stated clearly and in terms facilitating the evaluation of progress or achievement?
6. Does the statement of each school objective indicate
   a. the proposed level of performance?
   b. when the objective will be achieved?
7. Do the school objectives take into consideration individual differences among students as to backgrounds, abilities, interests, and aspirations?
8. Is there a school plan for the continuous development of students', teachers', parents', and important others' understanding of and their commitment to the objectives?
9. Is there a formal plan for periodic and systematic evaluation of progress toward or achievement of the school's objectives?
10. Are the objectives reexamined every two or three years to see whether modification, elimination, or the addition of new objectives is needed?

In too many schools, objectives are developed and published in the school district's or teacher's handbook, where they remain year after year, without critical examination as to their relevancy or accomplishment. Utilization of the preceding criteria should help school administrators maintain a set of relevant and appropriate objectives whose achievement is evaluated.

In carrying out an examination of a school's efforts in establishing, implementing, and evaluating its objectives, however, administrators should be aware of certain potentially negative consequences suggested by Larson:

1. Assessing effectiveness and efficiency on the basis of goal attainment may be misleading because multiple goals may be in conflict and hence inhibit single goal realization.

2. Frequent measurement of goal attainment may lead to an emphasis on more quantitative as opposed to important but more difficult to measure qualitative goals.
3. Unanticipated demands on an organization may require energy and resources to be expended on problem solving which, although necessary for survival, may not be directly related to any goal.
4. Unless goals are occasionally updated, over time public or official goals may be succeeded by new goals which, although important, may not be stated and thus may escape assessment. In such a situation it may seem that the organization is not performing effectively.
5. A commitment on official goals that is too narrowly focused may inhibit the organization from adopting new goals more appropriate for its mission.
6. Overemphasis on attainment of certain goals may divert resources from other vital organizational functions not as clearly linked with the stated goals (e.g., inservice education for staff may be neglected in favor of the official goal of instructional improvement). Also, official goals can divert management's attention from the more immediate personal needs of employees. Personnel relationships are seldom a publicly stated goal, yet failure to attend to them can lead to serious internal motivation and morale problems.
7. Certain goals although societally sanctioned, may, if publicly pronounced, be unpalatable to segments of the clientele served (e.g., the socialization function of education versus the 3 R's). An unproductive conflict may result which inhibits the attainment of related goals.[51]

A FINAL COMMENT

Administrators must take the initiative to utilize the ideas presented in this chapter in cooperation with teachers and parents to improve the formulation and evaluation of school objectives. Administrators could easily believe that they are too busy to engage in such efforts and that other priorities demand attention. Certainly, school administrators' jobs are demanding, and many problems and issues compete for their time. However, the development and evaluation of school objectives may very well be the most important task administrators can perform, because the objectives chart the direction that education should take in a school.

Review and Learning Activities

1. What are the distinguishing features of a school mission statement?
2. Explain how school effectiveness research contributes to the understanding of school objectives.
3. What are the main organizational and social factors an administrator needs to take into consideration in the development of school objectives?
5. Identify the groups an administrator should involve in the development of school objectives. Which contribution can each group be expected to make?
6. What are the major problems and obstacles to developing functional school goals and objectives? What are the implications for the administrator of these possible problems and obstacles?
7. What are the major factors that an administrator needs to consider in resolving the issue of whether or not the school should include the teaching of values and attitudes in its objectives? Now, choose a position and defend it.
8. State the arguments for and against behaviorally defined school objectives.
9. To what extent should the school and the school administrator be held accountable? What are the implications of your position on this matter?

Notes

1. For a concise discussion of the findings pertaining to school effectiveness research, see Thomas L. Good and Jere E. Brophy, "School Effects," in *Handbook of Research on Teaching,* 3d ed., ed. Merlin Wittrock, New York: MacMillan Publishing Company, 1986), 570–602.

2. G. Weber, *Inner-City Children Can Be Taught to Read: Four Successful Schools* (Washington, D.C.: Council for Basic Education, 1976); W. B. Brookover, C. Beady, P. Flood, J. Schweitzer, and J. Wisenbaker, *School Social Systems and Student Achievement* (New York: Praeger, 1979); M. Rutter, B. Maughan, P. Mortimore, J. Ouston, and A. Smith, *Fifteen Thousand Hours: Secondary Schools and Their Effects on Children.* (Cambridge, Mass.: Harvard University Press, 1979); Ronald R. Edmonds, "Effective Schools for the Urban Poor," *Educational Leadership* (1979): 15–27; and S. C. Purkey and M. S. Smith, "Effective Schools: A Review," *Elementary School Journal* (1983): 427–52.

3. Joseph Murphy, Philip Hallinger, and Richard P. Mesa, "Strategies for Coupling Schools: The Effective Schools Approach," *NASSP Bulletin* (February 1985): 8.

4. J. Howard Johnston, "Values, Culture, and the Effective School," *NASSP Bulletin* (March 1987): 81.

5. Ibid.

6. For interesting discussions regarding centralized versus decentralized planning see William D. McInerney, "Participation in Educational Planning at the School District Level," *Planning and Changing* (Winter 1985): 206–15; and Robert H. Beach and William D. McInerney, "Educational Planning Models and School District Practice," *Planning and Changing* (Fall 1986): 180–91.

7. McInerney, "Participation in Educational Planning," 207.

8. Good and Brophy, "School Effects," 585.

9. Olaf Helmer and Norman Dalkey, "An Experimental Application of the Delphi Method in the Use of Experts," *Management Science* (April 1963): 458–67.

10. Arlene Hartman, "Reaching Consensus Using the Delphi Technique," *Educational Leadership* (March 1981): 495–97.

11. Robert C. Erffmeyer, Elizabeth S. Erffmeyer, and Irving M. Lane, "The Delphi Technique: An Empirical Evaluation of the Optimal Number of Rounds," *Group and Organizational Studies* (March–June 1986): 120–28.

12. For a discussion of the original Nominal Group Technique, see A. L. Delbecq, A. H. Van de Ven, and D.H. Gustafson, *Group Techniques for Program Planning: A Guide to Nominal Group and Delphi Processes* (Glenview, Ill.: Scott, Foresman, 1975); and for a recent adaptation, see William M. Fox, *Effective Group Problem Solving: How to Broaden Participation, Improve Decision Making, and Increase Commitment to Action* (San Francisco: Jossey-Bass Publishers, 1987).

13. Norman Hale, "Problem-Solving Techniques for Administrators" (ERIC Report Ed-151–894). Also see Beverly Carver, "NGT Modified Delphi Technique: Convergence Patterns in Educational Goal Development" (Ph.D. diss., Arizona State University, 1980).

14. Joint Committee on Educational Goals and Evaluation, *Education for the People I,* "Guidelines for Total Community Participation in Forming and Strengthening the Future of Public Elementary and Secondary Education in California" (Sacramento: California Legislature, 1972), 21–26.

15. Thomas J. Sergiovanni, Martin Burlingame, Fred D. Coombs, and Paul Thurston, *Educational Governance and Administration* 2d ed. (Englewood Cliffs, N.J.: Prentice-Hall, 1987), 206.

16. Linda S. Lotto and David L. Clark, "Understanding Planning in Educational Organizations," *Planning and Changing* (Spring 1986): 9.

17. Ibid., 10.

18. Ibid.

19. Leroy V. Sloan, "Operative vs. Official Goals in Assessing the Effectiveness of Educational Systems" (Paper presented at the American Educational Research Association annual meeting, Los Angeles, 1981).

20. Robert Larson, *Goal Setting in Planning: Myths and Realities* (Burlington, Vt.: Center for Research, University of Vermont, 1980).

21. Ibid., 18–20.

22. For further discussion of this problem in organizations, see James G. March and Johan P. Olson, *Ambiguity and Choice in Organizations,* 2d ed. (New York: Oxford University Press, 1980).

23. For this problem and others related to goal setting, see Sloan, "Operative vs. Official Goals."

24. Richard A. Gorton, *School Leadership and Administration: Important Concepts, Case Studies, and Simulation* 3d ed. (Dubuque, Iowa: Wm. C. Brown, 1987), 17–26.

25. Herbert Spencer, *Education* (New York: D. Appleton and Co, 1880), 32.

26. Karl L. Alexander and Aaron M. Pallas, "Curriculum Reform and School Performance: An Evaluation of the 'New Basics'," *American Journal of Education* (August 1984): 391–420.

27. Alec M. Gallup and David L. Clark, "The 19th Annual Gallup Poll of the Public's Attitudes toward the Public Schools," *Kappan* (September 1987): 24.

28. Edward A. Wynne, "The Great Tradition in Education: Transmitting Moral Values," *Educational Leadership* (January 1986): 4–9; and Edward A. Wynne and Mary Hess, "Long-Term Trends in Youth Conduct and the Revival of Traditional Value Patterns," *Educational Evaluation and Policy Analysis* (Fall 1986): 294–308.

29. For a review of these views and the literature on teaching values, see Richard W. Paul, "Ethics without Indoctrination," *Educational Leadership* (May 1988): 10–19; and Steven Selden, "Character Education and the Triumph of Technique," *Issues in Education* (Winter 1986): 301–12.

30. Robert A. Wilkins, "If the Moral Reasoning of Teachers Is Deficient, What Hope for Pupils?" *Kappan* (April 1980): 548–49.

31. Charles Silberman, *Crisis in the Classroom* (New York: Random House, 1970), 9.

32. William Proefriedt, "Power, Pluralism and the Teaching of Values: The Educational Marketplace," *Teachers College Record* (Summer 1985): 543.

33. R. Pratte, "Cultural Pluralism: Can It Work?" *Theory into Practice* (Winter 1981): 1–72.

34. Pamela B. Joseph, "Like It or Not, Your Schools Are Teaching Values, So Emphasize These," *American School Board Journal* (May 1986): 35, 46; and Mary Ellen Saterlie, "Developing a Community Consensus for Teaching Values," *Educational Leadership* (May 1988): 44–47.

35. For an excellent and still relevant discussion of the problem and these four alternatives, see George E. Artelle, "How Do We Know What Values Are Best?" *Progressive Education* (April 1950): 191–95.

36. Robert Mager, *Preparing Instructional Objectives,* 2d ed. (Belmont, Calif.: Pitman Learning. 1975).

37. W. James Popham, "Two-Plus Decades of Educational Objectives," *International Journal of Educational Research* 11, no. 1, (1987): 33.

38. J. R. Calder, "In Defense of the Systematic Approach to Instruction and Behavioral Objectives," *Educational Technology* (May 1980): 21–25.

39. Popham, "Two-Plus Decades," 34.

40. For example, see *Educational Planning Model* (Bloomington, Ind.: Phi Delta Kappa, Commission on Educational Planning); and for an excellent review of research on the effectiveness of behavioral objectives, see the March 1981 issue of *Educational Technology.*

41. S. Allen, "Accountability Revisited," *Education Canada* (Winter 1980): 30–34. See also, Chris Pipho, "Accountability Comes Around Again," *Kappan* (May 1989): 662–63.

42. M. Wilson, "Planning for School Improvement Using Quantitative and Qualitative Data," *Planning and Changing* (Summer 1987): 106–19.

43. A. Silberman, "Accountability: A Horror Story," *Instructor* (November 1977): 28.

44. See Richard M. Jaeger and Carol Kehr Title, *Minimum Competency Achievement Testing* (Berkeley, Calif.: McCutchan, 1979), part I.

45. For a description of several of these, see Jaeger and Title, *Minimum Competency,* part IV; and Richard M. Jaeger, "The Final Hurdle: Minimum Competency Achievement Testing," in *The Rise and Fall of National Test Scores,* ed. G. R. Austin and H. Garber (New York: Academic Press, 1982); and Craig E. Richards, "A Typology of Educational Monitoring Systems," *Educational Evaluation and Policy Analysis* (Summer 1988): 106–16.

46. Edith L. Archer and Judith H. Dresden, "A New Kind of Dropout: The Effect of Minimum Competency Testing on High School Graduation in Texas," *Education and Urban Society* (May 1987): 269–79.

47. Edward L. McDill, Gary Natriello, and Aaron M. Pallas, "Raising Standards and Retaining Students: The Impact of the Reform Recommendations on Potential Dropouts," *Review of Educational Research* (1985): 415–33.

48. "Debra P.: The End of Competency Testing," *Education U.S.A.* (May 25, 1981): 309; and M. S. McClung, "Are Competency Testing Programs Fair? Legal?" *Kappan* (February 1978): 397–400.

49. For a concise discussion of evaluation measures and criterion-referenced versus norm-referenced tests see Popham, "Two-Plus Decades," 36–38. Descriptions of remedial programs may be found in Janella Rachal and Lee McGraw Hoffman, "The Effects of Remediation and Retention upon Basic Skills Performance among Elementary Students Participating in a State Basics Skills Test Program: (Paper presented at American Educational Research Association annual meeting, Chicago, 1985); and in Claudia Merkel-Keller, "At What Price Success?—Summer Basic Skills Remediation and Paid Employment" (Paper presented at the American Educational Research Association annual meeting, Washington, D.C. 1987).

50. Edward G. Buffie, "Accountability: The Key to Excellence," *Childhood Education* (November/December 1984): 107–14.

51. Larson, *Goal Setting in Planning, 3–4.*

2

• • • • •

Dimensions of Administration

———

3

. . . . .

The School Administrator:
Tasks and Administrative Process

The goals and objectives discussed in chapters 1 and 2 represent the desired outcomes of education in a school. These outcomes are not likely to materialize, however, without the organization and administration of human and physical resources. The essential job of school administrators is to organize and manage these resources efficiently and effectively so that school objectives can be successfully achieved. This involves administrators in the performance of many administrative tasks and in the utilization of an administrative process. The following sections introduce the tasks and process.

ADMINISTRATIVE TASK AREAS

Figure 3.1 presents an overview of administrative task areas and examples of their component activities; it is a synthesis of several studies concerned with identifying the major activities of school administrators.[1]

Because the literature and research on administrative tasks indicate that administrators engage in a multitude of activities usually characterized by brevity, variety, and fragmentation, they need to assign priorities and determine appropriate time allocations within these various task areas.[2] Reviewing the goals of the district and mission of their buildings and reflecting on their personal educational beliefs and values are useful activities that help administrators determine to which tasks to devote their time.[3] Richard Andrews and Jill Hearne noted that when they examined the importance administrators attached to various dimensions of their role, typically, administrators did not spend their time in a manner consistent with how they believed they should.[4]

Figure 3.1 Major Task Areas in School Administration.

I. **Staff Personnel**
A. Help formulate staff personnel policies.
B. Recruit staff personnel; attract able people to the school staff.
C. Select and assign staff personnel.
D. Schedule teachers' assignments.
E. Communicate the objectives of the school program to the faculty.
F. Observe teachers in their classrooms.
G. Diagnose the strengths and weaknesses of teachers.
H. Help resolve the classroom problems of teachers.
I. Evaluate the performance of teachers.
J. Improve the performance of teachers.
K. Coordinate the work of teachers.
L. Stimulate and provide opportunities for professional growth of staff personnel.
M. Maximize the different skills found in a faculty.
N. Develop *esprit de corps* among teachers.

II. **Pupil Personnel**
A. Provide guidance services.
B. Institute procedures for the orientation of pupils.
C. Establish school attendance policy and procedures.
D. Establish policy and procedures for dealing with pupil conduct problems.
E. Establish policy and procedures in regard to pupil safety in the building and on the school grounds.
F. Develop and coordinate the extracurricular program.
G. Handle disciplinary cases.
H. Arrange systematic procedures for the continual assessment and reporting of pupil performance.
I. Confer with juvenile court, police agencies, etc.

III. **Community-School Leadership**
A. Develop and administer policies and procedures for parent and community participation in the schools.
B. Confer with parents.
C. Handle parental complaints.
D. Assist PTA and other parent groups.
E. Represent the school in participation in community organizations.
F. Cooperate with other community agencies.
G. Make possible the continual reexamination of acceptable plans and policies for community improvement with particular reference to the services which the schools are rendering.

IV. **Instruction and Curriculum Development**
A. Help formulate curriculum objectives.
B. Help determine curriculum content and organization.
C. Relate the desired curriculum to available time, physical facilities and personnel.
D. Provide materials, resources, and equipment for the instructional program.
E. Provide for the supervision of instruction.
F. Provide for in-service education of instructional personnel.

V. **School Finance and Business Management**
A. Prepare school budget at local school level.

(continued)

Figure 3.1 Continued

B. Provide for a system of internal accounting.
C. Administer school purchasing.
D. Account for school monies.
E. Account for school property.
F. Keep the school office running smoothly.

VI. **School Plant**

A. Determine the physical plant needs of the community and the resources which can be marshalled to meet those needs.
B. Develop a comprehensive plan for the orderly growth and improvement of school plant facilities.
C. Implement plans for the orderly growth and improvement of school plant facilities.
D. Develop an efficient program of operation and maintenance of the physical plant.

E. Supervise the custodial staff.

VII. **General Tasks**

A. Organize and conduct meetings or conferences.
B. Handle delicate interpersonal situations.
C. Direct the work of administrative assistants.
D. Publicize the work of the school.
E. Diagnose the strengths and weaknesses of the school program.
F. Attend school functions, such as assemblies, plays, athletic contests.
G. Respond to correspondence.
H. Prepare reports for the district administration.
I. Attend principals' meetings.
J. Keep school records.
K. Schedule school programs.

For example, principals reported that although they believed that the improvement of the educational program and selection and evaluation of personnel were the most important tasks of their jobs, they spent the greatest amount of time on school management and supervision of students—aspects of their job perceived as least important.

A practical response to setting task priorities and allocating time is to point out that in most situations one administrator is not, and should not be, solely responsible for carrying out all of the activities in figure 3.1. Many of these responsibilities are shared between two or more administrators at the building level, or with other administrative or supervisory personnel at the district office. However, school administrators are either actually involved in carrying out most of the activities in figure 3.1, or are responsible for making sure the tasks are implemented if the activities have been delegated to someone else. Because the task areas of school administration are so important, later chapters contain an in-depth examination of each area.

ADMINISTRATIVE PROCESS: BASIC ELEMENTS

Henri Fayol is generally regarded as the father of the administrative process. In his book, *General and Industrial Management,* Fayol identified and defined

Figure 3.2 Administrative Process.

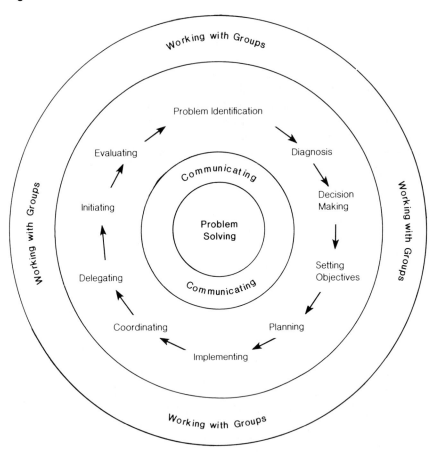

the basic elements of the administrative process.[5] Later, Luther Gulick and L. Urwick adapted Fayol's conceptualization to the job of the chief executive, and other writers on administration attempted to refine or further elaborate the process.[6]

The administrative process consists of the methods administrators utilize to achieve specific tasks and objectives. Writers vary as to the basic elements or methods in the process. However, based on an examination of the literature, the authors of this text believe that the thirteen elements identified in figure 3.2 make up the administrative process. The figure illustrates that to solve problems, administrators need to employ the various elements of the administrative process; each element relies on the administrators' ability to communicate effectively with others and work successfully with others within group settings.

With a thorough understanding of all the elements in figure 3.2 and with appropriate application of those elements, administrators should not only be able to accomplish administrative tasks more effectively but also experience greater success in achieving objectives. The effectiveness with which administrators utilize each element is greatly enhanced through the meaningful involvement of significant others, such as teachers.[7]

Rather than discussing all thirteen administrative processes in detail—since entire books have been devoted to most of them—a brief discussion of each establishes its functions and use. These processes are also discussed in later chapters as they apply to the task areas. In addition, most of these processes are discussed by Gorton in considerable depth in another text, *School Leadership and Supervision: Important Concepts, Case Studies, and Simulations.*[8]

PROBLEM IDENTIFICATION

There is no shortage of problems for which administrators are expected to provide solutions. In fact, some administrators—those on the firing line particularly—may feel that they need not concern themselves with identifying problems; other people such as students, teachers, and parents identify or present more problems than they may care to think about. These administrators' motto is, in essence, "Why seek trouble where none exists?" or, "Let sleeping dogs lie!"

Nevertheless, administrators who want to avoid going from crisis to crisis must begin to identify those underlying problems which eventually manifest themselves in troublesome behavior; they must begin to identify potential problem areas which, if not corrected, could ultimately lead to serious consequences for their schools. Of course, no one is recommending that administrators attempt to find or create problems where none exist. But neither can administrators sit back and wait for problems to land on their desks, since at that point such problems may have ripened into crises much more difficult to resolve. Instead, administrators should engage in the behavior observed by Arthur Blumberg and William Greenfield in their study of effective principals: "She doesn't wait for problems to come to her. Instead, she seeks them out."[9] Administrators who fail to engage in problem identification continue to be besieged with crises which seem to come on them suddenly and from which there appears to be no respite.

Although much has been written about the process of problem solving, until recently little attention has been given to the process of problem identification. Historically, theorists and writers assumed that a problem already existed, and the main question was how to define and solve it. Recent literature, however, has argued that the work of administrators is primarily one of problem identification (frequently referred to as problem finding) and subsequent problem solving.[10] Similarly, the authors' position is that school administrators should actually spend some of their time trying to identify problems that already exist, because without efforts by administrators to address them, they could eventually evolve into full-blown crises. In a related sense, Kent Peterson noted that, "The means by which administrators *identify* problems is perhaps as important as how they go about solving them, for if the key problem is not identified then energies are not expended on tasks which solve central organizational problems."[11]

To identify problems, administrators need to ask questions. As Bruce McPherson, Richard Crowson, and Nancy Pitner stated, "Problem finding is the act of transforming an uncomfortable or irritating situation into a question which can be answered, or into a hypothesis which can be tested."[12] Thus, asking the right questions is the key to uncovering potential problems which, if left uncorrected, could lead to serious consequences. However, whether the right questions are raised depends, at least in part, on one's criteria for satisfaction or success, and on whether an assessment is made of performance in a specific area.

For example, if only 35 percent of the parents show up for parent-teacher conferences, the level of attendance may not be perceived as a problem by anyone unless one of the criteria for judging the success of parent-teacher conferences is attendance greater than 35 percent. In addition, if the administrator or someone else does not attempt to ascertain the percentage of parents who participate in parent-teacher conferences, people have no basis for determining whether a problem exists. Therefore, before a problem can be identified, administrators must establish criteria for determining whether objectives have been attained and must collect information to document the degree to which the criteria were met. This involves the administrator in asking value and evaluative questions to identify problems.

Sample questions illustrating the kinds of inquiries that administrators, in cooperation with teachers, students, and parents, might pursue in attempting to identify problems are presented in figure 3.3.

DIAGNOSIS

Why are some students underachieving? Why don't more parents participate in school affairs? Why don't some teachers carry out their responsibilities fully? To answer any of these questions adequately, administrators must engage in the process of diagnosis—investigating the basic causes of the problem.[13] Diagnosis is concerned with ascertaining the underlying roots of a problem and distinguishing these from its mere symptoms or manifestations. It includes careful, thorough, and objective investigation into the conditions which have

Figure 3.3 Sample Problem-Identification Questions.

Criteria Questions	Assessment Questions
A. Students	
1. What *should* be the attitude of students toward the value and usefulness of their school program?	1. What *is* the attitude of students toward the value and usefulness of their school program?
2. What *should* be the level of performance achieved by the students in the school?	2. What *is* the level of performance achieved by students in my school?
3. To what extent *should* students be developing a positive self-concept, self-initiative, and problem-solving skills?	3. To what extent *are* students developing a positive self-concept, self-initiative and problem-solving skills?
B. Teachers	
1. To what extent *should* teachers know and understand the home background and learning strengths and disabilities of their students?	1. To what extent *do* teachers know and understand the home background and learning strengths and disabilities of their students?
2. To what degree *should* teachers individualize instruction and adapt the curriculum to meet the individual needs of students?	2. To what extent *do* teachers individualize instruction and adapt the curriculum to meet the individual needs of students?
3. To what extent *should* teachers go beyond teaching skills and subject matter to developing student attitudes and values?	3. To what extent *do* teachers go beyond teaching skills and subject matter content to developing student attitudes and values?
C. Parents	
1. To what degree *should* the parents understand clearly and accurately the objectives of the school and the programs and activities offered in order to reach those objectives?	1. To what degree *do* parents understand the objectives of the school and the programs and activities offered to reach those objectives?
2. What *should* be the extent and nature of parent participation and involvement in the school?	2. What *is* the extent and nature of parent participation and involvement in the school?
3. What *should* be the attitude of parents toward the school program and the professional staff?	3. What *is* the attitude of parents toward the school program and professional staff?

led to or created the problem.[14] If care is not taken in this stage of the process, symptoms may be confused with causes and the wrong corrective action may be initiated. Thus, the process of diagnosis, similar to problem identification, begins with the formulation of questions.

For example, administrators confronted by a growing student attendance problem might begin their investigations by asking,"Why are so many students truant?" One immediate response to that question could be that "these students are lazy, or they don't have good habits of attendance." Some administrators would stop at this point, satisfied that they have answered the question, and begin to try to change the students. Other administrators would continue to ask questions, seeking more fundamental causes of the students' misbehavior: "*Why* are the students lazy? *Why* don't they have good habits of punctuality? What is the home situation of these students? Is it possible that the attendance behavior of some or many of these students is affected by learning disabilities, such as reading problems, and would the school's cumulative records or diagnostic testing be helpful in checking out this possibility? Is the educational program that the school offers perceived by these students as relevant? Is there anyone in the school with whom these students relate well?"

These examples of diagnostic questions seek the basic causes for the students' misbehavior. Whether these specific questions uncover the root causes of the problem or whether, perhaps, other questions need to be raised is not the issue. If school administrators are to avoid dealing with only the symptoms of problems, they must raise questions to identify the underlying and basic causes of a situation.

Of course, these questions frequently are not easy to answer, nor are the answers always pleasing to the administrator. The easiest thing for an administrator to do—at least temporarily—is to refrain from asking basic questions or seeking their answers, and instead proceed through the school year, hoping that nothing serious erupts, and delaying any response to a situation until trouble actually develops. Unfortunately, the consequence of this behavior is that administrators seldom deal with problems until they manifest themselves in ways frequently difficult to resolve; as a result, these administrators' schools fail to function as well as they might. One book that should assist school administrators who would like to improve their school's problem-solving capacity has been written by Philip Runkel and his colleagues.[15]

School administrators should engage in the process of diagnosis before they attempt to solve any problem or implement any task. In a sense, administrators are asking a fundamental question: "What is really involved here?" Unless administrators employ appropriate diagnosis in solving the problems of a school and carrying out their administrative tasks, they are not likely to be successful.

SETTING OBJECTIVES

Administrators who wish to be reasonably effective must set objectives which represent the outcomes that they want to achieve—the targets at which they are aiming.[16] The function of objectives is to give an individual or group a direction, purpose, and reason for action.

Objectives may be categorized as individual, group, or program. For example, if administrators are to be productive, they must set *individual* objectives for themselves. If the faculty or PTA are to capitalize on their potentialities, administrators should work with them in establishing *group* objectives. If various programs or services the school offers are to meet the needs of those they are designed to serve, administrators should work with the personnel involved in the program, helping them to define *program* objectives. Each individual, group, and program in the school should have well-defined short- and long-range objectives.

Administrators need to ask two basic questions in establishing objectives: "What should we be trying to accomplish?" and, "Have we clearly defined what we want to accomplish?" The first question is designed to stimulate thinking about what the objectives of an individual, group, or program should be. The second question is intended to focus efforts on the precise specification of objectives for an individual, group, or program. In essence, administrators, with the assistance of appropriate others associated with the school, should be trying to arrive at more appropriate and more sharply defined objectives that can be clearly communicated and subsequently serve as standards against which progress or achievement can be measured. (Goal setting is also discussed in chapters 2, and 20.)

DECISION MAKING

Administrators engage in decision making perhaps more often than in any other process. For example, in one study conducted by Harvey Brightman, when asked to report the amount of time they spent in interpersonal, informational, and decisional roles, principals noted that 50 percent of their time was devoted to decision-making activities.[17] In a related sense, Kenneth Leithwood noted,

> The bulk of educational administration theory would support an image of school administration as decision making. . . . Principals are faced with a continuing series of choices to be made. Their job is to make those choices that best suit the context in which they find themselves. Alternative courses of action must be weighed against the purposes they are to serve, the beliefs, values, abilities and expectations of those touched by the choice.[18]

Decision making is basically the process of choosing among alternatives. In most situations, two or more alternative courses of action exist; administrators must decide which alternative to pursue. Before making a decision, however, administrators should engage in diagnosis to better understand the nature of the situation calling for a decision and the alternatives available as well.[19] Then they should assess the advantages and disadvantages of each alternative and the probabilities of success in each case. During the process of reaching a decision, administrators should involve teachers, parents, students, central office supervisors, or others as appropriate, to capitalize on any special insights and expertise they may be able to contribute.

Once a decision has been made, administrators need to concentrate on other administrative processes such as planning, implementing, and coordinating the decision. For an extended discussion of decision making, see *School Leadership and Supervision: Important Concepts, Case Studies, and Simulations;* the remaining chapters of this text also provide many opportunities to examine and apply the process of decision making.[20]

PLANNING

Similar to decision making, planning partially overlaps into several other administrative processes. Much of the planning process occurs, however, after goals have been established and decisions made.

Planning is concerned primarily with the question of how a goal is to be achieved or a decision implemented.[21] Consideration of the following questions is involved:

1.	What needs to be done?	→	*Task definition.*
2.	Which resources are needed to do the job, and within which period of time?	→	*Definition of resource needs and time parameters.*
3.	Who is competent, interested, and available to do the job?	→	*Selection of personnel.*
4.	What responsibilities need to be assigned to whom?	→	*Definition and assignment of responsibility.*
5.	Which tasks and people need to be related to each other in some manner?	→	*Identification of coordination needs.*

6. Who should be in authority over whom?	→	*Specification of authority relationships.*
7. Who should supervise whom and in which areas?	→	*Specification of supervisory relationships.*
8. Who should communicate with whom and about what?	→	*Specification of communication relationships.*
9. Which standards determine effectiveness?	→	*Establishment of evaluation criteria.*

The process of planning should begin with a definition of the tasks or activities needed to achieve previously approved goals and decisions and should conclude with the determination of criteria used to evaluate the extent to which the goals are achieved, or the decisions successfully implemented. Intermediate steps include specifying authority, supervisory, and communication relationships between people, and defining the resources required to carry out specific tasks within a certain period of time.[22]

IMPLEMENTING

Once a plan or program has been designed, it must be implemented. Essentially, implementing involves administrators in the process of making sure that the plan is carried out as intended. This includes providing resources, assistance, and monitoring progress.

Even though many administrators may believe that once a program is planned, it is easily implemented, research indicates that program implementation is frequently less than ideal.[23] Generally this is a result of failure to consider adequately one or more of the questions raised in the discussion on planning. For example, William Kritek found that efforts to implement innovations typically failed because of goals that were too vague and ambitious, minimal planning to operationalize the innovation and to integrate it into the school, resources that were too limited, and failure to anticipate adequately and deal constructively with the developments that occurred after the innovation was introduced.[24]

To avoid problems regarding the implementation of a proposed program, William Pink indicated that as a program is developed several factors critical to its successful implementation should be addressed.[25] Failure to attend to the following summarized issues can jeopardize the impact of the proposed program:

1. *Leadership.* An individual at the central office or building level should have responsibility for the program and sufficient time to provide adequate leadership.
2. *Support.* The program must receive the support of key persons in the central office.
3. *Technical assistance.* Teachers and administrators must receive sufficient help to accomplish the proposed tasks.
4. *Staff Development.* When teachers and administrators are asked to do something different, they need focused and ongoing staff development which allows them to learn the desired behaviors.
5. *Materials.* Schools must be provided with the required materials prior to their need to use them in the program.
6. *Monitoring and Evaluation.* Plans for monitoring the implementation of the program, as well as the summative evaluation of the program, should be made prior to the beginning of the program.
7. *Time.* Adequate time must be provided for teachers and administrators to learn about and implement the program. For greatest impact, activities should be conducted during the school day and teachers involved in new initiatives should have adjusted teaching loads.
8. *Governance.* Involving the major actors at the school-level in programmatic decision making raises the likelihood that implementation will be successful.
9. *Funding.* Providing sufficient funding for both the personnel and support costs of program initiatives is critical to the subsequent impact of the efforts.[26]

Difficulties in implementation can also result from inadequate monitoring of progress and problems after the program has been introduced, incorrect diagnosis of problems, and inadequate efforts to resolve problems.[27] Fortunately, most of these difficulties can be avoided or reduced if the administrator anticipates them and takes corrective action before the problems become major. In anticipating the kinds of problems that could occur during implementation, administrators would do well to remember two of Murphy's famous laws: "Most things are more complicated than they initially appear to be," and "Most things take longer than originally anticipated."

COORDINATING

Coordination is perhaps one of the most discussed but least developed concepts in organization theory. In terms of definition, "coordination concerns the degree of functional articulation (or unity of effort) between various parts of an organization. Coordinating process, on the other hand, concerns the mechanisms through which the various component parts of an organization are articulated with one another, such as mutual adjustment, organizational rules and schedules, and group problem-solving/meetings."[28] Therefore, a well-coordinated organization is characterized by a high degree of coherence; various work activities are performed to supplement and complement one another and directed toward a common objective.[29]

A potential need for coordination exists whenever two or more people, activities, resources, and/or time schedules either operate in conjunction with each other or should operate in conjunction with one another. The need for coordination is particularly evident when personnel with different specializations work toward the same or similar objectives. For example, when guidance counselors, nurses, social workers, psychologists, and other pupil personnel specialists are working in the school, there is usually a need for coordination. All of these individuals, along with the teachers, are trying to help students; for total effectiveness, their efforts should be coordinated.

The process of coordinating should occur not only during the planning process but also as a plan or decision is being implemented. At this latter stage the blueprint for action starts to take form—people begin to perform tasks, use resources, and interact with each other, based on some kind of a time schedule. In many situations prior planning for a task or program may obviate the necessity for further coordination; yet in other instances, administrators may need to become actively involved in the process of coordinating after a program has been introduced.

For example, administrators may have to redefine roles so that they complement each other better. They may need to restructure tasks so that they do not conflict with or overlap each other; new lines of communication may need to be designated for better coordination of activities or use of resources; and time schedules may need to be rearranged so individuals or groups can work together more easily. In all of these activities, administrators are engaged in the process of coordinating. They are reorganizing people, tasks, resources, and time so that functions proceed more smoothly. As a result, administrators can increase the extent to which an activity or program is carried out efficiently and effectively.

DELEGATING

No administrator can effectively perform all of the various administrative functions and tasks within a school.[30] Therefore, some duties must (or at least, should) be delegated to other people. Because of financial constraints in hiring assistants or additional staff, administrators may be faced with the problem that there is no one to whom responsibilities can be delegated. In many situations, however, administrators do not delegate responsibilities to an assistant or another person on the staff simply because they either do not know how to delegate or have reservations about relinquishing some of their duties.

According to Carl Heyel, who has studied the latter problem, administrators may be reluctant to delegate responsibility to others when they should, for one or more of the following reasons:

1. They have a strong need to be involved in every aspect of administration and cannot bear to delegate any of their responsibilities to others.
2. They are concerned that others may begin to wonder if they are really capable of handling the job if they delegate some of the responsibilities to other people.
3. They are not confident that others will do good jobs if they delegate certain responsibilities; or at the least, administrators doubt whether others could do as good a job as they would in carrying out a task.
4. They have a strong need to be recognized as the leader in the organization and are concerned with the possibility that delegation of some of the responsibilities will necessitate the sharing of leadership recognition.
5. They are concerned that by delegating responsibility to someone else, they may be facilitating the advancement of that individual to the point at which the situation could become competitive.[31]

The extent to which an administrator may be influenced by one or more of the considerations suggested by Heyel can be determined only by objective self-analysis. Certainly many, if not most of these factors could affect an individual in a subconscious way difficult to ascertain. At any rate, it seems reasonable to assume that in many instances the lack of additional staff due to financial constraints is not the only factor which would account for the administrator's failure to delegate responsibility.

For some administrators, uncertainty about when or under which circumstances to delegate responsibility may also be a problem. Figure 3.4 presents four general guidelines which should be of assistance to an administrator.

In delegating a task or responsibility, administrators should ask themselves, "What would I want to know if my superior were delegating the same kind of responsibility to me?" To answer this question adequately, administrators should define in considerable detail the nature and scope of the responsibility being assigned, the degree of authority that the individual should be given over others, the extent to which there are supervisory responsibilities associated with the assignment, and the people with whom the individual should

Figure 3.4 When to Delegate Responsibility.

---

1. When someone else can do the task as well as or better than you can.

2. When you don't have the time to do the job or you have other important priorities.

3. When someone else could do the job adequately, if not as well, but at less expense.

4. When you are attempting to provide orientation and training to someone else who is preparing for a similar position.

---

communicate in carrying out the new assignment. As a result of carefully defining these factors, administrators can avoid, or at least minimize, uncertainty and unsatisfactory performance on the part of the person to whom an assignment has been delegated.

INITIATING

Administrators engage in the process of initiating when they reach the point at which they are ready to take some kind of action individually or with a group. School administrators attempt to initiate actions by other people in a variety of ways. They request, instruct, direct, command, motivate, or try to persuade others to initiate desired action or activity.[32] In selecting the manner in which they attempt to initiate action, administrators need to examine the assumptions they may be making about their authority and power, other people's perception and acceptance of that authority and power, and the kind of an initiating approach most likely to be successful in bringing about the desired results.[33] For example, are administrators merely assuming that they have the authority or power to direct, command, or instruct people to do what they want done in particular circumstances? Or has the authority or power on which they are basing their attempts to initiate action been explicitly delegated to them through school board action or directives from their superiors?

In addition to examining their own assumptions about whether they have actually been delegated the authority to initiate action on the part of other people, administrators should also attempt to ascertain the extent to which other people perceive and accept the fact that they do, indeed, possess such authority and power. Even though they may, in fact, validly derive their authority and power from the organizations in which they serve, administrators undoubtedly experience difficulty in initiating action if the people from whom they are attempting to elicit action do not accept this fact.

And finally, administrators need to consider all feasible alternative methods for initiating action. Although they may believe it is easier simply to issue directives, give commands, and instruct others what to do, there may be additional approaches to initiating action that are ultimately more successful, particularly in specific situations with certain types of people. For example, requesting or asking others to do something is frequently a productive approach to initiating action. Also, trying to persuade people of the value of taking a particular action is often desirable and may be essential.

Although some administrators may recoil at the notion of trying to persuade individuals to take action rather than directing them to do it, circumstances can arise in which only the former approach is viable, particularly if administrators' authority or power is lacking or rejected. In addition, if people are persuaded of the merits of taking certain actions, they may be more likely to perform these actions with greater commitment than if they are merely responding to the administrator's authority or power. In any case, administrators should seriously consider the advantages and disadvantages of the various approaches they might use in attempting to initiate action on the part of others.

COMMUNICATING

School administrators probably engage in communicating more often than any other process, with the possible exception of decision making. To persuade, instruct, direct, request, present, stimulate, or develop understanding, administrators must communicate. To communicate, they must deliver a message via a medium which reaches a receiver (another person or group) and registers a desired response, such as action or understanding.[34] Administrators need to recognize that information dissemination is not synonymous with communication. Communication means that a message not only was sent but also received and responded to in a way indicating that it was understood. Gerald Ubben and Larry Hughes proposed five questions which administrators can utilize to assess their communication techniques:

1. If the message was received, was it read [heard]?
2. If it was read [heard], was it understood?
3. If it was understood, was it understood in the right spirit?
4. If it was understood in the right spirit, will it be acted on in a positive manner?
5. How do you know?[35]

To illustrate the communication process, consider the following: An administrator may wish to bring to the faculty's attention that there has been too much noise in the hallways during the week, and that the professional staff should increase their efforts to keep noise to a minimum. This, then, is the message the administrator wants to deliver to the staff. In delivering the message, there are several different media for communication from which to choose. The administrator could write a memo, present the message over the public address system, announce it at a faculty meeting, or have an administrative assistant pass the word to teachers. Each of these communication media may possess advantages for delivering this particular message, depending on the administrator's skill in communicating, the type of group to whom the message is delivered, and the nature of the circumstances surrounding the message.

Actual transmission of the message by some means, however, is not the end of the communication process. The message also must register with the receivers, in this instance the faculty, before the communication can be judged to be effective. They must become aware, first, of the noise problem in the hallway, and second, that the administrator wants them to take action to reduce the noise level. If, after the message is delivered, the faculty is not any more aware of the noise problem and the administrator's expectation that they take action to reduce the level of noise in the hallways, the administrator has not communicated effectively. The administrator may have attempted to communicate, but unless the message has registered, communication has not really taken place.

Whether the faculty will take action to reduce noise in the hallway, depends, of course, on factors beyond whether the administrator has communicated effectively with them. The faculty may clearly understand what the administrator wants and yet not accept it. On the other hand, if the purpose of the administrator's communication was to initiate action on the part of the faculty, then the message has not been successfully communicated with them unless they take such action.

The communication process need not be initiated in only a formal sense. Informal communication channels provide opportunities for staff members to talk to each other. Given the isolated nature of teachers' work, these opportunities certainly do not occur as often as they should. Administrators, therefore, should encourage staff members to engage in professional dialogues and learn more about each other's ideas and strategies for improving teaching and learning. Thus, administrators and teachers should be encouraged to be interested in the work of others; this will lead to innovation and new ideas while still maintaining the managerial control over necessary decisions.

John Naisbitt, in his book *Megatrends,* indicated that most organizations are adopting a decentralized organization structure. Furthermore, he views the traditional downward flow of communication as being obsolete; rising to take its place will be "smaller, decentralized units . . . linking informally with one another, and therefore relying far less on formal structures."[36] Similarly, in reviewing the studies of effective organizations James DeConinck and Dale Level found that the intensity of informal communication was of an extraordinary nature.[37] They noted that administrators in effective organizations allowed time for " 'no-holds-barred communications,' where discussion is encouraged from all participants, the exact opposite of what was found in other organizations where people who had worked together for a long time relied only on written communication."[38]

Whether formal or informal, communicating is one of the most important administrative processes. By the very nature of their jobs, administrators communicate with a variety of people, including students, teachers, parents, and central office personnel, about a wide range of items during the course of a school year. Administrators' success in working with these people and in productively carrying out their other responsibilities is greatly influenced by the extent to which they are effective communicators.[39] Examples of the use of communication concepts are provided in later chapters.

WORKING WITH GROUPS

Most school administrators spend a considerable amount of their time working with various groups in different settings. Administrators interact with the faculty, the parent organization, and the student body, as well as with other smaller groups, ranging from student clubs and organizations to the individual departments or grade units within a school.[40] These groups differ in many respects, particularly in size and degree of organizational structure and purpose, but they all possess certain basic common characteristics which the administrator needs to recognize. These characteristics are presented in figure 3.5.[41]

Because most school administrators are aware of the formal characteristics of the groups with whom they have contact, the informal characteristics are the ones to which administrators need to become more sensitive. Kenneth Bettenhausen and J. Keith Murnighan noted that

> Ad hoc committees and special work teams force people who have no history of prior interaction to work on often poorly defined tasks. If group members proceed deliberately, testing the appropriateness of their scripts, they will spend considerable time "getting to know" one another and establishing a shared understanding of the group's mission and the actions that are appropriate for its performance. . . . This process should lead to effective group functioning, as research has indicated.

Figure 3.5 Common Characteristics of Most Groups.

Formal Characteristics	Informal Characteristics
1. A group is originally organized to accomplish a particular objective(s).	1. The objective(s) which the members of the group presently feel to be important may not be the same as the one(s) for which they were originally organized.
3. A group has an appointed or elected leader.	2. There is usually one or more individuals in a group to whom the members of the group look for informal leadership.
3. A group has formally defined roles and tasks.	3. A group generally develops norms and expectations for what constitutes appropriate behavior for its members and others who interact with the group.
4. A group has a prescribed and defined system of communication among its members and its leader.	4. An informal system of communication usually develops within a group which may not be readily apparent to those who are not accepted members of the group.

> If, however, new group members assume that everyone has similar scripts, they will respond quickly and confidently. If group members do have similar scripts, the group's interactions will proceed without incident. . . . If their scripts are not similar, the members may proceed in pluralistic ignorance until someone questions the appropriateness of the group's actions.[42]

Thus, in working with groups, if administrators proceed only on their knowledge of the formal characteristics of groups, real problems could result.

For example, administrators may assume that a group has a certain organizational objective, the original one for which it was organized, when in reality the group may have developed a different objective. Or administrators may assume that the appointed leader of a group, such as a department head, is the actual leader of the department, when in reality there is another individual in the department to whom the members actually look for leadership. In another situation, administrators may determine the tasks for a group to perform, but if they fail to understand group norms and expectations toward the accomplishment of these tasks, they may not be performed well or may not get done at all. Knowledge of the informal characteristics of a group can facilitate administrators' efforts with that group; lack of such knowledge can constitute a major handicap.[43]

In addition to being knowledgeable about the informal characteristics of a group, school administrators need to be competent in functioning as group leaders and in helping groups to work together effectively, since they are the appointed leaders in many situations.[44] How administrators perform as group leaders is influenced in large part by their own conception of how leaders should behave, and their perceptions of the needs of a group. Administrators who see their leadership role in working with the members of a group as that of instructing, directing, or ordering them, probably would tend to play a very dominant, perhaps authoritarian, leadership role. In response to this type of leadership, the behavior of the group may tend to be passive, restive, or perhaps hostile to administrators' efforts to lead.[45]

If, on the other hand, administrators see their leadership role as being consultants, resource persons, or facilitators of group discussion and decision making, they are more likely to work with groups as members than as the individuals in charge. Under this leadership there is apt to be greater participation on the part of the members and more group cohesion and esprit de corps.

In working with groups, school administrators need to be aware that when first formed most groups go through certain stages in their development; at their meetings they enact particular behavior characteristic of their stage. These various stages are described in figure 3.6.[46]

During the first two stages, the members of a group do not really function very well together, and the cause can be detected from the nature of the comments made. In the last two stages, group members begin to perform better as they develop greater purpose and focus, become better acquainted with each other, resolve major differences, and define more functional relationships.

Figure 3.6 Stages in Group Development.

---

1. *The "Groping" Stage.* It is characterized by comments such as "What are we supposed to be accomplishing?" "Who is supposed to do what?" "Who is really in charge here?"
2. *The Griping Stage.* This is a period during which the members of a group find it difficult to adjust to the task of the group or the role which has been assigned to them.
3. *The Consolidation Stage.* This is the stage during which efforts are made to develop group harmony and avoid conflict. Members of the group begin to be more comfortable with each other and their roles in the group.
4. *The Solidifying Stage.* The group is now functioning well, and all members are performing their roles and cooperating easily with each other.

As administrators interact with groups, they should attempt to behave in ways that help the group to work together cooperatively and to accomplish their objectives. These behaviors, revealed in a study of group leadership, are enumerated and identified as follows:

Group Leadership Behavior

1. Help members of the group to define their goals and delineate their problems.
2. Establish a cooperative, permissive atmosphere which puts the participants at ease so that they contribute their best thinking to the solution of the group's problems.
3. Utilize the various talents and knowledge of the members of the group in arriving at decisions.
4. Show a genuine regard and appreciation for the worth of each individual and a willingness to understand and accept each person's level of growth.
5. Enlist the help of outside resources. Don't always give answers but help to provide experiences through which teachers and lay groups can find their own answers.
6. Plan the procedures, the timing, and the situation so that the group members are comfortable, have sufficient time, and have opportunity to participate.
7. Allow sufficient time for group thinking so that the participants do not have too many hurdles to surmount at one time.
8. Practice the technique of acceptable group procedures by becoming a listener, teller, questioner, and silent partner as your leadership and expertness merge with the best interest of the group.
9. Instill in others the desire to belong, to participate, and to take responsibility for, and pride in, the work of the group.
10. Discover skills, competencies, interests, and abilities so that each individual, while taking part in group processes, gains the maximum security which results from having a part to play and a contribution to make.
11. Relinquish leadership to other members of the group when appropriate, but continue to serve as consultant and adviser, to clear obstacles, and revive flagging enthusiasm.
12. Provide materials and resources and make available research studies and data to aid the group in their work.

13. Evaluate yourself continually to see that your purposes are valid, that human relationships are observed, that the steps in group processes are followed, that you are not moving too fast for the group, and that the work of the group is in keeping with the overall program of the school.
14. Be sensitive to group techniques and to human relationships between teachers and administrators, and among teachers, administrators, and supervisors.[47]

The behavior of effective group leaders identified in the preceding enumeration need not be restricted to school administrators. These behaviors can be initiated by any member of a group and should be so encouraged by administrators. The important factor is not who enacts the behavior but that it is initiated by someone in the group and at the appropriate moment. Stimulating other people in the group to engage in leadership behavior may be the most important group process skill administrators can exercise.

EVALUATING

Evaluating represents one of the most important processes that school administrators can employ, but one which, unfortunately, seems to be among the least frequently utilized. Evaluation can be defined as the process of examining as carefully, thoroughly, and objectively as possible an individual, group, product, or program to ascertain strengths and weaknesses.[48] School administrators should engage in the evaluative process in relation to the following three areas: (1) evaluation of others, such as a teacher evaluation; (2) evaluation of a school product, process, or program; and (3) evaluation of self.

Observation suggests that school administrators spend the greatest proportion of their evaluation time focusing on assessment of staff and the least time on self-evaluation. In response to pressures for greater school and administrator accountability, it appears that administrators are spending more of their time on product, process, and program evaluation. However, most of these efforts could be characterized as unplanned, superficial, and sporadic. Despite notable exceptions to this criticism, in most schools there is virtually no carefully planned, in-depth attempt to evaluate the various programmatic aspects of the school on a regular basis.[49] And the same criticism could be made about administrators' attempts to engage in self-evaluation.

Although a lack of evaluation skills may act as a deterrent, perhaps the main barrier to more extensive evaluating is that it is potentially threatening to administrators. Despite this obstacle, administrators need to recognize that in the absence of carefully planned, in-depth evaluation in the three areas previously identified, little significant improvement is possible. For this reason then, the need for evaluation and specific ideas for engaging in evaluation are stressed throughout the book.

PROBLEM SOLVING

Problem solving can be thought of as a separate process or, perhaps more appropriately, as the effective utilization of most if not all of the administrative elements previously described. Whether or not administrators employ all of these administrative elements depends in most circumstances on the nature of the problem. Before most problems can be solved, administrators need to take the steps of identifying and diagnosing the problem, setting goals and making decisions; and they also need to plan, implement, initiate, communicate, and coordinate the action. Additionally, in many situations administrators need to delegate responsibilities before a problem can be resolved, and frequently their problem solving involves them with groups. Finally, before they can know whether the problem has been successfully resolved, they have to evaluate.

So in a real sense, problem solving is not a separate or unique process but a synthesis of many different but related steps or subprocesses. When problems are not solved, the difficulty can frequently be traced back to a failure to engage in or enact effectively one or more of the subprocesses.

Administrators differ in their approaches to problem solving.[50] Some administrators respond to a problem by immediately jumping at a solution, while others take considerable time to seek information enabling them to define more adequately the nature of the problem as a basis for deciding on possible alternative solutions. Administrative styles in problem solving also differ and can range from authoritarian to democratic to laissez-faire.[51]

While no one best approach to problem solving could cover every problem, circumstance, and individual, the effective problem solvers base their actions on the following principles, extracted from a review of the educational and social science literature:

1. Do not wait for problems to manifest themselves. Try to anticipate problems or identify potential problem areas which, if not given attention, may result in significant trouble.
2. When faced with a problem, seek more information about its causes, nature, and severity. Avoid leaping to quick or easy solutions.
3. Search for more than one or two alternative solutions to a problem. Avoid settling on the first possible solution that is apparent, or viewing any proposed solution as the only one possible.

4. Evaluate carefully the consequences—both positive and negative—of each of the alternative solutions under consideration.
5. Utilize the insights, perceptions, and assistance of relevant others throughout the problem-solving process. Avoid the assumption that administrators possess all the wisdom and/or expertise for solving a problem successfully.
6. Recognize that adopted solutions to a problem must be thoughtfully implemented and eventually evaluated. Evaluation is particularly important if future mistakes are to be avoided and effective problem-solving approaches utilized.

Successful problem solving is rarely easy. It usually requires perceptive anticipation, careful analysis, thorough planning, and the involvement of people who can offer useful information, ideas, and constructive assistance. There is no shortcut or easy way to successful problem solving.

A FINAL NOTE

By now it should be clear that the job of school administrators is a multi-faceted one composed of many tasks and different elements. While some tasks or elements may be more important than others, depending on the nature of a situation, administrators should attempt to master all of them so that when the need arises, they can respond competently. Administrators who can effectively perform the tasks and elements identified in this chapter should be in a good position to meet the problems and challenges confronting their schools.

Review and Learning Activities

1. Compare the job description for the principal in your district with the task areas identified in figure 3.1. To which extent are certain task areas not reflected in the job description? Why not?
2. Read the following case study. Then assume that you are the principal and indicate how you would use each of the basic elements of the administrative process described in the text; for example, problem identification to help avoid or resolve the problems explicitly and implicitly presented in the case study. If you believe that a basic element of the administrative process could not be used, explain why.

FACULTY MEETING AGENDA

It was 15 minutes before the faculty meeting was scheduled to begin, and the principal quickly reviewed his agenda for the meeting:

Faculty Meeting Agenda
November 5

I. Announcements
   A. The deadline for nine-week grades (Principal)
   B. United Fund Drive (Principal)
   C. Request from PTA concerning the need for greater teacher involvement (Principal)
   D. Reemphasis of the Superintendent's Bulletin concerning physical examinations for teachers (Principal)
   E. Deadline for teachers' dues (Chairman of the Faculty Social Committee)
II. Topics for Discussion
   A. Is there too much noise in the corridors?
   B. Are we assigning too much homework?

The principal thought to himself that it looked like a rather lengthy agenda, but perhaps the announcements wouldn't take too much time. He hoped that he and the faculty could soon get down to the real problems which seemed to be affecting the operation of the school. Anyway, there didn't seem to be any good way to limit the number of announcements, and they all seemed quite important. He had considered putting the information in a written bulletin to the teachers, but when he had tried this procedure in the past, many of the teachers had apparently failed to read the bulletins carefully, if at all.

The principal glanced over the agenda a final time. He had spent at least an hour in the early part of the afternoon making up the agenda, and he didn't think that he had missed anything. The agenda appeared to be ready to distribute to the teachers at the beginning of the meeting.

As he walked toward the room where the faculty meeting was to be held, he hoped that he could develop more faculty interest and participation than in the past. For some reason, the teachers always seemed to be rather apathetic. In fact, he could count on the fingers of one hand those teachers who ever took the initiative to contribute anything to the discussions in the faculty meetings. He realized that teachers were often tired at the end of the day, but there should be some way to get them more involved. He felt that the topics to be covered during this afternoon's meeting were very important, as the hallways had been particularly noisy this week, and he had received several complaints from parents about the amount of homework being assigned. These were problems that affected every teacher in the school, and he certainly hoped that the faculty would respond with concern and involvement.

[For additional case studies that can be related to other concepts presented in the text, see Richard Gorton, *School Leadership and Supervision: Important Concepts, Case Studies, and Simulations* 3d ed. (Dubuque, Iowa: Wm. C. Brown Company Publishers.]

Notes

1. The following major sources of ideas were used in the development of figure 3.1: Robert S. Fisk, "The Task of Educational Administration," in *Administrative Behavior in Education,* ed. Roald F. Campbell and Russell T. Gregg (New York: Harper and Row, 1957), chap. 8; Jack A. Culbertson, Curtis Henson, and Ruel Morrison, eds. *Performance Objectives for School Principals,* (Berkeley, Calif.: McCutchan Publishing, 1974); Richard A. Gorton and Kenneth McIntyre, *The Effective Principal* (Reston, Va.: National Association of Secondary School Principals, 1978); Donald Walters, *Perceptions of Administrative Competencies.* (ERIC Report Ed–172–361); in addition, more recent discussions on administrative tasks may be found in *Effective School Principals: A Proposal for Joint Action by Higher Education, States, and School District* (Atlanta, Ga.: Southern Regional Education Board, 1986); Linda Grace, Robert Buser, and Dean Stuck, "What Works and What Doesn't: Characteristics of Outstanding Administrators," *NASSP Bulletin* (November 1987): 72–76; *Principal Selection Guide* (Washington, D.C.: Office of Educational Research and Improvement, 1987); and Karolyn J. Snyder, *Competency Development for Principals.* (ERIC Report Ed–279–067).

2. William L. Rutherford et al., *A New Perspective on the Work of Managers.* (ERIC Report Ed–250–812), 1983; and Harry Mintzberg, *The Nature of Managerial Work* (New York: Harper and Row, 1973).

3. For a useful discussion on time management, see James W. Guthrie and Rodney J. Reed, *Educational Administration and Policy: Effective Leadership for American Education* (Englewood Cliffs, N.J.: Prentice-Hall, 1987), 218–23.

4. Richard L. Andrews and Jill T. Hearne, "How Principals Perceive Their Jobs: A Comparison of High School, Middle School and Elementary School Principals," *National Forum of Educational Administration and Supervision Journal* 5, no. 2 (1988–89).

5. Henry Fayol, *General and Industrial Management,* trans. Constance Storrs (London: Pitman, 1949).

6. Luther Gulick and L. Urwick, eds., *Papers on the Science of Administration* (New York: Institute of Public Administration, Columbia University, 1937), 13; and Robert Owens, *Organizational Behavior in Education* (Englewood Cliffs, N.J.: Prentice-Hall, 1981). Also see *Principal Selection Guide,* (Washington, D.C.: Office of Educational Research and Improvement, June 1987).

7. P. C. Dutweiler, "Changing the Old Ways," *Journal of Research and Development in Education* (Winter 1989): 7–12.

8. Richard A. Gorton, *School Leadership and Supervision: Important Concepts, Case Studies, and Simulations* 3d ed. (Dubuque, Iowa: Wm. C. Brown Company Publishers, 1987).

9. Arthur Blumberg and William Greenfield, *The Effective Principal: Perspectives on School Leadership* 2d ed. (Boston: Allyn & Bacon, 1986), 11.

10. Kent Peterson, "Vision and Problem Finding in Principals' Work: Values and Cognition in Administration," *Peabody Journal of Education* (1987): 87–106.

11. Ibid., 90. For an additional discussions of problem solving, see M. Stager and K. A. Leithwood, "Cognitive Flexibility and Inflexibility in Principals' Problem Solving," *Alberta Journal of Educational Research* (September 1989): 217–36; and R. A. McWhirt, J. S. Reynolds, and C. M. Achilles, "You Can't Cure It If You Don't Know You Have It," *National Forum of Applied Educational Research Journal* 2 (1989/90): 35–41.

12. R. B. McPherson, R. L. Crowson, and N. J. Pitner, *Managing Uncertainty: Administrative Theory and Practice in Education* (Columbus, Ohio: Merrill, 1986), 273.

13. Harvey J. Brightman, "Improving Principals' Performance through Training in the Decision Sciences," *Educational Leadership* (February 1984): 51–56.

14. Jerry J. Herman, "External and Internal Scanning Identifying Variables that Affect Your School," *NASSP Bulletin* (November 1989): 48–52.

15. Philip J. Runkel, Richard A. Schmuck, Jane H. Arends, and Richard P. Francisco, *Transforming the School's Capacity for Problem Solving* (Eugene, Oreg.: Center for Educational Policy and Management, 1979).

16. Gerald C. Ubben and Larry W. Hughes, *The Principal: Creative Leadership for Effective Schools* (Boston: Allyn & Bacon, 1987), chap. 5; and W. James Popham, "Two-Plus Decades of Educational Objectives," *International Journal of Educational Research* 11, no. 1 (1987): 31–41.

17. Brightman, "Improving Principals' Performance, 52.

18. Kenneth A. Leithwood, "Differences in Problem-Solving Processes Used by Moderately and Highly Effective Principals" (Paper presented at the annual meeting of the American Educational Research Association, San Francisco, 1986, ERIC Report ED–018–484), 3.

19. I. L. Janis, *Crucial Decisions: Leadership in Policymaking and Crisis Management* (New York: Free Press, 1989).

20. Gorton, *School Leadership and Supervision,* chap. 1. See also, Jon Saphier, Tom Bigda-Peyton, and Geoff Pierson, *How to Make Decisions that Stay Made* (Alexandria, VA.: Association for Supervision and Curriculum Development, 1989).

21. William Cunningham, *Systematic Planning for Educational Change* (Palo Alto, Calif.: Mayfield Publishing, 1982). See also, Jerry J. Herman, "A Vision for the Future: Site-Based Strategic Planning," *NASSP Bulletin* (September 1989): 23–27.

22. The following references provide interesting discussions regarding educational planning: William D. McInerney, "Participation in Educational Planning at the School District Level," *Planning & Changing* (Winter 1985): 206–15; Linda S. Lotto and David L. Clark, "Understanding Planning in Educational Organizations," *Planning & Changing* (Spring 1986): 9–18; and Robert H. Beach and William D. McInerney, "Educational Planning Models and School District Practice," *Planning & Changing* (Fall 1986): 180–91.

23. William J. Kritek, "Lessons from the Literature on Implementation," *Educational Administration Quarterly* (Fall 1976): 86–102.

24. Ibid.

25. William T. Pink, "Facilitating Change at the School Level: A Missing Factor in School Reform," *The Urban Review* 18, no. 1 (1986): 19–30.

26. Ibid., 20–22.

27. Gorton, *School Leadership and Supervision,* 149–52.

28. Joseph L. C. Cheng, "Organizational Coordination, Uncertainty, and Performance: An Integrative Study," *Human Relations* (October 1984): 832.

29. Ibid., 833.

30. R. Rees, "Delegation: A Fundamental Management Process," *Education Canada* (Summer 1988): 26–32.

31. Carl Heyel, *Organizing Your Job in Management* (New York: American Management Association, 1960), 126–35. For further guidelines in delegating, see Richard Brown, "Delegating Authority," In *Encyclopedia of School Administration and Supervision,* ed. Richard A. Gorton, Gail T. Schneider, and James C. Fisher (Phoenix, Ariz.: Oryx Press, 1988), 89.

32. Gorton, *School Leadership and Supervision,* chap. 3.

33. For an excellent description of principals engaging in the process of initiating, see Blumberg and Greenfield, *The Effective Principal.*

34. Gorton, *School Leadership and Supervision,* chap. 2.

35. Ubben and Hughes, *The Principal,* 79–85.

36. John Naisbitt, *Megatrends* (New York: Warner Books), 190.

37. James DeConinck and Dale Level, "An Analysis of Current Perspectives of the Influence of Communication in Successful Organizations," *The Bulletin* (March 1987): 7–11.

38. Ibid., 9.

39. Gorton, *School Leadership and Supervision,* chap. 2.

40. James L. Doud, "The K–8 Principal in 1988," *Principal* (January 1989): 6–12.

41. On formal characteristics, see W. W. Charters, Jr., "An Approach to the Formal Organization of the School," in *Behavioral Science and Educational Administration,* ed Daniel F. Griffiths (Chicago: University of Chicago Press, 1964), 243–44. For informal characteristics, see Lawrence Iannaconne in the same source, 233–42.

42. Kenneth Bettenhausen and J. Keith Murnighan, "The Emergence of Norms in Competitive Decision-Making Groups," *Administrative Science Quarterly* (1985): 369.

43. For additional discussion of the informal characteristics of a group and the effects of these characteristics on the operation of the school, see Gorton, *School Leadership and Supervision,* 78–84.

44. For a useful discussion on working with groups, see Patricia J. Watson, "Effective Task Forces: Getting a Quality Product in Minimum Time," *Planning & Changing* (Winter 1987): 131–45.

45. Kurt Lewin et al., "Patterns of Aggressive Behavior in Experimentally Created Social Climates," *Journal of Social Psychology* 10 (1939): 271–99.

46. Adapted from material developed by Russell D. Robinson, professor of educational leadership, University of Wisconsin-Milwaukee.

47. Adapted from a list of leadership behavior performed by supervisors in a group setting. See *Group Processes in Supervision* (Washington, D.C.: Association for Supervison and Curriculum Development, 1958), 128.

48. Evaluation is emphasized throughout the book. However, the following references may provide supplementary sources of ideas: *Program Evaluation Kit* 2d ed. (Newbury Park, Calif.: Sage Publications 1987); *Standards for Evaluation of Educational Programs* (New York: McGraw-Hill Company, 1980); *Evaluating Teaching Effectiveness* 2d ed. (Newbury Park, Calif.: Sage Publications, 1984); and *The Personnel Evaluation Standards: How to Assess Systems for Evaluating Educators* (Newbury Park, Calif.: Sage Publications, 1989).

49. Robert E. Slavin, "PET and the Pendulum: Faddism in Education and How to Stop It," *Kappan* (June 1989): 752–58.

50. Keith A. Leithwood and Mary Stager, "Expertise in Principals' Problem Solving," *Educational Administration Quarterly* (May 1989): 126–61.

51. Jacob W. Getzels, James Lipham, and Roald Campbell, *Educational Administration as a Social Process* (New York: Harper & Row, 1968); Arthur Blumberg and William Greenfield, *The Effective Principal: Perspectives on School Leadership,* 2d. ed. (Boston: Allyn & Bacon, 1986); James W. Guthrie and Rodney J. Reed, *Educational Administration and Policy: Effective Leadership for American Education* (Englewood Cliffs, N.J.: Prentice-Hall, 1986), 199–208; and Joel L. Burdin, ed., *School Leadership: A Contemporary Reader* (Newbury Park, Calif.: Sage Publications, 1989).

4

. . . . .

The School Administrator
Roles, Expectations, and Social Factors

During a school year, administrators perform a number of different roles.[1] At one point they may act as instructional leaders, at another point as conflict mediators, and at a later date they may need to perform different roles. In each situation, the decision to adopt a particular role is greatly influenced by the following aspects: (1) the administrators' own needs and attitudes, (2) expectations of important others, and (3) various social factors.[2] In this chapter, the major roles which might be performed by school administrators are presented first, followed by a discussion of the various expectations and social factors that may influence an administrator's role behavior.

MAJOR ROLES OF THE SCHOOL ADMINISTRATOR

There is no shortage of opinions, proposals, or conceptualizations regarding the role of the school administrator.[3] A review of the literature on the subject reveals that, at one time or another, six major roles have been proposed: (1) manager, (2) instructional leader, (3) disciplinarian, (4) human relations facilitator, (5) evaluator, and (6) conflict mediator. While it is unlikely that administrators would be required to enact all six of these roles simultaneously, they should attempt to become competent in each role so that they can perform it effectively when and if the situation requires.

The following summary descriptions provide administrators with a brief introduction to each of the roles; other chapters of the book present related discussions of these roles, and references are listed at the end of this chapter for further study.

MANAGER

In the eyes of many people, school administrators are first and foremost managers. The position originated in the 1800s based on this general concept, and though other roles have since been proposed, the concept of the administrator as manager has persisted.[4] Recent literature pertaining to the educational reform movement has focused on the debate regarding the managerial versus instructional foci of school administrators' work.[5] This debate centers largely on the self-expectations of school administrators in performing their tasks and job functions. For example, as Larry Cuban noted in discussing the role of school principals,

> For those principals who imagine a direction for their schools, who wish to accomplish certain aims with students beyond those mandated by the district, the managerial and instructional roles intersect. However, for those principals whose orientation is to accomplish the school district's goals, who see their job as primarily maintaining the existing arrangements, the managerial and instructional roles are largely separate roles.[6]

As managers, school administrators are expected to procure, organize, and coordinate both physical and human resources so that the goals of the organization can be attained effectively.[7] Their main role is to develop or implement policies and procedures resulting in the efficient operation of the school. More specifically, the "administrative tasks associated with carrying out district and school policies, such as planning, gathering and dispersing information, budgeting, hiring, scheduling classes, grouping of students, completing reports, dealing with conflict between varied participants, and maintaining the building, constitute this role."[8] In fact, the popularized notion of a manager is one who keeps things running smoothly.

The term *manager* conveys a negative connotation for certain individuals.[9] Many administrators, in particular, do not like to think of themselves as managers; the term *leader,* which is discussed later, is perceived by them as a more attractive appellation. However, school administrators should recognize that when different people and resources are brought together in one location (in this case, a school building or district), there is a need for someone to organize, schedule, and coordinate the entire operation. That someone at the building level has typically been the school administrator.

Consequently, rather than resisting their role as managers, school administrators should accept and implement the role in such a way that the school is efficiently managed, yet they are in a position to be available for other role options. By successfully performing their role as managers, administrators can help others to accomplish tasks and goals; in the process they can generate a more positive attitude toward their contribution to their school. The school administrator's role as manager is further discussed in other chapters, particularly in chapter 6 on budget and plant management.

INSTRUCTIONAL LEADER

The role of the school administrator as an instructional leader has had a long history.[10] Although the school administrator was at first more a manager than a leader, it was not long before the instructional leadership dimensions of the position began to be emphasized in the educational literature and at various professional meetings which administrators attended.[11] It is probably safe to say that leadership, often referred to as educational leadership, or instructional leadership, has been widely accepted by administrators as the raison d'etre for the continued existence of their position at the building level.

One of the problems in connection with the proposed role of the school administrator as instructional leader is that people define the role in different ways and with varying degrees of precision, thereby creating confusion for administrators expected to carry out the role.[12] For example, to some, the principalship is a leadership position, and any activities in which the principal engages to improve instruction are leadership activities. To others, there are certain types of activities or actions, such as classroom observation, in which principals are expected to participate if they are to function as instructional leaders. Compounding the problem is the fact that principals are frequently encouraged to be instructional leaders and yet they may not be perceived by teachers as possessing the subject matter expertise necessary for helping them to improve.[13] In addition, the concept of instructional leadership has generally not been defined beyond such generic functions as protecting instructional time, coordinating curriculum, and monitoring student progress; thus, school administrators who desire to become instructional leaders are frequently uncertain as to how to fulfill this role.[14] These problems and other aspects of the role of the administrator as an instructional leader are explored in chapter 11.

DISCIPLINARIAN

The importance of the disciplinary role of school administrators has been revealed by several studies. For example, in Gallup poll after Gallup poll teachers and parents have indicated that discipline is one of the top five problems facing public schools.[15] Students also tend to see school administrators as disciplinarians (although there is some doubt as to whether they approve of this role).[16]

On the other hand, principals tend to reject the idea that being disciplinarians is their major role, and frequently assign this responsibility to assistant principals. However, research has shown that an increasing number of assistant principals and vice-principals also seem reluctant to accept the disciplining of students as the primary responsibility of their position.[17] Even when the responsibility for student discipline is delegated to assistant principals, they need to keep principals apprised of chronic or unusual problems because suspension or expulsion cases are usually assigned to the principals who are ultimately responsible for solving these problems.[18]

Generally, school administrators resist or reject the role of disciplinarian because of the negative connotation of the term and because the duties associated with the role are frequently frustrating, irritating, and unpleasant to perform. The term, *disciplinarian,* traditionally has implied one who punishes someone else; in this case, usually a student.

Punishing students can be a very vexing and frustrating job, as anyone who has had to assume this responsibility knows. Although modern concepts of discipline emphasize more positive approaches to improving student conduct, the fact remains that working with student misbehavior problems represents a difficult assignment with few rewards; this may explain administrators' negative reactions to the role. Nevertheless, because student misconduct still constitutes a major problem in many schools, important reference groups associated with the school will probably continue to expect the principal and/or an assistant to play the role of disciplinarian. This role is discussed in considerable depth in chapters 13 and 14.

FACILITATOR OF HUMAN RELATIONS

The human relations role of the school administrator originated in the early 1920s and was given initial impetus by the publication of a book by Mary Parker Follett entitled *Creative Experience.*[19] In this book and in her other writings, Follett emphasized the importance of administrators' concentrating as much on meeting the personal needs of employees and developing cooperative and harmonious relationships among them, as on achieving the productivity goals of the organization. Later studies by Elton Mayo provided empirical support for Follett's approach, and books by Daniel Griffiths and others attempted to incorporate concepts of human relations into the theory of school administration.[20]

School administrators should, of course, practice good human relations in all aspects of their jobs, and in relationships with people generally. However, the two areas in which this becomes particularly important are in the developing of high staff morale and a humane school environment. The specific human relations skills involved in achieving these two goals are identified in the chapter on staff relations.

EVALUATOR

Increased emphasis on school accountability has placed added importance on the role of school administrators as evaluators.[21] A large number of parents and other members of the public are apparently no longer satisfied with the opinion of administrators that everything is satisfactory with the schools; the public wants to see evidence of effectiveness or attempts to improve situations.[22]

To provide evidence of effectiveness or improvement, school administrators need to perform the role of evaluator. This role in most cases tends to center on the evaluation of staff and on program evaluation. In addition, administrators may be involved in the evaluation of student performance, as well. In many of these situations administrators need to utilize the expertise of others to help with the evaluation process.

Essentially the role of evaluator involves the following aspects:

- Clarifying the evaluation request and responsibilities and determining who should be involved in the evaluation.
- Developing a management plan.
- Establishing evaluation criteria and selecting methods of evaluation.
- Dealing with political, ethical, and interpersonal aspects of evaluation.
- Collecting, analyzing and interpreting data.
- Drawing conclusions and developing recommendations.
- Reporting findings and implementing recommendations.
- Evaluating the evaluation.[23]

The importance of evaluation and specific evaluation approaches are discussed throughout the text. See also an excellent text on evaluation by Edward F. DeRoche, *An Administrator's Guide for Evaluating Programs and Personnel* (Boston: Allyn & Bacon).

CONFLICT MEDIATOR

The role of school administrators as conflict mediator is of recent origin. Although administrators have always been faced with the need to adjust differences, it was not until the mid-1960s that the need to mediate conflict became a major aspect of the school administrators' role. Since that time they have been confronted with, among others, conflicts associated with student disruption, teacher militancy, and parental and community demands for greater involvement in school decision making.

At the present time, conflict resolution comprises a major part of the administrators' job. In the role of conflict resolver, school administrators act basically as mediators.[24] They attempt to secure all of the facts in a situation, as well as the perceptions each party to the dispute has of one another and of the issues in conflict. Generally, the administrator's major goal is for each side to recognize some validity in the other party's position, so that compromise can take place and the conflict can be resolved. Most studies of organizational roles have shown that ineffectiveness and inefficiency are due not so much to conflicts which are "out in the open and understood as to those that are unspoken and misunderstood."[25] As administrators work with all parties to a dispute, whether students, teachers, parents, or others, they need to develop an understanding that neither side is totally right, and that some give and take is necessary before the conflict can be resolved.

When one views the turmoil surrounding education today, it is clear that the role of conflict mediator is an essential one for the school administrator. For an extended discussion of conflict and the role of the school administrator as a conflict mediator, see Gorton.[26]

ROLE VARIABLES INFLUENCING AN ADMINISTRATOR'S BEHAVIOR

For every administrative position in an effectively managed organization, written job descriptions or policy statements emanate from a governing board; these embody the formal expectations of the organization. In addition, in every organization there are usually implicit, frequently unexpressed expectations for administrators' behavior; these originate with the various individuals or groups with whom they come into contact. Together, both sets of expectations comprise a behavioral definition of the role which different individuals or groups—both formal and informal—believe administrators should perform in a particular situation. As Jacob Getzels has observed, "The expectations define for the actor [administrator], whoever he may be, what he should or should not do as long as he is the incumbent of the particular role."[27] The expectations also serve as "evaluative standards applied to an incumbent in a position," and therefore can represent a powerful source of potential influence on any administrator's behavior.[28]

The Getzels model hypothesizes that the behavior of administrators is also affected by their own attitudes toward the roles they should play.[29] These attitudes constitute administrators' self-expectations and may be more important than the expectations of others in determining the roles they take in a given set of circumstances. For example, if administrators feel that they should play the role of manager, they may become involved in activities designed to bring about a more efficiently operated school, despite the contrary expectations for their role held by other individuals or groups.

Thus, administrative behavior results from two basic elements: (1) institutional-role expectations which emanate from the normative dimension of the organization; and (2) individual personality and need dispositions,

Figure 4.1 Major Factors Which Influence an Individual's Behavior.

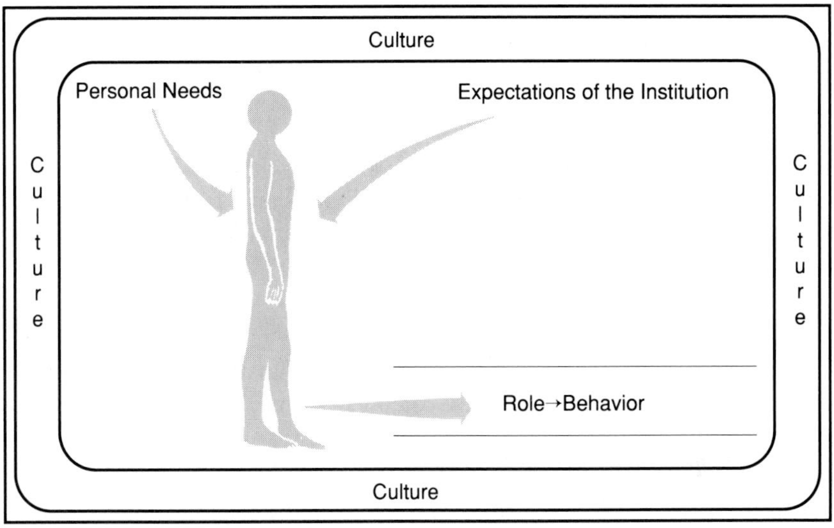

which together constitute the personal dimension. As James Lipham, Robb Rankin, and James Hoeh noted, "To understand, predict, or control observed behavior in a social system, one must understand the nature and interaction of these two basic dimensions."[30] Figure 4.1, based on the Getzels model, illustrates the major dimensions and role variables that can impact on an administrator.

In the following sections the potential effect of school administrators' personal dispositions on their role, the expectations of important reference groups, and the impact of certain social forces are discussed.

PERSONAL VARIABLES

Administrators possess certain needs, values, and attitudes which potentially can influence their role behavior.[31] These can perhaps be best illustrated by the thoughts expressed by several administrators, along with the attitude or value orientation each represents:

Personal Thoughts

Attitude or Value

1. "I wonder about the risks involved in pursuing this particular role."

   Risk orientation.

2. "If Hank recommends it, I am   *Attitude toward people.*
   sure that it is a role that needs
   to be performed."

3. "I question whether adopting a   *Educational philosophy.*
   far out innovation like the open
   classroom is good education."

4. "This is the type of role that   *Concern about status.*
   an educational leader would
   adopt."

5. "It seems to me that if I adopt   *Concern about authority and*
   this role, I can no longer call   *control.*
   the shots in that area."

These five examples, of course, are merely illustrative of a wide range of possible values and attitudes that could have a major influence on the type of roles administrators adopt.

As Lipham, Rankin, and Hoeh have perceptively observed,

> In the first place, values serve as a perceptual screen for the decision maker, affecting both the awareness of problems and the screening of relative information. Second, values affect the extent to which the possible alternatives will be congruent with the value systems of those who will be affected by a decision. Finally, values serve as the criteria against which higher-order goals are assessed and projected, since the principal serves simultaneously as a values analyst, values modifier, and values witness in the process of making decisions.[32]

Since administrators probably cannot avoid the influence of values and attitudes in making decisions about roles, they should attempt to become more aware of the ethical nature of those values. This proposition is deeply seated in the literature on administrative behavior. For example, Chester Barnard in his classic work, *The Functions of the Executive,* argued that the ethos of an organization and its success depended in part on the moral character of the chief executive.[33] And Robert Stout in discussing Barnard's perspective indicated that "administrative responsibility becomes manifest in action (or inaction as well), driven by personal codes of conduct or moral status."[34] In a corresponding manner, Carl Ashbaugh and Katherine Kasten interviewed school principals to evoke their reflections on decisions they viewed as troublesome or difficult and to determine the convictions salient at the time the decisions were made.[35] Their findings show that moral or ethical bases frequently undergird principals' decision-making process and underscore the complex nature of the influence of values in determining role behavior.

A related problem in regard to the influence of attitudes and values in decision making about roles is the extent to which they can be a dominant factor in compromising the objectivity of the decision maker and thereby short-circuiting the decision-making process. For example, the administrator who has the attitude that, "If Hank recommends it, I am sure that it is a role which needs to be performed," is revealing a strong, positive attitude or bias toward the person, Hank. Because of the administrator's attitude in this situation, the administrator will probably find it difficult to be objective about evaluating Hank's recommendation or any competing alternative. As a result, the administrator may not engage thoroughly in the various steps of the decision-making process, which should include identifying and evaluating objectively all possible alternatives.

Although the administrator's attitude in the preceding example is a positive one—at least toward Hank, in another situation involving someone else it may be negative, with the same potential results of compromised objectivity and a superficial decision-making process. Of course, it is not axiomatic that such a decision about roles is a poor one, and it is recognized that the press of time on an administrator may require a shortcut through the decision-making process. However, it is because of the bias of the decision maker and such shortcuts that poor decision making frequently results. Therefore, administrators should make every effort to become more aware of their attitudes and values and how these influence the decisions they make about the roles they should perform. Administrators must reduce that influence when it could compromise their objectivity or result in a less thorough and thoughtful decision-making process.

REFERENCE GROUPS' EXPECTATIONS FOR THE SCHOOL ADMINISTRATOR'S ROLE

If school administrators are to make wise decisions about the roles they should adopt in particular situations, they need to be knowledgeable about the expectations held by various reference groups. These groups include students, teachers, parents, and others who may be associated with the school. Figure 4.2 identifies a number of groups who hold expectations for the role of the school administrator.

While it may be impossible for school administrators to become knowledgeable about the role expectations held by all the different groups associated with the school, it would appear essential that they become so in the case of four of the groups with whom they have direct contact: students, teachers, parents, and the school administrator's superiors. Although the specific expectations of any of these groups may vary according to the nature of the groups and the local situation, research studies have provided useful information to help the administrators develop an understanding of the general orientation of these groups. (The following sections are presented so that an

Figure 4.2 Reference Groups Who Hold Expectations for the Role of the School Administrator.

At the Building Level

1. Teachers and other members of the faculty
2. Other administrative personnel in the school
3. Students
4. Clerical and maintenance staff

At the District Level

1. The superintendent
2. Central office administrative/supervisory staff
3. The school board
4. Administrators in other schools

Local and State Groups

1. Parents
2. Parents' organizations
3. Social, labor, and business organizations
4. State department of public instruction
5. Professional organizations
6. Accreditation agencies

---

administrator may better understand the expectations of groups; no inference should be drawn that administrators must conform to those expectations or that all the people in a specific reference group hold identical expectations.)

STUDENTS' EXPECTATIONS FOR THE SCHOOL ADMINISTRATOR'S ROLE

Many students have probably never even thought about the role of school administrators, while others may possess well-conceived ideas about what they should be doing in the school. In many instances, students' comments are often highly descriptive and insightful about administrators' roles.

A review of the research on students' expectations for the role of the school administrator shows that this area of inquiry has not attracted much interest from researchers. However, some indication of students' expectations can be gleaned from a study conducted by the Far West Laboratory for Educational Research and Development and reported by Carrie Kojimoto.[36] The students when interviewed indicated that helpful school administrators (1) create and maintain a safe and orderly environment; (2) enhance students' self-esteem, sense of responsibility, and ability to get along with others; and (3) help students grow academically. Generally students indicated that they expect school administrators to be highly visible. Circulating frequently connoted to students that the administrator knows what is going on in the school and is interested in what students are doing. School administrators (specifically principals) who remain in their offices, were characterized as unfriendly, lazy, and uninterested.

In addition to high visibility, students expressed a clear preference for principals who counsel and mediate, who actually listen to their ideas and evaluate that information before meting out punishments. Such administrators conveyed to students a message that safety and order were not their only concerns. Thus, qualities that further distinguished a good principal were "nice" and "caring."

Finally, and probably of most importance, students spoke highly of school administrators who contributed to their academic growth. When students considered one principal more helpful than another, it was often because of the praise and compliments paid them in their academic pursuits.

The importance of administrators' personal relationships with students was also verified by the National Study of School Evaluation, which found that the most prevalent concern of students regarding administrators was an uncertainty that administrators were interested in them as individuals.[37] These findings may be interpreted in various ways, but one point is certain: school administrators need to become more visible to students if they are to be perceived as performing an important role in the school.

TEACHERS' EXPECTATIONS FOR THE SCHOOL ADMINISTRATOR'S ROLE

Perhaps more than any other reference group, teachers have the opportunity for interaction with school administrators and are, therefore, in a better position to develop expectations for their role. As a consequence, research studies on teachers' expectations for the role of the school administrator have been numerous. These studies, in general, indicate four major expectations that teachers hold for the administrator's role:

1. **The school administrator should support teachers on issues and problems of student discipline.** Several studies have documented this particular expectation of teachers. Arthur Blumberg and William Greenfield, for example, noted that teachers often demand unwavering principal support in matters of discipline.[38] In a similar vein, Joseph Blase discovered that a significant teacher expectation focused on the extent to which school administrators stood behind teachers in matters involving discipline; and Edwin Bridges reported that the administrators' support of teachers in regard to their problems with pupils was more valued by teachers than anything else they could do.[39] Further, a study by Robert Brumbaugh and John Skinkus, as well as periodic surveys of teachers, provides additional evidence of the importance to teachers of their principal's support in situations involving student discipline.[40]

Studies on teachers' expectations reveal that teachers believe it is less crucial that school administrators be strong disciplinarians (although this may be important) than that they back or support the teachers regardless of the nature of their approach to discipline. However, meeting this latter expectation is not always possible or even desirable in certain situations, as further discussed in the chapter on student misbehavior.

2. School administrators should treat teachers as professional colleagues with different but equal roles, rather than as subordinates in a bureaucratic relationship. Teachers have improved their educational and professional status in recent years; and research studies have long pointed out that many do not recognize the traditional superior-subordinate relationship that existed in the past between the administrator and teachers.

Jack Lam, for example, conducted a study to examine determinants of teacher professionalism and found that mutual support was crucial to perceptions of their professional role. He concluded teachers expect school administrators to play a critical role in (1) increasing teachers' tendency toward engagement with their school activities; (2) improving teacher job performance by assisting with student issues and eliminating trivial paperwork; (3) bolstering teachers' professional commitment; and (4) increasing social satisfaction.[41]

Charles Bidwell's and Joseph Blase's studies discovered that teachers expect school administrators to set clear and fair standards for teachers' behavior.[42] Francis Chase's research revealed that teachers expected school administrators to show understanding and respect for their competency and work, and Russell Sharpe noted that teachers expected school administrators to communicate with them frequently and to refrain from curtailing their individual initiative or freedom.[43] These researchers' findings continue to be confirmed by opinion polls and articles in teacher association journals.[44]

In summary, the main implication of these studies is that teachers expect to be recognized as professionals and to be treated accordingly. To this end, Ann Lieberman noted that the current interest in improving teacher professionalism offers a real opportunity to change the teaching profession in profound ways. The possibilities she noted include:

1. Building collegiality among teachers who have long been isolated from one another.
2. Providing greater recognition and status for teachers who have suffered from mythological and oversimplified definitions of their work.
3. Enlarging the reward structure to allow for choice, renewal, and opportunities to grow and learn—for teachers as well as students.
4. Building a school structure that permits autonomy, flexibility, and responsibility, and provides resources for teaching and learning.
5. Building a professional culture in the schools that broadens the way they function and enables them to become more sensitive to the communities they serve.[45]

Each of these challenges implies expectations for school administrators if they are to be accomplished.

3. **School administrators should provide a meaningful opportunity for teachers to participate in school decision making and should include a significant role for teachers in the making of final decisions about those activities directly affecting them.** All of the studies on teacher expectations point to the desire of teachers for a significant role in school decision making. This desire for involvement in decision making is not new. Chase, for instance, found that teachers expected the school administrator to provide opportunities for their active participation in curriculum development, determination of grouping and promotion, and control of pupils.[46] In addition, teachers emphasized that if they were to serve on a committee, the committee must have the power to make decisions rather than mere recommendations on questions already decided by the principal. G. L. Sharma discovered in his study that teachers wanted shared responsibility in all areas of the school program except instructional activities, wherein they wanted total responsibility.[47]

Recent literature and studies continue to show a strong expectation by teachers that school administrators take an active role in involving them in those decisions affecting teachers in some professional way.[48] In addition, as with Sharma's study, teachers have indicated a desire to expand their decision-making involvement to include managerial, schoolwide issues in addition to instruction issues. Thus, as Dan Riley concluded, teachers expect school administrators to

> identify avenues for their active participation, such as building level curriculum committees; timetabling committees; greater involvement by teachers in grouping of students, the establishment of discipline policies, equipment replacement, and textbook selection. Such committees need not necessarily be permanent or extensive in their powers, but rather be identified as offering additional avenues for teachers to be actively involved in the running of their school.[49]

Involving teachers in decision making is advantageous to administrators, for as Gladys Johnston and Vito Germinario stated, "The most effective teacher-administrator relationship, in terms of both morale and productivity, is a participatory one."[50] Astute school administrators are expected to use discretion and determine which decisions are perceived by teachers as being most important for shared decision making. These efforts and the establishment of participative decision-making structures should pay dividends to school administrators in increased teacher loyalty to the administrator and increased levels of teacher job satisfaction.[51]

4. School administrators should assist teachers in attaining the instructional skills and curricular materials necessary to teach effectively. As Robert B. McCarthy noted, "School systems that claim excellence in instruction as their highest goal must provide their staff with the means to achieve that excellence."[52] He argues that in addition to involving teachers in decision making regarding critical issues, school administrators should be expected to provide teachers with the technological support and time necessary for them to fulfill their roles. Simply put, providing students with effective instruction is a sophisticated, complex process: teachers should expect administrators to challenge them to engage in appropriate staff development activities.

In addition, since curriculum cannot be created or maintained with vintage equipment, teachers should be provided with technologically advanced equipment to facilitate the instructional process. "In most schools, teachers are provided with primitive tools (manual typewriters, a ditto machine) and restricted use of the photocopy machine usually located in the main office. Schools have historically allocated clerical and technological resources according to station rather than purpose or need."[53]

And finally, teachers need to be afforded the time "to meet with colleagues, to share ideas, to visit each other, and to reduce the mind-numbing isolation of those who work in our schools."[54] The shared decision-making process previously advocated is time intensive; therefore, school administrators should be expected to develop organizational structures and arrangements demonstrating a sincere commitment to protecting teachers' time.

Whether or not school administrators should meet all or any of the four main expectations teachers hold for their role depends, of course, on many factors. Obviously, it is not always possible and may not even be desirable for administrators to meet all of the teachers' expectations. However, administrators need to be aware that important consequences are associated with the extent to which they meet teachers' expectations.

PARENTAL EXPECTATIONS FOR THE SCHOOL ADMINISTRATOR'S ROLE

Parents constitute an important third group that holds expectations for the role of the school administrator. Perhaps more than any of the other groups discussed thus far, parents are heterogeneous in their expectations. Therefore, it is more difficult to generalize about the expectations of any single parents' group, to say nothing of parents' groups in different communities. In addition, there has been surprisingly little research on the expectations of parents for the role of the school administrator. Still, some useful findings can be gleaned from the few studies that have focused on parents' expectations for the school administrator's role.

Thelbert Drake, for example, found in a study of PTA officers that they identified the following five expectations for the principal as carrying a high priority:

- Initiating improvements in teaching techniques and methods.
- Making certain that curricula fit the needs of students.
- Directing teachers to motivate students to learn at their optimal levels.
- Affording teachers the opportunity to individualize programs.
- Directing teachers to coordinate and articulate the subject matter taught on each grade level.

The low-priority expectations which PTA officers held for the principal included:

- Becoming involved in community affairs.
- Keeping a school maintenance schedule.
- Scheduling the activities of the school.
- Maintaining school records.
- Performing other administrative duties assigned by the superintendent.[55]

Examining these two sets of expectations, the PTA officers surveyed are clearly more concerned with the role of the principal as an instructional leader than as a school manager.

Another study focusing more on parents' expectations for the principal in regard to working with parents and students was conducted by Reed Buffington.[56] In his study of parental expectations for the role of the principal this researcher found that parents expected the principal to engage in the following kinds of behavior:

I. Developing relationships with parents' groups and the community
   A. Organizing parents' groups
   B. Working with parents' groups
   C. Interpreting the school to the community
II. Knowing and helping individual parents
   A. Meeting parents' complaints
   B. Establishing friendly relations with parents
   C. Reporting to parents on progress of children
III. Working with and caring for children
   A. Maintaining discipline
   B. Showing personal interest in children
   C. Protecting the health and safety of children
   D. Working with atypical children

As one can see from an examination of these expectations, they fall into three categories: (1) working with parents' groups, (2) interacting with parents on an individual basis, and (3) working with and showing concern for children. Although most administrators would probably believe that the kinds of behavior listed under each of these categories are desirable, many parents are not satisfied with the extent to which their expectations have been met by administrators. Although this problem is discussed more fully in the chapters on school-community relations, it seems that administrators—with few exceptions—need to become more aware of the expectations by parents for the role of the administrator, as well as more knowledgeable about the extent to which parents believe that administrators are not meeting their expectations. (For further evidence and discussion of the expectations of parents, consult the chapters on school-community relations.)

SUPERIORS' EXPECTATIONS FOR THE SCHOOL ADMINISTRATOR'S ROLE

Probably many school administrators consider the most important expectations for their behavior to be those held by their superiors who had an important role in hiring them and who play a major role in determining their salary, retention, and status in the district, as well as other matters. For these reasons alone, school administrators have a tendency to weigh heavily the expectations of their superiors.

In addition, in a bureaucratic organization such as the school, which is operated according to principles of line and staff, administrators are responsible to and accountable to their superiors. Therefore, it is only natural to give a higher priority to the expectations of superiors than to the expectations of other reference groups. A problem for school administrators arises when their own expectations conflict with those of their superiors. The nature of these conflicts and possible resolutions are discussed in other readings.[57]

Perhaps the best study of superiors' expectations for the role of the school administrator was conducted by Robert Moser.[58] His research showed that superintendents expected their principals to engage in the following behavior: (1) lead forcefully, (2) initiate action, (3) accomplish organizational goals, and (4) emulate the nomothetic behavior of their superiors. Recent efforts to further define the role of school administrators have not rescinded these expectations; however, as Philip Hallinger and Joseph Murphy noted, these global expectations have become more specific, particularly in the area of instructional leadership where administrators are expected to (1) define the school's mission, (2) manage the instructional program, and (3) promote a positive school learning climate.[59]

Nomothetic behavior can be defined as actions seeking to meet the expectations of the institution in which an individual works.[60] As applied to the school administrator-superior relationship, nomothetic expectations mean that the administrators' superiors expect them to pay greater attention to the expectations of the organization for which they work than to their own personal needs or the personal needs of others with whom they may be associated at the building level.

Whether school administrators will always be able to meet the expectations of their superiors depends on many factors, including the extent to which the expectations are realistic. Certainly they should consider trying to change the expectations of their superiors if administrators believe that they are not in their own best interests or in the best interests of their schools. Their success in this endeavor depends as much as their own skill and perseverance as on the receptivity of their superiors for change. In any event, school administrators should make sure that they accurately understand the expectations of their superiors and consider carefully the consequences of not meeting those expectations.

AGREEME..₁ AMONG REFERENCE GROUPS

Although there is considerable evidence that the expectations of others for the role of the school administrator frequently conflict, common ground does exist. A general review of the expectations of teachers, parents, PTA presidents, nurses, custodians, and secretaries for the role of the school administrator revealed that all of these groups agreed that the following behavioral characteristics were important for the administrator: (1) show interest in work, offer assistance; (2) praise personnel; (3) back up personnel; (4) assume authority, stand by convictions; (5) allow self-direction in work; (6) make feelings clear; (7) allow participation in decisions; (8) be a good disciplinarian; (9) be considerate of work loads; (10) possess good personal characteristics, and (11) be well organized.

Even though some of these expectations seem contradictory, and school administrators cannot realistically expect reference groups' expectations to always be in agreement, compatibility may be achievable to a large extent. The most important step administrators can take to reach this goal is to make sure that they understand accurately the expectations of reference groups.[61] For, as Roald Campbell perceptively pointed out,

> An understanding of these expectations, often conflicting in nature, may appear most frustrating. Only by such understanding, however, can the administrator anticipate the reception of specified behavior on his part. Such anticipation seems necessary if the area of acceptance is to be extended and the area of disagreement minimized. Moreover, such understandings are necessary if a program of modifying expectations is to be started.[62]

SOCIAL FACTORS AFFECTING THE SCHOOL ADMINISTRATOR'S ROLE

The job of the school administrator has, of course, seldom been without problems; but in the last two decades, several social factors have emerged to make this job one of the most challenging in education today. While observers may differ on the nature of the impact, there appears to be fairly general agreement that five factors in particular have affected the role of the school administrator: (1) demographic changes, (2) the state of the economy, (3) collective bargaining, (4) the influence of federal and state government, and (5) the influence of news media and educationally adapted technology.

DEMOGRAPHIC CHANGES

The role of the school administrator has frequently been influenced by demographic changes of one kind or another. For example, a major demographic change during the 1960s and 1970s was the significant decline in the birth rate which led to decreasing student enrollments in many school districts.[63] As a result, administrators were forced to reduce staff; close some school buildings; and deal with the problems of lower staff morale, an older staff, excess building space, and community opposition to the closing of schools. According to a study by the Association for Supervision and Curriculum Development, declining enrollments also resulted in administrator layoffs, reassignment of administrators to other schools, assignment of more than one school to an elementary school principal, cutback of in-service education, decreased use of student teachers, fewer courses in the curriculum, and excess buildings, or building space being sold or leased.[64]

By and large, school districts' elementary school enrollments are now coming out of the decline period; however, growth at the secondary levels has been and will continue to be sporadic throughout the 1990s. For some time now, student enrollments have been increasing at the preschool and elementary levels. While the reported birthrate in the United States is 2.1 births per woman—a rate that reflects a replacement level—the number of births is projected to continue to increase. This paradox is explained by the fact that although each couple is producing fewer babies than their counterparts of twenty years ago, there are more women available to have children. In essence, what we are experiencing are the arrival of children to the 1950s baby boomers who postponed childbearing until their late twenties or early thirties. Thus, although the birthrate is down, the number of births is rising.[65] As a result, there has been a large increase in the population under age five since 1980 (11.6 percent); this increase is a reflection of what has been coined the "echo effect" of the prior baby boom.[66] Similarly, although the five-to-thirteen-year-old population declined by 1.1 percent between 1980 and 1987, this age group is beginning to grow again as the echo effect babies enter this cohort in increasing numbers.[67]

Consequently, administrators need to monitor birthrates to be prepared for the changes the school system will undergo to meet the needs of an expanding student body. As enrollments begin to increase, administrators need to determine how to accommodate the additional students. For example, decisions regarding school facilities and staffing assignments need to be revisited. In essence, school district administrators will be faced with issues and decisions similar to those experienced during the 1960s and 1970s when enrollments increased sharply during the post-World War II baby boom; the literature discussing the lessons learned should be reexamined.

The characteristics of the family have also undergone major changes in the last decade or two. The divorce rate, which more than doubled between 1970 and 1980, is now declining; it dropped from 22.6 divorces per 1,000 married women in 1980 to 21.7 divorces per 1,000 women in 1985.[68] The percentage of children born out of wedlock increased; in 1984, 13 percent of white children and 59 percent of black children were born to unmarried mothers, compared with 6 percent and 38 percent respectively in 1970.[69] And, the proportion of single-parent households increased nearly 80 percent during the 1970s; in 1984, 15 percent of white children and 50 percent of black children under age 18 lived with their mother only, compared with 8 and 29 percent respectively in 1970.[70] As Sandra Hofferth noted, "If current trends continue, between 42 and 70 percent of white children and 86 and 94 percent of black children born around 1980 will spend some time in a one-parent family before reaching age 18."[71] In summary, families with a working father, a housewife mother, and two or more school-age children constitute only a very small percent of the U.S. households.[72]

In addition, over half of the females are in the work force (and almost 70 percent if you only consider working age women); thus the number of latchkey children—those who are home alone after school when adults are not present—has shown a dramatic increase and will continue to do so as more women choose to have children and work outside the home.[73]

These changes in family characteristics have had an impact on schools and their administrators. For example, Gerald Unks pointed out that schools must address the needs of single-parent families and working mothers.[74] He advocated that schools must provide services to children traditionally assumed to be provided by the mother (e.g., early breakfast programs, after-school child care programs). He also noted that John Goodlad advocated that children begin school at an earlier age for pedagogical reasons; however, there are also compelling social and economic reasons. Therefore, Unks believes that the school system should "embrace the day-care function in order to ensure that all children are afforded a stimulating cognitive, affective, and psychomotor environment . . . the school must not only assume custody for children at an earlier age; it must also keep them for a longer time each day."[75]

In addition, the high rate of divorce in families, the increased number of children born out of wedlock, and the trend toward both parents (or, in one-parent families, the family head) working outside the home have placed greater pressures on the students coming from these situations. In many circumstances, these factors have made it difficult for school administrators to communicate with and gain support from the home.[76] With particular reference to single-parent families, Patrick Lynch noted recent evidence indicating that

> what should be of most concern to teachers and administrators is that the known data illustrate that schools may define children of single-parents as disciplinary problems when in fact those children have attendance patterns no different from children of two-parent homes. School organizational structures may be punishing the one-parent child or withholding its support in many subtle ways.[77]

School administrators must recognize the needs of students from single-parent families without stigmatizing them. To this end, administrators should consider organizing support groups for single parents, providing after-school activities for children who would otherwise return to unsupervised settings after school, providing group counseling support sessions for children, placing boys from father-absent homes with male teachers to provide appropriate adult role models, and determining school policies for communicating with noncustodial parents.[78]

Other demographic changes have also affected the schools. For example, migration from the large cities to the suburbs, to rural areas, and from the East and Midwest to the Southwest and the West continues to increase, causing the paradox of increased enrollment in some school districts amidst an overall national decline in student enrollment.[79] Immigration, both legal and illegal, has increased greatly during the last decade, bringing with it children with problems of cultural assimilation and specific educational needs.[80] Harold Hodgkinson noted that "by around the year 2000, America will be a nation in which one of every three of us will be nonwhite. And minorities will cover a broader socioeconomic range than ever before, making simplistic treatment of their needs even less useful."[81]

The proportion of the population aged 65 and older has increased and is likely to grow substantially in the future, constituting a sizable percentage of the adult population in many communities, thereby compounding possible problems of financial support for the schools.[82] The increasing number of people whose children are no longer in community schools has, and will continue to, make it a high priority to communicate with these older citizens. School administrators must gain their understanding and support of the goals of the schools and the importance of education. The increased role of the school in adult education for senior citizens is another possible implication. The demographics regarding age reveal, "It is clear that for the next decade, the only growth area in education will be in adult and continuing education, with increases in elementary schools in certain regions."[83]

THE STATE OF THE ECONOMY

A second major social force that can affect the role of the school administrator is the state of the economy. Trends in unemployment, inflation, and taxes tend to influence the management, funding, and operation of school systems. For example, during periods of high unemployment and inflation, taxpayers' resistance to the increased costs of education rise tremendously. This resistance creates a serious dilemma for school boards and administrators who are not opposed to economizing but concerned that continued budget reductions could seriously damage the quality of education provided to students.

Although school boards and administrators have attempted to economize to maintain or reduce costs of education, they have been confronted with the reality of spiraling costs due to decreased federal support of categorical programs such as special education, increased state mandates for new programs (e.g., at-risk students, competency testing, etc.), and parental resistance to the elimination or reduction of favorite programs. Furthermore, since most of the school budget is concentrated in the area of personnel salaries and fringe benefits, budget cuts are hard to make because of contractual agreements.[84] In addition, many school board members and administrators believe that they have reached the point at which continued reduction in school costs would begin to severely erode the quality of education.

Unfortunately, no easy answers present themselves for the solution of these problems because most of the economic factors impacting on school administrators are beyond their control, although these factors can be changed by the actions of federal and state officials. What administrators can do, however, is to (1) manage the educational enterprise as efficiently as possible; (2) monitor closely the economic climate at the national, state, and local levels; (3) work to develop a better understanding on the part of the public regarding goals and values of education; and (4) identify clearly the consequences of arbitrary reduction in the financial support of education. These topics are further addressed in chapters 6, 9, and 18.

COLLECTIVE BARGAINING

There seems to be little doubt that collective bargaining has changed the role of school administrators, at least in their relationship to teachers. According to the Educational Research Service, "Many observers would agree that collective bargaining has affected the process of decision making and school governance more than any other single development in the mid-twentieth century."[85] Prior to collective bargaining, school administrators' relationships with teachers were frequently paternalistic. In most situations, administrators had a choice as to whether or not they should consider teachers' grievances, consult with them about work assignments, or involve them in school decision making; all too often—at least according to teachers' perceptions—they chose not to do so. The introduction of collective bargaining, however, has meant that in most situations administrators must consider teachers' grievances and must consult with teachers in regard to work conditions and other matters affecting their welfare.[86]

From an administrative perspective, collective bargaining undoubtedly offers both disadvantages and advantages as a technique or process for conflict resolution. For example, Gary Smit believes at least three aspects of the collective bargaining process are detrimental to school district governance: (1) teachers' associations gain decision-making authority over management prerogatives; (2) union demands illegally infringe on statutory duties of school districts; and (3) the conflict between laypersons and professionals for control of the schools intensifies.[87] Other perceived negative consequences have been the limitations placed on the initiative and flexibility of school boards and administrators to promulgate those personnel policies they believe to be in the best interest of the school district and the local community. However, on the positive side, collective bargaining has frequently led to a reduction in arbitrariness and insensitivity by some school districts regarding the needs, problems, and aspirations of teachers.

Collective bargaining has also tended to involve teachers more as partners in the management of school districts. As Susan Johnson noted, teachers have negotiated working conditions which have covered a wide range of provisions such as those that define teachers' job responsibilities, provide job security, and establish their roles in policy making.[88] In addition, Johnson found that teachers had "successfully reduced their nonteaching duties through bargaining and that they continued to try to restrict the limits of their formal responsibilities to classroom instruction."[89] This increased involvement of teachers in school governance coincides with current efforts to enhance the professional role of teachers and will necessitate the development of a new relationship between the school administration and the teachers' professional associations.[90] Whether this relationship is attainable or not is yet to be determined; clearly, school governance and the administration of school personnel policies in most school districts will continue to be influenced by collective bargaining.[91]

Although teachers have made noticeable financial gains, improved their job security, and influenced working conditions through collective bargaining, school administrators should not assume that they are powerless in leading their schools. Johnson's research indicated that "school site administrators in even the strongest union districts could manage their schools well. Principals were neither figureheads deferring to union representatives nor functionaries complying slavishly with the contract."[92] Thus, although administrators need to be mindful of the influence of collective bargaining, their leadership need not be significantly hindered by it. (The topic of collective bargaining and contract administration is further discussed in chapter 9; for concise treatments of these topics, which are beyond the intended scope of this text, see Delbert C. Clear, "Collective Bargaining," in *Encyclopedia of School Administration and Supervision,* ed. R. A. Gorton, G. T. Schneider, and J. C. Fisher (Phoenix, Ariz.: Oryx Press, 1988), 62–64; and Susan Moore Johnson, "Unionism and Collective Bargaining the Public Schools," in *Handbook of Research on Educational Administration,* ed. Norman J. Boyan, (New York: Longman, 1988), 603–22.)

INFLUENCE OF THE FEDERAL AND STATE GOVERNMENTS

A fourth major social force which has affected the role of the school administrator has been the intervention by the federal and state governments in educational affairs.[93] This intervention has taken several forms and has posed new problems for school administrators.

For example, historically the courts did not often attempt to substitute their judgment for that of school officials in the administration of the school unless, of course, a serious offense was committed.[94] In the 1960s and 1970s, however, acting in response to challenges by students, teachers, and parents to school authority and decision making, the courts laid down a number of rulings altering the role of administrators. These rulings covered a wide range of areas, including students' due process rights, racial and sexual discrimination, teacher evaluation, reduction in staff, and competency testing.[95]

These court decisions have had important impact on the roles of school administrators. Administrators' authority has been limited, and they are required to demonstrate that the school has acted fairly and prudently in relations with others. Although there appear to be many administrators who believe that the courts have "interfered" in school affairs and have made the administrator's job more difficult, the overall result in many situations has been to make the school and the relationships within the school less authoritarian and more humane. The extent to which the latter result has been achieved, however, has depended as much on the manner and spirit in which the school administrator has implemented the court decisions as on any other factor.[96]

During the 1980s, through President Ronald Reagan's appointments of Chief Justice William Rehnquist and Justices Sandra Day O'Connor, Antonin Scalia, and Arthur Kennedy, the conservative arm of the U.S. Supreme Court was strengthened. As a result, issues which had previously been decided within a liberal framework were viewed through a more conservative perspective. If this shift in the philosophy of the Supreme Court continues, in the 1990s the Court will likely accept cases involving critical issues such as: prayers in the classroom, public support of parochial education, affirmative action, freedom of speech, equal educational opportunities for handicapped students, and school desegregation/busing.[97] As in the past, decisions made by the Supreme Court will undoubtedly have a profound impact on the organization and operation of public schools; administrators will need to follow closely the actions and trends established through the Supreme Court decisions.

State and federal legislatures have also passed laws and regulations tending to increase the difficulty of the administrators' jobs and to alter their administrative roles. These laws and regulations have attempted to address such problems as segregation, disadvantaged students, handicapped students, students speaking English as a second language, and a variety of other perceived needs.[98] These efforts, although perhaps needed and commendable in their original intent, have complicated enormously the roles of school administrators. For example, a Rand Corporation Study on the effects of federal education programs on school principals revealed that in general, "Principals are now more constrained by rules, more subject to public scrutiny, and less in control of their own schedules, than they were five years ago."[99] Perhaps, in response to these problems, the executive branch of the federal government has recently attempted to reduce and simplify federal regulations, and both the executive and legislative branches of the federal government have tried to reduce the federal role in education through deregulation and the development of state-administered block grants rather than federally funded categorical aid.[100] Although these actions have been welcomed by many administrators, new problems of state control and unmet school and societal needs will likely emerge as a result.

Whether state and federal laws and regulations on education constitute interference in local school affairs can be debated, but it does seem evident that such laws and regulations have increased the difficulty of the administrator's role.[101] Administrators need to recognize however, that state and federal governments do not usually pass legislation affecting a local school situation unless local initiative is not being exercised to correct a serious problem. The best alternative for school administrators may be to move more quickly to identify and resolve problems on the local level so that state and federal legislative action is unnecessary.

INFLUENCE OF THE NEWS MEDIA AND EDUCATIONALLY ADAPTED TECHNOLOGY

The news media and several innovations in educationally adapted technology have affected the role of the school administrator, and the prospects are that they will continue to do so in the future.

The news media consist of newspapers, magazines, and radio and television stations which carry news programs. In recent years the news media have discovered education, and seldom does a week pass without some major news story on education. The news story may consist of a TV documentary on "What's Wrong with American Education," a magazine article on "Sex Education in the Schools," a radio talk-show interview of a proponent of "Back to Basics in Our Schools," or a newspaper article on "Violence in the Schools." Regrettably, the focus of much of the news media's coverage of the schools seems to concentrate on problems of American education, although there are exceptions. One reason for the lack of positive news coverage may be that lack of reliable outcome measures in education limits the amount of hard, positive educational news.[102]

The impact of this increased and largely critical news coverage of the schools has yet to be scientifically determined. However, many administrators believe that the news media's coverage of education impacts negatively on public opinion and places school officials in a defensive, reactive position.[103] Consequently, they often tend to perceive the news media, and reporters in particular, as adversaries and are ambivalent in responding to their news inquiries. This type of attitude and behavior by administrators, although understandable, is unfortunate and usually counterproductive. Given the increasing proportion of nonparents in communities, administrators must improve their relations with media personnel and use newspapers, radio, and television to build community support for education.[104]

Representatives of the news media have a job to accomplish and, while they frequently may not perform this job to the satisfaction of administrators, a negative attitude and reaction are only likely to make the situation worse. Instead, most administrators need to take the initiative to develop a better relationship with the news media, to understand the role of the press and how journalists do their jobs, and to initiate improved ways of communication with the public.[105] Ideas and recommendations for achieving those goals are presented in chapter 18.

Contrary to the news media's perceived negative impact on the role of the school administrator, several innovations in educationally adapted technology have exerted a largely positive influence. These innovations include the use of computers for school data processing and scheduling, hand-held calculators for mathematics, microprocessors for individualized instruction and learning, and videotape recorders, videodiscs, and cable television for instructional and self-improvement activities.

Although most of these innovations are too recent to determine their eventual use and value, potentially they could dramatically change administration, teaching, and learning. For example, computer-generated master schedules could drastically reduce the time administrators spend on scheduling the instructional program; split screen video recorders offer the possibility for improved staff evaluation and instructional supervision by providing the teacher and the administrator with an expanded visual record of a class session, with the opportunity for replay and analysis.[106] Microcomputers offer the possibility of diagnosis, remediation, and individualization in a variety of school subjects including English and social studies.[107] They are also being linked to videodiscs and other data sources to provide more individualized and enriched learning experiences for students at school and in the home.[108] And cable television offers schools not only the possibility of enriching their curriculum through various programs but also an opportunity to communicate more directly with their public and to obtain feedback more systematically.[109]

Whether many of these possibilities and opportunities are actually capitalized on depends in large part on school administrators. Projections indicate that by the mid-1990s students in kindergarten through grade nine will spend almost a quarter of the school day using computers or video technology, either alone or in small groups.[110] Thus, administrators need to develop a deeper understanding of the potential and the use of educationally adapted technology. They also need to develop skills in evaluating software for the educationally adapted technology, and to provide inservice education to help their faculties develop awareness of and skills for using the technology.[111] While most of these increased understandings and skills can be obtained through reading, course work, and special workshops, very little is likely to occur unless administrators have the vision and take initiative in this area. Many schools are already underutilizing traditional audiovisual aids, such as the overhead projector, and unless there is more enlightened leadership and initiative with respect to educationally adapted technology, schools could wind up with a lot of very expensive, underutilized equipment. (For further discussion on how to introduce program change and to plan in-service education for the staff, see chapters 11 and 12. Also, for additional reading in the area of educationally adapted technology, note the references at the end of this chapter.[112])

CONCLUDING NOTE

After finishing this chapter, it may appear that school administrators have an impossible job. This would represent an understandable but incorrect conclusion. There is little doubt that the job of school administrators is filled with challenges. However, each of those challenges represents an opportunity to exercise *leadership*. By thoroughly understanding the concepts and ideas presented throughout this text, and thinking about and practicing their application, administrators should be able to respond successfully to the various challenges and, in the process, exercise the kind of leadership needed in education.

Review and Learning Activities

1. Which of the six major roles of the school administrator described in the text are you currently most competent to perform? Which of the six are you least competent to perform? What is the basis of your self-assessment? What are the implications of those assessments?

2. What implications does Getzel's model hold for your role behavior as an administrator?

3. Based on the discussion in the text on personal variables, to what extent is your own behavior as a teacher or administrator influenced by your attitude and values?

4. Examine the reference group expectations presented in the text. How would you ascertain the expectations of the students, teachers, parents, and superiors associated with your own school?

5. To what extent should an administrator meet the expectations of students, teachers, parents, and superiors for her role? What are the advantages and disadvantages of meeting or not meeting the expectations of these groups?

6. After reading the presentation in the text on social factors, attempt to ascertain the extent to which these social factors are impacting on your own school situation. What are the implications for the role of the school administrator, insofar as these social factors are affecting your local situation?

Notes

1. Arthur Blumberg and William Greenfield, *The Effective Principal: Perspectives on School Leadership,* 2d ed. (Newton, Mass.: Allyn & Bacon, 1986).

2. Richard A. Gorton, *School Administration and Supervision: Important Concepts, Case Studies, and Simulations,* 3d ed. (Dubuque, Iowa: Wm. C. Brown Company Publishers, 1987).

3. For example, see Robert Owens, *Organizational Behavior in Education* (Englewood Cliffs, N.J.: Prentice-Hall, 1987); and Robert E. Wentz, "School Principals: The Emerging Community Heroes as the 1990s Unfold," *NASSP Bulletin* (September 1989): 40–43.

4. Paul R. Pierce, *The Origin and Development of the Public School Principalship* (Chicago: University of Chicago Press, 1935), 12.

5. See William D. Greenfield, ed., *Instructional Leadership: Important Concepts, Cases, and Controversies* (Newton, Mass.: Allyn & Bacon, 1987); W. L. Rutherford, "Styles and Behaviors of Elementary School Principals," *Education and Urban Society* 17 (1984): 9–28; and Philip Hallinger and Joseph Murphy, "Assessing the Instructional Management Behavior of Principals," *The Elementary School Journal* (November 1985): 217–45.

6. Larry Cuban, *The Managerial Imperative and the Practice of Leadership in Schools* (Albany, N.Y.: State University of New York Press, 1988): 74–75.

7. Karolyn J. Snyder, "Managing a Productive School Work Culture," *NASSP Bulletin* (October 1988): 40–43.

8. Cuban, *The Managerial Imperative,* 74.

9. M. Claradine Johnson, "The Principal in the 1980s: Instructional Leader, Manager," *NASSP Bulletin* (January 1981): 88–90. For a different point of view, see Cheryl Overy, "A Study of the Managerial Role of the Public School Principal" (Ph.D. diss., University of Nebraska-Lincoln, 1981).

10. See Ellwood P. Cubberley, *The Principal and His School* (Boston: Houghton-Mifflin, 1923).

11. Ibid., 43.

12. Sharon F. Rallis and Martha C. Highsmith, "The Myth of the 'Great Principal': Questions of School Management and Instructional Leadership," *Kappan* (December 1986): 300–304.

13. Deborah Burnett Strother, "The Many Roles of the Effective Principal," *Kappan* (December 1983): 291; and "The Principal's Role: How Do We Reconcile Expectations with Reality?" *R and D Perspectives* (Winter 1982): 1–8. Also see chapter 11 on instructional leadership for additional evidence on this point.

14. Hallinger and Murphy, "Assessing the Instructional Management," 218.

15. Larry W. Hughes and Gerald C. Ubben, *The Elementary Principal's Handbook: A Guide to Effective Action,* 2d. ed. (Boston: Allyn & Bacon, 1984), 162–66. The results of the annual Gallup Poll of the Public's Attitudes Toward the Public Schools appears each year in the September issue of the *Kappan.*

16. Carrie Kojimoto, "The Kid's-Eye View of Effective Principals," *Educational Leadership* (September 1987): 69–74.

17. William D. Greenfield, "Developing an Instructional Role for the Assistant Principal," *Education and Urban Society* (November 1985): 85–86.

18. James M. Lipham, Robb E. Rankin, and James A. Hoeh, Jr., *The Principalship: Concepts, Competencies, and Case Studies* (New York: Longman, 1985), 218–19.

19. Mary Parker Follett, *Creative Experience* (New York: Longmans, Green, 1924).

20. Elton Mayo, *The Human Problems of an Industrial Civilization* (Boston: Graduate School of Business Administration, Harvard University, 1946); and Daniel Griffiths, *Human Relations in School Administration* (New York: Appleton-Century-Crofts, 1956).

21. See Blaine R. Worthen and James R. Sanders, *Educational Evaluation: Alternative Approaches and Practical Guidelines* (New York: Longman, 1987), 3–10; and Robert J. Starratt, "Administrative Leadership in Policy Review and Evaluation," *Educational Evaluation and Policy Analysis* (Summer 1988): 141–50.

22. See discussion in chapter 2 for an additional review of the evidence supporting this point.

23. Worthen and Sanders, *Educational Evaluation,* chap. 12–21.

24. See Jackson M. Drake, "Navigating the Storms of Controversy," *NASSP Bulletin* (May 1984): 82–86; Geoffrey B. Isherwood, "Leadership Effectiveness in Cooperative and Counteracting Groups," *Journal of Educational Administration* (Summer 1985): 208–18; and C. T. Araki, "Managing Conflict in the Schools with System 4," *National Forum of Educational Administration and Supervision Journal* 7 (1990/1991): 18–30.

25. Lipham, Rankin, and Hoeh, *The Principalship,* 41.

26. Gorton, *School Leadership and Administration,* chap. 5. See also, F. M. Wirt and L. Christovich, "Administrators' Perceptions of Policy Influence: Conflict Management Styles and Roles," *Educational Administration Quarterly* (February 1989): 3–35.

27. Jacob W. Getzels, "Administration as a Social Process," in *Administrative Theory in Education,* ed. Andrew Halpin (Chicago: Midwest Administration Center, University of Chicago, 1958), 153.

28. Neal Gross et al., *Explorations in Role Analysis: Studies of the School Superintendency Role* (New York: John Wiley & Sons, 1958), 58.

29. James M. Lipham, "Getzels's Models in Educational Administration," in *Handbook of Research on Educational Administration,* ed. Norman J. Boyan, (New York: Longman, 1988): 171–84.

30. Lipham, Rankin, and Hoeh, *The Principalship,* 35.

31. This section and the previous one were adapted from material in Gorton, *School Leadership and Supervision,* 71–77.

32. Lipham, Rankin, and Hoeh, *The Principalship,* 87.

33. Chester Barnard, *Functions of the Executive* (Cambridge, Mass.: Harvard University Press, 1938).

34. Robert Stout, "Executive Action and Values," *Issues in Education* (Winter 1986): 199. For an additional discussion on values and decision making, see Gabriele Lakomski, "Values and Decision Making in Educational Administration," *Educational Administration Quarterly* (August 1987): 70–82.

35. Carl R. Ashbaugh and Katherine L. Kasten, "A Typology of Operant Values in School Administration," *Planning and Changing* (Winter 1984): 195–208.

36. Kojimoto, "The Kid's-Eye View," 69–74.

37. Clinton I. Chase, "Teenagers Are Mostly Positive about High School," *Kappan* (March 1981): 526.

38. Blumberg and Greenfield, *The Effective Principal,* 136–43.

39. Joseph Blase, "Dimensions of Effective School Leadership: The Teacher's Perspective," *American Educational Research Journal* (Winter 1987): 602; and Edwin M. Bridges, "Teacher Participation in Decision-Making," *Administrator's Notebook* (May 1964): 1–4.

40. Robert Brumbaugh and John Skinkus, *Organizational Control and the Middle School Principal.* (ERIC Report ED–180–053); and Joseph Sjostrom, "Teachers Want More Backing from Better Bosses," *Chicago Tribune* (May 3, 1981), section 2, p. 10.

41. Y. L. Jack Lam, "Determinants of Teacher Professionalism," *Alberta Journal of Educational Research* (September 1983): 168–79.

42. Charles E. Bidwell, "Some Causes of Conflict and Tensions among Teachers," *Administrator's Notebook* (March 1956); and Joseph Blase, "Dimensions of Effective School Leadership: The Teacher's Perspective," *American Educational Research Journal* (Winter 1987): 599.

43. Francis L. Chase, "The Teacher and Policy Making," *Administrator's Notebook* (May 1952); and Russell T. Sharpe, "Differences between Perceived Administrative Behavior and Role Norms as Factors in Leadership and Group Morale" (Ph.D. diss., Stanford University, 1955), 159.

44. For example, see recent issues of *Today's Education.*

45. Ann Lieberman, "Expanding the Leadership Team," *Educational Leadership* (February 1988): 8.

46. Chase, "The Teacher and Policy Making."

47. G. L. Sharma, "Who Should Make What Decisions?" *Administrator's Notebook* (April 1955). For a more recent discussion supporting this point, see Robert R. Spillane, "The Changing Principalship: A Superintendent's Perspective," *Principal* (January 1989): 19–20.

48. See Daniel Duke, Beverly K. Showers, and M. Imber, "Teachers and Shared Decision Making," *Educational Administration Quarterly* (Winter 1980): 93–106; Gail Thierbach Schneider, "Teacher Involvement in Decision Making: Zones of Acceptance, Decision Conditions, and Job Satisfaction," *Journal of Research and Development in Education* (Fall 1984): 25–32; Jon Saphier, Tom Bigda-Peyton, and Geoff Pierson, *How to Make Decisions that Stay Made* (Alexandria, Va.: Association for Supervision and Curriculum Development, 1989).

49. Dan Riley, "Teacher Utilization of Avenues for Participatory Decision Making," *Journal of Educational Administration* (Winter 1984): 45.

50. Gladys Johnston and Vito Germinario, "Relationship between Teacher Decisional Status and Loyalty," *The Journal of Educational Administration* (Winter 1985): 91.

51. Ibid., 101; and Schneider, "Teacher Involvement in Decision Making."

52. Robert B. McCarthy, "Technology, Time, and Participation: How a Principal Supports Teachers," *Education and Urban Society* (May 1985): 326.

53. Ibid., 328.

54. Ibid.

55. Reported in William H. Roe and Thelbert L. Drake, *The Principalship* (New York: MacMillan Publishing, 1980), 132–33.

56. Reed L. Buffington, "The Job of the Elementary School Principal as Viewed by Parents" (Ed.D. Diss., Stanford University, 1954), 943.

57. Gorton, *School Leadership and Supervision,* chap. 5.

58. Robert P. Moser, "A Study of the Effects of Superintendent-Principal Interaction and Principal-Teacher Interaction in Selected Middle-sized School Systems" (Ph.D. diss., University of Chicago, 1957).

59. Hallinger and Murphy, "Assessing the Instructional Management," 217–45.

60. J. W. Getzels, James Lipham, and Roald Campbell, *Educational Administration as a Social Process* (New York: Harper and Row, 1968), 145–49.

61. For discussions regarding reference groups' expectations, see William J. Banach and Jean A. Kasprzyk, "What Secretaries Say about Principals," *Principal* (January 1989): 42–43; J. Allen Queen, "What Does It Take to Be an Effective Principal?" *Principal* (January 1989): 34; and Muriel Stevenson, "Are You Listening?' *Principal* (January 1989): 49.

62. Roald F. Campbell, "Situational Factors in Educational Administration," in *Administrative Behavior in Education,* ed. Roald F. Campbell and Russell T. Gregg (New York: Harper & Row, 1957), 264.

63. *Statistical Abstract of the United States* (Washington, D.C.: U.S. Government Printing Office, 1981); *The Condition of Education* (Washington, D.C.: National Center for Educational Statistics, 1980).

64. See *The Effects of Declining Enrollments on Instructional Programs and Supervisory Practices in Public Elementary and Secondary Schools* (Alexandria, Va: Association for Supervision and Curriculum Development, 1980); James G. Cibulka, "Theories of Education Budgeting: Lessons from the Management of Decline," *Educational Administration Quarterly* (Winter 1987): 7–40; and Willard Duckett, "Using Demographic Data for Long-Range Planning," *Kappan* (October 1988): 166–70.

65. U.S. Bureau of the Census, Current Population Reports, Series P–25, No. 1022, *United States Population Estimates, by Age, Sex, and Race: 1980 to 1987,* (Washington, D.C.: U.S. Government Printing Office, 1988).

66. Ibid., 2.

67. Ibid.

68. *Marital Status and Living Arrangements: March 1980* (Washington, D.C.: Census Bureau, 1980); and Marvin J. Cetron, Wanda Rocha, and Rebecca Luckins, "Into the 21st Century: Long-Term Trends Affecting the United States," *The Futurist* (July–August 1988): 39.

69. Sandra L. Hofferth, "Implications of Family Trends for Children: A Research Perspective," *Educational Leadership* (February 1987): 79.

70. Ibid.

71. Ibid.

72. See Harold Hodgkinson, "The Right Schools for the Right Kids," *Educational Leadership* (February 1988): 10–14;; and Harold Hodgkinson, *All One System: Demographics of Education-Kindergarten through Graduate School* (Washington, D.C.: Institute for Educational Leadership, 1985): 1–18.

73. Hodgkinson, *One System,* 5.

74. Gerald Unks, "The New Demography: Implications for the School Curriculum," *Education and Urban Society* (August 1984): 449–51.

75. Ibid., 449–50.

76. John Ourth, "Children in One-parent Homes: The School Factor," *Principal* (September 1980): 40.

77. Patrick D. Lynch, "Single-Parent Families," in *Encyclopedia of School Administration and Supervision,* ed. R. A. Gorton, G. T. Schneider, and J. C. Fisher (Phoenix, Ariz.: Oryx Press, 1988), 237.

78. Ibid.

79. U.S. Bureau of the Census, *Statistical Abstract of the United States: 1988,* 108th ed. (Washington, D.C.: December 1987), 367.

80. Phoebe P. Hollis, "The Student of the Future." (ERIC Report Ed–195–507).

81. Hodgkinson, *All One System,* 7.

82. Michael W. Kirst and Walter I. Garms, *The Demographic, Fiscal and Political Environment of Public School Finance in the 1980s.* (Stanford, Calif.: Institute for Research on Educational Finance and Governance, 1980). Also see U.S. Bureau of Census, *Current Population Reports,* Series P–25, 1988, 5.

83. Hodgkinson, *All One System,* 3.

84. Based on an examination of numerous contractual agreements.

85. Joan P. Sullivan Kowalski, *Negotiating the Teacher Evaluation Issues* (Arlington, Va.: Educational Research Service, 1979), iii. See also, Frank Ambrosie, "Collaborative, Versus Negotiated, Decision Making," *NASSP Bulletin* (September 1989): 56–59.

86. Ronald W. Rebore, *Personnel Administration in Education: A Management Approach* (Englewood Cliffs, N.J.: Prentice-Hall 1987), 298–323.

87. Gary Smit, "The Effect of Collective Bargaining on Governance in Education," *Government Union Review* (Winter 1984): 28–34. See also, Gene Geisert, "Participatory Management: Panacea or Hoax?" *Educational Leadership* (November 1988): 56–59.

88. Susan Moore Johnson, "Unionism and Collective Bargaining in the Public Schools," in *Handbook of Research on Educational Administration,* ed. Norman J. Boyan (New York: Longman, 1988), 617.

89. Ibid, 619.

90. Robert Nielsen and Irwin H. Polishook, "Educational Reform and Teacher Professionalism," *Chronicle of Higher Education* (June 11, 1986): 45.

91. See Richard A. Gorton, "School Personnel Policy: in *Encyclopedia of Educational Research* ed. Harold E. Mitzel (New York: Macmillan Company, 1982); and Steven M. Goldschmidt and Suzanne R. Painter, "Collective Bargaining: A Review of the Literature," *Educational Research Quarterly* 12, no. 1 (1987–88): 10–24.

92. Johnson, "Unionism and Collective Bargaining, 619."

93. An excellent book on this topic by Arthur E. Wise is *Legislated Learning* (Berkeley, Calif.: University of California Press, 1979). For more recent discussions, see Vin Weber, "Federal Education Policy: How to Influence It, and Where We're Going in the 1990s," *NASSP Bulletin* (November 1989): 7–11; William A. Firestone, Susan H. Fuhrman, and Michael W. Kirst, "Implementation, Effects of State Education Reform in the '80s," *NASSP Bulletin* (February 1990): 75–84; and Susan H. Fuhrman, "State Politics and Education Reform," in J. Hannaway and R. Crowson, *The Politics of Reforming School Administration: Politics of Education Association Yearbook* (New York: Falmer Press, 1989): 61–75.

94. John C. Hogan, *The Schools, the Courts, and the Public Interest* (Lexington, Mass.: Lexington Books, 1974), chap. 2.

95. Thomas J. Sergiovanni, Martin Burlingame, Fred S. Coombs, and Paul W. Thurston, "Public Schools and the Law: Constitutional Standards," *Educational Governance and Administration,* 2d ed. (Englewood Cliffs, N.J.: Prentice-Hall, 1987), 308–37.

96. See, for example, "Districts' Compliance with Courts—Low," *Institute for Research on Educational Finance and Government* (Summer 1980): 3.

97. David G. Savage, "Watching a Changing Court: Will the Center Hold?" *Kappan* (October 1987): 135–37.

98. See Michael W. Kirst, "The Changing Balance in State and Local Power to Control Education," *Kappan* (November 1984); Lorraine M. McDonnell and Susan Fuhrman, "The Political Context of School Reform," in Van D. Mueller and Mary P. McKeown, *The Fiscal, Legal, and Political Aspects of State Reform of Elementary and Secondary Education* (Cambridge, Mass.: Ballinger, 1985); Anne C. Lewis, "The Party's Over," *Kappan* (September 1988): 4–7; and John F. Jennings, "Working in Mysterious Ways: The Federal Government and Education," *Kappan* (September 1988): 62–66.

99. Paul Hill et al., "The Effects of Federal Education Programs on School Principals." (ERIC Report ED–191–178). Also see Jackie Kimbrough and Paul Hill, *The Aggregate Effects of Federal Education Programs* (Santa Monica, Calif.: Rand Corporation, 1981).

100. See A. Harry Passow, "Whither (or Wither?) School Reform?" *Educational Administration Quarterly* (August 1988): 246–56; Barry G. Rabe and Paul E. Peterson, "The Evolution of a New Cooperative Federalism," and Richard K. Jung, "The Federal Role in Elementary and Secondary Education: Mapping a Shifting Terrain," in *Handbook of Research on Educational Administration,* ed. Norman J. Boyan (New York: Longman, 1988); and Thomas B. Timar and David L. Kirp, "State Efforts to Reform Schools: Treading between a Regulatory Swamp and an English Garden," *Educational Evaluation and Policy Analysis* (Summer 1988): 75–88.

101. Deborah A. Verstegen and P. Anthony, "Is There a Federal Role in Education Reform?" *Journal of Education Finance* (Summer 1988): 30–56.

102. Denis P. Doyle, "Education and the Press: Malign Neglect?" *American Educator* (Spring 1985): 28–33.

103. Richard A. Gorton, "What Do Principals Think of News Media Coverage?" *NASSP Bulletin* (December 1979): 116–18.

104. Albert E. Holliday, "Mobilizing the Media: Practical Ways to Work Effectively with Newspapers, Radio, and Television Stations," *Journal of Educational Communication* (December 1983): 4–7.

105. George Rhoades and Lynn Rhoades, "Meeting the Press: Challenge and Opportunity," *Clearing House* (October 1984): 77.

106. Thomas J. Gustafson, *Microcomputers and Educational Administration* (Englewood Cliffs, N.J.: Prentice-Hall, 1985), 78–82; and Alan Frager, "Video Technology and Teacher Training: A Research Perspective," *Educational Technology* (July 1985): 20–22; Keith A. Acheson and Meredith Damien Gall, *Techniques in the Clinical Supervision of Teachers: Preservice and Inservice Applications* 2d ed., (White Plains, N.Y.: Longman, 1987), 123–26; and J. M. Gould, "A School-Business Partnership that Yields Interactive Videodiscs, *Journal of Staff Development* (Fall 1989): 10–14.

107. Harold Miller, "Academic and Societal Uses of Microcomputers," *An Administrator's Manual for the Use of Microcomputers in the Schools* (Englewood Cliffs, N.J.: Prentice-Hall, 1988), 41–65.

108. Allen D. Glenn and Kent T. Kehrberg, "The Intelligent Videodisc: An Instructional Tool for the Classroom," *Educational Technology* (October 1981): 60–63. Also see "Videodisc Report," *New Technology* (April 1981): 1–4.

109. Dan J. Wedemeyer, "The New Age of Elecommunication: Setting the Context for Education," *Educational Technology* (October 1986): 7–13; and Eliza T. Dresang, "Communicating via Cable," *School Library Journal* (April 1987): 44–47.

110. For more information see *Preparing Schools for the Year 2000: The Impact of Technology on America's Classrooms in the Decade Ahead* (Chicago, Ill.: Society for Visual Education, 1988).

111. Miller, *An Administrator's Guide for the Use of Microcomputers in the Schools,* 67–76; and Lipham, Rankin, and Hoeh, *The Principalship,* 287–88.

112. John Lindelow, *Microcomputers in the School Office: Primer for Administrators,* School Management Series, no. 30 (Washington, D.C.: National Institute of Education, 1984); James A. Mecklenburger, "What the Ostrich Sees: Technology and the Mission of American Education," *Kappan* (September 1988): 18–31; a series of articles on technology in *NASSP Bulletin* (October 1989); and various issues of *Educational Technology* and *New Technology*.

5

· · · · ·

The Administrative Team
School Site and District Levels

___

The concept of *team* suggests a group of people working together cooperatively, rather than unilaterally, to achieve a common goal. The main goals of an administrative team should be to develop school policies and procedures, solve common problems, and, in general, to improve education in the schools by utilizing the collective talents and interests of team members.[1] The concept is based on the assumption that administrative decision making should be a joint effort rather than the sole responsibility or province of one individual, such as the principal or the superintendent. Educational problems are too complex for individual decision making; thus, it is becoming increasingly difficult for individuals to make sound decisions regardless of their levels of competence.[2]

Although it may not be possible to establish an administrative team in every school or school district (and evidence presented later shows that many school districts only pay lip service to the concept), the potential advantages of cooperatively pooling human resources to achieve school and district objectives strongly support the need to organize an administrative team, where feasible. An administrative team is particularly important as a means of facilitating school-based management—a concept premised on the assumption that the individual school is the fundamental decision-making unit within the district.[3] The following sections discuss, first at the building level and then at the district level, the various aspects of organizing and operating an administrative team.

THE ADMINISTRATIVE TEAM AT THE SCHOOL SITE LEVEL

COMPOSITION OF THE TEAM

With few exceptions, principals should make the final decision on the composition of the administrative team at the school site level. They are the ones who are administratively in charge of the school and should, consequently, determine the membership of the team. In determining team composition, they should keep in mind that its basic functions are leadership, communication, decision making, and shared power and authority.[4] Therefore, key communicators who are involved or should be involved in school decision making should be members of the team. These would include, in most situations, the people occupying the positions identified in figure 5.1.

Figure 5.1 shows the proposed composition of the administrative team and its main characteristics. It indicates that the composition of the administrative team at the building level consists of the principal; the assistant and/or vice-principal; department heads, unit leaders, or representative teachers; program directors; pupil personnel workers; and a central office representative. The latter might be the individual in charge of secondary or elementary school education in the district, or someone else who could represent the central administration's point of view, because a number of the topics that the administrative team discusses are likely to hold implications for the entire district. Care should be given that the team not become too large. James Guthrie noted that administrative teams "should probably be limited to no more than twelve members, since the awkward social dynamics of larger groups often pose problems."[5] (Consider also adding parent representatives to the team to obtain perceptions, insights, and other contributions to effective decision making and community support that the team might not otherwise receive.)

Note the recommendation that the pupil personnel workers (such as the school psychologist) and the program directors (such as the director of the instructional materials center) should be members of the administrative team. These persons may not actually be administrators or supervisors in the strictest sense of those terms, but at least some of their responsibilities are administrative or supervisory in nature. More important, because of their contacts with students, teachers, and parents, they offer a potentially rich source of insights and perceptions useful to the other members of the team. Even though it may not be possible or even necessary to include these specialists in all of the team meetings, each of them can make a valuable contribution and consequently should be included as members and attend meetings as appropriate.

Figure 5.1 Proposed Composition and Characteristics of the Administrative Team at the School Level.

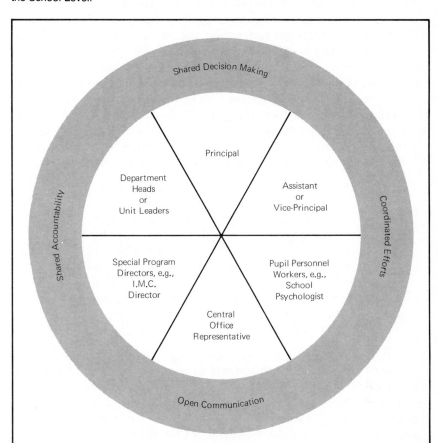

STRUCTURE OF THE TEAM

Once the composition of an administrative team has been determined, its structure should be defined, that is, how each component of the team should function individually and in relationship to the other components. If the principal has not already assigned responsibilities to each member of the team, this should be the first priority.[6]

The next objective should be to define the interrelationships between the various members of the team. If the administrative team is to operate effectively, each member must know about the responsibilities and roles of the other members, and how all team members can help each other and work together cooperatively. In essence, assisting one another and working cooperatively are the keys to a successful team. The type of structure which is initiated must arrive at these outcomes, or the concept of *team* degenerates into a group of individuals merely trying to promote and protect their own selfish interests or those of the people they represent, rather than the common good of the school.

Administrators should recognize that team members need assistance in learning their new roles if they are to be active, effective participants. Therefore, a series of in-service programs should be developed for building administrators, department heads, teachers, and parents. These programs would (1) educate all members about the concepts and practices of team management; and (2) begin to develop, build, and strengthen relationships among members of the administrative team. David Cavanaugh and Cynthia Yoder noted in describing a highly successful team model that

> in-service must focus on group processes in the areas of communication/problem solving, decision making/goal setting, and values clarification. Through such activities we have been able to break down barriers which, consciously and/or subconsciously, inhibit teaming. Additionally, the interaction has led to a building of trust and understanding between team members. This, in turn, has facilitated ownership of district goals and objectives (shared between team members) and resulted in a commitment to complete, or assist in completing those goals and objectives. The bottom line is increased productivity coupled with an increased sense of accomplishment and self-esteem.[7]

When establishing the structure of an administrative team, the issue of the authority relationships within the team should be faced squarely. An initial question which needs to be answered is, who should head the team? Although various arguments could be made in response to this question, it would appear that in most situations the head of the team will be—and should be— the principal. The principal is the one who has the overall responsibility for administering the school and is the one held primarily accountable for what goes on in the school.

This does not mean, however, that principals should play a domineering or controlling role on the administrative team, nor does it mean that they should exercise all of the leadership on the team.[8] On the contrary—the principal's main role should be that of facilitator and resource person for the other team members, as further discussed under "Group Leadership Behavior" in chapter 3. More precisely, as Roland Barth indicated, the new, emerging concept of shared leadership will rely on principals able to (1) articulate their goals and visions, (2) relinquish power, (3) involve teachers in decision making, (4) assign responsibilities wisely, (5) share responsibility for failure, (6) attribute success to others, and (7) recognize and believe in the competence of others.[9] Thus, principals should try to stimulate members' involvement and leadership, and should attempt to emphasize and encourage cooperation among all members of the team.[10] Although principals may retain the authority to assign responsibility and evaluate the performance of the team members, this should be done cooperatively as much as possible.

Once decisions have been made regarding who will serve on the administrative team, other logistical issues need to be addressed: first, the administrator needs to determine *how often* and *when* team meetings will be held. Weekly? Monthly? Before school? After school? During the school day? Administrators should not assume that these will be easy questions. To a certain extent, decisions regarding frequency, time, and duration of meetings depend on the composition of the team. Obviously, when teachers are involved (as they should be), the issues become far more complex than when the team is comprised of only administrators and support personnel. James Lipham found in his studies of effective secondary schools that schedules were typically arranged so that the team could meet at least weekly, usually during school time.[11]

Second, decisions need to be made regarding the *length of terms of membership.* In addressing this issue, James Guthrie noted that "council members should be elected for two- or three-year terms. To provide some continuity, council members' terms should be overlapping."[12] In addition, policies need to be determined regarding the replacement and/or reappointment of team members once their terms have expired.

Finally, and probably of greatest significance, is the issue of *compensation* for participation on the administrative team. For some members, such as assistant principals and program directors, participation is a necessary element of their job descriptions; therefore, compensation is not an issue. However, for others for whom participation is an added responsibility, such as teachers and counselors, the issue eventually surfaces if the team is to become a regular component of the school's organizational structure. A number of members are satisfied with the intrinsic rewards of recognition and status which their membership may provide; yet, at a practical level, administrators need to address questions regarding released time, load reductions, and financial compensation. Ann Lieberman indicated that the answers to these questions, and those previously raised, can be determined by the local context, available funding, and the level of administrative support for the team concept.[13]

ADMINISTRATIVE TEAM PROCESSES

An administrative team is functioning if all members are carrying out their responsibilities effectively, and the various members of the team are working cooperatively with each other. Although many of the activities of the team members take place outside of their formal meetings, most of the important discussions and decisions take place during team meetings; and members have their greatest opportunity to interact during meetings.[14]

Probably the most important step principals can take, to productively utilize the contributions members offer during a meeting and to help the group to function as a unit, is to maintain an atmosphere conducive to a spirit of cooperation and mutual respect with an absence of tension or nervousness. In such an atmosphere, each member of the team should feel free to contribute ideas and to question other members of the team, including the principal.

The atmosphere at the meetings depends primarily on what the principal says and does. An organizational structure for the team may have been defined which ostensibly permits a great deal of give and take in discussions. But if the principal dominates and controls discussion during the meetings, it is unlikely that the atmosphere will be conducive to a free exchange of ideas and thoughts by the other members of the team.[15]

The principal undoubtedly needs to exercise authority in certain situations. For example, the other members of the team may wish to make a decision that the principal opposes or one that is in the principal's area of primary responsibility and accountability.[16] The administrator can avoid most of these situations by specifying clearly at the outset the authority of the administrative team and the authority of the principal. In exercising their authority, principals should also adhere to the following guidelines developed by Gorton based on an analysis of the social science literature on authority:

1. In deciding on the need for a directive and in its formulation, presentation, and execution, principals should take into consideration how the order affects the recipients personally, recognizing that people are likely to question or resist directives which they believe are not in their best interest.

2. They should take into consideration the strengths and limitations of those expected to implement a directive. They should avoid issuing orders for which people lack the necessary motivation, skill, or training to carry out.

3. They should explain thoroughly the rationale behind each directive and its relationship to the goals of the organization. They should not assume that people will understand the reasons for an order or that they will necessarily see the logic or value of an order.

4. They should leave room for modifying the original order or its method of implementation. Flexibility and a willingness to compromise when appropriate are key factors in exercising administrative authority successfully.

Figure 5.2 Recommended Processes for Team Meetings.

A.	B.	C.	D.	E.
Soliciting input from team members for the development of the agenda	Preparing background material on agenda items and disseminating these materials and the agenda several days prior to the meeting	Maintaining a written record of important ideas and decisions made during the meeting	Disseminating written minutes to all appropriate parties after the meeting	Following through on decisions or actions taken during meetings

5. They should issue only directives they are relatively sure will either be obeyed or can be enforced if they are resisted. Orders which cannot be enforced in one situation weaken administrators' authority for successfully issuing orders in other circumstances.[17]

While it may be necessary for principals to exercise authority on occasion, their main role should be that of facilitator and resource person.

For administrative teams to function effectively, principals should also establish certain managerial procedures, such as those identified in figure 5.2.

The processes recommended in this section are designed to facilitate input from the various members of the team in the development of the agenda and to provide organization and continuity to the meetings. Although one can overemphasize the need for planning and the follow-through after a meeting, a certain degree of preparation and organization is necessary to avoid an aimless discussion and few concrete results. It is primarily the principal's responsibility to make sure that these outcomes do not occur.

SELECTED MEMBERS OF THE TEAM AT BUILDING LEVEL

For administrative teams to operate successfully, school administrators must understand the roles and problems of team members. Because some of these roles are presented in other chapters, this section concentrates on the role and problems of the assistant principal, the department chair, and the unit leader.

THE ASSISTANT PRINCIPAL

For the most part the assistant principalship has not received the attention it deserves in most administration and supervision textbooks and in the educational literature.[18] In recent years both national elementary and secondary school administrators' organizations have attempted to spotlight the role of the assistant principal; several studies have focused on ascertaining the role and problems of the assistant principal.[19]

For example, one study by Gorton and Robert Kattman surveyed assistant elementary school principals in large city school systems where assistant principals at the elementary level were more likely to be found.[20] Their analysis of the data revealed several interesting findings that shed light on the assistant principalship at the elementary level.

One somewhat surprising finding was that a slight majority of the assistant principals were women. Although historical data are not available, there has been a substantial increase in the number of women serving in the elementary school assistant principalship. An analysis of mean differences between male and female assistant principals participating in Gorton and Kattman's study showed that females were significantly more satisfied in the position than were males, and salary was a less important reason for women to enter administration than for men.

Almost 90 percent of the assistant principals in the study reported that they possessed Master's degrees or higher; approximately 25 percent of the assistant principals had earned Ed.S. or Ph.D. degrees. Most of the assistant principals had been teachers for thirteen or more years, and approximately 60 percent of them were over forty-six years old. The main reason most assistant principals had entered administration was to capitalize on the opportunity to help others, according to the respondents. Most of the assistants were serving in schools with student populations between 600 and 900.

Seventy percent of the assistant principals held full-time administrative positions; 30 percent of the assistants indicated that they also had teaching responsibilities and, of this number, about 19 percent had been given no released time to carry out their administrative assignments. The amount of released time from teaching allocated to the assistant principals was significantly related to the extent to which they actually performed important administrative tasks ranging from conducting orientation for new students to evaluating teachers.

Most assistant principals reported that their main responsibilities at the elementary level were (1) administering student discipline, (2) placing substitute teachers, (3) providing instructional materials, and (4) establishing teacher duty rosters. Student discipline appeared to be the dominant responsibility of assistant principals, with three-fourths of the assistants stating that they had been assigned major or total responsibility for discipline. However, in a related analysis, only about one-third of the assistants indicated that they desired to take that much responsibility for student discipline.

What would the assistant principals do if they were not heavily occupied with the responsibility for administering student discipline? Most of them wanted significantly more responsibility than they were currently assigned in the following areas: orienting new teachers, selecting textbooks, administering public relations programs, planning teacher in-service, conducting student orientation, developing the school calendar, administering special education programs, administering guidance programs, developing curriculum, and deciding school policy. The research data do not suggest that most assistant principals want to be totally responsible in each of these areas, but they definitely want more responsibility than they are currently assigned.

The elementary school assistant principals who participated in the study were asked to indicate their perception of the severity of certain problems occurring in their situations. Most assistant principals reported that the following possible problems were either nonexistent or very minor: few opportunities for on-the-job professional growth, no job description, poorly defined responsibilities, little appreciation for contributions, lack of information provided by principal, little or no involvement in decision making, uncooperative parents, and little or no feedback from superiors on areas in need of improvement. The percentage of assistant principals who felt that these problems were serious or very serious in their situations ranged from 10 to 30 percent. The two problems that were perceived by the assistant principals as most serious were (1) insufficient time to do the job, and (2) too many misbehaving students. A majority of the assistant principals viewed these as either moderate or very serious problems.

All of the problem areas were negatively correlated with job satisfaction. The more serious the assistant principal perceived the problems to be in the school situation, the more likely was that person to report a low level of satisfaction with the job. However, most assistant principals indicated considerable satisfaction with their jobs, although from 28 to 34 percent of them reported a low level of satisfaction with the salary they received, the recognition the job has given, and the assistance they received to improve their effectiveness.

Most assistant principals identified their principals as their main sources of help on their jobs; about 20 percent reported that their principals provided only some or no help. Approximately 60 percent of the assistant principals stated that they received only some or no help from other assistant principals, other principals in their town, or the central office staff. Over three-fourths of the assistant principals indicated that they received no on-the-job help from their university advisers, their state administrators' assocciations, or the national administrators' association. The latter results may be related to the finding that most of the assistant principals who participated in the study did not now belong to state or national elementary administrator organizations, nor did they plan to join these organizations in the future.

What did elementary assistant principals hope to be doing in the future? Almost half of the respondents hoped that in five years they would become principals; another 29 percent wanted to become central office administrators. Only 25 percent of the assistant principals wanted to continue in the same positions either in the same schools or different ones.

Even though the data from Gorton and Kattman's study of elementary school assistant principals show that most of them were currently satisfied with their jobs, the majority desired higher salaries, greater recognition, increased responsibility, and eventual promotion to higher-level administrative positions. These latter findings on the desires of assistant principals suggest that consideration needs to be given to improving the salary and recognition of elementary school assistant principals and redesigning the responsibilities of the position.

At the secondary level, several studies have been conducted on the assistant principal. In discussing the various tasks assistant principals typically perform, Lewis Roderick noted the following:

1. Supervising bus loading/unloading.
2. Listening to teachers' explanations of problems they are having with students.
3. Telephoning parents to check students' placement.
4. Informing teachers of changes in students' placement.
5. Hearing students describe their difficulties with teachers or students.
6. Consulting with guidance counselors or psychologists about the best way to approach or deal with students.
7. Writing notes responding to teachers' inquiries.
8. Talking with teachers about their schedules.
9. Sending notes to teachers requesting information about students' achievement, behavior, and attendance.[21]

These activities appear to be consistent with those reported in the past.[22]

An examination of the various activities reported by assistant principals reveals that student control and discipline are the basic responsibilities.[23] This is not surprising since traditionally and, perhaps, typically the main duties of the assistant principal have been in these areas. In schools having assistant principals, students who are discipline problems are referred to the assistant principal. The assistant principal is also the one who has the responsibility of checking on and working with students who have attendance problems. Although student discipline and attendance duties may be shared with the principal, the assistant principal usually shoulders the major responsibility for these two areas.

Supervising student discipline and attendance are not the only functions of assistant principals. In reality, their duties depend on what the principal assigns to them; most assistant principals are given other kinds of responsibilities in addition to student discipline and attendance.

For example, a study by Lee Stoner and William Voorhies found that a majority of assistant principals agreed that the assistant principal(s) in their schools perform the following responsibilities, in addition to handling student discipline and attendance:

- Supervise the student activity program.
- Supervise teachers through classroom visitations.
- Assist in the evaluation of teachers.
- Counsel teachers concerning personal or professional troubles.
- Prepare daily bulletins or announcements.
- Represent the school at community functions.[24]

Data from other aspects of this research and related studies, however, strongly indicate that handling student discipline and attendance problems continues to be the main responsibility of most assistant principals at the secondary school level.[25]

The responsibilities of working on problems of student discipline and attendance are important ones; assistant principals can make valuable contributions to school programs by carrying out these responsibilities effectively. Nevertheless, frequently these are onerous and frustrating tasks for them, particularly if assistant principals are primarily responsible. There are many days when assistant principals may not even be able to leave their offices during an entire morning or afternoon because they are seeing students or teachers in regard to student discipline or attendance problems. These typically are not pleasant experiences for assistant principals, even though they may derive some measure of satisfaction from the feeling that they are trying to help others. In fact, Catherine Marshall contends that new assistant principals experience a form of culture shock as they come to terms with the reality of their new positions.[26]

The job of the assistant principal at the secondary level would not seem to be a very satisfying position, but research is not conclusive on this point. One study by the National Association of Secondary School Principals found that assistant principals were much less satisfied with their current jobs than they were when they were teaching.[27] Other studies, however, have concluded that most assistant principals are reasonably well satisfied in their current jobs but, perhaps paradoxically, they do not see the assistant principalship as a lifetime career position.[28] One investigation found that assistant principals were dissatisfied when they were

- Placed on salary levels similar to those of instructional staff and counselors.
- Completing tasks that require a work day of ten hours or more.
- Functioning in a totally traditional (lacking any particular innovative quality) organizational structure.
- Lacking sufficient secretarial assistance, loyalty, and/or skills.
- Lacking adequate office space, equipment, and privacy.
- Lacking assistance from immediate superiors.
- Ignored by superiors.
- Having constraints placed on them by collective bargaining agreements.
- Perceived negatively by faculty members in reference to the handling of student discipline problems.
- Perceived by students merely as disciplinarians.
- Experiencing on-going constraints implicit in state and federal policies, in recent student rights and responsibilities documents, and in recent court decisions relative to due process and discipline.
- Having credit for work performed by the assistant principal attributed to superiors.[29]

Assistant principals who are not as satisfied with their current positions as when they were teaching are not apt to remain in their present situations if they receive opportunities to advance. Nor is it likely that these same individuals can operate at their maximum effectiveness in their present jobs if those jobs are not giving them the professional and personal satisfaction which they expect and need.

The findings from these studies have raised questions about whether the assistant principalship as it has been set up in many schools is meeting the needs of the individuals occupying the positions or the needs of the schools. Consequently, efforts have been made to improve the position; these include a number of conferences for assistant principals sponsored by the national elementary and secondary administrators' associations.[30] One approach has been to better define the nature of the position. A proposed job description for the assistant principal, which was developed after an examination of many job descriptions, appears quite comprehensive; it is presented in figure 5.3.[31] John Kreikard and Scott Norton have also developed a competency-based job description for assistant principals, which should be examined.[32]

One approach to making the job of the assistant principal more satisfying and effective has been to divide the responsibilities for student discipline and attendance among two or more assistant or vice-principals, rather than

Figure 5.3 Job Description for the Assistant Principal.
NASSP Bulletin, May 1980. Used with the permission of the National Association of Secondary School Principals.

Relationships

The assistant principal is directly responsible to the principal, and is expected to maintain an effective working relationship with other administrators, teachers, maintenance staff, clerical staff, and student personnel.

Duties

Administration

1. Assists in the general administration of the school and serves as the principal when the principal is absent.
2. Operates the school according to the policies established by the principal, superintendent, and the board of education.
3. Participates in the preparation of the annual budget.
4. Assists in preparing district, state, and county reports.
5. Has the responsibility for preparing orientation program for substitute teachers and for assigning them as the situation demands.
6. Prepares the school calendar in cooperation with those responsible for school activity programs.
7. Designs the master schedule for the school.
8. Issues and keeps an inventory of all keys to school property.
9. Supervises the maintenance and cafeteria personnel and originates maintenance requests with the proper authorities.
10. Supervises school security aides.
11. Arranges bus schedules for students.
12. Performs such other duties and assumes such other responsibilities as the principal may assign.

Teaching Personnel

1. Participates in the evaluation of teachers.
2. Assists in the preparation of the teacher handbook.
3. Assists in interviewing and recommending prospective staff members and substitutes.
4. Assists teachers in the improvement of teaching techniques after an assessment of teaching methods.
5. Develops a regular schedule for teacher observation and maintains an accurate record of the observation providing an opportunity for teacher reaction.
6. Serves as liaison, when necessary, between individual teachers and the school principal.
7. Maintains an "open door" policy to all teaching personnel.

Student Personnel

1. Assists those who are responsible for school discipline.
2. Makes disciplinary judgments for students, assigns school detention, or takes other appropriate measures.
3. Establishes a system for keeping detailed records of discipline problems.
4. Assists in the development of the student activities program and is responsible for securing sponsors and supervising the financial aspects of the program.

(continued)

Figure 5.3 Continued

5. Supervises guidance functions relating to counseling, testing, college information, etc.
6. Participates in the responsibility for the safety and security of students and all others participating in the educational programs of the school.
7. Schedules time to become known to the students by having visibility in the halls, classrooms, and at school activities.

Curriculum

1. Assists department chairpersons and teachers in curriculum revision and improvement.
2. Attends departmental meetings on a regular basis.
3. Participates in area, district, and other public and professional meetings that concern curriculum improvement.
4. Supervises the mandatory testing programs.
5. Participates in preparation of reports and maintenance of records pertaining to curriculum and instruction.
6. Maintains a constant effort to keep aware of curriculum innovations that surface in areas outside the school's local district.

External Relations

1. Establishes liaison with community agencies (not school financed) that are concerned with the health and welfare of citizens.
2. Attempts to develop good working relationships with the law enforcement and judicial personnel. Works cooperatively with the police and probationary officers.
3. Approves all news releases that deal with the school's operation and establishes a good relationship with the media.
4. Is responsible for developing good articulation programs with feeder schools.
5. Maintains good relationships with service groups that assist handicapped and economically deprived students.

assigning all student discipline and attendance problems to one individual. In this situation, other tasks such as classroom supervision, curriculum implementation, and administration of student activities are shared by two or more assistant principals, thereby providing them with some task variety while utilizing their individual special talents. Generally this kind of sharing of responsibilities occurs in schools where the administrative team concept is being fully implemented and assistant principals feel that "they are real working partners in the management of the school."[33]

Examples of this approach may be found in schools—particularly those with large enrollments—where assistant principals may be assigned the responsibility for a single grade level, such as tenth grade, or, in an elementary school, three grade levels. Typically included in these assignments are the maintenance of student discipline and attendance, and/or classroom supervision, curriculum development and implementation, and administration of student activities. Assistant principals are responsible for the total programs at their grade levels, and principals provide the overall coordination and leadership for their schools.

Whether a school can have an assistant principal for each grade level or set of grade levels depends, of course, on the size of a school and the financial circumstances of the school district. Apportioning the responsibilities of student discipline and attendance, as well as other administrative and supervisory tasks, among the administrators of the school is a desirable step toward improving the position of the assistant principal; and it is consistent with the team concept described earlier. In defining and allocating the responsibilities of the assistant principal, principals should keep in mind the following guidelines developed by the Utah Association of Secondary School Principals and reported in the *Bulletin of the National Association of Secondary School Principals:*

1. Project a clear picture of what the assistant will be doing and offer some suggestions about how it should be done.
2. Outline carefully how much responsibility and authority will be given: when responsibility is given, give your assistant equal amounts of authority.
3. Seek the other faculty members' willingness to cooperate with your assistant, and spell out for them the areas of responsibility you have given.
4. Your assistant will do a better job if informed of your plans and problems.
5. Add responsibility gradually. Let your assistant get the feel of the job, then give more responsibility in small doses, to continue to develop capabilities.
6. Hold a loose rein. Constant checking will make your understudy nervous and slow down development. It can also lead to loss of confidence and initiative.
7. If a time limit has been set for the completion of an assignment, expect your assistant to abide by it. Never ignore the failure to complete a task.
8. Praise excellence. When a job is well done or exceeds your expectation, express your compliments. Expressing appreciation motivates one to excel.
9. The accountability for the activities of an assistant cannot be reassigned or relinquished. If an assistant is ineffective, the principal is expected to take remedial action.
10. Periodically review and evaluate your assistant's progress. Be constructive. Your assistant has the right to know of weakness and strength as you see them.[34]

In the final analysis, the principal holds the key to the professional improvement, as well as the morale and satisfaction, of the person who occupies the position of assistant principal.[35] Generally the principal delegates to the assistant principal the latter's responsibilities and provides whatever supervisory help, support, and recognition the assistant principal receives. To maximize their assistant principals' leadership contributions, Gorton suggests that principals (1) expand the job to include activities beyond student discipline and attendance; (2) become an advocate for the position of assistant principal and stress its worth and importance publicly; (3) increase the rewards associated with the position by increasing the amount of public and private recognition given to the assistant principal; and (4) facilitate the professional growth of the assistant principal by encouraging and endorsing participation in classes, workshops, state conferences, and national conventions.[36]

Even though in too many instances principals still delegate to assistant principals only those activities and responsibilities that they find less desirable. Most principals now recognize that the assistant principalship must become more than just a dumping ground for those tasks that the principal does not want to handle.[37] Principals must provide the kinds of responsibility, support, and recognition which give assistant principals opportunities to make maximal contributions and meet their professional and personal needs as well if they are to become truly viable administrative team members.

THE DEPARTMENT CHAIR

A second important member of the administrative team of a school, more typically found at the secondary school level, is the department chair, often referred to as the department head.[38]

Similar to the position of assistant principal, the department chair was created in response to increases in the managerial and supervisory functions of the school, but was also a result of the growth of departmentalization in the secondary schools.[39] Once secondary schools became departmentalized, the next logical step was the appointment of individuals to administer the departments, and the position of the department chair came into existence. Although the position is more prevalent in large schools and in departments such as English, social studies, math, and science, many schools have a department head for every department in the school. Despite periodic predictions of its demise, the position continues to exist in the vast majority of secondary schools in the country.

Similar to the role and responsibilities of the assistant principal, those of the department head are no more or less than the principal defines them to be. Though often proposed by various educational authorities as a position of instructional leadership, in practice the department chair has frequently been grounded in the quicksand of administrative triva and handicapped by inadequate released time to carry out instructional improvement activities.[40]

In many schools a department head provided with only one period of released time is saddled with various administrative minutiae ranging from inventorying equipment and furniture to administering a department's supplies and requisition procedures. This is unfortunate; a department chair potentially can make a major contribution to the improvement of a school's instructional and curricular program because of the subject matter and methodological expertise of the individuals occupying those positions. Before that potential can be realized, however, schools must define the nature of the position and provide sufficient released time so that department heads can more reasonably carry out their leadership responsibilities.

Developing a Job Description

The first step toward improving the position of department head in a school is to develop a comprehensive job description.[41] Sample job descriptions for the department chair appear in an excellent book by Thomas Sergiovanni, *Handbook for Effective Department Leadership.*[42]

To be functional, a job description should be developed cooperatively by those working in the position and those supervising and evaluating its occupants. In the case of the department chair, this means that the department heads themselves should be directly involved with the principal in any process leading to the revision of a job description already in use or the introduction of a new one. If individuals who occupy the position of department chair are to accept fully their responsibilities, it is essential to obtain their involvement in defining those responsibilities.

Released Time and In-service Training

Although department chairs' job descriptions should meet the criterion of comprehensiveness, they cannot be considered realistic unless the individuals who occupy the roles are provided with both sufficient time to carry out their responsibilities and in-service training to help them to acquire the knowledge and skills necessary to function as the educational leaders of their departments.[43] How much released time should be provided for department heads is not an easy question to answer, but certainly one period is insufficient (except in very small departments) if the school really expects chairs to function as leaders of departments.

It would appear that chairs of small departments should be given at least one period of released time to carry out leadership responsibilities. In departments with more than six to eight teachers, two or three periods of released time should be provided, depending on the relative size of the department.[44] The administration of a school or school district must consider financial factors in deciding about released time; however, unless department chairs are given adequate time, it is unrealistic to assume or expect that they can truly function as educational leaders of their departments.

Providing sufficient released time will not, of itself, ensure that chairs use the time wisely and productively. Most department heads are good teachers, and some of them are masters of the art. The vast majority of them, however, do not possess the background nor have they received the training necessary to function as educational leaders. They may possess expertise in the methodology and content of their discipline, but they typically lack knowledge and skill in such areas as leadership, classroom supervision, human relations, and curriculum development and implementation.[45]

Before department chairs can make maximum contributions to the improvement of educational programs, they need to be involved in some type of in-service training in the areas just mentioned. Whether this training is conducted by the school district with university assistance or wholly by the school district is not important. What is important is that the school or school district provide department heads with developmental in-service programs that help them acquire the knowledge and skills they need to function as educational leaders.[46] As with released time, the provision of an in-service program has financial implications. But until department heads are given appropriate training for their responsibilities, they are unlikely to perform effectively.

Problems

Poorly defined role descriptions, insufficient released time, small salary increment for increased responsibilities, and little or no in-service training for the position represent the major problems that many department heads experience. However, an additional difficulty barely mentioned in the educational literature on department chairs is the problem of role conflict. Role conflict is created when chairs have imcompatible expectations placed on them by two or more individuals or groups. In the case of the department heads, they have expectations placed on them in regard to their behavior by both the principal and the teachers in the departments. These expectations may be—and frequently are—incompatible, thereby creating role conflict for the department heads.[47]

For example, the teachers in a department typically regard the department chair as their representative and expect the chair to be loyal to them and to promote their interests.[48] The principal, on the other hand, has usually appointed or selected the chair and consequently generally regards the chair as the administration's representative to the department, and expects the chair to be loyal and promote the administration's interests.

THE UNIT/TEAM LEADER

In elementary schools organized along multiunit lines, the unit leaders in the building should be included on the schools' administrative teams.[49] Each unit in a multiunit elementary school is headed by a unit leader who is also a member of the instructional improvement committee of the school. Although the Wisconsin Research and Development Center, which originated the position, has stated, "the responsibility of the unit leaders is instructional, not administrative or supervisory," they have gone on to say, "They serve as a liaison between the unit staff and the principal and consultants, and they coordinate the efficient utilization of the unit staff members, materials, and resources."[50] Because all of the latter tasks are administrative in nature, it is recommended that the unit leader be included in the administrative team at the elementary level.[51] (For further information on the responsibilities of the unit leader, write the Wisconsin Research and Development Center, Madison, Wisconsin.)

In elementary schools not organized by units, representative teachers from the various grade levels should be selected for participation on the administrative team. The critical issue is not the formal title bestowed on teachers, but rather that teachers be included on the administrative team and be allowed to demonstrate their leadership potential. However, Sharon Rallis noted that before teachers can undertake this leadership role two conditions must exist:

1. Policymakers and administrators must establish the structures and send the signals enabling teachers to undertake such leadership.
2. Teachers must become responsible professionals, willing to devote the time and energy that leadership requires, willing to be held accountable for the decisions they make, and willing to listen to one another and to accept leadership from within their own ranks.[52]

In general, the same concerns and problems experienced by department chairs at the secondary level need to be addressed and resolved at the elementary level by unit leaders as well. These issues include determining role expectations, released time, compensation, and in-service training. In many ways, given the restrictive nature of an elementary teacher's day, these issues are more complex and difficult to arrange at the elementary level than at the secondary level.

THE ADMINISTRATIVE TEAM AT THE DISTRICT LEVEL

Although our focus thus far has been on the concept of the administrative team at the building level, the idea originated at the district level, primarily in response to problems created by teacher militancy.[53] Beginning in the late 1960s, administrators began to find themselves being squeezed out of teachers' organizations. At the same time, more and more pressure was being placed on administrators by both school boards and superintendents to decide whether they were management or something else. This was not an easy decision for many administrators concerned that the lines of difference between management and teachers were being drawn too rigidly. For most school administrators, however, there was little choice: the teacher groups wanted them only on terms perceived as unfavorable by most administrators; superintendents and school boards moved quickly to introduce the concept of the administrative team, which seemed to offer a logical or useful home base in the district. Since that time the record of the administrative team at the district level has been a mixed one, and problems have surfaced that are discussed later. Because few people disagree with the concept of a district administrative team, and since the problems can be resolved, given the right kind of commitment and educational vision, we begin our examination of the district team by first looking at the proposed objectives of the team.

OBJECTIVES OF THE DISTRICT ADMINISTRATIVE TEAM

A review of the literature on the district administrative team suggests that it has two main objectives: (1) to develop and present a unified front in collective bargaining with teachers and in the implementation of the master contract, and (2) to utilize collectively the talents and interest of individual administrators and supervisors to solve problems and improve education within the district.[54] Even though writings on the concept of the district administrative team no longer emphasize the first objective, it remains undoubtedly an important goal of most district teams. More important to an administrative team, however, is the second one. The full sense of what the achievement of this goal implies, at least to building administrators, was stated in *Management Crisis: A Solution,* a booklet published by one of the national principals' associations; this statement continues to represent the most tenable rationale for a district administrative team.

> An administrative team represents a means of establishing smooth lines of organization and communication, common agreements, and definite patterns of mutuality among administrators and the Board of Education as they unite to provide effective educational programs for the community. There are two primary parties involved in the

leadership of a school district, namely, the board of education whose responsibility is policy making, and the administrative team (including all administrators) whose major responsibilities include first advising the board in establishing district policies and then guaranteeing their effective implementation. A close, harmonious working relationship between these two parties is obviously vital to the successful operation of a school district.

It should also be clear that an effective administrative team has, in addition to its assigned legalistic and primary role of policy implementation, a vital leadership function to perform. Never before has more interest and concern been raised about the need for strong and united educational leadership. An effective administrative team provides a collective means of strengthening school district leadership, giving individual administrators needed assistance, opportunities, and job satisfaction.[55]

COMPOSITION AND STRUCTURE OF THE DISTRICT ADMINISTRATIVE TEAM

A district administrative team should be composed of all of the principals and assistant principals in a district and all of the central office supervisors and administrators.[56] Department heads are not usually included on a district administrative team, nor are the other individuals identified as serving on a *school's* administrative team except as specifically mentioned in this section.

The district team is, of course, headed by the superintendent. Although the responsibilities of a district superintendent would vary somewhat depending on the size of the district and the expectations of the school board and community, the job description presented in figure 5.4 illustrates the duties expected of most superintendents.[57] (For additional information on the superintendent's role and relationships, see *Roles and Relationships: School Boards/Superintendents,* published by the American Association of School Administrators at Arlington, Virginia.)

The job of an administrator is seldom a particularly easy one, but various studies have shown that the position of superintendent is especially demanding and frequently of short duration. For example, Carl Dolce sees the superintendency under a great deal of stress because of numerous special interest groups.[58] And a study by Nancy Pitner and another by Rodney Ogawa found the superintendent frequently bogged down by telephone calls, petty problems, and mundane activities.[59] However, due to the size of the sample in these studies, we cannot be sure that the findings are representative of most superintendents. On the other hand, observation would suggest that the job of the superintendent is indeed a challenging one.

Figure 5.4   Job Description for the Superintendent of Schools.

Basic Responsibility

The Superintendent is Chief Executive Officer, responsible for overall planning, operation, and performance of the district. He provides staff support and recommendations to the Board with respect to decision-making policies and planning, and is the Board's agent in all relationships with the staff. He selects, organizes, and gives leadership to the management team, oversees planning, staff development, and reward systems throughout the district, and ensures adequate operational and financial control.

Reports to   Board of Education

Supervises   Associate Superintendent(s)
                      Director of Planning and Analysis
                      Director of Public Relations
                      Administrator of Business Services
                      Administrator of Educational Services
                      Principals

Primary Duties

1. Establish and maintain a constructive relationship with the Board of Education based on appropriate performance and financial information. Guide and aid the Board in its effective operation through competent staff support and through development of his and the Board's skills in working together effectively.
2. Establish programs and practices for the constructive relationship of the district with its community on a school and district level.
3. Direct and coordinate district planning to ensure educational programs and performance in line with community needs and desires. Ensure sound planning of financial, facility, and enrollment requirements for the future. Prepare and recommend an annual budget consistent with long-range plans and appropriate to community financial resources.
4. Recommend district purposes, objectives, policies, and decisions as required, supported appropriately with information, analysis and conclusions presented to the Board and to the public.
5. Organize, staff, and give leadership to the management team as required to meet district objectives. Plan and execute a management development program appropriate to realizing the district's educational objectives.
6. Establish and maintain constructive relationships throughout the district at all levels, including community, parents, students, teachers, staff, and Board.
7. Ensure the development and operation of adequate recruiting, selection, appraisal and compensation systems to meet district objectives.
8. Develop the competence of teachers, staff, and management to the maximum extent possible in the best interests of the individuals involved and to meet district objectives.
9. Establish a performance monitoring system incorporating test data results and consumer judgments to meet the needs for performance information throughout the organization.
10. Establish financial and operating controls adequate to safeguard the district against misuse of funds or unnecessary operations, and to ensure fair value for all expenditures.

Figure 5.4 Continued

11. Provide leadership to the district and community in developing, achieving, and maintaining high educational standards, sound programs, and good performance.
12. Ensure that district operations meet all legal requirements.
13. Oversee staff negotiation and contract administration.

Key Working Relationships

1. Work with the Board of Education to ensure effective Board operations, district policies, objectives, decisions, and performance in line with the public interest.
2. Maintain effective relationships with and among staff at all levels of the organization.
3. Ensure a healthy relationship of the district with its community.
4. Represent the district as required and appropriate in various community, association, and government activities.

Even though the superintendent is undoubtedly the most important member of the administrative team at the district level, other members such as the building principals, assistant superintendents, and program directors, also make up the team.[60] And, although it is difficult to generalize, other members of the team in many school districts are clearly not of equal status, regardless of what the promotional literature about the team may suggest. Central office administrators, such as assistant superintendents and directors, have greater status on the district administrative team than do principals, and principals are accorded greater status on the team than supervisors. The hierarchical nature of a district administrative team does not mean, however, that the team cannot work together cooperatively and effectively if the status differences between the various members of the team do not inhibit or restrict input from the members of the team, and if each person on the team is given a role in which to make useful contributions and from which to derive adequate satisfaction.

Although there are a large number of important principles to be followed in operating and evaluating a district administrative team, those presented in question form in figure 5.5 are basic. These same principles can be adapted for use in operating and evaluating the administrative team at the building level.

PROBLEMS OF THE DISTRICT ADMINISTRATIVE TEAM

Building administrators have much to gain from, and a great deal to contribute to, the district administrative team. However, the team concept at the district level is not without its problems, according to the reports of principals.[61] As implemented in some school districts, the administrative team has

Figure 5.5 Principles for Operating and Evaluating the District Administrative Team.

1. Are the roles and responsibilities of each member of the team, and of the team as a whole, clearly defined?
2. Does the team provide adequate involvement for all members in the development and evaluation of school and district objectives, policies, and procedures?
3. Does the team work on the problems that individual schools are experiencing, as well as on districtwide problems?
4. Does the team provide assistance and help, when needed, to the various members?
5. Do the team philosophy and objectives permit diversity and individual initiative when, in the eyes of the building administrator, such efforts would improve education in an individual school?
6. Is there periodic evaluation of team effectiveness?
7. Is there truly a spirit of good will and cooperation on the part of the various members of the team?

stifled creativity and initiative at the school building level and has provided individual school administrators with little or no involvement in developing, as contrasted with implementing, school policies and procedures.

For example, the objective of some district administrative teams seems to be to promote uniformity in school curriculum, teaching, and rules and regulations among all of the schools of the district. Individual differences are frowned on. School administrators attempting to develop a different curriculum for their students or trying to operate their schools in a somewhat different way are informed that they are not performing as team members should and that individuality is not desirable or possible under the team concept.

Of course, the issue of centralization and uniformity versus individualization and diversity is not a new problem in education. There has always been some tension, and sometimes a great deal, between the central administration and its desire to achieve district objectives with articulation and correlation among various schools, and school administrators who seek the autonomy to develop the best educational program possible for "their kids," even if that program differs from the educational program in the other schools of the district.[62] The team concept, as implemented in some school districts, has accentuated this tension and caused significant problems for some building administrators.

An equally important, but different kind of problem that has confronted some school administrators trying to work cooperatively on the district administrative team is their limited role. Building administrators may be regarded by other members of the administrative team as only the implementers of school board policies and procedures. Frequently they are not given an adequate opportunity to participate fully in the development of recommended policies and procedures, and often their involvement could be characterized as "too little, too late." As a result, building administrators in a number of states have pressured their state legislatures to pass collective bargaining laws.[63] A corollary development has been the establishment of administrative unions in a number of districts, particularly more populous ones.[64]

ADMINISTRATORS' UNIONS

According to the Educational Research Service, the main causes of middle management unionization are

1. Inadequate communication with the superintendent and the school board.
2. Unclear role information.
3. Desire for improvements in salaries and fringe benefits.
4. Lack of influence in decision making.
5. Erosion of authority through teacher negotiations.[65]

With regard to the fifth cause, in his study of the role of the principal on the school district management team Robert Sladky found that principals did not perform a significant role in decision making about teacher-board negotiations. In general, principals were limited to being reactors to the impact of contract language on administering the school; they were not involved at all in the decision-making process to establish school district priorities for bargaining with teachers.[66]

When middle management personnel have organized themselves into collective bargaining units, they have concentrated in their bargaining on securing protection from the adverse effects of unilateral and bilateral decisions by the school board and superintendent; these have tended to erode the authority and professional security base of principals and supervisors.[67] Roy Nasstrom and Craig Pier noted that through collective bargaining,

> Principals may secure higher salaries and fringe benefits, more extensive employment rights, seniority provisions in case of layoffs, better communications with other school district personnel, greater authority on the job, and opportunities to achieve quick resolution of internal disputes (chiefly through effective grievance procedures).[68]

A study by John Pisapia and Jack Sells on collective bargaining agreements between administrators and school boards found that these protections fell into three areas.

Administrator Collective Bargaining Protection	Example
1. Protection of middle management's traditional right to participate in decision making.	In staffing for a school, the principal has the right to define the position and shall have the primary responsibility for recommending the hiring of all personnel.
2. Protection against arbitrary or capricious actions affecting the job security of middle management personnel.	The school board will refrain from making involuntary transfers and when transfers are made, will transfer to a position of equal or higher status.
3. Protection against arbitrary or capricious acts against middle management personnel's character, integrity, physical well-being, and personal property.	The principal shall have the availability of grievance procedures and shall be given opportunity to become knowledgeable about all adverse items placed in his/her personnel file.[69]

As can be seen from these protections, most if not all of them should not require administrators' collective bargaining but should result from the full implementation of the concept of the administrative team discussed previously in the chapter. The fact that many administrators have felt a need to bargain for these protections suggests that in many school districts the superintendent and the school board are giving only lip service, if even that, to the concept of the administrative team. That this is occurring is suggested by a publication of the American Association of School Administrators, which states:

> The superintendent who tries to go it alone in this increasingly complex world is riding for a fall, and the school board that insists on it is only fooling itself. . . . Meanwhile administrator groups around the country are making noises ominously like those of teacher organizations. . . . They feel that they are "management" in name only. . . . They are turning more to the negotiations arena to resolve their identity crises.[70]

What the future holds for administrator collective bargaining is uncertain. Many people oppose it because of its potential divisiveness and the devastating effect it may have on the administrative team concept. Nasstrom and

Pier asserted that the "adversarial aspects of bargaining would make impossible the unity of purpose inherent in the concept of administrative team."[71]

Although national principals' associations would prefer the administrative team rather than collective bargaining as a vehicle for advancing their members' interests and securing their protections, their position is likely to change if the authority of the principal continues to erode in more and more districts, and school boards and superintendents do not use the administrative team to provide principals with necessary protections.[72] Specifically, what do school boards and superintendents need to accomplish? John Dillion recommends the following:

1. Extend to your principals and supervisors real and meaningful authority over the selection and direction of personnel for whom they are responsible.
2. Give your building administrators or others with similar responsibility an opportunity to participate in the budgeting/planning process and to develop priorities for the purchasing of equipment and supplies which they require to carry out the educational program.
3. Before making the concessions at the bargaining table, seek the advice and counsel of those who must serve on the front line administering and implementing the terms of the contract.
4. Finally, let the economic benefits which you offer them and the status and support which you give them be such that they will feel no need or reason to bargain collectively.[73]

Although it would seem that the implementation of these recommendations would give real substance to the concept of the district administrative team, the most important ingredient of all is the need for mutual trust and respect among administrators, the superintendent, and the school board. As Harold McNally perceptively observed, "An administrative team's success depends above all on the existence of an atmosphere of mutual trust, cooperation, and open communication among team members."[74] Unless the superintendent and the school board can create and maintain this type of an atmosphere, building administrators will likely choose to organize a separate bargaining unit, rather than to become members of a district's administrative team.

A FINAL NOTE

Undoubtedly, the administrative team approach is potentially a valuable mechanism for facilitating cooperation among administrators, teachers, and staff members, and for better utilizing their individual interests and talents.

Whether that potential is realized or not, however, depends in large part on the extent to which the concept is fully implemented in practice, and on the degree to which all members of the team strive to work together cooperatively in a spirit of mutual trust and confidence. To this end, Barth noted

> If the vision of shared leadership helps teachers and principals respond less randomly and more coherently and cooperatively to the thousands of situations they face every day in the school, it may matter less whether the schools become communities of leaders than that they are heading in the right direction.[75]

Review and Learning Activities

1. What are the purposes and advantages of the administrative team?
2. What factors should an administrator consider in defining the composition and structure of the team?
3. How can the administrator increase the effectiveness of team meetings?
4. Discuss the main duties and problems of the assistant principal. How can the problems perhaps be ameliorated?
5. What are the purposes, composition, and problems of the district administrative team? How can the problems be best solved?
6. Why have some administrators chosen collective bargaining rather than the administrative team to protect and promote their interests and concerns? What are the implications of collective bargaining for administrators, in regard to their relationships with the superintendent, the school board, and teachers?

Notes

1. For a review of the origins of team management, see J. S. Swift, "Origins of Team Management," *National Elementary Principal* (February 1971): 26–35.

2. Bryce W. Grindle, "Administrative Team Management: Four Essential Components," *Clearing House* (September 1982): 29–33.

3. See James W. Guthrie, "School-Based Management: The Next Needed Education Reform," *Kappan* (December 1986): 305–9; J. Lindlow and J. Hynderickx, "School-Based Management," in S. C. Smith and P. K. Piele, *School Leadership: Handbook for Excellence,* 2d ed. (Eugene, Oreg.: ERIC Clearinghouse on Educational Management, 1989), 109–34; Paula A. White, "An Overview of School-Based Management: What Does the Research Say?" *NASSP Bulletin* (September 1989): 1–8; Jerry J. Herman, "A Decision-Making Model: Site-Based Communications/Governance Committees," *NASSP Bulletin* (December 1989): 61–66; and Thomas Timar, "The Politics of School Restructuring," *Kappan* (December 1989): 265–75.

4. See Bryce W. Grindle, "Administrative Team Management"; and Philip Hallinger and D. Richardson, "Models of Shared Leadership: Evolving Structures and Relationships," *Urban Review* (Winter 1988): 229–45.

5. Guthrie, "School-Based Management," 307.

6. David P. Cavanaugh and Cynthia L. Yoder, "Team Management + Merit Pay = Effective Leadership: From Theory to Practical Application," *NASSP Bulletin* (February 1984): 93–99.

7. Cavanaugh and Yoder, 98.

8. See Roland S. Barth, "Principals, Teachers and School Leadership," *Kappan* (May 1988): 639–42; Sharon C. Conley and Samuel B. Bacharach, "From School-Site Management to Participatory School-Site Management," *Kappan* (March 1990): 539–44.

9. Barth, "Principals, Teachers, and School Leadership," 640–42.

10. For a good approach to achieving these goals, see Joseph A. Young and Jerry Sturm, "A Model for Participatory Decision Making," *NASSP Bulletin* (April 1980): 63–66.

11. James M. Lipham, "Administrative Arrangements," in Herbert J. Klausmeier, James M. Lipham, and John C. Daresh, *The Renewal and Improvement of Secondary Education* (Lanham, Md.: University Press of America, 1983), 199–224.

12. Guthrie, "School-Based Management," 307.

13. Ann Lieberman, "Teachers and Principals: Turf, Tension, and New Tasks," *Kappan* (May 1988): 648–53.

14. For an excellent discussion of the various administrative processes involved in operating a team outside of meetings as well as during meetings, see Richard Wynn, *Theory and Practice of the Administrative Team* (Washington, D.C.: National Association of Elementary School Principals, National Association of School Administrators, and National School Public Relations Association, 1973), 23–35.

15. Although focused on the informal leader, this article by Bradford is well worth reading, as the topic of a hidden agenda might apply to the principal and team meetings. See Leland P. Bradford, "The Case of Hidden Agenda," *National Elementary School Principal* (October 1957): 23–28.

16. For an interesting discussion of shared authority, see Guthrie, "School-Based Management," 307.

17. Richard A. Gorton, *School Leadership and Administration: Important Concepts, Case Studies, and Simulations* (Dubuque, Iowa: Wm. C. Brown, 1987), 59. For an expanded discussion of the concepts and issues associated with authority, power, and influence, see chapter 3.

18. Although some may associate the position of assistant principal primarily with the secondary school, it has long existed at the elementary level as well. For example, see Esther L. Schroeder, "The Status of the Assistant Principal in the Elementary School," in *The Elementary School Principalship: The Instructional and Administrative Aspects,* Fourth Yearbook of the Department of Elementary School Principals, ed. Arthur J. Gist (Washington, D.C.: National Education Association, 1925), 389–400.

19. Neal C. Nickerson, Jr., "Assistant/Vice-Principal," in *Encyclopedia of School Administration and Supervision,* ed. Richard A. Gorton, Gail T. Schneider, and James C. Fisher (Phoenix, AZ: Oryx Press, 1988), 35–36.

20. Dick Gorton and Bob Kattman, "The Assistant Principal: An Underused Asset," *Principal* (November 1985): 36–40.

21. Lewis Rodrick, "Working with Assistant Principals to Achieve Maximum Value," *NASSP Bulletin* (February 1986): 92.

22. See B. D. Austin and H. L. Brown, *Report of the Assistant Principalship, vol. 3: The Study of the Secondary School Principalship* (Washington, D.C.: National Association of Secondary School Principals, 1970); and John C. Croft and John R. Morton, "The Assistant Principal: In Quandary or Comfort?" (ERIC Report Ed–136–392).

23. Catherine Marshall and William Greenfield, "The Dynamics in the Enculturation and the Work in the Assistant Principalship," *Urban Education* (April 1987): 36–52.

24. Lee H. Stoner and William T. Voorhies, "The High School Assistant Principalship in NCA Schools in Indiana," *The North Central Association Quarterly* (Spring 1981): 408–13.

25. Ibid. Also see Alice Black, "Clarifying the Role of the Assistant Principal," *NASSP Bulletin* (May 1980): 33–38; and Croft and Morton, *The Assistant Principal: In Quandary or Comfort?*

26. Catherine Marshall, "Professional Shock: the Enculturation of the Assistant Principal," *Education and Urban Society* (November 1985): 28–58.

27. David Austin, *The Assistant Principalship* (Reston, Va.: National Association of Secondary School Principals, 1970), 72.

28. For example, see Stoner and Voorhies, "High School Assistant Principalship."

29. Robert Garawski, "The Assistant Principal: His Job Satisfaction and Organizational Potency," *Clearing House* (September 1978): 9.

30. See David Panyako and LeRoy Rorie, "The Changing Role of the Assistant Principal," *NASSP Bulletin* (October 1987): 6–8; Joseph A. Smith, "Assistant Principals: New Demands, New Realities, and New Perspectives," *NASSP Bulletin* (October 1987): 9–12; Kent D. Peterson, Catherine Marshall, and Terry Grier, "The Assistant Principals' Academy: Technical Training and Socialization of Future Leaders," *NASSP Bulletin* (October 1987): 32–38; and *The Assistant Principal of the 90s* (Madison: Association of Wisconsin School Administrators, 1990).

31. See "Job Description for the Assistant Principal," *NASSP Bulletin* (May 1980): 50, 51–55; and Association of Wisconsin School Administrators, *The Role of the Assistant Principal* (Madison, Wisc.: AWSA, 1985), 1–6.

32. John A. Kriekard and M. Scott Norton, "Using the Competency Approach to Define the Assistant Principalship," *NASSP Bulletin* (May 1980): 1–8; *The Role of the Assistant Principal* (Madison, Wisc.: Association of Wisconsin School Administrators, 1985); and M. Scott Norton and John A. Kriekard, "Real and Ideal Competencies for the Assistant Principal," *NASSP Bulletin* (October 1987): 23–30.

33. Richard A. Gross et al., "How the Management Team Concept Can Succeed," *NASSP Bulletin* (May 1980): 26; and Graham Kelly, "The Assistant Principalship as a Training Ground for the Principalship," *NASSP Bulletin* (October 1987): 13–20.

34. "Taking the Pressure Off," *NASSP Bulletin* (December 1980): 128.

35. See Richard Gorton, "Improving the Assistant Principalship: The Principal's Contribution," *NASSP Bulletin* (October 1987): 1–4 and "How to Increase the Assistant Principal's Effectiveness," *Tips for Principals* (Reston, Va.: National Association of Secondary School Principals, 1988).

36. Gorton, "Improving the Assistant Principalship," 2–4.

37. Molly J. Clemons, "The Assistant Principal's Responsibility in School-Based Management Systems," *NASSP Bulletin* (September 1989): 33–36.

38. Joseph J. Blase, "Political Interaction Among Teachers: Sociocultural Context in the Schools," *Urban Education* (October 1987): 286–309.

39. An early report of this process can be found in Preston W. Search, "The Larger High Schools," *School Review* (April 1900): 225–27. For an early study of the position of department chairs, see Harlan C. Koch, "Some Aspects of the Department Headship in Secondary Schools," *School Review* (April 1930): 263–75.

40. Thomas J. Sergiovanni, *Handbook for Effective Department Leadership*, 2d ed. (Boston: Allyn & Bacon, 1984), chap. 1a.

41. James F. Costanza, Saundra J. Tracy, and Roger Holmes, "Expanding Instructional Leadership through the Department Chair," *NASSP Bulletin* (November 1987): 77–82.

42. Sergiovanni, *Handbook for Effective Department Leadership,* chap. 1b and 2a.

43. James M. Gallagher, *How to Make Better Use of Department Chairmen.* (ERIC Report Ed–136–366).

44. For evidence on the importance of adequate released time so that the department chairman can perform effectively as an instructional leader, see James A. Hoeh, "The Effectiveness of Department Chairmen in the Improvement of Instruction" (Ph.D. diss., University of Michigan, 1969).

45. Frances Weaver and Jeffrey Gordon, *Leadership Competencies for Department Heads: Needed Areas for In-service Education.* (ERIC Report: Ed–168–197).

46. For an example of such a program, see Samuel Kostman, "On-the-Job Training for Classroom Supervisors," *NASSP Bulletin* (December 1978): 44–50.

47. Lieberman, "Teachers and Principals," 649–50.

48. Richard J. Konet, "Research-Based Method for the Selection of Department Chairpersons," *Clearing House* (May 1989): 384–86.

49. The multiunit school was pioneered by the Research and Development Center at the University of Wisconsin, and its operation is now rather widespread. For more information about the multiunit school, see Herbert J. Klausmeier, "The Multiunit School and Individually Guided Education," *Kappan* (November 1971): 181–84.

50. Herbert J. Klausmeier et al., *Individually Guided Education and the Multiunit Elementary School* (Madison, Wisc.: Wisconsin Research and Development Center, 1971), 31.

51. Ibid. 32–34.

52. Sharon Rallis, "Room at the Top: Conditions for Effective School Leadership," *Kappan* (May 1988): 643.

53. *The Administrative Team* (Washington, D.C.: American Association of School Administrators, National Association of Elementary School Principals, National Association of Secondary School Principals, and Association of School Business Officials, 1971).

54. J. Lindelow and S. Bentley, "Team Management," in S. C. Smith and P. K. Piele, *School Leadership: Handbook for Excellence,* 2d ed. (Eugene, Oreg.: ERIC Clearinghouse on Educational Management, 1989), 135–51.

55. *Management Crisis: A Solution* (Washington, D.C.: National Association of Secondary School Principals, 1971): 3–4.

56. For an earlier concept of the administrative team which excluded building administrators, see *Profiles of the Administrative Team* (Washington, D.C.: American Association of School Administrators, 1971).

57. Robert Crowson, "The Local School District Superintendency: A Puzzling Administrative Role," *Educational Administration Quarterly* (August 1987): 49–69.

58. Carl Dolce, *Superintendents Under Seige—Get the Leader.* (ERIC Report Ed–122–362).

59. Nancy J. Pitner and Rodney T. Ogawa, "Organizational Leadership: The Case of the School Superintendent," *Educational Administration Quarterly* (Spring 1981): 45–65.

60. *Selecting the Administrative Team* (Arlington, Va.: American Association of School Administrators, 1981), chap. 5.

61. Normal Hale, *The Management Team* (Eugene, Oreg.: ERIC Clearinghouse on Educational Management, 1978).

62. For an interesting discussion of "creative insubordination," see R. Bruce McPherson, Robert L. Crowson, and Patricia A. Brieschke, "Majorie Stallings: A Walk Through a Mine Field," *Urban Education* (April 1986): 62–85.

63. John Pisapia, "The Legal Basis of Administrator Bargaining," *NOLPE School Law Journal* (1980), no. 1: 61–84.

64. B. Cooper, "Collective Bargaining for School Administrators Four Years Later," *Kappan* (October 1979): 130–31.

65. Educational Research Service. *Collective Negotiation Agreements for Administrators: An Analysis of 100 Contracts* (Arlington, Va.: Educational Research Service, Inc., 1976); see also, Bruce S. Cooper and Robert T. Nakmura, *The Unionization of School Administrators: A Study of Public Policymaking and Labor Relations* (ERIC Report Ed–248–569).

66. Robert Sladky, "The School Principal and the District Management Team," *Association of Wisconsin School Administrators Bulletin* (May 1980): 22–26.

67. Roy R. Nasstrom and Craig D. Pier, "Bargaining and Nonbargaining Principals," *Planning & Changing* (Summer 1983): 101–8.

68. Ibid., 101.

69. John R. Pisapia and Jack D. Sells, "Administrator Protections in Negotiated Contracts," *NASSP Bulletin* (November 1978): 43–54.

70. The American Association of School Administrators, *The Administrative Leadership Team* (Arlington, Va.: AASA, 1979).

71. Nasstrom and Pier, "Bargaining and Nonbargaining Principals," 101.

72. "Management Team: An Idea Whose Time Has Passed?" *Education U.S.A.* (February 26, 1979): 200.

73. John Dillon, "Alleviating Administrator Unionism" (Paper presented at the 112th annual meeting of the American Association of School Administrators, Anaheim, California, 1980).

74. Harold J. McNally, "A Matter of Trust," *National Elementary Principal* (November/ December 1973): 33.

75. Barth, "Principals, Teachers," 642.

6

· · · · ·

BUDGET AND PLANT MANAGEMENT

———

In recent years budget and plant management have assumed greater importance in education. Although the economic situation and public opinion influence the priority an administrator gives to these two administrative responsibilities, in a period of increased expectations and reduced resources the efficient and effective management of the budget and the school plant becomes essential. Without prudent budget and plant management, a school district likely goes from one budget crisis to the next, and the physical facilities of the district are not used economically. Therefore, any administrator who wishes to manage the school's financial and physical resources efficiently and effectively must understand the major concepts of school budget and plant management.

BUDGET MANAGEMENT

To begin an exploration of budget management, it is necessary to define a budget. Most individuals have a common knowledge of what a budget is; yet, many are not aware of the distinction between a budget and budgeting. A budget is a product consisting of three elements: "(1) a description of the total educational program to be provided by the school district; (2) an estimate of the expenditures needed to carry out the desired program; and (3) an estimate of the revenues which will be available to pay for the expenditures."[1] Budgeting, on the other hand, is the process used to develop the budget document.

Therefore, budgeting is defined as "the sequence of activities involved in planning the district's educational program, estimating the needed expenditures and revenues to implement these programs, gaining the necessary approval, and using the budget to assist in managing the district's operations."[2] Thus, the school administrator's role in relation to the budget consists of three tasks: (1) developing the budget, (2) administering the budget, and (3) evaluating the efficiency and effectiveness of the services and products funded by the budget. A discussion of the concepts, practices, and problems associated with each of these tasks follows.

DEVELOPING THE BUDGET

The school administrator's role in developing a budget may be a limited or an important one, depending on the degree to which the budget process in a school district is centralized.[3] In a *centralized* budget process the school administrator's responsibility is typically restricted to asking teachers to submit a list of items needed for the next year on a prescribed form, reviewing the requests, submitting to the district office a combined list of requests, reporting to the district office data relative to the number of students and teachers assigned to the school for the following year, and identifying which capital improvements are needed for the building.[4] In this traditional budget process, most administrators make a modest effort to involve the instructional staff in the budgeting process, but "often this becomes simply a matter of asking the staff for their ideas about equipment and supplies."[5]

After receiving each building's requests, district central office personnel develop the budget for each school based on preestablished formulae which determine the allocations for the various budget categories.[6] For example, the district budget formula for library books may be $20 for each student enrolled in a school. Thereby, a school of 750 students would receive a budget allocation of $15,000 for the purchase of library books, whereas a school of 1,000 would receive $20,000. The superintendent consolidates all requests across all buildings and submits a detailed budget to the board of education.

Under a centralized budget-making process, the role of the school administrator is a very limited one. The advantages of this approach are that the allocation criteria are applied objectively and evenly, and the development of the budget proceeds efficiently.

For a *decentralized* budget, the process is reversed: The school board and central office personnel develop a total districtwide operating budget and determine a lump-sum allocation for each building.[7] This budget approach is frequently referred to as "school-based, or site-level, budgeting," and it seems to be on the increase in certain parts of the country.[8] Decentralized budgeting is based on the following principles:

1. The establishment of an overall district budget target.
2. The establishment of basic (nonschool site) costs.
3. The assignment of all remaining funds to individual schools on a per capita basis.
4. The development of individual school expenditure plans.
5. The assembly of individual school expenditure plans into a comprehensive district budget in accordance with item 1.[9]

After receiving their building allocation, school administrators are assigned responsibility for developing the budgets for their schools, based on the unique characteristics of the students and/or the educational program in the building.[10] This method of determining the district's budget "stems from a belief in the individual school as the fundamental decision-making unit within the educational system."[11] In this approach, administrators are encouraged to involve teachers, parents, and even students in developing the budget for their schools. Each of these groups may be requested to identify and define their needs relative to the replacement and/or addition of products and services. Throughout the process, the emphasis is on involving a wide variety of people and developing a budget reflecting the unique needs of a particular school. School administrators, working with advisory committees, produce detailed building budgets which specify the amounts to be "spent for certified and noncertified personnel, supplies, equipment, facilities operations and maintenance based on the committee's perception of the needs of the individual school."[12]

Once individual building budgets are determined, there could be many variations within a school district regarding how each building decides to allocate its funds. Probably of greatest significance, would be the impact the process might have on teacher assignments and hiring. Under a strongly decentralized model, school administrators are able to determine staffing patterns within their schools. For example, each school might receive a specified number of instructional units based on the school's projected enrollment, such as one unit for every 25 students.[13] For budgeting purposes, an instructional unit is a sum of money equal to the average teacher salary in the district. A school may be assigned 30 instructional units at an average of $30,000 for a total building allocation of $900,000. The school administrator and the advisory committee then determine the staffing arrangement for the school and how many teachers, aides, paraprofessionals, and other instructional support personnel to employ using the instructional allocation. Given the needs of a specific building, a decision might be reached to increase the teacher-student ratio and hire additional paraprofessionals or classroom aides rather than maintaining the traditional staffing arrangement.

Although budgets developed under a decentralized process are seldom accepted without some changes by the district administrations, proponents of this budgeting process generally believe that it is more likely to reflect the needs of each school than is a centralized approach. By encouraging greater involvement by teachers, parents, and students, a decentralized method capitalizes on their insights and helps them to understand the problems and parameters of budget making. As Thomas Glass observes, "Perhaps one of the most effective ways in which a district can obtain legitimate and direct participation in the school district is by involving them in the district budgeting process, preferably at the local neighborhood school level."[14] To further strengthen the participatory nature of this model, central office administrators should consider soliciting special building and program requests prior to determining the building allocation. By doing so, building administrators and staff members would have the opportunity to present their unique needs and future plans for inclusion into the budgeting process. Following a systematic review of the various building requests, differentiated building allocations could be made based on the needs presented.

Generally, the advantages attributed to school-based budgeting focus on the strong programmatic emphasis of the process. Jo Ann Spear, for example, noted that advantages of the system are (1) a cooperative examination of existing practices and programs (2) the involvement of teachers in determining the schools' financial status and spending limitations; (3) a closer relationship between parents and teachers; and (4) decision making closer to the students.[15]

One disadvantage of a decentralized budget process, according to Carl Candoli and associates, is that it may result in a situation in which, "Each school becomes a small kingdom within itself and cooperative efforts among and between schools can become difficult."[16] In addition, school administrators' responsibility and demands on their time are greatly increased when districts shift control of the school's budget to the school site.[17] And, teachers need to put in extra time and planning to make the system work. Thus, the intensity of this system which demands investments of time and personnel is frequently viewed as both a disadvantage and an advantage of the decentralized process.

School district officials need to determine the extent to which the district will be centralized or decentralized. The popularity of centralized budgeting has frequently focused on the "belief that budgets were best managed by centralization, and growth of executive authority which resulted from increased centralization and the ability of centralized funding plans to provide the best workable method for allocating resources during times of growth."[18] On the other hand, "the most important reason to decentralize is: when the school district is facing a persistent and substantial decline in resources or enrollment, or when the system is experiencing disruption in communications."[19] Thus, as Francis Theimann, and Penney Sanders posited, "the concept then is: in periods of growth, decisions should be made centrally so that all components grow at approximately the same rate. In periods of decline, decentralized units should determine what should be discontinued so that the essential elements can survive."[20]

Of course, the budget-building process in many schools is neither totally decentralized nor centralized, but a combination of the two. For example, one pattern is for the central office to determine the initial budget allocations for each school, based on preestablished formulae, giving each administrator an opportunity to present a case for raising the budget allocation to accommodate any specific category for a school. The salient advantage of this budget system is that it establishes a degree of equity among schools in budget allocations, while providing for additional financial support for any school which can demonstrate that due to certain conditions or circumstances it merits a higher budget allocation than the district standard formula allows. The disadvantages of this method are that (1) the budget is still formulated largely on the basis of the central office's assumptions about the needs of each school rather than on an assessment by the people at the building level, and (2) a tendency exists for building administrators to accept the district office's determination of their budgets to avoid the arguments and hassles which may be required to secure a higher budget allocation for their schools.

Any budget process has disadvantages as well as advantages; the only purpose of this analysis is to explore several alternatives.

PPBS

One systematic approach to budget building about which the school administrator should be knowledgeable is PPBS: planning, programming, budgeting system. This approach is sometimes called PPBES, where the E stands for evaluation.[21] Simply defined, PPBS "calls for resources to be aligned with organizational purposes, programs, or objectives instead of with actual objects to be puchased, personnel, or materials. If a purpose is agreed to by decision makers, then whatever expenditure is necessary to accomplish the purpose is permitted."[22] Although traditional approaches to budgeting also emphasize

Figure 6.1 PPBS versus the Traditional Approach: The Process.

PPBS	The Traditional Approach
Stages:	Stages:
1. Assess educational needs.	1. Ascertain teacher needs in the areas of supplies, books, etc.
2. Define educational objectives and the criteria and methods to be used in evaluating the objectives.	2. Determine the merits of teachers' budget requests on the basis of perceived need.
3. Determine programs and priorities to achieve objectives.	3. Estimate the cost of teacher requests.
4. Ascertain and cost-estimate the resources needed to carry out programs	4. Organize the budget around categories of needs, e.g., instructional supplies, books, etc.
5. Organize the budget around program areas and objectives.	

planning and programming, these budgeting processes are not organized to the same degree around programs and program objectives as are those in PPBS, nor is evaluation emphasized to the same extent.

Gerald Ubben and Larry Hughes noted that at its simplest PPBS involves five steps:

1. Establishing the general goals to be achieved.
2. Identifying the specific objectives defining this goal.
3. Developing the program and processes believed necessary to achieve the objectives and goals.
4. Establishing the formative and summative evaluation practices.
5. A review and recycle procedure that indicates whether or not, or the degree to which, the program and processes resulted in the achievement of the objectives and the goals; and, if not, to help determine other procedures, processes, and programs.[23]

Perhaps the best way for school administrators to understand PPBS is to compare this budget process with the traditional approach and to see an example of how the budget is organized under each. Figure 6.1 presents an outline of the process of PPBS along with the traditional approach.[24]

As one can see by comparing the two approaches shown in figure 6.1, PPBS places a much greater emphasis on defining and evaluating program objectives and on relating the funds which the school purportedly needs to achieve those objectives, rather than to the nature of the items being funded. For an example of how the budget is organized and presented under the two approaches, see figures 6.2 and 6.3.[25]

Although PPBS appears to represent a more logical and effective method of budget building, it has been adopted in only a minority of school districts

Figure 6.2 Traditional Budget Format.

School _____   Date _____

Current Enrollment _____   Anticipated Enrollment _____

Resources Needed

	Account No.	Current Costs	Projected Costs
Personnel Certified	_____	_____	_____
Personnel Noncertified	_____	_____	_____
Instructional Supplies	_____	_____	_____
Noninstructional Supplies	_____	_____	_____
Capital Equipment	_____	_____	_____
Maintenance	_____	_____	_____
Food Services	_____	_____	_____
Transportation	_____	_____	_____

Figure 6.3 PPBS Budget Format.

Program Title _____ Program Level _____ Program No. _____

For period beginning _____ and ending _____

Program objective(s) _____ (The space on this form is less than _____

_____ would be needed in actual practice) _____

Program Description _____

_____

Program Criteria and Evaluation Methods _____

_____

_____

Anticipated Enrollment _____ Personnel Assigned _____

Resource Requirements	Current Year	Next Year	Following Year	Following Year
Salary and Teacher Fringe Benefits				
Supporting Staff				
Textbooks				
Supplies				
A.V.				
Maintenance				
Capital				
Other				

and its use is not as common as it was in the 1970s.[26] Experience has shown that the process can be extremely time-consuming. Also, it places an emphasis on relating budget allocations to definable objectives, and defining certain educational objectives has proved to be a difficult and frustrating task.[27] Other potential problems as identified by Forbis Jordan and Dean Webb include agreement on the input data and decisions that are required for the operation of the process and the inherent reservations that some administrators have for systems-oriented decision techniques.[28] Still, when one considers both the advantages and disadvantages, it would seem that PPBS offers school administrators a very good conceptual tool for the budget-building process. The findings of a study conducted by Hughes and Ubben concluded that budgets prepared using the planned program budgeting system were superior to those using the traditional approach.[29] The declining availability of resources and increased pressure for school accountability will likely force more districts to adopt some variation of this budget model.

PROBLEMS OF BUDGET BUILDING

Because school administrators' responsibility in the budget-building process is greater when a decentralized approach is utilized, it would be advisable for them to be aware of problems they might encounter in implementing this method.[30] The problems noted are not necessarily inherent in the decentralized approach to budget building, nor do they occur in all schools, but they may arise if the administrators fail to take certain safeguards. These problems, and our recommended precautionary measures, fall into several areas.

BUDGET REQUESTS BASED ON ACQUISITIVENESS OR LACK OF KNOWLEDGE

School administrators who involve teachers and others in the budget-building process sometimes receive budget requests from people who do not actually need what they are requesting or who do not know very much about the item they are requesting or how they are going to use it. For example, the administrator may receive a request from a grade-level chairperson who would like an additional word processor to be used by six teachers who already have access to another word processor. Or, the administrator may receive a request from a social studies teacher to include in the next year's budget a computer terminal to be installed in one of the social studies classrooms. In this case, the social studies teacher may be convinced about the educational value of a computer terminal but may lack the knowledge or skills for effectively utilizing the computer terminal in the social studies program.

One of the best safeguards for preventing problems of acquisitiveness or lack of knowledge from affecting the budget process is to require those individuals who submit budget requests to state in writing the rationale for proposing each item, how it will be used, and the extent to which those who will be using the item possess or will need to acquire additional knowledge and/or skill for effective utilization. School administrators should also require any person making a budget request to indicate in the rationale whether the proposed item is desirable or essential.[31] A desirable item is one that would improve a situation, but failure to purchase it would not be detrimental to the educational process. An essential item could be defined as something necessary to prevent a deterioration of a situation, or to implement a particular program successfully. A suggested format for securing this kind of information is included in the discussion of the next problem in budget building.

LACK OF SPECIFICITY ON HOW THE PROPOSED BUDGET ITEM WILL INCREASE STUDENT LEARNING

Budget requests may be for replacement or additional items. Proposed additional items may reflect increased enrollment, or they may represent projected improvements in the program of the school. A problem is created when school administrators receive budget requests that are unrelated to increased enrollment or do not clearly specify either how the proposed item would improve student learning or how such an improvement in student learning would be assessed. The individuals or groups who propose improvement items as additions to the budget may believe that these items are necessary for a better

Figure 6.4 Budget Proposal Form.

Name _____   Subject _____   Date _____

Budget Classification No. _____   (Check appropriate spaces)

                                                _____ Replacement _____ Desirable

                                                _____ Enrollment   _____ Essential
                                                              addition

                                                _____ Improvement addition

Description of Item _____

_____

_____ Unit Price: _____

Justification: _____

_____

_____

(Include in your justification the reasons why the item is needed, why it is desirable or essential, how it will improve learning opportunities, and how the improvement can be assessed before the next budget year.)

school program. Unless that belief can be translated into a statement of how the improvement would come about and how it would be assessed, however, administrators are in poor positions to make judgments on the validity of such budget requests. Questions for which administrators must obtain answers from the proponents of new budget improvement items are, "How would the new item(s) help the students, and how would we determine whether or not the improvement has been achieved?"

A budget proposal form school administrators might consider using to ameliorate the problems discussed in the previous two areas is presented in figure 6.4.

Although the budget request form recommended in figure 6.4 may seem complicated and imposing, it asks only for the information that administrators need to evaluate a budget request properly. If individuals making budget requests have carefully and thoroughly considered all of the various implications of the requests, they should have little difficulty in completing the form. The advantage of this budget proposal form is that it increases the probability of adequate investigation and consideration supporting each budget request.

NEED FOR BUDGET REDUCTION

Legislative mandates, citizen initiatives, the state of the economy, and declining enrollment have, from time to time, created a need for reduction in the overall budget of a school or school district. For the foreseeable future, educators will probably have to cope with the reality of less available resources and greater pressures for accountability.

Reducing the budget from the level of previous years is seldom an easy task. When programs are modified or eliminated, staff members laid off, and maintenance work and capital improvements delayed, the potential for frustration, disillusionment, and low morale is great. Although not all of the debilitating effects of budget reductions can be avoided, their effects can be minimized if the budget approach utilized is rational and fair. One budget approach that seems to meet these criteria and which has proven to be very useful in situations involving the need for budget reduction is zero-base budgeting. (Zero-base budgeting is not limited to the need for budget reduction, but its applicability seems most relevant to this situation.)

Zero-base budgeting (ZBB) originated in the federal government and has now been introduced in a number of school systems.[32] As William Hartman noted, this approach "attempts to avoid incremental budgeting, in which the existing budget is not questioned and attention is focused only on the new amounts or additions to be added to each. Rather, zero-based budgeting considers the entire budget and requires comparisons among all budget areas."[33] In essence, each expenditure must be justified theoretically from a base of zero. This includes current expenditures, as well as proposed new expenditures. Barry Mundt, Raymond Olsen, and Harold Steinberg further defined ZBB as "a process in which 'decision packages' are prepared to describe the funding of existing and new programs at alternative service levels, both lower and higher than the current level, and funds are allocated to programs based on rankings of these alternatives."[34]

In other words, in ZBB school administrators must provide justification for every single item in the proposed budget each year. The justification should include a rationale, objectives, evaluation criteria, and needed resources for alternative levels of service for each program. An adaptation of figures 6.3 and 6.4 could be used for this purpose.

Generally ZBB includes five basic steps:

1. Identifying decision units (defined as any programs that consume resources).
2. Analyzing decision packages (documents that describe a decision's objectives, activities, resources, and costs).
3. Ranking decision packages.
4. Allocating funds.
5. Preparing official budgets.[35]

Even though ZBB may offer an excellent approach for providing needed information so that decision makers can make more rational and fair budget reductions, the system does require increased competency on the part of the budget makers; a lot of hard work lies ahead for individuals and groups involved in the process.[36] ZBB requires decisions on resource allocations based on "operational definitions of goals and objectives, and analysis of associated costs."[37] When certain programs are cut and/or staff reduced, these actions impact negatively on the people affected. However, despite these possible limitations, ZBB offers a potentially better approach to reducing a budget than across-the-board cuts or other less systematic or more political methods.[38]

Cale Hudson noted that budget reductions are generally in response to declines in enrollment and loss of revenue and that the common practice of across-the-board budget cuts to reduce budgets *are* indiscriminate and *do* not use the professional judgment of school officials.[39] In urging that budget reductions should be systematic, he suggested the following areas as a logical priority listing when reductions are necessary:

1. *Budget Pad.* "Good times" budgets often contain a substantial safety margin. When conditions require a budget reduction, this is an area to examine for possible savings.
2. *Reductions in classes.* When enrollment losses are concentrated in grade levels and result in less than desirable size units for instruction, the duplicate classes could be eliminated without downgrading program quality.
3. *Noninstructional service functions.* Regardless of the reason for a budget reduction, examine such areas as transportation, maintenance, insurance premiums, and purchasing procedures for ways to operate more efficiently without restricting the instructional program.
4. *Capital outlay plans.* When budgets are under stress for reduction, the need to review any plans for new buildings or major remodeling projects seems obvious.
5. *Instructional support services.* Enrollment declines may induce a reduction in the need for materials and/or personnel in such areas as counseling, media/library, and administration and should be considered without fear of reducing program quality.
6. *The instructional program.* Only when all other options have been explored should the instructional program be violated.

LACK OF EXPERTISE IN EVALUATING BUDGET REQUESTS

Typical school administrators are generalists working with groups of teachers who are subject matter specialists. Administrators may have specialized in some aspect of the school program such as social studies or mathematics as undergraduates. But it is unlikely that administrators possess a very thorough understanding of all subject disciplines comprising the educational program. Consequently, during the budget-building process, administrators receive requests to include in the proposed budget certain items about which they may know very little.

For example, an administrator may receive a request from the science teachers to order a number of lab kits. The administrator may have taken only one or two college courses in science and may have no idea whether these particular kits are essential or even desirable. The administrator may be able to ask the science teachers a few general questions about the lab kits, but unless the administrator is personally knowledgeable about the subject, the penetrating, probing questions which need to be raised in evaluating the request may not be asked.[40]

In this situation, administrators have three main alternatives: Because the teachers are in a better position to know what they need than administrators are, the science teachers' recommendation that they need the lab kits may be accepted, although this procedure can result in administrators becoming rubber stamps for budget requests rather than evaluators of them.

Another alternative for administrators is to try to become more knowledgeable in the area for which the budget request is being made. Even though this approach is feasible to a limited extent and should be utilized as much as possible, it is not a complete answer to the problem, in light of all of the other responsibilities that administrators must perform.

A third alternative for administrators is to utilize consultant help from a department chairperson, a subject-matter supervisor in the district office, or perhaps even someone at the university or state department level to help with evaluating budget requests of a specialized nature. Assuming that such consultant help is available—a condition not always present—administrators should be careful in selecting the consultant to make sure that the latter will be objective in making assessments. The contribution of a consultant is of inverse value if the consultant has a vested interest in "building an empire" in the subject area.

REQUESTS FOR A SPECIFIC BRAND OF AN ITEM VERSUS CENTRALIZED BIDDING

Many individuals who request a budget item do not want just any make of the item, but desire a particular brand or model. For example, the teacher who believes that a 3M overhead projector is superior does not want any other brand. Or the orchestra instructor may request a musical instrument manufactured by a certain company. The problem is that the desire to specify a particular brand of an item is antithetical to the purchasing procedures of many school districts which believe in, or are required to, solicit bids on budget items and then select the company submitting the lowest bids. Competitive bidding for necessary items can result in cost savings in a market where there are several suppliers.[41] Therefore, teachers are seldom encouraged to specify particular brands for items they request.

School districts are, of course, obligated to obtain the best price possible in purchasing products and services. However, the primary factor determining whether a particular product or service is purchased should be the extent to which the item will be effectively utilized. Durability and cost are other important factors. Still, it makes little sense for a school district to purchase low-priced items if teachers or students will not utilize them effectively. Also, as one budget expert observed, "It is a principle of good management, as well as of good human relations, that the people who are to use equipment and facilities be given some voice in suggesting the materials they believe would be most effective to carry out the job."[42]

On the other hand, teacher turnover makes the policy of always budgeting and purchasing the exact brand of an item that a teacher requests a risky one. Perhaps the best resolution of this overall problem is for a school district to involve teachers and students—users and consumers of the products and services—to a greater extent in establishing the criteria for budgeting and purchasing items. This procedure would increase the possibility that factors other than cost and durability would be given consideration in the budgeting and purchasing of products and services, and should result in greater utilization of these items.

INADEQUATE CONSULTATION BETWEEN THE DISTRICT OFFICE AND INDIVIDUAL SCHOOLS

Because the budget-building process is a complex operation, it requires a great deal of consultation. Consultation is, of course, important in all aspects of administration, but is of extreme importance in the budget-making process.

If the district's central office and the individual schools do not consult sufficiently and coordinate their efforts effectively, the process of developing the budget may become disjointed and frustrating for many of those involved. Unfortunately, in all too many cases the latter consequences are prevalent.

A lack of consultation between a district's central office and the individual schools can occur at two main points during the budget process: (1) at the beginning, and (2) after the school budget is delivered to the central administration. At the beginning of the budget process, school administrators need to know certain basic facts about the budget situation in the district. For example, they need to know of any financial parameters under which the district and/or school must operate for the coming year. They need to know the program priorities of the district and the expectations of the district's central office for program development in the school. And, they need to know the extent to which they are free to involve teachers, students, and parents in the budgeting process for the school, and whether there are any budget limits under which they must work. The problem is that, in many districts, school administrators are not consulted at all in regard to this information, or the consultation is such that the information given to them by the district is vague or inaccurate in light of what eventually happens when the proposed budget is sent to the district's central office.

After the budget is sent from the individual school to the district office for review and final approval, the second type of inadequate consultation may occur between district administrators and school administrators. At this point, in too many instances, the proposed school budget is modified and changed by the district administrators without anything more than pro forma consultation with the school administrator. Proposed items are cut and substitutions are made, but the school administrator may not discover that these changes have been made until the approved budget is returned later in the year. The inadequate consultation, if acknowledged at all by the district office, is typically justified on the basis of insufficient time and "no other choice."

It would be unfair to indict district administrators totally for the problem of inadequate consultation between them and school administrators. School administrators themselves have not always taken the initiative to consult with the district administration, or taken advantage of the opportunity to consult. For example, it is particularly important for school administrators to confer with district business managers during all aspects of the budget process.

Also, in regard to inadequate consultation, district administrators are not free agents in making budget decisions; they are subject to many pressures from the school board and other groups. Additionally, consultation with school administrators is difficult to achieve in districts with a large number of schools.

Despite these obstacles, greater effort should be made by all concerned to increase the extent of consultation between the central office and the individual school in all phases of the budget-building process. Through better consultation, the ambiguities and frustrations of the budget-building process could be considerably reduced, thereby contributing to a more constructive and acceptable budget.

ADMINISTERING THE SCHOOL BUDGET

RESPONSIBILITIES AND PROBLEMS

Once the proposed budget is finally approved by the school board, administrators' main responsibilities relate to purchasing and accounting procedures. Typically, these procedures are predetermined by the district office and implemented by the schools.

School administrators are usually given the responsibility of making sure that the schools operate within their allocated budgets and do not overspend in any of the budget categories. By definition, "budget management is the process of regulating expenditures during the budget year to ensure that they do not exceed authorized amounts and that they are for the proper purposes."[43] To carry out this responsibility effectively, administrators need to obtain periodic (at least monthly) budget status reports. These reports should provide information on how much money has been spent up to a certain date, how much money has been encumbered (designated for purchase of products or services but not actually spent), and how much is left in each budget account.

In most medium and large school districts a budget status report is provided periodically to each school administrator. In districts that do not provide this service for administrators, they need to instruct the school secretaries or bookkeepers to prepare budget status reports. Without such reports, school administrators cannot effectively monitor the spending of funds. Even in those districts which provide budget status reports to the school administrators, the reports are usually a month behind the expenditures. This means that toward the end of the budget year it may be necessary for the school administrator to keep some type of internal accounting of the money spent, so as to not exceed the allocated budget.

Fortunately, computer technology is now available to assist school administrators in managing their budgets.[44] Yet, as Kent Chabotar found, it is both disappointing and surprising how little computerization exists within public schools.[45] Frequently, financial records are kept manually; thus, making data retrieval time-consuming and expensive. Many districts rely on large mainframe computers for financial management operations; therefore, data entry is slow and reports are typically late and out of date.

These problems may be corrected through the use of microcomputers at school sites. Relatively inexpensive, yet powerful, computers are now available with the appropriate spreadsheet and data base software to maintain most, if not all, of each school's financial records. With such equipment, school administrators are able to initiate an accrual accounting system,

> which means that as soon as a purchase order is initiated or a requisition for anything is approved, it is encumbered in the account book [data base]. Through such a process, the principal knows immediately how much money remains to be expended in any particular account. Under such a system, it is not likely that financial obligations will be made beyond the actual amount of money available.[46]

Generally, once the computer system is up and running, entering the day-to-day transactions into the computer is no more difficult, and sometimes less so, than entering the data into a ledger of some kind.[47] Furthermore, as districts enhance their computer capabilities through networks linked by telephone, school-site information may be transferred to the central computer for districtwide use.

Although computers can be helpful as school administrators manage their budgets during the year, they may encounter problems which have occurred in many school districts. First of all, certain people in the school, perhaps even the administrator, may want to purchase an item which has not been included in the budget. Or individuals or departments may want to borrow from one budget account (e.g., capital expenditures) to supplement another budget account (e.g., instructional supplies) which was inadequately budgeted.

Generally, district accounting and purchasing philosophies and procedures tend to discourage, if not actually prohibit, budget transfers from one account to another. The rationale usually given to school administrators is that they should have budgeted for the item desired, and if permission is given for one school to engage in this practice, other schools may want to do the same thing, and budget planning would become meaningless. There may also be city or state governmental regulations which make budget transfers impermissible.[48]

Despite the need to exercise control over the expenditure of funds previously approved by the school board, insofar as possible there should be flexibility in the spending of those funds. School administrators should not be permitted to exceed the total amount budgeted for the school, but they should be allowed some flexibility to adjust the funding in budget categories to meet new situations. The sums of money in the various budget accounts should not be perceived as limits, but as guidelines which can be changed if the situation warrants revision, so long as administrators do not exceed the total amount in the budget.

This solution would also resolve another problem which has frustrated many school administrators. The difficulty occurs when funds left unspent by a school during one budget year must revert back to the agency that authorized the funds, such as the school board or city hall, instead of being credited to the school for the ensuing year. If school administrators were given greater flexibility in adjusting budget accounts, money not used during the year for one budget account could be applied in areas where the need is greater than anticipated, and the unused funds would not be lost, as far as an individual school is concerned. Of course, such flexibility could be misused, in that administrators might not plan their budgets carefully enough, knowing that they could adjust budget accounts later. This is not an inevitable disadvantage, however, and could be avoided with appropriate in-service education and close monitoring.

ADMINISTERING THE STUDENT ACTIVITIES ACCOUNT

The student activities account is one aspect of the budget which deserves special attention, because it is a potential trouble spot. This account usually is not a part of the educational budget previously discussed and is administered primarily at the school level with district supervision. The account involves the funds collected and disbursed for various extracurricular and student activities. Included are monies derived from classroom accounts, candy sales, athletic funds, club treasuries, petty cash, funds from charity drives, gifts, and so on. Ubben and Hughes noted that "individually, the accounts may be quite small, but collectively they often amount to a considerable sum."[49]

The total sum of money in the activities account in any one year can be large, and there have been criticisms of the way the money has at times been spent and the way the account has been administered. Even though the activities account is usually audited by an independent agency, school principals are relatively free to authorize the expenditure of funds for purposes they think important. This practice has led in some instances to the expenditure of money for items that would not have been approved if submitted in the educational budget. In other situations it has resulted in some very large activities funds, the monies of which were put into savings accounts, thereby earning interest. Although seldom has there been anything illegal about a principal's action in relation to a student activities account, administration of these accounts has frequently been sloppy; therefore better guidelines and supervision would appear to be needed.

First of all, school administrators need to recognize that the monies collected and disbursed are public funds; the courts have ruled that "the proceeds of those activities belong to the board of school directors and must be accounted for in the same manner that the other funds of the school district are accounted for."[50] School board members may delegate to school administrators the responsibilities of collecting and disbursing the funds, and if so, they are accountable for the manner in which they carry out these responsibilities.

Second, school administrators need to design and implement a responsible system for collecting, disbursing, and monitoring the spending of student activities monies. Such a system should include the following characteristics:

1. School board authorization for the collection of student activities fees.
2. Involvement of students and teachers in determining the establishment and size of student activities fees and in decisions about how monies are to be spent.
3. Maintenance of school records of monies collected and disbursed, showing that these procedures are being followed:
    a. A receipt is issued to the individual from whom money is received.
    b. A deposit receipt is obtained from the bank, indicating that on being received all monies have been deposited.
    c. The amount which is deposited is recorded in a student activities account under the appropriate fund.
    d. A requisition form, requiring the signature of the activity sponsor, is used to initiate purchases, with purchases involving large sums of money requiring the approval of the principal additionally.
    e. School checks are used to expend monies and to pay student activities bills.
    f. All expenditures are recorded in the student activities ledger, under the appropriate fund.
4. Provision of a monthly budget status report for each activity sponsor and for the school administrator.
5. A yearly audit and review of the purposes for which student activity monies have been spent, conducted by the district office with the involvement of the school administrator and activities' sponsors.

As one might suspect, administering the student activities account can be very time-consuming, and this responsibility might be delegated to the school's business manager or another member of the staff. Even if the responsibility is delegated, however, the final accountability is still that of the school administrator. The administrator is the one who is ultimately responsible, so the administrator must be sufficiently knowledgeable and involved to explain the transactions that occur.

EVALUATING BUDGET UTILIZATION: EFFECTIVENESS, EFFICIENCY

A third function of the school administrator in relation to the budget is to evaluate its effectiveness and efficiency.[51] Budget effectiveness is determined by evaluating the extent to which the funds allocated for each of the programs in the school are achieving their objectives. Budget efficiency is determined by evaluating the extent to which the products and services bought with budget funds are purchased at the lowest price consistent with the items' usability, durability, and reliability. It also involves the monitoring of products and services utiliziation. Budget effectiveness and efficiency should both be important concerns of school administrators, particularly in a time of limited funds.

Until recently it was difficult, if not impossible, to talk meaningfully about evaluating budget effectiveness and efficiency. Budgets were organized according to account categories which, in most cases, bore little if any relationship to school programs or objectives. With the advent of PPBS, the planning, programming, budgeting system, it is now possible for the administrator to evaluate more accurately the effectiveness and efficiency of the budget. Under PPBS, the budget is organized according to educational programs whose objectives have been defined, and for which criteria and methods of evaluation have been identified.

Under this system, if administrators want to find out whether or not the funds for a particular program are being utilized effectively, they can evaluate the extent to which the objectives are being achieved, and then make a judgment about whether or not that achievement is sufficient, considering the funds allocated.[52] It should be emphasized that part of the basis for that judgment must relate to whether or not increased funding of the same program or funding of a different program to reach the same objectives would result in greater achievement of those objectives. A program should not be judged as effective or ineffective by itself, but only in comparison to what an alternative may cost and achieve.

For an example of how PPBS can be used to evaluate budget and program effectiveness, see figure 6.5.[53]

Figure 6.5 Cost Effectiveness Analysis.

Program Alternatives for Teaching Remedial Reading to a Class of 9th Grade Students

	Class Size	Personnel	Equipment	Total Estimated Costs	Per Student Cost	Predicted Results
Program Option No. 1	10	1 teacher	None	$30,000	$3,000	Increase one grade level
Program Option No. 2	20	1 teacher	Overhead Projector	$30,500	$1,525	Increase ½ grade level
Program Option No. 3	40	1 teacher, 1 aide	None	$44,000	$1,100	Increase ¼ grade level

Once the budget has been approved by the school board, the school administrator's role in evaluating budget efficiency is generally limited to monitoring and preventing wasteful use of funds.[54] Any product or service which is inefficiently utilized, either because of wastefulness or underutilization, merits the administrator's attention. The administrator especially needs to watch for excessive use of supplies, underutilization of equipment, and inefficient use of time and personnel. Evaluating the efficiency of the expenditure of funds is never a popular task, but in situations of limited financial support for education, a school administrator cannot abdicate this important responsibility.

SCHOOL PLANT MANAGEMENT

Winston Churchill is said to have observed, "We shape our dwellings and then our dwellings shape us." The physical environment in which we work can and does influence what we do and how we feel. For example, it can affect our flexibility in teaching, our communication patterns, the amount of noise and extent of discipline problems in the school, and many other facets of the total educational enterprise.[55] A well-maintained, bright, sparkling, flexible. physical facility suggests a school that people care about. Such a school does something positive for the spirit of the individuals who occupy the building.

On the other hand, a school which is poorly maintained, institutional-looking and inflexible in its structure tends to dull the spirit of the people who must spend their workdays there. It suggests a school in which people have lost interest and lack pride. Although the importance of the school plant's appearance and flexibility can be overemphasized, they do affect the feelings and behavior of the people who occupy the building. In addition, a school building can, over the years, develop a special attraction for the people in the community, particularly parents. This loyalty is most evident when a school closing is being considered.

Three major responsibilities of the school administrator are discussed in the following sections: (1) maintenance of the school plant, (2) scheduling facilities, and (3) school plant planning.

MAINTENANCE OF THE SCHOOL PLANT

The administrator is not, of course, responsible for personally maintaining the school plant. The school district has hired custodians and related workers to perform the actual tasks of keeping the school clean, bright, energy efficient, and in good repair.[56] However, school administrators cannot assume that these tasks will be carried out effectively without some supervision on their part. In fact, an emerging school law issue for school administrators is tort liability regarding negligence in the proper maintenance of school buildings, property, and equipment.[57] Thus, administrators, or someone else to whom this responsibility is delegated, need to supervise custodians and maintenance personnel and monitor their work as it relates to the general appearance and condition of the building and grounds and energy conservation. If school administrators are fortunate enough to have conscientious head custodians, their supervisory responsibility is greatly reduced. Unfortunately, such custodians are not always available, and in many schools some supervision and monitoring by school administrators *is* probably required.[58]

Even though the nature and extent of the administrator's responsibilities for supervising the custodians and monitoring the maintenance of the school plant and grounds vary depending on local conditions, the following general responsibilities are proposed:

1. **Keep informed about the work schedule and specific responsibilities of each member of the custodial staff.** School administrators should know the work schedule of each person on the custodial staff and should be knowledgeable about who does what.

2. **Tour the school building and grounds regularly for the purpose of observing the extent to which they are being kept clean, neat, energy efficient, and in good repair.**[59] Admittedly, administrators may have other higher priorities, leaving limited time for this kind of activity. If they care enough about the appearance and energy efficiency of the school building and grounds, administrators schedule such tours every week or two. These tours can be veritable eye openers.

3. **Conduct, with the assistance of appropriate help, a comprehensive audit of the energy needs and excesses of the school/district, and design and implement energy conservation practices.** Energy to operate the schools is likely to be in short supply in the foreseeable future and therefore expensive. Administrators should take steps to improve the energy efficiency of their schools. These steps might include (*a*) carrying out a full energy use audit of all school facilities; (*b*) establishing appropriate temperature control in all classrooms; (*c*) conducting regular inspection and maintenance of all heating, cooling, and ventilating systems; (*d*) reducing all unnecessary lighting; and (*e*) eliminating all unnecessary use of water. Of course, these steps are just a beginning, and many other actions need to be considered, as identified in the references listed at the end of this chapter.[60] For most of these actions to be effective, the understanding and cooperation of teachers and students are needed, so orientation and in-service meetings should be initiated to achieve these objectives.[61]

4. **Design some method or procedure for students, teachers, or others to bring to the attention of the head custodian and/or the school administrator any problems in plant and grounds maintenance, appearance, or energy loss.** A form could be developed for this purpose, or perhaps administrators could simply point out to students and teachers the procedure to follow when a problem occurs. (Some students and teachers will be reluctant or will not take time to report a problem directly to the custodians.) Administrators may want to receive the reports, or at least a copy of the reports, so that they can become better informed about the maintenance and energy problems in the building.

5. **Develop a good working relationship with all of the custodial staff, particularly the head custodian.** The custodial staff should be treated with the same respect and human relations approach as any other group of employees in the school. They perform an important job and, if dissatisfied, can make things difficult for the school administrator and teachers.

The appearance and energy efficiency of the school plant and grounds should, of course, be the concern of everyone, including students and teachers. However, administrators must assume the overall responsibility for making sure that the school plant and grounds are kept clean, neat, in good repair, and energy efficient. This responsibility is one which administrators should not avoid and for which they should rightly be held accountable.

SCHOOL PLANT SCHEDULING

Facilities scheduling is a second major component of plant management. Someone must be responsible for scheduling facilities in a way that promotes appropriate and maximum usage. That person is frequently the school administrator, although the responsibility may be delegated to someone else in certain situations.

School facilities must be scheduled to accommodate (1) the regular educational program of the school; (2) the school's student activities program; and (3) requests of people who would like to use the building at night, on weekends, or during the summer for recreational or adult programs.

There are many different approaches to scheduling the regular educational program of a school, and references are provided for readers who wish to explore this subject in depth.[62] Scheduling has been defined by Hughes and Ubben as "the plan to bring together people, materials, and curriculum at a designated time and place for the purposes of instruction. Its basic purpose is to coordinate the requirements laid down by previously reached decisions regarding curriculum, instruction, grouping, and staffing."[63] To accomplish these purposes, school administrators need to be aware of the characteristics of a good schedule, the process of scheduling, the various types of schedules, and the technology available to support building the master schedule and preparing teacher and student schedules.

Based on his review of the criteria of effective schedules, Harry Bluhm sets forth the following criteria which a good schedule should meet:

1. Provide maximum support for the goals and objectives of the school.
2. Allow students to pursue the courses of study they need or desire.
3. Assign teachers to courses for which they are qualified and, when possible, for which they have a preference.
4. Involve teachers, specialists, administrators, and even parents and students at certain levels in the decision making.
5. Provide for optimum utilization of all rooms relative to the building capacity and student enrollment.

6. Meet all minimum standards for time allocations as designated by the state department of education and other accrediting agencies.
7. Provide planning time for each teacher every day.
8. Make provisions for special groups to accommodate the need for special education classes, ability groups, and the like.
9. Plan lunch periods in the most convenient way for students, faculty, and food service personnel.
10. Provide for a good balance in the distribution of class sections in the schedule, section size, and in the number of students and sections assigned to teachers.
11. Contain no conflicts between courses for more than a small percentage of students.
12. Be clear and complete so as to be ready by the first day of school.
13. Function with a minimum of confusion and change after the first few days of the school year.[64]

Fortunately, school administrators are now able to utilize computers in the scheduling process.[65] Though schools have a choice in scheduling students either manually or by computer, the latter method provides benefits that outweigh those of the former.[66] Generally, computers "reduce the time spent by professionals and nonprofessionals in scheduling, enroll students in additional courses without encountering undue course conflicts, improve student balance in courses of multiple sections, obtain better room and facility utilization, enhance the scheduling of special groups like team teaching and large and small group instruction, and meet teacher-requested special course designs."[67] Thus, school administrators should explore the possibility of acquiring scheduling software as they assess their possibilities of incorporating microcomputers in the mangement of their buildings.

Although considerable attention is generally placed on scheduling the school's educational program, relatively little attention has been paid in the educational literature to facility scheduling for extracurricular programs or for the recreational and adult programs at night and on weekends. Administrators who find that there is considerable demand for the use of the school facilities after the end of the school day probably need to assign to a staff member the responsibility for setting up and administering a system for handling requests and scheduling facilities. This system should be coordinated with the custodians' work load and schedule, if problems are to be avoided.

In small schools, individuals who have overall responsibility for facilities scheduling may well have to be the principals themselves. In larger schools, principals can delegate this responsibility to an assistant principal, or it may be assigned to the head custodian. And, in large districts, scheduling of district facilities may be centralized in the district offices.

Facility scheduling may or may not be regarded as a particularly interesting or rewarding aspect of school administration. Nevertheless, it is a task requiring effective performance, though it need not become a time-consuming or frustrating experience if approached in an organized manner and if administrators utilize available computer technology.

SCHOOL PLANT PLANNING

The administrator's major responsibilities for school plant planning are twofold: (1) planning for changes in the existing structure, such as remodeling or additions, and (2) planning for a new facility or the closing of a school.[68]

In a time of educational change, many school plants simply do not provide sufficient flexibility or comprehensiveness to accommodate the various proposals for improving the educational program of the school, and modernization of old buildings is a constant need. Not all communities can afford to build a new school, so administrators may need to consider ways in which present facilities can be remodeled or expanded.[69] For example, changes in facilities may be needed to accommodate handicapped students.[70] In addition, modification may be needed to increase the facility's energy efficiency.[71]

Because form should follow function, administrators should first determine, in cooperation with relevant others, the kind of educational program to be implemented in the school, and then consider needed changes in the physical plant.[72] Having ascertained the type of educational program which the school should implement, administrators can logically move to the next step—analyzing the physical facilities required by that program and then identifying the need for remodeling or expanding the present school plant. In taking this step, school administrators should consult with appropriate facilities specialists in the district office, at the university, and at the state department of public instruction. Assistance in estimating the cost of making changes in the physical plant should also be secured. As a result of conferring with various experts, school administrators should be in a position to submit to the school board for its consideration (1) a description of the educational program that will be possible with the modification of facilities; (2) preliminary sketches showing the proposed change; and (3) an estimate of the cost to the district.[73]

School plant planning for remodeling or expanding takes time and preparation. Many of our school plants need remodeling or expansion if they are to accommodate needed improvements in the educational program and energy efficiency.[74] Philip Piccigallo noted that the authors of the recent report titled *An Imperiled Generation* by the Carnegie Foundation acknowledged that "a good building does not necessarily make a good school"; however, the report also noted that the widespread neglect of inner-city schools impairs the learning process for students.[75] Furthermore, Piccigallo contends that the abysmal condition of the schools conveys a negative message to students regarding their self-worth and society's expectations for them.

In considering new building projects or renovation efforts, school administrators need to consider what the future needs of the school may be as educators rethink the working conditions of teachers and the organization of schools and as we move into a more technologically sophisticated educational era than we have known in the past.[76] For example, the concept of teacher professionalism will move teachers out of isolated classrooms and organize them in physical arrangements that facilitate collegial interaction. As a result, boxy classrooms will yield to spaces with more variety and flexibility. Similarly, as computer technology becomes more common within schools, facility designs will allow networking of educational systems requiring more elaborate wiring configurations than schools presently have.

In highlighting the urgency of building for tomorrow, William Brubaker stated:

> School design is a hot topic again. After years of dwindling student enrollments, both the U.S. and Canada are starting to experience enrollment increases caused by immigration and the so-called baby boomlet. Simultaneously, people are beginning to face the fact that many school buildings simply are too old or worn out.[77]

PLANNING A NEW FACILITY

Although most school administrators are more likely to participate in planning for facility remodeling or expansion, some administrators will be fortunate enough to become involved in planning for an entirely new school building. This task will challenge the creativity, patience, and endurance of any administrator. At the same time, it can be a very exciting and rewarding activity.

Instead of discussing the innumerable details of planning for a new building, we provide some general principles to be followed when planning.[78]

1. **Define the educational objectives to be achieved in the new school and the programs and activities to be implemented to achieve those objectives.** This effort should result in a document formally referred to as the educational specifications of the school.[79] These educational specifications should be as detailed and precise as needed to enable both the administrator and the architect to understand the type of educational program the new building is to house.

2. **Involve in the planning of the new facility as many of those people who will occupy the new building as possible: students and teachers.** It may be more convenient and efficient for an administrator to exclude these people, but this increases the risk that the new facility will not be functional for their needs. The administrator may choose to establish committees, solicit recommendations from individuals, or attempt some other alternative in securing input.

   Regardless of the approach chosen by the administrator, however, a determination should be made in advance that the ideas and recommendations generated from the involvement of teachers, students, and others will be carefully considered and not be rejected simply because they might be more expensive than other ideas. Obviously, there are financial parameters within which the school board and the administrator must operate. However, if the participants in the planning process, particularly teachers, get the impression that cost is going to be the main criterion in assessing the worth of a recommendation, they are unlikely to contribute their time and effort. A school district does not need to involve many people in the planning of a new facility if the basic objective is simply to build the least expensive plant possible.

3. **Study the educational literature on school plant planning.** It makes no sense to reinvent the wheel; many mistakes can be avoided by reviewing the recommendations and experiences of others.[80]

4. **Define the nature and scope of the responsibilities of the architect for the project.** In too many situations the architect's responsibilities, particularly regarding decisions about the educational program to be housed in the school and the type of physical facilities needed, are not clearly delineated. As a result, the architect may end up making decisions which are, in reality, educational decisions about the nature of the new building.

5. **Devise a master plan and time schedule to program within a specified timetable the planning and implementation activities that need to be accomplished by a certain date.** Unless an overall plan identifies and sequences the various steps to be carried out within a specific time frame, it is unlikely that the new facility will be completed on schedule. An excellent tool which the administrator should utilize in developing and implementing the master plan is PERT–CPM, Program Evaluation and Review Technique and Critical Path Method.[81]

6. **Develop criteria and procedures for evaluating the new facility after it is in operation.** Any new structure, regardless of how well conceived and planned, will have defects or deficiencies which may need to be corrected and which should be avoided in the planning of the next facility.[82] In evaluating a new facility, strong consideration should be given to involving the people who are most affected by it: students and teachers.

A FINAL NOTE ON BUDGET AND PLANT MANAGEMENT

The school budget and plant represent important vehicles for conserving resources and improving educational opportunities for students. Whether the full potential of these means is realized depends in large part on school administrators. They undoubtedly face problems and need to work within certain financial and physical constraints. However, in the final analysis, administrators' success in providing the best possible budget and physical facilities for the school depend for the most part on their *knowledge, resourcefulness,* and *persistence.*

Review and Learning Activities

1. What are the steps involved in, and the advantages and disadvantages of, the centralized budget process? The decentralized budget process?
2. Describe the main elements of the planning, programming, budgeting system (PPBS). What are its advantages and disadvantages? Compare it to zero-base budgeting (ZBB).
3. Discuss the major problems associated with the process of developing the school budget. What are the implications of these problems for the school administrator?
4. Identify those factors that characterize the effective administration of the budget.
5. Describe the major responsibilities of the administrator in maintaining the school plant, scheduling facilities, and school plant planning.
6. Assume that you have been requested to develop a plan for use by a school district considering the possibility of adding to some schools. Which factors and problems should your plan address?

Notes

1. William T. Hartman, *School District Budgeting* (Englewood Cliffs, N.J.: Prentice-Hall, 1988), 2.

2. Ibid., 3.

3. See Leonard L. Gregory and Roger R. Farr, "Involving the Principal in the Budget-Making Process," *School Business Affairs* (July 1988): 18; and Harry J. Hartley, "Budgeting," in *Encyclopedia of School Administration and Supervision,* ed. Richard A. Gorton, Gail T. Schneider, and James C. Fisher (Phoenix, Ariz.: Oryx Press, 1988), 40–41.

4. Ibid., 19.

5. Ibid.

6. David S. Honeyman and Rich Jensen, "School-Site Budgeting," *School Business Affairs* (February 1988): 13.

7. Ibid.

8. Tom McConaghy, "The Quiet Revolution: School-Based Budgeting," *Kappan* (February 1989):: 486–87; and W. T. Hartman, "Participatory Budgeting in High School," *Planning and Changing* (Spring 1989): 15–25.

9. Hartman, *School District Budgeting,* 39. Also see Ervin Decker et al., *Site Management, an Analysis of the Concepts and Fundamental Operational Components Associated with It* (ERIC Report ED–150–736).

10. Honeyman and Jensen, "School-Site Budgeting," 13.

11. James W. Guthrie, "School-Based Management: The Next Needed Education Reform," *Kappan* (December 1986): 306.

12. Honeyman and Jensen, "School-Site Budgeting," 13.

13. Guthrie, "School-Based Management," 307–8.

14. Thomas E. Glass, "Developing the District Budget through Direct Citizen Participation," *School Business Affairs* (February 1979): 12–14.

15. JoAnn Palmer Spear, *School Site Budgeting/Management: The State of the Art* (ERIC Report Ed–231–082).

16. I. Carl Candoli et al., *School Business Administration: A Planning Approach* (Boston: Allyn & Bacon, 1984).

17. Honeywell and Jensen, "School-Site Budgeting," 13–14.

18. Ibid., 13.

19. Francis C. Thiemann and K. Penney Sanders, "School Based Management (SBM): Modifying the Principal's Role," *Planning and Changing* (Fall 1986): 159.

20. Ibid.

21. Hartman, *School District Budgeting,* 28.

22. James W. Guthrie and Rodney J. Reed, *Educational Administration and Policy: Effective Leadership for American Education* (Englewood Cliffs, N.J.: Prentice-Hall, 1986), 261.

23. Gerald C. Ubben and Larry W. Hughes, *The Principal: Creative Leadership for Effective Schools* (Boston: Allyn & Bacon, 1987), 321.

24. PPBS process adapted from Robert F. Aliota and J. D. Jungherr, *Operational PPBS for Education* (New York: Harper and Row, 1971), 52.

25. Figure 6.2 was adapted from several school districts' budget worksheets; figure 6.3 was adapted from one school district's budget worksheets.

26. Leonard L. Gregory and Roger R. Farr, "Involving the Principal in the Budget-Making Process," *School Business Affairs* (July 1988): 20.

27. For an additional analysis of system theory application, see Harvey Bleecher, "System Theory Effects on Practices in Education," *Education* (Fall 1983): 67–71.

28. K. Forbis Jordan and L. Dean Webb, "School Business Administration," *Educational Administration Quarterly* (Summer 1986): 171–82.

29. Larry W. Hughes and Gerald C. Ubben, *The Elementary Principal's Handbook,* 2d ed. (Newton, Mass.: Allyn & Bacon, 1984), 289–309.

30. For some reason the role of school administrators and the problems they encounter in developing the budget are given limited attention in the educational literature. Therefore, the ideas presented in this section are based primarily on the experiences of a number of principals who have been interviewed, and a useful study by Brian Caldwell, *Implications of Decentralized School Budgeting* (ERIC Report Ed–161–148).

31. Michael L. Bowman, "Allocating Money for Priority Items—Easier with Participative Budgeting," *NASSP Bulletin* (November 1986): 5–10.

32. For a discussion of the origins of zero-base budgeting, see Allen Schick, "The Road from ZBB," *Public Administration Review* (March/April 1978): 177–79.

33. Hartman, *School District Budgeting,* 29.

34. Barry M. Mundt, Raymond T. Olsen, and Harold I. Steinberg, *Managing Public Resources* (New York: Peat Marwick International, 1982).

35. Sam W. Bliss, *Zero-Base Budgeting: A Management Tool for School Districts* (ERIC Report Ed–220–907).

36. Ross A. Hodel and G. Gruendel, "Budgeting—A Management Approach for the 80s," *School Business Affairs* (February 1980): 24–25.

37. P. A. Phyrr, *Zero-Base Budgeting* cited in Jordan and Webb, "School Business Administration," 179.

38. For additional information on ZBB and related management tools, see *Educational Management Tools for the Practicing School Administrator: A Handbook for School Programs* (Arlington, Va.: American Association of School Administrators, 1979).

39. C. Cale Hudson, "Reducing Budgets Not Quality," *School Business Affairs* (July 1986): 36–37.

40. For help in regard to this problem, see R. Louis Bright, *Should Educators Generate Specifications for the Purchase of Equipment?* (ERIC Report Ed–039–736).

41. Hartman, *School District Budgeting,* 190.

42. New York State University, *School Business Management Handbook: Budget* (Albany: State Education Department, 1956), 41.

43. Hartman, *School District Budgeting,* 227.

44. For a thorough review of computer applications in business management, see Craig E. Richards, *Microcomputer Applications for Strategic Management in Education: A Case Study Approach* (White Plains, N.Y.: Longman, 1989); and Harry P. Bluhm, *Administrative Uses of Computers in the Schools* (Englewood Cliffs, N.J.: Prentice-Hall, 1987).

45. Kent John Chabotar, "Problems and Opportunities in School Financial Management: A Consultant's Perspective," *Urban Education* (April 1987): 15–16.

46. Ubben and Hughes, *The Principal,* 328.

47. Harold Miller, *An Administrator's Manual for the Use of Microcomputers in the Schools* (Englewood Cliffs, N.J.: Prentice-Hall, 1988), 31–32.

48. C. Candoli, W. G. Hack, J. R. Ray, and D. G. Stollar, *School Business Administration: A Planning Approach* (Boston: Allyn & Bacon, 1984).

49. Ubben and Hughes, *The Principal,* 330–31.

50. See re German Township School directors, 465 and C, 562 (1942).

51. For a review of theory and research on this aspect, see Henry M. Levin, "Cost-Effectiveness and Educational Policy," *Educational Evaluation and Policy Analysis* (Spring 1988): 51–69.

52. For a good description of one model that appears to be useful in this area, see Jim E. Kim, *A Cost-Effectiveness/Benefits Analysis Model for Improving Educational Program Management.* (ERIC Report ED–170–870); W. K. Poston, "Curriculum-Driven Budgeting: Case Study of Recent Approach to Quality Control," *National Forum of Educational Administration and Supervision Journal* 7 (1990/1991): 56–69; and K. Penny Sanders and Francis C. Thiemann, "Student Costing: An Essential Tool in Site-Based Budgeting and Teacher Empowerment," *NASSP Bulletin* (February 1990): 95–102.

53. For further elaboration and discussion of the concepts leading up to figure 6.5, see I. Carl Candoli et al., *School Business Administration.*

54. Candoli et al., *School Business Administration.*

55. See Richard Niece, "The Impact of Environment on Teaching and Learning," *NASSP Bulletin* (May 1988): 79–81; and W. E. Hathaway, "Educational Facilities: Designing to Enhance Learning and Human Performance," *Education Canada* (Winter 1988): 28–35.

56. Ubben and Hughes, *The Principal,* 336.

57. Dennis Dunklee and Robert J. Shoop, "School Facilities' Negligence: A Mine Field Fraught with Litigation," *School Business Affairs* (June 1986): 36–39.

58. For an excellent discussion of administrative policies and procedures in this area, see Arthur Steller and Carroll Pell, *Clean Up Your School Custodial Program* (Alexandria, Va.: National School Boards Association, 1986).

59. David S. Honeyman et al., "The Fiscal Support of School Facilities in Rural and Small Schools," *Journal of Education Finance* (Winter 1988): 227–39.

60. Larry Beam, "Viewing Energy Conservation in the Proper Light," *School Business Affairs* (February 1987): 10–14; and William R. Minning, "Strategy Plan Strengthens Energy Conservation Program," *School Business Affairs* (February 1987): 18–20.

61. See the chapter on instructional leadership for in-service concepts and alternatives.

62. Richard A. Dempsey and Henry P. Travers, *Scheduling the Secondary School* (Reston, Va.: National Association of Secondary School Principals, 1982).

63. L. W. Hughes and G. C. Ubben, *The Secondary Principal's Handbook* (Boston: Allyn & Bacon, 1980).

64. Harry P. Bluhm, *Administrative Uses of Computers in the Schools* (Englewood Cliffs, N.J.: Prentice-Hall, 1987), 101.

65. For a thorough discussion of computer applications in scheduling, see Bluhm, *Administrative Uses of Computers,* 101–9; and Thomas J. Gustafson, *Microcomputers and Educational Administration* (Englewood Cliffs, N.J.: Prentice-Hall, 1985).

66. Bluhm, *Administrative Uses of Computers,* 105.

67. Ibid., 106.

68. Basil Castaldi, *Educational Facilities: Planning, Modernization and Management,* 3d ed. (Boston: Allyn & Bacon, 1987).

69. For a discussion of facility needs, see Joe D. Coley, "A Practitioner's Perspective on School Facilities Problems," *School Business Affairs* (August 1988): 20–24; Ted Schwinden, "What Are Schools For? *Kappan* (November 1986): 223–24; and Lyle R. Bruss, "Space Planning Guidelines for Elementary and Secondary Schools in the U.S. and Canada," *Educational Facility Planner* (July/August 1989): 6–8.

70. For suggestions, see Thomas L. Erekson, "Identifying, Removing Architectural Barriers for the Handicapped," *NASSP Bulletin* (January 1980): 102–8; and for an additional discussion of special education program needs, see Daniel D. Sage and Leonard C. Burrell, *Policy and Management in Special Education* (Englewood Cliffs, N.J.: Prentice-Hall, 1986).

71. Chuck Miles, "Energy Management," in *Encyclopedia of School Administration and Supervision,* ed. R. Gorton, G. Schneider, and V. Fisher (Phoenix, Ariz.: Oryx Press, 1988), 110.

72. See C. William Day, "Planning Is the Key to Excellence in Facilities," *School Business Affairs* (January 1986): 14–15; and David S. Honeyman, "A Growing Concern for School Buildings," *The Educational Facility Planner* (March/April 1989): 4–6.

73. See Castaldi, *Educational Facilities,* parts III and V.

74. Ibid., part III.

75. Philip R. Piccigallo, "Renovating Urban Schools Is Fundamental to Improving Them," *Kappan* (January 1989): 402–6.

76. For a creative discussion of building for tomorrow, see C. William Brubaker, "These 21 Trends Will Shape the Future of School Design," *The American School Board Journal* (April 1988): 31–36; and W. E. Hathaway, "Technology and Education: Designing Educational Facilities to Avoid Premature Obsolescence," *CEFP Journal* (November–December, 1988): 13–17; and Harold L. Hawkins, "Facilities and Learning: Essentials of Educational Reform," *National Forum of Applied Educational Research Journal* 3 (1989–90): 17–30.

77. Brubaker, "These 21 Trends," 31. For additional information on the impact of technology on facility planning, see A. Jones, E. Scanlon, and T. O'Shea, *The Computer Revolution in Education* (New York: St. Martin's Press, 1987) and W. E. Hathaway, "Technology and Education: Designing Educational Facilities to Avoid Premature Obsolescence," *CEFP Journal* (November/December 1988): 13–17.

78. Useful literature on new school plant planning includes Castaldi, *Educational Facilities,* parts II and III; and Donald Gross, James E. Morrell, and Joseph S. Yarworth, "New Construction: A Guide for Principals," *NASSP Bulletin* (October 1988): 101–2.

79. For a comprehensive review of the literature on this topic, with sources on ideas for developing educational specifications for the elementary, middle, junior high, and high schools, see Philip K. Piele, *Educational Specifications.* (ERIC Report Ed–058–620). In addition, see W. E. Hathaway, "Educational Facilities: Designing to Enhance Learning and Human Performance," *Education Canada* (Winter 1988): 28–35.

80. The ERIC Clearing House on Educational Management at Eugene, Oregon, is a good source for reviewing the literature on school facilities and school plant planning.

81. For a good explanation of PERT–CPM, see "Network Models: CPM and PERT–Methods for Planning, Coordination, and Control," *Small Business Report* (Feburary 1986): 37–40.

82. C. William Day and James P. Groten, "How Well Do You Know School Construction? *School Business Affairs* (November 1986): 44–47.

7

• • • • •

Staff Recruitment, Selection, and Induction

▬

As D. E. Davis and N. C. Nickerson have observed, "The education of children is the central purpose of any school, and the teacher is the most important single resource in producing a quality education."[1] Therefore, every school administrator should be interested in improving the quality of the professional staff. Three important processes by which an administrator can take a major step toward the achievement of this goal are personnel recruitment, selection, and induction. Although the availability and turnover of personnel influence the priority given to these three processes, they still represent significant means by which an administrator can improve the quality of the staff.

STAFF RECRUITMENT

Staff recruitment may be defined as the active pursuit of potential candidates for the purpose of influencing them to apply for positions in the school district. The goal of a school's or district's staff recruitment program should be to attract applications from the best people available, both beginning and experienced.

During the 1970s, school districts experienced a dramatic decrease in pupil enrollment. This decline in enrollment forced many districts to lay off a large number of teachers. The reductions in staff which school districts experienced affected the number of students entering teacher preparation programs. As high school students and early college entrants assessed the job market and their career potential in education, the dismal employment forecast discouraged many from pursuing careers in education.[2]

This problem has been compounded by the large number of teachers leaving the profession because of retirement, those seeking employment in fields other than education, and those leaving because of dissatisfaction with work conditions.[3] In a study investigating attrition rates of teachers, Richard Murnane found that within a group of 13,000 beginning teachers, 15 percent of the group stopped teaching before completing two years in the classroom. Another 9 percent left before completing three years and only 56 percent, slightly more than half, were still teaching six years after they had begun.[4] Murnane attributed the increase in teacher attrition to a number of factors including a lack of commitment by young people entering the profession, the failure of schools to retain talented teachers, low salaries compared to salaries in alternative occupations, and overwhelming responsibilities. The result is that more teachers are leaving the profession than entering it.

Furthermore, schools are now experiencing an increase in student enrollment. This increase, combined with the teacher attrition rate, may produce a severe teacher shortage especially for certain subject areas and parts of the country.[5] To illustrate this point, Arthur Wise, Linda Darling-Hammond, and Barnett Berry stated that

> Most of the teachers who will be teaching in American classrooms in 1995 have not yet been hired. Over the next decade, our public school systems will need to hire nearly 2 million new teachers to meet a growing demand being created by increasing student enrollments, teacher turnover and retirements, and reform initiatives. At the same time, the supply of new entrants to teaching has been declining for the past 15 years.
>
> The potential teacher shortage is exacerbated by public concern over teaching quality and increasing calls for the schools to attract, select, and retain the most talented recruits. With these conditions in mind, how well are current teacher selection procedures likely to serve school district needs over the next decade?[6]

To enhance the pool of candidates from which to recruit, school administrators and teachers need to recognize the role they might play in encouraging able students to pursue careers in education. For example, based on an analysis of interviews held with thirty Harvard College students admitted to the undergraduate teacher education program, Jerome Murphy found that (1) students are attracted to teaching by their desire to provide a service to others and society; (2) early teaching experiences played an important role in motivating the students to become teachers; and (3) high school teachers played a major role in the lives of students and in their decisions to become teachers.[7] Thus, school personnel obviously play a critical role in recruiting students into the field of education by providing opportunities for youngsters in elementary and secondary schools to teach and by hiring high-quality teachers who may serve as role models and communicate to students the rewards within the profession.

Teacher shortages are expected to be severe in urban school districts. To illustrate this point, Vernon Clark and Rochelle Clemson stated that, "Large urban school systems which are surrounded by suburban school systems with higher teacher salaries and a smaller percentage of hard-core problems—e.g., drug use, gang activities, teacher abuse, limited human and technological resources and support services—will lose a portion of their best teachers and administrators to these surrounding school systems."[8] Therefore, administrators within urban school systems need to develop aggressive, creative recruitment strategies to secure the best teachers for these challenging assignments. Two urban systems, Houston, Texas, and Milwaukee, Wisconsin, have initiated programs to encourage and prepare college-bound students for careers in education. The primary mission of each program is to make teaching attractive to talented students of various ethnic and socioeconomic backgrounds. The programs' objectives are (1) to present students with a positive image of the teaching profession; (2) to increase students' awareness of the range of career opportunities available in education; (3) to acquaint students with the cultural diversity of an urban high school; and (4) to encourage students who might not otherwise do so to go on to college.[9]

Other districts have employed enterprising enticement or incentive systems to recruit candidates during strong demand periods. Clark and Clemson indicated that notable enticements and incentives have included the following:

1. Securing attractive living quarters for new teachers with guarantees of low-interest loans and gratuitous rent for the first month of apartment occupancy.
2. Guaranteed summer employment.
3. Low-interest automobile loans for teachers.
4. Tuition assistance for teachers pursuing further study in the area of their contract responsibilities and for those retooling in high-need content areas.
5. Orientation sessions for new teachers to help acclimate them to the community and the school system.
6. Bimonthly or monthly professional in-service training based on teacher-selected needs, skills, or subjects.
7. Teacher option to use one or two days each month to visit the instructional materials/staff development center where teachers can develop learning materials for their use, view materials developed by other teachers, or consult with staff on appropriate, commercially produced materials.[10]

In a more traditional sense, school administrators need to be involved in developing a dynamic recruitment process to locate the best candidate to fill each vacancy within their districts. Because most staff recruiting programs are centralized at the district level, either in a personnel office or under the jurisdiction of a central office administrator, the focus in this section is on ways in which school administrators can most effectively work with the central office in the recruitment of staff.

ASSESSING NEEDS

The first important way in which school administrators can help the district administration in the recruitment of staff is by providing them with data on personnel needs for the school.[11] There are at least three major categories of staff personnel needs for which school administrators should provide data to the central office:

1. Increased or decreased enrollment which creates a need for more staff or a reduction in staff.
2. Changes in the educational program which necessitate additional or differently trained staff.
3. Staff resignations or transfers which may create a need for new personnel.

For recruitment to be effective, the district office must receive data about all three categories of staff needs, at the earliest possible date during the school year. By studying the enrollment figures for their schools and feeder schools, and by estimating from census figures and the previous years' student turnover, administrators should be able to project to the central office by January any staff needs related to potential increases or decreases in the student enrollment in the school for the following year.

Estimating the need for new staff due to changes in the educational program is not easy. If school administrators approach the change process systematically and establish target dates, they can indicate to the district office by early spring the existence of vacancies for additional or specially trained staff. Although they may find it difficult to meet these target dates, administrators should recognize that the later they report personnel needs to the district office for the purpose of recruiting, the harder it is to find highly qualified staff still available.

Administrators may also encounter considerable difficulty in estimating staff needs created by resignations or transfers. Some districts require that staff transfers from one school to another within the district take place by a certain date, but resignations can and frequently do occur late in the spring, and even into late summer.[12] Some administrators try to survey their staffs in March or April to ascertain who may be leaving but the data obtained are not always valid or reliable. Teachers who eventually resign may not want administrators to know that they are even thinking about resigning until they have actually secured other jobs. The best school administrators can do in these circumstances is to "keep their ears to the ground" and report staff needs to the district office as soon as they can.

AVOIDING EMPLOYMENT DISCRIMINATION

In the development of personnel recruitment and selection policies and procedures, it has become increasingly important for school district administrators to take into consideration federal laws, regulations, and court cases on discrimination in employment.[13] School district administrators should take certain steps to avoid any charges of employment discrimination in the recruitment and selection of applicants. First of all, school district personnel should develop a clear policy statement regarding equal employment opportunities. An example of such a statement is provided by Ben Harris and his colleagues.[14]

Second, school district supervisors should develop and implement an affirmative action employment program. As defined by Ronald Rebore, affirmative action programs are

> detailed, result-oriented programs, which, when carried out in good faith, result in compliance with the equal opportunity clauses found in most legislation and executive orders. Affirmative action, therefore, is not a law within itself but rather an objective reached by following a set of guidelines that insure compliance with legislation and executive orders. Thus, an organization does not "violate" affirmative action: it violates the law.[15]

In delineating the process, an affirmative action plan should include a statement of policy and purpose, a work force utilization analysis, a set of procedures for identification and modification of present procedures and practices having a discriminatory impact or perpetuating past discrimination, and a statement establishing affirmative action goals and timetables. Public employers are required by Equal Employment Opportunity Commission (EEOC) rules and regulations, and by the existing employment laws, to use job-related, standardized, and valid selection methods.[16] Selection regulations are presented in the *Uniform Guidelines on Employee Selection Procedures,* which govern all employment decisions. The *Uniform Guidelines* state: (1) any criteria used to screen or select applicants, or to promote employees, must be reasonably related to the entry-level requirements of the position for which the applicant is applying; and (2) there should be empirical evidence demonstrating the validity of the selection criteria.[17]

The main purpose of an affirmative action plan with regard to personnel recruitment should be to ascertain the need to correct past discrimination in employment and, if discrimination is found to have been present, to take positive corrective steps to aggressively recruit women and minority members for staff vacancies. Although a high priority should be given to developing a policy on nondiscrimination in employment and an affirmative action plan to carry out that policy, an equal amount of attention should also be directed toward monitoring and assessing the degree to which the policy and plan are actually being implemented. Even though governmental laws and regulations addressing this problem may be reduced, no administrator should be comfortable with less than a vigorous program to eliminate employment discrimination.

THE ADMINISTRATOR'S ROLE IN RECRUITING

The actual recruitment of staff is typically organized by a personnel office in larger school districts or by a district administrator, such as the superintendent or an assistant, in smaller school districts. Two methods are generally used by school districts to recruit personnel: (1) the dissemination to university, state, and private placement bureaus of brochures describing the district and its employment opportunities; and (2) visitations by district recruiting teams to personnel placement offices. The latter approach tends to be used primarily by those districts with increased enrollment and personnel needs.

School administrators could make a useful contribution to both of these recruiting approaches. Certainly administrators should, at the minimum, be involved in reacting to the strengths and weaknesses of the district's current brochures, or in helping to develop proposed brochures to be sent to teacher placement bureaus and to candidates who inquire about the district. For most potential candidates, the district's brochures are the first tangible information they receive about the school system, and the likelihood that they might be interested in exploring staffing opportunities at a particular school will be influenced by the quality of the brochures.

School administrators should also be involved in orienting the district's recruiting team to the school's particular staffing needs. In the past, building administrators were often included on district recruiting teams, but currently this practice is less typical. Even though the school system's team is recruiting for the entire district (not just for one administrator's school), to be maximally effective the team must give attention to the specific staffing needs of individual schools. To accomplish the latter objective, the recruiting team needs to be oriented by the principal and, to the extent possible, by the faculty, about the school in which the vacancy has occurred. If the district's philosophy or procedures do not provide an opportunity for such orientation, school administrators should take the initiative to bring about changes. A perspective must be developed to the effect that the district should be recruiting teachers to meet the needs of individual school programs, staff, and clienteles, rather than just hiring teachers at large, or as interchangeable components.

Perhaps the best way building administrators can develop this perspective is to work closely with the district recruiting team in the development of position descriptions pertaining specifically to the vacancies in their schools; these descriptions can then be disseminated to all interested candidates and subsequently used in the interviewing process. According to Harris,

> A job description should contain all of the essential information that a prospective employee would need in order to "size up" the job, including the following: job title, relevant background information on the community and school, general description of the position, responsibilities of the position, relationships to others in the school system, benefits associated with the position, qualifications desired or required, and terms of employment (type and length of contract, vacations, salary, etc.).[18]

There need not necessarily be a separate position description for each vacancy in an administrator's school. However, to the extent to which a vacant position is unusual, a position description should be developed. A sample position description is shown in figure 7.1.[19] Vaughn Phelps provides some excellent guidelines for developing job descriptions.[20]

THE ADMINISTRATOR'S MAJOR CONTRIBUTION

Probably the most important contribution school administrators can make to the effective recruitment of staff is to help their schools develop excellent educational programs and good working conditions. (Obviously, potential candidates may also weigh other factors in deciding whether to pursue a staff vacancy, such as the size of the school and community, and cultural opportunities). A school or district which becomes recognized in the state as a leader in education and a good place to work (or one known to be striving toward these goals) thereby does more to improve its success in staff recruiting than perhaps anything else it could do.

Figure 7.1 A Sample Position Description.

Title: Diagnostic Teacher (Certificated)
Suggested Position Level: Teacher Basis
Days Per Year of Employment: 200 (Full-time)
Reports to: Project Director, Educational Resource Team, and the Principal
Supervises: Project Teacher and Aides (Functionally)
Major Duties and Responsibilities:

1. Diagnoses children referred for learning problems.
2. Assists in diagnosis of children referred for behavior problems.
3. Assesses the needs of children referred for learning problems.
4. Trains project teachers in the use and interpretation of individual standard and nonstandard tests.
5. Trains project teachers and paraprofessionals in individual analysis of student needs.
6. Correlates educational activities of cooperating school teachers with those of project teachers relative to referred children.
7. Works with individual children referred with the intention of confirming diagnoses.
8. Works with the language curriculum specialist in developing recommendations of specific educational programs and techniques.
9. Provides relevant information based on observation and evaluation to the behavioral counselor, to facilitate planning of behavioral approaches.
10. Attends all staffings on referred children both in cooperating school and project setting.
11. Maintains written records on all referred children.
12. Conducts, together with the language/curriculum specialist, in-service sessions.
13. Assists with functional responsibilities in the absence of the project director.
14. Assists in maintaining ongoing internal program continuity and acts as liaison between cooperating school and project director.
15. Assists project director in planning and developing orientation and program structure of proposed implementation of P.E.R.T.

On the other hand, a school or district with a fair or poor reputation— or possibly one with no image or reputation—as a good place to work or for offering a quality educational program is probably hampered in its recruiting efforts. Therefore, the most important steps that school administrators can take in helping the district office to recruit staff is to concentrate initially and continuously on the improvement of the educational program and working conditions within the school. Even though this may seem obvious to many, it needs to be emphasized, since regardless of what else a school administrator or school district might do by way of recruitment, there must be a solid basis in working conditions and in educational accomplishments before recruitment of quality candidates shows significant success.

STAFF SELECTION

Although school administrators are generally involved to only a limited extent in staff recruitment, they should play a major role in staff selection. However in some school districts—usually those in large cities—the school administrator's role in staff selection can be described as peripheral. In these situations, the personnel department of the district selects new staff for the schools, and building administrators may not find out who will be joining their staffs until just before classes begin. While in many of these circumstances, school administrators have been given opportunities to specify to the personnel department the kinds of new staff needed, it is the personnel department rather than school administrators that ascertains and decides whether or not candidates for particular vacancies meet the appropriate prerequisites.

In spite of seeming advantages in efficiency when a personnel department (or, for that matter, other central office administrators) select the staff, as long as building administrators are held accountable for the performance of the staff, they should be directly involved in the staff selection processes. There is a sound rationale for the proposition that building administrators should be given an opportunity to interview and recommend candidates for employment and assignment at their school.[21] Building administrators should also be able to appeal to the superintendent any directives from the personnel office to assign to their schools individuals they do not want.

In addition to building administrators, Harris and his colleagues have advocated that "other individuals who are affected by the person chosen for a given job should have considerable involvement in decisions concerning selection criteria and the procedures that will be followed."[22] For example, in teacher selection, representatives of the teachers, parents, and students might well assist the school administration in determining the selection criteria and procedures. Although the final decision to forward a hiring recommendation to the school board frequently rests with the superintendent and principal, it is advisable to obtain input from those individuals who will be "working side by side with the individual being considered."[23]

The preceding recommendations define a major role for school administrators, teachers, and staff members in staff selection and, by implication, a lesser role for the personnel department. However, the contributions of all are important, and the expertise of the personnel department should be capitalized on whenever possible.

Figure 7.2 The Staff Selection Process.

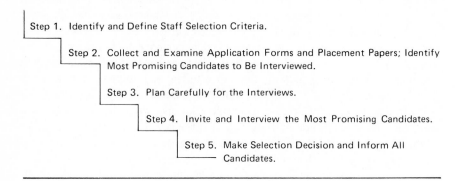

Step 1. Identify and Define Staff Selection Criteria.

Step 2. Collect and Examine Application Forms and Placement Papers; Identify Most Promising Candidates to Be Interviewed.

Step 3. Plan Carefully for the Interviews.

Step 4. Invite and Interview the Most Promising Candidates.

Step 5. Make Selection Decision and Inform All Candidates.

STAFF SELECTION PROCESS AND TEAM

Staff selection can be conceptualized as a process consisting of a series of sequentially interdependent steps, as depicted in figure 7.2. The first step in the staff selection process is to define the characteristics of new staff members the school seeks to employ. Ideally, this should have been accomplished at the beginning of the recruitment process, but many schools and districts limit themselves to merely identifying the grade level or subject to which the teacher will be assigned, such as, third grade or science. They may have other criteria in mind when they identify the vacancy, and they frequently apply additional criteria in making the final selection decision, but initially there appears to be a lack of specificity or comprehensiveness.

A major problem associated with the first step in the selection process is the determination of relevant and valid selection criteria. The basic question is, "Which personal qualities and professional capabilities should candidates possess?" Research suggests that little consensus exists among school districts on this matter. In addition, a study conducted by Beverly Browne and Richard Rankin found that "being bright may be a hindrance in obtaining a job."[24] Generally high academic achievement does not seem to be regarded as an essential selection criterion. As Daniel Duke has noted, if teacher effectiveness is to be improved (and growing concern about teacher competency ameliorated), individuals possessing subject matter expertise, communications skills, pedagogical abilities, and sound judgment—need to be selected.[25]

The tentative conclusion emerging from an examination of various studies on personnel selection criteria in education is that a wide range of variables is considered important, with an emphasis on personal factors. The basic problem with personnel selection criteria utilized by school districts is that they seem to be based on subjective impressions rather than on valid research and theory. As questions continue to be raised about research on teacher effectiveness, a number of recent studies reviewed in chapter 10 on staff evaluation have produced findings which should be considered by school districts in the development of personnel selection criteria.[26]

To help identify and define the selection criteria, administrators should consider establishing a *staff selection team.* The team might include such individuals as a department head or unit leader, a team leader or grade level coordinator, and an assistant principal. Identification of those for whom involvement on the team would be relevant depends on the nature of the vacancy, but for certain openings, guidance counselors, students, and even parents could make a valuable contribution to defining the selection criteria, interviewing candidates, and even making staff selection recommendations.[27] The school board has the authority to make final decisions on staff selection, and the building administrator may want to reserve the final determination on whom to recommend to the superintendent and, ultimately, the school board. This should present no real barrier to the nonadministrative members of the staff selection team as long as they understand their role and that of the building administrator.

In defining staff selection criteria, the school administrator and the selection team should give consideration to the following questions.

1. Is it important that the candidate believe in a particular kind of educational philosophy? If so, what are the specifics of that philosophy?
2. Should the candidate have the same basic personality and values as the rest of the staff?
3. What kinds of teaching techniques should the candidate be qualified to use, such as, inquiry method, discussion leader?
4. What should be the candidate's approach to student discipline and control?
5. How important is it that the candidate be able to work effectively with others, for example, colleagues, students?
6. Which personal characteristics do we want the candidate to possess, such as, type of personality, appearance?
7. What kinds of educational background and training do we expect the candidate to possess, for example, degree, teaching experience?
8. How much weight should be placed on recommendations?
9. What evidence is available that would provide significant support of the staff selection team's answers to the first eight questions?[28]

The final question is undoubtedly the most difficult and frustrating one for the school administrator and staff selection team to answer, but it is an extremely important question and should be raised at each point at which responses to the other questions are being considered. Most schools or districts define their staff selection criteria on the basis of personal preference and experience rather than on a systematic investigation of research on teacher effectiveness. Even though the former factors are not unimportant, the staff selection criteria should, so far as possible, be based on factors which research has demonstrated are related to teaching effectiveness. And Browne and Rankin's research indicates that all too frequently this is not the case.[29]

ANALYZING PLACEMENT PAPERS

After the selection criteria have been defined, the staff selection team needs to identify and employ procedures for collecting and examining candidates' data which pertain to the criteria. The two procedures most typically utilized by schools or districts are an examination of applicants' placement papers and personal interviews with candidates. Although these procedures possess certain advantages, each also has certain weaknesses of which the school administrator needs to be more aware. In reading the following discussion of these weaknesses, bear in mind that there are no perfect screening procedures and the weaknesses of each procedure can be ameliorated through careful planning, design, and execution.

An examination of placement papers has as its main purpose the screening of applicants to determine which ones should be invited for personal interviews. A candidate's placement papers may contain a great deal of useful information, depending on how the forms are designed. But the person or team examining this information needs to keep in mind that an applicant's primary objective is to project a favorable image. For example, it is unlikely that a candidate would knowingly reveal in a statement of philosophy anything which might impair the possibility of securing a job. Certain information requested on an application form is factual, of course, such as the number of years taught; but most of the content of an application form or placement papers is subjective and, therefore, should not be accepted at face value.

In addition, application forms have often contained sensitive, personal items. As Harris et al. noted, until the 1970s school districts could ask employment applicants for virtually any type of biographical information.[30] Since the enactment of the Equal Employment Opportunities Act of 1972, school districts which receive federal funds must scrutinize their procedures to ensure that they do not discriminate against minority groups and women. Therefore, school administrators need to exercise care about legal restrictions governing what information can and cannot be elicited on an application form. According to Rebore, data that should not be requested include such items as national origin, age, race, religion, sex (except when a bona fide occupational qualification exists), marital and family status, credit ratings, and nonjob related handicaps (including alcohol or drug consumption).[31]

Transcripts of a candidate's academic work are also generally requested as part of placement papers. However, Harris and his colleagues question whether they are really trustworthy indicators of academic performance or predictors of job success because of the problem of grade inflation and the variability in grading among individual professors, departments, and institutions of higher learning.[32] Generally, transcripts are more useful in screening out the clearly inferior candidates than they are for selecting the superior applicants.[33]

Letters of recommendation are probably perceived with greater confidence in the initial screening process than any other factor, but their utility has also been questioned by Harris and others.[34] Because letters of recommendation are beset by so many limitations, are used so often in the initial screening process, and seldom mention weaknesses or provide a comprehensive analysis of a candidate's strengths, Rebore suggests that school administrators must "write, telephone, or contact in person those individuals who have sent in reference letters supporting an applicant."[35] These contacts can help clarify and validate the information provided by a candidate or another party.

Rebore further indicates the three basic types of reference letters: (1) the glowing letter affirming the candidate's potential, (2) the negative letter indicating the applicant's performance was inferior, and (3) the neutral letter which is vague and does not provide a qualitative judgment of the applicant's performance.[36] The vast majority of the letters submitted are highly positive and, therefore, they offer little basis for differentiating among applicants. In addition, most letters contain hidden messages. Thus, school administrators would be wise to follow up on all letters of recommendation submitted on behalf of candidates to obtain more insight regarding the candidates' potential for success than their recommendation letters might reveal.

Moreover, any assessment or description of a candidate's strengths is usually limited by a lack of knowledge of the frame of reference and value system of the individual who has provided the recommendation. Evaluating recommendations has also been potentially limited by the Buckley Amendment, which permits candidates access to their placement files and to letters of recommendation therein.[37] Individuals writing letters of recommendation are aware of which persons have access to their own files, and may, therefore, temper analyses of those candidates' weaknesses. Many employees seem to be aware of the possible impact of the Buckley Amendment on letters of recommendation because a general preference exists for confidential letters.

While examining recommendations or ratings of candidates, keep in mind that the frame of reference of the person writing the statement or making the recommendation is generally unknown and consequently, one can seldom be absolutely sure what the ratings or recommendations mean. Also, a rater or person writing a letter of recommendation for an employee may not convey true feelings for fear of losing—or not losing—the employee. For these reasons, administrators should carefully scrutinize the data contained on application forms and placement papers, and exhibit considerable caution in drawing firm conclusions about candidates, based only on such data. Perhaps the best use of placement credentials is to develop hypotheses and questions about candidates, which can later be explored during a personal interview. This recommendation is buttressed by evidence from a study by Paul Arend, who found that, for the most part, candidates' placement papers did not differentiate between effective and ineffective teachers.[38]

Recently, the development and submission of a teaching portfolio has been suggested as a relatively new method for assessing the entry-level competencies of beginning teachers.[39] Such a portfolio might include a student teaching notebook, a slide/narrative program detailing significant experiences of the candidate, audiocassette tapes of lessons taught during student teaching, a videotape showing the candidate in practice teaching, and examples of unit/lesson plans. The portfolio assembled by the candidate could be requested by a school district. Administrators interested in this rather promising approach should initiate exploratory discussions with university placement officers.

THE PERSONNEL SELECTION INTERVIEW

The key technique in the selection process is the interview.[40] Many employers believe such important characteristics as personality and attitude are best observed and ascertained during a personal interview with the candidate.[41] However, despite its extensive use in personnel selection, the interview has come in for its share of criticism. According to Harris and his colleagues, the personal interview represents the most used and abused selection technique.[42] The problems apparently stem from inadequate planning, unconscious bias during the interview, and the absence of follow-up after the interview for the purpose of validating the interviewer's procedures and conclusions.[43]

Based on research and criticism of job selection interview techniques, a number of recommendations have been offered for improvement.[44] J. E. Greene, for example, has suggested that administrators exclude those variables or characteristics difficult to assess reliably and validly during an interview, such as leadership; that the number of variables assessed be few; that more than one person conduct the interview; and that a rating scale or written checklist be used by the interviewers for recording comments and judgments about a candidate.[45] A number of authors have identified the basic steps that an interviewer should take in planning for an interview; Phillip Young's research has indicated that interviewers need to be cognizant of the halo effect that candidates' interpersonal performance style has on the interviewers' perceptions of employability; and J. Roberts has provided guidelines for conducting a structured interview, offering examples of questions that might be used.[46] A type of structured interview referred to as a *Teacher Perceiver* has been used in many school districts and has been described by Donald Chalker.[47]

In addition, school districts need to consider the federal laws and various court cases which apply to interviews. As previously indicated in the discussion on application materials, due to federal laws and court cases, several areas or specific aspects of a candidate's background are no longer valid areas for inquiry during an interview. These include, but are not limited to, the candidate's marital and family status, age, religion, national origin, arrest, pregnancy, and nonjob-related handicaps. The latter prohibition is particularly important, inasmuch as Public Law 93–112, Section 504, disallows discrimination in the employment of any handicapped person.[48] To reject a handicapped candidate, an employer must not only demonstrate that the person is unqualified but also show that the reasons why the person is not qualified are unrelated to the person's handicap, and that those reasons could not be removed by restructuring the job, changing the facilities, purchasing new equipment, or employing an aide. G. R. Weisenstein provides a good discussion of traditional barriers and myths that have led to the unemployment and underemployment of the handicapped.[49]

PLANNING AND CONDUCTING THE INTERVIEW

After application forms and placement papers have been examined by the staff selection team, a decision should be made to invite for interviews those individuals who seem to meet the selection criteria to the greatest extent. The team may interview each candidate, the administrator may decide to conduct the interview unilaterally, or another interviewing arrangement may be implemented. Regardless of who is conducting the interview, however, careful planning is a key to its success.

A survey of hiring practices conducted by Joseph Braun found that the median length of an interview was approximately sixty minutes, the average number of candidates interviewed is four, and 72 percent of interviewers used

Figure 7.3 Key Questions in Planning for an Interview.

1. What are the objectives of the interview? What do we hope to accomplish?
2. How can we best establish rapport with the candidate at the beginning of the interview, to facilitate communication and candor?
3. What kinds of questions should be asked during the interview to ascertain what we want to know or confirm about the candidate? How should these questions be sequenced?
4. What are likely to be the objectives of the candidate during the interview? What does he/she hope to achieve?
5. What kinds of questions is the candidate likely to ask?
6. What kinds of information or knowledge do we want to be sure that the candidate has been given before leaving the interview?

a specific pool of questions that they asked applicants.[50] Researchers also found that the types of questions used were either designed by the district or individual administrator (54.4 percent) or the commercially obtained Perceiver instrument (45.5 percent).

The importance of planning for the interview was also underscored by Barry Farrell who found that "research performed over the past twenty years does not paint a favorable picture of the employment interview. The research has indicated that, compared to other selection procedures, the interview is least standardized, is most subject to bias, and has little or no value in predicting success."[51] Apparently, more thorough planning for the staff selection interview is needed if it is to accomplish its intended purpose. Planning for staff selection interview should include consideration of questions identified in figure 7.3.

During the interviews, the staff selection team should attempt to convey an atmosphere of friendliness and warmth, but team members should recognize that their primary objective is to determine candidates' suitability for a particular staff vacancy. This means that the selection team needs to ask penetrating questions of each candidate to reveal individual strengths and weaknesses, because many if not most candidates project their best images and seldom volunteer information or are very open about their limitations.

In asking questions administrators should try to avoid six common errors in interviewing: (1) posing questions that can be answered by "yes," or "no," thereby eliciting little information from the candidate; (2) asking unimaginative questions for which the astute applicant already has prepared answers; (3) asking leading questions which suggest the "correct answers;" (4) asking questions which reveal the interviewer's attitude on the questions; (5) asking questions unrelated to the task; and (6) asking questions already answered on the candidate's application form or resume.[52] Instead, the administrator and the staff selection team should concentrate on asking questions which require candidates to discuss in depth their background, qualifications, and interest in the vacancy.[53]

After an interview, the members of the staff selection team should discuss their impressions, and then rate the candidates on the extent to which they met the previously defined selection criteria. Perhaps at this point a decision can be made to hire or reject a particular candidate, although there is value to interviewing all candidates scheduled for conferences before a final decision is made. The selection team should maintain a written record summarizing impressions of the rating given to each candidate. Such a record is helpful later, when a final decision on hiring must be reached, or in the eventuality that any question may be raised about the selection process. A video or audio tape of each interview would be even more desirable.

When all of the candidates scheduled for conferences have been interviewed and evaluated, the selection team should be ready to make a final decision on the individual whom they recommend for employment. At this stage, the administrator and the selection team should be aware of the degree to which their own personal biases may potentially influence their decisions.

For example, a study by Daniel Merritt disclosed that principals are more attracted to candidates with attitudes about education similar to their own than to candidates with dissimilar attitudes.[54] This finding would not appear to possess any special significance unless one also knows that the principals in the study preferred candidates with attitudes similar to their own regardless of whether the candidates had high or low qualifications. Highly qualified candidates were selected by principals only when they possessed attitudes about education similar to their own, and candidates with low qualifications were selected over more highly qualified candidates when the former possessed attitudes about education similar to those of the principals.

A major implication of Merritt's study is that an interviewer's attitude can exert an important influence on the evaluation of a candidate—an influence which could result in the rejection of a highly qualified individual in favor of one who may be less qualified. Awareness of this possibility by the administrator and the selection team, and a conscious attempt toward greater objectivity should help a great deal to avoid this pitfall. Even though it is certainly important that there be a reasonable degree of attitude similarity between new staff and the administrator in regard to how they view education, improved educational opportunities for students can hardly be achieved by rejecting highly qualified candidates in favor of those with lower qualifications but with attitudes more similar to those of the administrator. In selecting staff, a certain amount of diversity in thinking is desirable and perhaps should even be deliberately sought by a school administrator.

In addition, Phillip Young and Herbert Heneman indicated that administrators need to be conscious of the decisions made by candidates during the selection process.[55] When administrators are seeking staff members for employment during periods of teacher shortages or in areas of high demand (math, science, computer technology, bilingual education, etc.), candidates often use the interview as a means of selecting the district in which they prefer to work. In their study, Young and Heneman found that teachers' reactions to the selection process were more positive when "interviewers tended to be aware of the feelings of interviewees, tended to work all the way through before reaching a conclusion, and were perceived to project personal warmth toward the candidate."[56] These findings suggest that the personality characteristics of the interviewer can significantly influence the applicant's decision to accept or reject a job offer. Therefore, to build trust and rapport during the interview process, administrators should:

1. Give the candidate the impression that the interview is the day's top priority. Hold the interview in private, and tell the secretary—in the presence of the candidate—to hold all but emergency phone calls.
2. Show respect for the candidate's ideas, even if they differ from the school's philosophy.
3. Make candidates feel that what they say is important by taking notes. Note taking is threatening to some candidates, however, so explain the need to record accurate information for later referral.
4. Repeat the advantages of the position, using different examples and expanding on a basic idea each time the information is repeated.[57]

TEACHER COMPETENCY TESTING

The perceived inadequacy of previously described personnel selection procedures has led to the use of competency or performance testing for the selection of teachers.[58] Although the use of competency testing in the selection of school personnel has been limited, its use may spread if public concern about the quality of teachers continues.[59] As educators face the issue of teacher competency testing, decisions need to be made regarding who should be tested and what testing instruments should be used.

The debate on who should be tested tends to focus on issues regarding the competence levels of both preservice, prospective teachers and in-service, experienced teachers. Generally, there is less resistance to testing teachers as they exit training programs than there is to the testing of veteran teachers.[60] In part, this is due to concerns regarding the validity of the tests and the relationship between successful test performance and effective teacher performance.[61] Yet, as James Popham and W. N. Kirby asserted, "Every child in the U.S. public schools has the right to be taught by a literate teacher."[62] To this end, they argue that "although in the future tests of basic skills should be routinely administered to prospective teachers, it is also necessary—unfortunately—to administer such tests to individuals who are currently teaching in U.S. schools."[63]

The National Teacher Examination (NTE) is the most frequently used teacher testing instrument.[64] It is designed to measure academic preparation in four domains: basic skills, general education, professional education, and subject field specialization.[65] Unfortunately, conflicting evidence exists regarding the appropriateness of using the NTE in assessing teacher competence. On the one hand, a study conducted by J. W. Andrews and his colleagues, found significant relationships between supervisors' ratings of practice teachers and these prospective teachers' scores on the National Teacher Examination.[66] And research by M. K. Piper and P. S. O'Sullivan also tended to support the value of the NTE in the selection of teachers.[67] On the other hand, D. Owen found that the NTE tests do not provide direct evaluation of teaching performance.[68] William Webster, in his study of teacher testing, found that another test, the Wesman Personnel Classification Test (WPCT), which tests verbal and quantitative ability, was highly correlated with the NTE and is, therefore, as good a predictor of rated teaching effectiveness as the NTE.[69]

In part, in response to criticisms raised regarding the use of the NTE with experienced teachers and the continued need for competency testing of experienced teachers, the Educational Testing Service recently announced that it is creating a broader measurer of teacher competence to replace the standard multiple-choice, paper-and-pencil NTE.[70] The new test will be administered during three separate phases in a teacher's education and training:

Stage I, to be given during or after students' sophomore year in college, would measure their basic skills; it would use a computerized diagnostic assessment to identify strengths and weaknesses.

Stage II, to be taken at the completion of college or a teacher training program, would measure how well students know their subject matter and the principles of teaching.

Stage III, to be given after a prospective teacher has spent time in a supervised teaching situation, would measure the ability to teach a subject in the classroom, often as "pedagogical content knowledge."[71]

The test developers have indicated that they intend to make use of such technological developments as interactive video, computer simulations of typical classroom events, and portfolios documenting a teacher's accomplishments.

Although a small body of research is available on the effectiveness of using tests in the selection of school personnel, the weight of evidence to date suggests that standardized tests may provide useful information about candidates, particularly when combined with other kinds of selection approaches.[72] The available research on this selection method, however, does not justify relying solely on tests in hiring school personnel. Serious concerns exist regarding the use of competency testing. These include "questions about cost, content validity, control (who determines what should be tested), limited response format (paper and pencil), and the inability of current tests to measure critical dimensions of teacher behavior (e.g., interpersonal skills)."[73] Thus, those districts or educational agencies considering using tests in personnel selection need to seek information about the reliability, validity, and potential racial or cultural bias of any test; they should make sure that the examination utilized for personnel selection is clearly job-related.[74] Several courts have ruled that unless a test has been proven to be directly related to important aspects of a job, it should not be used in personnel selection.[75] One testing program that appears to meet these standards has been described by William Webster.[76]

Due to concern about the validity of personnel selection procedures and prior discrimination in personnel selection, the federal government published *Uniform Guidelines on Employee Selection,* which was previously discussed.[77] An addendum to the original publication includes certain questions raised in regard to the guidelines; it should be studied by every school district and educational agency involved in personnel selection.[78] The guidelines apply to all personnel selection procedures, including application forms, tests, interviews, and evaluation of performance. The guidelines do not require validated selection procedures, but if the procedures are legally challenged as discriminatory, employers must then present validation evidence supporting the selection procedures, as well as proof that they did not discriminate on the basis of race, color, sex, religion, or national origin. In the event of such a legal challenge, employers are required to do more than assert the validity of their procedures; they must provide evidence as to that validity. To provide evidence of the validation of personnel selection procedures, employers must demonstrate the job-relatedness of their selection procedure as outlined in the *Uniform Guidelines.*

Even though the extent to which school districts attempt to validate their personnel selection procedures is uncertain, research suggests that much remains to be done. Barbara Grohe found, for example, that most school districts in her study had established no procedures or plan for validating their selection criteria or process.[79] Arend and Merritt, in studies discussed earlier, uncovered findings about school districts' selection procedures raising serious questions about their reliability and validity.[80] Consequently, as the available research illustrates, most school districts and other educational agencies involved in personnel selection could benefit from a careful study of the appropriate government documents on employee selection procedures and from an assessment of the current selection procedures, developing more valid ones where the need is evident.

STAFF INDUCTION

After new members of a staff have been hired, the process of induction or orientation should begin immediately. Staff induction is a process by which recently employed individuals are helped to become oriented to a new environment, which includes the community, the school system, the teaching position, and the people with whom they will be working.[81] The importance of the process is underlined by the observations of Lloyd McCleary and Stephen Hencley:

> Orientation requires sensitive planning and careful execution. It is during the orientation period that new staff members gather their first impressions concerning the school's policies, objectives, leadership, and method of operation. Moreover, it is at this time that initial acquaintance is made with colleagues and with the community inhabitants, characteristics, agencies, and services. Since first impressions are often lasting, every effort should be expended during orientation to assure that new staff members gain correct understanding of the many facets of school and community life.[82]

In recent years, attention has been focused on developing induction or mentorship programs to assist beginning teachers entering the teaching profession.[83] As Elizabeth Ashburn noted,

> Since 1980, many state legislatures have mandated an "Entry Year Assistance Program," "Beginning Teacher Helping Program," "Assistance/Assessment," and "Teacher Mentor Program." A few states have gone so far as to specify program content and to design the delivery system. Most programs have been established so recently that effectiveness studies are not yet available.[84]

In general, induction programs contain the following elements: (1) a group of experienced teachers willing to work with beginners; (2) a set of specified activities defining the mentor-mentee relationship; and (3) a clear outline of a plan for the professional development of beginning teachers.[85] A study of one mentor program suggested five themes for emphasis during the year: classroom management, instructional delivery, home-school relationships, professional concerns, and extracurricular activities.[86] To address these themes, participants heard guest speakers, participated in guided discussions, engaged in role-playing, and participated in simulations.

Breda Murphy Bova and Rebecca Phillips found that mentors were generally influential persons who helped entry-level teachers achieve their professional goals.[87] Obviously, the success of induction/mentorship programs relies heavily on the quality of the mentors involved in the programs. L. A. Wagner identified the following skills as necessary for a mentor to possess: communication, modeling of exemplary teaching, leadership, ability to build a trusting relationship, and completion of mentoring tasks.[88]

To entice the most desirable staff members to participate in an induction program, school administrators should be able to identify the benefits which a mentor might expect to receive as a result of their participation in the program. Larry Godley, Donald Wilson, and Beverly Klug, in a review of the research on the teacher consultant role, identified the professional benefits accompanying mentoring or assisting relationships. These benefits included

> sharing of materials and techniques, developing collegial relationships, and being treated as professionals. Individuals acquired new knowledge of materials and strategies, clarified their own instructional goals and objectives, and grew in their understanding of the circumstances under which students learned through participation in these associations.[89]

PROBLEMS OF NEW STAFF

To plan an effective orientation program, administrators need to be knowledgeable about the problems new staff members may encounter. An analysis of research on the problems of beginning teachers in adjusting to their new environments suggests that they can experience difficulties in the following major areas during their first year of teaching: (1) knowing what is expected of them, (2) planning and organizing for teaching, (3) motivating and evaluating students, (4) controlling and disciplining students, (5) establishing friendly and cooperative relationships with other members of the school or district, (6) communicating with parents and the community, and (7) achieving personal and professional self-confidence.[90]

Whether the problems experienced by new teachers during their first year result from their own deficiencies or from a poor induction program, or

Figure 7.4 Questions of New Teachers During the First Semester.

1. "What, exactly, is my total assignment in this school?"
2. "Why don't I have any permanent classroom or office of my own?"
3. "Is everyone as busy during the day and as exhausted at the end of the day as I am?"
4. "What do I do to motivate the kids to learn what I am teaching? And how do I evaluate and grade these kids?"
5. "What do I do about the kids who can't learn? How do I handle the troublemakers in my classes?"
6. "How do I handle this angry parent who keeps calling me to complain about the way I'm treating her child?"
7. "How does one get accepted in this school by the older teachers?"
8. "I am unsure. Do the students and the other teachers really like me, accept me, and think I am a good teacher?"

both, is not certain. All too frequently, school and district induction programs can be characterized as "too little, too late." Most school districts give considerable emphasis, before school starts, to orienting new staff members to the school district itself; but orientation to the community (particularly the community adjacent to the school), and to teaching in the assigned school, seems lacking. With the exception of those school districts that have initiated induction programs, there is little or no follow-through during the year, once initial orientation activities have been concluded.[91] As a result, many new teachers continue to develop questions and feelings similar to those reported in a survey of beginning teachers after the third week of school, and identified in figure 7.4.[92]

Questions such as those presented in figure 7.4 support the need for a continuous induction program. As the National Education Association has pointed out, "The orientation of teachers is something that cannot be done in a single day or single week or in a matter of weeks."[93]

A FINAL NOTE

In many school systems, the building administrator's involvement in staff recruitment, selection, and induction is limited. This is regrettable because of the long, continuing tradition of holding administrators accountable for the performance of the professional staff in their schools. If building administrators are to be held accountable, they should play significant roles in the recruitment, selection, and induction of the professional staff. Certainly no other administrator is in a better position to know the needs of the school. Therefore, an important prerequisite for any effective staff recruitment, selection, and induction program is the major involvement of the building administrator.

Review and Learning Activities

1. What is the main purpose of the district's recruiting program? Describe the ways in which an administrator can make an important contribution to that program.
2. Why is it important for the building administrator to be involved directly in the process of staff selection?
3. Identify the steps involved in the staff selection process. How might the use of a staff selection team help with the process?
4. Describe the factors an administrator should consider in determining staff selection criteria and in analyzing placement papers.
5. Discuss the factors an administrator should consider in planning for and conducting the staff selection interview.
6. What is the main purpose of a staff induction program? Which problems do many beginning teachers encounter, and which steps should a school take to prevent and/or ameliorate these problems?
7. Interview the beginning teachers in your school to ascertain the problems and concerns they have and the extent to which the program of induction recommended in the text has been implemented.

Notes

1. D. E. Davis and N. C. Nickerson, *Critical Issues in School Personnel Administration* (Chicago: Rand McNally, 1968), 17.

2. Ronald W. Rebore, *Personnel Administration in Education: A Management Approach* (Englewood Cliffs, N.J.: Prentice-Hall, 1987), 70.

3. Ernest J. Middleton, Emanuel J. Mason, William E. Stilwell, and William C. Parker, "A Model for Recruitment and Retention of Minority Students in Teacher Preparation Programs," *Journal of Teacher Education* (January–February 1988): 14–18.

4. Richard Murnane, "Understanding Teacher Attrition," *Harvard Educational Review* (May 1987): 177.

5. J. N. Fox, "The Supply of U.S. Teachers: Quality for the Twenty-First Century," in *Eighth Annual Yearbook of the American Education Finance Association,* ed. K. Alexander and D. Monk (Cambridge, Mass.: Ballinger 1988): 49–68.

6. Arthur E. Wise, Linda Darling-Hammond, and Barnett Berry, "Selecting Teachers: The Best, the Known, and the Persistent," *Educational Leadership* (February 1988): 82.

7. Jerome T. Murphy, "Attracting Talented Students to Teaching," *Harvard Educational Review* (May 1987): 183–84.

8. Vernon Clark and Rochelle Clemson, "Teacher Staffing in Urban Schools: Beyond the Question of Supply and Demand," *Metropolitan Education* (Spring 1987): 11–12.

9. Jay Alison Spuck, "What Teacher Shortage? In Houston, We're Growing Our Own," *American School Board Journal* (October 1987): 39, 47. Information on the Milwaukee Y.E.S. (Young Educators' Society) is available through the Center for Teacher Education, School of Education, at the University of Wisconsin-Milwaukee.

10. Clark and Clemson, "Teacher Staffing in Urban Schools," 12.

11. Ben M. Harris et al., *Personnel Administration in Education,* 2d ed. (Boston: Allyn & Bacon, 1985), 131–33. See also, Blake Rodman, "Teacher Recruitment, Selection Procedures Outdated, Study Says," *Education Week* (March 18, 1987): 20.

12. Wise et al., "Selecting Teachers," 84.

13. For a review of these, see Richard A. Gorton, "Personnel Policies," in *The Encyclopedia of Educational Research,* ed. Harold E. Mitzel (New York: Macmillan, 1982). A major part of this chapter has been adapted from this source. In addition, see Robert J. Weiss, "Affirmative Action: A Brief History," *Journal of Intergroup Relations* (September 1987): 40–53; I. Phillip Young and H. Schmidt, "Effects of Sex, Chronological Age, and Instructional Level of Teacher Candidates on Screening Decisions Made by Principals," *Journal of Research and Development in Education* (Summer 1988): 41–48; and William M. Gordon, "The New Direction of Affirmative Action," *Record* (Fall 1989): 29–30.

14. Harris et al., *Personnel Administration in Education,* 223.

15. Rebore, *Personnel Administration in Education,* 38.

16. William R. McKinney, "Public Personnel Selection: Issues and Choice Points," *Public Personnel Management* (Fall 1987): 243–57.

17. Equal Employment Opportunity Commission, "Uniform Guidelines in Employee Selection Procedures," *Federal Register* (August 25, 1978), 38290–315.

18. Harris et al., *Personnel Administration in Education,* 149–50.

19. Adapted from a position guide of Milwaukee Public Schools, Milwaukee, Wisconsin.

20. Vaughn Phelps, *How to Develop Job Descriptions* (ERIC Report Ed–154–526).

21. This principle has long been supported by the American Association of School Administrators, which has stated "Since principals have a big stake in the outcome, they should have a voice in the selection of candidates." American Association of School Administrators, *Staff Relations in School Administration* (Washington, D.C. 1955), 35.

22. Harris et al., *Personnel Administration in Education,* 116.

23. George M. Arnold, "Sound Techniques, Good Fortune Ensure a First-Rate Teaching Staff," *NASSP Bulletin* (February 1988): 61.

24. Beverly A. Browne and Richard J. Rankin, "Predicting Employment in Education: The Relative Efficiency of National Teacher Examinations Scores and Student Teacher Ratings," *Educational and Psychological Measurement* (Spring 1986): 191–97.

25. Daniel L. Duke, *School Leadership and Instructional Improvement* (New York: Random House, 1987), 67.

26. N. L. Gage, "What Do We Know about Teaching Effectiveness?" *Kappan* (October 1984): 87–96; and Theodore Coladarci, "The Relevance of Educational Research for Identifying Master Teachers," *NASSP Bulletin* (January 1988): 90–98.

27. See, for example, Nicholas A. Fischer, "Parents: Effective Partners in Faculty Selection, Hiring," *Kappan* (February 1981): 442; and Harris et al., *Personnel Administration in Education,* 116.

28. Arnold, "Sound Techniques," 59–61.

29. Browne and Rankin, "Predicting Employment in Education."

30. Harris et al., *Personnel Administration in Education,* 108.

31. Rebore, *Personnel Administration in Education,* 103–4.

32. Harris et al., *Personnel Administration in Education,* 110.

33. Ibid.

34. Joseph A. Braun, Jr.; Arnie Willems; Max Brown; and Kathy Green, "A Survey of Hiring Practices in Selected School Districts," *Journal of Teacher Education* (March/April 1987): 45; and Harris et al., *Personnel Administration in Education,* 108–9.

35. Rebore, *Personnel Administration in Education,* 105.

36. Ibid.

37. James A. Tidwell, "Principals' Liability for Negative Letters of Recommendation," *NASSP Bulletin* (December 1987): 61–70.

38. Paul Arend, *Teacher Selection: The Relationship between Selected Factors and the Rated Effectiveness of Second Year Teachers* (ERIC Report Ed–087–102).

39. Braun et al., "A Survey of Hiring Practices," 48.

40. I. Phillip Young, "The Effects of Interpersonal Performance Style in Simulated Teacher Selection Interviews," *Journal of Research and Development in Education*, no. 4 (1984): 43. See also Robert W. Eder and Gerald R. Ferris, eds., *The Employment Interview: Theory, Research, and Practice* (Newbury Park, Calif.: Sage, 1989).

41. Braun et al., "A Survey of Hiring Practices," 45–49.

42. Harris et al., *Personnel Administration in Education*, 110–11.

43. R. Dipboye et al., "Equal Employment and the Interview," *Personnel Journal* (1976): 520–22.

44. Allan S. Vann, "A Principal's Guide to the Hiring and Induction of New Teachers," *Principal* (September 1989): 26–29.

45. J. E. Greene, *School Personnel Administration* (Philadelphia: Chilton Book Co., 1971), 137.

46. R. A. Engel and D. Friendrichs, "The Emergence Approach: The Interview Can Be a Reliable Process," *NASSP Bulletin* (January 1980): 85–91. See also Dorothy Molyneaux and Vera W. Lane, *Effective Interviewing* (Rockleigh, N.J.: Allyn & Bacon, 1981); "The Interview Process: A Systematic Approach to Better Hiring," *Small Business Report* (August 1984): 57–62; Young, "The Effects of Interpersonal Performance Style," 43–51; and Jo Roberts, "How to Make the Most of Teacher Interviews," *NASSP Bulletin* (December 1987): 103–8.

47. Donald M. Chalker, "The Teacher Perceiver Interview as an Instrument for Predicting Successful Teaching Behavior" (Ed.D. diss., Wayne State University, 1981).

48. Public Law 93–112, Section 504 (Washington, D.C.: U.S. Department of Health, Education, and Welfare, 1975). See also Philip R. Voluck, "Recruiting, Interviewing and Hiring: Staying within the Boundaries," *Personnel Administrator* (May 1987): 45–52.

49. G. R. Weisentein, "Barriers to Employment of the Handicapped: Some Educational Implications," *Journal of Research and Development in Education* (Summer 1979): 57–70. Also see *Educators with Disabilities; A Resource Guide* (Washington, D.C.: U.S. Government Printing Office, 1981).

50. Braun et al., "A Survey of Hiring Practices," 47.

51. Barry M. Farrell, "Recruitment: The Art and Science of Employment Interviews," *Personnel Journal* (May 1986): 91.

52. Richard H. Magee, "The Employment Interview—Techniques of Questioning," *Personnel Journal* (May 1962): 241–45.

53. Everett W. Nicholson and William D. McInerney, "Hiring the Right Teacher: A Method for Selection," *NASSP Bulletin* (November 1988): 88–92.

54. Daniel L. Merritt, "Attitude Congruency and Selection of Teacher Candidates," *Administrator's Notebook* (February 1971); and a study by Perry suggests this situation persists: Nancy Perry, "New Teachers: Do 'the Best' Get Hired?" *Kappan* (October 1981): 113–14.

55. I. Phillip Young and Herbert G. Heneman III, "Predictors of Interviewee Reactions to the Selection Interview," *Journal of Research and Development in Education* (Winter 1986): 29–36.

56. Ibid., 35.

57. "The Interview Process: A Systematic Approach to Better Hiring," *Small Business Report*, 58.

58. W. E. Hathaway, "Testing Teachers," *Educational Leadership* (December 1980): 210–15; see also Arnold M. Gallegos, "Competency Testing, Teachers," in *Encyclopedia of School Administration and Supervision*, ed. R. A. Gorton, G. T. Schneider, and J. C. Fisher (Phoenix, Ariz.: Oryx Press, 1988): 70–71.

59. Samuel Brodbelt, "Issues in Teacher Testing," *Clearing House* (January 1988): 197–201.

60. Ibid.

61. Ibid., 198.

62. W. James Popham and W. N. Kirby, "Recertification Tests for Teachers: A Defensible Safeguard for Society," *Kappan* (September 1987): 46.

63. Ibid.

64. George F. Madaus and Diana Pullin, "Teacher Certification Tests: Do They Really Measure What We Need to Know?" *Kappan* (September 1987): 31–38.

65. *No Panaceas: A Brief Discussion of Teacher Selection Instruments* (ERIC Report Ed–252–569); see also R. E. Carlson, "The Impact on Preparation Institutions of Competency Tests for Educators" (Paper presented at the annual meeting of the American Educational Research Association, Chicago, Illinois, 1985).

66. J. W. Andrews et al., "Preservice Performance and the National Teacher Exams," *Kappan* (January 1980): 358–59.

67. M. K. Piper and P. S. O'Sullivan, "The National Teacher Examination: Can It Predict Classroom Performance?" *Kappan* (January 1981): 401.

68. D. Owen, *None of the Above: Behind the Myth of Scholastic Aptitude* (Boston: Houghton Mifflin, 1985).

69. William J. Webster, *Five Years of Teacher Testing: A Retrospective Analysis* (ERIC Report Ed–276–769), 1984.

70. Lynn Olson, " 'Different' Tests of Teaching Skill Planned by Firm: NTE to be Replaced with High-Tech Format," *Education Week* (November 2, 1988): 1, 27.

71. Ibid., 27.

72. Harris et al., *Personnel Administration in Education,* 113. See also William J. Webster, "Selecting Effective Teachers," *Journal of Educational Research* (March/April 1988): 245–53.

73. Gallegos, "Competency Testing, Teachers," 71.

74. W. B. Castetter, *The Personnel Function in Educational Administration* (New York: Macmillan Co., 1981).

75. Harris et al., *Personnel Administration in Education,* 112.

76. Webster, *Five Years of Teacher Testing.*

77. Equal Employment Opportunity Commission, "Uniform Guidelines," 38290–315.

78. Equal Employment Opportunity Commission, "Adoption of Questions and Answers to Clarify and Provide a Common Interpretation of the Uniform Guidelines on Employee Selection Procedures," *Federal Register* (March 2, 1979): 11996–12009.

79. Barbara Grohe, "School Districts' Teacher Selection Criteria and Process in Wisconsin and Related Demographic Factors" (Ph.D. diss., University of Wisconsin-Milwaukee, 1981).

80. Arend, *Teacher Selection;* and Merritt, "Attitude Congruency."

81. Harris et al., *Personnel Administration in Education,* 133–34.

82. Lloyd E. McCleary and Stephen P. Hencley, *Secondary School Administration: Theoretical Bases for Professional Practice* (New York: Dodd, Mead and Co., 1965), 287.

83. See *Perspective on Teacher Induction: A Review of the Literature and Promising Models* (ERIC Report Ed–258–857); and Merlin Manley, Lee Siudzinski, and Leonard J. Varah, "Easing the Transition for First-Year Teachers," *NASSP Bulletin* (March 1989): 16–21.

84. Elizabeth A. Ashburn, "Current Developments in Teacher Induction Programs," *Action in Education* (Winter 1986–87): 41–44.

85. Rochelle L. Clemson, "Mentorship in Teaching," *Action in Teacher Education* (Fall 1987): 85–90.

86. Jane Ann Zaharias and Thoms W. Frew, "Teacher Induction: An Analysis of One Successful Program," *Action in Teacher Education* (Spring 1987): 49–55.

87. Breda Murphy Bova and Rebecca R. Phillips, "Mentoring as a Learning Experience for Adults, *Journal of Teacher Education* (1984): 16–20.

88. L. A. Wagner, "Ambiguities and Possibilities in California's Mentor Teacher Program," *Educational Leadership* (1985): 23–29.

89. Larry B. Godley, Donald R. Wilson, and Beverly J. Klug, "The Teacher Consultant Role: Impact on the Profession," *Action in Teacher Education* (Winter 1986–87): 66–67.

90. See Kevin Ryan et al., *Biting the Apple: Accounts of First Year Teachers* (New York: Longman, 1980); Sandra J. Odell, Catherine E. Loughlin, and Douglas P. Ferraro, "Functional Approach to Identification of New Teacher Needs in an Induction Context," *Action in Teacher Education* (Winter 1986–87): 51–57; Joseph C. Sommerville, "Principals' Perceptions of Beginning Teacher Behavior: A Challenge," *National Forum of Educational Administration and Supervision Journal* (1988–89): 48–58; Robert J. Krajewski and Lamont Veatch, "Orienting New Staff for Instructional Leadership," *NASSP Bulletin* (November 1988): 62–66; and Thomas J. DeLong, "Teachers Need Principals' Guidance in Career Development," *NASSP Bulletin* (March 1989): 23–28.

91. Carl A. Grant et al., "In-service Support for First Year Teachers: The State of the Scene," *Journal of Research and Development in Education* (November 1981): 99–111.

92. Richard A. Gorton, "Questions of New Teachers after the Third Week of School" (study revised in 1980). Also see Hane H. Applegate et al., "New Teachers Seek Support," *Educational Leadership* (October 1980): 74–76.

93. "Editorial: Welcome to the New Teacher," *National Education Association Journal* (October 1963): 10.

8

· · · · ·

Special Personnel Problems

■

Not all members of a school's staff experience the problems discussed in this chapter. However, in recent years problems associated with issues such as teacher absenteeism, drug and alcohol abuse, merit pay, differentiated salary plans, fringe benefits, and sexual harassment have occurred on an increasing basis. When these problems occur, they not only affect the lives of the individuals involved but they can also have an impact on the rest of the school. Certainly, they represent major personnel challenges for school administrators. While there are no easy answers to these problems, an important first step for administrators is to understand better the nature of each problem. Then they need to develop policies and programs to deal with the current problems and prevent their future occurrence. The following sections should assist administrators with those objectives.[1]

EMPLOYEE ABSENTEEISM

Employee absenteeism surfaced as an issue in education in the 1980s after many years of concern about the problem's prevalence outside the field of education.[2] Available evidence suggests that employee absenteeism will continue to challenge school administrators as one of the major school personnel issues of the 1990s.

The primary reason that employee absenteeism has become a problem is that many people, including school administrators and school board members, believe that sick leave provisions are being abused by increasing numbers of employees.[3] The abuse has brought about several negative consequences: greater costs for substitute teachers, a feeling that the quality of education decreases when substitute teachers are utilized more frequently, and a concern about the additional time principals must spend in monitoring teacher absences and arranging for substitute teachers.[4] One state, for example, estimated that $888 million per year was being spent for total professional salaries directly attributable to teacher absences.[5] This amount represented a greater percentage of the total budget than was allocated by that state for school health services, student activities, capital outlay, community services, or food services.

A second reason employee absenteeism is likely to develop into a major policy issue is that teachers' associations question whether serious abuses are prevalent in the area of teacher sick leaves. They have contended that most statistics on teacher absences are misleading because they do not distinguish between excused absences for professional meetings, legitimate absences for illness, and unexcused absences.[6]

Unfortunately, it has been difficult to ascertain objectively whether absenteeism by school employees represents a serious problem or not. The records maintained by most school districts are not useful in making such an assessment; consequently, there is a paucity of hard data on the extent and severity of the problem. In addition, questions have been raised regarding the varied methods for measuring absenteeism. For example, three different ways to calculate absenteeism have been identified.[7] The first counts the total number of lost days or hours (minus absences designated as exceptions); the second tracks the number of incidents of absence (a two-day absence is recorded as one incident); and the third combines the first two approaches by assigning penalty points based on the degree of disruptiveness which the absence causes. Thus, given the differences in measuring employee absenteeism, studies have often encountered difficulty in identifying reliable and valid techniques by which to measure absenteeism.

School district administrators consider abuses as falling into two categories: the first is for violating district rules (misconduct) and the second is for excessive absenteeism. Regarding misconduct, the reason for the absence is assessed in accord with those reasons identified as "excused." For example, school districts assess whether employees are actually sick, rather than taking the day off because they do not feel quite up to teaching. Within the excessive absence category, attention is placed on the number of absences without regard to their reason. Excessive absenteeism, therefore, is defined as "a performance situation which can be improved rather than a misconduct problem which should be punished."[8] Although certain techniques and forms have been developed to help school districts keep better records of teacher absenteeism, the problem of verification remains a touchy one.

Even when reasonably useful and objective data on staff absenteeism have been collected, a decision must still be made regarding the level at which employee absences constitute a serious problem. School districts may vary in that determination, but at least two authorities on the subject suggest that a monthly absentee rate exceeding 5 or 6 percent constitutes a matter of great concern.[9] Regardless of the level of staff absences defined as a problem, local determinations are based on value judgments as much as on absentee data; consequently, differences of opinion persist regarding whether or not a serious problem actually exists in a locality.

Acknowledging any difficulties involved in obtaining data regarding the severity of employee absenteeism, the fact remains that many people perceive it to be a problem, and that perception has stimulated much discussion and investigation into the causes of employee absenteeism. For example, over 400 articles and studies on the topic of employee absenteeism have been identified by Educational Research Service (ERS).[10] In a comprehensive review of that literature, ERS concluded that research findings have been inconsistent on the relationship between employee absenteeism and education level, salary level, tenure, satisfaction with pay, satisfaction with promotion, employment status, job autonomy and responsibility, satisfaction with sense of achievement, marital status, or family size. ERS's analysis of the literature further revealed no relationship between absenteeism and satisfaction with organizational policies and practices, employee control and participation, organizational climate, group cohesion/satisfaction with coworkers, or satisfaction with the supervisor and employer. However, ERS did find research showing a consistent association between employee absenteeism and increased stress and anxiety, job satisfaction, organization size, lenient personnel policies on absenteeism and leave usage, bargaining and union activity, and dissatisfaction with the work itself.

In a more recent review of the literature, David Ralston and Michael Flanagan identified a number of factors identified as antecedents to absenteeism. These factors include family size and responsibility, role clarity, job autonomy and level, role orientation, role stress, and interrole conflict. To address the issue of interrole conflict, their study of employee absenteeism found that men and women who were afforded flextime arrangements (establishing their own work schedules within basic parameters) were absent significantly less often than women who were not afforded flextime. Thus, they concluded that "the work hours discretion provided by flextime helps to reduce work/family interrole conflict differences between females and males, and as such minimizes absenteeism difference for females due to family role demands."[11] Furthermore, the lack of difference in absences between men and women under flextime support the notion that interrole conflict is a function of the number of roles one holds and not one's sex.

In regard to the relationship between absenteeism and job satisfaction, Edwin Bridges concluded that such a relationship was more likely under conditions of high work interdependence than under moderate or low interdependence.[12] In this connection, Robert Thompson suggests that teachers are less likely to take unwarranted leave days when they know others are depending on them.[13] Thus, he suggests that school administrators foster this feeling of interdependence by developing organizational and instructional arrangements which encourage faculty members to work together.

Specific studies on teacher absenteeism provide additional insights into possible causes. For example, Sharon Conley, Samuel Bacharach, and Scott Bauer found that role ambiguity, student behavior problems, routinization of work, and class size were positively correlated with teacher absenteeism.[14] Thus, they concluded that clarifying teachers' jobs and improving the managerial structure of schools are critical in enhancing teacher motivation and retention.

Regarding district policies, a relationship between the number of teachers using their sick leave and the nature of teacher personnel policies on teacher absenteeism was documented by at least two studies. Researchers investigating fifty-six Pennsylvania school systems discovered a positive relationship between liberal personnel policies on sick leave and employee absenteeism.[15] Those school districts that granted sick leave in addition to that required by the state were plagued by higher employee absentee rates than the school districts which provided no additional sick leave days. A related study showed that the monitoring and reporting techniques used on teacher absences make a difference.[16] When teachers were required to phone in their sick leave request to their principals, they were much less likely to make the request than when they could simply call an answering service or another supervisor.[17] The type of sick leave policy established by a school district has also been found to be related to the level of absenteeism in that district.[18]

Although studies on teacher absenteeism can be helpful, usually the research on causes of employee absenteeism has consisted of correlational studies that imply but do not demonstrate causality. The samples employed by researchers have also tended to be small and limited, which make generalization difficult; and frequently controls for other relevant variables have not been used. Nevertheless the research findings here presented are probably at least as reliable and valid as the personal opinion and subjective experiences which seem to form the basis for most personnel policies on this topic. Administrators

Figure 8.1 Major Factors Influencing Employee Attendance.

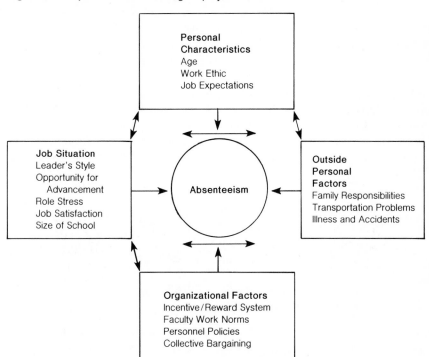

who question the validity of research findings in regard to their particular school setting should conduct their own studies rather than simply dismissing the findings of others and falling back on personal inclinations.

One model which could be helpful to the administrator in understanding the causes of employee absenteeism was developed by R. M. Steers and S. R. Rhodes, and has been adapted by Gorton in figure 8.1.[19]

Figure 8.1 suggests that essentially four major sources of factors could influence an employee's attendance: (1) personal characteristics of the employee, such as work ethic; (2) the particular aspects of the job situation itself, such as the amount of stress experienced by the employee; (3) organizational factors, such as the type of personnel policies governing employee absenteeism; and (4) outside personal factors, such as illness or accidents.[20] The factors identified in each part of the figure exemplify the nature of the category and are not intended to depict its full scope.

Although the causes of employee absenteeism are complex and not well understood, there has been no shortage of proposals to control or reduce the problem. These proposals have ranged from "Let's-get-tough" programs to humane approaches to teacher absenteeism. Both alternatives have been criticized for a variety of reasons including: (1) management's approach to attendance was punitive and policing; (2) policies often penalize legitimate needs while abuse continues; (3) little recognition of good or even perfect attendance; (4) supervisory favoritism; and (5) inconsistent interpretation of absenteeism policies.[21] In light of these criticisms, one proposed approach developed by the American Association of School Personnel Administrators seems especially worthy of consideration. It recommends that a school district

1. Establish an employee monitoring system to ascertain whether the district is experiencing an absentee problem.
2. Develop a policy that sets standards and procedures for governing all aspects of employee absenteeism.
3. Design a program to provide assistance and counseling for those employees whose absenteeism may indicate a particularly serious problem.
4. Offer an incentive program to motivate employees to reduce their absenteeism.[22]

Generally, experts agree that the starting point in any attempt to improve employee absenteeism is the development of a school board policy on employee attendance. An example of such a policy is "The board recognizes that good attendance is necessary and expected in order to maintain an efficient school system. Therefore, the board encourages its employees to develop satisfactory attendance performance in pursuance of that goal."[23]

Once a general school board policy has been developed, the next step is to promulgate specific administrative regulations that set forth management's expectations of employee attendance, identify indicators of unacceptable absenteeism, incorporate the use of progressive discipline, employ impartial investigation into the cause of absences, promote proper communication of the attendance policies, and establish procedures for handling employee absenteeism.

Crucial to the success of any school board policy and/or administrative regulations on employee absenteeism is the building principal. Unless principals are committed to the school board's policy and the administrative regulations, the possibility of their success is uncertain at best. To develop this commitment, school districts need to involve their principals in the development of policies and regulations on employee attendance, and principals need to be provided with in-service education to help them carry out the policy and regulations. For example, the following guidelines may be useful for principals in improving their employee attendance.

- Gain current knowledge of the problem.
- Recognize excessive and chronic patterns of absence.
- Establish school objectives regarding staff absence.
- Concentrate efforts on employees with excessive absence.
- Review with supervisors cases requiring special attention.
- Make absence records part of the personnel records system.
- Stress the importance of attendance in the pre-employment stages.
- Consider using incentives to encourage good attendance.
- Conduct research dealing with employee working conditions, attitude, and other factors relating to good attendance.
- Check the school calendar to avoid fracturing the school schedule.

Although principals may need to initiate disciplinary procedures with certain employees who have absentee problems, the recommended approach is to try to provide assistance and counseling for those whose absenteeism may indicate a particularly serious problem. The initial step in this approach should be to try to better understand the nature of the problem. To achieve that objective, administrators should schedule personal conferences with employees who have apparent absentee problems and seek answers to the following questions:

- Is anything about your assignment making the work less enjoyable these days?
- Are any health or personal problems affecting your attendance at school?
- Are you satisfied with your relationships with students and your colleagues?
- Is anything else in your work environment affecting your attendance at school?
- Is there anything that I can do to help the situation?

The purpose of such questions would be to gather information about the causes of the absences and to show concern about the problem, as well as a willingness to be a source of assistance. Of course, if the administrator's help is rejected and/or the situation does not improve, then it may be necessary to take more direct measures to deal with the problem, including disciplinary measures. With regard to the latter, administrators should check the master contract and board policies before taking action, to make sure of the extent of administrative authority.

Employee absenteeism can be a serious problem in some cases that is not easily resolved. However, the extent and severity of the problem can be reduced as a result of an accurate understanding of the causes of employee absenteeism, a clear school board policy on attendance and absenteeism, specific and reasonable regulations on the implementation of the policy, in-service training for building principals, and a persistent and positive effort by the principal to improve employee attendance.

EMPLOYEE DRUG AND ALCOHOL USE

Chemical dependency, particularly alcoholism, is believed to be a serious employee personnel problem in private industry. According to Larry Pace and Stanley Smits, "Substance abuse affects an estimated 12 percent of today's work force. When combined with the estimated 6 percent who suffer from emotional disorders, the problems of the affected employees can reduce productivity by 25 percent and cause tremendous monetary losses to organizations."[24] In an attempt to deal with these ever-pressing employee issues, Employee Assistance Programs (EAP) were developed from the efforts of private industry during the 1950s to address the problem of alcohol abuse. The initial foci of these programs were to reduce absenteeism and improve employee productivity. Since the early stages of program development, there has been a radical expansion of these programs and the problems they address. For instance, Peter Jaffe, Richard Stennett, and Raymond Gladwell noted that

the initial concentration on alcoholism has been expanded to a number of human crises and conflicts, including depression, anxiety, and family or marital difficulties. Although alcohol continues to exist as a major problem area, the issues of the 1980s have grown in importance: drug abuse, AIDS, death and dying in an aging employee group, and economic hardships in various employee groups.[25]

Fortunately, a number of publicly funded institutions have followed the lead of private industry in addressing the drug, alcohol, and personal problems of their employees.[26] These programs generally provide free, confidential, professional assistance to employees to help them resolve problems affecting their work. In their study, Peter Jaffe et al. found that large districts are much more likely to have employee assistance programs than small districts, and they found that budgets supporting these programs ranged from $1,000 to $283,000.[27]

Regrettably, in too many instances, administrators unable to deal with the direct causes of substance abuse and personal problems decide that their choices are limited to living with the problem and accepting it as a cost of doing business in modern society or to addressing the problem through a re-active approach often leading to disciplinary action.[28] In contrast, proactive employee assistance programs concentrate on work-site prevention and cost-effective intervention.

Even though evaluation and research on drug abuse prevention and treatment programs are limited, the National Institute on Alcohol Abuse and Alcoholism states that an effective program should include the following com-ponents: (1) a written policy and plan; (2) explicit labor-management involve-ment and cooperation in program development and operation; (3) description of key organizational personnel to identify and refer employees for appropriate diagnosis; (4) orientation and in-service training for all supervisors and teacher representatives; (5) dissemination of information about the program to all em-ployees; (6) the provision of health insurance coverage for the treatment of alcoholism and related drug abuse; and (7) the assurance of total confiden-tiality for those identified and referred through the program.[29]

As with employee absenteeism, the initial starting point in drug abuse prevention and treatment is the development of formal, written, school board policies on the matter. These policies should

> define the parameters of the problem in terms of performance expectations, attendance requirements, on-the-job behavior, safety and so forth. Such policies must include a clear statement of the employer's rights and responsibilities when an employee's behavior or performance is unacceptable. It [they] also must address the rights and responsibilities of the employee when his or her behavior or performance has been judged unacceptable.[30]

Substance abuse policies are often difficult to develop; thus, administrators are advised to seek the help of specialized legal counsel. Although some school districts appear to have an informal policy on employee drug abuse, only a formal, written policy is likely to express clearly the school district's attitude and expectations about this problem. In developing a policy on employee chemical dependency, the issue of drug testing needs to be addressed. For an extended discussion of this issue see two excellent articles in the *Journal of Law and Education.*[31]

Once a school district has developed a policy on employee drug abuse—and we recommend that the policy be jointly developed by management and employees—the role of the building administrators in implementing the policy should be specified. Unless the building administrator's role in preventing drug abuse is made clear and given a high priority, the policy holds little likelihood of being successful. Unfortunately, there is a scarcity of information on this role in an educational setting. However, a proposed supervisor's role in a non-educational setting is applicable to a school district and has been adapted for the latter purpose.

1. Chemically dependent employees interpret administrative acceptance of their work records as evidence that their drug abuse is not recognized or is still within acceptable limits. Therefore, as soon as administrators notice substandard or deteriorating job performance (but well before the situation has worsened to the point that probation, suspension, or termination is needed) they should discuss the problem with involved employees in private conferences.

2. At the end of each individual's conference, the administrator should inform the employee that, if the decline in performance is caused by a personal problem, the employee may wish to seek counseling and diagnostic services offered by the school district or its health agent.

3. If, after a reasonable time, the employee refuses the school district's help (or declines to seek another source of help with the problem), and if job performance continues to be unsatisfactory, the administrator should provide a choice of either accepting the service available or accepting the consequences of a negative job performance evaluation. If the employee continues to refuse help and job performance continues to be unsatisfactory, dismissal procedures should be initiated.

4. If the employee is willing to accept the school district's help, a referral to a medical agency for diagnosis should be made by the administrator.

5. If the diagnosis does not indicate drug abuse, but the poor performance seems to result from other personal problems, the administrator should offer counseling assistance or referral.

6. If the diagnosis does indicate a chemical dependency problem, such as alcoholism or drug abuse, the administrator should provide information about the school district's plan for rehabilitation or, if the district has no plan, about an outside agency's plan. The school administrator should strongly encourage the employee to seek rehabilitation.

7. During rehabilitation, the administrator should attempt to provide continuous encouragement and support and try to help the employee in any way that seems reasonable and feasible.

8. If, for some reason, the employee does not seek rehabilitation, drops out of the rehabilitation program, or is not successfully rehabilitated, and the employee's job performance continues to be unsatisfactory because of chemical dependency, the school administrator should initiate dismissal procedures.[32]

This approach appears to provide a necessary balance between counseling employees with possible drug abuse problems which impair their job performance and taking punitive steps if the offered assistance is declined or rehabilitation is unsuccessful. Even though the policy examples and proposed role make it appear that the school district does not need to become concerned about the employee's drug abuse problem until that problem begins to impair job performance, we recommend that school districts adopt a more humane policy. The district should offer, at the minimum, counseling assistance to any employee experiencing a drug abuse or personal problem (whether or not that problem has yet impaired the employee's job performance). In addition, the district should provide in-service education to all employees regarding the dangers of drug abuse and the importance of personal physical and emotional wellness. Despite the financial implications this recommendation carries, in the long run the suggested activities would be a good investment in human resources.

MERIT PAY, SALARY, AND FRINGE BENEFITS PROBLEMS

Three other special personnel problems either have or will be confronting many school administrators: public pressure for some type of merit pay for teachers, differentiated staffing and salary plans, and growing concern about the increasing cost of employee benefits. An initial factor that administrators in most states need to take into consideration in resolving these problems is the reality of collective bargaining. In states which permit collective bargaining, salary and fringe benefits are usually perceived as part of the working conditions, subject to negotiation between employees and the governing board of a school district. Even in states without collective bargaining legislation, frequently some type of informal negotiations influences decisions about personnel salary and fringe benefits.

One major policy issue that has surfaced periodically over the years in regard to employee salaries is whether or not employee salary standardization is desirable. Generally, employee salaries and benefits are standardized within a school district on what is referred to as a single-salary schedule.[33] For example, each teacher receives the same fringe benefits provided by the school district, and teachers with identical levels of education and length of teaching experience receive the same salary, regardless of any differences in teaching effectiveness. The assumptions underlying this salary structure include the following: (1) salaries for teachers are scheduled and paid solely on the basis of professional preparation and experience; (2) teacher effectiveness increases with experience and preparation; and (3) all positions are equal in importance and responsibility.[34] The absence of any attempt to take into consideration distinctions in job performance when deciding on individual salary levels has troubled a number of people over the years. Consequently, from time to time, merit pay proposals, incentive plans, and career ladders for teachers have been advocated and, in a few districts, implemented.

MERIT PAY SYSTEMS

Simply defined, merit pay means determining teachers' salaries according to the effectiveness of their performance. Definitions in practice of merit vary from "stringent (excellence, superior performance) to vague (effective performance). To some individuals, merit implies a monetary reward, or an increase in salary, while to others it means nonmonetary recognition, or little more than a pat on the back."[35] The basic assumption underlying merit pay is that more effective teachers are more valuable to the school and to students than less effective teachers, and the former deserve to be compensated more for their services. Although this seems to be a reasonable assumption, merit pay plans in education have aroused controversy.

Major reasons given by teachers opposing merit pay include the belief that the criteria for determining merit were not valid; the evaluators were not competent; the comparisons between teachers were invidious, resulting in lower morale; and salary should be negotiated rather than determined by an evaluator.[36] Merit pay for teachers has, on the other hand, been endorsed by a number of school boards, administrators, and managerial groups, although it appears to be more prevalent as a means for determining administrators' salaries.[37] Advocates of merit pay for teachers believe that employees should be paid according to their effectiveness, that valid criteria of effectiveness can be developed, that competent evaluators can be trained, and that invidious comparisons and low morale are not inevitable consequences of merit pay.[38]

As a result of the controversy over merit pay, most school systems have not adopted merit pay plans.[39] Nevertheless, pressures from the public for school accountability, improved teacher competency, and overall cost-effectiveness could change this situation. One basic issue needing to be resolved before merit pay for teachers could be successfully introduced into a large number of school districts is whether or not the general salary for all teachers in a school district is commensurate with their responsibilities and the cost of living. Studies have consistently shown that the beginning salaries of teachers have been lower than for other college graduates except social workers, and that because of inflation, teachers' salaries overall have increased very little in constant dollar terms during the past decade.[40] John Wright noted that in towns and cities, both large and small, starting salaries are usually between $14,000 and $16,000 with maximums after twenty years (with a master's degree) between $28,000 and $33,000.[41] The national average of approximately $25,000 is an accurate measure of the country as a whole. He also observed that

> as with nurses, librarians, and social workers, the principal reason why teachers earn less than other white-collar workers with college educations has more to do with the historical role gender has played in determining wage rates than with anything else. About 50 percent of all secondary school teachers are women, while 80 percent of all elementary school teachers are. So, while teachers' unions may be standardizing pay rates within the profession, the monetary rewards of the job remain a severe handicap in attracting and holding the most talented people.[42]

As long as these conditions exist, merit pay proposals are unlikely to receive serious consideration by most teachers.

Another difficulty precluding more favorable consideration of merit pay is the perceived lack of valid and acceptable criteria and procedures for evaluating the merits of teachers.[43] (Criteria and procedures presented in chapter 10 on staff evaluation appear worthy of consideration.) Teachers would also need to become persuaded of the validity of the premise that more effective teachers should be paid higher salaries than their less effective colleagues. In addition, in those states which require collective bargaining, teacher associations are likely to want something in return for their approval of merit pay, and the outcome could be a more costly endeavor than many communities will approve. However, pressures for teacher and school accountability are likely to continue to raise the question of why teachers cannot be paid according to their merit.

In the few, documented cases where merit systems have been successfully implemented, the following supporting factors have been identified:

1. Merit reward systems were based on effective, objective, and consistent evaluation procedures; decisions were based on valid and verifiable measures of superior performance. Teachers understood the criteria by which they were evaluated, and they received feedback from the evaluation process.
2. The superintendent was an effective leader who sold the plan to the staff and worked to win board approval. School board members and administrators were committed to making the merit plan work.
3. Merit plans were developed with input from individuals from all levels of the hierarchy and were not perceived as being pushed from the top down. Teachers were involved in the development of the merit system, and adequate time was allowed for development and implementation of merit plans.
4. Teachers were allowed to create individual performance objectives. Rewards which were personally and professionally satisfying to teachers were determined. Merit systems allowed for differential acquisition of rewards based on individual needs.
5. Merit plans defined a teacher's role in the broad sense and allowed for recognition in areas outside of instructional performance.
6. Adequate financing existed. Rewards were available to all who qualified. The amount of money offered provided a real incentive to improve immediate performance.[44]

INCENTIVE PAY PLANS

In some instances, in part due to difficulties associated with the implementation of a pure merit system, districts have adopted incentive pay programs. The term *incentive pay* is used to "represent the wide variety of plans and programs for providing extra compensation to deserving school personnel."[45] Incentive pay may be provided for a number of reasons, including exemplary teacher attendance; excessive class size; difficult class assignments (that is, a large portion of low-achieving students); extra duties such as in-school suspension supervision; development of special programs; critical staffing needs (math, science, bilingual, or special education); advanced educational training; or schoolwide improvement of academic achievement. In general, these programs either amount to extra pay for extra work or are forms of premiums paid to teachers in high-demand certification areas. Incentive pay plans tend to differ from merit pay systems in that judgments regarding quality or effectiveness are generally not made, and the determination of whether or not employees are eligible to receive incentive pay is usually based on specific criteria (that is, they accepted the position or they did not; they completed the training or they did not; they were absent or they were not, etc.).[46]

CAREER LADDERS

Somewhere between the two concepts of merit pay and incentive pay are career ladder programs. In such systems, teachers advance "up the career ladder" by fulfilling specified level objectives. Generally, each career step or level contains a combination of quantitative (completed course work, attended workshops) and qualitative (demonstrated instructional effectiveness) measures. Teachers progress through various stages until they ultimately apply for master teacher recognition. This recognition is based on certification or demonstration of important knowledge and skills.

> For example, at the basic level, state licensure certifies the mastery of a knowledge base and technical proficiency in teaching. Direct observation of teaching under structured clinical settings can be used to diagnose and evaluate the mastery of necessary techniques and the ability to apply them in the classroom. More experienced and proficient teachers demonstrate the mastery of a variety of techniques, plan much of their own work, and evaluate the outcomes of their teaching, applying increasingly stringent standards. Precision judgments about the appropriateness of their professional decisions, the skillful use of a broader range of techniques, knowledge in their subject area, and application of developmental psychology reflect the quality of their teaching. Their curriculum units, contributions to schoolwide quality, and involvement in the profession can serve as evidence of professional growth.
>
> Master teachers demonstrate all of the foregoing qualities. In addition, they may be involved as mentors for new teachers and in leadership and evaluation decisions in the school. They make difficult decisions, quickly adapt to contextual factors, and apply professional standards and ethics to the school setting.[47]

A primary differentiating feature between merit plans and career ladders is that the burden of proof of meeting the program's objectives often rests with the teacher. The major benefit of career ladder programs is that they make it possible for teachers to receive public recognition as they advance and progress through their teaching careers.

Regardless of the ultimate form and structure, it appears that school administrators must continue to examine and restructure existing teacher salary plans if teaching is to continue as a viable career option. Creative salary plans and career development programs need to be developed if education is to attract high-quality, entry-level teachers and retain experienced, effective teachers.

FRINGE BENEFITS

A related area just beginning to surface as a major problem in school administration is the cost of fringe benefits. In recent years the number and cost of fringe benefits in education have increased greatly.[48] In many school districts, teachers' associations have concentrated as much on adding to or improving fringe benefits for members as they have on increasing salaries. Fringe benefits can include pension plans, annuity plans, disability insurance, sick leave, personal day(s), life insurance, legal assistance, and health care consisting of medical, dental, vision insurance, and child care.[49] An examination of a number of fringe benefit plans revealed that they can also include tuition reimbursement, longevity payments, severance payments, sabbatical leave, and maternity leave. Given the wide array of possible benefit packages, James Ferris and Donald Winkler noted that

> it is unlikely that all teachers value each of these fringe benefits at its cost to the school district. In order to continue to take advantage of this nontaxable form of compensation, yet increase the individual teacher's choices and welfare, cafeteria benefit plans are an option. A cafeteria plan allows the individual to select a combination of fringe benefits that does not exceed some specified monetary limit.[50]

Cafeteria plans are covered under Section 125 of the Internal Revenue Code and, according to the code, allowable expenses are nontaxable benefits.[51] Thus, although employees who take advantage of such plans reduce their gross salaries, they generally realize an increase in their disposable or net income because of the before-tax savings.[52] In a related sense, employers also stand to profit through these plans because as employees' taxable income is reduced, payroll taxes (FICA, unemployment, disability, workers' compensation) also drop. The advantages of choice plans are most pronounced for families with two wage earners where fringe benefit packages may often be redundant. For example, Ferris and Winkler noted that "there is relatively little benefit from double health care benefits. With the flexibility of a cafeteria plan, the teacher in the dual earner family could choose child care benefits or some other form of in-kind compensation not available in the spouse's fixed fringe benefit package."[53]

In general, as school districts attempt to attract high-quality teachers, attention will focus on constructing creative compensation packages which provide attractive salary and fringe benefits plan. Ferris and Winkler suggest the following alternatives for consideration: (1) increase starting pay and reduce rate of pay increases; (2) institute sign-up bonuses; (3) change compensation plans by possibly increasing pay and decreasing retirement benefits or by adopting a cafeteria fringe benefit plan; (4) make greater use of pay differentials for critical needs or shortage areas (math, science, bilingual); or (5) provide financial incentives for improved performance through rewarding merit and innovation and promoting professional development.[54] Before implementing any of these alternatives, administrators must consult and work with teachers and their union representatives to ensure that the selected plan meets the needs of the teachers as well as the school district.

SEXUAL HARASSMENT

Although sexual harassment is as old as the workplace, it has only been recognized as a serious personnel problem within the last decade. Showing its concern, the Equal Employment Opportunity Commission (EEOC) issued guidelines that define sexual harassment and made it a form of sex discrimination under Title VII legislation.[55] The guidelines state that

> unwelcome sexual advances, requests, or demands for sexual favors and other verbal or physical conduct of a sexual nature are defined as sexual harassment when (1) submission to such conduct is made either explicitly or implicitly a term or condition of an individual's employment; or (2) submission to or rejection of such conduct by an individual is used as the basis for employment decisions affecting such individuals; or (3) such conduct has the purpose or effect of unreasonably interfering with an individual's s work performance or creating an intimidating, hostile, or offensive working environment.[56]

This definition and other evidence suggest that sexual harassment may and does occur within the school setting. Victor Ross and John Marlowe noted that sexual harassment "touches teachers and administrators, male and female alike, just as frequently as it does students and parents, and dealing with sexual harassment can be both difficult and emotionally draining."[57] To emphasize their point, they ask whether

> any school employee can argue that none of these activities exist within his or her particular school system: (1) generalized sexist remarks (à la Archie Bunker); (2) inappropriate and offensive but essentially sanction-free sexual advances (such as placing one's hand on another's lower back or other "unsafe" touching area); (3) solicitation of sexual activity or other sex-linked behavior by promise of rewards; (4) coercion of sexual activity by threat of punishment; and (5) sexual assaults.[58]

In addition to the moral outrage which districts should experience related to such activities, school districts may in fact be found liable for damages for sexual harassment. Thus, for both moral and legal reasons, school administrators need to develop clear policies prohibiting all forms of sexual harassment—"from outright solicitation of sex to unwarranted touching and verbal advances."[59]

In *Meritor Savings Bank v. Vinson,* the court held that sexual harassment constitutes a form of sex discrimination under Title VII of the Civil Rights Act of 1964; as a result, schools may be "sued for damages by an employee even if the harassment is not linked directly to 'job status'—in other words, even when no one promises a promotion, threatens to fire, or grants a salary increase in exchange for sexual favors."[60] Specifically, a school district's obligations as employer regarding sexual harassment include:

1. *Supervisory personnel.* Districts are not automatically liable for sexual harassment committed by a supervisor. On the other hand, an employer may be held liable for charges of sexual harassment if top supervisory employees knew about or should have known about the behavior and took no immediate or corrective action.
2. *Fellow employees.* Districts are responsible for sexual harassment occurring between fellow employees in the workplace in situations where the employer knows or should have known of the behavior and no immediate or corrective action was taken.

3. *Nonemployees.* Districts may be held responsible for the actions of nonemployees who sexually harass employees in the workplace in situations in which supervisory personnel knew or should have known of the behavior and no reasonable, corrective action was taken.[61]

A critical component of the concept of sexual harassment is that the sexual advances must be unwelcome. When relationships develop between consenting adults, administrators find that as long as the relationship remains private and does not diminish the effectiveness or role performances of the staff members involved, there is little they can do in terms of legal or negative sanctions. In such instances, administrators may still address the involved parties directly, transfer one of the individuals if possible, or explain the district's views regarding the sexual involvement of faculty members; however, in most cases they are not able to discipline or dismiss the individuals involved. As a case in point,

Can a teacher be fired for having sexual intercourse with another man's wife (she was also a teacher) in the back seat of a car (particularly when the woman's husband is hiding in the trunk of the car)? No, said the Iowa Supreme Court (Erb v. Iowa State Board of Education, 1974). The court ruled the incident was unlikely to have an adverse effect on the erring teacher's effectiveness, since the sex tryst happened away from school and at night and was an activity of his private life; he was reinstated.[62]

Administrators may, nonetheless, pursue a dismissal action and be successful even if the employee has been judged innocent in court if they can show that the employee can no longer be effective in his or her job.[63] In some instances when formal charges have been initiated, the publicity attached to the case and the community's subsequent knowledge of the allegations of sexual harassment or involvement may impair the employee's future job effectiveness. This is particularly true in the case of teachers who have historically been viewed as role models of appropriate behavior for students.

A different and equally serious problem is the sexual harassment of students by faculty or staff members. Ross and Marlowe note that "most pedophiles—those who seek out children for sexual purposes—are men, but there is increasing evidence that many are women; further, rape is generally a crime against women by male attackers but females also rape men and boys."[64] Arlene McCormack noted that because "teachers have positions of authority from which they evaluate the performance of the student, the initiating of sexual demands can leave the student unsure of the teacher's reaction to a refusal."[65]

Her investigation of sexual harassment of students indicated that "approximately one in every six women, regardless of family background, will be likely to experience sexual harassment from teachers."[66] And, she reported that this finding is consistent with past claims by the National Advisory Council on Women's Education that 10 to 20 percent of women students experience sexual harassment sometime during their education experiences. As the age of the involved student increases, the issue becomes more complex, particularly when the student reaches the legal age of consent and is considered an adult—possibly a consenting adult.

Richard Titus and Carol DeFrances indicate that preemployment screening is receiving increased attention in response to growing concern regarding the increase in sexual harassment and exploitation within schools and to protect districts from potential liability lawsuits.[67] They contend that reference checks, networking, and other forms of preemployment screening can often identify applicants who are not suitable for work around children because of histories of alcoholism, mental illness, drug abuse, or violence. They propose that screening techniques be conducted not only for teachers and administrators but also for clerical, security, bus driver, custodian, or lunchroom worker applicants because support staff generally have as much contact with students as the professional, certified staff.

Obviously, the sensitive and potentially volatile nature of the problems of sexual harassment indicate a need for administrators to develop policies, training activities, and guidelines to prevent the occurrence of sexual harassment and to ensure that if and when it occurs, they are prepared to deal with it. To do so, Robert Decker recommends the following steps:

1. **Develop a clear policy statement prohibiting sexual harassment.** The board policy should include definitions of objectionable advances, prohibitions on such behavior, and guidelines for employees that include information on how to file complaints and a discussion of the standards to be used when complaints are investigated.

2. **Create guidelines to implement the policy.** Check the school system's grievance procedure to make sure it applies to sexual harassment cases; if it does not, amend it accordingly.

3. **Publicize policy statements and grievance procedures.** Publish the information in appropriate publications, such as the school system's policy handbook, school staff handouts, and the local teacher union newsletter. All employees should receive a copy of the policy and be made aware of what is considered appropriate and inappropriate conduct.

4. **Determine the extent of the problem.** Try to assess the extent of the problem in school systems using questionnaires, informal discussions, interviews, or even systemwide surveys. This process not only brings valuable information to light but it also lets victims of sexual harassment know board members and administrators are concerned about it.

5. **Discuss the topic with supervisors.** Supervisors need to be aware of the legal ramifications of sexual harassment both for themselves and for the school system. Suggested topics include; how to identify sexual harassment, the requirements of the EEOC guidelines, the school system's policy and guidelines, and internal procedures for handling sexual harassment complaints.

6. **Understand and make sure others understand the consequences of losing a sexual harassment case.** Because school people often are viewed as community role models, school systems harboring or tolerating sexual harassment by employees tarnish their public images.

7. **Designate a key administrator to oversee and ensure compliance with the law related to sexual harassment.** The district's affirmative action officer might be the appropriate person to serve this function.

8. **Investigate all complaints thoroughly and speedily.** Administrators should be advised to take quick action and keep records of complaints and administrative follow-up actions.

9. **Alert employees to the resources available for resolving complaints and help them to become aware of how to conduct themselves if they are harassed sexually.** Among other things, employees who are victims of sexual harassment should be told to make it clear to their harassers that they disapprove of such behavior, to talk to others at home and in the workplace about it, and to keep a diary if the harassment continues.

10. **Make sure employees know the complaint filing deadlines set by state and federal agencies.** The deadline for filing an EEOC sexual harassment complaint is 180 days after it has gone through an in-house complaint procedure; state human rights commission deadlines vary.[68]

In addition, school districts should provide needed psychological help—perhaps through an employee assistance program—for the victims of sexual harassment. For victims, sexual harassment can be not only embarrassing but also traumatic; administrators should make every effort to help these persons recover from such unfortunate experiences.

Attending to these recommended steps, administrators should be able to establish a comprehensive, defensible process for dealing with sexual harassment within their schools. In a broader sense, in addressing issues pertaining to sexual harassment administrators should keep uppermost in their minds that one of their primary obligations is to ensure that schools are safe, protective environments for students and faculty members alike and, thus, all policies, guidelines, and procedures should support this primary goal.[69]

A FINAL NOTE

The special personnel problems discussed in this chapter are all too frequently not addressed until they develop into serious crises. The approach we recommend is early problem identification, diagnosis, and appropriate corrective action. The following Review and Learning Activities should provide experience in utilizing such an approach.

Review and Learning Activities

1. How does your school district determine whether staff absences are legitimate? How reliable and valid are those methods?
2. Discuss the causes of employee absenteeism presented in this text. What implications do these causes carry for the school administrator?
3. Develop a district policy and plan, based on the ideas presented in the text, for decreasing employee absenteeism. Which obstacles would the policy and plan have to overcome before they could be implemented successfully?
4. Develop a district policy and plan, based on the ideas presented in this chapter, for addressing the possible problem of chemical dependency on the part of employees. Which obstacles would the policy and plan have to overcome before they could be implemented successfully?
5. Differentiate between merit pay systems, incentive pay plans, and career ladders. Discuss the arguments, pro and con, of each salary system.
6. Develop a district policy and plan for preventing sexual harassment. Which obstacles would the policy and plan need to overcome before they could be implemented successfully?

NOTES

1. Major sections of this chapter represent an adaptation and expansion of an entry by Richard A. Gorton entitled, "School Personnel Policy," in *The Encyclopedia of Educational Research,* ed. Harold E. Mitzel (New York: Macmillan, 1982).

2. K. Dow Scott, Steven E. Markham, and G. Stephen Taylor, "Employee Attendance: Good Policy Makes Good Sense," *Personnel Administrator* (December 1987): 98.

3. American Association of School Personnel Administrators, *Conference Reports: Employee Absenteeism* (Seven Hills, Ohio: American Association of School Personnel Administrators, 1979).

4. D. C. Manlove, "Absent Teachers . . . Another Handicap for Students?" *The Practitioner* 5, no. 4 (1979): 3–6.

5. Pennsylvania School Boards Association, *Teacher Absenteeism: Professional Staff Absence Study* (Harrisburg, Pa.: Pennsylvania School Boards Association, 1978).

6. "Here's How to Reduce Teacher Absenteeism," *The Executive Educator* (April 1979): 11–12.

7. Scott, Markham, and Taylor, "Employee Attendance," 102.

8. Ibid., 99.

9. R. D. Johnson and T. O. Peterson, "Absenteeism or Attendance: Which Is Industry's Problem?" *Personnel Journal* (1975): 568–72.

10. Educational Research Service, *Employee Absenteeism: A Summary of Research* (Arlington, Va.: Educational Research, Inc., 1980).

11. David A. Ralston and Michael F. Flanagan, "The Effect of Flextime on Absenteeism and Turnover for Male and Female Employees," *Journal of Vocational Behavior* 26 (1985): 215.

12. Edwin M. Bridges, "Job Satisfaction and Teacher Absenteeism," *Educational Administration Quarterly* (Spring 1980): 41–56.

13. Robert Thompson, "Teacher Absenteeism," in *Encyclopedia of School Administration and Supervision,* ed. R. A. Gorton, G. T. Schneider, and J. C. Fisher (Phoenix, Ariz.: Oryx Press, 1988): 268–69.

14. Sharon C. Conley, Samuel B. Bacharach, and Scott Bauer, "The School Work Environment and Teacher Career Dissatisfaction," *Educational Administration Quarterly* (February 1989): 58–81.

15. *Teacher Absenteeism and Related Policies for Supplementary Remuneration,* produced by the Philadelphia Suburban School Study Council and the South Penn School Study Council Group (Philadelphia: University of Pennsylvania, Graduate School of Education, 1970).

16. Pennsylvania School Boards Association, *Teacher Absenteeism.* Also see *Teacher Absenteeism: Experience and Practices of School Systems* (Arlington, Va.: Educational Research Service, 1981).

17. Thompson, "Teacher Absenteeism," 268.

18. D. R. Winkler, "The Effects of Sick Leave Policy on Teacher Absenteeism," *Industrial and Labor Relations Review* (January 1980): 232–40.

19. R. M. Steers and S. R. Rhodes, "Major Influences on Employee Attendance: A Process Model," *Journal of Applied Psychology* (August 1978): 391–407.

20. Ibid.

21. Richard L. Bunning, "A Comprehensive Approach to Improving Attendance," *Personnel Journal* (August 1988): 44–49.

22. American Association of School Personnel Administrators, *Conference Reports: Employee Absenteeism.* For a similar, more recent discussion, see Bunning, "A Comprehensive Approach to Improving Attendance."

23. *Teacher Attendance Improvement Program: A Joint Business-Education Project* (Newark, N.J.: Greater Newark Chamber of Commerce, 1975), 10. See also S. E. Jacobson, "Pay Incentives and Teacher Absence: One District's Experience." *Urban Education* (January 1989): 37–39.

24. Larry A. Pace and Stanley J. Smits, "Employee Assistance; Workplace Substance Abuse: A Proactive Approach," *Personnel Journal* (April 1989): 84.

25. Peter Jaffe, Richard Stennett, and Raymond Gladwell, "Employee Assistance Programs in Canada," *School Business Affairs* (October 1988): 14.

26. Ibid., 15.

27. Ibid., 16.

28. Pace and Smits, "Employee Assistance," 84.

29. National Institute on Alcohol Abuse and Alcoholism, *Alcohol and Health* (Rockville, Md.: National Institute on Alcohol Abuse and Alcoholism, 1978): 77.

30. Pace and Smits, "Employee Assistance," 85.

31. J. I. Crystal and R. L. Samson, "Drug Testing of Public Employees: A Managerial Perspective"; and B. A. Miller and R. S. Linden, "Drug Testing of Public Employees: The Union Perspective," *Journal of Law and Education* (Fall 1988): 703–29.

32. Richard M. Weiss, *Dealing with Alcoholism in the Workplace* (New York: The Conference Board, 1980), 10–11.

33. R. Warren Eisenhower, "Teacher Salaries," in *Encyclopedia of School Administration and Supervision,* ed. R. A. Gorton, G. T. Schneider, and J. C. Fisher (Phoenix, Ariz.: Oryx Press, 1988), 279.

34. Ibid.

35. Gail Thierbach Schneider, "Merit Pay," In *Encyclopedia of School Administration and Supervision,* ed. R. A. Gorton, G. T. Schneider, and J. C. Fisher (Phoenix, Ariz.: Oryx Press, 1988), 168.

36. Gail Thierbach Schneider, "Schools and Merit: An Empirical Study of Attitudes of School Board Members, Administrators, and Teachers toward Merit Systems," *Planning and Changing* (Summer 1984): 89–105.

37. Educational Research Service, *Merit Pay for School Administrators* (Arlington, Va.: 1979). See also *Merit Pay for School Administrators: Procedural Guide* (Arlington, Va.: Educational Research Service, 1984).

38. See Educational Research Service, *Merit Pay for Teachers* (Arlington, Va.: Educational Research Service, 1979): 4–7. See also *Merit Pay Plans for Teachers: Status and Descriptions* (Arlington, Va.: Educational Research Service, 1983).

39. Jay R. Schuster and Patricia K. Zingheim, "Merit Pay: Is It Hopeless in the Public Sector?" *Personnel Administrator* (October 1987): 83–84.

40. National Center for Educational Statistics, *The Condition of Education* (Washington, D.C.: National Center for Educational Statistics, 1979). For more recent, yet similar, statistics see John W. Wright, *The American Almanac of Jobs and Salaries* (New York: Avon, 1987–88).

41. Wright, *The American Almanac,* 127.

42. Ibid., 128.

43. J. Aaron Hoko, "Merit Pay—In Search of the Pedagogical Widget," *Clearing House* (September 1988): 29–31.

44. Schneider, "Merit Pay," 169.

45. M. Scott Norton and William W. Hegebush, "Incentive Pay Programs: Does Participation Change Viewpoints?" *Clearing House* (December 1988): 149.

46. For interesting discussions regarding the issues behind incentive pay plans, see Vernon Clark and Rochelle Clemson, "Teacher Staffing in Urban Schools: Beyond the Question of Supply and Demand," *Metropolitan Education* (Spring 1987): 1–16; Robert H. Evans, "Factors Which Deter Potential Science/Math Teachers from Teaching; Changes Necessary to Ameliorate Their Concerns," *Journal of Research in Science Teaching* (January 1987): 77–85; and Deb Kortokrax-Clark, "The Minority Teacher Shortage: An Overview and a Solution," *Action in Teacher Education* (Winter 1986–87): 7–13.

47. Ann Weaver Hart, "Career Ladders," in *Encyclopedia of School Administration and Supervision,* ed. R. A. Gorton, G. T. Schneider, and J. C. Fisher (Phoenix, Ariz.: Oryx Press, 1988): 48.

48. Educational Research Service, *Fringe Benefits for Teachers in Public Schools,* 1987–88 (Arlington, Va.: Educational Research Service, 1988).

49. James Ferris and Donald Winkler, "Teacher Compensation and the Supply of Teachers," *The Elementary School Journal* (March 1986): 398.

50. Ibid., 398.

51. Rob Johnson, "Flexible Fringe Benefit Plans Save You Money and Keep Employees Happy," *American School Board Journal* (May 1987): 30.

52. Ibid.

53. Ferris and Winkler, "Teacher Compensation," 396.

54. Ibid., 399.

55. Robert H. Decker, "Eleven Ways to Stamp Out the Potential for Sexual Harassment," *American School Board Journal* (August 1988): 28.

56. Ibid., 28. For additional definitions, see Gary N. Powell, *Women and Men in Management* (Newbury Park, Calif.: Sage Publications, 1988), 115–18.

57. Victor J. Ross and John Marlowe, *The Forbidden Apple* (Palm Springs, Calif.: ETC Publications, 1985), 76.

58. Ibid., 77.

59. David A. Splitt, "Sexual Harassment," *The Executive Educator* (October 1986): 12.

60. Ibid.

61. Julie Underwood, "End Sexual Harassment of Employees, or Your Board Could Be Held Liable," *American School Board Journal* April 1987): 43.

62. Ross and Marlowe, *The Forbidden Apple,* 98.

63. Ibid., 97.

64. Ibid.

65. Arlene McCormack, "The Sexual Harassment of Students by Teachers: The Case of Students in Science," *Sex Roles* 13 (1985): 22.

66. Ibid., 28.

67. Richard M. Titus and Carol J. DeFrances, "Is There a Pedophile on Your Payroll? Princpals Must Be Alert to Hidden Danger When Hiring Staff," *Principal* (September 1989): 14–16.

68. Decker, "Eleven Ways," 28, 38.

69. For additional background information on sexual harassment and child sexual abuse, see Diana E. H. Russell, *Sexual Exploitation: Rape, Child Sexual Abuse, and Workplace Harassment* (Newbury Park, Calif.: Sage Publications, 1984).

9

• • • • •

Administrator-Staff Relations

School administrators work with a variety of people, including students, teachers, and parents. Although no single individual or group should be considered to be more important than another, there is little doubt that administrators' relationships with staff members significantly influence their effectiveness as leaders. Even though a positive relationship does not guarantee effective administrative leadership, it is difficult to conceive how administrators could continue to function successfully as leaders if their relationships with staff members were negative.

In the sections that follow, two aspects of administrator-staff relationships are explored: (1) staff satisfaction and morale, and (2) collective bargaining and contract administration.

STAFF SATISFACTION AND MORALE

Definition and Purpose

Most administrators recognize the importance of developing and maintaining high staff satisfaction and morale, even if they are not sure how to achieve these goals. Satisfaction and morale are attitudinal variables reflecting positive or negative feelings about a particular situation or person. The two concepts are often used synonymously in the educational literature, and it is easy to understand why. The state of one's morale reflects the extent of his or her satisfaction with a situation or person. Satisfaction can also refer to people's feelings about themselves or the situations in which they find themselves, although most studies of the concept have concentrated on the latter. Both terms can refer to the attitudinal characteristics of either a group or an individual. (While research seems to focus on teachers, school administrators should take a broader view of their staffs to include support personnel as well as noncertificated workers—whose morale and satisfaction are also important.)

Many attempts have been made to define the terms *satisfaction* and *morale.* Satisfaction, as it applies to the work context, seems to refer to the degree to which individuals can meet their personal and professional needs in the performance of their roles.[1] Morale, on the other hand, as defined in the educational literature seems to hold a broader meaning. Wayne Hoy and Cecil Miskel, for example, indicate that morale is a function of identification, belongingness, and rationality. In their explanation of morale, "*identification* refers to the communality of goals, that is, the extent to which individual needs are congruent with organizational goals; *belongingness* is the congruence between bureaucratic expectations and personal needs; and *rationality* is the congruence between bureaucratic expectations and organizational goals."[2]

In other words, for morale to be high, (1) individuals must be able to identify with the goals of the organization; (2) based on an assessment of their skills and personal needs, they must sense that they belong within the organization; and, (3) in an overall evaluation of the organization, its goals, objectives, and expectations must appear rational and make sense to them.

However one chooses to define satisfaction and morale, they are clearly desirable goals for school organizations. A basic principle of personnel relations has long been the idea that a satisfied emplyee, one with high morale, is likely to get along better with coworkers, is more accepting of management's directives, is more committed to achieving organizational goals, and in general is more productive. This belief persists despite rather limited supportive research.[3] Studies generally have been correlational in nature, and little hard evidence supports the basic premise regarding the purported outcomes of high staff satisfaction and morale. In fact, at present no conclusive evidence documents that a satisfied employee with high morale is necessarily a motivated or productive employee.[4] Nevertheless, it seems reasonable to assume that a dissatisfied employee with low morale is not likely to be a maximally motivated and productive worker.

High staff satisfaction and morale can be considered either as ends in themselves or as necessary conditions for achieving the educational objectives of a school. If the two are considered as ends in themselves, administrators are assuming that high staff satisfaction and morale are intrinsically valuable. Although, high satisfaction and morale are certainly desirable, in some circumstances administrators may have to actually create some temporary dissatisfaction to improve a stagnant situation. Such action would be based on the realization that important and needed changes generally do not occur as long as people are satisfied with the status quo; it should be initiated only on a selective basis, and with considerable thought and care.

We believe that high staff satisfaction and morale may be desirable as ends in themselves, but their primary value is in helping to achieve other worthwhile goals. These goals would include staff stability, cohesiveness, and increased effectiveness. Although research on the consequences of high or low staff satisfaction and morale is not conclusive, it would appear that the extent of staff satisfaction and morale can influence the degree to which the goals previously mentioned can be achieved.[5] For these reasons then, administrators need to understand better the factors contributing to low or high staff satisfaction and morale; based on that understanding they should develop conditions which build and maintain the latter.

CONCEPTUAL BACKGROUND

The question of how to develop and sustain high morale and satisfaction on the part of workers is one that has long attracted the attention of theorists. No single conceptual framework can totally answer such a complex question; several theories or models however, have been advanced which administrators ought to consider.

Perhaps the most important initial factor influencing administrators' priorities and approaches to developing staff members' morale and satisfaction is their attitudes toward staff members and what motivates them. In this connection, D. McGregor has formulated a useful theory that is relevant to this discussion about administrators' attitudes toward people. He postulated that administrative behavior is influenced by two basic attitudes which he referred to as theory X and theory Y. The main characteristics of these two attitudes, as they apply to decision making, follow:

Theory X

1. "The average human being has an inherent dislike of work, and avoids it if he can."
2. "Because of this human characteristic of dislike of work, most people must be coerced, controlled, directed, and/or threatened with punishment in order to get them to put forth adequate effort toward achievement of organizational objectives."
3. "The average human being prefers to be directed, wishes to avoid responsibility, has relatively little ambition, and wants security above all."

Theory Y

1. "External control and the threat of punishment are not the only means for bringing about effort toward organizational objectives. Man will exercise self-direction and self-control in the service of objectives to which he is committed."

2. "The average human being learns, under proper conditions, not only to accept but to seek responsibility. Avoidance of responsibility, lack of ambition, and emphasis on security are generally consequences of experience, not inherent human characteristics."

3. "The capacity to exercise a relatively high degree of imagination, ingenuity and creativity in the solution of organizational problems is widely, not narrowly, distributed in the population."[6]

Obviously, theory X and theory Y administrators differ markedly in their attitudes toward people. A major implication of McGregor's theory and the supporting research is that administrators' attitudes toward other people are likely to influence their selection of approaches to motivating them. (The attitude of many administrators is a synthesis or combination of theories X and Y, referred to by some authorities as theory Z.)

A second conceptual model, which has greatly influenced the thinking of many educators, was developed by Abraham Maslow who asserted that everyone seeks to satisfy basic needs.[7] These needs are identified in figure 9.1.

The two central ideas in Maslow's theory are (1) that a hierarchy of needs exists in which low-level needs, such as physiological needs, must be satisfied before higher-level needs, such as self-esteem or self-actualization, assume importance for an individual; and (2) that once a need is satisfied, it becomes less important as a motivator. Even though the terms utilized in Maslow's theory are often sprinkled in the conversations of school practitioners,

Figure 9.1 Maslow's Need Hierarchy.

Self-actualization Needs
↑
Self-esteem and Respect from Others Needs
↑
Love and Belonging Needs
↑
Safety Needs, e.g., Security, Order
↑
Physiological Needs, e.g., Food, Shelter

Figure 9.2 Basic Needs of Teachers.

Basic Needs	*Desired Fulfillment*	*Actual Fulfillment*
• **Self-actualization:** the teacher-perceived need for personal and professional success, achievement, peak satisfaction, and working at full potential	_____	_____
• **Autonomy:** the teacher-perceived need for authority, control and influence	_____	_____
• **Esteem:** the teacher-perceived need for self-respect, respect by others as a person and as a professional	_____	_____
• **Social:** the teacher perceived need for acceptance, belonging, friendship, and membership in formal and informal work groups. Affiliation is another term for this need	_____	_____
• **Security:** the teacher-perceived need for money, benefits, and tenure associated with one's job	_____	_____

there is little evidence that school personnel policies are based on the theory to any great degree. A review of the research on Maslow's theory conducted by M. A. Wahba and L. G. Bridwell concluded that reasearch had not confirmed the theory, although the reviewers emphasized that the lack of evidence did not necessarily invalidate the theory.[8]

A useful reformulation of Maslow's theory has been proposed by Lyman Porter, and was later adapted by T. J. Sergiovanni and F. D. Carver for use with teachers.[9] The latter researchers defined the basic needs of teachers as those presented in figure 9.2.[10] (In this particular conceptualization, physiological needs have been dropped and autonomy needs added.)

This model of needs advances the idea that need deficiency is determined by ascertaining the differences between the desired level of need fulfillment in a particular area and the actual level of fulfillment. The lower the difference, the greater the satisfaction; the higher the difference, the greater the dissatisfaction. Several studies using this model have found that need deficiencies tend to be greater for the higher level needs, especially esteem and self-actualization.[11]

Figure 9.3 Factors Influencing Teacher Satisfaction.

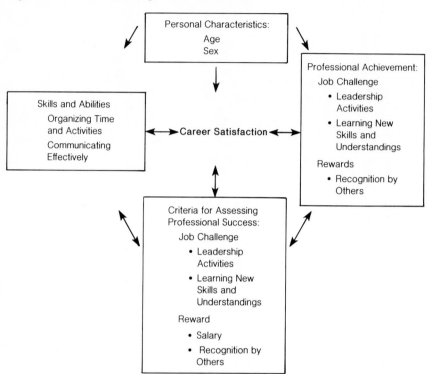

A somewhat different model of teacher satisfaction has been proposed by David Chapman and Malcolm Lowther.[12] Based on earlier research, they have concluded that teacher satisfaction (or the lack of it) is influenced by four major factors. These factors are identified in figure 9.3, which has been adapted from their model.

Figure 9.3 suggests that the career satisfaction of a teacher is influenced by (1) the teacher's personal characteristics, (2) the teacher's skills and abilities, (3) the criteria a teacher uses to evaluate his or her professional success, and (4) the teacher's actual career accomplishments. The model also indicates that several of these factors influence each other. For example, the criteria for assessing professional success could influence how much professional achievement is attempted, and the actual achievement could cause one to revise the criteria for determining professional success.

Research by Chapman and Lowther has tended to support the model, although further evidence is needed.[13] One finding of particular interest was revealed by these researchers; namely, that while actual achievement by a teacher had a strong positive relationship to satisfaction, career satisfaction was also significantly related to assigning little importance to possible activities and accomplishments that might be difficult to achieve because of the structure of a school.[14] The latter finding suggests that acceptance and realism may be important personal characteristics related to career satisfaction.

Another major theory on employee satisfaction which has influenced many school administrators was developed by Frederick Herzberg and his colleagues.[15] Herzberg theorized that the factors which satisfy employees and the factors which dissatisfy employees are mutually exclusive and are not aligned along a continuum. For example, in his study of accountants and engineers he found that the factors presented in figure 9.4 contributed to satisfaction or dissatisfaction, but not to both.

Herzberg found that the existence of the five factors listed in figure 9.4 under "Satisfaction" tended to affect the employees' attitudes in a positive direction. Interestingly, a reduction of these same factors did not result in job dissatisfaction. On the other hand, an improvement in one or more of the eleven factors listed under "Dissatisfaction" in figure 9.4 tended to reduce employee dissatisfaction, but this change did not ensure employee satisfaction. In essence, he contended that individuals could be simultaneously satisfied and dissatisfied with their jobs.

Figure 9.4 Herzberg's Satisfaction/Dissatisfaction Factors.

Satisfaction Motivators	*Dissatisfaction Hygienes*
1. Achievement	1. Salary
2. Recognition	2. Possibility of growth
3. Work itself	3. Interpersonal relations (subordinates)
4. Responsibility	4. Status
5. Advancement	5. Interpersonal relations (superiors)
	6. Interpersonal relations (peers)
	7. Supervision—technical
	8. Company policy and administration
	9. Working conditions
	10. Personal life
	11. Job security

A major implication of Herzberg's research is that administrators cannot assume that modification of a factor creating dissatisfaction will automatically result in job satisfaction, nor can it be assumed that failure to maintain a satisfactory condition will inevitably result in staff dissatisfaction. Different factors seem to be involved in creating satisfaction or dissatisfaction on the part of employees.

Following Herzberg's work, several studies in education have been initiated in an attempt to verify his findings.[16] Sergiovanni, for example, conducted a study of 3,382 teachers and discovered that achievement, recognition, and responsibility contributed predominantly to staff satisfaction.[17] Advancement was not a factor associated with teachers' satisfaction or, for that matter, with dissatisfaction. The work itself was a potential source of either satisfaction or dissatisfaction.

As revealed in Sergiovanni's investigation, those factors which seemed to contribute primarily to teacher dissatisfaction were poor relations with peers and students, unfair or incompetent administrative and supervisory policies and practices, and outside personal problems. The remaining factors associated with dissatisfaction in Herzberg's study (see figure 9.4) turned out to be potentially significant for creating either satisfaction or dissatisfaction. The conditions affecting satisfaction or dissatisfaction, or both, as reflected in Sergiovanni's study, did not vary with the sex, teaching level, or tenure status of the teacher.

By and large, the same factors do not hold equal potential for creating staff satisfaction or dissatisfaction: the conditions which create staff satisfaction seem to be intrinsic factors associated with the work itself; the conditions contributing to dissatisfaction seem to be associated with the environment of work, particularly the interpersonal relations aspect of that environment. These findings are consistent with Maslow's theory that individuals have a hierarchy of needs and that lower level needs such as security must be met before the higher level needs such as achievement or responsibility become important. Some theorists have attempted to refine and elaborate on Herzberg's theory. For example, Hoy and Miskel modified the theory in several respects. First, they reformulated the theory to include three factors instead of two: motivators, hygienes, and ambients.[18] Ambients, which function as either satisfiers or dissatisfiers, may include such variables as salary, professional growth possibilities, status, relationships with superiors, and risk opportunities. Second, Hoy and Miskel suggested that, while the motivators contribute more to job satisfaction than to job dissatisfaction, a lack of adequate motivators can contribute to dissatisfaction. Finally, they contend that, although hygiene factors contribute more to job dissatisfaction than to satisfaction, an abundance of hygiene factors can contribute to job satisfaction.

Chris Argyris and Victor Vroom have proposed additional theories on motivation, satisfaction, and morale, providing useful ideas worthy of further investigation.[19]

RESEARCH FINDINGS

SYMPTOMS OF DISSATISFACTION AND LOW MORALE

A review of the literature reveals that possible symptoms of teacher dissatisfaction and low morale include questioning and criticizing school goals and policies, lack of enthusiasm for teaching, rejection or lack of follow-through on administrative directives, absenteeism, and fragmentation, that is, a general feeling of being pulled in different directions.[20] J. C. Stapleton and his colleagues, who also identified some of these symptoms in their study, reported a positive relationship between teacher job dissatisfaction and brinkmanship, which they defined as teacher behavior that attempts to challenge the authority structure of the school while at the same time trying to avoid negative sanctions.[21]

Ronald Sylvia and Tony Hutchinson identified the need configurations which underlie the dissatisfaction of teachers and found six clear factors.[22] These included a lack of social variables and collegial support; negative supervisor relations; insufficient gratification from intrinsic work elements and dissatisfaction with extrinsic elements such as pay and benefits; uninteresting work and inappropriate responsibility levels; lack of opportunities for learning and development combined with negative attitudes about day-to-day duties; and inadequate job security, unclear expectations, and excessive workloads.[23]

In addition, Mel Schnake, Stephen Bushardt, and Curran Spottswood explored the effects of goal clarity, goal difficulty, participation in goal setting, and task complexity on work motivation and job satisfaction.[24] Their study found that intricate relationships existed among these variables. Low levels of goal clarity and participation in goal setting led to lower levels of work motivation for individuals on simple, low-complexity jobs. Thus, participation in goal setting allowed individuals to interact with superiors, which may have accounted for the increase in goal clarity. Furthermore, the researchers indicated that the results might have strong implications for traditional goal-setting programs which tend to involve only middle- and upper-level administrators and do not include teachers at the technical level of the organization's operation.

Dissatisfaction and low morale are also manifested by employee stress and burnout. A. Werner perceives psychological stress as a combination of such feelings as frustration, great pressure, and a lack of control over one's emotions and environment, whereas C. Maslach has defined burnout as emotional exhaustion caused by the stress of the job.[25] Herbert Freudenberger, who first coined the term *burnout,* identified it as

> cynicism, negativism, inflexibility, rigidity of thinking, unhappiness, boredom, psychosomatic symptoms, and a condition in which helping professionals wear out in their pursuit of impossible goals. Burnout has also been seen as exhaustion, depersonalization, a sense of reduced personal accomplishment, chronic fatigue, depression, and a desire to withdraw.[26]

The Maslach Burnout Inventory, an instrument originally developed by Maslach for measuring burnout, has been adapted by Edward Iwanicki and Richard Schwab for use with teachers.[27]

Among the more important indicators of teacher burnout are the following characteristics: loss of concern about and detachment from the people with whom one works; a cynical and dehumanized perception of students, accompanied by a deterioration of the quality of teaching; depression; increased use of sick leave; and efforts to leave the profession.[28] According to C. Maslach and S. Jackson, the development of burnout is progressive. In the initial stage, the affected personnel develop increased feelings of emotional exhaustion and fatigue; as emotional resources become depleted, they feel that they are no longer capable of giving of themselves as in the past. In the second stage, they develop negative, cynical attitudes toward their students. Finally, affected personnel turn against themselves and begin to evaluate themselves very negatively.[29]

A study conducted by K. Dawani found that levels of burnout among teachers tended to fall into the moderate category according to the Maslach Burnout Inventory. They did find that burnout appears to be higher among "young, less experienced teachers, as opposed to their older, more experienced counterparts."[30] These findings indicate that more experienced teachers may eventually become better able to cope with the problems of their profession or better able to control their own feelings.

POSSIBLE CAUSES

Not only are the causes of employee stress and burnout frequently difficult to ascertain; they are also not easily distinguished from the symptoms. Nevertheless, numerous ideas have been advanced on possible causes. Four factors contribute to stress at work: (1) role factors, (2) job factors, (3) physical factors, and (4) interpersonal factors. A number of techniques for reducing stress created by the various factors have been recommended.[31] Milbrey McLaughlin et al. found that the dominant motivation and source of reward for teachers lies in promoting student growth and development; yet, they also found that school conditions prevent teachers from obtaining the rewards which drew them to teaching in the first place.[32] As one teacher indicated,

> Things are set up these days so that teachers never feel they can do a good job. The classes are too large, the materials aren't there, and the students come to school with incredible needs that teachers can't meet. We are constantly pushed. We are constantly told by the superintendent that teachers have to do this, and we are constantly told by parents that teachers have to do that. Everyone expects the schools to take care of social problems. I think that schools could be a very progressive force— but not with the resources they currently have. I feel angry; I feel depressed; I feel frustrated. It is a very difficult situation for those teachers who care.[33]

McLaughlin indicated that to minimize their feelings of failure, teachers often (1) withdraw emotionally from the classroom; (2) place increased value on material rewards; (3) become hostile toward school officials; (4) work for promotion to other positions; or (5) leave the profession altogether.[34] Stuart Palonsky provides a vivid account of the culture which many new teachers experience when they first encounter the reality of work within schools.[35] New teachers reported that in addition to the press of time, lack of resources, precarious personal relationships, and inadequate income, they also felt that significant aspects of their work situation were out of control.

In a study by Fred Feitler and Edward Tokar, the five most frequent sources of stress reported by teachers were individual pupils who continually misbehaved, too much work, trying to uphold/maintain values and standards, noisy pupils, and a difficult class.[36] In a study of working conditions in urban schools, the more important causes of teacher stress centered on problems of governance and leadership; budget cuts; staff relations; student issues; and disruption and threats to the teachers' physical, professional, and personal well-being.[37]

Suggested causes of teacher burnout are generally believed to be similar to those associated with stress.[38] Richard Schwab and Edward Iwanicki, for example, found that role conflict and role ambiguity were significantly related to teacher burnout.[39] Mary Anderson and Edward Iwanicki discovered that teacher burnout was significantly related to the extent to which teachers felt that their needs for professional respect and self-actualization were not being met; Daniel Duke indicated that teachers often find themselves in unsafe schools striving to fulfill ambiguous expectations with diminishing resources.[40]

Sharon Conley, Samuel Bacharach, and Scott Bauer noted that working conditions may be related to teacher dissatisfaction.[41] Their study found that teacher dissatisfaction and career commitment were highly correlated with the decisional climate of the school. And McLaughlin et al. discovered that the following factors contributed to teacher frustration and disillusionment:

1. Lack of teacher input into decisions that directly affect their work.
2. Administrative decisions that undermine teachers' professional judgment and expertise.
3. Absence of the opportunity for collegial exchange to examine new and alternative practices.
4. Lack of recognition for accomplishments.[42]

Thus, the failure of schools to provide a true professional environment may have an adverse effect on new and experienced teachers.[43]

Based on a review of the literature on school culture, certain aspects of school culture impact negatively on teacher satisfaction and morale.[44] These cultural elements included physical, emotional, and psychic demands of teaching; uncertainty of teaching because of a lack of validated technical procedures; and isolation from other teachers, which can result in loneliness. Seymour Sarason and Daniel Lortie have treated the topic of isolation in great depth, and Ann Lieberman and Lynne Miller have addressed the inability of teachers to find time and collegial support to engage in reflective practice.[45]

An additional cause of employee dissatisfaction and low morale may be the different frames of reference that administrators and teachers possess. This is typically conceptualized as a conflict between the bureaucratic orientation of the administration and the professional orientation of the staff.[46] A bureaucratic orientation emphasizes staff compliance with rules and regulations, and loyalty to the administration; on the other hand, a professional orientation emphasizes a desire for autonomy, control over one's work environment, and allegiance to one's subject matter and/or clients rather than to the organization itself. In this conceptualization teachers are assumed to be professionally oriented, while administrators are believed to have a bureaucratic orientation.[47] However, some writers have questioned whether all teachers possess a professional orientation and all administrators are characterized by a bureaucratic orientation.[48]

The relationship between personal satisfaction and motivation, and the extent of bureaucracy in school organizations has been the focus of several studies; thus far, confirming evidence of such a relationship has been limited. M. S. Patton and Cecil Miskel found no significant relationship between teacher motivation and school district bureaucracy; but in a related study, Miskel and his colleagues discovered that increased centralization of decision-making power reduces job satisfaction while increased formulation of school rules improves teachers' attitudes toward their jobs.[49] Ted Schackmuth's findings also failed to support the hypothesis that, as the level of bureaucracy increases, teachers' work satisfaction decreases.[50] Apparently the relationship between the level of bureaucracy and job satisfaction (if one exists) is complex and yet to be defined by research. In this connection, J. S. Packard has even questioned whether the concept of bureaucracy is appropriate for schools and school districts because, he points out, classroom teaching seems to be regulated little by administrators, rules, or other formal operating procedures. He also contends that the job of teaching does not possess the characteristics normally included in defining a profession.[51]

PROPOSED PROGRAMS

Although research on the causes of employee dissatisfaction, low morale, stress, and teacher burnout is still in progress and it is premature to draw any definite conclusions about causality, a number of suggestions have been offered to help cope with these negative conditions. Katherine Kasten believes, as do Lieberman and Miller, that teachers need to become more aware of the overall nature and working conditions of the teaching profession, particularly those factors that pertain to their specific areas of responsibility.[52] These writers also recommend that teachers develop more open and supportive interaction with colleagues and superiors and set realistic goals and expectations for themselves and their students.

In-service programs and counseling services should be provided by school districts for teachers who may experience or are experiencing stress or burnout, according to Yvonne Gold.[53] The role of the principal in ameliorating such distress on the part of teachers has been put forth by Werner as (1) gaining more awareness of indicators of stress and burnout on the part of teachers; (2) communicating to the staff that asking for and accepting assistance in times of stress does not indicate weakness; (3) providing emotional support to teachers in times of stress; and (4) taking appropriate action wherever possible.[54] A. G.

Boudewyn has described a useful meeting format for employees to voice their concerns and frustration.[55] In addition, Alfred Alschuler has offered numerous ideas for conducting workshops on teacher burnout; Patricia Hanley and Kevin Swick's workshop ideas have also focused on reducing teachers' stress.[56] Even though many writers have emphasized the role of school administrators with respect to developing high satisfaction and morale, the research on the relationship between that role and the satisfaction and morale of school personnel has been limited. E. M. Duncan found that teacher morale was significantly higher in schools with employee-oriented administrators than in schools with task-oriented administrators, but he recommended that a combination of the two styles be utilized by administrators in working with teachers.[57] E. B. Ingle and R. E. Munsterman observed that teachers in high-satisfaction schools described their principals as more democratic than did teachers in low-satisfaction schools; and Kathy Leslie found that those categories that had the greatest influence on overall job satisfaction were teaching decisions, school working conditions, professional recognition, salary, benefits, and job status.[58] Based on a review of the literature on managing motivation, group-centered leadership has been advocated by P. Degenfelder as most effective in promoting a healthy motivational climate for teachers.[59] She also concluded that teachers needed employment security, high interaction opportunity, institutional supportiveness, and high perceived contribution opportunity, for a healthy motivational climate to be maintained. One study found, however, that while teachers tended to rate the potential costs of decision-making involvement as low and the potential benefits as high, many teachers were reluctant to become involved because they saw little likelihood that the administration would provide them with meaningful involvement in which they could make a significant contribution.[60]

An often recommended approach to increasing staff satisfaction is that of providing greater incentives and recognition. Dennis Spuck has contended, however, that administrators exercise little control over organizational incentives for school personnel.[61] He has pointed out that most extrinsic rewards, such as salaries, are limited by legal and collective bargaining constraints, and that intrinsic rewards or incentives are controlled for the most part by the teachers' colleagues, students, and the teachers themselves. In this connection, Susan Johnson believes that teaching continues to be rather limited in the extrinsic rewards that can be made available, and that if teacher satisfaction is to be increased, then efforts need to be applied to improving the teaching situation itself and the *intrinsic* rewards available to teachers.[62] She states that the problematic nature of teaching makes this objective challenging because goals are intangible and unclear, assessment difficult, and the expectations and behavior of the clientele diverse. Susan Rosenholtz noted that, when asked, teachers have seldom mentioned salary as the most rewarding aspect of their jobs.[63] Instead, they value rewards that come from students' accomplishments and recognition of their ability to help students.

In recent years, various incentive plans designed to recruit, reward, and retain effective teachers have been initiated. These plans have been labeled as either career ladder plans or merit pay systems; they were intended to provide financial incentives, varied work, and advancement opportunities for teachers.[64]

Career ladders and differentiated staffing reforms are designed to enrich teachers' work opportunities and responsibilities. The reasons given most often for the implementation of career ladders are the following:

1. Establishes career patterns in teaching, making promotion in teaching possible.
2. Breaks the lockstep salary schedule and provides new ways to encourage competent people to remain in teaching.
3. Provides teachers with a choice of roles.
4. Is consistent with the free enterprise system.
5. Stimulates teachers to be more critical of their teaching.
6. Promotes competition.
7. Incorporates a pay for performance approach.[65]

Plans differ in respect to their adherence to the preceding factors and their reliance on objective versus subjective criteria for movement up the ladder. Generally, the plans contain a combination of criteria which address teachers' involvement in classroom, school-based, district, and professional activities.[66]

Merit pay plans, unlike career ladder programs, focus primarily on teaching effectiveness and have an implied emphasis on productivity. The application of what appears to be a pure business model has been questioned and criticized as being inappropriate in education. Bacharach and Conley indicated that

> numerous studies have shown merit pay to be effective only in those occupational settings in which cooperation among workers is not necessary and the contribution of each individual worker (or group of workers) can be differentiated from the contributions of others. Furthermore, merit pay is most effective in those occupational settings in which the enhanced efforts of workers directly increase the monetary resources of the organization. Teaching fails to meet both of the prerequisites for successful implementation of merit pay.[67]

In terms of efforts to enhance teacher professionalism, the concept of merit pay, in its pure sense, would appear dysfunctional when the concepts of collegiality and cooperation are being promoted.

Administrators should note that not all incentives need to be costly.[68] In fact, often the cost-free incentives are the most valuable. These might include (1) writing a commendation letter for a teacher's personal file; (2) complementing a teacher on an exceptional lesson or a general task; (3) taking the time to interact informally with a teacher; (4) recommending a teacher for a special recognition award; (5) appointing a teacher to a prestigious committee; and (6) involving teachers in goal setting and decision making within the school.

RECOMMENDATIONS

Research studies on staff satisfaction and morale can be instructive. Unless the findings are translated into recommended courses of action, however, they represent little more than interesting reading. Therefore, based primarily on the findings presented in the previous sections, the following guidelines are offered to administrators who wish to develop and maintain high staff satisfaction and morale in the school:

1. **Attempt on a regular basis to obtain systematic feedback from the staff, as individuals and as a group, on their perceptions of the problems, concerns, and issues which they feel affect them personally or the school generally.** Administrators cannot hope to develop and maintain high satisfaction and morale on the part of their staffs unless they know what is on the staff members' minds; and they cannot realistically hope to arrive at this knowledge without actually asking the staff periodically for this information. Two procedures for achieving this goal would be the administering of anonymous questionnaires each semester, asking the staff to identify what they see as the main problems and issues affecting the school, and a principal-teacher *open discussion* scheduled at least monthly for teachers who want to discuss problems and issues on a more direct basis. An important prerequisite to the provision of feedback by staff is their belief that the administrator is sincerely interested in obtaining it, and that there will be constructive follow-up.[69]

2. **Exert a major effort toward improving the satisfaction which staff derive from their work.** The research on teachers' satisfaction and morale indicates that when they feel a sense of accomplishment from teaching and receive due recognition for their efforts and performance, staff satisfaction and morale are high.

Improving the conditions under which the staff works—size of class; type of facilities; quantity and quality of teaching materials; problem nature of the class; the quality of administrative and supervisor supporting services; and increasing opportunities for initiative, responsibility, and achievement—are administrative contributions which should increase the likelihood that staff can obtain a sense of accomplishment from their endeavors.

In many school districts the master contract and/or local financial circumstances limit or reduce the opportunity for an administrator to improve working conditions, but the key factor is administrator effort. If an administrator is perceived by the staff as at least trying to improve working conditions, that effort is likely to positively affect staff morale. Certainly, at the minimum, administrators can provide appropriate recognition and positive reinforcement to staff members for their accomplishments. Such recognition could take the form of a personal tribute at a faculty or PTA meeting, an individual letter with a copy for the teacher's personnel file, or a recommendation for advancement on the salary scale. All too often teachers complain that administrators take them for granted. Almost all human beings need periodic expressions of appreciation of their worth, and this frequently requires no more than simply providing verbal positive reinforcement.

3. **Strive to improve the operation of the school and the overall quality of the educational program of the school.** People feel pleased and proud to work in a school that is efficiently administered and that offers a quality educational program. A poorly organized school with a limited or mediocre educational program is bound to affect adversely the morale and satisfaction of its teachers. According to Frederick Redefer, one of the major factors associated with faculty morale is the quality of the school's educational program.[70] Consequently, the administrator who improves the quality of a school's educational program concurrently improves the morale of the faculty. Again, the key is for the administrator to be striving to improve the operation of the school and the quality of the educational program. Not every administrator is in a situation where it is possible to have an outstanding program, but every administrator can at least be aspiring to this standard of excellence and striving to achieve it.

4. **Try to be sensitive to problems of an interpersonal nature between and among teachers, students, and parents, and try to mediate these problems when appropriate.** Problems of interpersonal relations seem to be one of the main factors contributing to low teacher satisfaction and morale, according to research. Administrators will probably experience difficulty in ascertaining these kinds of problems, however, because in many instances the people involved may be reluctant to talk to them. Administrators can partially overcome this handicap by becoming more aware of what is going on in the school and by showing understanding and compassion when such problems are brought to their attention. Administrators themselves may not always be in the best possible position to mediate these problems, but they should at least be knowledgeable of appropriate agencies for purposes of referral.

5. **Provide meaningful participation for teachers in the decision-making processes of the school.** Considerable evidence indicates that teachers desire a more active and meaningful role in school decision making. Research evidence also suggests that increased teacher involvement can result in higher faculty morale. Harold Leiman, for example, concluded in his study that teachers who participated in school administration manifested:
   a. Higher morale than teachers who did not participate.
   b. More positive attitudes toward their principals, their colleagues, and their pupils.
   c. Higher regard for themselves and for the teaching profession.[71]

In addition, studies by Gail Schneider, and Norman Benson and Patricia Malone found that job satisfaction was related to the perceived level of influence in decision making and to the extent to which teachers were participating in school decision making at the level they desired.[72] And Wayne Hoy and B. L. Brown found that elementary teachers reported a large zone of acceptance, or range of behavior within which they are willing to accept decisions made for them by their principals, when principals demonstrated a leadership style which combined both structure and consideration for individuals.[73]

The key word in this fifth recommendation is "meaningful" participation.[74] It makes little sense for administrators to involve staff members in school decision making unless they are prepared to fully utilize staff members' knowledge and expertise, involve them at their expected level of involvement, and accept the consensus of the group, provided their decision does not result in a violation of school board policy, the master contract, or the law. Lesser involvement, while perhaps necessary in certain situations, runs the risk of being perceived unworthy of teachers' time and efforts, and can result in reduced morale and satisfaction. An in-depth discussion of concepts, methods, problems, and issues associated with staff involvement in school decision making may be found in Gorton's *School Leadership and Administration: Important Concepts, Case Studies, and Simulations.*[75]

6. **Practice good human relations in your own interactions with the faculty as a whole and with individual faculty members.** The relationship between the faculty and the school administrator is probably one of the most important factors affecting faculty morale. If that relationship is perceived as a good one, faculty morale is likely to be high; if it is perceived as a poor one, faculty morale is likely to be low.

A major factor influencing the relationship between faculty members and administrators is the kind of human relations that they practice. Although obviously many different ingredients contribute to good human relations, the following seem essential for any administrator:

a. Be sensitive to the needs of others.
b. Attempt to explain the reasons for your actions.
c. Try to involve others in decisions about the school.
d. Be open to criticism; try not to be defensive.
e. Be willing to admit mistakes and to make changes.
f. Be honest and fair in your interactions with others.

A critical review of twenty-five years of research on morale concluded that whether or not teachers were satisfied depended primarily on the quality of the administrative relationships in which teachers were involved and the quality of the leadership they received.[76] Therefore, a major key to high faculty morale and satisfaction seems to be the leadership behavior of the school administrator.

COLLECTIVE BARGAINING AND CONTRACT ADMINISTRATION

Beginning in the 1960s, a new element entered into the relationship between the faculty and the school administrator: collective bargaining.[77] Previously, on their own initiative, many school boards and administrators had informally consulted with teachers about conditions of employment and the operation of the school; then, the introduction of collective bargaining meant that the school board and administrators were required to consult and negotiate with teachers about these matters. As a result, school boards and administrators were no longer as free to make unilateral decisions affecting the faculty's welfare, but had to share decision-making authority with the teachers. Since most, if not all of the decision-making authority which teachers wanted to share had traditionally been considered management's prerogative, teachers' attempts to gain and expand their rights under collective bargaining were certain to affect the role of school administrators, particularly the school principal.[78]

For building administrators, collective bargaining has raised four basic questions: (1) What should be the role of school principals in collective bargaining? (2) What should be their role in contract administration? (3) What should be their role in grievance procedures? and (4) What should be their role in a teachers' strike? The following sections discuss recommendations and problems associated with each of the four roles.

THE PRINCIPAL'S ROLE IN COLLECTIVE BARGAINING

At the outset of collective bargaining between school boards and teacher groups, most principals seemed uncertain as to whether or not they should participate.[79] Early opinions among principals ranged from a desire to remain detached from collective bargaining for fear of jeopardizing their relationship with teachers, to a preference and concern that building administrators be involved in all aspects of collective bargaining lest they lose significant decision-making authority to the faculty. Eventually, the latter conception of the role of the building administrator in collective bargaining prevailed, as evidenced by a statement by Benjamin Epstein in an official document of the National Association of Secondary School Principals: "The members of NASSP feel very strongly that principals and other administrators must be included in every phase of elective decision making whenever their fate and that of the schools for which they are responsible are to be determined."[80]

Statements published by the National Elementary Principals Association during the 1960s showed that it, too, supported the concept of involving principals in all aspects of collective bargaining that would affect their roles.[81]

While the official position of the principals' associations and the eventual opinion of most principals was that principals should be involved in all aspects of collective bargaining between school boards and teachers that affect their role, this concept was not immediately accepted by either of the latter two groups.

In the early years of collective bargaining, many teachers and school boards believed that building administrators should be excluded from the process of collective bargaining; surprisingly, most superintendents seemed to concur.[82] Later, district administrators and school boards began to recognize the desirability of involving principals in the process of collective bargaining. Not only could principals contribute useful ideas and perceptions to the formulation of a district's bargaining proposal, but their reactions to the teachers' bargaining demands were also essential for the development of an educationally sound and enforceable master contract.

Although the degree to which building administrators receive opportunities to become involved in the collective bargaining process may vary, the following guidelines would make the greatest and most effective utilization of building administrators' experiences and insights:

1. Building administrators should be involved in the formulation of the school board's bargaining position. Specifically, all building administrators should be asked (prior to the development of the board's bargaining proposal to teachers) to submit suggested items which relate to education at the school building level for consideration during the bargaining process.
2. Building administrators should be represented on the negotiation team for the school board or on an advisory committee which gives counsel to the negotiation team during the bargaining process. The most appropriate way of involving building administrators in the bargaining process is not easy to determine and depends to a large extent on school board and administrative philosophies, along with conditions within the local district. Obviously, not all building administrators can be involved equally, and different forms of participation may be appropriate. The key factor is that regardless of the form of involvement, it is essential that the building administrators' points of view be presented and adequately considered during the bargaining process.

3. Building administrators should, as a group or through their representative, be given an opportunity during collective bargaining to evaluate the implications of any item which may affect the operation of the school, their role in the school, or their relationship with others associated with the school. Building administrators are usually the ones primarily responsible for interpreting and enforcing the provisions of the master contract. Many of the items which are negotiated affect them and the operation of the school. They should, therefore, be given an opportunity to evaluate the effect of these factors on the school and its administration.

The extent to which building administrators are involved in one or more of the ways just identified depends on local conditions and personalities. Clearly, building administrators can and should play an important role in the formulation of the school board's bargaining position and during the bargaining process itself.[83] Unfortunately, experience and observation suggest that their role may be a limited one. Nevertheless, if a school board and a superintendent choose to ignore the building administrators' abilities and perceptions, they potentially run the risk not only of alienating an important component of their management team but also of failing to capitalize on a valuable source of ideas and insights. (Entire books have been devoted to the topic of collective bargaining; thus, this chapter cannot possibly do justice to the subject. An excellent analysis of the literature is William G. Webster's *Effective Collective Bargaining in Public Education* [Ames: Iowa State University Press, 1988.])

THE PRINCIPAL'S ROLE IN CONTRACT ADMINISTRATION

The final product of the bargaining process is a master contract between the school board and the teachers' group. The master contract contains in essence the various agreements reached during collective bargaining to which management and employees alike are expected to adhere. Webster noted that "Contract administration involves the processes of interpretation, implementation, and enforcement of collective bargaining agreements. It is the means by which the objectives of the contractual relationship are fulfilled. To that extent, it is as important as the entire bargaining process that yielded the contract."[84]

School principals are usually viewed by the school board and the district administration as their main agents in administering master contracts because the vast majority of the teachers are located at the school building level. Principals are the chief administrators at this level, so they are the ones expected to interpret and enforce master contracts for management. JoAnn Mazzarella in examining the role of the principals in contract administration found that 48 percent of policy provisions concerned curriculum, 64 percent concerned student placement, and 96 percent concerned teacher placement.[85] Obviously, principals need to be knowledgeable about these policy provisions, and their role in assuring the implementation of the policies. Although principals may need assistance from the district office when significant questions or problems arise, typically they have the main responsibility at the building level for administering master contracts.

Contract administration at the building level usually consists of two major tasks: interpreting the language and intent of the provisions of the contract, and enforcing the terms of the contract. A third task, implementing grievance procedures, can be considered a part of contract administration but is sufficiently important to warrant separate treatment in the next section.

Interpreting

The role of principals in interpreting the language and intent of the provisions of master contracts can be a difficult or easy one, depending on the precision with which the contracts were written and the degree to which the principals received adequate orientation about the contracts before they were expected to begin administering them.

Master contracts containing such phrases as, "if at all possible," "when feasible," and "every effort will be made," provide the school board and/or teachers with desired flexibility but also place a large interpretative responsibility on school principals. If in doubt, they can seek guidance from the district administration. However, the guidance which they receive from this source, although usually helpful, may not arrive in time, may not be useful, or may not agree with the teachers' interpretation of the contract. As a result, in too many situations school principals are forced to make their own interpretations of the language of the contract or else they find themselves in the middle between the district office's interpretation and the teachers' interpretation of master contracts.

A related problem which some principals have encountered in administering master contracts arises from the fact that they received inadequate orientation to the provisions and intent of the contracts prior to implementation.[86] Given copies of the master contract, sometimes even after the teachers in the building received their copies, they were then instructed to administer the contracts to the best of their ability. On occasions, principals did not even receive copies of the master contract until after the opening of school in the fall, although the master contract had been available earlier.

If principals are to administer the master contract effectively, they should receive comprehensive orientation to contracts prior to implementation, and they should have an opportunity to ask questions about any features. An orientation of this nature would minimize incorrect interpretations of the contract and should result in more uniform and consistent application of its provisions. Certainly, such an orientation program would make it easier for principals to effectively administer master contracts in their schools.

Enforcing

Interpreting the master contract is one aspect of contract administration. Enforcing the provisions of the contract, particularly in regard to teachers, is a second important responsibility of the school principal. Some may assume that there is only one way to enforce the rules of a contract; however, a research study of rule enforcement by principals revealed three approaches, each with specific consequences for adminstrator-faculty relations.[87]

Utilizing the Gouldner model of bureaucratic administration, Frank Lutz and Seymour Evans investigated the effects of three types of rule administration by principals: mock, representative, and punishment-centered. *Mock* administration was defined as nonenforcement of the rules when teachers failed to observe them. *Representative* administration was defined as the cooperative acceptance of the rules by principal and teachers, accompanied by enforcement by the principal and obedience by the teachers. *Punishment-centered* rule administration was characterized by the principal's use of threats or punishment to achieve rule adherence by teachers. No school, however, was run solely through the use of one type of rule administration.

After spending a considerable length of time making observations, conducting interviews with the personnnel, and collecting questionnnaire data in six schools, the researchers succeeded in documenting the effects of each type of rule enforcement.

Positive feelings between principals and teachers seemed to be associated in most instances with mock administration of the rules. Nonenforcement was usually associated with such rules as board policy on smoking, the use of school telephones, teacher time cards, and the use of sick leave. In most of the situations when principals ignored rules, they believed that extenuating circumstances surrounded its violation by teachers. Nevertheless, in some cases administrators were concerned about the lack of rule enforcement.

In those instances when principals engaged in representative rule administration, tension between teachers and principals developed initially but subsided over time. With few exceptions, warmth and friendliness were observed in the relationship between principals and staff members, and a high rating of principal leadership was given by teachers whose principals exhibited representative rule administration as their dominant style. The researchers further discovered that when principals engaged in representative rule enforcement, they initiated considerable informal, as well as formal, contact with teachers. As a result, complaints and problems frequently were resolved informally before they ever reached the grievance stage.

The key to effective representative rule enforcement seemed to be *intensive and extensive communication,* that is, explaining the rule and the reasons for it, and working with teachers on interpretation of the rule. Regular meetings between the principal and the teachers' building representative also appeared to be particularly helpful in reducing initial tensions and avoiding problems.

Data from the study indicated that punishment-centered administration was likely to produce negative consequences. Principals who adhered to every rule and used or threatened punishment to enforce the rules were regarded as "running a tight ship" but were usually given low leadership ratings by their teachers. More important, perhaps, was the tension and hostility which developed as a result of punishment-centered rule enforcement and persisted beyond the original disagreement, thereby creating an atmosphere for potential future conflict between the administrator and the teachers.

Although the results of any study cannot be generalized to different situations, school principals should realize that the quality of the relationship between themselves and their staffs is affected by the approach they take in enforcing the provisions of their master contracts. Whether or not they should enforce every rule may, of course, depend in many instances on factors beyond their control. Available research suggests that representative rule administration, as defined earlier, results in the most positive consequences in principal-staff relations.

THE PRINCIPAL'S ROLE IN GRIEVANCE PROCEDURES

A major objective of collective bargaining by teacher groups has been to secure the inclusion of grievance procedures in the master contract of the district. Although prior to collective bargaining, many school districts had informally mediated teacher grievances, these procedures did not, in the eyes of the teachers, sufficiently safeguard or guarantee their rights to fair hearings and appeals.[88] Therefore, teachers' associations and unions have concentrated on gaining formal grievance procedures in their master contracts; at the present time, most master contracts contain some formal grievance procedure for teachers. These procedures have been viewed as necessary since without them employers have few incentives to comply with agreements which create benefits for employees.[89]

A grievance procedure is, essentially, a method or process requiring the parties to a dispute to discuss and try to resolve the dispute, with an opportunity for appeal to a higher authority by either of the parties disagreeing with the initial resolution of the matter.[90] The two main purposes of such a procedure are to prevent either party to a dispute from acting unilaterally to resolve the matter and to guarantee the right of appeal. When master contracts contain grievance procedures, administrators must respond to teachers' grievances by attempting to work out cooperative solutions.

Although there can be considerable disagreement over what constitutes a grievance under a master contract, grievances typically arise under the following conditions:

1. A misinterpretation or incorrect application of the provisions of the master contract.
2. An intentional violation of the provisions of the master contract.
3. A practice contrary to school board policy.
4. Unfair or discriminatory behavior which may not be prohibited by the contract or school board policy, but which causes individuals to believe that they have been wronged.[91]

The latter condition is, in many contracts, defined as a complaint rather than a grievance, and it may be handled informally by the administrator rather than by going through formal procedures and appeal.

Whether a teacher actually files a grievance with the administration depends on many factors. First of all, one of the four conditions previously identified needs to be alleged. Second, the teacher must believe strongly enough about the grievance to lodge a formal protest to the administration. At this point the role of the building representative for the teachers' group becomes very important. The teacher with a grievance normally goes to the teachers' building representative in matters involving the master contract before registering a protest to the principal. If the building representative is supportive, then the teacher is likely to file the grievance. On the other hand, if the building representative indicates to the teacher that a legitimate grievance does not exist, or if the building representative attempts to persuade the teacher to resolve the matter informally rather than going through formal procedures, the teacher may never initiate the grievance with the administration. The role of the building representative can be crucial in determining whether or not a grievance should be or will be filed with the administration.

In examining research on the role of the building representative, whether or not a building representative encourages a teacher to file a grievance depends to a large extent on the building representative's relationship with the administration of the school.[92] A study of this relationship showed that building representatives who believed that the administration had not communicated with them sufficiently and had not consulted with them frequently enough in school decision making tended to file more teacher grievances than those building representatives satisfied with the communication and participation provided by the administration. A negative attitude by the building representative toward the administration was also likely to increase the teacher grievances filed. The main implication of this research is that the school principal would be well advised to develop a good working relationship with the building representative for teachers. A positive relationship may not prevent all grievances, but it should do much to reduce unnecessary ones.

If a teacher and the building representative decide to file a grievance, they should follow the procedures specified in the master contract; these usually include the following steps:

1. The teacher submits the grievance directly to the principal, within five days after the teacher knows about or experiences the conditions giving rise to the grievance. (The time limitations specified in the contract may vary slightly from one district to another.)
2. If the grievance is not resolved to the satisfaction of the teacher within five days, the teacher can appeal the principal's decision to the superintendent or a district-level representative.
3. Within five days of receipt of the written appeal, the superintendent or district representative, the teacher, and all other relevant parties, such as the principal and building representative, meet in an attempt to resolve the matter. The administration must give its position on the grievance within five days after the meeting.
4. If the administration's response is not satisfactory to the teacher, the matter may be appealed to the school board. The school board or a subcommittee of the board then meets and must render a written decision within twenty days of the hearing.[93]

Finally, arbitration by an outside agency may be part of the grievance procedure if the school board and the teachers have agreed to this previously, or if it is required by law.

The principal's role during grievance procedures, particularly in the initial stages, is crucial.[94] Many, if not most grievances can be resolved at the building level without going through additional steps of appeal—if school principals perform their roles effectively. While their roles vary somewhat, depending on the specific circumstances, principals should carry out the following steps in relation to grievance procedures:

1. **Study all the provisions of the master contract to understand them completely and accurately.** Resolving teacher grievances requires that principals possess a good understanding of their master contracts. If principals are not knowledgeable about their master contracts, they may give the teachers incorrect interpretations, or, worse yet, challenge teachers' correct interpretations of the contracts. During a grievance procedure, principals must be able to interpret master contracts correctly; to do this, they must be knowledgeable about all aspects of those contracts.

2. **Attempt to resolve teacher concerns prior to their reaching the stage of formal grievances if possible.** Many grievances can be resolved before they are formally filed with the principal of a school. Principals should try to be aware of teacher complaints and attempt to resolve them before they develop into formal grievances.

   They should also be sensitive to the concerns of the teachers and make every feasible effort to improve working conditions and education in general in the building. These actions not only help to reduce the grievances filed in a building but also create a more positive attitude toward the principal on the part of the teachers and the teachers' representative if a situation ever reaches the formal grievance stage.

3. **Maintain your poise on receiving a teacher's grievance and do not automatically assume that the filing of a grievance constitutes a personal attack on you.** If principals view grievances in personal terms, they are less likely to be objective in their responses to them, and their emotions may adversely affect the possibility of successfully resolving the grievances. (In some instances, the filing of a grievance does constitute a personal attack on the principal; even in these cases, becoming defensive is unlikely to contribute to the effective resolution of a grievance.)

   No district administration or school board should use the number of grievances filed in a school during the year as a major basis for evaluating a building administrator's effectiveness. A large number of grievances in a building could indicate something about a principal's effectiveness, but then again, it may only reflect a very militant faculty in that particular building. Grievances are filed for many reasons; more investigation and study would be needed before a fair conclusion could be reached about their relationship to administrative effectiveness.

Administrators should recognize that grievances are not necessarily bad. They can represent positive opportunities to correct misunderstandings and to improve school conditions.

4. **Try to understand the grievance from the teacher's point of view.** This does not mean that a principal should necessarily agree with a teacher or forget to represent management during a grievance proceeding. However, if principals are to avoid any invalid assumptions or interpretations about the teachers' grievances, they must do everything possible to understand how teachers view the situations which caused the grievances. Even though this type of understanding may not in itself resolve the grievances, it can reduce unnecessary conflict and appeals of the principals' proposed resolutions of grievances, and it should result in a more positive attitude on the part of the teachers toward principals.

5. **Consult with the district administration if there is doubt about how to proceed before and during the grievance conference.** Usually someone in the district administration has the responsibility of helping principals when grievances arise. This individual can be a source of considerable assistance to principals unsure about some aspect of their master contracts or about which course of action they should take in dealing with teachers' grievances. Consultation between principals and the district administrators when grievances arise is usually desirable and sometimes essential for appropriate resolution of the grievances.

6. **Create an atmosphere conducive to communication during the grievance conference; provide and seek information to help both parties decide on the best course of action to take.** Principals should provide quiet, private settings for the grievance conferences; during conferences they should facilitate communication as much as possible by not interrupting teachers or responding defensively. If appropriate, principals should consider letting the teacher and the teacher's representative tell their view of the grievance first.

Under no circumstances should principals attempt to negotiate with the teacher or make any precipitous decisions during the conference. Principals should offer whatever remedy is available under their master contracts, but should not go beyond that. Their basic task should be to provide and seek information enabling them to make proper decisions on the disposition of the grievances. This also gives the teacher and the teacher's representative an adequate basis on which to reach a decision about how they will proceed with the grievance.

7. **Give a response in writing to the teacher, concerning the disposition of the grievance after the conference.** Principals should not attempt to communicate to teachers any final decisions about the disposition of grievances until there has been time after the grievance conference to think about the situation and, perhaps, to consult with the central administration. Then, a final decision should be communicated in writing to the teacher, to minimize any inadvertent or intentional misinterpretations of the principal's decision. A written record of the principal's disposition of a grievance could become very important should the teacher decide to appeal the decision.

8. **Make every effort to maintain a positive relationship with the teacher and the building representative, even if the grievance is appealed by the teacher to your supervisor.** Obviously, this recommendation will frequently be difficult to implement. No one likes to have a decision challenged and appealed; it would be perfectly normal for principals to experience some negative feelings toward the teachers and building representatives if they should appeal the decision. However, principals should remember that they will probably still be working with both of them long after the grievance is finally settled. For this reason, principals should attempt to maintain a positive relationship with teachers and building representatives during the appeal process, regardless of behavior on their part which may be upsetting at the time.

9. **Make sure that the solution is implemented fully, no matter what the final resolution of the teacher's grievance may be.** Regardless of whether the final resolution of the teacher's grievance supports or rejects the original decision by the principal, it is the principal's responsibility to see that the solution is implemented promptly and fully. Lack of follow-through, particularly if the grievance is decided in favor of the teacher, can negatively affect relationships between the principal and other teachers and may result in unnecessary future grievances.

In some situations it may be difficult to implement all of the guidelines recommended. At times, the grievance filed is frivolous or represents a personal attack on the administrator. Certainly, most grievances hold potential for being personally upsetting to an administrator. Nevertheless, in such situations administrators must maintain their poise and perspective, and resist adopting the tactics of the other party or viewing the latter as an enemy. Such self-control may not come easily but it is necessary to avoid exacerbating the problem.

THE ADMINISTRATOR'S ROLE IN A TEACHERS' STRIKE

Not all teacher grievances and collective bargaining matters can be resolved to the satisfaction of the teachers; in some cases, they may use the strike as their ultimate strategy for achieving their objectives. Although binding arbitration of the issues unresolved by collective bargaining may avoid a strike, strikes are likely to continue to occur, if for no other reason than one or more of the relevant parties may not accept the concept of binding arbitration.

Teachers' strikes usually put a severe strain on the relationship between school administrators and their faculty members. Unfortunately, in most cases building administrators are placed in an adversary relationship with teachers in the school. Although building administrators may not be without sympathy for the teachers' cause, they are expected by the school board and the district administration to represent management during the strike. Their main expectation for principals is to carry out all the school board's directives, even if their implementation may impair principals' current or even future relationships with their staffs.

Although the specific roles of school administrators in teachers' strikes vary depending on particular circumstances, in most situations they need the ability to anticipate problems accurately, to plan thoroughly, to be resourceful, and to maintain a sense of humor and perspective. In addition, the administrators' school systems ideally will have developed a strike contingency plan to guide administrators during the prestrike, strike, and poststrike stages. While the presentation of the many details of such a plan go beyond the intended scope of this text, several sources contain a number of excellent recommendations, largely from people who have been through strikes.[95]

Obviously, the various problems that may occur during teachers' strikes cannot always be accurately anticipated in advance. However, to the extent that administrators can accurately anticipate problems and plan thoroughly for avoiding or ameliorating problems, strikes are less likely to be disruptive forces. If unanticipated problems do occur during a teachers' strike, administrators are dependent on their ability to respond quickly to rapidly moving events. Certainly, they should not act impetuously. But failure by administrators to move quickly and imaginatively during a teachers' strike could put them on the defensive and limit their options. In many situations, administrators need a high degree of resourcefulness to avoid being overcome by events they did not adequately anticipate.

Finally, an administrator needs to possess a good sense of humor and a long-range perspective to come through a strike successfully. Many events during the strike are frustrating and irritating.[96] Teachers' motives may seem questionable, and it may be difficult not to perceive the teachers and anybody who agrees with them as "the enemy." Nevertheless, administrators should avoid taking themselves too seriously or questioning the motives of others.

They should, of course, do whatever they think is right in strike situations, but before they act, they should remember that they will be working with many of those same teachers long after the strikes have been terminated. While administrators may be forced during the strike to take steps that temporarily impair their relationship with teachers, they should refrain as much as possible from taking any action that permanently makes it difficult to work successfully with the faculty after the strike.

A FINAL PERSPECTIVE

With the advent of collective bargaining and grievance procedures, the relationship between school administrators and their staffs has changed. The relationship is now frequently a frustrating and uneasy one in which both the administrators and staff members are unsure of each other's intentions and reliability. As a result, polarization and conflict between administrators and staff have increased in many schools. Fortunately, a few examples of cooperative efforts exist, giving rise to the hope that a new era of administrator-staff relations may be beginning.[97]

The current reform movement in education necessitates a new working relationship between the school administration and the teachers' union. In many ways, teachers' unions may ultimately control the outcomes and successes of the reform movement.[98] If a new professionalism in teaching is to emerge, both sides need to recognize that roles must be redefined and that administrators need latitude and flexibility in interpreting the roles of their professional staff members. Yet, administrators should not forget that teachers represent the most important resource in the school for helping to educate students, and without their support and commitment there is very little administrators can accomplish in bringing about educational improvement.

Therefore, administrators need to work to build and maintain high staff satisfaction and morale while respecting the contractual rights of their faculty members. Obviously not always easy, this is necessary for a cooperative, productive relationship.

Review and Learning Activities

1. Why are high staff morale and satisfaction thought to be important in personnel relations? When would high staff satisfaction and morale be undesirable, and how should the administrator respond?
2. What are the implications for the administrator of each of the theories of satisfaction, morale, or motivation presented in the text?
3. Assess proposed programs to deal with employee dissatisfaction and low morale. Indicate how you would change current staff personnel practices in your school as a result of the research on the extent, symptoms, and possible causes of staff dissatisfaction and low morale.
4. What is the role of the principal in the collective bargaining process in your school district? Is that role capitalizing sufficiently on the contributions that principals could make to this process?
5. What should be the role of the building administrator in administering the master contract? Which problems might be encountered, and how should these problems be approached?
6. Discuss those factors that may influence a teacher to file or not file a grievance. What should be the role of the administrator in responding to a grievance?
7. Identify those characteristics an administrator should possess before, during, and after a strike.

Notes

1. Douglas E. Mitchell, Flora Ida Ortiz, and Tedi K. Mitchell, *Work Orientation and Job Performance: The Cultural Basis of Teaching Rewards and Incentives* (Albany: State University of New York Press, 1987), 31.

2. Wayne K. Hoy and Cecil G. Miskel, *Educational Administration: Theory, Research, and Practice,* 3d ed. (New York: Random House, 1987), 74.

3. J. F. Cooper, *The Relationship of Morale and Productivity: A Historical Overview* (ERIC Report Ed–147–985); see also, Cecil Miskel and Rodney Ogawa, "Work Motivation, Job Satisfaction, and Climate," in *Handbook of Research on Educational Administration,* ed. Norman J. Boyan (New York: Logman, 1988), 279–304.

4. Miskel and Ogawa, "Work Motivation," and Richard A. Gorton, "Job Satisfaction and Morale," in *Encyclopedia of Educational Research,* ed. Harold Mitzel (New York: Macmillan, 1982). A major portion of this section on staff satisfaction and morale has been adapted from this latter source.

5. Ibid.

6. Douglas McGregor, *The Human Side of Enterprise* (New York: McGraw-Hill, 1960), 33–34, 47–48.

7. A. H. Maslow, *Motivation and Personality* (New York: Harper & Row, 1970).

8. M. A. Wahba and L. G. Bridwell, "Maslow Reconsidered: A Review of Research on the Need Hierarchy Theory," *Organizational Behavior and Human Performance* (April 1976): 212–40. For an additional discussion of the subsequent research on Maslow's theory, see Hoy and Miskel, *Educational Administration,* 180–82.

9. Lyman W. Porter, "A Study of Perceived Need Satisfaction in Bottom and Middle Management Jobs," *Journal of Applied Psychology* (1961): 1–10.

10. Thomas J. Sergiovanni and Fred D. Carver, *The New School Executive: A Theory of Administration,* 2d ed. (New York: Harper & Row, 1980).

11. For example, see G. Goldsberry, R. Henderson, and T. J. Sergiovanni, *Perceived Need Deficiencies of Teachers in 1978 as Compared with 1968* (Urbana: Department of Educational Administration and Supervision, University of Illinois, Urbana-Champaign, 1978).

12. David W. Chapman and Malcolm A. Lowther, "Teachers' Satisfaction with Teaching" (Paper presented at the annual meeting of the American Educational Research Association, Los Angeles, 1981).

13. Ibid., 8–9.

14. Ibid., 12.

15. Frederick Herzberg et al., *The Motivation to Work* (New York: John Wiley & Sons, 1959), 114.

16. Charles R. May and Robert H. Decker, "Putting Herzberg's Two Factor Theory of Motivation in Perspective," *Planning and Changing* (Fall 1988): 141–49.

17. Thomas Sergiovanni, "Factors which Affect Satisfaction and Dissatisfaction of Teachers," *Journal of Educational Administration* (May 1967): 66–82. For a more recent review of research pertaining to Herzberg's theory, see Paula Silver, "Job Satisfaction and Dissatisfaction Revisited," *Educational and Psychological Research* (Winter 1987): 1–20.

18. Hoy and Miskel, *Educational Administration.*

19. C. Argyris, *Personality and Organization* (New York: Harper & Bros., 1957); and Victor R. Vroom, *Work and Motivation* (New York: John Wiley & Sons, 1964).

20. D. H. Cook, "Teacher Morale: Symptoms, Diagnosis and Prescription," *Clearing House* (April 1979): 355–58; Educational Research Service, *Employee Absenteeism: A Summary of Research* (Arlington, Va.: Educational Research Service, 1980); and E. Klugman et al., *Too Many Pieces: A Study of Teacher Fragmentation in the Elementary School* (ERIC Report Ed–178–515). See also, Linda M. McNeil, "Contradictions of Control, Part 1: Administrators and Teachers," *Kappan* (January 1988): 333–39.

21. J. C. Stapleton, J. C. Croft, and R. G. Frankiewicz, "The Relationship between Teacher Brinkmanship and Teacher Job Satisfaction," *Planning and Changing* (Fall 1979): 157–68.

22. Ronald D. Sylvia and Tony Hutchinson, "What Makes Ms. Johnson Teach? A Study of Teacher Motivation," *Human Relations* (September 1985): 841–56.

23. Ibid., 841.

24. Mel E. Schnake, Stephen C. Bushardt, and Curran Spottswood, "Internal Work Motivation and Intrinsic Job Satisfaction: The Effects of Goal Clarity, Goal Difficulty, Participation in Goal Setting, and Task Complexity," *Group and Organization Studies* (June 1984): 201–19.

25. A. Werner, "Support for Teachers in Stress," *The Pointer* (Winter 1980): 54–60. For an extensive discussion of burnout, see Anthony Gary Dworkin, *Teacher Burnout in the Public Schools: Structural Causes and Consequences for Children* (Albany: State University of New York Press, 1987). See also C. Maslach, "Job Burnout: How People Cope," *Public Welfare* (1978): 56–58.

26. Dworkin, *Teacher Burnout in the Public Schools,* 25.

27. Edward F. Iwanicki and Richard L. Schwab, "A Cross Validation Study of the Maslach Burnout Inventory" (Paper presented at the annual meeting of the American Educational Research Association, Los Angeles, 1981).

28. D. Walsh, "Classroom Stress and Teacher Burnout," *Kappan* (December 1979): 253.

29. C. Maslach and S. Jackson, "The Measurement of Experienced Burnout" (Research report, Department of Psychology, University of California, Berkeley, 1979).

30. K. Dawani, "Teacher Burnout and Its Relation to Sex, Age, and Years of Experience," *National Forum of Educational Administration and Supervision,* (1987/1988): 99–110.

31. J. C. Quick and J. D. Quick, "Reducing Stress through Preventative Management," *Human Resources Management* (Fall 1979): 15–22; and Mibrey Wallin McLaughlin, R. Scott Pfeifer, Deborah Swanson-Owens, and Sylvia Yee, "Why Teachers Won't Teach," *Kappan* (February 1986): 420–26.

32. McLaughlin et al., "Why Teachers Won't Teach," 420.

33. Ibid., 421.

34. Ibid., 422.

35. Stuart Palonsky, *900 Shows a Year: A Look at Teaching from the Teacher's Side of the Desk* (New York: Random House, 1986).

36. Fred C. Feitler and Edward B. Tokar, "Teacher Stress: Sources, Symptoms and Job Satisfaction" (Paper presented at the annual meeting of the American Educational Research Association, Los Angeles, 1981).

37. D. J. Cichon and R. Koff, "Stress and Teaching," *NASSP Bulletin* (March 1980): 91–103; and R. Ginsberg et al., "Working Conditions in Urban Schools," *Urban Review* (1987): 3–27.

38. See D. W. Russell, E. Altmaier, and D. Van Velzen, "Job-Related Stress, Social Support, and Burnout among Classroom Teachers," *Journal of Applied Psychology* (May 1987): 269–74; and Jane S. Brissie, Kathleen V. Hoover-Dempsey, and Otto C. Bassler, "Individual, Situational Contributors to Teacher Burnout," *The Journal of Educational Research* (November/December 1988): 106–12.

39. Richard L. Schwab and Edward F. Iwanicki, "The Effect of Role Conflict and Role Ambiguity on Perceived Levels of Teacher Burnout" (Paper presented at the annual meeting of the American Educational Research Association, Los Angeles, 1981).

40. Mary B. Anderson and Edward F. Iwanicki, "The Burnout Syndrome and Its Relationship to Teacher Motivation" (Paper presented at the annual meeting of the American Educational Research Association, Los Angeles, 1981); and Daniel L. Duke, *School Leadership and Instructional Improvement* (New York: Random House, 1987), 17.

41. Sharon C. Conley, Samuel B. Bacharach, and Scott Bauer, "The School Work Environment and Teacher Career Dissatisfaction," *Educational Administration Quarterly* (February 1989): 58–81. See also, S. B. Bacharach, S. C. Bauer, and J. B. Shedd, *The Learning Workplace: The Conditions and Resources of Teaching* (Ithaca, N.Y.: Organizational Analysis and Practice, 1986).

42. McLaughlin et al., "Why Teachers Won't Teach."

43. See David A. Erlandson and Sandra Lee Bifano, "Teacher Empowerment: What Research Says to the Principal," *NASSP Bulletin* (December 1987): 31–36; and Buck Adams and Gerald D. Bailey, "School Is for Teachers: Enhancing the School Environment," *NASSP Bulletin* (January 1989); 44–48.

44. See J. F. Rugus and M. Martin, "The Principal and Staff Development: Countering the School Culture," *Clearing House* (September 1979): 27–31; Ann Lieberman and Lynne Miller, *Teachers, Their World, and Their Work: Implications for School Improvement* (Alexandria, Va.: Association for Supervision and Curriculum Development, 1984); K. K. Kumwalt, "Are We Improving or Undermining Teaching?" in L. N. Tanner, *Critical Issues in Curriculum: Eighty-Seventh Yearbook of the National Society for the Study of Education, Part I* (Chicago: University of Chicago Press, 1988): 148–74.

45. Seymour B. Sarason, *The Culture of the School and the Problem of Change* (Boston: Allyn & Bacon, 1971); Daniel C. Lortie, *Schoolteacher: A Sociological Study* (Chicago: University of Chicago Press, 1975); and Lieberman and Miller, *Teachers, Their World, and Their Work.*

46. P. M. Blau and W. R. Scott, *Formal Organizations: A Comparative Approach* (San Francisco: Chandler, 1962).

47. R. G. Corwin, "Professional Persons in Public Organizations," *Educational Administration Quarterly* (1965): 1–15; and Hoy and Miskel, *Educational Administration;* 156–58.

48. A. J. DeYoung, "Professionalism and Politics: Toward a More Realistic Assessment of the Issue," *Clearing House* (February 1980): 268–70.

49. M. S. Patton and C. Miskel, "Public School Districts' Bureaucracy Level and Teachers' Work Motivation Attitudes" (Paper presented at the annual meeting of the American Research Association, Washington, D.C., 1975). See also C. G. Miskel, R. Fevurly, and J. Stewart, "Organizational Structure and Processes, Perceived School Effectiveness, Loyalty, and Job Satisfaction," *Educational Administration Quarterly* (Fall 1979): 97–118.

50. Ted Schackmuth, "Creating Job Satisfaction in a Static Teacher Market." *Clearing House* (January 1979): 229–32.

51. J. S. Packard, "A Questionnaire Method for Measuring the Autonomy/Equality Norm" (Paper presented at the annual meeting of the American Educational Research Association, San Francisco, 1976).

52. Katherine Kasten, "Redesigning Teachers' Work," *Issues in Education* (Winter 1986): 272–86; and Lieberman and Miller, *Teachers, Their World, and Their Work.*

53. Yvonne Gold, "Stress Reduction Programs to Prevent Teacher Burnout," *Education* (Spring 1987): 338–40. See also, Walter H. Gmelch, "Educators' Response to Stress: Toward a Coping Taxonomy," *Journal of Educational Administration* (July 1988): 222–31.

54. A. Werner, "Support for Teachers in Stress." *The Pointer* (Winter 1980): 54–60.

55. A. G. Boudwyn, "The Open Meeting in a Confidential Forum for Employees," *Personnel Journal* (April 1977): 192–94.

56. Alfred S. Alschuler, *Teacher Burnout* (Washington, D.C.: National Education Association, 1980); and Patricia Hanley and Kevin J. Swick, *Stress and the Classroom Teacher* (Washington, D.C.: National Education Association, 1980).

57. E. M. Duncan, *Task and Employee-Oriented Styles of Behavior in Selected Minnesota School Administrators* (ERIC Report Ed–116–279). Also see Martha Leveilbe, "Characteristics of High and Low Teacher Morale" (Ed.D. diss., University of Southern California, 1981).

58. E. B. Ingle and R. E. Munsterman, "Relationship of Values to Group Satisfaction" (Paper presented at the annual meeting of the American Educational Research Association, New York, 1977); and Kathy Leslie, "Administrators Must Consider and Improve Teacher Satisfaction," *NASSP Bulletin* (January 1989): 20.

59. P. Degenfelder, "Managing Motivation," *Planning and Changing* (Spring 1979): 7–11.

60. Daniel L. Duke, Beverly K. Showers, and Michael Imber, "Teachers and Shared Decision Making: The Costs and Benefits of Involvement," *Educational Administration Quarterly* (Winter 1980): 93–106. See also Carnegie Foundation for the Advancement of Teaching, *Teacher Involvement in Decision Making: A State-by-State Profile* (New York: Carnegie Foundation, 1988).

61. Dennis W. Spuck, "Reward Structures in the Public Schools," *Educational Administration Quarterly* (1974): 18–34.

62. Susan Moore Johnson, "Incentives for Teachers: What Motivates, What Matters," *Educational Administration Quarterly* (Summer 1986): 54–79.

63. Susan J. Rosenholtz, "Political Myths about Education Reform: Lessons from Research on Teaching," *Kappan* (January 1985): 349–58.

64. Johnson, "Incentives for Teachers," 54.

65. H. Jerome Freiberg, "Career Ladders: Messages Gleaned from Experiences," *Journal of Teacher Education* (July–August 1987): 49.

66. For interesting discussions regarding career ladder plans, see Lynn M. Cornett, "Trends and Emerging Issues in Career Ladder Plans," *Educational Leadership* (November 1985): 6–10; and Bettty Malen and Ann Weaver Hart, "Career Ladder Reform: A Multi-Level Analysis of Initial Efforts," *Educational Evaluation and Policy Analysis* (Spring 1987): 9–23.

67. Samuel B. Bacharach and Sharon C. Conley, "Education Reform: A Managerial Agenda," *Kappan* (May 1986): 641.

68. For concise discussions of teacher incentives, see Cresap, McCormack, and Paget, *Teacher Incentives: A Tool for Effective Management* (Reston, Va.: National Associations of Elementary School Principals, School Administrators, and Secondary School Principals, 1984); Pedro Reyes, "Schools Must Match Incentives to Value Structure," *NASSP Bulletin* (October 1989): 133–34; and Lloyd Campbell and John Williamson, "Principals' Perceptions and Control of Teacher Stress," *NASSP Bulletin* (February 1989): 123–26.

69. C. John Tarter, James R. Bliss, and Wayne K. Hoy, "School Characteristics and Faculty Trust in Secondary Schools," *Educational Administration Quarterly* (August 1989): 294–308.

70. Frederick L. Redefer, "Factors that Affect Teacher Morale," *Nation's Schools* (February 1959): 59–62.

71. Harold Leiman, "A Study of Teacher Attitudes and Morale as Related to Participation in Administration" (Ph.D. diss., New York University, 1961). For more recent research on this point, see Michael Buckley, "The Relationship of Philosophical Orientation, Participation in Decision Making, and Degree of Fulfillment of Expectations about Participation in Decision Making to Elementary School Teachers' Attitudes toward Leaders, Leader-Teacher Interaction and Membership in the Organization" (Ph.D. diss., University of Connecticut, 1981); and Harry Bernstein, "Supervisors Can Wreck Power Sharing if They're Ignored," *Los Angeles Times* (July 25, 1989): part IV, p. 5.

72. Gail T. Schneider, "Teacher Involvement in Decision Making: Zones of Acceptance, Decision Conditions, and Job Satisfaction," *Journal of Research and Development in Education* (Fall 1984): 25–32; and Norman Benson and Patricia Malone, "Teachers' Beliefs about Shared Decision Making and Work Alienation," *Education* (Spring 1987): 244–51.

73. Wayne K. Hoy and B. L. Brown, "Leadership Behavior of Principals and the Zone of Acceptance of Elementary Teachers," *Journal of Educational Administration* (March 1988): 23–38.

74. Pedro Reyes, "The Relationship of Autonomy in Decision Making to Commitment to Schools and Job Satisfaction: A Comparison between Public School Teachers and Mid-Level Administrators," *Journal of Research and Development in Education* (Winter 1989): 62–69.

75. Richard A. Gorton, *School Leadership and Administration: Important Concepts, Case Studies, and Simulations* (Dubuque, Iowa: Wm. C. Brown Company Publishers, 1987), chap. 1.

76. C. E. Blocker and R. C. Richardson, "Twenty-Five Years of Morale Research—A Critical Review," *Journal of Educational Sociology* (January 1963): 200–210. For more recent research on this point, see Miskel and Ogawa, "Work Motivation."

77. Thomas W. George, "The Principal and Collective Negotiations," in *The School Principal and the Law*, ed. Ralph Stern (Topeka, Kans.: National Organization on Legal Problems of Education, 1978).

78. Jo Ann Mazzarella, "Collective Bargaining: How Does It Change the Principal's Role?" *NASSP Bulletin* (May 1985): 75–81.

79. William G. Webster, Sr. *Effective Collective Bargaining in Public Education* (Ames: Iowa State University Press, 1988).

80. Benjamin Epstein, *The Principal's Role in Collective Negotiations between Teachers and School Boards* (Washington, D.C.: The National Association of Secondary School Principals, 1965), 6.

81. See, for example, Department of Elementary School Principals, *Professional Negotiations and the Principalship* (Washington, D.C.: Department of Elementary School Principals, 1969), 126; see also "Proposed 1970 Resolutions," *National Elementary Principal* (February 1970): 64–65.

82. See John A. Thompson, "The Principal's Role in Collective Negotiations between Teachers and School Boards" (Ph. D. diss., University of Wisconsin, 1968). For a somewhat more positive but generally similar perception of the role of the principal in collective negotiations, see Stephen Milton Poort, "Attitudes of Selected Kansas Superintendents, Principals, and Teachers toward the Involvement of Principals in a Collective Negotiations Environment" (Ed.D. diss., University of Kansas, 1968).

83. H. L. Schachter, "Win-Win Bargaining: A New Spirit in School Negotiations?" *Journal of Collective Negotiations in the Public Sector* 18, no. 1 (1989): 1–8.

84. William G. Webster, Sr., *Effective Collective Bargaining,* 187.

85. Jo Ann Mazzarella, "Collective Bargaining: How Does It Change the Principal's Role," *NASSP Bulletin* (May 1985): 75–81.

86. Gregory Benson, *The Principal and Contract Management* (ERIC Report Ed–175–151).

87. For the total report of this study, see Frank W. Lutz and Seymour Evans, *The Union and Principal Leadership in New York City Schools* (ERIC Report Ed–029–400). For later studies on the topic, see Susan Moore Johnson, "Collective Bargaining and Leadership," *R and D Perspectives,* University of Oregon (Summer 1981): 3.

88. Jerome E. Brendel, "The Hardest Part of Negotiations," *School Business Affairs* (October 1987): 11–12.

89. Delbert K. Clear, "Teacher Grievance Procedure," in *Encyclopedia of School Administration and Supervision,* ed. R. A. Gorton, G. T. Schneider, and J. C. Fisher (Phoenix, Ariz. Oryx Press, 1988): 275–76.

90. Marc Gaswirth, *Administering the Negotiated Agreement* (Trenton, N.J.: New Jersey School Boards Association, 1980), chap. 1; see also Clear, "Teacher Grievance Procedure."

91. Gaswirth, *Administering the Negotiated Agreement,* chap. 2.

92. Alan M. Glassman and James Belasco, "Grievance Procedures in Public Education: An Empirical Case Study" (Paper presented at the annual meeting of the American Educational Research Association, 1972). Also see Estella Gahala, "An Ethnographic Study of Grievance Handling Procedures by Principals and Teachers' Association Representatives" (Ph.D. diss., Northwestern University 1980).

93. Adapted in part from William Smith, "Coping with Grievances: Guidelines for Administrators," *NASSP Bulletin* (May 1981): 80–83; and Clear, "Teacher Grievance Procedure."

94. Kenneth T. Murray and Barbara A. Murray, "Principals Are Evaluated during Teacher Grievances Procedures," *NASSP Bulletin* (October 1989): 123–24.

95. Samuel L. Dolnick, "What to Do in the Event of a Strike," in *The School Principal and the Law,* ed. R. D. Stern (Topeka, Kans.: National Organization on Legal Problems in Education, 1978); Robert Heller, "The Principal's Role in Planning for a Teacher's Strike," *NASSP Bulletin* (May 1978): 98–105; *Contingency Planning for Teacher Strikes* (Arlington, Va.: Educational Research Service, 1976).

96. J. M. Gonroff, "The Effects of a Teachers' Strike on Principal Behavior," *Texas Study of Secondary Education Research Journal* (Fall 1979–80): 45–48.

97. See Patricia Smith and Russell Baker, "An Alternative Form of Collective Bargaining," *Kappan* (April 1986): 605–7; Burton M. Nygren, "Union/Adminstrator Cooperation that Works," *ERS Spectrum* (Spring 1988): 12–14; and Louis Peck, "Today's Teacher Unions Are Looking Well Beyond Collective Bargaining," *The American School Board Journal* (July 1988): 32–36.

98. Susan Moore Johnson and Niall C. W. Nelson, "Teaching Reform in an Active Voice," *Kappan* (April 1987): 591–97.

10

. . . . .

Staff Evaluation and Supervision

■

Staff evaluation and supervision represent two interdependent means for improving the professional resources of a school. Staff evaluation is a process whereby the strengths and limitations of an individual or group are identified and defined. Supervision is a process designed to capitalize on the strengths and correct any weaknesses of an individual or group.

Evaluation and supervision are interdependent, in that one cannot usually achieve maximum effectiveness without the other.[1] Staff evaluation without supervision can lead to anxiety, frustration, and resistance on the part of the recipient of the evaluation. The individual or group may have been informed through evaluation about certain areas which need to be improved but, in the absence of appropriate follow-up supervision, may not be able to remedy the deficiencies. On the other hand, staff supervision without adequate prior evaluation tends to lack focus and is often misdirected. In such a situation, the individual (or group) receives assistance which is not based on an accurate diagnosis of need; as a result, the recipients are not likely to accept or profit from the supervision.

In recent years, the educational reform movement has focused considerable attention on teacher performance; as a result, evaluation and supervision processes are undergoing some important changes.[2] For example, according to Joan Buttram and Bruce Wilson, associates at Research for Better Schools, progressive districts are

1. Linking evaluation systems to research on effective teacher practices.
2. Providing improved training for evaluators.
3. Holding administrators more accountable for conducting evaluations.
4. Using evaluation-identified teacher deficiencies to focus staff development.
5. Making teachers active partners in the evaluation process.[3]

The sections that follow discuss various aspects of staff evaluation and supervision; the next chapter focuses on instructional leadership in greater depth.

PHILOSOPHY, GOALS, AND OBJECTIVES

A comprehensive program of staff evaluation should "include the school district's philosophy of staff evaluation, evaluation goals, and specific evaluation objectives. The main purpose of providing this information is to make clear to all concerned why the school district believes staff evaluation is important and what the district is attempting to achieve."[4]

A recent study conducted by Arthur Wise and his colleagues concluded that:

1. A successful teacher evaluation system must suit the educational goals, management style, conception of teaching, and community values of the school district.
2. The school district should decide the main purpose of its teacher evaluation system and then match the process to the purpose.
3. Philosophical commitment to and resources for evaluation produce more useful information than do checklists and procedures.
4. To sustain resource commitments and political support, teacher evaluation must be seen to have utility, which in turn depends on the efficient use of resources to achieve reliability and cost-effectiveness.
5. Teacher involvement and responsibility improve the quality of teacher evaluation.[5]

They further contend that districts' philosophies and objectives need to differentiate between bureaucratic and professional conceptions of teacher evaluation. In *bureaucratic* models, the district (1) relies primarily on administrators to design and operate a uniform teacher evaluation process; (2) bases evaluation on generalized criteria such as generic teaching skills or other context-free teaching behaviors; (3) recognizes a fixed set of learning outcomes; and (4) treats all teachers alike.[6]

In general, bureaucratic models are designed to monitor conformance with uniform criteria of effective teaching. A *professional* orientation, on the other hand, (1) involves teachers in the development and operation of the teacher evaluation process; (2) bases evaluation on professional standards of practice that are client-oriented; (3) recognizes multiple teaching strategies and learning outcomes; and (4) treats teachers differently according to their teaching assignments, stages of development, and classroom goals.[7] Thus, Arthur Wise and Linda Darling-Hammond see professional evaluation as clinical, practice-oriented, and analytic. The implication of these findings is that evaluation without supervision is only meeting bureaucratic purposes and does not meet the professional needs of the teacher.

Clearly, the evaluation and supervision processes which administrators and supervisors use should be related to their districts' philosophies. If a district adopts an evaluation philosophy which embodies a professional perspective, the supervisory arrangements and resources needed differ considerably from a district which views evaluation as strictly a routine, bureaucratic, compliance process. Unfortunately, in too many instances, although a professional perspective is asserted, the resources available and behaviors exhibited do not support the publicly attested philosophy.

PROBLEMS AND ISSUES OF STAFF EVALUATION AND SUPERVISION

Staff evaluation/supervision programs are perceived by many teachers and administrators as a mixed blessing.[8] Most teachers and administrators accept evaluation and supervision as inevitable and potentially valuable, but many question their usefulness and value in practice because of the presence of certain basic problems and issues that we discuss shortly.[9] These problems and issues do not, of course, exist in all schools, but wherever they are prevalent, they impair the usefulness of the staff evaluation/supervision program. The point that needs to be emphasized, however, is that such problems are not inevitable or irresolvable. Administrators can, by concentrating on developing a better understanding of the problems and issues associated with staff evaluation and supervision, and by initiating needed reforms, maintain an effective program of staff evaluation and supervision. (Moreover, the public's emphasis on school accountability undoubtedly requires school administrators to give a high priority to maintaining such a program.) After reflecting on and discussing the ideas presented in the following sections, school administrators and other concerned parties should view the various problems and issues as challenges and opportunities for leadership.

PURPOSES

The main purposes of the district evaluation program are (1) to identify needs for supervisory assistance, and (2) to reach a determination about whether or not a staff member should be retained, nonrenewed, or dismissed.

In the eyes of many teachers, these objectives are incompatible and in direct conflict. To achieve the first objective, staff members should be open, candid, and cooperative about revealing or confirming their limitations with their administrator. On the other hand, however, if staff members want to be retained or promoted, they naturally want to be seen in the best light; it may be to their disadvantage to willingly reveal their limitations or confirm the perceptions of the administrator about specific deficiencies.

Several consequences can result from this conflict in the purposes of the district's staff evaluation program. First of all, achieving the objective of identifying needs for supervisory assistance is impaired because of the reluctance of staff members to identify their weaknesses, for fear that they will not be retained or promoted. And, a second consequence of conflict in the purposes of the district evaluation program is that the evaluation process has a poor image in the eyes of many teachers. They view the process as threatening, punitive, of little help, and not in their best interests. Consequently, they are often not very receptive to attempts by administrators to evaluate them. Similarly, evaluators share these concerns regarding the separation of the formative and summative tasks.[10] Yet, the fact is that in most schools administrators are placed in the position of conducting both evaluations.

As a means of elaborating on the issue of these role conflicts, Howard Knoff presented an interesting discussion of the different role relationships which exist within supervision/evaluation (hierarchical), consultation (collegial, nonhierarchical), and counseling (personal problem solving) processes.[11] He maintained that each process, while directly related to the overall evaluation program, demands unique skills and that supervisors should not engage in activities for which they are not trained. Knoff concluded that supervisors should be wary of confounding these three models and that they should not hesitate to involve others in evaluation programs when appropriate.

If administrators are to avoid problems, they must concentrate on resolving the apparent conflict in purposes in many staff evaluation programs. One possible solution to resolving the conflict may be to separate, to the extent possible, the main purposes through the use of separate personnel. If teacher evaluation is designed to serve both supportive (improvement, enhancement, growth) and decision-making (hiring, retention, advancement) purposes, it is not likely that a single evaluator can simultaneously perform the collaborative role of assisting and the detached role of decision making.[12]

Instead of using one person as both the supervisor and the evaluator, some suggest that the evaluation program involve a wide array of individuals in the various stages of the program. For example, Joyce Epstein noted that, while principals and curriculum specialists have long been recognized as appropriate evaluators of teachers, suggestions have been made to involve teachers in self-appraisal and peer-appraisal.[13]

SUMMATIVE AND FORMATIVE PROCESSES

No uniform process of staff evaluation and supervision could operate in all school districts. Yet, the staff evaluation and supervision processes in most districts are formally designed; that is, their purposes, procedures, and schedules are usually officially established and approved by the school board. Generally the official evaluation program includes both formative and summative purposes. The main purpose of formative or professional supervision is to identify needs for teacher improvement; whereas, the primary purpose of summative evaluation is to reach a determination on whether staff, particularly new members, should be retained, nonrenewed, or dismissed.[14] These conclusions are realized through a process of evaluating the staff on the extent to which they meet criteria for effectiveness, as previously defined by the district and through the development of a process of supervision which has as its purpose helping an individual to improve. Thus, in an ideal sense the evaluation and supervision processes become cyclical with one logically following the other.

Unfortunately, the typical evaluation program tends to emphasize primarily a summative approach. The evaluation process is usually initiated in the late spring or early fall in every building in the district and is conducted by the principal, perhaps with the assistance of another administrator or supervisor. The principal visits the classroom of each staff member who is to be evaluated during the year, and then holds an individual follow-up conference to present and discuss observations and conclusions. During the conference, the principal reviews with the staff member the district's rating scale on which the principal has recorded the evaluation of the strengths and weaknesses of the individual. The rating scale, along with comments and recommendations, forms the basis for identifying needs for supervision and for reaching a determination on whether or not a staff member should be retained for the following year.

When used professionally, the summative conference becomes a goal-setting conference for the remainder of the year and for the forthcoming school year. Therefore, based on the principal's assessment of the teacher's performance, the principal and teacher identify and determine appropriate short-term and long-term goals and objectives for the teacher to achieve. These goals and objectives thus become the foundation of the teacher's developmental supervision plan.[15]

Critics of the pure summative evaluation process contend that all too often most of the conclusions drawn by principals are based on the "principals' ratings of teachers that result from infrequent (sometimes just *one*) observations in teachers' classrooms; on cronyism, patronage, or other prejudicial decisions; or on seniority, credentials, and accumulated credits that do not involve the evaluation of teaching skills."[16] In addition, studies have indicated that teachers receive relatively little valuable feedback about their performance from principals; when they do receive feedback based on a single in-class visit once every two or three years, they often view the feedback as useless.[17]

STAFF INVOLVEMENT

A major complaint of many teachers is that they have not been involved to any significant degree in the development of the district staff evaluation program, particularly as it relates to criteria and the process of evaluation. As a result, the evaluative criteria and procedures designed by administrators in such districts do not reflect teachers' ideas. In these situations, professional staff members are being evaluated by criteria and a process on which they had little to say and about which they may disagree. Because teachers possess knowledge which would be beneficial to the development of a total evaluation program and the outcomes of the program are personally and professionally relevant to them, Carl Ashbaugh and Katherine Kasten have concluded that teachers should be integrally involved in the development and subsequent implementation of the evaluation program if they are to accept it.[18]

Furthermore, as Gene Huddle noted, "teacher involvement in the evaluation program creates a sense of ownership and improves the legitimacy, focus, and meaning of the activity."[19] One of the benefits of staff involvement in developing evaluation criteria and procedures is a supportive climate where school administrators can suggest improvements to faculty members. If staff members have participated in the development of the evaluation criteria and process, the likelihood is increased that many of them will accept or be receptive to both. Also, there is evidence that teacher organizations play an important role in the design and ongoing implementation of the evaluation process. Arthur Wise and Linda Darling-Hammond found that teacher participation has taken various forms such as "involvement in joint oversight committees, union appointments of teachers who assist in the evaluation process, and consultation between top administration officials and union leaders."[20] Furthermore, they found that the shift from an adversarial to a participatory approach required administrators to share their power but gave them more freedom and legitimate authority to implement decisions when they were made jointly.

Thus, to facilitate acceptance of the district's evaluation program and to improve the program, staff members should be involved in the formulation, assessment, and appropriate revision of the total district evaluation program, including the definition of evaluative purposes, criteria, and procedures. The key word in this recommendation is *involvement;* the administration and the school board should retain final authority in these matters.

To implement this idea, administrators should establish a standing committee of the faculty to examine the present evaluation program and to suggest revisions. The committee should be composed of nontenured as well as tenured teachers, and administrators should chair the committee. Its recommendations would probably be only advisory to the central office, but if its members did their homework, the committee could be a powerful force for changing and improving the staff evaluation program in the district. Part of its function should be to secure periodic and systematic feedback from the entire staff on the perceived strengths and weaknesses of the evaluation program, with recommendations for improvement. The alternative to encouraging this kind of voluntary involvement could be required involvement negotiated by the teachers through collective bargaining.

SELF-ASSESSMENT

The primary emphasis in many school districts' evaluation programs has been on external evaluation. The implicit assumption seems to be that teachers are either unwilling or unable to participate in a program of self-evaluation. Possibly administrators in most districts believe that the perceptions of teachers about their strengths and limitations are not important. However, with the onset of emphasis on the professionalization of teaching, attention has been placed on the ability of educators to engage in self-assessment or reflective practice for professional growth.[21]

The basic premise of self-assessment is that all teachers to be evaluated by the administrator should be given the opportunity to evaluate themselves on the criteria used by the district. If the other recommendations in this chapter are implemented, then the administration should have the trust and confidence of the teachers, necessary prerequisites for any program of self-evaluation. Inservice training to help teachers become more competent and objective in analyzing their behavior may also be necessary.

Ideally, teachers would be continuously engaged in self-evaluation, but formal efforts in this regard should begin at and proceed through the same time period during which administrators are conducting evaluations of the teachers. At the end of the self-evaluation process, teachers' evaluative perceptions should be shared with the administrators who, in turn, should discuss their perceptions with the teachers. As a result of this sharing of evaluative data, the principal or the teacher, or both, may decide to revise their original perceptions and conclusions or engage in further investigation and analysis.

To engage in self-assessment, teachers may find audiotapes or videotapes provide useful classroom data for analysis. Jerome Freiberg provided a number of practical suggestions for ways teachers might analyze their audiotapes or videotapes.[22] In each application, as teachers become more comfortable with viewing their teaching through different perceptual lens, their analytic skills improve and they begin to investigate the less obvious aspects of their teaching skills. Consequently, as teachers' self-assessment skills become more sophisticated, supervisors need to alter their interaction patterns.

The potential advantages resulting from self-evaluation as a parallel activity to external evaluation are (1) a lessening of defensiveness by teachers regarding evaluation, and (2) the identification of areas in need of improvement and/or strengths which external evaluation might not ascertain. However, whether teachers would be willing and able to engage in a program of self-evaluation for professional growth would depend on their degree of trust and confidence in the administration, and the extent to which the administration has provided in-service training for the teachers to help them become more competent and objective in analyzing their own behavior. If these conditions can be met, then self-evaluation by teachers can and should be a valuable activity for teachers and administrators alike.[23]

EVALUATION CRITERIA

The selection of the criteria for staff evaluation is undoubtedly one of the most important decisions in designing an evaluation program. The criteria are standards against which the teachers are to be evaluated and can usually be found in the district's instrument for evaluating members of the staff.

Many teachers question a district's evaluation form; they ask to what extent are the criteria presented based on personal preference and to what degree are they based on research supporting their importance in teaching effectiveness and student learning? Although the answer to these questions may vary depending on the school district, an examination of numerous evaluation forms reveals that the selection of criteria in many districts is based more on personal preference than on any research evidence or theoretical foundation.[24]

Part of the problem is that administrators who select the staff evaluation criteria frequently have not adequately investigated the research on teacher effectiveness. However, another equally important aspect is the likelihood that uniform criteria penalize teachers with different personalities who can teach effectively with different classes, using different methods and/or materials, under different classroom conditions. Lee Shulman contends that

> research on effective teaching has been translated into multiple-choice tests for teachers or checklists used by administrators to rate teachers according to an unchanging scale of uniform behaviors. . . . On the face of it, it seems absurd. How could someone go in with a generic rating scale, someone whose own training may be in industrial arts or in history, and make sense of the teaching in a Spanish class, or a trigonometry class, or a poetry class?[25]

Thus, there should either be different evaluation criteria for different teachers and situations, or the criteria should emphasize the outcomes of teaching more than the personality of the teacher or the process of teaching.[26]

In any regard, administrators need to realize that, to a large extent, the criteria used in the district evaluation program are probably based more on personal preference than on research or theory. The disadvantages of this subjective approach to teacher evaluation were pointed out by Donald Medley who found that, "teachers who looked most effective to supervisors were not actually the most effective in helping pupils learn."[27]

To lessen the perception of subjectivity, school administrators need to investigate the research on teacher effectiveness with appropriate staff involvement and then to propose to the central office a revision in staff evaluation criteria based more on research and less on personal preference. This does not mean that the criteria cannot reflect some philosophical orientation, but the majority of the criteria should not rest on a subjective foundation.

For the most part, research has not been very productive in identifying the characteristics of effective teachers. As Benjamin Bloom has noted, "In general, the relationship between teacher characteristics and student learning has typically been represented by correlations of less than +.20. [Therefore] we may conclude that the characteristics of teachers have little to do with the learning of students."[28] On the other hand, there have been some major breakthroughs when the focus has been on the behavior of teachers, meriting the administrator's consideration.[29]

For example, several studies have shown that effective teachers demonstrate the following behaviors to a far greater degree than do ineffective teachers.

1. Set high expectations for student achievement.
2. Ascertain students' current skill levels and knowledge and understanding levels before establishing learning objectives and assigning work.
3. Set and articulate specific learning goals for each lesson.
4. Plan carefully and thoroughly for each lesson, taking into consideration students' needs and involving them in planning when appropriate and feasible.
5. Make presentations at the most appropriate level of difficulty for most pupils.
6. Assign tasks to students appropriate to their ability levels so that chances of success are high and failures low.
7. Spend more time than ineffective teachers on the actual task of teaching. Spend more time structuring the lesson, giving directions, clarifying what needs to be learned, and how best to perform the work and illustrating how to do the assigned work.
8. Assess regularly student progress.
9. Keep students focused on and engaged in the task at hand.
10. Provide regular feedback to students which informs them of their progress and indicates how they can improve.
11. Reinforce correct student behavior and responses with positive rewards, for example, teacher praise.[30]

Although it might appear that this list of behaviors describes the "super teacher," such is not the case. As William Salganik has emphasized, "Contrary to popular myths, most teachers at schools that are effective are not charismatic figures generating unforgettable experiences. They are simply hard-working, organized teachers moving crisply through a well-planned day."[31]

Most of the behaviors of effective teachers identified in this section have been categorized under the term, *direct instruction,* which stresses being well-organized and task-oriented and has a very strong orientation to "drill and practice."[32] However, direct instruction may not be appropriate for all kinds of teaching situations. Penelope Peterson states that the central question is, "For what educational outcomes is direct instruction most effective, and for what kinds of students?"[33] She believes that direct instruction is most effective if one intends to teach basic skills, but it may not be as effective in teaching, for example, inquiry skills. Also, she asserts that direct instruction may be less effective in working with high-ability students who may need less direction, than with average and low ability students. Perhaps Ullik Rouk expressed it best: "Teaching strategies and methods that work best with all pupils all the time simply don't exist."[34] Nevertheless, the research reviewed for this section strongly suggests that the teaching behaviors previously identified are associated with effective teaching in most situations.

One of the more important variables research has shown to be associated with increased learning is "active learning time" or ALT.[35] Often referred to as time-on-task, ALT is the time that a student actually is engaged in learning new material.[36] Therefore, teaching styles or behaviors that involve the student in the task of learning and keep the student engaged are likely to be effective in increasing student learning.[37] In implementing ALT, teachers must avoid extreme teaching styles. As one researcher noted, "Perhaps this teacher (one whom fosters the highest levels of academic engagement) actually is undermining academic achievement because, with such high engagement, students are becoming cognitively fatigued."[38] Pressing the issue further, Herbert Walberg indicates that "we can help students learn by increasing time-on-task, but we can achieve more learning if we expect 'productive time,' where students engage in lessons adjusted to their differences in learning rate and background knowledge."[39]

While it might appear that the teacher's behavior is the only critical variable associated with effective teaching (and clearly, it is the most important variable), the teacher's attitude about the subject matter and toward students is also very important. Teachers who believe strongly that instructing students in the curriculum of the school is basic to their role and who believe that students under their charge are capable of learning new skills or subject matter are more likely to be successful in increasing student learning.[40] That this type of teacher held students' interest is supported by Gordon Sabine's study which found that students rated an educator's two most important characteristics as: (1) the teacher was demanding, and (2) the teacher cared.[41] Apparently most students want a teacher who not only challenges them and makes them work but also is interested in them as individuals. Certainly, a teacher's attitude about teaching and students is a crucial variable likely to influence a teacher's predisposition and decision to utilize those behaviors previously identified as associated with effective teaching.[42]

The studies reviewed for this section uncovered a number of research-based indicators of staff effectiveness that should be considered for inclusion in a district's staff evaluation criteria and evaluation instruments. In developing and deciding on these criteria, administrators should avoid including any high-inference variables. For example, a high-inference variable such as teacher enthusiasm, requires considerable judgement by the observer as to whether or not the behavior has occurred; low-inference behaviors require little or no inference by the observer regarding whether or not the particular teaching behavior has occurred. Although the criteria for evaluating teaching should contain as few high-inference behaviors as possible (because of the resulting problem that observations of the same teacher behavior may lead to different inferences), high-inference variables can be useful in staff evaluation if they are further analyzed into more precise measures.[43]

In addition to the importance of the relevance and validity of the criteria for staff evaluation, the instrument or rating scale used to apply the criteria to teacher performance should possess the following characteristics: it should be (1) reliable, that is, responses to it should be consistent; (2) reasonable in cost; (3) efficient to use and easy to understand; and (4) diagnostic in nature, that is, provide information to help the teacher to improve rather than information confined to identifying weaknesses.[44] The last factor is exceedingly important because a teacher's receptivity and perception of the evaluation's value are likely to be limited if the evaluation instrument only makes judgments about performance without helping the teacher to understand how to improve.[45]

Based on our examination of many school district evaluation instruments, major improvements are clearly needed. However, school administrators need to realize that bringing about changes in staff evaluation criteria and evaluation instruments will not be an easy task. This is particularly true where central office administrators and supervisors view the selection of criteria and instruments as their responsibility, and where they have considerable emotional investments in the use of existing criteria and instruments. Nevertheless, a major premise of this chapter is that teachers deserve to be evaluated by criteria and instruments directly related to their effectiveness in the classroom, and school administrators should exert leadership toward the achievement of that objective.

COMMUNICATION

In many schools the purposes, criteria, and process of staff evalution are not adequately communicated to the staff.[46] It is not unusual in those schools for the staff, particularly new members, to be uninformed about the criteria and process of the district evaluation program until they actually encounter them. Although most staff members are aware that the process of evaluation involves observation by an evaluator and a follow-up conference to discuss the results of the evaluation, questions about the nature, time, and frequency of observations and conferences are often not resolved. And, in many cases, teachers are observed for the purpose of evaluation without their possessing first-hand knowledge of the criteria on which they are to be evaluated.

Poor communication about the evaluation process can result in uncertainty and anxiety on the part of staff members. Not knowing exactly what to expect from the evaluation, they may not participate cooperatively in the process or accept the administrator's findings. Therefore, administrators should not assume that staff members are familiar with or will remember from year to year the evaluation purposes, criteria, and procedures. At the very least, new members of the staff should be informed of these elements before evaluation proceeds.

The most desirable approach would be for administrators to schedule a meeting, after the first few weeks of school, with all staff members who are to be evaluated during the year and review with them the purposes, criteria, and procedures to be used in the evaluation program. At that meeting certain points can be emphasized or clarified, and questions can be answered. The objectives of such a meeting would be to develop understanding and acceptance of the evaluation program, and to relieve anxiety and apprehension, particularly on the part of new staff members.

EVALUATION EXPERTISE

In recent years, teachers have become better prepared and more specialized in their subject matter and teaching methodology. Many teachers now question whether administrators, who typically have been out of the classrom for several years and may have specialized in only one aspect of the curriculum as undergraduates, have the expertise to evaluate them. As a result, administrators have sometimes experienced difficulty in evaluating teachers and, in particular, in getting them to accept administrative judgments about their strengths and weaknesses.[47]

We cannot overemphasize the importance of expertise in evaluating a professional staff. If administrators are to competently evaluate teachers and obtain acceptance of their findings, they need to be knowledgeable and expert in the various areas of curriculum, teaching methods, learning theory, and other facets of the educational program. They should also capitalize on and utilize as much as possible the expertise possessed by department heads, unit leaders, and other sources of assistance within the school and school district.[48] Staff evaluation today can no longer depend on the expertise of one individual, such as the principal.

Some people may believe that school administrators possess all of the expertise they need to evaluate teachers. However, we believe that school administrators cannot conduct evaluations with maximal effectiveness by themselves, and that the staff evaluation program is improved if they capitalize on the expertise of others in the school or school district.

The specific approach we recommend is that the principal organize a staff evaluation team, composed of the principal, the central office subject supervisor, and appropriate department heads or unit leaders.[49] The latter individuals normally possess specialized expertise in the curriculum and teaching methods of a particular subject area and should complement the administrator, who is a generalist and whose in-depth knowledge of those aspects is likely to be limited. Administrators have much to contribute to the evaluation process, particularly in the areas of class management and total-school perspective; and of course, they are responsible for making the final evaluation decisions at the building level.

Even though the team approach to evaluation has much to recommend it, problems may arise depending on the purposes for which administrators use the team. If they want the team to evaluate teachers for personnel decisions as well as for staff improvement, they are likely to experience difficulty in securing the cooperation of department heads (or unit leaders) and central office supervisors. Both will probably be interested in staff evaluation for improvement, but they may not want to participate in personnel decisions for fear of losing the confidence of the teachers with whom they work. Paradoxically, if administrators use the team only for the staff improvement objective, they lose their expertise for the other purpose of staff evaluation. There is no easy answer to the problem, and its final resolution depends on administrators' assessments of conditions in their own schools and school districts. However, it seems likely that there will be difficulties in utilizing the same personnel and approach for both objectives of staff evaluation.

DUE PROCESS

The two types of due process in staff evaluation are procedural and substantive.[50] *Procedural* due process means, at the minimum, that before any adverse action is taken against a staff member (such as dismissal or denial of salary increase), the individual is given written notification and documentation of the reasons for the action and is provided an opportunity to present evidence that might reduce the severity of the action or eliminate its need entirely.[51] It also usually means that before adverse action is taken, the individual must be given sufficient opportunity to remedy the identified weaknesses, and the supervisor must make every reasonable effort to help the person accomplish this goal.[52]

Substantive due process means that the criteria used in evaluating an individual are not arbitrary and are directly related to the job.[53] Although no complete record documents the extent to which schools follow standards of due process, when teacher dismissal cases reach the courts, judges rule more often against schools that have failed to follow standards of due process than for any other reason. As a result of collective bargaining,[54] more and more school districts are being required to provide due process. While schools are legally required to provide due process to tenured teachers, the law regarding nontenured teachers has not been conclusively established. Be that as it may, due process is clearly consistent with professional standards, even if it is not legally required, and should be considered by the school administrator for nontenured as well as tenured teachers. Thus, due process should be followed in the evaluation of all staff members, nontenured as well as tenured, whenever it appears that an evaluation may result in an adverse personnel decision for an individual.

The main purpose of due process is to ensure that an individual has received a fair and just decision. In staff evaluation, this means that the criteria must be legitimate, the individual must be informed of shortcomings, must be given sufficient opportunity to correct them, and must be provided with adequate supervision and assistance to do so. These four conditions (legitimate criteria, notification of weakness, sufficient time to correct weakness, and adequate supervision) represent professionally sound practices—regardless of whether or not they are legally required. Neglect by the administrator of any of these aspects may not be prohibited by law for nontenured teachers, but it is surely a professional inadequacy. Administrators who insist that due process be followed in all staff evaluations not only avoid possible legal entanglements at a later date but also meet high professional standards in regard to staff evaluation.

The basic due process procedures recommended for all staff members being considered for dismissal are the following:

1. Written identification of strengths and diagnosis of weaknesses with specific recommendations on how to improve. The diagnosis and recommendation for improvement should be given to the staff member in sufficient time before any final personnel ratings or decisions are made for the year so that the individual has adequate opportunity to correct or ameliorate the weaknesses.

2. Intensive follow-up supervisory assistance by the administrator and others working with the administrator, to help the staff member improve. The administrator should maintain written documentation on all efforts made to improve the staff member and the latter's response to those efforts. Both kinds of information are needed if, at a later date, the staff member should challenge a decision of the school district regarding a dismissal or salary consideration.

3. Advance notice in writing to the staff member of the reasons for an adverse personnel decision, and notification of an opportunity to have a hearing with the administrator to review the decision and the reasons for it.

4. A hearing with the administrator, if requested, to review an adverse personnel decision with the opportunity to appeal the administrator's decision to an immediate superior and, if necessary, to the school board and to the courts.

5. Publication to all staff members of the previous four procedures. A major principle of due process is that those affected by an adverse decision should be informed of their right to these procedures. Although an administrator may be willing to adopt these procedures if requested, due process does not become a reality in an evaluation program unless administrators take the initiative to explain these procedures to all staff members and emphasize their availability.

Some administrators may regard the use of these recommended procedures as controversial, particularly as they apply to nontenured teachers. Many administrators may believe that due process is awkward, time-consuming, and very inefficient; and that they should provide no more due process, at least for nontenured teachers, than required by law. Yet, some boards of education have been accused of constitutional violations due to their arbitrary and capricious nonrenewal of nontenured personnel.[55] Therefore, the right to due process in the case of a decision perceived as unfair or invalid is basic to our democratic heritage and should cause administrators no overwhelming concern if their personnel decisions are based on solid evaluation practices.

SUPERVISORY TECHNIQUES

One step in due process is informing individuals of their weaknesses; however, informing staff members of the need to improve usually is not helpful without adequate assistance to reach their improvement goals. And, of course, helping others to improve is not merely a part of due process but an essential component of any effective supervisory program.

CLINICAL SUPERVISION

The supervisory techniques used most frequently by supervisors are classroom visitations, preceded by and followed by individual conferences. Although these techniques can be treated as separate supervisory activities, they are usually employed in conjunction with each other; seldom does a classroom visitation hold much value for a teacher without a preobservational conference and a follow-up consultation. The entire process has been referred to as clinical supervision. L. F. Goldsberry indicated that the major characteristics of proper clinical supervision are as follows:

1. Observations are related to the teacher's goals.
2. Observations and conferences are cyclical and part of a continuous process.
3. A database is gathered through the observation process.
4. The teacher and supervisor jointly form final interpretations.
5. Subsequent teaching and observation sessions are based on hypothesis generation and testing.[56]

The following discussion is an introduction to the concept, process, and activities of clinical supervision. The three components of clinical supervision, conceptualized as a cycle, are depicted in figure 10.1.

Figure 10.1 The Process of Clinical Supervision.

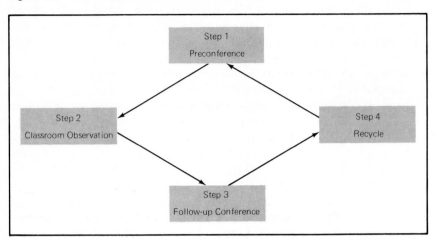

Preobservational Conference

The preobservational conference between the supervisor and the teacher to be observed is very important to the effectiveness of the classroom observation.[57] The objectives and activities of the preobservational conference include:

1. Developing rapport between the supervisor and the teacher to be observed.
2. Establishing the purposes and function of the classroom observation.
3. Agreeing on which aspects of the instructional program are to be observed.[58]
4. Developing procedures used during the observation.
5. Identifying the roles that the supervisor and the teacher perform during the observation.
6. Indicating the purposes and nature of the follow-up conference to be held after the classroom observation.
7. Answering the teacher's questions about the classroom observation and the follow-up conference.

Items one through six should be agreed on cooperatively rather than imposed by the supervisor. At the end of the preobservational conference, teachers should believe that they have been meaningfully involved in the supervisory process and that the supervisor has the teachers' best interests at heart. In most cases, the interpersonal relationship that develops between the supervisor and the teacher significantly influences the effectiveness of the supervision, perhaps more than any other factor. As Arthur Blumberg has noted, "The results of research on supervisory behavior styles in the school support the notion that the more open, collaborative and nondefensive is the interpersonal climate created by the supervisor, the more teachers are satisfied with their supervision and feel that it is productive for them."[59]

Classroom Observation

Following the preobservational conference, the supervisor should initiate the classroom observations. The classroom observation or visitation should be used to identify and diagnose strengths and areas in need of improvement. Through classroom visitation the supervisor can identify teacher and classroom improvement needs and can observe conditions impairing student learning. The supervisor should also use the classroom visitation to identify effective teaching and to gain a more complete and accurate picture of the total instructional program in the school. (Several observational systems or instruments to help supervisors are described by Keith Acheson and Meredith Damien Gall in *Techniques in the Clinical Supervision of Teachers.*)[60]

The supervisor needs to recognize, however, that classroom observations may not be viewed by many teachers as positive and constructive contributions to their effectiveness.[61] Poor planning by the supervisor for the classroom visitation, little or no follow-up on the observation, and a lack of constructive suggestions on how to improve have all cast considerable doubt on the value of the classroom visitation for many teachers. Added to these factors is the anxiety created by the classroom observation conducted for the purpose of teacher evaluation.

Most of these negative factors associated with the classroom observation can be corrected by supervisors, who should not reject the classroom visitation as one of their supervisory alternatives, despite possible teacher opposition. Supervisors aware of the attitude of many teachers about classroom visitations should try to make the visitations positive experiences. (An excellent source for ideas on the purposes of classroom observations and how to conduct them is *Responsive Supervision for Professional Development: An Overview of the Process,* by Nicholas Rayder and Trent Taylor.)[62]

A problem in trying to improve the instructional program encountered by most supervisors at one time or another is created by the difference in the way that the teacher and the supervisor perceive what has occurred in the classroom. One approach to this difficulty is for the supervisor to utilize, in cooperation with the teacher, a videotape machine to help both of them analyze the classroom situation.[63] This equipment can capture on tape for both the teacher and supervisor the actual dynamics of what has happened in the classroom, thereby enabling them to review and study the tape, and to analyze it for the identification of strengths and areas needing improvement in the instructional program. Recent developments utilizing split-screen video-taping, allowing both the teacher and the students to be observed on the screen at the same time, make this technology even more valuable for improving instruction.[64]

In addition to helping a supervisor and teacher develop a better understanding of and agreement on the specific aspects of the instructional program needing improvement, the videotape machine can also be used by a teacher to examine videotapes of colleagues or outside experts demonstrating effective instructional techniques and procedures. Through this kind of study a teacher can observe a model of how a particular teaching technique should be employed and learn how to use the same technique in the classroom. While many teachers could undoubtedly benefit from studying the videotapes without supervisory assistance, at least in the beginning the supervisor should work with the teacher in analyzing the tapes.

Although studying videotapes should prove to be of value to teachers trying to improve their methods and skills, a supervisor of a teacher may believe there is a need to practice a teaching skill before it is incorporated in classroom procedures. Again, the videotape equipment can play an important role in increasing the effectiveness of the teacher's practice sessions. Prior to use of the video equipment, the major problem individuals faced in deriving significant benefit from practice was that they normally could not observe how well they had accomplished a task while it was being performed. Once the event had occurred, it was too late to observe it; therefore, teachers were dependent on the perceptions of others who described it to them. However, by utilizing a video camera, teachers can now tape practice sessions with students and then view the tape to see how well they performed a particular skill and how they might improve in the next practice session. This process is referred to as microteaching.

The video recorder's essential function in supervision is to capture the reality of a situation for later study, analysis, and evaluation. It can be used by the supervisor and teacher to identify strengths and limitations in the instructional program, to analyze model teaching to gain ideas for self-improvement, and to provide feedback on progress that is being made in developing a particular teaching skill. It is without question a very useful supervisory tool for improving the instructional program, and any school lacking access to a videotape machine should investigate the possibility of obtaining one.

Follow-up Conference

After a classroom observation has been completed and a teaching problem which is impairing the effectiveness of the instructional program has been identified and diagnosed, a follow-up conference with the teacher is needed to improve the situation. A follow-up conference can be useful for discussing a teacher's strengths and should not be limited only to the discussion of the teacher's weaknesses.

As supervision without adequate prior evaluation tends to be misdirected, evaluation without immediate and constructive follow-up supervisory assistance can lead to anxiety, frustration, and resistance on the part of its recipients. Judging from the reports of many teachers, too frequently no immediate and constructive supervisory assistance follows the evaluation process. In such situations, teachers are informed of their weaknesses or limitations but are given no specific help in improving. Informing a teacher that "better class control" or "greater student participation" is needed may identify a shortcoming, but unless the individual is given supervisory assistance in achieving better class control or greater student participation, improvement may not be possible. Worse yet, informing an individual of a weakness without providing adequate help in correcting it may harm the person's self-concept and lead to a negative attitude toward evaluation.

A staff evaluation program designed to point out only strengths and weaknesses without helping to correct the limitations or to capitalize on the strengths is professionally inadequate. To improve, a person usually needs to receive specific and constructive assistance and support, as well as appropriate time in which to make the necessary changes. A possible format for a personnel improvement plan accomplishing these objectives is presented in figure 10.2.

Figure 10.2 Personnel Improvement Plan.

Objectives of the Plan
    What are the specific changes that are to occur?

Prescribed Activities
    What are the *specific* activities that the individual should engage in so as to accomplish the needed improvements?

Time Frame
    At what point should *progress* in accomplishing the objectives of the plan be apparent? At what point should the objectives of the plan *be accomplished?*

Supervisor's Role
    What kinds of assistance and monitoring activities will be provided by the supervisor?

Whether the evaluation program is perceived by the staff in a positive light will probably depend, as much on the adequacy of follow-up supervisory activities as on the perceived fairness and validity of the evaluation itself.

The follow-up conference can be a useful supervisory technique for accomplishing the following objectives:

- Developing a better understanding on the part of the participants in the conference of the way each person sees the classroom situation, and the reasons for those perceptions.
- Exploring possible solutions to an instructional problem.
- Designing and agreeing on a plan of action to improve the classroom situation.
- Reviewing progress made by the teacher in attempting to improve the classroom situation.

Whether any particular follow-up conference between a supervisor and a teacher should include all four of these objectives depends on the conditions that brought about the conference. However, accomplishing all four purposes will obviously, in most cases, take more than a single meeting.

The success of the follow-up conference depends in large part on the extent to which the teacher feels secure with and trustful of the supervisor, and the amount of planning invested by the supervisor in preparation for the meeting. A teacher who does not feel comfortable with the supervisor and does not believe that the supervisor has his or her best interest at heart is unlikely to be very cooperative. Also, factors such as the time and location of the conference, the seating arrangement, establishing and maintaining rapport during the conference, the objectives of the meeting, identifying and sequencing questions to be asked, anticipating questions the teacher may raise, and deciding how to close the conference—all need to be considered by the supervisor.[65] Successful conferences cannot take place without adequate planning; and evidence shows that many supervisory conferences need to be planned carefully to be successful.[66]

The value of the supervisory conference is not restricted to its use in conjunction with the classroom visitation. An individual conference can be used by the supervisor to discuss with the teacher a variety of items which may be impairing instruction: class scheduling, the homework policy, grading, or nature of the text material, for example. However, because the classroom observation and the preobservational conference and follow-up conference are generally linked in people's minds as well as in practice, the discussion has focused for the most part on the purpose and planning for those types of conferences.

INTERCLASS AND INTERSCHOOL VISITATIONS

Too many supervisors attempt to improve instruction by telling the teacher what needs to be changed in the classroom situation. While the technique of telling may work in some cases, a much more successful supervisory approach is to show the teachers a more effective way of conducting instruction. In some cases the supervisor might demonstrate the change which is being advocated. It may be more realistic and likely, however, for the supervisor to identify individuals in or outside the school who can most appropriately and effectively demonstrate a new technique or procedure.

For example, one teacher in the school may be particularly skillful in leading a class discussion, another person might be good in the area of establishing student self-discipline, and another in evaluation techniques. The supervisor should attempt to capitalize on the talents of these people and others by organizing a program of interclass and interschool visitation for teachers who would like to improve their skills in these particular areas. Interclass visitations might take place during a teacher's released period, or another type of accommodation might be made by the supervisor. Interschool visitations could take place during an in-service day or, if feasible, a substitute teacher might be hired to allow a member of the staff to view a class in another school. (A good example of an intervisitation program is described in Leon Gersten's article in *Phi Delta Kappan*.)[67]

Organizing a program of interclass and interschool visitations is not an easy task for the school supervisor; it requires effort and resourcefulness. Scheduling problems must be resolved, and the cooperation of those who are to be visited must be secured. However, interclass and interschool visitations are two excellent means by which teachers can actually see a technique or procedure demonstrated, instead of listening to a supervisor talk about it. For this reason, then, both kinds of visitations are recommended as desirable components of a good supervisory program.

PEER SUPERVISION

Another promising process which may be incorporated into a comprehensive evaluation/supervision program is peer supervision. Huddle, for example, noted that peer supervision or peer coaching can provide support to ongoing supervisory practices by decreasing teacher isolation and providing a supportive climate in which teachers may improve their teaching.[68] His conclusion was based, in part, on research conducted by Bruce Joyce and Beverly Showers who found that teachers make excellent peer coaches and are able to provide companionship and mutual reflection while focusing on improving teaching practices.[69] Joyce and Showers found that student achievement improved in

situations where teachers were placed on support teams and afforded opportunities to observe each other, model effective teaching strategies, and discuss
instructional improvement efforts.

While informal peer supervision can be helpful, its effectiveness is limited by its sporadic and isolated nature. The one important advantage of collegial interaction is that it typically possesses few risks for staff members, and
it can give teachers assistance which they may not be receiving from the districts' evaluation program. Yet, to establish a purposeful system of peer supervision, administrators need to provide the organizational arrangements and
supportive scheduling that allows for training, peer observation, and feedback
opportunities.[70]

In many respects, peer coaching or collegial support teams may be a
useful mechanism for minimizing the conflict between supervision and evaluation processes. In their study of effective evaluation practices, Wise and
Darling-Hammond found that all of the successful districts they studied had
involved highly expert teachers in some aspect of the evaluation process as
well as in other professional development activities. They concluded that the
"use of peer review or peer assistance in these districts greatly strengthens
their capacities for effective teacher supervision by providing additional time
and expertise for this function."[71]

A disadvantage of this approach is that it may appear to exclude school
administrators and their insights from the use of evaluation for staff improvement. Although peer supervision appears to be a promising strategy for enhancing the evaluation program, Tom McGreal noted that the average teacher
still does not want to be involved in evaluating other teachers.[72] Thus, he concluded that despite extraordinary examples of peer supervision, the real hope
for improving instructional supervision is going to come from improving the
interaction between the supervisor and the teacher. Furthermore, McGreal
believes it is "wrong to move toward a model that forces administrators to be
responsible only for summative evaluations and asks teachers to make formative evaluations."[73] Therefore, peer supervision or coaching should only comprise one element of the total evaluation/supervision program.

THE PROFESSIONAL LIBRARY

Most schools have some type of professional library, although it is probably
seldom perceived as a source of supervisory assistance. The primary purpose
of the professional library, however, should be to provide an opportunity for
staff members to improve themselves through reading or viewing various print
and nonprint materials.

Undoubtedly some members of the staff use the professional library on their own initiative and derive great benefit from it. However, observation and experience suggest that many members of the faculty of a school infrequently, if ever, use the professional library except in completing a university course or for other special reasons.[74] In most schools the professional library plays a minimal role in the improvement of instruction.

Whether the professional library can play an important role in improving instruction in a school depends on many factors, but two factors appear to be critical.[75] First of all, selecting and organizing materials and resources for instruction are schoolwide problems that the entire staff should consider. Second, supervisors must demonstrate to the faculty that they feel the professional library is an important part of the school. If they tend to ignore the library in their own reading or are unfamiliar with the collection, they not only fail to provide a good model for the faculty but also are in a poor position to utilize the library's resources in working with the staff.

The materials in a professional library can, if properly selected, be useful in helping teachers to improve themselves. But before they receive much use, supervisors must show that they are interested in the professional library's resources, and they must become sufficiently familiar with the resources to recommend them appropriately to others. Under these conditions the professional library can function as a useful supervisory resource for those interested in improving the instructional program.

STAFF DISMISSAL

A major responsibility of school administrators is to ensure an adequate learning environment for the students. If a member of the staff is not performing adequately in spite of supervisory efforts, then steps must be taken to remove that individual from the staff. This is never easy, but the responsibility for initiating action is clearly that of the school administrator. It makes little sense to have a good evaluation program in all other respects if such a program permits incompetent or unsatisfactory teachers to remain on the staff. When supervisory efforts are not successful in improving sufficiently the performance of an incompetent or, for some other reason, an unacceptable teacher, the school administrator needs to initiate dismissal steps which include due process.

An important problem, of course, is defining valid criteria for incompetent or unsatisfactory behavior; the research reviewed in the previous sections should be helpful in that regard. Also, state statutes should be examined for the legal grounds for dismissal in the school administrator's state.

A review of successful dismissal cases indicated that the courts have supported the following grounds for dismissal: (1) incompetent teaching methods, including failure to adapt to current teaching techniques, poor lesson organization, and failure to maintain classroom control; (2) negative impact on students, including inability to get along with pupils, failure to maintain self-control, and low pupil achievement; (3) negative teacher attitude, including insubordination, and (4) inadequate knowledge of subject matter, including lack of knowledge of English grammar, spelling, and punctuation.[76] Also, Larry Bendow identified eight of the most frequently effective administrative factors associated with successful teacher dismissal: (1) observations were numerous and well documented; 2) definite goals for improvement were established and a specific timetable was formed for the attainment of goals; (3) the administrator was willing and able to assist the teacher in areas that needed improvement; (4) the administrator informed the teacher early of incompetency, both verbally and in writing; (5) central administration was consistently informed of the situation; (6) the administrator held to initially established expectations; (7) the administrator was factual, truthful, consistent, and followed district policies and laws to the letter; and (8) the teacher was told, verbally and in writing, after all administrative support had failed, that termination was being recommended.[77] While dismissal of a staff person is seldom easy, the previous guidelines should be helpful in achieving the objective.[78]

EVALUATOR TRAINING

Most administrators who evaluate and supervise the staff have received only limited professional training as evaluators or supervisors and little if any on-the-job training for evaluating or supervising staff.[79] Because of a lack of preparation, many administrators approach the task of evaluating or supervising staff with some apprehension, or with a false sense of security, feeling that they know everything there is to know about evaluating and supervising school personnel while inwardly they know they are ill prepared.[80] Specifically, in S. B. Stow and S. J. Frudden's study, identified areas of training needs included conferencing, analyzing teacher behavior, and facilitating behavior changes; administrator training in interpersonal skills, listening skills, and cooperative skills was found by Larry Taylor et al to be effective in improving supervisory performance.[81] In a related sense, McGreal indicated that the first stage of appropriate evaluator training would be to provide teachers, administrators, and others involved in the evaluation program with an introduction to a set of skills that every teacher ought to possess.[82] He suggested beginnning with topics such as Barak Rosenshine's teaching functions, increasing student involvement, and appropriate use of feedback, and, then moving on to more complex topics, such as learning styles and thinking skills. He maintains that understanding a set of fundamentals provides teachers and evaluators or supervisors with a common language.

Regardless of the approach taken or the topics explored, administrators and district officials need to recognize that personnel evaluation and supervision is a complex process involving technical skills, and educational and legal concepts.[83] Therefore, evaluators and supervisors should be involved in an ongoing professional training process. All evaluators/supervisors should receive in-service training at least every three years to sharpen their technical skills and to update the knowledge base which they rely on in their evaluation/ supervision programs.

ASSESSMENT OF THE PROGRAM

The staff evaluation/supervision program, like any other program, needs to be assessed regularly if it is to improve and meet the needs of the people involved.[84] Regrettably, assessment of the strengths and weaknesses of the staff evaluation and supervision program is frequently haphazard and sporadic. Whatever assessment does occur tends to rely on the random impressions of administrators and usually includes limited or no feedback from staff members. Therefore, school administrators should assess the evaluation/ supervision program systematically every year or two to identify areas for improvement.
number of different forms, but one condition is essential: Those who are being evaluated or supervised should be surveyed on their perceptions of the progam's strengths and weaknesses and their ideas on how it could be made more effective.

A FINAL PERSPECTIVE

The staff evaluation and supervision program has had a checkered past and continues to be perceived by many as a necessary evil. However, recent trends indicate that a more positive perception of the benefits of staff evaluation and supervision is emerging; it views evaluation and supervision as important means not only for reaching specific personnnel decisions but also for improving the staff. Evaluation and supervision will likely continue to be major responsibilities of the school administrators; it is essential that they work to improve their programs. The discussion presented in this chapter was designed to help achieve that goal.

Review and Learning Activities

1. Ascertain the objectives of your district's staff evaluation program and examine the achievability of those objectives in light of the discussion in the text on cross-purposes.

2. To what degree are staff members involved in the development of staff evaluation purposes, criteria, and procedures? To what extent in your district is a low priority given to staff self-evaluation? To peer or collegial supervision? How could these situations be improved?

3. Assess the degree to which your district's staff evaluation criteria and form are based on research and recommendations presented in this chapter. Attempt to draft an improved staff evaluation form and criteria for your district.

4. Describe the extent to which your district differentiates between supervision and evaluation processes.

5. What are your school district's policies and procedures for evaluating tenured teachers and dismissing teachers? Draft an improved policy for each of these situations, based on the recommendations and ideas presented in the text.

6. Ascertain your school district's policy and plan for helping teachers to improve after the need for such improvement has been identified through teacher evaluation. What are the strengths and weaknesses of the policy and plan? How could they be made better?

Notes

1. J. Hiller, "Teacher Evaluation: Issues, Practices, and a Semiotic Model," *Education* (Winter 1986): 144–48.

2. See Lee S. Shulman, "A Union of Insufficiencies: Strategies for Teacher Assessment in a Period of Educational Reform," *Educational Leadership* (November 1988): 36–41; and Thomas L. McGreal, "Evaluation for Enhancing Instruction: Linking Teacher Evaluation and Staff Development," in Sarah J. Stanley and W. James Popham, *Teacher Evaluation: Six Prescriptions for Success* (Alexandria, Va.: Association for Supervision and Curriculum Development, 1988): 1–29.

3. Joan L. Buttram and Bruce L. Wilson, "Promising Trends in Teacher Evaluation," *Educational Leadership* (April 1987): 5.

4. Richard A. Gorton, "Staff Evaluation," in *Encyclopedia of School Administration and Supervision* ed. R. A. Gorton, G. T. Schneider, and J. C. Fisher (Phoenix, Ariz.: Oryx Press, 1988), 244.

5. Arthur E. Wise, Linda Darling-Hammond, Milbrey W. McLaughlin, and Harriet T. Bernstein, *Teacher Evaluation: A Study of Effective Practice* (R-3139-NIE) (Santa Monica, Calif.: The Rand Corporation, 1984).

6. Arthur E. Wise and Linda Darling-Hammond, "Teacher Evaluation and Teacher Professionalism," *Educational Leadership* (January 1985): 30.

7. Ibid.

8. See Gene Huddle, "Teacher Evaluation—How Important for Effective Schools? Eight Messages from Research," *NASSP Bulletin* (March 1985): 58–64; Hans A. Andrews and John H. Knight, "Administrative Evaluation of Teachers: Resistance and Rationale," *NASSP Bulletin* (December 1987): 1–4; Richard L. Sullivan and Jerry L. Wircenski, "Clinical Supervision: The Role of the Principal," *NASSP Bulletin* (October 1988): 34–39; Milbrey W. McLaughlin and R. Scott Pfeifer, *Teacher Evaluation: Improvement, Accountability, and Effective Learning* (New York: Teachers College Press, 1988); and R. J. Stiggins and D. Duke, *The Case for Commitment to Teacher Growth: Research on Teacher Evaluation* (Albany: State University of New York Press, 1988).

9. One of the main sources for identification of the problems and issues associated with teacher evaluation is the periodic review of the literature and survey of the field conducted by Educational Research Service, Washington, D.C.

10. James R. Weber, *Teacher Evaluation as a Strategy for Improving Instruction: Synthesis of the Literature* (ERIC Report Ed–287–213).

11. Howard M. Knoff, "Clinical Supervision, Consultation, and Counseling: A Comparative Analysis for Supervisors and Other Educational Leaders," *Journal of Curriculum and Supervision* (Spring 1988): 240–52.

12. Carolyn H. Denham, "Perspective on the Major Purposes and Basic Procedures for Teacher Evaluation," *Journal of Personnel Evaluation in Education* 1 (1987): 29–32.

13. Joyce L. Epstein, "A Question of Merit: Principals' and Parents' Evaluations of Teachers," *Educational Researcher* (August–September, 1985): 3–10. See also, Michael Koehler, "Back to the Basics of Supervision," *Clearing House* (January 1989): 220–21.

14. See Carl D. Glickman, *Supervision of Instruction: A Developmental Approach* (Newton, Mass.: Allyn & Bacon, 1985, 270–72; and W. James Popham, "Judgment-Based Teacher Evaluation," in Sarah J. Stanley and W. James Popham, *Teacher Evaluation: Six Prescriptions for Success* (Alexandria, Va.: Association for Supervision and Curriculum Development, 1988): 56–77.

15. Neal J. Powell, "A Plan for Principals: School Supervision that Works," *NASSP Bulletin* (March 1988): 42–49.

16. Joyce L. Epstein, "A Question of Merit," 3.

17. John T. Seyfarth and Elaine M. Nowinski, "Administrator Feedback Can Improve Classroom Instruction," *NASSP Bulletin* (December 1987): 47–50; and Donald McCarty, JoAnna Kaufman, and Julie Stafford, "Supervision and Evaluation," *Clearing House* (April 1986): 351–53.

18. Carl R. Ashbaugh and Katherine L. Kasten, "Should Teachers Be Involved in Teacher Appraisal?" *NASSP Bulletin* (September 1987): 50–53.

19. Huddle, "Teacher Evaluation," 59.

20. Wise and Darling-Hammond, "Teacher Evaluation," 33.

21. For an in-depth presentation of reflective practice, see Donald A. Schon, *The Reflective Practitioner: How Professionals Think in Action* (New York: Basic Books, 1983).

22. H. Jerome Freiberg, "Teacher Self-Evaluation and Principal Supervision," *NASSP Bulletin* (April 1987): 85–92.

23. For a specific example of an evaluation program which incorporates self-assessment, see Ken Peterson and Anthony Mitchell, "Teacher-Controlled Evaluation in a Career Ladder Program," *Educational Leadership* (November 1985).

24. Bruce W. Tuckman, "Judging the Effectiveness of Teaching Styles: The Perceptions of Principals," *Educational Administration Quarterly* (Winter 1979): 104–15; See also, Donald M. Medley and Homer Coker, "The Accuracy of Principals' Judgments of Teacher Performance," *The Journal of Educational Research* (March–April 1987): 242–47; and Daniel L. Duke and Richard J. Stiggins, *Teacher Evaluation: Five Keys to Growth* (Washington, D.C.: National Education Association, 1986).

25. "Teacher Assessments Too Simplistic, Shulman Contends," *ASCD Update* (May 1988): 1.

26. See, Medley and Coker, "The Accuracy of Principals' Judgments," and Lee S. Shulman, "Assessment for Teaching: An Initiative for the Profession," *Kappan* (September 1987): 38–44.

27. Donald Medley, *Indicators and Measures of Teacher Effectiveness: A Review of Research* (ERIC Report Ed–088–844), 6.

28. Benjamin S. Bloom, "The New Direction in Educational Research: Alterable Variables," *Kappan* (February 1980): 384. For similar findings, see Medley and Coker, "The Accuracy of Principals' Judgments," 242.

29. Kinnard White, Marvin D. Wyne, Gary B. Stuck, and Richard H. Coop, "Assessing Teacher Performance Using an Observation Instrument Based on Research Findings," *NASSP Bulletin* (March 1987): 89–95.

30. For a description of a number of these studies, see *Research on Teaching: Concepts, Findings and Implications,* ed. Penelope L. Peterson and Herbert J. Walberg (Berkeley, Calif.: McCutchan, 1979); *Handbook of Research on Teaching,* ed. Merlin Wittrock (New York: Macmillan, 1983). Also see Bloom, "The New Direction in Educational Research"; Thomas L. Good, "Teacher Effectiveness in the Elementary School," *Journal of Teacher Education* (March–April 1979): 52–64; Steven T. Bossert, "School Effects," in *Handbook of Research on Educational Administration,* ed. Norman J. Boyan (New York: Longman, 1988): 341–52; Andrew C. Porter and Jere E. Brophy, *Good Teaching: Insights from the Work of the Institute for Research on Teaching* (ERIC Report Ed–283–795); Jason Millman and Linda Darling-Hammond, *The New Handbook of Teacher Evaluation: Assessing Elementary and Secondary Teachers* (Newbury Park, Calif.: Sage Publications, 1989); and Herbert J. Walberg, "Productive Teaching and Instruction: Assessing the Knowledge Base," *Kappan* (February 1990): 470–78.

31. M. William Salganik, "Researchers Team with Reporter to Identify Schools that Work," *Educational R and D* (Winter 1980): 3.

32. Lawrence C. Stedman, "The Effective Schools Formula Still Needs Changing: A Reply to Brookover," *Kappan* (February 1988): 439–42.

33. Penelope L. Peterson, "Direct Instruction: Effective for What and for Whom?" *Educational Leadership* (October 1979): 46.

34. Ullik Rouk, "Separate Studies Show Similar Results of Teacher Effectiveness," *Educational R and D* (Spring 1979): 6.

35. *Time to Learn* (ERIC Report Ed–192–454).

36. Nancy Karweit, "Time-on-Task: The Second Time Around," *NASSP Bulletin* (February 1988): 31–39.

37. Irene R. Virgilio, "An Examination of the Relationships among School Effectiveness, Time-on-Task, and Teacher Effectiveness in Elementary and Junior High Schools," (Ph.D. diss., University of New Orleans, 1987).

38. Theodore Coladarci, "The Relevance of Educational Research for Identifying Master Teachers," *NASSP Bulletin* (January 1988): 95.

39. Herbert J. Walberg, "Synthesis of Research on Time and Learning," *Educational Leadership* (March 1988): 76.

40. Jere F. Brophy, "Teacher Behavior and Student Learning," *Educational Leadership* (October 1979): 33. Also see Harris M. Cooper and Reuben M. Baron, "Academic Expectations, Attributed Responsibility and Teachers' Reinformation Behavior," *Journal of Educational Psychology* (April 1979): 274–77.

41. Gordon A. Sabine, *How Students Rate Their Schools and Teachers* (ERIC Report Ed–052–533). Also see Robert Wright and Robert Alley, "A Profile of the Ideal Teacher," *NASSP Bulletin* (February 1977): 60–64.

42. Nate L. Gage, *The Scientific Basis of the Art of Teaching* (New York: Columbia University, Teachers College Press, 1978); and Nate L. Gage, "What Do We Know About Teaching Effectiveness," *Kappan* (October 1984): 87–96.

43. For a good discussion on how to reduce the high inference variables, see M. L. Land, "Low Inference Variables of Teacher Clarity: Effects on Student Concept Learning," *Journal of Educational Psychology* (December 1979): 795–99; and, Glickman, "Observing Skills," in *Supervision of Instruction: A Developmental Approach* (Newton, Mass.: Allyn & Bacon, 1985), 207–31; Keith A. Acheson and Meredith Damien Gall, *Techniques in the Clinical Supervision of Teachers; Preservice and Inservice Applications* (New York: Longman, 1987).

44. For further discussion of these points, see Gaea Leinhardt, "Modeling and Measuring Educational Treatment," *Review of Educational Research* (Fall 1980): 404–14.

45. For examples of several diagnostic instruments currently being used in teacher evaluation, see G. D. Borich and S. K. Madden, *Evaluating Classroom Instruction: A Sourcebook of Instruments* (Reading, Mass.: Addison-Wesley, 1977); and Acheson and Gall, *Techniques in the Clinical Supervision of Teachers.*

46. Donald Grossnickle and William B. Thiel, "The Etiquette of Evaluation—What's Often Forgotten but Not to Be Ignored," *NASSP Bulletin* (February 1981): 1–4. Also see June Thompson et al., *Failure of Communication in the Evaluation of Teachers by Principals* (ERIC Report Ed–105–637).

47. See Marv Nottingham and Jack Dawson, *Factors for Consideration in Supervision and Evaluation* (ERIC Report Ed–284–343, 1987); Arthur Blumberg and R. Stevan Jonas, "Permitting Access: The Teacher's Control Over Supervision," *Educational Leadership* (May 1987): 59–62; and Hans A. Andrews and John H. Knight, "Administrative Evaluation of Teachers: Resistance and Rationale," *NASSP Bulletin* (December 1987): 1–4.

48. Barnett Berry and Rick Ginsberg, "Creating Lead Teachers: From Policy to Implementation," *Kappan* (April 1990): 616–21.

49. See, for example, Donald W. Dubois, *Teacher Evaluation: The Salem Public Schools Model* (Eugene, Oreg.: Oregon School Study Council, 1980).

50. Martha M. McCarthy, "Due Process," in *Encyclopedia of School Administration and Supervision* ed. R. A. Gorton, G. T. Schneider, and J. C. Fisher (Phoenix, Ariz.: Oryx Press, 1988), 101–3.

51. Theodore P. Remley, Jr., and Virginia B. MacReynolds, "Due Process in Dismissals: A Reflection of Our Values," *NASSP Bulletin* (January 1988): 41–44.

52. W. P. Claxton, "Remediation: The Evolving Fairness in Teacher Dismissal," *Journal of Law and Education* (Spring 1986): 181–93.

53. Delon and Bartman, "Employees."

54. Claxton, "Remediation," 181–93; and S. B. Rynecki and J. H. Linquist, "Teacher Evaluation and Collective Bargaining: A Management Perspective," *Journal of Law and Education* (Summer 1988): 487–506; and K. L. Zerger, "Teacher Evaluation and Collective Bargaining: A Union Perspective," *Journal of Law and Education* (Summer 1988): 507–25.

55. D. H. Henderson, "The Constitutional Rights of Probationary Teachers: Improper Assessment May Be Costly to School Boards," *Journal of Law and Education* (January 1985): 1–21.

56. L. F. Goldsberry, "The Realities of Clinical Supervision: Polaroid Snapshot or Star Wars Movie?" *Eduational Leadership* (April 1984): 12–15.

57. Acheson and Gall, *Techniques in the Clinical Supervision of Teachers,* 71–76.

58. For a particularly good discussion of goal setting during the preobservational conference, see Thomas L. McGreal, "Helping Teachers Set Goals," *Educational Leadership* (February 1980): 414–19; and Thomas L. McGreal, "Goal Setting As the Major Activity of Evaluation," *Successful Teacher Evaluation* (Alexandria, Va.: Association for Supervision and Curriculum Development): 44–69.

59. Arthur Blumberg, *Supervisors and Teachers: A Private Cold War,* 3d ed. (Berkeley, Calif.: McCutchan, 1988).

60. Acheson and Gall, *Techniques in the Clinical Supervision of Teachers.*

61. D. John McIntyre, "Teacher Evaluation and the Observer Effect," *NASSP Bulletin* (March 1980): 36–39; see also Dennis Harry, "Relationships between Teacher Perceived Instructional Improvements and Teacher Evaluation Characteristics" (Ph.D. diss., University of Wisconsin-Milwaukee, 1987).

62. Nicholas Rayder and Trent Taylor, *Responsive Supervision for Professional Development: An Overview of the Process* (San Francisco: Far West Laboratory for Educational Research and Development, 1979).

63. C. H. Gardner, *Videotaping in a Naturalistic Classroom Setting* (Austin: Texas University Research and Development Center for Teacher Education, 1980).

64. William Moritz and Jo Anne Martin-Reynolds, "The Genie in the Bottle," *Educational Leadership* (February 1980): 396–99.

65. For an earlier, but still relevant, discussion of these points, see George C. Kyte, *The Principal at Work* (New York: Ginn): 274–76. Also see, Acheson and Gall, *Techniques in the Clinical Supervision of Teachers,* 153–86; and Kenneth M. Sorrick and Donald R. Grossnickle, "Beyond the Post-Observation Blues," *NASSP Bulletin* (December 1989): 112–16.

66. Judith Warren Little and Tom Bird, "Instructional Leadership 'Close to the Classroom,' in Secondary Schools," in *Instructional Leadership: Concepts, Issues, and Controversies,* ed. William Greenfield (Newton, Mass.: Allyn & Bacon, 1987): 118–37.

67. Leon Gersten, "Intervisitation: A Process of Growth and Enrichment," *Kappan* (March 1979): 532–33. Also see Thomas W. Clapper, "The Effects of Peer Clinical Supervision on In-Service Teachers" (Ph.D. diss., Pennsylvania State University, 1981).

68. Huddle, "Teacher Evaluation," 58–63.

69. See Beverly Showers, *Peer Coaching: A Strategy for Facilitating Transfer of Training* (Eugene: Center for Educational Policy and Management, University of Oregon, 1984 and Bruce Joyce and Beverly Showers, *Student Achievement through Staff Development* (New York: Longman, 1988).

70. Huddle, "Teacher Evaluation," 62.

71. Wise and Darling-Hammond, "Teacher Effectiveness," 32.

72. Ron Brandt, "On Teacher Evaluation: A Conversation with Tom McGreal," *Educational Leadership* (April 1987): 20–24. For an additional discussion of teachers' preferences regarding evaluators, see John T. Seyfarth and Elaine M. Nowinski, "Administrator Feedback Can Improve Instruction," 47–50.

73. Brandt, "On Teacher Evaluation," 24.

74. In fact, there is evidence that teachers are neither regular readers of professional literature or aware of what is written. See Thomas George, "Teachers Tend to Ignore Professional Journals," *Kappan* (September 1979): 69–70.

75. Marks et al., "How to Select, Organize, and Facilitate the Use of Instructional Media and Library Materials," *Handbook of Educational Supervision: A Guide for the Practitioner,* 3d ed. (Boston: Allyn & Bacon, 1985): 333–90.

76. Shirly Neill and Jerry Curtis, *Staff Dismissal: Problems and Solutions* (Arlington, Va.: American Association of School Administrators, 1978); Max A. Bailey and Nancy W. Sindelar, "Teacher Incompetence: An Old Problem with Some New Solutions," *NFEAS Journal* 1, (1987–88): 12–23; and James A. Gross, *Teachers on Trial: Values, Standards, & Equity in Judging Conduct and Competence* (New York: ILR Press, Cornell University, 1988).

77. Larry K. Bendow, "Factors in Teacher Dismissal Situations" (Ed.D. diss., Walden University, 1979).

78. For additional information on teacher dismissal, see Edwin M. Bridges, *Managing the Incompetent Teacher* (Eugene, Oreg.: ERIC Clearinghouse on Educational Management, 1984).

79. Buttram and Wilson, "Promising Trends in Teacher Evaluation," 5.

80. S. B. Stow and S. J. Frudden, "Teacher Evaluation: School Administrators' Perceptions of Their Competence at Teacher Performance Evaluations," *National Forum of Educational Administration and Supervision* 2/3 (1985): 49–54.

81. Ibid.; and Larry K. Taylor, Paul F. Cook, Edward E. Green, and J. Keith Rogers, "Better Interviews: The Effects of Supervisor Training on Listening and Collaborative Skills," *The Journal of Educational Research* (November–December 1988): 89–95.

82. Brandt, "On Teacher Evaluation."

83. See Robert L. Buser and Vernon D. Pace,"Personnel Evaluation: Premises, Realities, and Constraints," *NASSP Bulletin* (December 1988): 84–86; and Elizabeth K. Rice, "The Changing Principalship: A Principal's Perspective," *Principal* (January 1989): 21–22.

84. Daniel L. Stufflebeam, *The Personnel Evaluation Standards: How to Assess Systems for Evaluating Educators* (Newbury Park, Calif.: Sage Publications, 1988).

11

• • • • •

Instructional Leadership

Instructional leadership may be defined as those "actions undertaken with the intention of developing a productive and satisfying working environment for teachers and desirable learning conditions and outcomes for children."[1] This definition, although broad in nature, implies a focus on development or improvement, not merely maintenance, and on instructional leadership, as opposed to other kinds of leadership. Rick Ginsberg indicated that "it is hard to pinpoint the exact birth of the term instructional leadership"; yet, as Brad Mitchell and Luvern Cunningham noted, "the phrase *instructional leadership* is popular among many researchers, policymakers, and school reformers due to current pressures for accountability and excellence."[2] In part, the attention to this concept has emanated from the initial studies of school effectiveness which identified the "principal as instructional leader" as one of several critical factors in effective schools.[3] Even though at the building level, an administrator is usually involved in a variety of situations that call for leadership, probably the most important area for which an administrator has leadership responsibilities is the instructional program.[4]

The instructional program comprises all of the factors and conditions within a school that influence student learning. Although the teacher is perhaps the most important instructional variable affecting student learning, other factors and conditions also play a role. They include the size of the class, the quantity and quality of curricular materials available, and the educational and socioeconomic characteristics of the students.[5] Because the evaluation and supervision of individual staff members was discussed in the previous chapter, some of the other aspects of the role of the administrator in improving the school's instructional program and in working with groups of individuals are emphasized in this chapter.

CAN THE ADMINISTRATOR FUNCTION AS AN INSTRUCTIONAL LEADER?

Administrative Considerations

The role of school administrators as instructional leaders has frequently been espoused, particularly by administrator organizations.[6] However, for some time now, questions have been raised regarding (1) the discrepancy between the level of importance attributed to the function of instructional leadership and the actual amount of time allocated to the task, and (2) the amount of instructional expertise school administrators possess.

First, although principals have repeatedly reported that instructional leadership is their top priority within their job responsibilities, the amount of actual time they allocate to instructional leadership activities has not coincided with this purported level of importance.[7] In a review of the literature pertaining to the behavior of school administrators, Philip Hallinger and Joseph Murphy indicated that

> Principals believe that they should be highly involved in instruction and spend a large portion of their time in classrooms working with students and teachers. However, research indicates a discrepancy between this norm and actual principal behavior. At least in the recent past, principals have not allocated a significant portion of their time to managing instructional activities.[8]

In part, this discrepancy between desired involvement and actual involvement may be explained by the very nature of the school administrators' role and the competing expectations for their role performance. As Larry Cuban noted, "job descriptions for principals invariably lean heavily upon managerial duties that carry out the intentions of the school board and superintendent."[9] Thus, Cuban concluded that these competing expectations held by superiors result in the image of "principal as bureaucrat" rather than "principal as professional" leading teachers to improve instruction. Cuban's description of the gap between the images and descriptions of performance has been supported by numerous studies which have indicated the chaotic nature of principals' work.[10]

In fact, John Eisenhauer, Donald Willower, and Joseph Licata summarized the everyday work activities of school administrators as "fast paced, unrelenting, and composed of many brief, varied, fragmented, and interrupted segments."[11] The implications of these types of work pressures can be seen from a study by Mitchell and Cunningham that found

> principals expend significantly more of their time on activities that promote the overall school operation (e.g., recordkeeping, pupil services, and school facilities maintenance) than on functions related to the educational program. Responsibilities such as teacher observation, curriculum development, and program evaluation receive less attention. In fact, secondary school principals spend about 20 percent less time on the education program than on operational maintenance activities. Moreover, parallel research indicates that administrators are in their offices four to six times more than in classrooms.[12]

Second, although administrators ascribe a high level of importance to their role as instructional leaders, evidence has been surfacing that teachers—the main recipients of administrators' instructional leadership—do not always recognize them as instructional leaders of their schools.[13] For example, Sharon Rallis and Martha Highsmith recounted one principal's comments which indicated that teachers often view administrators' instructional expertise as limited:

> Most of my teachers know they couldn't manage the school as I do—they wouldn't want to. But because they recognize my skills as a manager, they doubt my skills as a teacher. Therefore, they don't want me to be the person supervising them or telling them about how to instruct. Even if I were up on the latest in instructional techniques—and I don't have enough time to read thoroughly in that area—they wouldn't want to listen.[14]

In a related sense, Anneka Bredo observed that, "Many teachers feel that no administrator can understand as well as they do what really goes on in the classroom, and that they themselves can judge what teaching practices are best suited to the particular group of students in their classes."[15] This perspective is not surprising; as Hallinger and Murphy noted, "the instructional skills most principals possess upon entering administration atrophy over time, further weakening their knowledge base for instructional leadership."[16] As a result, Nancy Pitner argued that administrators should interact differently with teachers who have a great deal of expertise or training than those with limited experiential bases and less education or training.[17] Thus, administrators may be well advised to look for assistance in resolving classroom problems from persons such as colleagues, subject matter specialists, supervisors, and professors.

For instance, John Croft found that teachers more often solicit help from colleagues rather than administrators on important professional issues.[18] Terrance Deal and Lynn Celotti discovered that, "Methods of classroom instruction are virtually unaffected by organizational or administrative factors at the school or district levels."[19] And, studies by R. G. Corwin, G. L. Sharma, and Bredo indicate a lack of acceptance on the part of many teachers of the administrator's role as an instructional leader.[20] Furthermore, Pitner noted that teachers see themselves as professionals and as such are not inclined to accept directives regarding how to improve their performance.[21] She contends, based on a review of related literature, that teachers will look to their "professional peer group for advice and informal evaluations, not to the hierarchical leader for recognition."[22]

Apparently the main problem many school administrators face in this regard is that their instructional leadership is perceived as (and may actually be) no longer based on an expertise differential.[23] Most teachers are as well—and perhaps better—prepared on subject matter and teaching methodology as the administrator. Articulating this view best is L. B. Ball, who states: "They [the teachers] know their subject matter, they know how to teach, they know a great deal about pupil behavior and motivation, and are in the best sense professionals. Many teachers today know a great deal more about their jobs than even the best principal can, and it's been a long time coming for principals to recognize this fact."[24]

As a result of their increased expertise, many teachers have become more militant in their expectations for professional autonomy and less receptive to attempts by administrators to exercise instructional leadership.[25] Their attitude is characteristic of the problems with which many administrators must cope if they try to exercise leadership over professionals without expertise as a source of leadership.[26] However, evidence shows that those administrators perceived by teachers as possessing instructional expertise are sought out by teachers if they have an instructional problem.[27]

Although the problems of role conflicts and limited acceptance of an administrator's instructional expertise are serious for many administrators, there exist, unfortunately, additional constraints or obstacles. These additional constraints or obstacles are not inevitable but, if present in administrators' school districts, could restrict their motivation and/or their efforts to perform as instructional leaders. Although these potential constraints or obstacles may vary somewhat from one situation to another, the most typical ones appear to be the following:[28]

The Press of Other Duties. Exercising instructional leadership takes time and energy over and above that which must be spent on administering a school or school district. Responsibilities other than instructional leadership frequently press for administrators' time and drain their energy, leaving them with the feeling that they are spread too thin and, though they would like to be instructional leaders, they really do not have the time.

The Nature of the Situation. Some situations involve more instructional problems, crises, and major issues necessitating the instructional leadership of the administrator than do others. If administrators are in very stable, problem-free situations with excellent instructional programs and staff, there may be less opportunity or need for instructional leadership.[29]

The Extent of Resources. A lack of resources—financial, physical, or human—can be a serious obstacle to instructional leadership. Administrators may want to lead, and the situation and expectations of others may call for their leadership. But, if the resources necessary to implement their leadership are inadequate, administrators face a significant constraint.

The Degree of Incentive. Administrators should not need much incentive to adopt the role of instructional leader, and yet, in school districts where one or more of the previously mentioned obstacles are operant, some compensatory incentive or reward probably is needed. Unfortunately, in all too many school districts, there is very little incentive for administrators to function as instructional leaders. Those who make the attempt seldom receive much recognition or sustained encouragement from their superiors and, in many cases, are subject to subtle (and sometimes not so subtle) pressure from colleagues to behave in a way not too much different from the other administrators.[30] Also, when one considers the risks frequently associated with instructional leadership, incentives appear meager in comparison.

The Personal Qualities of the Administrator. Administrators' own personalities, visions, extent of commitment, human relation skills, and so forth can constrain the exercise of effective leadership. When administrators do not possess the appropriate personal qualities needed (more will be said about this later), the absence of those characteristics can be self-constraining.

It is unlikely that any administrator would experience all of the previous constraints or obstacles, nor is it likely that any administrator works in a constraint-free situation. The extent of constraints for any administrator who wishes to exercise instructional leadership will probably vary from one situation to another; what may be viewed as a serious constraint by one administrator may be perceived as only a minor restriction by another. The approach an administrator should take when confronted by an apparent constraint is to seek more information about its nature and extent, and to attempt to diagnose and modify its causes. Constraints are frequently not insurmountable, and if administrators really want to exercise instructional leadership, they find some way to ameliorate the limiting influence of constraints on their leadership. This is not easy, but administrators with strong commitments to functioning as instructional leaders find a way to overcome or at least reduce the constraints operating in a situation. Available evidence indicates that administrators can function as instructional leaders.

For example, David Clark and his colleagues, after a review of 1,200 studies of urban schools and urban education, concluded that in successful schools, "The behavior of the designated school or program leader is crucial in determining school success. Principals are particularly important."[31] Ronald Edmonds, in his classic investigation of elements that make schools effective, discovered that such schools have strong administrative leadership.[32] He stated that effective schools must "have strong administrative leadership without which the disparate elements of good schooling can neither be brought together nor kept together."[33] In general, as Steven Bossert noted in his review of effective schools research, "studies consistently report that in addition to other characteristics, successful schools have administrators who are strong programmatic leaders and who set high standards, observe classrooms frequently, maintain student discipline, and create incentives for learning."[34] What these, and several other studies mentioned later, strongly suggest is that an administrator can be an instructional leader, and that such leadership is necessary if a school is to be successful.

Which qualities should administrators possess if they are to function effectively as instructional leaders, and in which activities should they engage? The rest of this chapter addresses these important questions.

RESEARCH ON EFFECTIVE INSTRUCTIONAL LEADERS

Research has not been notably successful in determining the personal qualities a leader should possess.[35] Based on a review of the literature on leadership, however, certain basic personal characteristics are important.

One important personal quality needed for effective instructional leadership appears to be the extent to which an administrator perceives accurately the existence of an instructional problem or area in need of improvement.[36] Leadership is usually stimulated by an awareness of the existence of a problem. Consequently, administrators who perceive few problems or tend to minimize or ignore their existence are unlikely to see the need for instructional leadership. Of course, this does not mean that administrators who aspire to leadership should find or create problems where none exists. However, they should try to be accessible and nondefensive to the people who bring problems to their attention, and they should take the initiative to seek feedback periodically from students, teachers, and parents on possible instructional needs. As one study revealed, "Effective principals understand the school's education program inside out. . . . [They] spend about half their time in the school's halls and classrooms, often teaching classes themselves. They are 'high visibility' leaders rather than spending most of their time in their offices."[37]

Closely related to the accurate identification of instructional problems is the need for an administrator to possess or develop educational vision.[38] As Kent Peterson noted, "the degree to which principals have a clear and strongly held set of long-range goals (vision) of their schools increases the clarity of their problem-finding. When principals have a clear and strongly held set of long-range goals, their problem-finding will be more effective at solving endemic problems."[39]

Thus, administrators' analyses of local problems certainly provide one clue about the changes that are needed. If they are to function as instructional leaders, administrators must go beyond solving the daily problems they encounter to considering and implementing more basic changes which offer the potential for improving education throughout the organization, and which may represent significant departures from the status quo. Such a vision can be developed through a program of continuing professional improvement (as recommended in the last chapter), travel, and consultation with various leaders in education. The importance of educational vision to instructional leadership is underscored by numerous researchers who have found that principals in successful schools have clear points of views about schooling, instruction, and educational goals, and possess definite ideas about which kinds of improvements are needed in instruction.[40]

Knowledge about the different aspects of the instructional and curricular program, and skill in introducing change in that program, as well as in the people who staff it, are key elements in the expertise that administrators need if they intend to exercise effective instructional leadership.[41] Earlier, research was presented which showed that many teachers did not accept administrators in the role of the instructional leader because of a perception (or the reality) that administrators lacked the necessary expertise to help them. On the other hand, research has shown that teachers accept the instructional leadership of principals who can demonstrate appropriate expertise, and that such administrators are associated with effective schools. As noted by Charles Guditus and Perry Zirkel, "The influence of principals depends to a considerable degree on their possession of special knowledge and skills which enable them to help teachers achieve their goals."[42]

A factor greatly influencing the type of leadership administrators exhibit is the kind of needs they possess. Do they have strong drives to set and achieve new goals? Do they seek out opportunities to exercise leadership? Do they derive satisfaction from solving problems?

James Lipham's study, which was indirectly concerned with leadership, found that effective administrators possess strong needs to develop good interpersonal relations with others; to engage in different problem-solving situations that call for considerable emotional control; and to be well organized, active, and directed toward achievement of success or status. By contrast, ineffective administrators had low needs in these areas.[43] Lipham's study implies that administrators who attempt to perform as instructional leaders possess a different set of needs than those who do not initiate leadership.

A strong commitment to improving instruction is another personal prerequisite to exercising effective instructional leadership. As mentioned earlier, obstacles and constraints must frequently be overcome if administrators are to function successfully in the role of instructional leaders. Pressures may divert them from instructional leadership activities to managerial duties, and often there will seem to be insufficient time to focus on improving instruction. Nevertheless, administrators with strong commitments to improving instruction take the initiative and work hard to ameliorate those obstacles and find the time to exercise leadership in the instructional program.

That a strong commitment is important has been demonstrated by several studies, particularly those focusing on school cultures and the principals' roles in shaping organizational cultures through their interactions with others within and outside the organization. Thus, vision, goal direction, and commitment are closely related to administrators' ability to influence their schools' cultures for effectiveness, productivity, motivation, and commitment of personnel to organizational goals. Citing the work of Edgar Schein, Peterson indicated that "the culture of the school is a difficult concept to describe, for it involves the patterns of values, norms, beliefs, and roles that people take on within an human organization."[44] Nonetheless, because school cultures vary considerably—"some are positive, child oriented, and growth producing, and others negative, teacher oriented, and stultifying"—leaders are important for they embed and reinforce cultures and, thus, they must read, shape, and change the basic features of their cultures.[45] They may do so by modeling, teaching, and coaching and by filling their schools with professionals who share their visions and commitment and the norms and values of their school cultures.

If administrators only believe that it would be nice or desirable to be instructional leaders, they are not likely to initiate much leadership. They usually feel that there are too many obstacles or constraints. Administrators must really have a strong commitment to improving instruction if they are to function effectively as instructional leaders.

Even with strong commitments to improving instruction, however, administrators may not succeed as instructional leaders unless they possess high energy levels. Instructional leadership is hard work, and it is time consuming. Administrators who do not have high energy levels may lack the stamina necessary to do the job. A careful reading of the publication, *High School Leaders and Their Schools,* reveals the importance of high energy, drive, and long hours on the part of those principals who are exercising instructional leadership.[46] As noted by Clark and his colleagues, "Effective leaders did more; they framed goals and objectives, set standards of performance, created a productive working environment, and obtained needed support."[47] All of this requires a high level of energy; an administrator deficient in this regard is unlikely to sustain the effort necessary for effective instructional leadership.

Another factor which observation and experience suggest is related to the probability that administrators will engage in leadership is their willingness to take risks. As Lipham has pointed out, leaders are disrupters of the status quo.[48] As disrupters, they run the risk of alienating people and even losing their jobs. If the changes they seek to introduce affect the basic ways people think and behave, educational leaders will undoubtedly threaten certain existing values and vested interests. George Michel indicated that, "The administrator who is a risk taker is sensitive to human problems and is quite willing to take a risk to implement a decision to solve those problems."[49] Yet, many people dislike and even fear change, particularly when it upsets their way of thinking, life-style, or work pattern. Administrators who perceive the need for change but are unwilling to run the risk of alienating some people are unlikely to engage in leadership behavior to try to bring about needed change. And, as Lorri Manasse suggests "if school districts and communities are serious about supporting effective principals, they must be prepared for principals who may be 'boat-rockers,' not satisfied to keep a low profile and maintain the status quo."[50]

Exercising instructional leadership frequently requires the courage to assume certain risks, sometimes at great personal and professional cost. The alternative of not attempting to exert leadership no doubt results in fewer risks and greater security for the administrator, but it may also mean the loss of opportunity to bring about needed improvement in education.

Finally, an important personal prerequisite which an administrator needs, particularly in risk situations, is the ability to work well with people.[51] Effective leaders possess human relation skills and are generally likable individuals, even though their actions may not always be popular. Manasse asserted that the "combination of personal vision, information sensing and analysis skills, and interpersonal skills that generate commitment to a common set of values seems to distinguish effective leaders in a variety of settings."[52] People generally respond to these kinds of leaders with trust and confidence.[53] Although researchers and theorists are not of one mind about the particular attributes and skills which generate this type of reaction, it appears that effective leaders

- Are sensitive to the needs of others.
- Explain the reasons for their actions.
- Involve others in important decisions.
- Are open to criticism, without being defensive.
- Are willing to admit mistakes and to make changes.
- Are honest and fair in interacting with others.[54]

It is probable that no one possesses to a high degree all of the qualities necessary to be an effective instructional leader, and there is no reason why a single administrator should have to possess every quality described previously. In most schools and school districts a number of people can make a contribution to improving the instructional program in one way or another. An important leadership responsibility of the administrator is to identify and then organize these people into an instructional improvement team.

THE INSTRUCTIONAL IMPROVEMENT TEAM

An important objective of any administrator trying to improve instruction should be to organize and utilize effectively all appropriate and available sources of expertise. Personnel in a school or district who could be assigned supervisory responsibilities for improving instruction include the assistant principal, the department head or unit leader, and the central office subject matter supervisor.[55] The degree to which all of these individuals are assigned supervisory responsibilities may vary somewhat from one district to another. However, each of these persons generally possesses special knowledge, skill, or insight which an administrator should attempt to utilize in improving instruction. Administrators can capitalize on the talents of these individuals in two ways: (1) by making explicit to them (and to the people with whom they associate) the nature and extent of their supervisory responsibilities; and (2) by organizing them into an instructional improvement team.

The instructional improvement team is a relatively recent concept in education and it has not been implemented in many schools.[56] Its basic purpose is to improve instruction by mobilizing and organizing the various kinds of expertise in a school. The team usually includes the principal and the department heads (or unit leaders) but can—and perhaps should—also include district supervisors if the latter are available.[57]

The main activities of the team should be to evaluate the effectiveness of the instructional program and to study, develop, and implement ways in which it can be improved. Larry Anders, Edward Centofante, and James Orr indicated that "The instructional team provides a way for teachers to obtain instructional services. At the same time, the process allows instructional leaders—principals and supervisors—to grow professionally through their cooperative involvement in team activities."[58]

The team should not, however, become directly involved in the evaluation of staff for the purpose of making personnel decisions. That function should be left to the staff evaluation team discussed in the previous chapter.

An example of the activities in which an instructional improvement team may become involved is shown by the team agenda in figure 11.1. The agenda for meetings of the instructional improvement team should be developed on the basis of members' input and should be distributed several days before the meeting to give participants an opportunity to consider it and prepare for the meeting.

The instructional improvement team should be involved in all aspects of the supervisory process. Supervision no longer should be the sole province of one person, the principal.[59] Even though principals may be held ultimately responsible for supervision and the improvement of instruction in their schools, they cannot accomplish the job alone. Therefore, in the rest of the chapter, references are made to the role of supervisor, a role which can (and if feasible should) be performed by various members of the instructional improvement team.

Figure 11.1 Instructional Improvement—Team Meeting Agenda.

1. Presentation of the Iowa Test results.
2. Discussion of how the test results relate to the achievement of the educational objectives of the school or organizational units within the school.
3. Identification of needed improvements.

A PROPOSED PROCESS OF INSTRUCTIONAL LEADERSHIP

The ultimate goal of instructional leadership should be to improve student learning, but its more immediate objective is to improve the instructional program. To achieve the latter purpose, the supervisor should engage in a number of activities. If these activities are interrelated and sequential rather than random, they constitute a process. The process of instructional leadership is really the supervisor's design to accomplish the objective of improving the instructional program.

The process of instructional leadership recommended in this chapter is the problem-solving approach. This approach is not new, of course, but its utilization as the main process of instructional leadership has been limited, at least insofar as discussion in the educational literature is concerned.[60] The main steps in the process are presented in figure 11.2. To help the supervisor better understand and utilize the problem-solving approach to instructional leadership as outlined in figure 11.2, the major aspects of the process are discussed in some detail.

IDENTIFICATION OF A PROBLEM OR A NEED FOR IMPROVEMENT

The supervisors' goals are to improve instruction. However, to accomplish that objective they must first determine which elements of the instructional program need to be improved. To arrive at that determination supervisors should

Figure 11.2 A Problem-Solving Approach to Instructional Supervision.

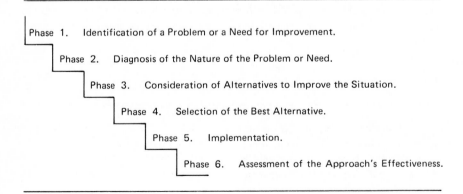

Phase 1.   Identification of a Problem or a Need for Improvement.

Phase 2.   Diagnosis of the Nature of the Problem or Need.

Phase 3.   Consideration of Alternatives to Improve the Situation.

Phase 4.   Selection of the Best Alternative.

Phase 5.   Implementation.

Phase 6.   Assessment of the Approach's Effectiveness.

consider at least three major sources of assistance in the identification of problems or needs of the instructional program: (1) people associated with the school, (2) professional standards and/or recommendations, and (3) local research.

PEOPLE WHO ARE ASSOCIATED WITH THE SCHOOL

Students, teachers, parents, and the central administration all represent potentially excellent sources of assistance for identifying instructional program needs and problems. Because most of these groups are closely involved with the instructional program, they are in a good position to suggest areas needing improvement. Although some of these people may, on their own initiative, recommend instructional improvement needs to supervisors, they should not depend on or limit their sources of feedback to only those few individuals.

If supervisors are really interested in securing input from students, teachers, parents, and the central office, they should survey these groups regularly to ascertain their perceptions and ideas on which aspects of the instructional program need to be improved.[61] Such a survey would not have to be long and complicated; it could provide useful information if it included only several questions. An example is presented in figure 11.3.

Although national survey results are frequently available, supervisors may feel that the results of a national survey are not valid for their schools. If so, they should conduct local surveys. Whether or not they agree with the perceptions of teachers on which aspects of the instructional program need to be improved, feedback can help them to have a better understanding of their attitudes. For example, if a majority of teachers see too many discipline problems as a major impediment to teaching, it would probably be to the supervisor's advantage to investigate the validity of their perception.

Figure 11.3   A Teacher Survey to Identify Instructional Problems.

---

1. What are the three *most* important classroom problems which you believe impair your effectiveness as a teacher?
2. What are three ways in which *each* of the problems listed above could be ameliorated?
3. Would you be willing to work on a committee to help resolve these problems?

PROFESSIONAL STANDARDS AND RECOMMENDATIONS

A second important source for helping to identify instructional improvement needs is the body of recommendations and standards proposed by professional organizations and educational authorities. For example, regional accrediting associations such as the North Central Association publish standards that member schools are expected to meet; these standards can be used by an administrator to identify areas for instructional improvement.[62] The National Association of Secondary School Principals, the National Association of Elementary School Principals, and the Association for Supervision and Curriculum Development also publish recommendations for improving instruction in the schools. In addition, articles and books are written each year by educational authorities who advocate various improvements in the instructional program.

Another publication that contains helpful ideas for improving instruction is *Research on Teaching: Concepts, Findings and Implications,* commissioned by the National Society for the Study of Education.[63] This book presents a comprehensive review of research regarding the improvement of instruction and is full of good ideas. For example, Barak Rosenshine's analysis of the research on instructional time and student achievement suggests that the concept and activities of direct instruction seem to have merit. Although the concept is not easily defined, it seems to focus on those teacher behaviors that directly attempt to improve learning in reading and mathematics, and includes the following elements: (1) making clear to students the goals of the lesson, (2) spending sufficient time on instruction, (3) extensively covering content, (4) continuous monitoring of student performance, (5) asking questions that are within the capacity of the student to answer, and (6) providing immediate and academically oriented feedback to the students.[64] While Rosenshine's ideas on direct instruction are certainly worth examining, other chapters in this book provide additional ideas and approaches to improving instruction.[65] Another equally valuable source of ideas is the *Handbook of Research on Teaching,* which contains many clues and hypotheses for instructional improvement.[66]

LOCAL RESEARCH

A third source of assistance for identifying instructional improvement needs is local research, initiated or coordinated by supervisors. The purpose of this type of research is to ascertain the effectiveness of the instructional program and the various conditions which influence its effectiveness. Although some supervisors may shudder at the mere mention of the term *research,* it can legitimately include a variety of activities which most supervisors should be able to conduct with appropriate assistance.

Three suggestions for local research are

1. A follow-up study of graduates; follow-up study of dropouts. Both studies can yield useful information about the effectiveness of the instructional program and the conditions affecting it. These studies should be initiated on a regular basis and can be conducted through the use of questionnaires and in-depth interviews.
2. A study of how much time is spent in the classroom on direct teaching and learning as opposed to other classroom activities. Considerable research now suggests that instructional time is an important variable associated with student learning.[67] A research question the supervisor could explore through classroom observation is, "Which kinds of activities, such as direct teaching, are occurring in the classroom, and how much time is actually being spent on instruction?" A useful technique for answering that question has been developed by the Wisconsin Research and Development Center, and readers are encouraged to pursue additional information about the method.[68]
3. An analysis of test data to ascertain progress toward or the achievement of the educational objectives of the school. Although an evaluation of the extent of achievement of educational objectives should not be limited to an examination of test data, these data can be helpful in suggesting possible areas in need of instructional improvement. The supervisor should, of course, be cautious in drawing firm conclusions about the instructional program based solely on test data, and it probably would be well to secure consultant assistance in interpreting the relationship between the test results and the achievement of educational objectives.

These are only a few examples of local research which could be helpful. By organizing such research efforts, a supervisor can begin to pinpoint weaknesses in the instructional program so that corrective action can be taken. In the absence of this kind of research activity, the supervisor frequently lacks the data necessary to ascertain the effectiveness of the instructional program.

In concluding this section on the identification of needs for improving instruction, we emphasize that the improvement of instruction depends on ideas of what instruction should be and data on what it is. Supervisors who do not possess or seek both kinds of information are dependent on their own subjective preferences for improving instruction, surely a weak basis for exercising professional judgment.

DIAGNOSIS OF THE NEED FOR IMPROVEMENT

Identification of a need for improving instruction should be followed by diagnosis of that need. Diagnosing a need simply means determining its nature and the reasons for its existence.

For example, suppose a supervisor observes that a teacher does not seem to provide much direct instruction, and students appear to be left on their own to a large extent. The initial question that should be asked in attempting to diagnose the situation is, why is the teacher behaving this way? To obtain an answer to that question, the supervisor may need to explore several alternative explanations and questions:

1. The subject matter or skill being taught does not lend itself to direct instruction but, rather, requires a more indirect teaching style that provides for considerable student self-instruction. (Is this the case? Why?)
2. The students are quite mature, responsible, and have a high level of ability; therefore, a more open classroom with less direct instruction is appropriate. (Do data support this hypothesis?)
3. The teacher's particular approach to teaching is meeting certain needs of the teacher's personality or value system. (Is this possible? What specific teacher needs are being met, and how likely is it that they could be changed?)
4. There are few or no rewards or incentives for the teacher or the students to participate in a more structured situation.

In examining a problem situation, the supervisor may find that a single factor explains the undesired behavior or condition. Frequently, however, there is more than one reason. Therefore, in the initial stages of diagnosis, the supervisor should concentrate on identifying a broad range of possible explanations for a problem and then attempt to focus on the more important and relevant factors that best explain why the problem exists. Once a problem has been completely and accurately diagnosed, the supervisor is in a position to consider possible solutions.

Accurate diagnosis of a problem is an important prerequisite for successful problem solving, because a proposed solution to a problem is likely to be based on its diagnosis. Inaccurate diagnosis is frequently the reason why an instructional problem is not satisfactorily resolved. Usually in such a situation the wrong solution has resulted from failure to properly diagnose the problem. Until instructional problems are properly diagnosed, the supervisor cannot expect to improve instruction to a significant degree.

INSTRUCTIONAL IMPROVEMENT: IN-SERVICE EDUCATION

Once a need for instructional improvement has been properly diagnosed, alternative means of achieving that improvement could be explored. Instructional improvement can be brought about in a variety of ways. Those approaches that involve the supervisor in working with individual staff members were discussed in the previous chapter in connection with staff evaluation and supervision. Other approaches to instructional improvement usually involve the supervisor working with groups and are typically referred to as in-service education. James Lipham, Robb Rankin, and James Hoeh define in-service education as "all professional development activities in which one engages after initial certification and employment and does not conclude until there is a termination of services."[69] They believe that, "The in-service program should focus on increasing professional expertise and remedying identified weaknesses of an individual or group of teachers."[70]

Although in-service education has been frequently advanced by educators as a corrective to many problems, like so many other aspects of education, it comes under periodic attack.[71] L. J. Rubin, for example, says quite simply, that "much in-service activity has been a disaster."[72]

Beverly Showers, Bruce Joyce, and Barrie Bennett, on the other hand, take a more optimistic view toward staff development activities, based on a fairly comprehensive review of the effectiveness of in-service programs.[73] They feel that research has shown that in-service education can be successful under the right conditions. (These are discussed later.)

Whether or not in-service education has been successful is a debatable question. What is clear, however, is that, "Significant improvement of education cannot be accomplished, it would seem, without a major programmatic effort at the in-service education of personnel in all elementary and secondary schools and colleges."[74] As Ben Harris emphasizes in connection with the need for in-service education, "The staff is the heart of the operation of the schools. Money, materials, time, space, facilities, and curricula—all of these are important, too. But initially, in process, and ultimately, the ability of the staff to perform is crucial."[75]

If in-service education is important but in need of improvement, how can it be improved? Based on an analysis of various recommendations for improving in-service programs, the following conditions must be met:

1. The staff needs to be involved in the establishment of the need for in-service education and in the development, implementation, and evaluation of the program.
2. The in-service program eventually initiated must be viewed by teachers as contributing to their professional growth rather than only meeting administrative needs.
3. The school board, administrators, and supervisors of the school/district much be committed to the importance of in-service education, and the latter two groups must plan carefully with the staff for the development, implementation, and evaluation of in-service activities.
4. Objectives of the in-service program need to be stated clearly and specifically, and be reasonably attainable, given the constraints of the situation.
5. In-service activities need to be varied and should involve the participants actively, as opposed to the more passive role of listener, observer, or reader.
6. In-service activities should be planned and scheduled so there is continuity and articulation between what goes on in the program and what occurs before and after the instructional program.
7. The leader or presenter of the in-service activity needs to show how (by demonstrating, if possible) new content, materials, or skills can be applied to the staff member's situation.
8. The incentives for participating in an in-service program should emphasize both intrinsic (e.g., professional improvement) as well as extrinsic rewards (e.g., credit on the salary schedule).
9. Participants in in-service education need periodic feedback during the program on their progress.
10. Adequate time and funds must be provided by the administration to plan, carry out, and evaluate the in-service activities.[76]

Although the presence of these ten conditions may not guarantee a successful in-service program, their absence would seem to limit its chances of success. Additional factors that supervisors need to take into consideration in planning and implementing particular in-service activities are discussed in the following sections.

DEPARTMENTAL OR UNIT MEETINGS

Most schools hold departmental or unit meetings periodically during the year. These meetings offer important opportunities for a supervisor to improve instruction by working with a group of teachers. Unfortunately, such meetings usually take place after a long day of school, and frequently only items of a housekeeping nature are discussed. However, the potential for discussing and exploring issues, problems, and new approaches to instruction is definitely present at a departmental or unit meeting. The key people for capitalizing on that potential are the supervisor and the department heads or unit leaders.

If the departmental or unit meeting is to become an important means of improving instruction, the supervisor needs to work with the department heads or unit leaders to extend their vision of the purposes and uses of these meetings, and should hold the department chairs or unit leaders accountable for focusing their meetings to a larger extent on instructional improvement purposes. Most department heads and unit leaders, because of a lack of training or vision, do not take the initiative to utilize their meetings for discussion of instructional improvement activities. They need help and encouragement from the supervisor.

A wide variety of possible instructional improvement topics could be explored during department or unit meetings. The following four examples illustrate the range of possibilities:

1. Examination of departmental or unit objectives to ascertain the degree of understanding and consensus on overall objectives and the objectives for each grade level.
2. Consideration of an assessment program to provide data on the extent to which departmental or unit objectives are being met.
3. Presentation and demonstration of available supplementary resources from the instructional materials center.
4. Development of a uniform grading or homework policy for the department or unit.

These four topics are only suggestive of the instructional improvement activities a department or unit could consider during its meetings.[77] This does not mean that the supervisor can realistically expect that all departmental or unit meetings can be devoted entirely to instructional improvement topics. There are admittedly legitimate housekeeping tasks, such as requisitioning and budgeting, which a department or unit must accomplish during its meetings. However, one of the primary purposes of these meetings should be to focus on instructional improvement.

FACULTY MEETINGS

The faculty meeting is probably one of the most abused and most often criticized of all group supervisory activities. It is generally scheduled at the end of the school day when teachers are tired, it is frequently informational in nature and dominated by the principal, and it seldom permits much teacher participation and involvement. Also, since the advent of the master contract for teachers, the time allowed for faculty meetings is frequently of such short duration that little of an instructional nature can be discussed. On the other hand, the faculty meeting represents one of the few vehicles available to the supervisor during the year for bringing the total faculty together to consider instructional concerns. By correcting the abuses of the faculty meeting, it can be used profitably for instructional improvement purposes.

One of the major constraints a supervisor must overcome to utilize the faculty meeting effectively is that, with the exception of very small schools, the size of the faculty usually limits the amount of participation which can take place.[78] Recognizing this limitation, it would appear that faculty meetings should be used primarily for problem identification and decision making, and that the investigation of a problem and exploration of alternative solutions should be carried out by subcommittees of the faculty, who would report their recommendations to the total faculty and administration for a final decision. This would make possible more effectively conducted faculty meetings, and yet the administrator (with the faculty, if appropriate) could make the final decision on matters. The alternative is for 40 to 100 people to attempt to determine the nature of a problem, the reasons for its existence, and possible alternative solutions—under conditions of apathy, fatigue, large group size, and a limited time frame.

If supervisors are to utilize faculty meetings more productively, they should try to follow rather simple but important principles.[79]

1. The meeting should be scheduled during school time, if possible, rather than at the end of the day. Some schools dismiss students early on one afternoon every week or two to provide greater time for faculty consideration of a topic. If this is not feasible, to the extent possible, the group should decide on the time and place of meetings, and should decide on a definite adjournment time.

2. Faculty input should be sought in developing the agenda. This may mean establishing a faculty meeting planning committee (required by some master contracts) or simply requesting the faculty to submit items for the agenda. In any regard, faculty members' input is important in the development of the agenda if they are to play more than a passive role at the meetings.

3. The agenda and all related materials for the faculty meeting should be distributed to the staff at least two days before the date of the meeting. If faculty members are to react, discuss, and make decisions on agenda items at the meeting, they need an opportunity to become aware of and think about the topics to be discussed, and to study related material prior to the meeting. It is conceded that some faculty members—perhaps even a large proportion—will not take or find time to consider the agenda and related materials before the meeting, even if they receive them in advance. However, many teachers will find this procedure helpful.

4. Supervisors should employ as much as possible group leadership skills and, throughout the meeting, teacher participation and activity should predominate. The supervisor's role during the faculty meetings should be to
   a. Create an atmosphere which is friendly and nonthreatening but task-oriented.
   b. Guide the discussion in such a way that as many people as possible who would like to and should participate during the meeting have an opportunity to do so.
   c. Clarify questions, comments, or statements so that intentions, meanings, and implications are not left ambiguous.
   d. Keep the group focused on the topic under consideration, and limit wandering from the subject.
   e. Summarize periodically where the group appears to be, relative to the topic, and what remains to be done.
   f. Mediate differences of opinion.[80]

5. Minutes of the meeting should be maintained that indicate important points made, questions raised that are yet to be resolved, commitments made, and decisions reached. The minutes are a useful record of what transpired during the meeting and can be used for self-improvement analysis and for providing continuity from one meeting to another.

6. Minutes of the meeting should be disseminated to the total faculty and other relevant parties, such as the immediate superior in the central office. Each member of the faculty needs a record of what transpired during the meeting, if understanding of and commitment to decisions reached during the meeting are to be maintained. It is also useful to provide space at the end of the minutes for reactions by faculty members for the purpose of obtaining feedback from individuals who, for one reason or another, did not comment during the meeting itself.

7. Follow-up activities need to be initiated after the faculty meeting to implement decisions reached and to investigate questions or problems raised. A fairly common complaint of many teachers about faculty meetings is that there is no follow-through afterwards. If the faculty are to believe that their meetings are worthwhile, the supervisor needs to initiate and coordinate appropriate follow-up activities after the meetings.

8. Each meeting should lead to improved competency and morale.

Faculty meetings can be a valuable group activity for the improvement of instruction if the previously described principles are followed. New approaches to teaching can be demonstrated; instructional problems can be identified; and/or recommendations from subcommittees on school philosophy, objectives, grading, and grade-level articulation, for example, can be considered and decided on. The value of the faculty meeting is limited mainly by the size of the faculty and the degree of resourcefulness and organizational skills possessed by the supervisor.

COMMITTEE WORK

Committee work is an appropriate problem-solving procedure for improving instruction as well as an excellent group activity for staff development. As a result of committee interaction and investigation of an instructional problem, each member of a committee can benefit through increased awareness, understanding, and possibly new skills.

Supervisors should utilize committees to improve instruction whenever a situation would be more thoroughly investigated and considered if several people were involved rather than only one individual. The primary rationale for establishing a committee, rather than assigning only one person, should be that the other people whom the supervisor might involve possess additional knowledge, skill, or insight which would be helpful in the accomplishment of a task. That task may be investigating a possible instructional problem, identifying alternative solutions, or gaining acceptance from the entire faculty on a recommended course of action.

Although committee work can be an excellent method for improving instruction and capitalizing on the expertise of various staff members, the experience of those involved with committees has not always been positive. Frequently, teachers have felt that they were not "meaningfully involved" on a committee, and that the supervisor's "mind was already made up" before the committee was appointed. Supervisors, on their part, have sometimes felt that teachers expected too much from their involvement and tried to exceed their authority. And, of course, there frequently arise problems of insufficient time, role ambiguity, and inadequate incentives for committee work.

Even though they would probably not be able to avoid all problems in regard to committee work, supervisors can minimize difficulties if these procedures are followed:

1. Clearly define and communicate to all committee members, in advance, the objectives, function, scope, and authority of the committee. If it is only an advisory committee to develop recommendations to submit to the supervisor, that function should be made clear to all participants.
2. Keep all members of the committee well informed before, during, and after meetings, as to what is transpiring. Advance agendas and minutes of each meeting are minimum requirements.
3. Utilize to the greatest extent possible the individual interest and talents of the members of the committee. There is little to be gained by either the school or the participants if the latter's potential contributions are not fully utilized.
4. Reward members of the committee for their individual and total contributions at every available opportunity. Committee work is frequently tedious, and periodic recognition of the value of the committee's work can pay important dividends.

A significant factor which has contributed to ineffectiveness of committees and the disillusionment of committee members is the ambivalence or vagueness of the supervisor in regard to the objectives and role of the committee, and the role of the supervisor in relationship to the committee. A precise understanding of these points on the part of everyone involved can avert serious problems at a later date.

(For additional ideas and conceptual tools for working with groups, see Richard A. Gorton, "Curriculum Committee," in *Encyclopedia of School Administration and Supervision* and Richard A. Gorton, *School Leadership and Administration: Important Concepts, Case Studies, and Simulations,* chapter 4.[81]

WORKSHOPS AND INSTITUTES

Three main types of school workshops or institutes are: (1) the preschool workshop for staff before classes formally begin in the fall; (2) the in-service workshop held during the school year on in-service days or Saturdays; and (3) the summer workshop.[82] Because the preschool workshop has already been discussed in conjunction with orientation for new staff, this section concentrates on the other two workshops.

The primary purpose of in-service workshops during the school year should be to explore a problem, topic, or new approach to instruction in greater depth than would be possible during a faculty or committee meeting. A workshop can include a combination of activities for the total faculty, small groups, or individuals; however, as Peter Oliva indicated, "the term *workshop* conveys the notion of hands-on experiences through which teachers may gain or improve specific knowledge."[83] Figure 11.4 presents a typical format for an inservice workshop scheduled during the year.

The success of an in-service workshop depends in large part on the degree of administrative planning, organization, and faculty input which have been invested in the design and implementation of the workshop. The last factor, faculty input, is tremendously important. If faculty members or their representatives have not been involved in choosing the theme and in planning for the workshop, its success is uncertain. Supervisors need faculty involvement so that in planning the workshop they can capitalize on the thinking and insight of staff members and increase their receptivity to it. In most cases, the faculty will not be very receptive to unilateral administrative decision making and planning in regard to an in-service workshop.

Figure 11.4 Sample Format for In-Service Workshop.

Workshop Theme: Improvement of Reading

8:15-8:30	Coffee and socializing in Room 201
8:30-8:45	Welcome and an overview of the Workshop
8:45-9:45	Presentation by Dr. Hiller, "Data on the Effectiveness of the School's Reading Program and Ways to Improve It."
9:45-10:00	Break
10:00-11:45	Small Group Discussions about the implications of Dr. Hiller's presentation
11:45-1:00	Lunch
1:15-3:30	Team and individual teacher planning of instructional techniques and materials that might improve our Reading Program
3:30-4:00	Workshop Evaluation

The first step in planning for an in-service workshop is to conduct a needs assessment.[84] Ideally, this procedure is not initiated only prior to a workshop, but as an ongoing process, utilizing the sources for identifying needs described in an earlier section, "Identification of a Problem or Need for Improvement." The essential question that a needs assessment is trying to answer is, "Which aspect of the instructional program needs to be improved?" The typical approach to answering that question has been simply to survey teachers as to their perceptions of areas to be improved in the instructional program, or in other aspects of the school program. Unfortunately, in many instances this approach has led to a superficial assessment of needs which has tended to reflect current interests and fads, rather than basic needs of the instructional program.[85] While teachers should be involved in any needs assessment, the approach to determining the needs for improvement should include additionally related sources for identifying needs. The approach should also foster objectivity in identifying needs and should emphasize basic and future needs, as well as apparent and current needs.

Once a comprehensive needs assessment has been completed, the supervisor (working with others involved in planning, implementing, and evaluating the workshop) should initiate a series of planning and organizing steps which are necessary if the workshop is to be successful. These include (1) specification of the objectives to be achieved; (2) analysis of the extent to which the proposed objectives are clear and reasonably attainable, given the limits of time, resources, and so forth; (3) identification and assessment of relevant workshop formats and activities to facilitate achieving the objectives; (4) identification of relevant and available resources needed; (5) identification and assessment of possible problems or obstacles which could impair the chances of conducting a successful workshop; (6) decisions on the most effective workshop format and activities, given the availability of resources, and the possibility of certain obstacles or problems; (7) identification and assignment of needed personnel for implementing the workshop; (8) preparation of a master schedule of events, detailing when, where, and for how long activities are to occur; (9) agreement, before implementing the workshop, on criteria and methods for evaluating its activities; (10) review of Murphy's Laws that "Most things are more complicated than they initially appear to be," and that "Most things take longer than originally anticipated"; and a reexamination of the previous nine steps before beginning the workshop.

While the steps just recommended may seem like a lot of work and perhaps an overemphasis on detail, they should be viewed as only general guidelines for planning and organizing a workshop.

After the workshop has been conducted, it should be evaluated; herein lies one of the major weaknesses of workshops or institutes.[86] Frequently they are not evaluated at all, or they are evaluated in terms of what the participants thought of the speeches, materials, or activities. Seldom is there an evaluation of the extent to which the workshop has achieved its objectives. Michael Fullan stated that, "The absence of follow-up after workshops is without a doubt the greatest single problem in contemporary professional development."[87] In addition, it seems that, regardless of the ideas, questions, or discussions explored during a workshop, there is very little indication two days later that it has had any discernible effect on what is taking place in the school. Part of the problem, of course, may be that little was accomplished during the workshop; but another hypothesis is that no one has assumed the responsibility of following through on what was achieved.

Certainly, all school personnel have a professional responsibility for workshop follow-up activities. But the supervisor must shoulder the major responsibility for initiating, coordinating, monitoring, and evaluating the activities. If the supervisor does not assume this responsibility, it is unlikely that anyone else will, and the value of the workshop will be quite minimal.

Evaluation methods are beyond the scope of this text; even so, some sample evaluation questions that should be asked following a workshop or institute are

1. To what extent were the workshop objectives achieved? What is the evidence for this?
2. To what degree did the workshop improve the knowledge, understanding, attitudes, or skills of the participants? What is the evidence for this?
3. How effective were the speakers and materials utilized during the workshop? What is the evidence for this?
4. How effective were the workshop format, activities, and schedule? What is the evidence?
5. Which problems or obstacles were encountered that had not been anticipated, and why?
6. What was learned from this workshop experience that should be taken into consideration in planning and organizing the next workshop?
7. How can changes in the participants' understanding, attitudes, or skills be best sustained?

These evaluation questions are, of course, only a representative sample of the kinds of questions that need to be addressed, but they should give supervisors some useful ideas for evaluating a workshop or institute.[88]

The points which have been made about in-service workshops held during the year also apply to summer workshops. Recently, participants in summer workshops have been remunerated, and problems of motivation and receptivity to workshop topics and activities have been correspondingly reduced. Careful planning, systematic organization, considerable faculty input, and adequate follow-through after the workshops are just as important for summer workshops as for those held during the year. Both types offer an excellent mechanism for staff development and for improving instruction if the conditions recommended in this section are present.

STAFF DEVELOPMENT CENTERS

In reaction to the poor quality of the typical in-service education program, a different type of in-service for teachers has come on the scene in recent years. Referred to as "staff development centers" or "teaching centers," the in-service education activities which take place in or through these centers emphasize teacher decision making on policy matters, self-direction, and colleague assistance, in regard to improvement; participation is voluntary as contrasted with required.[89] The centers are based on several assumptions, according to David Burrell:

> First, there is the notion that basic and effective innovation and reappraisal of work in the classroom will come about mainly through the efforts and activities of practicing teachers, assisted by whoever can contribute in some way. The second assumption is that there exists among teachers a vast reservoir of untapped expertise and experience. If they are given the opportunity, good teachers are capable of drawing on these and using them as a starting point for professional renewal and growth. The good practitioner is seen to have great potential as the trainer of other teachers. Third, it is assumed that centers can be effective instruments for reconsideration or development of current practice in the schools. The fourth assumption is that centers can provide a neutral arena in which teachers can work relatively free of constraints and pressures and the hierarchical assumptions often present in other training institutions. Many would argue that the rejection of the latter is the initial decisive factor in the development of true professionalism among teachers. It is certainly associated with the idea of teacher control of in-service planning, for the fifth assumption is that centers should be organized and controlled as far as possible by the teachers themselves through the centers' programs and other decision-making committees.[90]

Staff development centers have been implemented in a variety of locales, but they tend to be established in larger school districts, in regional centers, and/or near universities.[91] Their programs usually deal with the basic concerns and issues facing teachers.[92] The centers are often supported by external funds, although school district funding is not unusual. The effectiveness of staff development centers is still being ascertained and their merits debated.[93] Some people are concerned about the centers' heavy emphasis on teacher control of policy making, the voluntary nature of participation, and the assumptions behind self-directed improvement.[94] Despite these important issues, staff development centers or some variation of them are probably here to stay because they provide promising opportunities for cooperative learning and collegial interaction.[95] To pursue this topic further, read the additional material identified at the end of the chapter.[96]

A FINAL NOTE

The last step in the recommended approach to instructional supervision is assessment. No program can be significantly improved without assessment, and there is considerable evidence that the instructional leadership currently in operation in many schools is badly in need of improvement. Therefore, in addition to implementing the various suggested procedures described in this chapter, supervisors should periodically assess the effectiveness of the different components of the school's instructional leadership process with the involvement and help of the faculty.

Review and Learning Activities

1. Which factors limit and which factors enhance the role of the administrator as an instructional leader? Based on these factors, which improvements would have to take place before you could be an instructional leader in your current school or district?
2. Evaluate the concept of an instructional improvement team. What are its advantages and disadvantages? Does an instructional improvement team operate in your school? If not, why not?
3. What sources of assistance can a supervisor utilize in identifying a need for instructional improvement? Assess the utility of each source of assistance. To which extent are the sources of assistance recommended being used in your school?
4. Using the recommendations for improving in-service education, ascertain the extent to which each of the suggested guidelines is being implemented in your school. Also, attempt to diagnose reasons for a lack of implementation of guidelines.
5. Evaluate each type of in-service education described in this chapter. What are its advantages and disadvantages?

Notes

1. William D. Greenfield, ed., *Instructional Leadership: Concepts, Issues, and Controversies* (Boston: Allyn & Bacon, 1987), 60.
2. Rick Ginsberg, "Principals as Instructional Leaders: An Ailing Panacea," *Education and Urban Society* (May 1988): 276; and Brad L. Mitchell and Luvern L. Cunningham, "State Policy and the Pursuit of Instructional Leadership," *Theory into Practice* (Summer 1986): 207.
3. Rolf K. Blank, "In What Areas Do Principals Provide School Leadership? Evidence from a National Sample of Urban High Schools," *ERS Spectrum* (Summer 1987): 24–33.

4. See Ginsberg, "Principals as Instructional Leaders," 276–93; and Wilma F. Smith and Richard L. Andrews, *Instructional Leadership: How Principals Make a Difference* (Alexandria, Va.: Association for Supervision and Curriculum Development, 1989).

5. For an excellent review of research on the impact of these variables, see Herbert J. Walberg, ed., *Educational Environments and Effects* (Berkeley, Calif.: McCutchan, 1979). Also see Mark A. Smylie, "The Enhancement Function of Staff Development: Organizational and Psychological Antecedents to Individual Teacher Change," *American Educational Research Journal* (Spring 1988): 1–30; Jerry J. Herman and Gail M. Stephens, "The Four Keys Necessary for Instructional Leadership," *NASSP Bulletin* (March 1989): 55–59; and J. R. Weber, "Leading the Instructional Program," in S. C. Smith and P. K. Piele, *School Leadership: Handbook for Excellence* 2d ed. (Eugene, Oreg.: ERIC Clearinghouse on Educational Management, 1989), 191–224.

6. Owen Kiernan, testimony given to Senate Select Committee on Equal Education Opportunity, 1974. Also see National Association of Secondary School Principals, *Performance-Based Preparation of Principals: A Framework for Improvement* (Reston, Va.: NASSP, 1985); Bill Clinton, *Speaking of Leadership* (Denver, Colo.: Education Commission of the States, 1987); and National Commission on Educational Administration, *Leaders for America's Schools* (Tempe, Ariz.: University Council of Educational Administration, 1987).

7. See Professional Standards Commission. *The Principal: A Crucial Element in Quality Education* (Atlanta, Ga.: Professional Standards Commission, 1983), 49–52; J. N. Mangieri and J. W. Arnn, Jr., "Excellent Schools: The Leadership Functions of Principals," *American Education* 21 (1985): 8–10; and M. D. Richardson, "The Tennessee Principal: A Self-Perception" (Ph.D. diss., University of Tennessee-Knoxville, 1986).

8. Philip Hallinger and Joseph Murphy, "Assessing the Instructional Management Behavior of Principals," *The Elementary School Journal* 86 (1985): 219.

9. Larry Cuban, "Principaling: Images and Roles," *Peabody Journal of Education* (Fall 1986): 109.

10. See Kent D. Peterson, "The Principal's Tasks," *Administrators' Notebook* 26, (1977); W. J. Martin and Donald J. Willower, "The Managerial Behavior of High School Principals," *Educational Administration Quarterly,* no. 2 (1981); V. C. Morris, R. L. Crowson, E. Horwitz, and C. Porter-Gehrie, *The Urban Principal: Discretionary Decisionmaking in a Large Educational Organization* (Chicago: University of Illinois at Chicago Circle, 1981); A. Lorri Manasse, "Improving Conditions for Principal Effectiveness: Policy Implications of Research," *Elementary School Journal* 85 (1985): 439–63; and L. O. Pellicer, L. W. Anderson, J. W. Keefe, E. A. Kelley, and L. W. McCleary, *High School Leaders and Their Schools, Vol. I: A National Profile* (Reston, Va.: National Association of Secondary School Principals, 1988), 16–18.

11. John E. Eisenhauer, Donald J. Willower, and Joseph W. Licata, "Role Conflict, Role Ambiguity, and School Principals' Job Robustness," *Journal of Experimental Education* (Winter 1984–85): 86.

12. Brad L. Mitchell and Luvern L. Cunningham, "State Policy," 208.

13. Dan C. Lortie, "Built-In Tendencies Toward Stabilizing the Principal's Role," *Journal of Research and Development in Education* 22, no. 1 (1988): 85.

14. Sharon F. Rallis and Martha C. Highsmith, "The Myth of the 'Great Principal': Questions of School Management and Instructional Leadership," *Kappan* (December 1986): 302.

15. Anneka E. Bredo, "Teacher Legitimation of Principal Control as a Situational Contingency in Principal-Teacher Influence Relations" (Paper presented at the annual meeting of the American Educational Research Association, San Francisco, California, April 1979), 2.

16. Philip Hallinger and Joseph F. Murphy, "Assessing and Developing Principal Instructional Leadership," *Educational Leadership* (September 1987): 55–56.

17. Nancy J. Pitner, "Substitutes for Principal Leader Behavior: An Exploratory Study," *Educational Administration Quarterly* (Spring 1986): 23–42.

18. John C. Croft, "The Principal as Supervisor: Some Descriptive Findings and Important Questions," *Educational Administration Abstracts* (Spring 1969).

19. Terrence E. Deal and Lynn D. Celotti, "How Much Influence Do (and Can) Educational Administrators Have on Classrooms?" *Kappan* (March 1980): 471.

20. R. G. Corwin, "Teacher Militancy in the United States: Reflections on the Sources and Prospects," *Theory into Practice* (April 1968): 96–102; G. L. Sharma, "Who Should Make What Decisions?" *Administrator's Notebook* (April 1955); and Bredo, "Teacher Legitimation of Principal Control," 7–12.

21. Nancy J. Pitner, "Substitutes for Principal Leader Behavior," *Educational Administration Quarterly* (Spring 1986): 23–42.

22. Ibid., p. 41.

23. Ibid.

24. L. B. Ball, "Principal and Negotiations," *High School Journal* (October 1968): 22–29.

25. Edward H. Seifert and John Beck, "Elementary Principals: Instructional Leaders or School Managers?" *Kappan* (March 1981): 528. Also see Gordon Cawelti and Charles Reavis, "How Well Are We Providing Instructional Improvement Services?" *Educational Leadership* (December 1980): 236–40.

26. A. Etzioni, "Administrative and Professional Authority," in *Complex Organizations: A Sociological Reader* (New York: Holt, Rinehart and Winston, 1961).

27. Richard A. Gorton, "The Importance of Administrative Expertise in Instructional Leadership" (Paper presented at the annual meeting of the American Educational Research Association, 1971).

28. Identified in part from Ginsberg, "Principals as Instructional Leaders," *Education and Urban Society* (May 1988): 276–93; and Hallinger and Murphy, "Assessing and Developing Principal Instructional Leadership."

29. Kent D. Peterson, "Vision and Problem Finding in Principals' Work: Values and Cognition in Administration," *Peabody Journal of Education* (Fall 1986): 87–106.

30. William D. Greenfield, "Moral, Social, and Technical Dimensions of the Principalship," *Peabody Journal of Education* (Fall 1986).

31. David L. Clark et al., "What Aids Success in Urban Elementary Schools?" *Kappan* (March 1980): 467.

32. Ronald Edmonds, "Effective Schools for the Urban Poor," *Educational Leadership* (October 1979): 16–17.

33. Ibid.

34. Steven Bossert, "School Effects," in *Handbook of Research in Educational Administration,* ed. Norman J. Boyan (New York: Longman, 1988): 346.

35. Erwin Miklos, "Administrator Selection, Career Patterns, Succession, and Socialization," in *Handbook of Research in Educational Administration,* ed. Norman J. Boyan (New York: Longman, 1988): 54–55.

36. Andrew Halpin, "A Paradigm for Research on Administrative Behavior," in *Administrative Behavior in Education,* ed. Roald F. Campbell and Russell T. Gregg (New York: Harper & Row, 1957): 166–67. See also Peterson, "Vision and Problem Finding"; and Laura A. Cooper, "The Principal as Instructional Leader," *Principal* (January 1989): 13–16.

37. Institute for Educational Leadership, *What Makes an Effective School?* (Washington, D.C.: George Washington University, 1980), 89.

38. For discussions on educational vision, see Linda Tinelli Sheive and Marian Beauchamp Schoenheit, "Vision and the Work of Educational Leaders," *Leadership: Examining the Elusive* (Alexandria, Va.: Association for Supervision and Curriculum Development, 1987): 93–104; M. E. Dantley, "A Critical Perspective of Leadership Vision: Its Source and Influence upon the Educational Reform Movement," *Urban Education* (October 1989): 243–62; and Roland S. Barth, "A Personal Vision of a Good School," *Kappan* (March 1990): 512–16.

39. Peterson, "Vision and Problem Finding," 88.

40. See A. Lorri Manasse, "Principals as Leaders of High-Performing Systems," *Educational Leadership* (February 1984): 42–46; Larry Cuban, "Principaling: Images and Roles," *Peabody Journal of Education* (Fall 1986): 107–19; Cynthia J. Norris and C. M.

Achilles, "Intuitive Leadership: A New Dimension for Education Leadership," *Planning and Changing* (Summer 1988): 6–19; and Glen F. Ovard, "Leadership: Maintaining Vision in a Complex Arena," *NASSP Bulletin* (February 1990): 1–17.

41. See Philip Hallinger and Joseph Murphy, "Assessing the Instructional Management Behavior of Principals," *The Elementary School Journal* 86 (1985): 217–45; David C. Dwyer, "Understanding the Principal's Contribution to Instruction," *Peabody Journal of Education* (Fall 1986): 3–18; and William L. Johnson and Karolyn J. Snyder, "Instructional Leadership Training Needs for School Principals," *Journal of Educational Administration* (Summer 1986): 239–53.

42. Charles W. Guditus and Perry A. Zirkel, "Bases of Supervisory Power among Public School Principals" (Paper presented at the annual meeting of the American Educational Research Association, 1979), 16.

43. James Lipham, "Personal Variables of Effective Administrators," *Administrator's Notebook* (September 1960): 1–4. See also Erwin Miklos, "Administrator Selection, Career Patterns, Succession, and Socialization."

44. Kent D. Peterson, "Mechanism of Culture Building and Principals' Work," *Education and Urban Society* (May 1988): 251.

45. Ibid. 252.

46. Pellicer et al., *High School Leaders and Their Schools.*

47. Clark et al., "Success in Urban Elementary Schools," 467.

48. James M. Lipham, "Leadership and Administration," in Daniel Griffith, ed., *Behavioral Science and Educational Administration,* Sixty-third Yearbook of the National Society for the Study of Education (Chicago: University of Chicago Press, 1964), 122.

49. George J. Michel, "The Risk-Taking Dimension of Educational Leadership," *Record* (Spring 1986): 38.

50. Manasse, "Principals as Leaders," 45.

51. Richard A. Gorton and Kenneth J. McIntyre, *The Effective Principal* (Reston, Va.: The National Association of Secondary School Principals, 1978).

52. Manasse, "Principals as Leaders," 44.

53. Wayne K. Hoy and L. B. Brown, "Leadership Behavior of Principals and the Zone of Acceptance of Elementary Teachers," *Journal of Educational Administration* (Winter 1988): 23–37.

54. Gorton, *School Leadership and Administration,* 274.

55. Edward Pajak, *The Central Office Supervisor of Curriculum and Instruction: Setting the Stage for Success* (Boston: Allyn & Bacon, 1989).

56. For examples of successful instructional improvement teams, see Herbert J. Klausmeier, James M. Lipham, and John C. Daresh, *The Renewal and Improvement of Secondary Education* (Lanham, Md.: University Press of America, 1983); and Philip Hallinger, "Developing Instructional Leadership Teams in Secondary Schools: A Framework," *NASSP Bulletin* (May 1989): 84–92.

57. Sir James Robert Marks, Emery Stoops, and Joyce King-Stoops, *Handbook of Educational Supervision: A Guide for the Practitioner,* 3d ed. (Boston: Allyn & Bacon, 1985), 55–66.

58. Larry W. Anders, Edward F. Centofante, and James T. Orr, "Building the Instructional Team for Effective Leadership," *NASSP Bulletin* (November 1987): 61.

59. Robert O. Slater and Jameson W. Doig, "Leadership in Education: Issues of Entrepreneurship and Environment," *Education and Urban Society* (May 1988): 294–301.

60. For a somewhat similar attempt to utilize the problem-solving approach, see Leslee J. Bishop, *Staff Development and Instructional Improvement* (Boston, Mass.: Allyn & Bacon, 1976); and Gail Chase Furman, "School District Approval for Staff Development: 'Garbage Can' Decision Making," *Urban Education* (July 1987): 238–54.

61. For a more detailed description of the needs assessment process, see R. Lloyd Ryan, *The Complete In-service Staff Development Program* (Englewood Cliffs, N.J.: Prentice-Hall, 1987), 60–76.

62. North Central Association, 5454 South Shore Drive, Chicago, Illinois.

63. Penelope L. Peterson and Herbert J. Walberg, eds., *Research on Teaching: Concepts, Findings and Implications* (Berkeley, Calif.: McCutchan, 1979).

64. Ibid., 28–53.

65. Peterson and Walberg, *Research on Teaching.*

66. Merlin Wittrock, ed., *Handbook of Research on Teaching* 3d ed. (New York: Macmillan, 1986).

67. Herbert J. Walberg, "Synthesis of Research on Time and Learning," *Educational Leadership* (March 1988): 76–86.

68. "Timely Techniques: How Teachers Can Tell Where the Time Goes," *Wisconsin R and D Center News* (Spring 1980): 2.

69. James M. Lipham, Robb E. Rankin, and James A. Hoeh, Jr. *The Principalship: Concepts, Competencies, and Cases* (New York: Longman, 1985): 183.

70. Ibid.

71. Ryan, *The Complete In-service Staff Development Program,* 12–15.

72. L. J. Rubin, "The Case for Staff Development," cited in Gail Chase Furman, "School District Approval for Staff Development: 'Garbage Can' Decision Making," *Urban Education* (July 1987): 238–54.

73. Beverly Showers, Bruce Joyce, and Barrie Bennett, "Synthesis of Research on Staff Development: A Framework for Future Study and a State-of-the-Art Analysis," *Educational Leadership* (November 1987): 77–88.

74. Ben Harris, *Improving Staff Performance Through In-service Education* (Boston: Allyn & Bacon, 1980), 13.

75. Ibid.

76. Bruce Joyce and Beverly Showers, "Improving In-Service Training: The Message of Research," *Educational Leadership* (February 1980): 379–85; and Bruce Joyce and Beverly Showers, *Student Achievement through Staff Development* (New York: Longman, 1988). See also books by Harris, Lipham et al., and Ryan identified earlier.

77. For a description of several innovative approaches to making these meetings more interesting and productive, see Harris, *Improving Staff Performance,* chapters 7 and 8. Also see Vicki S. Dean, "Simulation: A Tool for In-service Education," *Educational Leadership* (April 1981): 550–52.

78. Association for Supervision and Curriculum Development, *Group Processes in Supervision* (Washington, D.C.: National Education Association, 1948), 49. Also see Steven H. Larson, "The Behavioral Side of Productive Meetings," *Personnel Journal* (April 1980): 292–96.

79. Anthony P. Williams, "Management for More Effective Staff Meetings, *Personnel Journal* (August 1979): 547–50. See also, Marks et al., "How to Provide Successful Faculty Meetings," *Handbook of Educational Supervision,* 199–221.

80. Association for Supervision and Curriculum Development, *Group Processes in Supervision,* 128.

81. Richard Gorton, "Curriculum Committee," in *Encyclopedia of School Administration and Supervision* (Phoenix, Ariz.: Oryx Press, 1988): 82–83; and Richard Gorton, *School Leadership and Administration: Important Concepts, Case Studies, and Situations* (Dubuque, Iowa: Wm. C. Brown Company Publishers, 1987) chap. 4.

82. Since there are more similarities than differences between workshops and institutes, the discussion focuses on workshops and refers specifically to institutes only when appropriate.

83. Peter Oliva, "Faculty Workshops," in *Encyclopedia of School Administration and Supervision,* ed. R. A. Gorton, G. T. Schneider, and J. C. Fisher (Phoenix, Ariz.: Oryx Press, 1988), 117.

84. Ibid.

85. Harris, *Improving Staff Performance,* 218–19.

86. Donald Grossnickle, "In-service Follow-Up—What to Do After the Expert Leaves," *NASSP Bulletin* (March 1987): 11–16.

87. Michael Fullan, *The Meaning of Educational Change* (New York: Teachers College Press, 1982).

88. For further ideas, see Leslee Bishop, *Staff Development*, 153.

89. Roy Edelfelt and Tamar Orvell, *Teacher Centers: Where, What, and Why?* (Bloomington, Ind.: Phi Delta Kappa, 1978). See also Susan Gould and Esther Letven, "A Center for Interactive Professional Development," *Educational Leadership* (November 1987): 49–52.

90. David Burrell, "The Teacher Center: A Critical Analysis," *Educational Leadership* (March 1976). For a more recent discussion of similar concepts, see Terry M. Wildman and Jerry A. Niles, "Essentials of Professional Growth," *Educational Leadership* (February 1987): 4–10.

91. For examples of staff development centers, see Gould and Letven, "A Center for Interactive Professional Development;" and Diana Leggett and Sharon Hoyle, "Preparing Teachers for Collaboration," *Educational Leadership* (November 1987): 59–62.

92. See Dennis Sparks, "A Teacher Center Tackles the Issue," *Today's Education* (November–December 1979): 37–39.

93. Roy A. Edelfelt, "Critical Issues in Developing Teacher Centers," *Kappan* (February 1982): 390–92.

94. Rubin, *In-Service Education of Teachers*, 14–18.

95. David W. Johnson and Roger T. Johnson, "Research Shows the Benefits of Adult Cooperation," *Educational Leadership* (November 1987): 27–30; and Allan A. Glatthorn, "Cooperative Professional Development: Peer-Centered Options for Teacher Growth," *Educational Leadership* (November 1987): 31–35.

96. Kathleen Devaney, ed., *Building a Teachers' Center*, (San Francisco: Far West Laboratory, 1979). In addition, see Roy Edelfelt, ed., *Teacher Centers and Needs Assessment*, (Washington, D.C.: National Education Association, 1981); Robert Luke et al., Teacher-Centered In-Service Education: Planning and Products (Washington, D.C.: Institute of Education, 1980); and Mary Paguette, "Voluntary Collegial Support Groups for Teachers," *Educational Leadership* (November 1987): 36–39.

12

. . . . .

Administrator's Role in Curriculum Improvement

An understanding of the administrator's role in curriculum improvement is essential for any administrator who wishes to increase educational opportunities for students. *Curriculum improvement* refers to any change in the subject matter content or in its organization and objectives which results in increased student learning.[1] The emphasis on curriculum improvement rather than administration of the curriculum reflects the priority given in this book to the leadership dimensions of the administrator's role.[2] However, effective leadership also requires in-depth study of the curriculum itself, which is beyond the intended scope of this text. Therefore, administrators should include in their education at least one, or preferably, two or three curriculum courses dealing with the content and design of the elementary and/or secondary school curriculum.[3]

The following sections focus on the role of school administrators in bringing about curricular improvement. Three aspects of this role are analyzed: (1) assessing the need for curricular improvement, (2) planning for curricular improvement, and (3) implementing curricular improvement.

DISTRICTWIDE VERSUS SCHOOL-SITE APPROACH TO CURRICULUM IMPROVEMENT

THE DISTRICT APPROACH

The districtwide approach to curricular improvement usually involves teacher and administrator representatives from different schools within a district, serving on a committee or curriculum council to investigate and develop ways in which some aspect of the district's curriculum can be improved.[4] As a part of this method, subcommittees are established for each discipline in the curriculum, and members of the superintendent's staff provide direction and supervision for the various committees. Generally, the major intended outcome of the districtwide approach to curriculum improvement is to bring about needed curricular change in all of the schools within the district. A concern for curriculum articulation and correlation among subjects, grades, and schools also characterizes this method.[5]

The extent to which school administrators become involved in districtwide curriculum improvement efforts varies with their own visions and capabilities, the size of the districts, and their districts' concepts of curriculum improvement and perceptions of the administrators' role. In situations where an individual administrator's potential contribution to curriculum improvement is recognized, a district may expect the administrator to perform a number of responsibilities. These include (1) serving as a member of the district's curriculum council or on one of the district's curriculum subcommittees; (2) keeping informed about major curricular trends and innovations; (3) working on curriculum improvement projects with the curriculum director and/or the director of elementary or secondary education; (4) involving the school's teaching staff in problem identification and curriculum committee work at the district level; and (5) working in a staff relationship with K–12 subject matter area coordinators and with fellow elementary and secondary principals in the exchange of curriculum improvement ideas.[6]

The districtwide approach to curriculum improvement offers several advantages.[7] It results in greater coordination of activities and promotes better curricular articulation and correlation between subjects, grades, and schools. It also provides access to a broader array of resources and expertise than might be possible with another method. And, because the superintendent's staff is usually directly involved in the curriculum council and committees, there is greater likelihood that a proposed curricular change will receive the superintendent's and the school board's ultimate approval.

On the other hand, the districtwide approach to curriculum improvement has several weaknesses, according to its critics.[8] It can stifle creativity and diversity at the building and classroom levels because of its emphasis on coordination and uniformity of curriculum in all schools. In addition, as a result of limited involvement in the districtwide approach, it can lead to teacher apathy about curriculum improvement at the building level and a belief that little can be accomplished unless the central office directs the change. In response to these criticisms, the school-site approach has been advanced as an equally valid means of curriculum improvement.

SCHOOL-SITE APPROACH

The school-site approach to curriculum improvement differs from the districtwide approach primarily in that the impetus for change occurs at the school rather than at the district level. As Hollis Caswell and his colleagues have pointed out:

> the "grass roots" [school site] approach which views the individual school as the operational and planning unit . . . means that problems which are dealt with on a systemwide or partial-system basis should arise out of work done by individual staffs and feed back into use through these staffs. The channel is from the individual school to the system and back to the individual school, rather than from the top down as under the traditional systemwide approach.[9]

It is generally assumed in the school-site approach that a curricular change which is initiated in one school in a district need not always be implemented in the other schools in that district. The premise is that, to some extent, the schools of a district serve different student clienteles and, for that reason, should be permitted to develop different curricula if appropriate. This does not mean, however, that each school should be permitted to "go it alone." Rather, individuals responsible for curriculum improvement should attempt to ensure that the district's curriculum is articulated vertically and horizontally. Vertical articulation refers to the coordination of curricular content from grade level to grade level within subject fields, and horizontal articulation focuses on interrelating the various subject fields within grade levels.[10] Underscoring this point, the Association for Supervision and Curriculum Development emphasized in one of its yearbooks:

> Building principals, however, must not assume that the individual schools within a school system are completely autonomous. Some

attention must be given to the need for a systemwide program. . . . The problem to be solved is how the building units can be stimulated to develop the best program possible for the neighborhoods which they serve, and at the same time, make their appropriate contributions to the total system of which they are parts.[11]

The school-site approach also affords opportunities for enhancing teacher involvement in the improvement of their school's curriculum. A number of recent studies have indicated that teachers desire more involvement in resolving issues which they believe are directly relevant to their lives as professional educators.[12] In addition, as John McNeil pointed out:

Teachers are not mere implementors of curriculum, but rather are crucial in making curriculum policy. They have considerable freedom to employ their own notions of what schools ought to be, even when subjected to external pressures of state textbooks, curriculum guides, and mandated testing. Teachers who decide which students get particular curriculum content and learning opportunities are engaging in a political act.

So, too, are principals when they involve department heads and teachers in developing curriculum courses and instructional units; selecting concepts, value processes to be emphasized; and designing learning opportunities that match student backgrounds and local concerns. By such activity, principals help teachers become better informed about the aims of education, better able to interpret the school's program to the public, and more willing to act upon newer views of subject matter, learners, and societal needs.[13]

Thus, school administrators would be well advised to utilize the expertise of their teachers in determining directions for curriculum improvement.

Despite several advantages to the school-site approach to curriculum improvement, including greater involvement of personnel, more responsiveness to the needs of the local student clientele, and improved opportunities for the proposed curricular change to be implemented in the classrooms, the method is not without its limitations. The performance of school-site administrators and staffs in generating and maintaining the impetus for curricular change has been spotty.[14] In addition, sole reliance on the building-level approach to curriculum improvement has in many instances resulted in a patchwork district curriculum with poor articulation and correlation between grades and among schools.

Although the potential disadvantages, like those of the districtwide approach, are not necessarily inherent in the school-site approach, clearly administrators should not rely on a single method.[15] Both the districtwide and the school-site approaches are needed for effective curriculum improvement, and the goal for administrators should be to capitalize on the strengths of each method while minimizing its disadvantages.

Regardless of which approach to curriculum improvement is utilized, the involvement of school administrators would appear to be essential. Perhaps Howard Spalding put it best when he said,

> The principal has much to contribute to the curriculum program. He is the one person who is concerned with every aspect of the life of his school. His interest in its success provides a strong and direct motivation for his efforts to secure curriculum improvement. He is better able than anyone else to discover the needs of his school. He knows best the contributions that the members of his staff can make . . . .His interest in the growth of his teachers requires that he should have responsibilities for the best single means for securing that growth—work on the curriculum.[16]

THE IMPORTANCE OF ADMINISTRATIVE COMMITMENT

Although Spalding obviously felt that school administrators could make important contributions to curriculum improvement, others question whether that is possible because of various obstacles and the lack of certain personal qualities. These obstacles and personal qualities have already been discussed in the chapter on instructional leadership, but the factors of available time and competency in curriculum improvement merit additional attention in this section.

Certainly, available time can be an important potential constraint limiting curricular leadership initiatives by school administrators. At least one study found that it was not so much whether or not principals felt they had the time to devote to curriculum improvement that determined the extent of their involvement, but the degree to which principals perceived that their superiors wanted them to give a very high priority to improving the school curriculum.[17] In addition, while competency in curriculum evaluation and planning is undoubtedly an important prerequisite to whether or not a school administrator becomes involved in efforts to improve the curriculum, Patricia Novotney asserts that commitment may be even more important.[18] For example, if principals believe that it is essential that they become involved in efforts to improve the school curriculum, they are likely to take steps to become more competent in curriculum evaluation and planning. On the other hand, if principals think that it would just be nice or desirable to become involved in curricular improvement, they are not as likely to increase their competency; perhaps more important, they are likely to get sidetracked into routine administrative tasks that should have a lower priority or be delegated to someone else.

Commitment is the crucial factor. School administrators must feel that it is essential that they become involved in curriculum improvement efforts. If they possess this commitment, perceived insufficient time and competency or other constraints become obstacles that they will strive to overcome, rather than resigning themselves to accept them as insurmountable barriers. Administrators with sufficient commitment become competent through study and application of the ideas in this chapter and related activities and find the time to become involved in curriculum improvement. The question next becomes, in which ways can they make their best contributions?

ASSESSING THE NEED FOR CURRICULUM IMPROVEMENT

School administrators interested in curricular improvement should, with the assistance of relevant others, initially concentrate their efforts on assessing the need for improvement. There is little reason to begin changing the curriculum until the nature of the need for improvement has been fully and accurately assessed. All too frequently, proposals for curriculum improvement are advanced and implemented without an accurate assessment of the real need for such improvement. As a result, curricular change occurs but not necessarily improvement.[19] The only valid criterion for ascertaining whether a curricular change results in significant improvement is whether the change better enables the school to achieve previously defined educational objectives. As Caswell has noted, "No matter how elaborate a program may be or how enthusiastic the staff, unless in the end the experiences of pupils are changed so that the educational outcomes are better than before, the work cannot be considered successful."[20]

Administrators can assess the need for improvement in at least two ways: (1) by evaluating a school's current program of studies, utilizing previously defined and accepted criteria; and (2) by studying and evaluating various proposals which are offered for the improvement of the curriculum. In either case, administrators must develop or utilize a comprehensive set of evaluative criteria for assessing the need for curricular change. Without previously defined criteria, administrators' assessment of the need for curricular improvement is likely to be unsystematic, idiosyncratic, and superficial. Using well-defined, comprehensive criteria, administrators are better able to assess the need for improvement in a current program of studies as well as to evaluate the potential of curriculum improvement proposals advanced by others.

Fortunately, there is no shortage of recommended criteria for assessing the need for curricular improvement. Over the years, a number of educational authorities have proposed criteria for evaluating the school curriculum.[21] The following synthesis of their main points has been developed in question form, with accompanying discussion:

1. **Has the school established clearly stated, operationally defined, educational objectives?** The school curriculum should be based on the educational objectives of the school.[22] If a school lacks clearly stated, operationally defined educational objectives, its curriculum is more likely to be based on tradition and/or fad than on desired student learning outcomes. Most schools have educational objectives of one kind or another, but these objectives are frequently not stated in a form which facilitates assessment of the need for curricular improvement. Therefore, administrators should begin their efforts to improve the curriculum by working with others to develop clearly stated, operationally defined educational objectives for the school. (See chapter 2 for further discussion of these tasks.)

2. **Is each course in the curriculum related to and supporting the achievement of school objectives?** No course in the curriculum is an end in itself. It should relate in some demonstrable way to the achievement of school objectives. Undoubtedly, some courses exist in a curriculum for reasons other than their contribution to achieving the objectives of the school. Administrators need to identify these courses and attempt to develop their relationship with overall school goals or to consider the elimination of the courses from the curriculum.

3. **Does the planned curriculum sufficiently take into consideration the hidden curriculum of the school?** Teachers, supervisors, curriculum developers, and relevant others plan the curriculum—facts, concepts, generalizations, and skills—that they want or intend students to learn.[23] However, students may have needs and experiences which result in learning facts, concepts, generalizations, and skills other than those intended, representing a hidden curriculum in that school personnel may not be aware of these learnings.[24] Two excerpts from the writing of a former student illustrate the nature of the hidden curriculum.

In First grade, all I remember is that a new lady came To
our Room for awhile and then went away and I learned
years Later that was because she was only a practice
teacher and She didn't like us much anyway you could tell
but we'd sit On the floor in front of her while she sat on a
chair sort of Board reading us a story and we could see up
her dress.

In eighth grade I wrote a funny theme about money
and read It in front of English class and the kids liked it a
lot but Mono Rynning told the teacher I copied it from
Life Magazine And he believed him and when he got to be
a high school Teacher years later I still hated him and
wondered how he Got promoted and that year I broke a
drill bit in shop class And went to the dime store to buy a
new one because Mr. Noble The teacher used to work in a
reform school and he scared me Because I saw him hit
Suggy one day really hard and Suggy Didn't cry but I was
glad it wasn't me.[25]

It will, of course, be difficult at best to anticipate the exact
nature of the hidden curriculum because of the individual
differences of students. However, in identifying the need for
curriculum improvement, school administrators must attempt to
ascertain the extent to which the planned curriculum is
compatible with the hidden curriculum because incongruities are
bound to negatively affect the successful implementation of the
planned curriculum.[26]

4. **Does the curriculum meet the needs of all students? Is it
comprehensive?** A comprehensive curriculum should meet the
needs of the noncollege-bound as well as the college-bound
students. It should provide for the needs of low-ability and
average students, as well as the academically talented. It should
also provide for the needs of students with special handicaps, as
well as the needs of other kinds of exceptional students. In
addition, the school should recognize that students have
immediate as well as long-range needs, and that both should be
accommodated through the curriculum. For example, the
immediate need of students to develop healthy self-concepts is as
important as the long-range need to gain knowledge and skills for
their careers. (Perhaps the most useful conception of the needs of

students has been advanced by Robert Havighurst who postulates that people have particular tasks which need to be mastered at certain stages in their development.[27])

A second way of raising the question about the comprehensiveness of the school curriculum is to ask, "To what extent does the curriculum help students to deal successfully with the various social influences which are or will be affecting their lives?" These social influences may include but are not limited to television, racial problems, poverty, war and peace, marriage and divorce, interpersonal relations, and urbanization.[28] For example, in a society in which the typical student spends almost as much time watching television as studying in school, the curriculum should help students to utilize more effectively this important medium of information and attitude change.[29]

The essential point is that if the school is to prepare students for a constructive and productive life, the curriculum should reflect the realities of that life. When this does not appear to occur, critics often claim that the curriculum is irrelevant. As Allan Ornstein noted, "When people say that the curriculum is irrelevant, they often mean either that it does not meet the needs of the social situation or the students, or that the subject matter should be modified."[30]

5. **Does the curriculum reflect the needs and expectations of society, as well as the needs of the students?** The school does not operate in a vacuum. As an agent of society, its curriculum must reflect to a reasonable degree societal expectations and needs.[31] Although our society is a pluralistic one and is frequently in a state of flux, it is still possible for an administrator to ascertain general expectations in regard to what the school should be teaching. The Gallup survey presented in chapter 1 is an example of the information administrators should obtain.[32]

6. **Does the content of the curriculum provide for the development of student attitudes and values, as well as knowledge and skills?** Whether this question can be answered affirmatively depends largely on whether or not the educational objectives of the school emphasize the development of student attitudes and values, as well as knowledge and skills. While some authorities believe that the school should limit its role to developing knowledge on the part of its students, others assert with equal conviction that the school can and should help students develop attitudes and values.[33]

In reality, of course, the school already teaches attitudes and values, directly and indirectly, through its emphasis on punctuality and neatness, its penalties for cheating, and its response to certain styles of dress and grooming.[34] The pertinent question would appear to be not *whether* the school should teach attitudes and values but *which* attitudes and values should the school attempt to develop, and how should the school curriculum provide for their development?

7. **Are the curriculum materials appropriate for the interests and abilities of the students?** The major assumption behind this question is that, for successful learning to occur, the curriculum materials must be at the interest and ability level of the students using them. When materials are too difficult for students to read or understand, learning is impaired; if the materials are too easy and insufficiently challenging, teachers have difficulty in motivating students to learn.[35] Moreover, when the curricular materials fail to match students' interest levels and attention spans, learning is adversely affected.[36]

One approach administrators can take is to utilize the help of a reading consultant to ascertain the reading level of materials used by each grade, and compare those levels with the reading levels of the students. Gorton once conducted such a study and discovered that in a ninth-grade class the biology materials had a twelfth-grade reading level. Due to the range of student reading abilities in any class, there are problems in learning for a number of students when only one textbook is used for the entire class.

A possible solution to this problem is the use of multiple texts and nonprint media to accommodate the different interests and abilities of students within a class. A good indicator of the need for curricular improvement in a school is the extent to which a single text approach is being utilized in the classrooms.

In selecting curricular materials the administrator needs to keep close watch on the free and inexpensive items that are frequently made available to the school. Seldom are such materials without bias.[37] Even textbooks may be a source of bias, particularly racial and sexual bias, and the administrator should make sure that the resource guide provided by the Commission on Civil Rights is utilized before selecting any materials for the curriculum.[38]

8. **Are the educational objectives for each subject in the curriculum clearly stated and operationally defined?** Earlier, the point was made that the school curriculum should be based on the overall educational goals of the school. Even though the subjects included in the curriculum should relate directly to overall school objectives, each subject should have specific objectives of its own which represent interpretations of the more general school goals.

   The objectives for each subject should be stated clearly and operationally defined if they are to provide direction and guidance to both teachers and students in the learning situation, and if the objectives are to be helpful in evaluating the extent to which a subject is achieving preestablished goals.[39] The achievement of educational objectives, whether they be school or subject objectives, is very difficult to assess if the objectives are stated vaguely or if, as is the case in some situations, they are nonexistent.

9. **Is there subject matter articulation between grade levels, and correlation among the various subjects of the curriculum?** The curriculum content introduced at each grade level (at each phase in nongraded schools) should be built on and be articulated with the subject matter introduced in the previous grade. Gaps or omissions in the sequencing of the content of the curriculum tend to cause problems for the learner. In each curricular area, the subject matter content should be composed of sequentially linked building blocks which the learner masters as he proceeds through the school system.

   In addition, efforts should be made to correlate wherever possible the subjects offered at a particular grade level. The correlation may take the form of core curriculum or it may only represent an effort to relate certain topics within two or more subjects.[40] The school curriculum has often been criticized for its fragmentation, and there is little doubt that there needs to be better correlation between its various subjects.

10. **Are the various subjects in the school curriculum achieving their proposed objectives?** Probably one of the most important efforts that an administrator can make in identifying the need for curricular improvement is to investigate the extent to which each of the subjects in the curriculum is achieving its proposed objectives. While administrators cannot do this alone, they can initiate the investigation and can organize and coordinate the

expertise of others in an evaluation of the achievement of course objectives. Methods of assessment could include the use of criterion-referenced tests, teacher-constructed tests, interviews, and questionnaires. Even though each of these evaluation methods possesses certain limitations as well as strengths, the most serious deficiency of all would be incurred as the result of an administrator's failure to initiate *any* assessment merely because an evaluation tool could not be found that would accomplish exactly what was wanted.

CURRICULUM EVALUATION

Identifying appropriate criteria is only the first step in evaluating the curriculum. The second step is to apply the criteria, which involves the collection, analysis, and interpretation of data. In many situations administrators lack technical skills and/or the time necessary to carry out these evaluation processes; therefore they need to identify and involve people who do have the skills and time for evaluation. They also need to become familiar enough with the basic concepts and techniques of evaluation so that they can monitor the work and its outcomes. In regard to methods, the approaches for carrying out curricular evaluation include the use of tests, interviews, questionnaires, and content analysis studies. A discussion of the various concepts and techniques of curriculum evaluation is included in several good sources listed at the end of this chapter.[41]

One curriculum evaluation method that merits attention—and tends to be overlooked—is the technique of curriculum mapping.[42] Curriculum mapping is essentially a process of verifying the curriculum that is actually being presented in the classroom of a school, as contrasted with the curriculum supposed to be implemented in the school. Too often the curriculum of a school is viewed as a written document or set of curriculum guides that specify the objectives and content to be taught. Any administrator who attempts an evaluation based on curriculum guides is unlikely to obtain a very realistic or valid picture of the school's curriculum.

To ascertain the actual curriculum—the one really being implemented in a school—the administrator needs to engage teachers and others in the technique of curriculum mapping. It can occur in two ways: (1) involving teachers and/or students in recording on paper the actual curriculum content being taught; and (2) involving independent observers in the classroom recording the kind of curriculum actually being implemented.[43]

The primary advantage of curriculum mapping is that it provides the evaluator with a more accurate picture of the actual curriculum in use, so that there is a more valid basis for determining the extent to which the criteria for needed improvement are being met. As mentioned earlier, this approach is only one of various tools for curriculum evaluation; it represents a very useful technique, particularly in the initial stage of evaluation.

The concept of curriculum mapping may be extended to that of curriculum alignment if, in addition to evaluating the congruence between the stated curriculum and what is being taught, the tests which are being used to determine the mastery of the curriculum are also evaluated for congruence with the material presented to students.[44] William Savard and Kathleen Cotton contend that the alignment of objectives, actual teaching, and the means and content of testing are essential to effective schooling.[45] To accomplish curriculum alignment, Roger Scott indicated that four attitudinal approaches were necessary:

1. Teachers and administrators need to know what they are responsible for teaching.
2. Teachers need to make decisions about time, materials, and teaching strategies appropriate for helping students learn the skills specified in the objectives.
3. Teachers should monitor the progress they are making on implementing the plan.
4. Teachers and administrators must assess the results of the school year, identify strengths and weaknesses, and incorporate the assessment into planning for the next year.[46]

In selecting a particular approach to be used in evaluating the curriculum, at the outset the administrator should ask certain basic questions: "What do I need to evaluate? Why do I want to evaluate? What do I intend to do with the results of my evaluation?"[47] As E. R. House points out, "For the evaluation to be effective [the administrator] must know precisely what she wants from it."[48] Unless administrators are clear in their own minds as to the answers to these questions, they are unlikely to be satisfied with the results of the evaluation.

THE ADMINISTRATOR'S ROLE IN PLANNING CURRICULUM IMPROVEMENT

In many school situations school administrators are too busy with other aspects of managing the school to become directly involved in planning curriculum improvement.[49] Also, their major role in relation to curriculum is too often perceived as implementing a proposed curricular change which has been prepared or planned by someone else. Be that as it may, school administrators can still play an important role in planning for curricular improvement if they possess commitment, educational vision, group leadership skills, and initiative. A twofold role is recommended: (1) working directly with groups or committees planning curriculum improvement; and (2) encouraging and evaluating proposals for improving the curriculum.

THE COMMITTEE APPROACH TO PLANNING CURRICULUM IMPROVEMENT

Planning for curricular improvement can be accomplished by individuals, and sometimes the best way to begin planning for a curricular change is on a limited scale, with one individual. However, most of the planning for curricular improvement probably is done by committees, so the concepts and issues discussed previously in chapter 3 in conjunction with group leadership skills, should be considered.[50]

In utilizing the committee approach to curricular improvement, the administrator needs to adopt a plan of action to guide the committee's efforts. Although there are undoubtedly several ways to proceed, a proposed process for an administrator and a curriculum improvement committee to follow is presented in figure 12.1.[51]

The process identified in figure 12.1 intentionally goes beyond planning for curricular improvement to present an overview of the total recommended process of curriculum improvement. There may be additional steps that could be added to the process, but an attempt has been made here to focus on the most important components. Although the proposed process emphasizes the group approach, the method proposed can be utilized on an individual basis as well.

As Francis Hunkins and Allan Ornstein noted, the administrator's role in working with a curriculum improvement committee should be that of consultant and facilitator.[52] Generally administrators interact with committee members who possess greater expertise than they do in the particular curricular area under consideration. Therefore, they are unlikely to contribute much

Figure 12.1 A Curriculum Improvement Process.

Steps	Committee's Activities
1 ⟶	Identify and define the need for curriculum improvement (Needs Assessment).
2 ⟶	Identify or develop proposed curriculum change alternatives that meet the need for improvement.
3 ⟶	Analyze the advantages, disadvantages, and costs of different proposals for improving the curriculum. Select the best alternative
4 ⟶	Identify and define what kinds of activities, resources, time, and other changes will be needed in order to implement the curriculum improvement.
5 ⟶	Prepare written document detailing proposed curriculum improvement and seek approval from appropriate individuals or agencies.
6 ⟶	Plan and initiate pilot project to test the validity of the proposed curricular improvement and to identify the need for revision before final implementation. Agree on evaluation criteria and methods before implementation of the pilot project.
7 ⟶	Determine the success of the pilot project and decide whether or not to revise the curriculum improvement proposal, implement "as is," or reject it.
8 ⟶	Implement the curriculum improvement change on a broader scale if the pilot project was successful. This step should include in-service education for those who are to implement the proposal and orientation for others who will be affected by the change.
9 ⟶	Evaluate the curriculum improvement change (using criteria and methods agreed upon prior to the implementation of the change) periodically after its implementation, to ascertain the need for further refinements.

subject matter knowledge. However, administrators can assist other people on the committee by helping them to define their function, to follow a process such as the one presented in figure 12.1, and to work together cooperatively and productively as a committee. They can also facilitate their actions by securing necessary resources, removing obstacles, and helping them to increase their problem-solving capabilities.

PROBLEMS

In establishing a committee for curriculum improvement, administrators should be aware of teacher attitudes toward committee work. While not all teachers can be assumed to possess identical attitudes, studies have revealed that many teachers have had negative experiences while serving on committees. For example, Allan Ornstein and Francis Hunkins indicated that teachers encountered a number of basic problems in trying to perform committee work. These problems included (1) lack of time, (2) lack of recognition or rewards, (3) lack of knowledge, and (4) lack of follow-through on the committee's recommendations.[53]

Perhaps the most serious of these problems is lack of time, which is one problem that must be resolved if the committee is to be successful. During the school year, teachers, students, and parents are busy and, for all practical purposes, their only available time is after school or on weekends. Neither of these times is particularly desirable, due to the fatigue factor in late afternoon and evening, or to potential conflicts with other commitments. A practical resolution of the time problem, as it affects teachers and students, is to dismiss school early one day each week, if feasible, to permit curricular planning and other kinds of professional activities to take place. A number of schools have adopted this procedure, apparently with good results. Other possibilities include preschool workshops, better use of faculty and departmental meetings, utilization of substitute teachers, in-service days during the year, and the implementation of flexible teaching/instructional arrangements.

Another partial solution to the problem of inadequate time is to schedule committee meetings during the summer to plan for curricular improvement. This can be an ideal time because school is not in session, and people are more available to work on the curriculum. Administrators should keep in mind that some of the individuals whom they might select to work on committees may prefer to attend summer school or take vacations. Administrators should also consider the possibility that they may be unable to secure a very high level of participation without remunerating committee members for their summer work for the school. Assuming that these problems can be avoided or resolved with careful advance planning and resourcefulness by administrators, the summer months may indeed provide an excellent opportunity for a school administrator and a curriculum committee to engage in planning for curricular improvement.

CONSULTANTS

In formulating a curricular improvement committee, administrators should give some attention to the need for outside help. Teachers, students, and parents on the committee and even the administrator may be familiar with the current program and associated problems, but they may not be fully aware of new approaches to the improving of a particular curricular area. A consultant from the district's central office, a university, the state department of public instruction, or another agency or organization might be able to offer valuable ideas and insights.

If administrators and committee members decide that a consultant would be useful, they should define as precisely as possible, before employing the individual, the nature of the consultant's contribution and the relationship to the committee. Frequently, when these factors are not adequately defined by the committee or communicated to the consultant, the consultant's expertise is not properly utilized or the performance does not meet the expectations of the committee. Consultants can often make an excellent contribution to a committee, but the expectations of the committee and the role of the consultant must be clearly defined in advance.

APPROVAL

School administrators should recognize that any proposed curricular changes which result from committee work must ultimately be approved by the superintendent and the school board before implementation can proceed. It is important, therefore, to keep the superintendent and school board informed at each stage of the planning process. This might be done through periodic progress reports and/or by actually including a representative from the central office and/or the school board on the committee planning for curricular improvement. Regardless of the method used to keep the superintendent and the school board informed, the importance of effective communication cannot be overemphasized. Many potentially good curricular improvement plans have encountered resistance or have even been rejected because they caught the superintendent or school board by surprise.

ENCOURAGING AND EVALUATING PROPOSALS FOR CURRICULUM IMPROVEMENT

A second major role of administrators in planning for curriculum improvement should be to encourage and evaluate proposals from various individuals or groups, both inside of and outside of the school system. Administrators can encourage proposals for the improvement of the curriculum from people within the school system by (1) making known their interest in receiving such proposals, (2) trying to secure released time for individuals or small groups to work on curriculum improvement proposals, and (3) giving recognition to those who develop curricular improvement proposals. To be effective, these kinds of encouragement cannot be limited to a single announcement or indication of interest. Instead, administrators must demonstrate an active, ongoing, visible commitment to receiving proposals for curriculum improvement.

In addition to encouraging the generation of curriculum proposals from within the school or district, administrators need to become better informed about those proposals advanced from the outside, by state and national organizations, agencies, and groups. As mentioned earlier, much curriculum change has originated with national curriculum committees. If administrators are to capitalize on the ideas and thinking of people outside the school in regard to curricular reform, they need to make a conscious effort to keep well informed about new proposals for improving the curriculum.[54]

Encouraging others to develop proposals and attempting to become better informed themselves about various ideas proposed for improving the curriculum, however, are not the only dimensions to the administrators' role in curriculum improvement. They also have a responsibility to evaluate curriculum improvement proposals carefully as to their appropriateness and feasibility. A sample work sheet which should be helpful to administrators in determining the merits of curricular improvement proposals is presented in figure 12.2. D. C. Anderson provides additional help for evaluating curriculum proposals.[55]

Although the suggested work sheet is recommended especially for evaluating the merits of curriculum improvement proposals, it could be used to assess the strengths and weaknesses of various other proposals, as well. It is primarily designed for helping administrators and others involved in curriculum improvement to focus on a number of important questions that should be addressed by any proposal. By seeking answers to these questions, administrators should be better able to assess the strengths and weaknesses of a proposal and make a judgment about its overall worth. (Administrators who adopt this work sheet should distribute copies of it in advance to those who are preparing proposals so that they may be aware of how their proposals will be evaluated, and so they can use the work sheet themselves, in evaluating their proposals.)

THE ADMINISTRATOR'S ROLE IN IMPLEMENTING CURRICULAR IMPROVEMENT

A major obstacle to curriculum improvement, from the teacher's point of view, is the lack of follow-through on committee recommendations. This problem is often a result of the administrator's failure to understand the process of and barriers to implementing a proposed curriculum change.

Implementing curricular improvement usually necessitates a modification in the attitudes and role of the staff, as well as in subject matter or its organization. For example, a proposed social studies curriculum which emphasizes student analysis and discussion of major problems and issues in

Figure 12.2 A Proposal Assessment Work Sheet.

Name _____ Date _____

Title of Proposal _____

1. What diagnostic methods or procedures were used to identify and define the problem or need?
2. What are the characteristics of the target population to which the proposal is addressed?
3. To what extent are the understandings, skills, attitudes, or values which the proposed program seeks to improve (the desired outcomes) clearly identified and stated in terms that will make evaluation possible?
4. To what degree does the proposal make clear *how* the recommended program will accomplish the objectives which are set forth?
5. To what degree is there evidence that potential problems (as well as strengths) of the proposed program have been identified, assessed, and possible solutions recommended?
6. To what extent does the proposal recognize the need for and make provision for in-service education for faculty and/or orientation activities for students and parents, to help ensure successful implementation of the proposed program?
7. Have the costs of the different aspects of the proposed program been fully assessed?
8. What procedures have been included in the proposal for ascertaining the progress/effectiveness of the program on a nine-week, semester, or yearly basis?

Summary

Strengths of the Proposal

Limitations of the Proposal

Priority Rating Assigned the Proposal

American history may require—if the new curriculum is to be successfully implemented—that teachers change their attitudes about how American history is best taught and learned, as well as their conceptions of the roles of teachers and students in classrooms.

Teachers who continue to lecture and limit the students' role to merely responding to questions may implement the proposed curricular change to the extent that they use different subject matter and the materials, but full effectiveness cannot be achieved unless teachers' and students' roles also change.

Therefore, in attempting to implement curricular improvement, administrators must recognize that curricular change also involves people change to be totally successful.[56] Too often this point has been ignored, or given insufficient consideration, and the implementation of curricular improvement has correspondingly suffered.

POSSIBLE BARRIERS TO CURRICULAR CHANGE

When implementing a proposed curricular improvement, administrators should perform the role of change agent. In this role, administrators should try to bring about a modification both in the curriculum and in people's attitudes and roles in regard to the curriculum. People whose attitudes and roles may need to be modified and who may present resistance or obstacles to change include faculty, students, parents, central office staff, and school board members. Of course, different people resist change for different reasons, and it is often rather difficult to ascertain the real reasons for their opposition. The major barriers to implementing curricular change (or, for that matter, most kinds of change) may be inherent in a specific situation. The major barriers of which administrators should be aware include the following:

Habit. Habit is the tendency of people to behave in the same way that they have always behaved. Proposed change challenges habit, and the challenge is frequently met with resistance.

The bureaucratic structure of the school district. The school district as a bureaucratic institution emphasizes the maintenance of order, rationality, and continuity. Uniformity of educational programs and procedures among the schools of the district seems to be valued, whereas diversity does not. Attempts by individual schools to introduce new programs or procedures are often viewed with suspicion. Because of these attitudes and the hierarchical structure of the district, proposed change may be diluted before it is finally approved, or it may be rejected because it threatens the stability of the institution.

The lack of incentive. Change can be a difficult and frustrating experience for the individuals or groups involved. Although administrators may be personally convinced of the benefits which can accrue if a proposed change is adopted, they can seldom guarantee those benefits or offer incentives (monetary or otherwise) to persuade others to adopt the innovation. As a result, they are dependent on their own abilities to influence others to adopt a proposed change for which there may be high personal costs in time and frustration and no immediate gain.

The nature of the proposed change. Innovations can vary according to complexity, financial cost, compatibility with the other phases of the schools' operation, and ease of communicability. Some innovations, because of these factors, are more difficult to introduce into a school system than other proposed changes. Therefore, the characteristics of the innovation itself may constitute a major obstacle or problem in securing its adoption.

Teacher and community norms. Teacher and community norms can act as significant barriers to innovating in the schools. Evidence shows that a teacher may receive disapproval from colleagues for adopting an innovation; and efforts by the administrator to bring about change in a teacher's role or methods may be viewed as a challenge to that teacher's professional autonomy. Research has further revealed that community groups may feel threatened by change because of its implications for upsetting the stability of the power relations within the community. Both sets of norms—teacher and community—can act as a powerful source of resistance to the administrator trying to introduce a particular innovation.

Lack of understanding. People may resist a proposed change because they do not possess an adequate or accurate understanding of it. Their deficiency may be caused by a failure on their part to pay close attention at the time the proposed change was explained or, on the other hand, information about the change may have been poorly or inaccurately communicated. In any respect, a lack of understanding of a proposed change can act as a significant deterrent to its successful implementation.

A difference of opinion. A proposed change may be resisted because of an honest difference of opinion about whether it is needed, or whether it will accomplish all that its proponents claim. The difference in opinion may be based on conflicting philosophies and values of education in regard to teaching and learning, or it may result from variant assessments of how much improvement would actually occur if the proposed change were implemented. If the difference of opinion centers on the amount of improvement that will take place, resistance may be reduced with the introduction of new evidence of potential success. However, if the difference of opinion is based on conflicting educational philosophies and values, the administrator will probably find it extremely difficult to remove this source of resistance.

A lack of skill. A proposed change may be resisted by any individual or group required to perform new skills and roles. The change from traditional roles and skills to new ones is an unsettling experience to many people.

Therefore, any innovation requiring new skills or roles on the part of the participants should be accompanied by an in-service program enabling them to develop the new skills or roles.[57]

Resistance to change is a complex phenomenon, and administrators should spend a considerable amount of time in diagnosing its sources before drawing any conclusions about how it might best be reduced.[58] In many situations there is more than one reason for resistance to change; administrators should assess the validity of each of the possible factors just identified. By accurately diagnosing the reasons for resistance, administrators are in a better position to ameliorate the resistance and smooth the way for successful implementation of proposed curricular improvement.

THE PILOT PROJECT APPROACH TO CURRICULAR CHANGE

If administrators are unable to overcome resistance to a proposed curricular change, they might initiate a pilot project, that is, a scaled-down version of the originally proposed change. The proposed innovation might be reduced in size, length of operation, or number of participants involved. For example, rather than introducing a new schoolwide language arts curriculum, the change could be implemented on a pilot basis at only one grade level. Or, perhaps, rather than implementing a curricular change at one grade level, several units of the curriculum could be introduced by all of the teachers of the school during the first semester of the school year. Other variations of the pilot project approach are also possible.

The pilot project approach to curriculum improvement implementation has several definite advantages. It can be conducted with fewer participants and can involve those more willing to try out new curricular ideas. If the pilot project is successful, its results may favorably influence other people who initially resisted the proposed change.

A pilot project can also be useful in identifying and correcting defects or weaknesses in the original curriculum proposal not perceived earlier. Most proposed curricular changes, whether emanating from study and planning within a district or from other school situations, require adaptation and refinement before they can be used successfully by an entire grade level, department, or school. And finally, a pilot project may prove useful in demonstrating that a proposed change will not work, either because of a defect in the proposal's concept or because local conditions make it impossible to implement.

The pilot project approach is not the only approach to curriculum implementation, nor is it a panacea for resistance to change. But because it offers important advantages, it should be considered by administrators.

KEY FACTORS IN CURRICULUM IMPLEMENTATION

Despite thousands of dollars and untold hours expended each year by districts in the development of curricular improvement plans or guides, the limited evidence available indicates that those plans are poorly implemented. For example, in Robert Krey's study of thirty-six elementary schools, thirteen junior high schools, and five senior high schools, teachers reported very little classroom implementation of district curriculum guides.[59] The modal response of the teachers about the extent of curricular implementation was, "No implementation."

Krey discovered in his investigation that four major factors were directly related to the degree in which curricular plans for improvement were actually implemented in the classroom:

1. The extent to which teachers felt a need for some kind of orientation and in-service activities to help them implement curricular plans.
2. The extent to which teachers received an opportunity to participate in the planning of orientation and in-service activities to help them implement curricular plans.
3. The extent to which teachers received an opportunity to participate in the evaluation of those orientation and in-service activities.
4. The extent to which teachers felt they had a professional obligation to participate in curriculum implementation.

Krey's study emphasizes the need for orientation and in-service activities to help teachers implement curriculum improvement proposals and plans. It also suggests the importance of faculty involvement in the planning and evaluation stages if orientation and in-service activities are to be perceived by teachers as worthwhile.

An important implication of the study is that school administrators should not assume that a curriculum improvement proposal or plan can be successfully implemented in the classroom without appropriate orientation and in-service activities for the teachers of the school. Such activities might include (1) workshops to familiarize teachers with all aspects of the curricular plan; (2) clinics to provide teachers with an opportunity to practice using the materials or techniques contained in the curricular plan before implementing them in the classroom; and (3) evaluation sessions for teachers, held after the curricular plan has been implemented in the classroom, for the purpose of identifying strengths and weaknesses of the plan and making appropriate revisions. Although the degree of implementation of proposed curricular improvement would also seem to depend on the merits of the particular proposal or plan (a factor not studied in the research), it would appear from Krey's investigation that little curriculum implementation occurs without adequate orientation and in-service activities for the staff.

In working with teachers on implementing proposed curricular improvements, administrators should also be aware that teachers' perceptions of their principals' attitudes toward implementing a particular plan are important. Conan Edwards, for example, found in his study of essentially the same schools examined in Krey's research, that the more the teachers perceived their principals as personally accepting the curriculum improvement plans and holding teachers responsible for implementation, the more likely they were to report a higher level of curriculum implementation in their classrooms.[60] The key factor seemed to be the teachers' perceptions of the administrator's attitude, rather than the administrator's actual feelings about the importance of curriculum implementation. Teachers who perceived that their principals personally accepted the curriculum improvement plans and intended to hold teachers accountable for implementing the plans, reported a higher implementation level than those teachers who perceived the opposite—regardless of how their principals actually felt about the implementation of the curriculum plans.

If administrators are interested in increasing classroom adoption of proposed curricular improvement plans, they cannot simply hold a positive attitude about those plans; they must accurately communicate to teachers their feelings about the importance of implementing the proposed curriculum improvement.

A FINAL NOTE

The main thrust of this chapter has been on the administrator's role in curricular improvement. Curricular improvement is seldom an easy task, and it is difficult for school administrators to resist pressures to concentrate on more manageable activities. However, school administrators are pivotal people in any attempt to improve the curriculum. School administrators can either be initiators and facilitators, or they can be resisters and rejectors. In the end, curriculum improvement should be viewed as a unique opportunity not only to revitalize programs but also to provide new directions in education. As Donald Monroe noted,

Curriculum development is a powerful and visible means for breathing new life into the profession. It is through the curriculum development process that educators can fashion for themselves and their constituents an understanding of who we are, where we have been, where we are now, and where we want to go. It provides a one-of-a-kind opportunity for educators to give expression to new understanding of learning and of what constitutes good teaching; to new ways to enrich the professional lives of teachers and enhance the credibility of the profession; to new ways of forging school and community partnerships; and to a new view of schools as thoughtful, forward-looking organizations unwilling to settle for anything but the best practice based on the most reliable and current information.[61]

Review and Learning Activities

1. Discuss the main characteristics, and the advantages and disadvantages of the district approach to curriculum improvement; then, the school-site approach. Describe your district's approach.
2. Attempt to apply the criteria for determining the need for improvement (as presented in this chapter) to the curriculum in your school or school district. Then draft recommendations for improvement.
3. Describe the committee process used in your school or district to improve the curriculum. How does it compare with the process identified in figure 12.1? Draft a new committee process for your school or district, taking into consideration the ideas and problems described in this chapter.
4. Ascertain the approach your administrator employs to encourage and evaluate curriculum improvement proposals. How does it compare with the ideas presented in the text? Specifically, how would you improve the approach used by your administrator?
5. To what extent are the barriers and obstacles to implementing curriculum improvement that are described in the text present in your own school or school district? How might you use the pilot project approach to help ameliorate these problems?
6. Utilize the findings in the studies by Krey and Edwards to evaluate your own district's approach to curriculum implementation. How would you improve this approach?

Notes

1. See Douglas Christensen, "Curriculum Development: A Function of Design and Leadership." (ERIC Report Ed–207–13); Daniel Tanner, "Improving the Curriculum—Guidelines for Principals," *NASSP Bulletin* (April 1987): 30–34; and Allan A. Glatthorn, *Curriculum Development* (Reston, Va.: National Association of Secondary School Principals, 1990).
2. Allan A. Glatthorn, *Curriculum Leadership* (Glenview, Ill.: Scott, Foresman and Company, 1987).
3. For a good introduction to this study, see Thomas S. Popkewitz, "Curriculum Studies, Knowledge and Interest: Problems and Paradoxes" (ERIC Report Ed–267–478).
4. Curriculum improvement efforts can also take place at the county, state, and national levels, but the emphasis in this chapter is on intradistrict approaches. For discussions regarding other levels and reform efforts, see Larry Cuban, "State-Powered Curricular Reform, Measurement-Driven Instruction"; Franklin Parker, "School Reform: Recent Influences"; and Ralph W. Tyler, "Examining the Current Demands for Curricular Reforms from a Historical Perspective," *National Forum* (Summer 1987); and Betty E. Steffy, "Curriculum Auditing as a State Agency Tool in Takeovers of Local School Districts," *National Forum of Applied Educational Research Journal,* no. 1 (1989–90): 5–16.
5. Marlene I. Strathe and Catherine W. Hatcher, "Curriculum Development by Consensus: An Evaluation Study of Model Implementation," *Planning & Changing* (Summer 1986): 79–89.
6. Barney M. Berlin, Jack A. Kavanagh, and Kathleen Jensen, "The Principal as Curriculum Leader: Expectations vs. Performance," *NASSP Bulletin* (September 1988): 43–49.
7. Dennis Kelly, "The Effects of Curriculum Organization Structure on Curriculum Innovation" (Paper presented at the annual meeting of the American Educational Research Association, 1977) (ERIC Report Ed–137–94). See also Tamara E. Avi-Itzhak and Miriam Ben-Peretz, "Principals' Leadership Styles as Change Facilitators in Curricular Related Activities," *The Journal of Educational Administration* (Summer 1987): 231–47.
8. For added discussion of these criticisms, see Daniel Tanner and Laurel Tanner, *Curriculum Development* 2d ed. (New York: Macmillan, 1980), 589–92; and Carl D. Glickman, *Supervision of Instruction: A Developmental Approach* (Boston: Allyn & Bacon, 1985): 314–17.
9. H. L. Caswell et al., *Curriculum Improvement in Public School Systems* (New York: Columbia University Teachers College Bureau of Publications, 1950), 72.
10. See Daniel Tanner, "Improving the Curriculum," *NASSP Bulletin* (April 1987): 30–34; and Francis P. Hunkins and Allan C. Ornstein, "Designing the Curriculum," *NASSP Bulletin* (September 1988): 50–59.
11. Association for Supervision and Curriculum Development, *Leadership for Improving Instruction, 1960 Yearbook* (Washington, D.C.: Association for Supervision and Curriculum Development, 1960), 62–63.
12. See Gail T. Schneider, "The Myth of Curvilinearity: An Analysis of Decision-Making Involvement and Job Satisfaction," *Planning & Changing* (Fall 1986): 146–58; J. L. Small and J. H. Young, "Teachers' Motivations for Participating in Curriculum Development Committees," *Alberta Journal of Educational Research* (March 1988): 42–56; David S. Martin, Philip S. Saif, and Linda Thiel, "Curriculum Development: Who Is Involved and How?" *Educational Leadership* (December 1986/January 1987): 40–48; and Michael W. Apple, "Curricula and Teaching: Are They Headed Toward Excellence?" *NASSP Bulletin* (September 1988): 14–25.
13. John McNeil, "Curriculum Politics: Local, State, and Federal," *NASSP Bulletin* (September 1988): 65.

14. Fenwick W. English, "Management Practice as a Key to Curriculum Leadership," *Educational Leadership* (March 1979): 412. See also, Gail McCutcheon, "Curriculum Theory and Practice: Considerations for the 1990s and Beyond," *NASSP Bulletin* (September 1988): 33–42.

15. Hollis L. Caswell, "Persistent Curriculum Problems," *Educational Forum* (November 1980), 108. See also Walter Dick, "Instructional Design and the Curriculum Development Process," *Educational Leadership* (December 1986–January 1987): 54–56; and Raj K. Chopra, "Synergistic Curriculum Development: An Idea Whose Time Has Come," *NASSP Bulletin* (September 1989): 44–50.

16. Howard G. Spaulding, "What Is the Role of the Principal in Curriculum Work?" *NASSP Bulletin* (April 1956): 388.

17. Allan Vann, "Can Principals Lead in Curriculum Development?" *Educational Leadership* (March 1979): 404–5. See also Barney M. Berlin, Jack A. Kavanagh, and Kathleen Jensen, "The Principal as Curriculum Leader: Expectations vs. Performance," *NASSP Bulletin* (September 1988): 43–49.

18. William Georigiades, "Curriculum Change: What Are the Ingredients?" *NASSP Bulletin* (March 1980): 70; and Patricia B. Novotney, "Principal as an Instructional Leader," *Educational Leadership* (March 1979): 405.

19. Gordon Cawelti, "Strategic Planning for Curricular Reform," *National Forum* (Summer 1987): 29–31; and Terrance L. Walker and Judith F. Vogt, "The School Administrator as Change Agent: Skills for the Future," *NASSP Bulletin* (November 1987): 41–48.

20. Caswell et al., *Curriculum Improvement.*

21. See Edward F. DeRoche, *An Administrator's Guide for Evaluating Programs and Personnel: An Effective Schools Approach* 2d ed. (Newton, Mass: Allyn & Bacon, 1987).

22. See W. James Popham and Eva L. Baker, "Establishing Instructional Goals," in *Curriculum Development: Issues and Insights,* ed. Donald E. Orlosky and B. Othanel Smith (Chicago: Rand McNally College Publishing Company, 1978): 14–16; and Naftaly S. Glasman, "School Leadership and Instructional Objectives," *Evaluation-Based Leadership: School Administration in Contemporary Perspective* (Albany: State University of New York Press, 1986), 71–81.

23. M. Francis Klein, "A Study of Schooling: Curriculum," *Kappan* (December 1979): 244–45.

24. Henry Giroux and David Purpel, eds., *The Hidden Curriculum and Moral Education: Deception or Discovery* (Berkeley, Calif.: McCutchan, 1983); and Gail McCutcheon, "Curriculum Theory and Practice," 33–42.

25. Richard Larson, "Curriculum Scope and Sequence," *Forward* (Spring 1980): 53.

26. Vincent Rogers, "Assessing the Curriculum Experienced by Children," *Kappan* (May 1989): 714–17.

27. Robert J. Havighurst, *Developmental Tasks and Education* (New York: David McKay, 1972), 43–82.

28. Ira Jay Winn, "Civilizing the Dialogue in the Forgetting Society," *Kappan* (April 1989): 630–31.

29. Marie Winn, *The Plug-in Drug: Television, Children and the Family* (New York: Viking, 1977). For an additional discussion of the influences of television on students' behaviors, see J. L. Singer and D. G. Singer, "Family Experiences and Television Viewing as Predictors of Children's Imagination, Restlessness, and Aggression," *Journal of Social Issues* 42 (1986): 107–24.

30. Allan C. Ornstein, "The Irrelevant Curriculum: A Review from Four Perspectives," *NASSP Bulletin* (September 1988): 26.

31. For further discussion of some of these influences, see Harold Hodgkinson, "Today's Curriculum—How Appropriate Will It Be in Year 2000?" *NASSP Bulletin* (April 1987): 2–7.

32. George H. Gallup, "The 20th Annual Gallup Poll of the Public's Attitudes toward the Public Schools," *Kappan* (September 1988): 33–46.

33. See McCutcheon, "Curriculum Theory and Practice."

34. Michael Apple and Nancy King, "What Do Schools Teach?" in Giroux and Purpel, *The Hidden Curriculum and Moral Education.*

35. For help in this area, see Meredith D. Gall, *Handbook for Evaluating and Selecting Curriculum Materials* (Rockleigh, N.J.: Allyn & Bacon, 1981).

36. An excellent resource which every administrator should utilize to help determine the effectiveness of curriculum materials, particularly those commercially produced, is the Educational Products Information Exchange Institute, New York City. Also see Gerald D. Bailey, "Guidelines for Improving the Textbook/Material Selection Process," *NASSP Bulletin* (March 1988): 87–92.

37. See Sheila Harty, *Hucksters in the Classroom* (Washington, D.C.: Center for Responsive Law, 1980).

38. U.S. Commission on Civil Rights, *Fair Textbooks: A Resource Guide* (Washington, D.C.: U.S. Commission on Civil Rights, 1980).

39. For assistance in doing this, see Robert J. Kibler et al., *Objectives for Instruction and Evaluation* (Rockleigh, N.J.: Allyn & Bacon, 1981).

40. Orlosky and Smith, *Curriculum Improvement: Issues and Insights,* chap. 11 and 12. Also see Theodore J. Kowalski, "Organizational Patterns for Secondary School Curriculum" *NASSP Bulletin* (March 1981): 5–6.

41. A good beginning source for the administrator would be Sharon Tumulty, *Curriculum and Instruction: Planning Improvement* (Philadelphia: Research for Better Schools, 1978). Then turn to Bruce W. Tuckman, *Evaluating Instructional Programs* 2d ed. (Boston: Allyn & Bacon, 1985); and John J. Bowers, *Planning a Program Evaluation* (Philadelphia: Research for Better Schools, 1978). For a good example of the application of evaluation methods to an actual evaluation of the curriculum, see Donald C. Wilson, "Curriculum Evaluation" (ERIC Report Ed–175–928). Also, Sage Publications of Newbury Park, California, offers a number of good publications on program evaluation.

42. E. M. Jarchow, and E. Look, "Curriculum Mapping Works!" *Education* (Summer 1985): 417–22; Donald F. Weinstein, *Administrator's Guide to Curriculum Mapping* (Englewood Cliffs, N.J.: Prentice–Hall, 1986); and Thomas Maglaras and Deborah Lynch, "Monitoring the Curriculum: From Plan to Action," *Educational Leadership* (October 1988): 58–60.

43. Fenwick W. English, *Quality Control in Curriculum Development* (Arlington, Va.: American Association of School Administrators, 1978).

44. See Ronald Crowell and Paula Tissot, "Curriculum Alignment" (ERIC Report Ed–280–874); and Fenwick W. English, "It's Time to Abolish Conventional Curriculum Guides," *Educational Leadership* (December 1986/January 1987): 50–52.

45. William G. Savard and Kathleen Cotton, "Curriculum Alignment: Topic Summary Report. Research on School Effectiveness Project" (ERIC Report Ed–265–631).

46. Roger Scott, "Curriculum Alignment as a Model for School Improvement" (ERIC Report Ed–252–508).

47. D. A. Erlandson, "Evaluation and an Administrator's Autonomy," in *School Evaluation: The Politics and Process,* ed. E. R. House (Berkeley, Calif.: McCutchan, 1973), 22. Also see Naftaly S. Glasman, *Evaluation-Based Leadership: School Administration in Contemporary Perspective* (Albany: State University of New York Press, 1986).

48. E. R. House, "A Tenuous Relationship," in *School Evaluation,* 8.

49. *National Elementary School Principals Study* (Arlington, Va.: National Association of Elementary School Principals, 1979); Leonard O. Pellicer, Lorin W. Anderson, James W. Keefe, Edgar A. Kelly, and Lloyd E. McCleary, "Tasks and Problems of School Leaders," *High School Leaders and Their Schools, Vol. I: A National Profile* (Reston, Va.: National Association of Secondary School Principals, 1988): 15–25.

50. Also see an older but still relevant work by Kenneth D. Beanne and Bozidar Muntyan, *Human Relations in Curriculum Change* (New York: Dryden Press, 1951). This book presents excellent ideas on working with groups in introducing change. Also see Carl D. Glickman, *Supervision of Instruction: A Developmental Approach* (Boston: Allyn & Bacon, 1985), chap. 17; and Richard A. Gorton, *School Leadership and Administration: Important Concepts, Cases and Simulations* (Dubuque, Iowa: Wm. C. Brown Company Publishers, 1987), chap. 4.

51. For further discussion on utilizing a needs assessment for curriculum improvement, see Fred D. Williams, "School District Needs Assessment for Curriculum Development" (ERIC Report Ed–137–95). Also see Willard Crouthamel and Stephen Preston, "Needs Assessment, User's Manual" (ERIC Report Ed–181–562).

52. Hunkins and Ornstein, "Designing the Curriculum," 57.

53. Allan C. Ornstein and Francis P. Hunkins, "Implementing Curriculum Changes— Guidelines for Principals," *NASSP Bulletin* (November 1988): 67–72.

54. An excellent way to accomplish this is by joining the Association for Supervision and Curriculum Development. This organization publishes many valuable articles and books on curriculum improvement and proposals.

55. D. C. Anderson, *Evaluating Curriculum Proposals: A Critical Guide* (New York: John Wiley and Sons, 1980).

56. For a discussion on teacher resistance and ability to change, see Francis P. Hunkins and Allan C. Ornstein, "Implementing Curriculum Changes—Guidelines for Principals," *NASSP Bulletin* (November 1988); 67–72.

57. Richard A. Gorton, *School Leadership and Administration: Important Concepts, Cases, and Simulations,* chap. 7; and Walker and Vogt, "The School Administrator as Change Agent."

58. For further ideas and discussion about how to diagnose the reasons for resistance to change, and how to introduce and implement successful changes in the curriculum, see Gorton, *School Leadership and Administration,* chap. 7.

59. Robert D. Krey, "Factors Relating to Teachers' Perceptions of Curriculum Implementation Activities and the Extent of Curricular Implementation" (Ph.D. diss., University of Wisconsin, 1968). For more recent evidence on this problem, see Fenwick W. English, "It's Time to Abolish Conventional Curriculum Guides," *Educational Leadership* (December 1986–January 1987): 50–52.

60. Conan S. Edwards, "The Principal's Relationship to the Implementation of Official Curriculum Plans" (Ph.D. diss., University of Wisconsin, 1968). That curriculum implementation continues to be a problem is made clear in an article by Fenwick W. English, "Educational Administration and Curriculum Management," *NFEAS Journal* 4 (1986–87): 22–41.

61. Donald S. Monroe, "Curriculum Development: The Medium Is the Message and the Message Is Crucial," *NASSP Bulletin* (September 1988): 1.

13

. . . . .

Student Discipline: Organizational Considerations

▬

The majority of students in most elementary and secondary schools do not misbehave. However, a minority of students do misbehave and their behavior is one of the major problems that confront administrators and their professional staffs. Because an examination of a number of books on school administration revealed limited attention to this topic, we treat this important subject in some detail.

FACTORS AFFECTING THE PREVENTION AND REDUCTION OF STUDENT MISBEHAVIOR

The prevention and resolution of student discipline problems have long been responsibilities of school administrators. In the early days of education these were major responsibilities.[1] Through the years, other duties—particularly in the area of instructional improvement—have been added to the administrator's job, but maintaining appropriate student behavior has continued to rank as one of the administrator's more important responsibilities. Recent surveys of both the public and educators have identified student discipline as one of the most significant problems facing our schools; such studies suggest that it will continue to occupy much of administrators' time.[2]

The amount of time that administrators should spend on discipline problems depends on many variables, including the nature of the student population, the capability of the faculty, and the willingness of teachers to work with their administrators in a team approach. However, two factors influence the effectiveness of administrators and faculty members: (1) their perception of the causes of discipline problems, and (2) the approaches they utilize to prevent or resolve them. In this chapter, we emphasize careful classification and diagnosis of student discipline problems, as well as organizational considerations for preventing and reducing them. Although the focus of most of the discussion is on student misbehavior, administrators and staff should always keep in mind that their ultimate objective should be to develop students' self-discipline. In this connection, the place to begin the process of careful classification and diagnosis of student discipline problems and the development of self-discipline is in the elementary school. By beginning at this level, many potential and actual student discipline problems can be identified, diagnosed, and ameliorated before they become worse in the secondary school.

DEFINING THE PROBLEM

All schools do not experience the same discipline problems, but the differences seem to be mainly a matter of degree rather than type. For example, at one time, vandalism was thought to be a problem only for large city schools and was of little concern to rural, suburban, or elementary schools. Recently, however, this particular problem has been encountered in a variety of locales and schools appear to be experiencing an increase in the general severity of crime in the school environment.[3] At present, probably few student discipline problems are unique to only one kind of school or school setting; in general, however, elementary schools probably encounter fewer overt discipline problems than do secondary schools.

Although schools report a wide variety of student discipline problems, they seem to fall into four general categories: (1) misbehavior in class; (2) misbehavior outside class, but in school or on school grounds; (3) truancy; and (4) tardiness. These categories are identified in the classification system presented in figure 13.1.

A difficulty encountered in designing any system of classifying problems is that one's definition of what constitutes a problem largely determines what is included in the system.[4] In the classification system presented in figure 13.1, the areas included are those most typically reported by the schools as student discipline problems.[5] However, administrators can narrow or broaden the scope of problems included in a classification system (thereby reducing or increasing the administrator's responsibilities) merely by changing the definition of what constitutes student misbehavior.

For example, under the category "Misbehavior in Class," many schools have a rule against gum chewing. Even though gum chewing may be objectionable to some people, the question that needs to be raised is, "Is this the type of student behavior that teachers and administrators should be spending

Figure 13.1 Types of Student Discipline Problems.

Misbehavior in Class	Misbehavior Outside Class (But in School or on School Grounds)	Truancy	Tardiness
1. Talking back to the teacher	1. Fighting	1. Cutting class	1. Frequently being late to class
2. Not paying attention	2. Vandalism	2. Skipping school	2. Frequently being late to school
3. Distracting others	3. Smoking		
4. Gum chewing	4. Using illegal drugs		
5. Vandalism	5. Student dress		
6. Profanity	6. Theft		
7. Cheating	7. Gambling		
8. Assault	8. Littering		
	9. Located in unapproved area		

time and energy to eliminate?" If the answer to the question is "Yes," the scope of responsibility for disciplining students has been broadened, and some of the time and energy of teachers and administrators is less available for other activities. Although it is true that the amount of time and energy devoted to the elimination of gum chewing is probably not great, the cumulative effect of a number of such rules can be considerable. A reasonable guideline for determining whether certain student behavior should be considered a problem is whether or not the behavior is disruptive or only distractive. (These terms are defined later in this chapter.) The former, rather than the latter, merits the time and energy of the administrator and the faculty.

For many years, administrators had wide-ranging control over student discipline. Administrators were generally viewed as acting in place of parents (frequently referred to as the *in loco parentis* doctrine) while students were in school. However, in the 1960s, as the courts began to increase the recognition given to the individual rights of students, administrators began to question the scope of their authority. In recent years this situation has changed, and the courts have increasingly supported administrators in their exercise of school board-derived authority in coping with student misbehavior.[6]

In considering the types of student misbehavior for which the school should assume responsibility for disciplining, administrators and staff members should also try to make a distinction between student misbehavior within the appropriate jurisdiction of the school and student misbehavior more properly handled by outside agencies. Vandalism and using illegal drugs, for example, are student behaviors which in most schools are subject to disciplinary punishment. These particular student actions are also violations of the law; therefore it is debatable whether the school has a legitimate role in disciplining students, in addition to whatever consequences are imposed on them by the police or the courts. As New York State's *Guidelines for Student Rights and Responsibilities* point out, "Standards of Conduct . . . need not prescribe school discipline for offenses committed within the school which are already adequately provided for by criminal law, unless the presence of the student in school would constitute a danger to the student himself, to other members of the school community, or to the continuation of the educative process."[7]

The school should play a role in *referring, counseling* and *educating* students who break the law; but whether a school should also act as an institution for determining guilt and administering punishment is doubtful. The school that decides to determine guilt and administer punishment for students' unlawful misbehavior not only adds immeasurably to the number and difficulty of the discipline problems with which it must deal but may also be subjecting students to double jeopardy. Therefore, in fairness to the student and in the best interest of the school, administrators and faculty members should limit themselves to defining and punishing only student behavior that tends to disrupt education, and which would not be handled more appropriately by some outside agency, such as the police or the courts.

DIAGNOSING DISCIPLINE PROBLEMS

After a school has defined which behaviors are considered student discipline problems, the faculty's and administration's initial approach when encountering such behavior should be to diagnose the reasons for it. Admittedly, in some cases diagnosis of a problem must follow punishment for the misbehavior. But if the intent is to prevent that misbehavior from occurring again, punishment alone is probably not very effective in most situations. All behavior is caused, and until the administration and faculty can better understand and deal with the causes of student misbehavior, it is likely to recur in the future.

In attempting to diagnose the causes of a student's misbehavior, the administrators are really trying to understand the reasons for the student's actions. Such reasons are typically complex and may not be understood even by the student. Administrators and staff members should conduct a thorough investigation into the causes of the problem if it is to be resolved successfully. The conclusions administrators and staff draw about why the student acted in a particular way greatly influence their decision on whether or how the student should be punished; they also determine which further steps should be taken to prevent the problem from happening again.

POSSIBLE CAUSES

To diagnose a discipline problem accurately, administrators and staff should investigate the validity of several alternative hypotheses or explanations for the student's misbehavior. Although the nature of the hypotheses will vary for different discipline and attendance problems, a taxonomy of hypotheses is presented in figure 13.2.

Figure 13.2 Diagnosing Student Misbehavior: Some Alternative Hypotheses.

School-Related Factors	Personal Factors	Home and Community Environment
1. Poor teaching	1. Student doesn't understand the rules	1. Poor authority figures and relationships within the home
2. Irrelevant curriculum	2. Student doesn't understand why the rules exist	2. Crime-infested neighborhood
3. Inflexible school schedule		3. Student's activities after school, e.g., work, other activities that keep him up late at night
4. Insufficient adaptation and individualization of school's programs to a student's educational background	3. Poor educational background	
	4. Undesirable peer relationships	
	5. Student is psychologically disturbed	
	6. Personality conflict between student and teacher	

As an examination of figure 13.2 shows, diagnosing the causes of student misbehavior is a complex task. Any or several of the factors listed could contribute to a student's misbehavior in a particular situation. Because administrators cannot hope to investigate all of the possible hypotheses at the same time, they must make some decisions about how to proceed. In general, their first line of approach should be to investigate the first three hypotheses listed under "Personal Factors" and then those under "School-Related Factors." These factors are subject to the influence of the administration and faculty and within the responsibilities of the school.

For example, the following school-related factors may account for a student's behavior and should be investigated:

1. The subject matter may be too difficult.
2. The subject matter may be too easy.
3. The subject matter or the class activities may not be relevant to the student's interests or needs.
4. The class assignment may be too heavy, too light, badly planned, poorly explained, or unfairly evaluated.
5. The course content or activities may not be properly sequenced for this student.
6. The seating arrangement for the student may be poor from a learning point of view.
7. There may be a personality conflict between the student and the teachers.[8]

Each or any combination of these conditions may cause considerable frustration, boredom, anxiety, or hostility in a student and could be expressed in misbehavior. Administrators who can ascertain the particular underlying reasons for a student's misbehavior are in a position to know which approach to take in remedying the problem.

Although one or more of the other hypotheses listed in figure 13.2 under "Personal Factors," such as items 4 or 5, and under "Home and Community Environment," may be valid for a given situation, the school frequently has little or no control or influence over these conditions. This is particularly true in respect to the factors associated with "Home and Community Environment." The school seldom has much control over students' situations in either their homes or neighborhoods. Both factors may be important in causing a student's misbehavior in school, but school authorities find it difficult to bring about change in these areas.

On the other hand, in some situations the school has a responsibility to respond immediately to a student problem caused by the home or the community. For example, some children misbehave in school because of their neglect or abuse in the home. Child abuse is now recognized as a serious problem in the United States; each year an estimated 1 million children suffer from abuse in the home and 4,000 children die of their abuse and neglect.[9] As Vincent Fontana noted,

> One need not break a child's arm to abuse that child. One may break the child's spirit through the constant use of verbal and psychological batterings. This type of abuse often is just as damaging as a physical beating. By definition, therefore, child abuse includes physical abuse, emotional or verbal abuse, sexual abuse, physical neglect, medical care neglect, abandonment, and emotional neglect.[10]

Public Law 93–247, the Child Abuse Prevention and Treatment Act, requires that individuals or agencies suspecting possible child abuse report it to the proper authorities. In every state and the District of Columbia, educators are required by this law to report suspected child abuse. Educators with this mandate to report include administrators, teachers, counselors, and school nurses.[11] To abide by their legal responsibilities and to prepare staff members for working with students who are victims of child abuse, Lynn Fossum and Lauralee Sorensen recommend that school districts provide in-service education for all personnel to help them recognize symptoms of child abuse and to obtain knowledge of resources available in the community to deal with the problem.[12] Several national organizations that provide literature on the topic of child abuse are identified at the end of this chapter; administrators are encouraged to keep well informed about this problem.[13] (Possible approaches for working with parents and community groups on other kinds of student misbehavior are described in the next chapter.)

Even though in some situations the school should look at the home or the community for possible causes of a student's misbehavior, in most instances administrators and staff members find the most productive approach is to concentrate initially on diagnosing those possible causes of a student's misbehavior within the school and for which the school can offer a remedy. As Daniel Duke and William Seidman point out, educators need to

> entertain the possibility that the ways schools are organized influence student behavior. The implications of such a possibility are great, given current concern over student disobedience, criminal conduct, and lack of motivation to work. Conceivably these dysfunctional behaviors can be lessened by altering school organization, rather than by attempting the difficult and frequently counterproductive task of changing students directly.[14]

PROCESS OF DIAGNOSIS

Although diagnosis in situations involving student discipline problems has yet to be fully developed as a concept or skill, it would seem to include the following behaviors on the part of administrators and staff members:

1. Conferences with students to ascertain their attitudes toward school and their feelings about those aspects of the school environment making it difficult for them to perform as they should and as they would like.
2. Conferences with the students' teachers to ascertain the teachers' analyses of the problem.
3. Examination of students' cumulative records for clues suggesting possible learning problems that might be frustrating them and causing their misbehavior. Examples of such clues would be low reading scores, poor grades in the past, and underachievement.[15]
4. Examination of the students' programs and schedules. Are programs and schedules appropriate, considering students' backgrounds, interests, and attitudes?
5. Review of the curriculum and teacher lesson plans in those areas of the students' programs where they appear to be experiencing the greatest difficulty, academically and behaviorally.
6. Conferences with students' parents to ascertain their attitudes and perceptions of the problems and to evaluate the extent to which they may provide assistance.
7. Observation of students and their interactions with others in various school settings, such as in the classroom or cafeteria or during an extracurricular activity.[16]

Engaging in all of these procedures for one student would admittedly represent a major investment of an administrator's and/or faculty's effort and time. (They should by all means utilize the help of the school counselor, psychologist, or other pupil personnel workers.) In many situations it is not necessary for the administrator and staff to complete all of the preceding steps in diagnosing the causes of a discipline problem. Sometimes the root of a problem may be uncovered after completing only two or three steps.

Administrators and staff members who want to avoid an inaccurate diagnosis of problems will be as thorough and comprehensive as possible. They should always bear in mind that if they fail to invest sufficient time and effort in diagnosing the causes of a problem, the time and effort that they have saved will need to be reinvested as the problem recurs time and again. There is no good educational substitute or shortcut to a comprehensive, in-depth diagnosis of a problem.

In engaging in the process of diagnosis, administrators and staff should be aware that certain subjective factors could compromise the objectivity and effectiveness of the process. According to attribution theory, individuals who are judging other people tend to attribute the actions of the latter to their personal characteristics and attitudinal dispositions rather than to situational factors.[17] Therefore, the physical characteristics, appearances, or attitudes of a student who has misbehaved could subconsciously affect an administrator and/or staff member, limiting the process of diagnosis as well as influencing the final disposition of the problem. For example, Edward Porter found that the disciplinarians' view of the circumstances surrounding student misbehavior and their choice of disciplinary responses were more influenced by the students' physical appearance than by the students' previous disciplinary record or even the violation of rules for which the punishment was supposedly being given.[18] James Frasher and Ramona Frasher report similar findings in regard to the influence of a student's attitude during a conference with the assistant principal and the severity of punishment recommended by the assistant principal, irrespective of the nature of the offense.[19] These findings, based on attribution theory, suggest that the individuals participating in the process of diagnosis need to pay special attention to how the characteristics of the student who has misbehaved are influencing their diagnosis and selection of corrective measures.

ORGANIZATIONAL CONSIDERATIONS

Responding to student misbehavior has thus far been viewed from a problem perspective. There is value, however, in examining student discipline from an organizational point of view. To maintain appropriate order in the school, roles need to be defined, procedures specified, relationships between roles coordinated, and the effectiveness of these various organizational elements needs to be assessed periodically.

RESPONSIBILITY FOR DISCIPLINARY POLICIES AND PROCEDURES

Disciplinary policies and procedures tend to be promulgated at both the school board and the building levels. Policies and procedures at the school board level are frequently rather general and may be no more specific than to delegate to the building administrator the authority to make those rules and regulations facilitating learning and maintaining order and safety in the school. Some school boards, however, are very specific in defining disciplinary policies and procedures, even to the extent of specifying the type of student conduct permitted, or not permitted, in the school district. Such specificity is usually for the purpose of maintaining a degree of uniformity throughout the district. It also results in lessening the authority of the administrator and staff in defining rules and regulations appropriate for their students.

If the responsibility for defining specific disciplinary policies and procedures is delegated by the school board to building administrators, they have greater flexibility in developing particular policies and procedures appropriate for their own student clientele.[20] But they should always keep in mind that policies and procedures at the building level must be logically related to the initial mandate given by the school board at the time of delegation. So, if the school board has delegated to building administrators the authority to "make those rules and regulations facilitating learning and maintaining order and safety in the school," the specific policies and procedures defined at the building level should not go beyond this delegation of authority. Administrators are not totally free to make whatever rules and regulations they think are best for their schools; all school rules and regulations must be based on school board policy and be compatible with state and federal laws.

THE TEACHER AND STUDENT DISCIPLINE

While administrators are primarily responsible for administering a school's disciplinary program, classroom teachers perform one of the most important roles in the program. Teachers are the key persons to interpret and implement the school's rules and regulations concerning student behavior; they are the ones that typically first identify, define, and react to a particular student behavior as a problem. Also, as Edwin Brown and Arthur Phelps have pointed out, classroom teachers can play a major role in reducing student misbehavior. The better the teachers' preparation, teaching techniques, personality, and other classroom aspects, the less likely are student misbehavior problems to arise.[21]

Probably the most important step that administrators can take to decrease the discipline problems referred to their offices by teachers is to work with the staff—particularly new teachers—in regard to their role in student discipline. Apparently, the first three weeks of class represent a critical time for teachers to establish appropriate classroom management. Edmund Emmer and his colleagues found that effective classroom managers establish their credibility as well as classroom procedures during the first three weeks rather than waiting until a crisis develops.[22] Specifically, these teachers

- Developed a workable system of rules and procedures that they then spent time teaching to their students.

- Made explicit the consequences of inappropriate classroom behavior.
- Stopped inappropriate behavior quickly and were consistent and predictable in their response to inappropriate behavior.
- Gave careful directions to students and monitored their behavior carefully.

Other research reviewed by Edmund Emmer and Carolyn Evertson underscores the importance of teacher behaviors that help students keep engaged in the task of learning.[23] A number of these teacher behaviors are identified in chapter 10 on staff evaluation and supervision.

Administrators can work individually or in groups with teachers who need help in classroom management. The latter approach can take the form of in-service activities beginning with a review of the school's student discipline policies and procedures and the rationale on which they are based. Such a review at the beginning of the year would be helpful for clearing up any misunderstandings and might even identify the need to revise some of the policies and procedures. Included in the review could be a discussion with the faculty on their expectations for student behavior.[24]

A good approach to stimulating faculty thinking on discipline would be to give out a short questionnaire to secure teachers' perceptions of various factors affecting how they react to different student behaviors. Administrators could develop their own questionnaires or use one of several available instruments, such as the Pupil Control Ideology instrument.[25] This questionnaire is composed of twenty statements suggesting factors that may be related to student control and discipline problems. Four sample statements from the instrument are:

- Teachers should consider revision of their teaching methods if these are criticized by their pupils.
- Being friendly with pupils often leads them to become too familiar.
- Pupils can be trusted to work together without supervision.
- Pupils often misbehave to make the teacher look bad.

Respondents to the Pupil Control Ideology instrument indicate the extent to which they agree or disagree with each statement. The instrument does not take long to administer, but can provide considerable useful information about the attitudes and philosophies of the faculty toward students; it may pinpoint the direction that an in-service program for the faculty should take. For example, responses to the instrument might show that many of the faculty are either creating discipline problems through their own actions, or that they are overly concerned about certain student behavior and insufficiently concerned about other kinds of student behavior. (Numerous studies through the years have suggested that teachers tend to overemphasize control problems and give inadequate attention to problems of a more psychological nature.) A major objective of an in-service program for the faculty, then, might be to develop a more positive philosophy and attitude toward student behavior, with emphasis on the role that a teacher needs to play in promoting student self-discipline. Excellent approaches for teaching students self-discipline have been developed by Judith Dobson and Russell Dobson, and by William Wayson and Gay Pinell.[26]

Although research has shown that most school districts do not provide in-service training for teachers to help them manage discipline problems more effectively, there is no shortage of in-service materials on the topic.[27] The following examples illustrate several materials and approaches:

1. *Assertive Discipline in the Classroom, Assertive Discipline in Action,* and *Assertive Discipline for Secondary School Educators* (for additional information on Assertive Discipline contact Canter and Associates, P.O. 64517, Los Angeles, California 90064, 213–395–3221 or 800–262–4347).

2. *T.E.T.: Teacher Effectiveness Training* (information about how school districts can offer the Teacher Effectiveness Training Course to their teachers may be obtained from School Programs, Effectiveness Training, Inc., 531 Stevens Avenue, Solana Beach, California 92075.

3. *Effective Classroom Management for the Elementary School* (videotape) can be purchased or rented from the Association for Supervision and Curriculum Development, 1250 N. Pitt Street, Alexandria, Virginia 22314–1403.

4. *Classroom Discipline* (case studies and viewpoints book) can be ordered from the National Education Association, NEA Professional Library, P.O. Box 509, West Haven, Connecticut 06516.

These references are useful resources in working with staff members to develop school discipline programs. Administrators should be warned, however, that the appeal of packaged programs is also their major drawback.[28] Richard Curwin and Allen Mendler noted that the "quick results they yield come at the expense of developing responsible students who understand the important principles on which rules are based."[29] Thus, administrators are encouraged to use these programs only if they fit preidentified needs within their schools' discipline program.

In-service activities for teachers should concentrate on the use of case studies, role playing, simulations, and videotape analysis (rather than more traditional methods such as guest speakers or open group discussions) to provide teachers with greater opportunities to practice the application of new concepts and techniques.

REFERRAL PROCEDURES

Students should not be referred to administrators for disciplinary action until teachers have first conferred with them about their behavior, unless it is such that class cannot continue as long as the student is in the room (i.e., disruptive behavior). The person best able to resolve discipline problems arising in the classroom setting is the teacher, and administrators should attempt to foster this approach with the faculty.

Experienced administrators know that not all discipline problems can be resolved at the classroom level, however; some student behavior problems have to be referred to administrators for appropriate action. Before this stage, administrators need to call on their organizational and administrative abilities to develop procedures facilitating careful consideration of the problems and accurate and full communication to all concerned.[30] Usually some type of a referral and feedback form is necessary. Although there are many examples of such forms, the one presented in figure 13.3, on the next page, has much to commend it.

Several provisions of the form presented in figure 13.3 should be included in any referral procedure. First of all, there should be a written record of the initial diagnosis of the problem and the action taken by the teacher and the administrator. Written communication, as opposed to verbal, tends to be more thoughtfully prepared and is less subject to misinterpretation and forgetfulness at a later date. Written communication is particularly important as part of the documentation that may be required later, if more severe disciplinary action taken by the school is challenged at a school board hearing or in the courts. (An option to reduce the amount of writing would be to identify and code the various student misbehaviors on the back of the referral forms, and request the teachers to use the appropriate code.)

Second, referral procedures should require the teacher to specify in as much detail as possible the nature of the problem and the action the teacher has taken to remedy the situation. These two requirements not only encourage the teacher to give some thought to why the problem has occurred and how it might be resolved at the classroom level but also provide the administrator with information on these aspects. Unless administrators have this information when a student is referred, they are likely to waste time or take the wrong

Figure 13.3 Referral and Feedback Form.

Student _____ Section _____ Time _____

Teacher _____ Date _____

Nature of Problem _____

_____

Action Before Referral	Teacher/Student/ Administrator Conference	Action by Administration
Conference with pupil _____	My planning period	Date _____
Detention _____	is _____	Conference with pupil (warning/reprimand)
Phone call home _____	Student is in room	_____
Parent conference _____	_____	Detention _____
Letter to parents _____		Phone call to parents
Guidance _____		_____
Other _____		Formal letter (copy in your mailbox) _____
		Conference with parent being requested _____
		Referral to pupil personnel department _____
		Suspension (until conference) _____
		Corporal punishment
		_____
		Other _____

Initials _____

approach with the student. Therefore, before administrators are in a reasonable position to take disciplinary or remedial action with students, they must obtain information about the nature of the problem based on the teacher's perception and learn what the teacher has already tried to do about the situation.

The school's referral procedures should also include a mechanism by which the administrator can communicate to the teacher the action that has been taken. Most administrators have good intentions in this regard, but for one reason or another the job frequently does not get done, at least according to teacher reports.

Probably the most efficient and certain way for an administrator to communicate back to the referring teacher is to use a procedure similar to the feedback portion of the form in figure 13.3. This system not only provides feedback to the teacher but also creates a written record of the action taken, which can be very useful in building documentation or in conducting an analysis of trends in discipline problems and the actions initiated by the administrator.

After receiving the referral and communicating its disposition to the teacher or teachers involved, administrators should establish a recordkeeping system for storing, retrieving, and analyzing the data contained on the referral forms. Administrators who have access to microcomputers with data base programs and software find that the computers provide a convenient means for consolidating and analyzing schoolwide data.[31] The reports which can be generated through these systems allow critical analyses of discipline data providing useful profiles regarding the types of discipline problems, frequency of occurrence, patterns of behavior, and profiles of offenders. These data can be valuable in predicting areas of potential discipline problems and determining preventive strategies.

UTILIZING SPECIALIZED RESOURCES

In attempting to prevent and ameliorate student behavior, administrators should organize all of the professional resources available to the school. School counselors, psychologists, social workers, and nurses, as well as personnel in law enforcement and family assistance agencies, all possess specialized knowledge and skills which administrators should try to utilize in working with students who are discipline problems. These specialists should not be involved in administering punishment to the student, but they certainly can make valuable contributions to diagnosing the nature of a problem and recommending remedial action.[32]

For these specialists to make a maximum contribution, administrators should consider organizing them into a pupil personnel committee for the purposes of studying and diagnosing severe student disciplinary problems and for offering suggestions about possible remediation. A deficiency in most approaches to student misbehavior is that they do not capitalize in an organized way on various professional expertise within the school and the community. The recommended approach to student misbehavior is one in which administrators take responsibility for organizing and utilizing all of the available expertise. Until administrators assume this organizational responsibility, their schools' approach to student discipline problems is likely to be piecemeal, lacking in coordination, and not very effective.

EVALUATING DISCIPLINARY POLICIES AND PROCEDURES

The disciplinary policies and procedures of many schools have been attacked periodically by students, parents, and the courts. Ironically, the number and severity of discipline problems in many schools have been increasing for some time. Both of these factors have made the job of trying to prevent or deal constructively with discipline problems a very difficult and frustrating one for school administrators. As Edward Ladd has noted, "Being an administrator trying to keep order in school must sometimes seem like being a modern physician trying to practice medicine in a country that has outlawed scalpels and hypodermic needles."[33]

Although some administrators may believe that, on the basis of court rulings, they can regulate little student misbehavior, the courts have never taken the position that the schools have no authority in this area. In fact, in the famous Blackwell case the court reaffirmed that "It is always within the province of school authorities to provide regulation, prohibition, and punishment of acts calculated to undermine the school routine."[34] In ruling against school disciplinary policies and procedures, the main thrust of court decisions has been that the policies and procedures were not fair, reasonable, or clear. Therefore, every administrator (with the assistance of relevant others) should periodically evaluate the school's disciplinary policies and procedures to ascertain the extent to which they meet these criteria.

Because specific discipline policies and procedures are frequently made at the building level, school administrators are most likely to be concerned with evaluating the validity and effectiveness of these policies and procedures, rather than the ones established by the school board. However, there may be situations in which they are requested to evaluate school board policies on student discipline and suggest changes. In either case, administrators need defensible criteria on which to make their evaluation. Due to the paucity of research on disciplinary policies and procedures, the following criteria are primarily based on a synthesis of recommendations in the professional literature and should, therefore, be discussed and analyzed before they are accepted.

CRITERIA FOR EVALUATING STUDENT DISCIPLINE POLICIES AND PROCEDURES

1. **A school's discipline policies and procedures should be based on school board policy.**[35] School building policies and procedures, particularly those presented in student and faculty handbooks, should be examined to determine the extent to which they are in conformity with school board policies.[36] In situations where there is doubt about a school policy or procedure, clarification should be obtained from the district administration and, if necessary, from the school board.

2. **There should be overall agreement among students, teachers, parents, and administrators about the philosophy and objectives of the disciplinary policies and procedures of a school.** If most people do not agree about the purposes of a school's disciplinary policies and procedures and why they must exist, they are very difficult to enforce. This is particularly true for classroom misbehavior. Unless administrators have secured from staff members an agreed-on, uniform, explicit designation of the kinds of behavior legitimately considered discipline problems, some members of the faculty may feel free to provide their own interpretations. In the latter case, undoubtedly some teachers will view students who question and argue as disrespectful and arrogant, while other faculty members perceive the same behavior as stimulating and challenging. In circumstances involving student tardiness, some teachers may believe that if a student is late to class two or three times, the student's behavior is excessive; other teachers may not concern themselves at all with this behavior. In the absence of a definitive discipline policy developed with faculty, student, and parent involvement, identical student behavior may be viewed by some people as a problem and by others as unimportant; as a result of this inconsistency, students may be treated unfairly.

Discipline policies and procedures are seldom popular. If those affected by the policies and procedures and those expected to implement them can understand and generally agree with their purpose and justification, then the possibility of adherence to them should be significantly increased.

3. **The school should maintain only disciplinary policies and procedures which have an educational purpose, are administratively feasible, and are legally enforceable.** The more rules and procedures, the more difficult it is to gain acceptance and adherence by students and teachers, and the more likely it is that administrators will have to devote larger and larger portions of their time to interpreting and enforcing disciplinary rules and procedures.

In the past, schools have attempted to enforce rules on such items as hair length and style of clothing. For one reason or another, these rules were unacceptable to many students and parents and ultimately, through court actions, have proved to be unenforceable in most situations. Therefore, it is important for the school to confine its regulations and procedures to those that are generally accepted and can be enforced. The New Jersey School Board has recommended that three criteria be applied to every proposed rule considered by administrators: "(1) Is the rule necessary for the orderly and effective operation of the school? (2) Does the rule involve some suppression of freedom? (3) If so, is the incidental restriction on . . . freedom any greater than is reasonably necessary for the orderly functioning of the school?"[37]

In determining which student behaviors should be regulated, the faculty and administration should initially try to make a distinction between behavior which is disruptive and behavior which is distractive.[38] *Disruptive* behavior is any action which prevents the continuation of an activity currently in process, such as teaching or learning. Fighting in class, throwing erasers, or refusing to keep quiet are examples of behavior which disrupts a class.

Distractive behavior, on the other hand, may temporarily slow down a class activity but does not actually prevent it from continuing. Chewing gum while the teacher is lecturing, is an example of behavior which may be distractive but certainly not disruptive.

Although schools may choose to regulate and punish distractive behavior, administrators should recognize that this decision significantly increases the number of discipline problems with which they and their faculty members must cope. In discipline cases the courts have, by and large, tended to apply the criterion of disruption rather than distraction. Even though a school could, if it chose, administer minor punishments, such as chastening, to those students who engage in distractive behavior, more extreme measures such as suspension would probably not be upheld by the courts.

4. **Policies and procedures on student behavior should be stated in a positive form as much as possible, and student responsibility rather than misbehavior should be stressed.** The emphasis should be on student behavior that is desired, not on unacceptable behavior. Two examples of this kind of emphasis are a statement entitled "Bill of Rights and Duties" in a student handbook disseminated by Barrington Consolidated High School and a statement by the Detroit Public Schools on elementary students' rights and responsibilities.[39]

5. **The policies and procedures governing student behavior should be written in clear, understandable language and be presented in student, teacher, and parent handbooks which are reviewed at the beginning of each school year.** Rules and procedures which are not written are more easily misunderstood or forgotten. And, rules and procedures not written in clear and understandable language can be misinterpreted or incorrectly applied.

Compounding these problems would be failure by a school to periodically review its rules and procedures with students, teachers, and parents. Every school should review its policies and procedures on student behavior at the beginning of each school year to refresh people's memories, clear up misunderstandings, and identify the need for change in current policies and procedures.

6. **The consequences of violating a rule or regulation should be made explicit and commensurate with the nature of the violation.** Students should not have to guess or infer what the consequences will be for violating a rule or regulation. The consequences should be made explicit at the time that the rule or regulation goes into effect. Students need to know what will happen if they violate a rule or regulation so they have the opportunity to take

that information into consideration. Administrators may want to leave themselves a certain amount of latitude in stating the consequences of minor offenses for first-time violators by using such words as "could result in" but for serious offenses and for repeated violations, language such as "will result in" is more appropriate.

The consequences of violating a rule or regulation need to be commensurate with the nature of the violation. Consequences that are too lenient do not generate sufficient respect, but overly severe consequences raise questions of harshness and fairness. Also, there is the problem that what is too lenient or too harsh to one person may appear otherwise to another individual. Obviously, administrators are not able to satisfy everyone as to the appropriateness of a specific punishment. However, by involving representative teachers, students, and parents in the development of a statement of consequences, administrators are more likely to end up with a defensible and acceptable statement.

7. **The rationale supporting the rules, procedures, and consequences governing student behavior should be clearly communicated to students and should be enforced fairly and consistently.** An understanding of the rationale behind the rules, and fairness and consistency in enforcement of rules and consequences are essential prerequisites to students' acceptance and compliance. In a study by Lawrence Vredevoe, students reported that the following factors (in order of frequency) were important:
   a. Interpreting the reasons and purposes of the rules.
   b. Fairness in enforcement.
   c. Treatment which recognizes the maturity of the student.
   d. Consistency in enforcement.
   e. Enforcement without embarrassment, whenever possible.
   f. Observance of rules by teachers.
   g. Opportunity to participate in making rules in areas where students are capable.[40]

It is interesting that students believed that if there were to be rules, they should be observed by the adults working in the school as well as the students. Of course, this may not always be feasible in school, but clearly it is a factor important to the students.

After administrators have utilized the seven general criteria for evaluating the school's discipline policies and procedures, they may want to make certain changes in them. The types of changes depend on their particular situation, but should not be made without faculty, parent, student, and school board involvement.[41] Participation by all parties who may be affected by revisions in a school's disciplinary policies and procedures is the key to successful implementation of needed changes.

A FINAL NOTE

Studies show a dramatic increase in recent years in certain criminal acts, such as assaults, vandalism, narcotics, and gang violence in the schools.[42] In response to this troubling situation, a growing number of schools have employed their own security officers and some have experimented with various forms of technology, such as closed-circuit television and walkie-talkies.[43]

Even though the "good old days" were far from idyllic, there is little doubt that school discipline problems are becoming more numerous and severe.[44] Whether school security officers or technological aids will be successful in the long run in preventing student misbehavior is open to question. These measures may be temporarily necessary in some schools to control a bad situation. A book by Peter Blauvelt is probably the most useful in that regard.[45] By their very nature, however, these techniques tend to deal more with the symptoms of the problem than with its basic causes, and such methods run the danger of infringing on the civil rights of students.

If a school is to make a significant reduction in student misbehavior, the administrator and faculty need to identify and correct the basic causes of that misbehavior. Diagnosis is the first step; then alternative approaches to preventing misbehavior should be instituted. These approaches are discussed in the next chapter.

Regardless of the approach employed, schools with effective discipline programs utilize the following elements in planning and implementing their programs:

- Agreed-on discipline philosophy
- Communication of the standards of proper conduct
- Supportive staff
- Enforced consequences for misbehavior
- Commitment to helping solve problems of students with special needs
- A variety of skills useful in managing class behavior
- A vital curriculum and effective teaching
- Respectful and dignified treatment of students[46]

The incorporation of these fundamental aspects of program design in determining school discipline policies and procedures increases the likelihood that administrators and their faculty members will experience long-term success in improving student behavior within their schools.

Review and Learning Activities

1. Explain how it is possible for administrators to narrow or broaden the scope and nature of their responsibilities by changing the definition of what constitutes student misbehavior in school.
2. What are the purpose and steps of diagnosis in responding to student misbehavior?
3. Identify the main hypothesized causes of student misbehavior. What is the rationale for investigating certain of these causes first, and others later?
4. How can an administrator work with teachers and other specialized personnel to reduce or prevent student discipline problems?
5. Apply the criteria recommended in the text to an evaluation of your own school's disciplinary policies and procedures.
6. What are the implications of Vredevoe's findings on student expectations insofar as your own school's disciplinary policies and procedures are concerned?

Notes

1. Ellwood P. Cubberly, *Public Education in the United States,* rev. ed. (Boston: Houghton Mifflin, 1934), 328.
2. See recent September issues of *Kappan* for Gallup poll data on this topic.
3. National Institute of Law Enforcement and Criminal Justice, *School Crime: The Problem and Some Attempted Solutions* (Washington, D.C.: Department of Justice, LEAA, 1979). See also, National School Safety Center, *School Discipline Notebook* (Malibu, Calif.: Pepperdine University Press, 1986): 5–9. See James R. Wetzel, "Kids and Crime," *School Safety* (Spring 1988): 4–7; Brenda Turner, "Violent Juvenile Crime Knows No Boundaries," *School Safety* (Spring 1988): 18–19; "The Escalating Toll of Violence at Schools: A Five-Year Chronology," *Education Week* (January 25, 1989): 4; Suzanne Harper, "LA's Gang Busters— Lessons Learned," *School Safety* (Fall 1989): 12–15; Ronald D. Stephens, "Gangsters: Back to the Future," *School Safety* (Fall 1989): 16–17; and Julius Menacker, Ward Weldon, and Emanuel Hurwetz, "Schools Lay Down the Law," *School Safety* (Winter 1990); 27–30.
4. Robert A. Stebbins, "The Meaning of Disorderly Behavior: Teacher Definition of a Classroom Situation," *Sociology of Education* (Spring 1971); 217–36. See also Joan S. Safran and Stephen P. Safran, "Teachers' Judgments of Problem Behaviors," *Exceptional Children* (November 1987): 240–44.

5. George M. Usova, "Reducing Discipline Problems in the Elementary Schools: Approaches and Suggestions," *Education* (Summer 1979): 419–22. See also Stanley T. Dubelle, Jr., and Carol M. Hoffman, *Misbehavin': Solving the Disciplinary Puzzle for Educators* (Lancaster, Pa.: Technomic Publishing Co., 1984).

6. "Disciplining Students for Out-of-School Misconduct," *A Legal Memorandum: National Association of Secondary School Principals* (September 1988): 1–6.

7. *Guidelines for Student Rights and Responsibilities* (Albany, N.Y.: New York State Education Department, n.d.), 30.

8. This list represents an adaptation and extension of factors suggested by George V. Sheviakov and Fritz Redl in *Discipline for Today's Children and Youth* (Washington, D.C.: Association for Supervision and Curriculum Development, 1956).

9. Vincent J. Fontana, "Child Abuse—One Sign of a Troubled Society," *Momentum* (September 1987): 25.

10. Ibid., 40.

11. "Child Abuse and Neglect: What to Watch for, What to Do," *Education Week* (November 25, 1987); 9.

12. Lynn Fossum and Lauralee Sorensen, "The Schools See It First: Child Abuse/Neglect," *Kappan* (December 1979): 274. Also see Stephen W. Stile, *The School's Role in the Prevention of Child Abuse* (Bloomington, Ind.: Phi Delta Kappa, 1982); Sandy K. Wurtele, "School-Based Sexual Abuse Prevention Programs: A Review," *Child Abuse & Neglect* 2 (1987): 483–95; and Linda Graham and Marilyn Harris-Hart, "Meeting the Challenge of Child Sexual Abuse," *Journal of School Health* (September 1988): 292–94.

13. Clearinghouse on Child Abuse and Neglect Information, P.O. Box 1182, Washington, D.C. 20013; National Committee for Prevention of Child Abuse, P.O. Box 94283, Chicago, Ill. 60690; National Child Abuse Hot Line, Hollywood, California, 800–422–4453; and the National Education Association's 1987 handbook for teachers, *How Schools Can Help Combat Child Abuse and Neglect,* N.E.A. Professional Library, P.O. 509, West Haven, Connecticut 06516.

14. Daniel L. Duke and William Seidman, "Are Public Schools Organized to Minimize Behavior Problems?" in *Helping Teachers Manage Classrooms,* ed. Daniel L. Duke (Alexandria, Va.: Association for Supervision and Curriculum Development, 1982), 140.

15. For a description of how such records might be used, see William S. Amoss, "The Use of School Records in the Identification of Juvenile Delinquents" (Ed.D. diss., University of Tulsa, 1970).

16. Most of the conceptual work on diagnosis in the school has occurred in the field of counseling; its application to administration has been extracted from the pioneer work of Francis P. Robinson. See Francis P. Robinson, "Modern Approaches to Counseling Diagnosis," *Journal of Counseling Psychology* (Winter 1963): 325–33. See also G. A. Koester, "The Study of the Diagnostic Process," *Educational and Psychological Measurement* (1954): 473–86; and for a more recent discussion, see Paul R. Lescault, "Guidelines for Developing a Discipline Code for an Effective Learning Environment," *NASSP Bulletin* (January 1988): 45–49. For a good discussion of how diagnosis can be used in responding to classroom discipline problems, see Boron Gil and Philip Heller, "Classroom Discipline: Toward a Diagnostic Model Integrating Teacher Thoughts and Actions." (ERIC Report Ed–167–514).

17. E. E. Jones et al., *Attribution Perceiving: The Causes of Behavior* (Morristown, N.J.: General Learning Press, 1972). For an additional discussion, see Mary M. Rohrkemper, "Teacher Self-Assessment," in *Helping Teachers Manage Classrooms,* ed. Daniel L. Duke, (Alexandria, Va.: Association for Supervision and Curriculum Development, 1982), 77–96.

18. Edward Porter, "The Effects of the Type of the Offense Committed, Appearance, and Previous Behavior on Discipline Decisions Rendered by Public School Disciplinarians," *Dissertation Abstracts International* (1927-A) (1973): 34. See also Safran and Safran, "Teachers' Judgments of Problem Behaviors."

19. James M. Frasher and Ramona S. Frasher, "Attribution Theory and Disciplinary Action in Schools" (Paper, Georgia State University, n.d.).

20. For an excellent study of the discretionary authority of the principal in this area, see Edward Casimis, "The Exercise of Administrative Discretion in Secondary Schools" (Diss., University of Chicago, 1976). For a more recent discussion, see Morris Van Cleave, *Principals in Action: The Reality of Managing Schools* (Columbus, Ohio: Merrill Publishing Co., 1984).

21. Edwin J. Brown and Arthur T. Phelps, *Managing the Classroom—The Teacher's Role in School Administration* (New York: Ronald Press, 1961), 121–24. See also Charles Dedrick, Donna Raschke, and Marlene Strathe, "Taming the Young and the Restless: Strategies for Positive Classroom Control," *Middle School Journal* (July 1988): 20–21; Thomas J. Lasley, "A Teacher Development Model for Classroom Management," *Kappan* (September 1989): 36–38; and G. G. Pestello, "Misbehavior in High School Classrooms," *Youth and Society* (March 1989): 290–306.

22. Edmund T. Emmer et al., "Effective Classroom Management at the Beginning of the School Year," *The Elementary School Journal* (May 1980): 219–31. See also Edmund T. Emmer, Carolyn M. Evertson, Julie P. Sanford, Barbara S. Clements, and Murray E. Worsham, "Getting Off to a Good Start," *Classroom Management for Secondary Teachers,* 2d ed. (Englewood Cliffs, N.J.: Prentice-Hall, 1989), 73–96.

23. Edmund T. Emmer and Carolyn M. Evertson, "Synthesis of Research on Classroom Management," *Educational Leadership* (January 1981): 342–47.

24. See Donald R. Grossnickle and Frank P. Sesko, *Promoting Effective Discipline in School and Classroom: A Practitioner's Perspective* (Reston, Va.: National Association of Secondary School Principals, 1985).

25. John S. Packard, *Pluralistic Ignorance and Pupil Control Ideology* (ERIC Report Ed–055–054), 109–11. Another instrument specifically designed for the elementary school which might be of interest to the elementary school administrator is described by Priscilla Pitt Jones, "A Method of Measuring Discipline Expectations," *Journal of Experimental Education* (February 1967): 39–45. See also "Clarifying Teachers' Beliefs about Discipline," *Educational Leadership* (March 1980): 459–62; and the "Beliefs on Discipline Inventory," described in Charles H. Wolfgang and Carl D. Glickman, *Solving Discipline Problems: Strategies for Classroom Teachers* (Newton, Mass.: Allyn & Bacon, 1986), 10–12.

26. Judith E. Dobson and Russell L. Dobson, "Teaching Self-Discipline: An In-Service Model," *Humanist Educator* (June 1979): 172–81; and William W. Wayson and Gay Su Pinnell, "Creating a Living Curriculum for Teaching Self-Discipline," in *Helping Teachers Manage Classrooms,* ed. Daniel L. Duke.

27. *Student Discipline, Problems and Solutions* (Arlington, Va.: American Association of School Administrators, 1979); and for a thorough discussion of various training models, see Wolfgang and Glickman, *Solving Discipline Problems.*

28. For example, see Gary F. Render, Je Nell Padilla, and H. Mark Krank, "What Research Really Shows about Assertive Discipline"; Sammie McCormack, "Response to Render, Padilla, and Krank: But Practitioners Say It Works"; Thomas R. McDaniel, "The Discipline Debate: A Road through the Thicket"; and Richard L. Curwin and Allen N. Mendler, "We Repeat, Let the Buyer Beware: A Response to Canter," *Educational Leadership* (March 1989): 72–83.

29. Richard L. Curwin and Allen N. Mendler, "Packaged Discipline Programs: Let the Buyer Beware," *Educational Leadership* (October 1988): 68.

30. Real G. Boivin and James R. Hammond, "Administering the School Discipline Policy Need Not Be Overwhelming," *NASSP Bulletin* (January 1988): 4–9.

31. Gail Thierbach Schneider and Fermin Burgos, "The Microcomputer: A Decision-Making Tool for Improving School Discipline," *NASSP Bulletin* (February 1987): 104–13. See also Harry P. Bluhm, *Administrative Uses of Computers in the Schools* (Englewood Cliffs, N.J.: Prentice-Hall, 1987).

32. Phil C. Robinson and Gail Von Huene, "Meeting Students' Special Needs," in *Helping Teachers Manage Classrooms* ed. Daniel L. Duke (Alexandria, Va.: Association for Supervision and Curriculum Development, 1982), 70–76.

33. Edward T. Ladd, "Regulating Student Behavior without Ending up in Court," *Kappan* (January 1973): 305.

34. *Blackwell* v. *Issaquena,* 363F. 2 and 749 (5th Cir. 1966).

35. The National School Boards Association has periodically published surveys of school board policies and procedures on discipline and attendance; these are worthy of administrators' consideration. For more information, write National School Boards Association, 1680 Duke Street, Alexandria, Virginia 22300.

36. Johnny R. Purvis and Rex Leonard, "Student Handbooks: An Analysis of Contents," *NASSP Bulletin* (March 1988): 93–96.

37. *Policies that Clarify Student Rights and Responsibilities* (Waterford, Conn.: National School Boards Association, 1970), 6. Also, for minimum legal essentials of enforceable rules, see E. Edmund Reutter, "Student Discipline: Selected Substantive Issues," in *The School Principal and the Law,* ed. Robert Stern (Topeka, Kans.: National Organization on Legal Problems of Education, 1978), 68–69; and John J. Lane, "Rights: Teachers' and Students' " in *Encyclopedia of School Administration and Supervision,* ed. Richard A. Gorton, Gail T. Schneider, and James C. Fisher (Phoenix, Ariz.: Oryx Press, 1988), 213–14.

38. William Thomas, "To Solve 'the Discipline Problem,' Mix Clear Rules with Consistent Consequences," *American School Board Journal* (June 1988): 30–31.

39. *The Roundup* [Student Handbook] (Barrington, Ill.: Barrington Consolidated High School, n.d.); and Detroit Public Schools, *Elementary School Student Responsibilities and Rights* (ERIC Report Ed–193–359). For an additional discussion of student rights and responsibilities, see National School Safety Center, *School Discipline Notebook* (Malibu, Calif.: Pepperdine University Press, 1986).

40. Lawrence E. Vredevoe, *Discipline* (Dubuque, Iowa: Kendall/Hunt Publishing Company, 1971), 24.

41. Paul R. Lescault, "Guidelines for Developing a Discipline Code for an Effective Learning Environment," *NASSP Bulletin* (January 1988): 45–49.

42. See National School Safety Center, *School District Notebook* (Malibu, Calif.: Pepperdine University Press, 1986); Alina Tugend, "Mayors Discuss Surge in Youth-Gang Violence," *Education Week* (January 29, 1986); and "Student Gangs Pose New Threat," *Education USA* (April 11, 1988).

43. Peter Blauvelt, "School Security," *Encyclopedia of School Administration and Supervision,* ed. R. A. Gorton, G. T. Schneider, and J. C. Fisher (Phoenix, Ariz.: Oryx Press, 1988): 228–29.

44. In Clifton Johnson's, *Old Time Schools and Schoolbooks* (New York: Macmillan Co., 1907), 21, it is reported that in 1837 over 300 schools in Massachusetts alone were broken into by rebellious pupils.

45. Peter D. Blauvelt, *Effective Strategies for School Security* (Reston, Va.: National Association of Secondary School Principals, 1981). See also Peter Blauvelt, "School Security."

46. Donald R. Grossnickle and Frank P. Sesko, *Promoting Effective Discipline in School and Classroom* (Reston, Va.: National Association of Secondary School Principals, 1985), 25.

14

• • • • •

Student Discipline: Punitive and Nonpunitive Approaches

By implementing the recommendations discussed in the previous chapter, school administrators should be able to gradually reduce the number and the severity of the student misbehavior problems with which they are confronted. But despite this improvement, most schools will continue to have student misbehavior of some type and degree. Two basic questions, then, are how should administrators respond to student misbehavior after it occurs, and how can it be prevented from occurring again? The following sections address these questions by analyzing punishment alternatives typically utilized by school administrators and by presenting several nonpunitive approaches for ameliorating student misbehavior and preventing its recurrence.

ANALYSIS OF PUNITIVE APPROACHES

In making decisions about punishing students, administrators generally choose among several alternatives identified in figure 14.1.*

There are several reasons why administrators might choose one of the alternatives identified in figure 14.1. They may believe that given the violation of a rule, they should punish the student—if for no other reason than to indicate that the student's behavior is not condoned. Or, administrators may face strong expectations by teachers or parents that students be punished for their misbehavior. Teacher and parental expectations that administrators be

---

*Although other alternatives could also be listed, those mainly utilized by administrators are identified. Such actions as holding a parent conference or referring students to a social agency should not be considered as punishment but as nonpunitive approaches to helping students to deal with the causes of their misbehavior.

Figure 14.1 Punitive Responses to Student Misbehavior.

1. Verbal Punishment ("Chewing Out")
2. Detention (Student Must Stay After School)
3. Assigned Work Around the Building After School
4. Suspension
5. Corporal Punishment
6. Recommendation of Expulsion

strong disciplinarians undoubtedly influence the decisions of many administrators regarding discipline alternatives.[1] Also, administrators may punish students based on the belief that punishment deters students from violating rules again.

School administrators should understand that, whatever else is achieved by punishment (and its effectiveness is debatable), it does not treat the basic causes of student misbehavior. While punishment may repress misbehavior temporarily—and that may be necessary in certain situations—it does not deal with its underlying causes such as the following identified by Irwin Hyman and John D'Alessandro:

1. Poor school organization
2. Inadequate administrative leadership
3. Inappropriate curricula
4. Overuse of suspensions/other punishments
5. Poor self-esteem and frustration with learning
6. Racism
7. Peer pressures
8. Overcrowding[2]

Administrators may need or want to punish students to set an example or to meet teachers' or parents' expectations. But they should not operate under the illusion that punishment somehow removes the roots of a problem or that student misbehavior will not recur. There is little affirmative evidence to show that punishment is an effective technique for preventing misbehavior from recurring, and much evidence to show the contrary.[3] In addition, punishment may possibly lead to undesirable side effects, such as an even more negative attitude by the student toward school.[4]

On the other hand, removal of all negative consequences associated with the violation of a rule or regulation could, over time, render such rules and regulations meaningless. Also, students need to know that they are accountable for their behavior and that negative consequences result from inappropriate behavior. Therefore, the imposition of certain punitive measures may be necessary. The decision as to whether to punish should be based on an accurate diagnosis of the cause of the student's behavior. In addition, of course, an investigation should be made of whether the student actually was in the wrong in violating the rule. The selection of the type of punishment should take into consideration the following factors: (1) the cause of the misbehavior; (2) the severity of the offense; (3) the number of times the student has committed the offense; and (4) the personality of the offender, for example, certain individuals may respond to punishment better than others. Also, in punishing students, school administrators would do well to heed the recommendations of Daniel O'Leary and Susan O'Leary:

1. Use punishment sparingly.
2. Make clear to students why they are being punished.
3. Provide students with an alternative means of meeting their needs.
4. Reward students for utilizing alternative means.
5. Avoid punishing while you are in a very angry or emotional state.[5]

Moreover, for punishment to be effective, it needs to be applied as soon after the offense as possible. Delay in administering the punishment tends to reduce the association between the punishment and the violation of the rule.

The following sections discuss some of the more significant punishments used in response to student misbehavior and the subject of due process.

CORPORAL PUNISHMENT

Corporal punishment is

the purposeful infliction of pain or confinement as a penalty for an offense committed by a student. The use of a wooden paddle is the most frequent method of administering it. Corporal punishment also takes the form of confinement in closets, bathrooms, or other closed spaces or forcing students to assume painful bodily postures or engage in excessive exercise. The use of electrical shock and forced eating or exposure to noxious substances falls with the definition as well.[6]

The U.S. Supreme Court has ruled in *Ingraham* v. *Wright* that corporal punishment does not constitute cruel or unusual punishment to students.[7] However, the court also pointed out in its ruling that persons imposing corporal punishment could be sued for liability if they used unreasonable force. Unfortunately, the Supreme Court did not define unreasonable force, and state and federal courts have had difficulty with this concept.[8] The court did indicate three general categories of corporal punishment:

1. Punishments that do not exceed the traditional common law standard of reasonableness are not actionable.
2. Punishments that exceed the common law standard without adequate state remedies violate procedural due process rights.
3. Punishments that are so grossly excessive as to be shocking to the conscience violate substantive process rights, without regard to the adequacy of the state remedies.[9]

More recently, in *Garcia* v. *Miera,* the high court cleared the way for a lawsuit by letting stand a 10th U.S. Circuit Court of Appeals ruling which said that at some point excessive punishment violates the substantive due process rights of students.[10] This ruling, in essence, overturned a previous federal district court ruling that school officials had qualified immunity from suit because it was unclear whether corporal punishment was a violation of substantive due process.[11] Thus, Richard Blackbourn concluded that "school officials should refrain from viewing governmental immunity as their security blanket and should be extremely careful to avoid excessiveness in this area."[12]

The use of corporal punishment in schools has been a controversial issue and will in all probability continue to be so.[13] According to a recent Gallup poll, only a slight majority of respondents say they approve of physical punishment (50 percent for, 45 percent against, 5 percent undecided).[14] These results indicate that since 1970 the opposition to physical punishment has gained considerable ground. In that year, "when the question was asked in the poll, 62 percent approved of physical punishment, and 33 percent disapproved of it."[15] As of June 1, 1988, eleven states prohibit corporal punishment under state law: California, Hawaii, Maine, Massachusetts, Nebraska, New Hampshire, New Jersey, New York, Rhode Island, Wisconsin, and Vermont.[16] In addition, as of that same date, seven states had bills in the legislative process banning corporal punishment, while five other states had stalled antipaddling bills which will presumably be reintroduced.[17] Paula Possin noted that the increase in legislative interest in corporal punishment is consistent with states' broader efforts to protect children and eliminate the use of physical violence against them.[18] Still, according to studies conducted by Temple University's National Center for the Study of Corporal Punishment and Alternatives in the Schools,

> the most frequent use of corporal punishment occurs in the South, Southwest, and rural areas of the country. Minority and/or poor children are the most frequent recipients of corporal punishment. Recent research suggests that corporal punishment is least likely to be administered by educators who experienced it infrequently or not at all in their own childhoods. Teachers who are the most frequent users tend to be more authoritarian, less experienced, and more impulsive than their peers.[19]

Although the use of corporal punishment in the schools may be legal if state law and school board policy permit it, there continues to be considerable disagreement on the part of the teachers, parents, and educational authorities about its desirability and effectiveness. The arguments supporting the use of corporal punishment usually contain the following points: (1) nothing else has worked, and something with more impact is needed; (2) some students only respond to physical punishment, usually because that is what they experience in the home; (3) physical punishment is effective because it makes students think twice before committing the same offense, and (4) the use of physical punishment can be a deterrent to other students who might violate a rule in the absence of such punishment.[20] Those opposing physical punishment often present the following reasons: (1) regardless of what the Supreme Court said, corporal punishment is cruel and inhumane, and the fact that it is no longer permitted in prisons and in most other countries of the world confirms its impact; (2) "unreasonable" corporal punishment is too difficult to prove in court, and many affected students and parents lack either the knowledge of court remedies or the resources to pursue them; (3) corporal punishment holds considerable potential for child abuse; (4) the use of corporal punishment tends to be discriminatory, in that it is used more often with younger students, non-white students, and with boys; (5) there are more effective nonphysical alternatives to correcting student misbehavior.[21]

It is unlikely that the debate over corporal punishment will be easily resolved. Firm evidence supporting the effectiveness of corporal punishment is lacking, although it is conceded that corporal punishment may act as a temporary suppressor of behavior in certain situations.[22] In spite of the lack of evidence supporting its effectiveness, corporal punishment continues to be used in many schools in a wide variety of situations. One study for example, found that corporal punishment was being used as a solution to nineteen different student discipline problems, ranging from chewing gum to bodily assault on teachers.[23] Obviously, if corporal punishment is to be employed as a disciplinary technique, it should be used on a more selective basis and only for very serious offenses. To avoid the risk of legal action, Mike Simpson suggests that school employees

1. Be familiar with and follow school district policies on the imposition of corporal punishment.
2. Always have an adult witness present.
3. Never hit any part of the student's body other than the buttocks.
4. Never use excessive force or administer more than a few blows.
5. Never use corporal punishment for petty infractions of rules or for a student's inability or unwillingness to perform schoolwork.[24]

Although the data previously presented have shown that more than two-thirds of the states authorize school districts to utilize corporal punishment in the schools, no school district is required to permit corporal punishment, and districts in such states which decide to use corporal punishment must first promulgate a policy. Certainly, no teacher or administrator should apply corporal punishment in the absence of a policy or go beyond the spirit and letter of the policy.

In developing a policy on corporal punishment, the administration and school board should involve representative students, teachers, and parents, and should consider the following guidelines extracted from various court decisions and recommendations by educational authorities:

1. Corporal punishment should not be used at all except when the acts of misconduct are so antisocial in nature or so shocking to the conscience that extreme punishment seems warranted.
2. The particular offenses that will result in corporal punishment should be specified. Also, the nature of the corporal punishment which will be permitted should be made explicit.
3. Evidence that other nonphysical methods were used earlier in an attempt to help the student improve his or her behavior should be required before corporal punishment is employed.
4. Corporal punishment should be not used in those situations where physical restraint is more properly called for. For example, teachers or administrators should not employ corporal punishment, but should be permitted to use physical restraint to protect themselves, the pupil, or others from physical injury; to obtain possession of a weapon or other dangerous object; and to protect property from serious damage.

5. If possible, a neutral party should administer the punishment, rather than the person in conflict with the student. The person who is to administer the corporal punishment should be specifically identified.
6. Corporal punishment should be administered only in the presence of another teacher or administrator as witness, an individual who was not in conflict with the student.
7. Exempt from receiving corporal punishment those students who have psychological or medical problems.
8. Provide due process before administering the corporal punishment, including informing the student of the rule that has been broken, presenting the student with the evidence indicating that the student has violated the rule, and providing the student with an opportunity to challenge the allegation and/or the evidence.
9. Specify the kinds of documentation required for administering corporal punishment, including those items specified in 8, and the details of the situation, such as the student's name, age, racial background, nature of the offense, nature of the corporal punishment, and so forth. Provide the option for parents to request a written explanation of the reasons for corporal punishment and the reasons why nonphysical alternatives were not appropriate or sufficiently effective.
10. Forbid corporal punishment to be used on a continuing basis for those students whose behavior does not improve after it has initially been administered.

In addition, administrators or teachers who employ corporal punishment should follow the legal prescriptions offered by Robert Hamilton: (1) act from good motives, and not from anger or malice; (2) inflict only moderate punishment; (3) determine what the punishment is, in proportion to the gravity of the offense; (4) convince themselves that the contemplated punishment is not excessive, taking into account that age, sex, and physical strength of the pupil to be punished; (5) assume the responsibility that the rule they seek to enforce is reasonable.[25]

Although these particular guidelines were written for teachers, they also apply to school administrators.

SUSPENSION AND EXPULSION

Suspension and expulsion are two other punishment alternatives utilized by school administrators in cases involving extreme misbehavior. *Suspension* can be defined as the temporary removal of a student from school for a certain period of time, generally from one day to several weeks, depending on the offense. *Expulsion* involves removing a student from school on a more permanent basis, usually for at least a semester or longer, depending on the severity of the misbehavior.

Administrators employ the procedure of suspension in cases of repeated minor offenses by students and for more serious student misbehavior such as smoking in school or truancy. Expulsion is usually applied only to the most serious student misbehavior and is generally used by administrators as a last resort. In the case of either suspension or expulsion, however, there is considerable doubt about the effectiveness of removing a student from school as a method of discipline. As Robert Phay and Jasper Cummings have observed, "School separation is a poor method. Students who misbehave usually are students with academic difficulties, and removal from the school almost inevitably adds to their academic problems."[26] Therefore, although suspension and expulsion may occasionally be necessary to protect the well-being of other students, these methods are probably counterproductive in their effect on the students removed from school.

Even though suspension and expulsion are disciplinary methods which may adversely affect students who are removed, there undoubtedly are times when administrators may need to initiate these procedures in the case of emergency or extreme situations. These situations, as defined by the National Juvenile Law Center at St. Louis University, include the following student misbehaviors:

1. Assault or battery on any other person on the school grounds.
2. Continual and repeated willful disobedience of school personnel legitimately acting in their official capacities, resulting in a disruptive effect on the education of the other children in school.
3. Possession or sale of narcotics or hallucinogenic drugs or substances on school premises.

The center also suggests that consideration for suspension be given to occurrences of the following student behaviors: (1) academic dishonesty, such as cheating or plagiarism; (2) theft from or damage to the institution's premises or property; (3) intentional disruption or obstruction of the educational function of the school; and (4) possession of firearms.[27]

Most of the student misbehavior identified by the National Juvenile Law Center represents violations of the law; in such cases law enforcement agencies should administer punishment rather than the schools. In general, administrators should suspend students from school only when there would be clear and present danger to the student or others in the school if the student remained in school.

Administrators should also proceed very carefully in making a decision to suspend or expel special education students. Two legal questions can arise with such punishments: first, is a student being punished for misconduct that is related in some way to a handicap? And second, does the punishment result in a change in the educational placement of the student?[28] If the answer to the first question is affirmative, the suspension or expulsion may not be legal unless the administrator can demonstrate a clear and present danger to keeping the student in school. If the answer to the second question is affirmative and the suspension is a lengthy one or the punishment is expulsion, the school may need to provide the due process safeguards mandated by federal law, as well as a new individualized educational plan.[29] The Supreme Court in *Honig* v. *Doe* ruled that the maximum length for short-term suspension is 10 days.[30] The Court, however, "observed that the stay-put provision [of the Education for All Handicapped Children Act] does not preclude disciplining handicapped students using 'normal' procedures, including the use of study carrels, timeouts, detentions, restricted privileges, or suspensions of up to ten days."[31] Larry Bartlett noted the Court's position was that "the ten-day period provides school officials time to plan alternative placements or to seek court approval for an extended period of time from the school."[32]

If the suspension of a special education student is a very brief one and the school is sure that the behavior of the student is unrelated to his or her handicap or can demonstrate that the student's removal from school is necessary to protect the student or others, the suspension will be on firmer legal grounds, although a question may still be raised regarding whether other less punitive alternatives might have been more appropriate.[33] Furthermore, the Department of Education (ED) has taken the position that Public Law 94–142 prohibits serial short-term suspensions and, since the Court based its ruling on short-term suspensions on the ED's interpretation of the law, it is likely that the Court would support the department's ban of serial suspensions.[34] Therefore, administrators would be advised to avoid using multiple, short-term suspensions that add up to more than ten days in a year.

In those situations involving a suspension or expulsion of a special education student from school, additional due process safeguards will probably be required. Generally, these are specified in state law; administrators are encouraged to examine these laws and to consult with the school district's attorney before proceeding with any action.

IN-SCHOOL SUSPENSION

Because of the limitations and general ineffectiveness of the procedure of suspension from school, enlightened administrators and educators have developed the concept of in-school suspension. This program differs from traditional suspension in that the latter procedure resulted in a student's removal from school for a specific number of days, while the former procedure removes the student from the regular school schedule while keeping the student in school, usually in a self-contained room under adult supervision. The characteristics of an in-school suspension program vary considerably among schools, ranging from a small isolation room where the student is not permitted to do any school work, to a large, well-equipped room staffed by professionals who provide academic assistance and personal counseling.[35]

The type of in-school suspension program found in a school seems to depend primarily on the purpose it is meant to serve.[36] If the main purpose is to punish the student for some offense or to use the program as a deterrent to misbehavior, the isolation aspects of the program are emphasized. If, on the other hand, the main purpose of the program is to diagnose and remediate the cause of the misbehavior, the nature of the facility where the program is housed, the nature of the activities, and the staffing emphasize student appraisal as well as educational and psychological counseling. Some in-house suspension programs, of course, attempt to achieve both the purpose of isolation and the goals of academic and social assistance.[37] However, according to Leslie Chamberlain, "The main emphasis during the in-school suspension time should be to assist the student to analyze his previous behavior, to consider alternative behaviors available to him, and to select a more appropriate behavior to be implemented after returning to the normal school setting."[38]

Research findings on the effectiveness of in-school suspension programs are limited and inconclusive, revealing both successes and failures.[39] Paula Short and George Noblit, in their study of ten programs identified as good by state juvenile and education officials, revealed that in-school suspension (ISS) programs were falling short in achieving what the literature proposes the programs should achieve.[40] They found that nine of the ten programs they studied were essentially punitive with a minimal academic component. Generally, they observed that

1. Students were isolated while working on class assignments.
2. ISS students were isolated from other students in the cafeteria, usually eating when the other students had gone.
3. The average length of assignment was three to five days.
4. Privileges were restricted and talking was not allowed.
5. Teachers sent students assignments to complete.

Short and Noblit found that these

> ISS programs were conducted in restrictive, coercive environments that used academic seatwork to fill the day. Of course, having sufficient academic assignments to actually fill the day was a problem, and the seatwork was often supplemented with silent reading of the students' choice. . . . Only one of the programs actually incorporated activities to improve self-image, enhance communication skills, participate in decision making, complete classwork as a "success" experience, and develop appropriate means to deal with the school environment.[41]

Interestingly, the educators they interviewed were quite satisfied with their ISS program and viewed it as an effective punishment option, especially when compared with out-of-school suspension. Short and Noblit conclude by noting that if an ISS program is simply a replacement for out-of-school suspensions then its primary contribution is to keep students off the street and doing some homework. To move beyond that purpose, in-school suspension programs must be part of a comprehensive, preventative/educational program that adequately addresses the needs of students.

Those programs which serve primarily as isolation rooms with little or no thought or activities designed to help a student understand and change behavior are apparently not likely to succeed. However, those programs that emphasize helping the student, which are capably staffed in well-equipped rooms, have greater potential for success. Norma Radin has described effective and humane alternatives to suspension including in-school suspension, assignments to alternative schools, timeout procedures, behavior contracting, peer and parental support, and social/cognitive skills training.[42]

DUE PROCESS

Suspension and expulsion from school are severe punishments. Although they may be necessary in certain situations, the decision to impose these punishments generally must be preceded by a careful and thorough process of investigation into the factual basis for the alleged offense with an adequate opportunity for the student to refute the charges, or to challenge the legitimacy of the violated school rules. This is referred to as due process. It means that an individual is entitled to a certain specified process or set of procedures, the objective of which is to assure that the individual is treated fairly and justly. Although some educators may view due process as unnecessarily burdensome, its essential rationale follows:

> A basic tenet of the American system of government as provided by the United States Constitution is that any individual who is threatened or becomes subject to serious or adverse action by public authorities must be provided with full rights of due process of law. Such procedures provide to the individual the opportunity to contest the proposed action within a series of proceedings which insure that fairness and good judgment govern the entire decision-making process.[43]

The two types of due process are termed substantive and procedural. Martha McCarthy indicated that "substantive due process rights can be impaired if disciplinary action is arbitrary or unnecessary as a means of attaining legitimate school objectives."[44] *Substantive due process* examines the question of whether the purpose of the rule or regulation which the student violated is fair, reasonable, and just. *Procedural due process* focuses on the question of whether the procedures used to remove the student from the school were fair, reasonable, and just.

Prior to 1975, due process was required primarily for expelling a student, but in some instances it had been required for suspension as well, particularly if the suspension was for an extended period of time. In 1975, the U.S. Supreme Court in *Goss* v. *Lopez* ruled that school administrators could not suspend students for any periods up to ten days without "minimum due process."[45] Minimum due process was defined by the Court to consist of the following elements:

- Students should be given oral or written notice of the charges against them.
- If students deny the charges, they are entitled to an explanation of the evidence the school has as the basis of the charge.
- Students shall have an opportunity to tell their sides of the story.
- There need be no delay between the time notice is given and the time of the hearing. In a majority of the cases, the principal may informally discuss the alleged misconduct with the student minutes after it has occurred.
- Because the hearing may occur almost immediately following the misconduct, generally the notice and hearing should precede the suspension.
- In cases where the presence of the student poses a continuing danger to persons or property, or an ongoing threat of disrupting the academic process, the student may be immediately removed from school.
- In such cases, the notice and hearing should follow as soon as practicable.

In the case of short-term suspension, the major import of the Court's decision was a change in the status of due process for students from a recommended practice to a legal requirement. Recognizing that this legal requirement could pose unforeseen problems for some administrators, Justice Byron White (speaking for the majority of the Court) stated, "We have imposed requirements which are, if anything, less than a fair-minded school principal would impose upon himself in order to avoid unfair suspension."

In a recent case focusing on the due process protection of students, *Newsome* v. *Batavia Local School District,* the Sixth Circuit Court of Appeals decision "reflects the return swing of the pendulum from the rights of individual students toward the collective rights of the school."[46] In this case, Newsome, a high school junior, filed suit in federal court claiming that his due process rights had been violated when he had been expelled for selling marijuana on school property without being allowed to cross-examine his accusers and the administrators who investigated the charges and recommended expulsion. Furthermore, he claimed that the administrators had violated his rights by participating in the board's closed deliberations and by introducing new evidence during the closed session.

The court concluded that, in the turbulent atmosphere of drug use and violent crime in schools, "the necessity of protecting student witnesses from ostracism and reprisal outweighs the value of the truth-determining process of allowing the accused student to cross-examine [or know the identity of] his accusers." In addition, although the court acknowledged the fact-finding value to cross-examining the administrators, it was outweighed by the burden of "diverting school board members' and school administrators' attention from their primary responsibilities in overseeing the educational process to learning and applying the common law rules of evidence."

The Sixth Circuit, however, remanded the case to the district court for trial because it agreed with Newsome that the disclosure of new evidence to the board during the closed session did violate his constitutional rights. The school district will need to prove that Newsome would have been expelled even without the additional evidence. For damages, Newsome will have to show that he suffered actual injury, such as mental or emotional distress. The case is still pending; however, the general tone of court's ruling on Newsome's right to know and cross-examine his accusers and administrators might indicate a changing spirit within the courts regarding the due process rights of students in disciplinary cases.

After the *Goss* decision, there were various reactions and predictions as to how the "minimum due process" requirements would impact on the schools. Reports differ, yet observational evidence suggests that the due process requirements have not unduly complicated the lives of most school administrators, and the procedures have brought an increased degree of fairness and

Figure 14.2 A Model for Responding to Student Misbehavior.

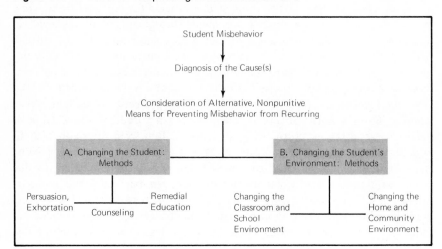

equality to disciplinary decisions.[47] Research in this area is very difficult to conduct, however, and generally depends on the self-reports of participants. Since whatever due process that occurs generally takes place behind a closed office door or in some other relatively private setting, it is difficult to obtain objective data on how due process for students is working in the schools.

NONPUNITIVE APPROACHES TO STUDENT MISBEHAVIOR

A major implication of the data and statements discussed in the previous sections is that school administrators and faculty members need to concentrate more on the in-depth diagnosis and remediation of student discipline problems and less on the punishment of student misbehavior. While punishment may still have to be utilized at times to temporarily control or suppress misbehavior, or to meet teachers' or parents' expectations, it is at best a short-term solution to a problem which requires alternative methods. A model designed to provide administrators with an overview of several alternative approaches to student misbehavior is presented in figure 14.2.

As figure 14.2 indicates, the first step that administrators should take cooperatively with teachers, parents, and others in response to student misbehavior is to try to diagnose the causes of the misbehavior. (Possible causes of student misbehavior and the process of diagnosis were discussed in the preceding chapter.) Student misbehavior does not just happen; it is caused by some condition(s).

Administrators must recognize that their diagnosis of the causes of student misbehavior greatly influence their choice of approaches to preventing the problem from recurring. If administrators decide that the causes of problems rest within the students, attempts to change the students will probably be made through one or more of the means identified in figure 14.2, part A. If, on the other hand, administrators diagnose the causes of the problems as lying within the students' environment (either the school environment or the home and community environment), administrators try to change that environment. The essential point is that administrators' perceptions of the causes of the misbehavior determine to a large extent their selection of an approach to be employed in an effort to prevent the misbehavior from recurring.

A second factor influencing administrators' choices of the best approach to prevent student misbehavior from recurring is their awareness of alternative methods of responding to student misbehavior. Since punishment has already been discussed, we now analyze nonpunitive approaches.

CHANGING THE STUDENT

PERSUASION AND EXHORTATION

Most administrators confronted with the first instance of a student's misbehavior (if minor in nature) respond with an approach other than punishment. Even in the case of repeated misbehavior, many administrators attempt to change the students by trying to persuade them that it is not in their best interests to misbehave and by exhorting them to do better.

An investigation of the educational literature uncovered no research evidence on the effectiveness of these disciplinary tactics. Undoubtedly, for some administrators, these approaches work—at least with certain students. For the most part, however, persuasion and exhortation do not appear to be very effective with students who are discipline problems, if one can judge by their repeated misbehavior. These methods typically are employed by administrators because the "let us reason together" approach is commonly valued in American society, and frequently they are unaware of any other type of nonpunitive techniques.

Before persuasion and exhortation could be effective in preventing student misbehavior from recurring, a correct diagnosis of the factors causing the misbehavior would have to be made, and administrators employing these tactics would have to be perceived by the student as possessing a high degree of credibility.[48] If the causes of the student's problem have been incorrectly diagnosed, administrators may be trying to persuade or exhort a student to do something which will not remove the basis of the misbehavior. And if administrators are not perceived by students as individuals who can be believed and trusted, students are unlikely to be persuaded or exhorted to do anything the administrator wants (if the student can avoid it).[49] Therefore, while persuasion and exhortation by administrators in response to student misbehavior may be preferable to punitive measures, the former techniques are dependent on certain conditions which may or may not be present in a specific situation.

COUNSELING

Many administrators attempt to counsel students who have misbehaved. Desirable as that approach may appear, its success depends on the administrator's possession or acquisition of adequate knowledge and skill in counseling techniques, and on the student's perception that the administrator is a counselor rather than a disciplinarian. Unfortunately, seldom is either of these conditions met. This does not mean that a school administrator should not use counseling techniques in working with student discipline cases. Gail Schneider and Fermin Burgos describe one administrator who has attempted to utilize counseling techniques in working with students who misbehave.[50]

Most school administrators probably need to become more knowledgeable about these techniques before they can achieve much success. Perhaps a more realistic and effective approach for an administrator would be to utilize whatever counseling resources exist within the staff or school district.

Counselors and teachers have been utilized in individual counseling and group guidance situations to work with students who engage in misbehavior. In a study designed to focus on students with self-defeating academic behaviors and in an attempt to reduce the rate of recidivism to their in-school-suspension program, Menchville High School in Newport News, Virginia, initiated a pilot counseling program called "Beat It."[51] Every other student who was referred to ISS was alternatively assigned to an experimental group which received counseling intervention or to a control group which received no specific counseling. Counselors participated in in-service sessions to refresh their group counseling skills. Subsequently, students were involved with counselors in a series of activities designed to help students get more direction, purpose, and meaning in their lives. The six counseling sessions focused on:

1. Getting acquainted during which time group rules were decided on and agreed to by the members.
2. Developing enthusiasm, helping students to define enthusiasm, and deciding on which problem areas students needed to work.
3. Analyzing self-defeating behavior and making a commitment to accomplish something during the week.

4. Setting goals and developing plans of action.
5. Exploring issues of self-confidence and identifying students' strengths, talents, and abilities that made them feel worthwhile.
6. Looking to the future and describing how they hoped to change and what their future plans would be.

The results were fairly dramatic. Stephen Hochman and Wayne Worner reported that

> in the 27 weeks following the experiment, the control group (those who were not involved in the counseling) were 15 times more likely to be referred to the principal's office, 13 times as likely to be returned to in-school suspension, more likely to be suspended out of school (none of the experimental group were suspended), and more likely to repeat the kind of behavior that led them to be assigned to in-school suspension in the first place.[52]

In addition, while the grade point averages of neither group showed significant increases, the grades of those who did not receive counseling continued to decline while the grades of those who received counseling stabilized.

There are other examples of successful counseling programs aimed at reducing student misbehavior. The After School Discussion (ASD) program at Decatur High School in Indianapolis is based on "the assumption that students' school-related problems are tied to their personal problems and learning to cope with situations in their personal lives is necessary if students are to succeed in school."[53] The program focuses on ten topics believed to be relevant to students' needs: decision making, interpersonal communication, stress management, personal responsibility and accountability, crisis management, peer relationships, organizational management, self-examination, self-concept, and planning for success. The topics may be modified, eliminated, or replaced by each group. The students agreed that as a result of completing the program, they were better able to cope with problems.

A different approach was reported at Waukesha North High School in Waukesha, Wisconsin.[54] The program which employed one-on-one counseling was designed to "prevent dropouts, reduce antisocial behavior, increase academic achievement, and stimulate students' self-concepts."[55] With rare exceptions, only one student per faculty member was permitted. Participating faculty members met with the counseling staff for an in-service session which focused on (1) the nature of the self-concept; (2) techniques of building a caring relationship, such as: listening, restatement, reflection, and empathic understanding; and (3) time management. Of the eighteen students who participated in the program, four dropped out of school; the rest improved their attendance and grades and showed a positive change in attitudes toward school and school-related interpersonal relationships.

Debra Viadero described a particularly innovative counseling program which involved the use of a mediation center at Coolidge High School in Washington, D.C., where students involved in misbehavior met with classmates trained in the art of negotiation to resolve student conflicts and determine the disposition of students referred for misbehaving.[56] As a result of the success of the program, a peer-mediation program was expanded to include a junior high school and an elementary school near Coolidge. These reports at the high school levels strongly suggest that individual counseling and group guidance can be successful in improving student behavior. Robert Bowman and Robert Myrick found that a systematic group guidance program at the elementary level could be effective in improving classroom behaviors and school attitudes of elementary students.[57]

The degree of expertise of the pupil services team, the availability of their time, proper facilities, and the extremity of the student misbehavior problems seem to be important considerations in determining counseling effectiveness. Probably the most significant factor is the degree to which the counselors and other members of the pupil services team understand and accept the principle that they possess specialized expertise which can make a valuable contribution to ameliorating student behavior problems. Unless pupil personnel workers wholeheartedly accept this concept, they are unlikely to make any significant contributions to improving student behavior.

Because the attitude of the pupil personnel specialists may be the most significant variable affecting the success of a counseling program for students who misbehave, school administrators must help the pupil services team develop an appropriate understanding of and attitude toward the contribution they can make to ameliorating student misbehavior. To achieve this objective, administrators need to study and utilize the concepts in the next chapter focusing on pupil personnel services.

REMEDIATION OF LEARNING PROBLEMS

Learning problems of one kind or another are probably associated with most student misbehavior. Whether the learning problems result from the misbehavior or cause it has long been a subject of debate among educators. Unfortunately, research has not resolved the debate.

It does seem reasonable to assume, however, that learning problems play some role in regard to student misbehavior. The process occurs in either of the two ways presented in figure 14.3.[58]

Figure 14.3 Some Possible Relationships between Learning Problems and Misbehavior.

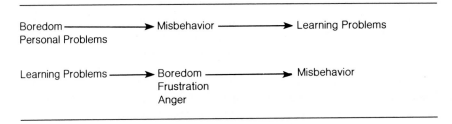

As figure 14.3 suggests, learning problems might cause, as well as result from, student misbehavior. Students who do not initially engage in misbehavior or encounter learning problems may eventually become discipline problems if sufficiently bored with school or if experiencing personal problems. As a result of conflict with the school or of a loss of time, they may develop learning disabilities. Also, students who possess learning disabilities of one kind or another and experience resultant failure in the classroom are more likely to feel frustration, anger, or boredom, and then engage in misbehavior to vent their emotions. The misbehavior may consist of talking back to the teacher, fooling around in class, or skipping class or school. That the latter misbehavior has its roots in learning disabilities was poignantly brought out by one probation officer: "I found that the biggest problem with youngsters getting into trouble, boys in particular, was that they didn't want to face not being able to read in class. They would stay out of school, and their truancy would lead them into more serious trouble."[59]

A constructive approach to ameliorating student misbehavior, therefore, would be for administrators to investigate the possibility that students engaging in misbehavior are handicapped by learning disabilities or motivational problems.[60] This investigation should include reading and special education specialists as well as other pupil personnel workers to screen and diagnose the students' problems.[61] Depending on the nature of the problems and their diagnoses, students may require individual and small-group work, different materials, special classes, or other remedial alternatives.[62]

Remediation of student learning problems may be a long-term solution to a student misbehavior problem that demands an immediate response from the administration. Administrators could also be pressured by the expectations of teachers and others to take more immediate and punitive action when student misbehavior occurs. However, administrators who hope to have any significant success in preventing student misbehavior from recurring must investigate the possibility that student learning problems are causing or are a result of the misbehavior and organize remedial assistance to correct these conditions.

CHANGING THE STUDENT'S ENVIRONMENT

Thus far, attention has been focused on nonpunitive approaches to changing the student to reduce or eliminate misbehavior. Nonetheless, it may be difficult or even impossible for students to change unless their environments change. And, for many students, their environments may be the basic cause of their misbehavior.

A student's environment can be considered as composed primarily of two elements: (1) classroom and school conditions, and (2) home and community conditions. Figure 14.4 presents some possible variables in the students' environment which individually or collectively may be causing their misbehavior and which may need to be changed before the misbehavior can be reduced or eliminated.

The list of variables identified in figure 14.4 does not, of course, exhaust all of the possibilities, but it should give administrators a good indication of the numerous environmental factors which may be causing a particular student's misbehavior.

Figure 14.4 Environmental Variables Affecting Student Misbehavior.

Classroom and School Environment	Home and Community Environment
1. Teacher's attitude toward and expectations for the student	1. Parents' attitude toward and expectations for the student and for the school
2. Teacher's style or methods of teaching	2. Extent of crowdedness in the home
3. Classroom rules and policies	3. Attitude toward school held by siblings in the family and by the neighborhood peer group
4. Content of the subject being taught	4. Availability of alternative pursuits which are more attractive and rewarding to the student than is school
5. Textbook and other reading materials	
6. Size and composition of the class	
7. Student's seating assignment in the class	
8. School's schedule and total program of studies	

In general, administrators are more likely to achieve success in trying to modify a student's classroom and school environment than the home and community environment. Administrators have more contact with and control over the school environment; in many cases, they can do very little about a student's home and community environment. This does not mean that efforts should not be made to influence the student's home and community environment in positive ways; specific suggestions are discussed later in the chapter. Nevertheless, the highest priority for changing a student's environment (if that is what is needed) should be given to attempts to bring about changes in the classroom and school environment. The nature of the changes would depend on the school's diagnosis of the causes of the problem; two particularly promising approaches for changing the student's school environment are discussed in the following sections.

CHANGING THE STUDENT'S SCHOOL ENVIRONMENT: BEHAVIORAL MODIFICATION

One approach to preventing student misbehavior from recurring is behavioral modification. Defined simply, behavioral modification is an attempt to change the behavior of an individual who has misbehaved by changing the response of the person or persons reacting to the misbehavior.[63] The method is based on the premise that the response to the misbehavior determines whether or not the misbehavior persists, rather than any antecedent or internal cause.

In the school situation, a student's misbehavior typically provokes a response from a teacher or administrator. The response may range from a punishment to a suggestion of possible rewards for correct behavior. The behavioral modification method is based on the assumption that certain responses to student misbehavior tend to prevent the misbehavior from recurring, while others only encourage the student to persist in misbehaving.

The behavioral modification approach changes the role of the teacher or administrator from that of punishing misbehavior to one of reinforcing correct student behavior. As Michael Palardy and Thomas Palardy noted, "The key to behavior modification is not the use of punishment, but the use of reward."[64] Advocates of the approach do not entirely reject the use of punishment, but question its effectiveness unless used sparingly. They also believe in clear and consistently applied rules, preferably kept to a minimum.

Perhaps the best means of understanding the behavioral modification method is to examine the instructions given to classroom teachers asked to employ this approach in working with student discipline cases:

General Rules for Teachers

1. Make explicit the rules as to what is expected of students for each period. (Remind of rules when needed.)
2. Ignore (do not attend to) behaviors which interfere with learning, unless a child is being hurt by another. Use punishment which seems appropriate, preferably withdrawal of some positive reinforcement.
3. Give praise and attention to behaviors which facilitate learning. Tell students what they are being praised for. Try to reinforce behaviors incompatible with those you wish to decrease. Example of how to praise: "I like the way you're working quietly." "That's the way I like to see you work." "Good job, you are doing fine." Transition period: "I see Johnny is ready to work." "I am calling on you because you raised your hand." "I wish everyone were working as much as 'X,' " and so forth. Use variety and expression. In general, give praise for achievement, pro-social behavior, and following the group's rules.[65]

As can be seen by examining the instructions given to teachers, behavioral modification places a great emphasis on the teacher's rewarding students for behaving correctly, rather than paying attention to and punishing misbehavior. One of the underlying premises of the behavioral modification approach is that when teachers or administrators react negatively to a students' misbehavior, that response only provides students with the attention they are seeking; therefore, their misbehavior is likely to be repeated. On the other hand, if students' misbehavior is ignored and teachers' attention is focused instead on identifying (and rewarding) the response that is desired, the misbehavior will eventually be eliminated and the correct response strengthened.

The behavioral modification approach offers school administrators a method they might use in working with students or one which they might encourage their teachers to utilize. The approach has been tested empirically in a number of classroom situations, and it seems to be generally effective.[66] Moreover, several studies have shown that the principal can use behavioral modification techniques in reducing student misbehavior.[67]

Behavioral modification has also been criticized in some circles.[68] Probably the greatest obstacle to its effective utilization is that, when faced with student misbehavior, teachers and administrators do not find it easy to accentuate the positive and to ignore rather than punish the misbehavior. Nevertheless, there is now sufficient evidence of the merits of this approach to student misbehavior to motivate school administrators to at least investigate it further for possible use in their schools. (For further readings in this area, see *Behavior Modification: What It Is and How to Do It,* by Garry Martin and Joseph Pear.)[69]

CHANGING THE STUDENT'S SCHOOL ENVIRONMENT: ALTERNATIVE EDUCATIONAL PROGRAMS

The use of behavioral modification is an attempt to change the school environment of a student who has misbehaved by changing the teacher's or administrator's immediate response to the misbehavior. Even though this approach shows promise, many schools have tended to turn to alternative education programs for those students who persistently engage in misbehavior. Three educational alternatives are work-study programs, alternative classes or schools for chronic misbehavers, and the development of individualized educational programs.

Work-Study.   Participation in work-study programs is, of course, not restricted to students who have misbehaved; many types of students participate in this forward-looking educational alternative combining study in school with work on the job. For students not motivated by standard classroom activities, who get into trouble because of their boredom and frustration, a work-study program offers an alternative way of learning from which they can derive greater meaning and satisfaction. Students in such a program usually attend formal academic classes in the morning and work at their jobs in the afternoon. An attempt is often made to relate their academic activities in school, to their jobs and vice versa.

The basic program strategies of the Job Training and Partnership Act (JTPA), a federal training initiative to educate students for employment, provide useful guidelines for the development of effective work-study programs. The common elements of programs related to JTPA include

1. Career exploration and establishment of career goals.
2. Development of employability skills and attitudes.
3. Emphasis on academic skill development and remediation.
4. Supervised work experiences.
5. Academic credit for participation.
6. Establishment of school, business, and community member advisory committees to assist with program design and implementation.[70]

Although the work-study program seems to be a constructive alternative to punishment as a means of reducing student misbehavior, it has limitations. Sometimes, due to child labor laws, participation in the program cannot begin until the junior year of school; by that time students may have dropped out of school, or their misbehavior may have become so chronic that they could not qualify for the program. Also, because applicants for work-study programs are carefully screened to maintain cooperative relationships with employers, problem students most in need of this experience may not qualify for admission because of their extreme behavior. In addition, programs suffer because there are frequently insufficient jobs available in which to place students, or insufficient funds and other resources to do an adequate job of administering and supervising a large program.

For these reasons work-study programs have not totally met the need for alternative educational experiences for students who are turned off by school and engaged in misbehavior. But work-study programs still represent valid options in reducing student misbehavior and should be explored and utilized by administrators to the greatest extent possible.[71]

Alternative Classes or Schools.   Another approach to changing the school environment of students who have engaged in misbehavior is to provide them with alternative classes or, in some instances, placement in an alternative school. In general, many alternative programs are suited to the interests or learning styles of students who find regular academic classes "irrelevant, unstimulating, or impossible. An explicit or implicit purpose of these alternatives is to keep such students in high school."[72]

Ability-grouping has in many circumstances resulted in alternative classes for students who misbehave, because of the strong relationship between learning problems and student misbehavior. In other situations, alternative classes or in-school suspension programs have been specifically designed for problem students. Many of these classes and programs emphasize the development of reading and study skills, and frequently include opportunities for individual and group counseling and discussion of vocational opportunities.[73] The classes are generally smaller than regular classes and are taught by teachers trained to work with these students. In addition, the school schedule set up for the students is usually more flexible. (The same characteristics are true of alternative schools for chronic misbehavers.) According to Ronald Garrison, field services director for the National School Safety Center, successful alternative programs for disruptive students share several characteristics, including:

1. Placement by choice from several options provided by the school district, human services, probation, or the courts.
2. Daily attendance and progress reports.
3. Continual monitoring, evaluation and formalized passage from one step or program to another.
4. Direct supervision of all activities on a closed campus.
5. Administrative and community support for the program.
6. Parent and student counseling.
7. Full-day attendance with a rigorous workload and minimal time off.
8. High standards and expectations of student performance both academically and behaviorally.
9. Curricula addressing cultural and learning style differences.
10. Clear and consistent goals for students and parents.
11. A motivated and culturally diverse staff.
12. A democratic climate.[74]

In some situations it may not be necessary for each and every condition to exist for a special class or school to succeed, but in general most of the conditions should be viewed as prerequisites to success. There are no doubt problems (particularly, financial ones) that must be resolved in providing these conditions, but school administrators are responsible for resolving these problems and moving ahead with the introduction, maintenance, and improvement of the alternative program. The ultimate effectiveness of an alternative program should be judged according to the percentage of students who can successfully be integrated back into the regular school program. A resource paper on alternative schools is available from the National School Safety Center, 7311 Greenhaven Drive, Sacramento, California 95801.

Individualized Educational Programs. The concept of individualized education has been discussed in educational circles for many years. However, with the passage of the Education of All Handicapped Children Act (Public Law 94–142), the concept took on new importance and became much more widely implemented in the schools. Public Law 94–142 mandates that each school district desiring to receive federal funds must develop written individualized education programs for each handicapped student.[75] Obviously not all handicapped students misbehave, nor are all students who misbehave handicapped in some way; however, the passage of the law has forced school districts to take a closer look at students for possible handicaps than had been thus far attempted. In the process many students who had misbehaved were found to possess handicaps of one kind or another.

In those cases in which a student has been diagnosed as possessing a handicap, the law requires that the school district, in cooperation with the parents, develop an individualized educational program (IEP) for the student. An IEP consists of a written statement of the objectives, content, implementation, and evaluation of a student's educational program and process. Daniel Sage and Leonard Burrello noted that "the individual education planning process is analogous to curriculum planning for the individual student rather than classes of students."[76] The basic rationale for the IEP has been summarized by Maynard Reynolds and Jack Birch:

> Most pupil behaviors called learning disabilities and behavioral disorders are best acknowledged as the consequences of failure to provide enough high-quality individualized instruction. The problem does not reside in the child, hidden in some mysterious physiological or psychological recess. It sets squarely in the hands of teachers, and its resolution depends on the degree to which they design and carry out personalized teaching.[77]

(The specific details of the IEP and possible problems in developing and implementing it are discussed in the next chapter.)

The law does not presently require an IEP for students without handicaps, even if they misbehave frequently. However, most—if not all—students who misbehave could benefit from an individualized education program. Even though the development and implementation of such a program for those misbehaving students lacking handicaps could add greatly to the time demands and responsibilities of school personnel, an effective IEP could reduce significantly the time and energy currently being invested by school personnel in dealing with repeated student misbehavior. In any regard, the IEP does offer the school a worthwhile nonpunitive alternative for responding to student misbehavior.

CHANGING THE STUDENT'S HOME AND COMMUNITY ENVIRONMENT

Many educators believe that the causes of student misbehavior can be found in the student's home and/or community environment.[78] Despite a certain amount of evidence to support this theory, frequently administrators who try to change students' home or community environments are likely to encounter difficulties.[79] For example, administrators and professional staff members are typically occupied with myriad tasks at their schools and may not have sufficient time to become well-acquainted with students' home and community environments. In addition, in many situations, some administrators and teachers do not even live in the community from which their schools draw students.

Probably the basic difficulty that administrators face in trying to change students' home and community environments is that schools have very little control or influence over those environments. The following conditions in students' homes and communities may contribute to their misbehavior in school, but school administrators and staff members are limited in what they can do about any of these conditions:

1. Large families living in crowded homes.
2. Both parents work and do not have much time to supervise children.
3. Older brothers and sisters did not finish school.
4. Street gangs exist in the neighborhood.
5. Undesirable influences on students, such as drugs, exist in the neighborhood.[80]

Any or all of these home and community conditions may be causing students' misbehavior at school, but the likelihood that administrators and the professional staff can change any of them is small. This is not to minimize the importance of efforts to work with parents and various neighborhood groups to improve conditions in the home and/or community. For example, individual and group counseling of the parents of children with behavioral problems has been effective in some situations and ultimately improved school behavior.[81] Lawrence DeRidder notes that school dropouts are most frequently the children of parents in the lowest socioeconomic underclass or especially from specific ethnic or racial groups and that by the third grade approximately 70 percent of eventual dropouts can be identified; therefore, he maintains that intervention must begin in the early elementary grades.[82] Furthermore, efforts need to be maintained in working out cooperative programs with community groups to improve the conditions of the community.

In addition, Anker has identified at least fifteen ways that schools can work with the community to provide students with more positive opportunities such as

• Additional recreational facilities with longer hours.
• Conferences with parents.
• Meetings with local political, religious, and civic leaders, as well as representatives from influential citizen and ethnic groups.

- Street workers to provide a bridge between school and community.
- Community relations programs to keep schools aware of local problems, including an intelligence network to alert administrators to gang activities.[83]

The American Friends Service Committee has published a book listing fifty approaches to improving home-school cooperation.[84]

One approach in particular that could be of potential assistance in reducing student misbehavior if the program was initiated in the elementary school[85] would be parenting classes. Many of today's parents need help in raising their children, and schools could assist parents in identifying students' emerging problems at an early stage and offer appropriate assistance.

Although schools can do much in working with parents and the larger community to reduce student misbehavior, administrators need to recognize that, in attempting to change students' home and community environments, progress may be slow and limited. Consequently, their main efforts and those of the professional staff should be focused on diagnosing and taking action on possible environmental conditions within the classroom and the school that may be causing students' misbehavior and over which administrators and teachers have better control and can more easily bring about change.

OTHER APPROACHES

In addition to the methods discussed thus far, some schools have experimented with several other approaches to preventing and reducing student misbehavior. For further information on these approaches, consult the sources listed at the end of the chapter.[86]

A FINAL NOTE

Edward Ladd has observed that "A sad but no longer rare spectacle is the school principal who used to keep order with reprimands, threats, and punishment but who finds them ineffectual today and becomes frustrated and angry."[87] The discussion and analysis in this chapter should have shown school administrators that punitive responses to student misbehavior are largely ineffective in preventing that behavior from recurring—even though they may be temporarily necessary—and that nonpunitive remedies are available to prevent and reduce student misbehavior. Although the nonpunitive methods suggested may be perceived by some administrators as too time-consuming or not immediate enough in their impact, administrators need to recognize that there are few shortcuts to or panaceas for the prevention and reduction of student misbehavior. The nonpunitive approaches recommended in this chapter may not eliminate student misbehavior, but if implemented they could eventually reduce its recurrence significantly. And as Graham emphasizes, the key is leadership by the principal: "By far the most significant factor with regard to school discipline is the leadership role of the principal. Weak leadership is likely to produce increased discipline problems, and strong leadership is likely to reduce them."[88]

Review and Learning Activities

1. Define the function of punishment. What are its advantages and disadvantages?
2. Identify the punishment alternatives that an administrator has available. Which guidelines should an administrator follow in deciding on and implementing a punishment alternative?
3. Discuss those factors and guidelines an administrator should consider in using corporal punishment with students who misbehave.
4. Under which circumstances are suspension and/or expulsion appropriate or inappropriate methods of responding to student misbehavior?
5. Define the terms *substantive due process* and *procedural due process* as they apply to student suspension or expulsion. Explain what is meant by *minimum due process*.
6. Identify several nonpunitive approaches to changing a student who has misbehaved. Describe the advantages and disadvantages of each approach.

Notes

1. For an example of this type of influence by teachers, see Donald Willower, *The Teacher Subculture and Curricular Change* (ERIC Report Ed–020–588).

2. Irwin A. Hyman and John D'Alessandro, "Good, Old-Fashioned Discipline: The Politics of Punitiveness," *Kappan* (September 1984): 42.

3. Anthony F. Bongiovanni, "An Analysis of Research on Punishment and Its Relation to the Use of Corporal Punishment," in *Corporal Punishment in American Education,* ed. Irwin A. Hyman and James H. Wise (Philadelphia: Temple University Press, 1979). Also see Mike Simpson, "Let the Paddler Beware," *NEA Today* (February 1988): 27. For a contrary view, see R. G. Gaddis, "Punishment: A Reaffirmation," *Clearing House* (September 1978): 5–6.

4. Timothy Heron, "Punishment: A Review of the Literature with Implications for the Teacher of Mainstreamed Children," *Journal of Special Education* (Fall 1978): 243–52.

5. K. Daniel O'Leary and Susan G. O'Leary, *Classroom Management: The Successful Use of Behavior Modification* (Elmsford, N.Y.: Pergamon Press, 1972), 152. For a more recent discussion, see J. Michael Palardy and Thomas J. Palardy, "Classroom Discipline: Prevention and Intervention Strategies," *Education* (Fall 1987): 90.

6. Irwin Hyman, "Corporal Punishment," in *Encyclopedia of School Administration and Supervision,* eds. Richard A. Gorton, Gail T. Schneider, and James C. Fisher (Phoenix, Ariz.: Oryx Press, 1988), 79.

7. *Ingraham* v. *Wright,* 430 U.S. 651, 1977.

8. For example, see *Leblanc* v. *Tyler,* 381 So. 908, 1980. See also Perry Zirkel, "Judicial Decisions," in *Encyclopedia of School Administration and Supervision,* eds. R. A. Gorton, G. T. Schneider, and J. C. Fisher (Phoenix, Ariz.: Oryx Press, 1988), 153–54.

9. Richard Blackbourn, "Tenth Circuit Clarifies Defense of Immunity Relative to Corporal Punishment," *National Forum of Educational Administration and Supervision Journal* 5, no. 2, (1988–89): 12.

10. *Garcia* v. *Miera,* 817 F. 2d 650 (10th Cir. 1987).

11. Perry A. Zirkel and Ivan B. Gluckman, "Constitutionalizing Corporal Punishment," *NASSP Bulletin* (March 1988): 105–9.

12. Blackbourn, "Tenth Circuit Clarifies Defense," 13.

13. Nathan L. Essex, "Corporal Punishment: Ten Costly Mistakes and How to Avoid Them," *Principal* (May 1989): 42–44.

14. Alec M. Gallup and Stanley M. Elam, "The 20th Annual Gallup Poll of the Public's Attitudes toward the Public Schools," *Kappan* (September 1988): 42.

15. Ibid.

16. See Paula Possin, "Legislature Bans Corporal Punishment in Wisconsin Public Schools," *Education Forward* (September 1988): 12; and Simpson, "Let the Paddler Beware."

17. Possin, "Legislature Bans Corporal Punishment."

18. Ibid.

19. Irwin A. Hyman, "Corporal Punishment," in *Encyclopedia of School Administration and Supervision,* eds. R. A. Gorton, G. T. Schneider, and J. C. Fisher (Phoenix, Ariz.: Oryx Press, 1988), 79–80.

20. Lansing K. Reinholz, *A Practical Defense of Corporal Punishment* (ERIC Report Ed–132–733).

21. Roosevelt Ratliff, "Physical Punishment Must Be Abolished," *Educational Leadership* (March 1980): 474–76. For a more extended discussion of these issues and considerable background in the history of punishment, see "Practice and Alternatives to Corporal Punishment," in *Corporal Punishment in American Education,* ed. Hyman and Wise.

22. Adah Mauer, "All in the Name of the 'Last Resort'," *Inequality in Education* (September 1978): 21–28. Also see Bongiovanni, "Analysis of Research on Punishment."

23. William T. Elrod, "Discipline and Corporal Punishment in Indiana Public Secondary Schools" (unpublished paper n.d.).

24. Simpson, "Let the Paddler Beware," 27.

25. Robert Hamilton, *Legal Rights and Liabilities of Teachers* (Laramie, Wy.: Laramie Printers, 1956), 36. For an additional discussion of essentially the same guidelines on administering corporal punishment, see Joseph J. Cobb, *An Introduction to Educational Law for Administrators and Teachers* (Springfield, Ill.: Charles C. Thomas, 1981), 88–89.

26. Robert E. Phay and Jasper L. Cummings, Jr., *Student Suspension and Expulsions* (Chapel Hill, N.C.: Institute of Government, 1970), 9. See also Eve E. Gagne, "Disruptive Students," in *Encyclopedia of School Administration and Supervision,* eds. R. A. Gorton, G. T. Schneider, and J. C. Fisher (Phoenix, Ariz.: Oryx Press, 1988), 95–96.

27. Ralph Faust, *Model High School Disciplining Procedure Code* (St. Louis, Mo.: National Juvenile Law Center, 1971), 4–5. Also see Phay and Cummings, *Student Suspensions and Expulsions,* 15–23.

28. Terry L. Rose, "Current Disciplinary Practices with Handicapped Students: Suspensions and Expulsions," *Exceptional Children* (November 1988): 230–39.

29. *Education for All Handicapped Children Act,* P.L. 94–142, and Section 504 of the Rehabilitation Act of 1973.

30. *Honig* v. *Doe,* 108 S. Ct. 592, 605 (1988).

31. Perry A. Zirkel, "Disciplining Handicapped Students: Jack and John Went Up the Hill," *Kappan* (June 1988): 772.

32. Larry Bartlett, "Disciplining Handicapped Students: Legal Issues in Light of *Honig* v. *Doe,*" *Exceptional Children* (January 1989): 357.

33. "U.S. Supreme Court Limits Authority of School Officials to Exclude Disabled Students," *Newsnotes* (Cambridge, Mass.: Center for Law and Education, Inc., August 1988), 3–4.

34. Benjamin Sendor, "You Can't Act Unilaterally in Disciplining the Disabled," *American School Board Journal* (May 1988): 24–25.

35. Antoine M. Garibaldi, "In-School Alternatives to Suspension," *The Urban Review* (Summer 1979): 97–103. See also Frank J. Fischel, "In-School Suspension Programs— Questions to Consider," *NASSP Bulletin* (November 1986): 100–103.

36. Judy S. Sullivan, "Planning, Implementing, and Maintaining an Effective In-School Suspension Program," *Clearing House* (May 1989): 409–10.

37. See Norma Radin, "Alternatives to Suspension and Corporal Punishment," *Urban Education* (January 1988): 476–95; and Mary Louise Mickler and Barbara Martin, "Saturday School: One Alternative to Suspension," *NASSP Bulletin* (October 1989): 117–19.

38. Leslie J. Chamberlain, "How to Improve Discipline in Ohio Public Schools," *American Secondary Education* (December 1980): 6–13.

39. See C. W. Stessman, "In-School Suspension," in National Association of Social Workers, *Spare the Rod?!* (Silver Spring, Md.: National Association of Social Workers, 1986): 152–55; and Joanne S. Johnston, "High School Completion of In-School Suspensions Students," *NASSP Bulletin* (December 1989): 89–95.

40. Paula M. Short and George W. Noblit, "Missing the Mark in In-School Suspension: An Explanation and Proposal," *NASSP Bulletin* (November 1985): 112–16.

41. Ibid., 113.

42. Radin, "Alternatives to Suspension and Corporal Punishment,"

43. *Federal Register* (December 30, 1976), 56972.

44. Martha M. McCarthy, "Due Process," in *Encyclopedia of School Administration and Supervision,* eds. R. A. Gorton, G. T. Schneider, and J. C. Fisher (Phoenix, Ariz.: Oryx Press, 1988), 102.

45. *Goss* v. *Lopez,* 419 U.S. 565, 1975.

46. *Newsome* v. *Batavia School District,* 842 F.2d 920 (6th Cir. 1988); and Perry A. Zirkel, "The Pendulum Swings on Expulsion Hearings," *Kappan* (December 1988): 335. For an additional discussion of students' rights, see Perry A. Zirkel and Ivan B. Gluckman, "Due Process for Student Suspensions," *NASSP Bulletin* (March 1990): 95–98.

47. See T. Page Johnson, "Procedural Due Process and Fairness in Student Discipline," in *A Legal Memorandum* (Reston, Va.: National Association of Secondary School Principals, January 1990).

48. Behaviors that might convey the credibility are identified in a study by Rosa Baggett, "Behaviors that Communicate Understanding as Evaluated by Teenagers" (Ed.D. diss., University of Florida, 1967).

49. The norms of the reference group to which the student belongs are a major factor in this regard. See Albert K. Cohen, *Delinquent Boys* (Glencoe, Ill.: Free Press, 1955), chap. 4.

50. Gail Thierbach Schneider and Fermin Burgos, "The Microcomputer: A Decision-Making Tool for Improving School Discipline," *NASSP Bulletin* (February 1987): 104–13.

51. Stephen Hochman and Wayne Worner, "In-School Suspension and Group Counseling: Helping the At-Risk Student," *NASSP Bulletin* (October 1987): 93–96.

52. Ibid., 95.

53. Walter Bourke and Ronnie D. Furniss, "After-School Discussion Helps Problem Students," *Kappan* (November 1987): 241.

54. Ryan Champeau, "One-to-One: A Counseling Relationship," *NASSP Bulletin* (December 1983): 124–25.

55. Ibid. 124.

56. Debra Viadero, "Peer Mediation: When Students Agree Not to Disagree," *Education Week* (May 25, 1988): 1, 23; and Bernice Hamberg, "Peer Counseling Can Identify and Help Troubled Youngsters," *Kappan* (April 1980): 562–63.

57. Robert P. Bowman and Robert D. Myrick, "Effects of an Elementary School Peer Facilitator Program on Children with Behavior Problems," *The School Counselor* (May 1987): 369–78.

58. For the model's theoretical basis, see John Dollard et al., *Frustration and Aggression* (New Haven, Conn.: Yale University Press, 1939). A review of relevant research suggests that this misbehavior is not the only outcome for aggression; see Gerald Adams, "Classroom Aggression: Determinants Controlling Mechanics and Guidelines for the Implementation of a Behavior Modification Program," *Psychology in Schools* (April 1973): 155–67.

59. Statement of former probation officer Jessie Jackson, reported in *Ebony* (November 1972); 67.

60. Palardy and Palardy, "Classroom Discipline," 88.

61. Samuel M. Deitz and John Hummel, "*Discipline in the Schools: A Guide to Reducing Misbehavior* (Englewood Cliffs, N.J.: Educational Technology Publications, 1978).

62. Antoine Garibaldi, ed. *In-School Alternatives to Suspension: Conference Report* (Washington, D.C.: National Institute of Education, 1979).

63. For an easily understandable introduction to this topic, see Saul Axelrod, *Behavioral Modification for the Classroom Teacher* (New York: McGraw-Hill, 1977). See also Jack Harris and Gary L. Short, "An Introduction to the Comprehensive Behavior Management System," *NASSP Bulletin* (January 1988): 28–35.

64. Palardy and Palardy, "Classroom Discipline," 91.

65. Wesley C. Becker et al., "The Contingent Use of Teacher Attention and Praise in Reducing Classroom Behavior Problems," *Journal of Special Education* (Summer–Fall 1967): 287–307. See also Bob Algozzine, *Problem Behavior Management: Educator's Resource Service* (Frederick, Md.: Aspen Publishers, 1983 [updated annually]).

66. Axelrod, *Behavioral Modification.*

67. Howard A. Rollins, Jr., and Marion Thompson, "Implementation and Operation of a Contingency Management Program by the Elementary School Principal," *American Educational Research Journal* (Spring 1978): 325–30. Also, James S. Cangelosi, *Classroom Management Strategies: Gaining and Maintaining Students' Cooperation* (White Plains, N.Y.: Longman, 1988).

68. *Classroom Discipline* (Eugene, Oreg.: ERIC Clearinghouse on Educational Management, August 1979), 2–3.

69. Garry Martin and Joseph Pear, *Behavior Modification: What It Is and How to Do It,* 3d ed. (Englewood Cliffs, N.J.: Prentice-Hall, 1988), 37.

70. Wayne Haasl, "Education for Employment Partnerships: A Program for Dropouts," *NASSP Bulletin* (January 1989): 58.

71. For a description of what appears to be a particularly worthwhile program, see Reagan Walker, "In Fresno Job Program, Students' Workday Begins in the Classroom," *Education Week* (August 3, 1988): 35.

72. James S. Catterall and David Stern, "The Effects of Alternative School Programs on High School Completion and Labor Market Outcomes," *Educational Evaluation and Policy Analysis* (Spring 1986): 78.

73. Jeffrey Robbins et al., "Alternative Programs," *NASSP Bulletin* (May 1981): 48–56.

74. Ronald Garrison, "Alternative Schools Get New Recognition, Results," *School Safety* (Fall 1987): 22.

75. See *Federal Register* (December 30, 1976), 56966–98.

76. Daniel D. Sage and Leonard C. Burello, *Policy and Management in Special Education* (Englewood Cliffs, N.J.: Prentice-Hall, 1986), 194.

77. Maynard C. Reynolds and Jack W. Birch, *Teaching Exceptional Children in All America's Schools* (Reston, Va.: Council for Exceptional Education, 1977), 351.

78. For a review of the theoretical basis for that point of view, see Clinard B. Marshan, *Sociology of Deviant Behavior,* rev. ed. (New York: Holt, Rinehart & Winston, 1964).

79. See R. Lynn, "Personality Characteristics of the Mothers of Aggressive and Unaggressive Children," *Journal of Genetic Psychology* (1961): 159–64. Also see Naomi M. Serot and Richard C. Tevan, "Perceptions of the Parent-Child Relationship and Its Relation to Child Adjustment," *Child Development* (February 1961): 363–78.

80. Extracted from Sheldon Glueck and Eleanor Glueck, *Unraveling Juvenile Delinquency* (Cambridge, Mass.: Harvard University Press, 1950).

81. Lucretia G. Robinson, "Volunteer Counseling, Not Suspension," *Kappan* (October 1978): 131. See also Robert P. Bowman and Robert D. Myrick, "Effects of an Elementary School Peer Facilitator Program on Children with Behavior Problems," *The School Counselor* (May 1987): 369–78.

82. Lawrence M. DeRidder, "School Dropout Prevention Begins in the Elementary Years," *Education* (Summer 1988): 488–92.

83. Reported in "Principal Roles and School Crime Management," by Lewis M. Ciminillo, *NASSP Bulletin* (February 1980): 83.

84. *Everybody's Business: A Book about School Discipline* (Columbia, S.C.: Southeastern Public Education Program, 1980).

85. Margaret R. Rogers Wiese and Jack J. Kramer, "Parent Training Research: An Analysis of the Empirical Literature 1975–1985," *Psychology in the Schools* (July 1988): 325–30.

86. Daniel L. Duke, ed., *Helping Teachers Manage Classrooms* (Alexandria, Va.: Association for Supervision and Curriculum Development, 1982); Charles H. Wolfgang and Carl D. Glickman, *Solving Discipline Problems: Strategies for Classroom Teachers,* 2d ed. (Boston: Allyn & Bacon, 1986); Edmund T. Emmer, Carolyn M. Evertson, Julie P. Sanford, Barbara S. Clements, and Murray E. Worsham, *Classroom Management for Secondary Teachers* (Englewood Cliffs, N.J.: Prentice-Hall, 1989); Alex Molnar and Barbara Lindquist, *Changing Problem Behavior in Schools* (San Francisco: Jossey-Bass, 1989); and Richard L. Curwin and Allen N. Mendler, *Discipline with Dignity* (Alexandria, Va.: Association for Supervision and Curriculum Development, 1989).

87. Edward T. Ladd, "Regulating Student Behavior without Ending up in Court," *Kappan* (January 1973): 308.

88. Quoted in an article by Stanley Fagan et al., "A Principal's Checklist for School Behavior Management," *The Pointer* (Fall 1979): 33.

15

· · · · ·

Administration of Special Education and Pupil Personnel Services

Many different kinds of students attend school, ranging from the academically talented student to the special education student. The major objective of education should be to help all students achieve their maximum potential; the primary function of special education and pupil personnel services should be to provide a set of specialized services which aid the school and, ultimately the students, to accomplish that objective.

Because a special education and pupil personnel services program may be found in most schools and school administrators usually have overall administrative responsibility at the building level, they need to be well informed about the many facets of this very important program. This chapter can help administrators better understand the objectives, personnel roles, administrative responsibilities and issues, and problems of the special education program, as well as the two main components of pupil personnel services: (1) the counseling and guidance program; and (2) the social, psychological, and health program.

THE SPECIAL EDUCATION PROGRAM

Special education has been part of the educational scene for many years.[1] Until 1975, however, special education in most states was separate from the general school program.[2] Public Law 94–142, the Education for All Handicapped Children Act, was passed by Congress in 1975; among other things, it mandated the increased integration of special education with general education where appropriate.[3] The law, according to Martha McCarthy, has been characterized in a variety of ways: "A bill of rights for handicapped children, an administrative nightmare, a disaster, a paradigm of educational perfection, a remarkable piece of legislation, and a bombshell."[4]

Since 1975, this federal law has had its share of critics, as well as supporters. Thus, school administrators must understand the basic concepts of Public Law 94–142 to communicate its main tenets to educators, parents, and community members; in all likelihood, this law will continue to play an important role in American education. Also, by understanding the basic concepts of the law, school administrators learn a great deal about special education.

The Education for All Handicapped Children Act requires that:

- Handicapped children receive a free and appropriate public education at no cost to parents or guardian.
- State education agencies (through individual school districts) locate and aid all handicapped children who presently are not receiving public education.
- Nondiscriminatory, comprehensive testing and evaluation be used in determining a person's handicap and eventual placement in an educational program.
- An individualized educational program (IEP) be developed and maintained for each handicapped child.
- Special education be provided for each handicapped child in the least restrictive environment for that child.
- There be regular parent or guardian consultation in the handicapped student's assessment, program placement, and IEP development process.
- The child's parents be guaranteed due process.[5]

The term *handicapped* in the federal law is defined very comprehensively:

> the term *handicapped children* means mentally retarded, hard of hearing, deaf, speech impaired, visually handicapped, seriously emotionally disturbed, orthopedically impaired, or other health impaired children, or children with specific learning disabilities who, by reason thereof, require special education and related services.[6]

Perhaps the most innovative concept in the law is the individualized educational program, more commonly referred to as the IEP. The IEP is a "written commitment of resources necessary to enable a handicapped child to receive needed special education and related services."[7] The IEP is not a binding legal contract between the school and the child/parents, but an explicit, systematic, cooperative planning process designed to provide the best education possible for the handicapped child.[8]

According to LeRoy Aserlind and Ellen Browning, when completed the IEP should contain the following information:

1. Statements of the student's present levels of performance in each educational area.
2. Statements of the annual goals for the student.
3. By curriculum area, statements of the short-term instructional objectives leading to attainment of the annual goals.
4. The anticipated dates for initiation and completion of each objective.
5. The methods to be utilized to teach each objective (although not mandated, it is strongly encouraged that the materials to be used be included in this section).
6. An outline of the time the student will be in regular and special services (i.e., speech and language, occupational therapy, resource room, etc.).
7. The persons responsible for attaining each short-term objective.
8. The criteria and evaluation procedures and schedules for determining whether the short-term objectives have been attained.[9]

The overall process leading to the development of an IEP includes the following:

Phase I

1. Referral of the student to a multidisciplinary team to ascertain whether or not a handicap exists.
2. Assessment of the skills, abilities, interests, and present level of performance.
3. Diagnosis and decision on whether or not the student is handicapped.

Phase II

1. Evaluation of the child's present program placement and appropriate alternative placements and a decision to place the student in the least restrictive educational program for that child.
2. Development of an educational program which best serves the child.
3. Establishment of an effective monitoring system for ascertaining the extent to which the educational program is being implemented and maintained.
4. Identification of criteria and methods for ascertaining student achievement and program effectiveness.[10]

Participants in Phase II of the process should include a representative of the educational agency, such as a school district, to supervise the administration of the plan; the child's teacher; one or both parents or guardians; the child, if appropriate; and one or more persons knowledgeable about the child or evaluation procedures.[11] As a result of the varied contributions of the participants involved in the process described, an individualized educational program for each handicapped student should be produced, containing (1) the child's present level of performance; (2) a statement of annual goals and short-term instructional objectives; (3) a description of special education and related services for the child, plus the extent of participation in regular educational programs recommended for the child; (4) specified dates for initiation of services and their duration; and (5) identification of objective criteria and evaluative procedures for assessing whether the instructional objectives are being achieved, on at least an annual basis.[12]

Although the federal mandate of required IEPs for all handicapped children has been criticized for a number of reasons—including the allegation that it is confusing, expensive, and time-consuming—that aspect of the IEP most in need of improvement is the involvement of parents.[13] One study, for example, showed that parents generally knew their children had IEPs, but only 20 percent were thoroughly familiar with what was in them. In the same study, parents were less familiar with the IEPs of their children than the teachers believed they were.[14] Another study discovered that only about half of the parents actually attended the meetings in which IEPs were developed; interestingly IEPs were more accurate when parents were involved.[15] And, in a third study, 71 percent of the parents with learning disabled children remembered being informed about an IEP, but only one-fourth helped write it, and only one-fourth were satisfied with their involvement.[16] A recent review of the literature found no evidence to refute these findings; thus, these studies strongly suggest the need for school administrators, in cooperation with the IEP team, to develop a better system of involving parents in the development of the IEPs. Such a system is further described by Lawrence Gaines.[17]

Parent involvement is also important because if parents are not satisfied with the school district's response to the needs of their handicapped children, they have a right to due process. The specific procedural guarantees to parents include

- The right to a timely, written notice of the place and time of the hearing.
- The right to review all records and information that the school has available on the child.
- The right to be represented by counsel, to bring witnesses, to cross-examine witnesses, and to present evidence.

- The right to obtain an independent evaluation of the data being used to evaluate the child's possible handicap and eventual placement at the expense of the school.
- The right to a complete written report of the hearing proceedings and findings.
- The right to appeal the assessment decision and the placement decision.[18]

Obviously, this aspect of the law on the handicapped is complex and potentially troublesome. For further information, see an excellent monograph discussing major problems and issues with regard to due process, published by Research for Better Schools.[19]

Another important aspect of Public Law 94–142 is the requirement that special education be provided for each handicapped child in the least restrictive environment for the child. This has been interpreted to mean that a handicapped child is entitled to an environment that provides the greatest interaction with other, nonhandicapped, students in which satisfactory performance can still be assured. A decision to take a handicapped child from a special education setting and place the child in a regular classroom has been termed *mainstreaming*.[20] The rationale for mainstreaming has been best expressed in a statement by the Council for Exceptional Children:

> Mainstreaming is a belief which involves an educational placement procedure and process for exceptional children, based on the conviction that each such child should be educated in the last restrictive environment in which his educational and related needs can be satisfactorily provided. This concept recognizes that exceptional children have a wide range of special educational needs, varying greatly in intensity and duration; that there is a recognized continuum of educational settings which may, at a given time, be appropriate for an individual child's needs; that to the maximum extent appropriate, exceptional children should be educated with nonexceptional children; and that special classes, separate schooling, or other removal of an exceptional child from education with nonexceptional children should occur only when the intensity of the child's special education and related needs is such that they cannot be satisfied in an environment including nonexceptional children, even with the provision of supplementary aids and services.[21]

Certainly, mainstreaming a handicapped child requires much more than merely placing that child in a regular classroom. Several studies have shown that even though handicapped students are physically in the mainstream, they often continue to be socially isolated.[22] As Ganelda Sowers points out, successful mainstreaming in a school requires

- New perspectives and new skills for the staff.
- Increased awareness and sensitivity on the part of each individual.
- In-service for teachers, with emphasis on acquiring diagnostic and observational skills.
- Supportive resources for the classroom teacher.
- Acceptance by the faculty.
- Understanding by resource teachers of their role.
- Acceptance of children with special needs by other pupils.
- Variety of instructional materials.
- Efficient methods in diagnosing and prescribing for individual pupils.[23]

Consultation models whereby special and regular education teachers work together on informal, school-based, problem-solving teams are becoming popular.[24] This collaborative process provides special and regular education teachers with a strategy by which they might identify and deal with the needs of special students at the prereferral stage and during the IEP development and implementation phases. The special education teacher can play a key role in assisting the regular classroom teacher should mainstreaming be contained within the student's IEP. Assistance that the special education teacher should provide includes (1) discussion with the regular teacher on how the student will be prepared for the change in classes; (2) description of techniques used by the special education teacher that have proved to be useful in teaching the student to manage behavior and to establish work habits; (3) identification of limits and controls used by the special education teacher to help students manage their behavior; (4) description of behavioral and academic expectations used in the special education setting and how they could be adjusted for use in the regular classroom; and (5) provision of materials used in the special education classroom that might be used or adapted for the regular classroom.[25] The goal of the special education teacher should be to make the transition from the special to the regular classroom and the integration within the regular classroom as smooth as possible for both the student and the regular classroom teacher.

The classroom teacher also plays an important role in the success of a mainstreaming endeavor. The attitude of the teacher is apparently the key variable.[26] If the classroom teacher holds a positive attitude, the chances of success for a mainstreamed child are probably high. On the other hand, if the classroom teacher is negative or even ambivalent toward mainstreaming, the chances of successful mainstreaming are, at best, uncertain. Barbara Larrivee and Linda Cook, in their study of variables affecting the teacher's attitude toward mainstreaming found three factors had the greatest import: (1) the teacher's perception of the degree of success possible with special education students; (2) the availability of supportive services to the teacher, such as special reading teacher assistance or appropriate instructional materials; and (3) the level of administrative support received.[27]

That school administrators can make a significant contribution to the success of mainstreaming seems obvious. For example, a study by Cheryll Duquette and Robert O'Reilly found that the behavior of school administrators was positively related to the positive attitudes of teachers toward mainstreaming.[28] Specifically, they found that an effective administrator "makes clear the rationale and objectives of mainstreaming; clarifies the roles of teachers, consultants, and themselves; and makes known the support of mainstreaming by senior administrative officials. In addition, the principal maintains a flexible organization to meet the requirements of mainstreaming and gives attention to solving problems which individual teachers may have concerning mainstreaming."[29]

As far as school administrators' specific responsibilities in administering a special education program are concerned, a review of the literature suggests that the primary and support responsibilities of building principals include:

- Helping to design a special education services delivery plan.
- Helping to formulate long-term policies and objectives for special education programs.
- Helping to recruit and select special education personnel.
- Providing in-service training for professional staff.
- Evaluating special education professional personnel.
- Coordinating due process procedures for students and parents.

With regard to evaluating special education personnel and programs (a frequently neglected task), Daniel Sage and Leonard Burrello present a thorough discussion of possible strategies for evaluating all aspects of special education services, and they provide descriptions of exemplars in special education evaluation.[30] And, Gary Borich and Deborah Nance present a program evaluation model which assesses:

Compliance: adherence to local, state, and federal rules and regulations which designate programmatic expectations related to legal and funding constraints.

Coordination: the degree of overlap and/or gaps in service existing among special education program components and between special education programs and external (parallel and overarching) educational programs which provide services to the same population of students.

Change: the measurement of student progress (or lack thereof), parents' attitudes, and staff competencies, which may be compared periodically to determine the program's effectiveness.[31]

Even though the role description of the Council for Exceptional Children defines considerable involvement for school administrators in supervising special education programs, research suggests that the actual role may be more limited. For example, a study by Jeremy Leitz and Maxine Towle found that the school administrators in their sample wanted more responsibility for directing the special education program than was occurring in actual practice.[32]

In carrying out their responsibilities for the special education program, school administrators should keep abreast of federal and state requirements concerning special education, establish reasonable expectations of the staff in implementing the requirements of the law, and provide supportive services and staff development. Perhaps most important, they should provide a model of behavior indicating to all observers that the education of the handicapped in the least restrictive environment is an important and desirable educational priority, rather than an unnecessary legal mandate.

The concept of mainstreaming handicapped students is one of the more controversial ideas in American education; even some special educators question whether academically and socially many handicapped children benefit from integration with nonhandicapped students.[33] In recent years, a major proposal to better unify regular and special education has gained prominence among researchers and practitioners. According to John O'Neil, "the 'Regular Education Initiative,' as it has come to be known, questions many of the assumptions underlying the education of mildly disabled students in special settings."[34] The national attention and interest regarding this initiative indicates that educators are looking carefully at the quality of services and the educational programs afforded special education students.

The preceding discussion is merely a short introduction to the major concepts of exceptional education; we invite you to pursue the references at the end of the chapter for further background.[35]

THE COUNSELING AND GUIDANCE PROGRAM

Although the counseling and guidance program is only one of the two components of pupil personnel services, it may constitute the only pupil personnel services offered in many schools. Counseling and guidance programs are more

Figure 15.1 Counseling and Guidance Services.

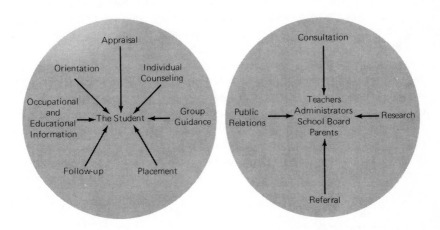

typically found in the secondary schools, yet a strong case can be made that they are needed as much, if not more, at the elementary level.[36] Younger students tend to be more receptive to counseling and guidance, and problems can be addressed in their early stages before they become more complex and difficult. A young person does not suddenly develop a need for counseling and guidance when entering junior high school; often the need develops much earlier but does not receive the attention it deserves.

The basic purposes of the counseling and guidance program are to assist students to better understand themselves and to realize their potentialities more fully.[37] To achieve these objectives, the program should provide to the student, and to others working to help the student, the services identified in figure 15.1.[38]

As figure 15.1 shows, the counseling and guidance program provides services to five groups. The first and undoubtedly the most important group is the student body. The counseling and guidance program offers a set of services designed to help students understand themselves (appraisal), as well as their immediate and future environments (orientation, educational, and occupational information), and to reach decisions that fully utilize their present and future capabilities (individual and group counseling and guidance). In addition, a good counseling and guidance program provides assistance to those students seeking a job or a college appropriate for them (placement), and checks with them periodically after they have left school to ascertain the effectiveness of the school's assistance to them and their need for further help (follow-up).

While students are probably the primary recipients of counseling and guidance services, the program also tries to provide help to other groups, as figure 15.1 indicates. These services include *consultation* on ideas for maximizing students' potentialities, a *referral* source on ways to prevent and ameliorate student problems; *research* on student aptitudes, interests, and problems; and *public relations* activities to help people better understand the counseling and guidance program. Teachers, administrators, school board members, and parents can and should utilize these services to help them do a better job in working with students. Frequently these groups do not make adequate use of the specialized resources which the counseling and guidance program can offer. Although the reasons for such underutilization are often complex, it is the responsibility of building administrators, in cooperation with the guidance staff, to develop appropriate understanding and use of counseling and guidance services on the part of teachers, parents, the school board, and other administrators.

THE ROLE OF THE COUNSELOR

Central to the effective utilization of counseling and guidance services is a broad understanding of the role of the counselor. The counselor is the transmitter of counseling and guidance services, much as the teacher is the transmitter of the curriculum. Though there have been many formulations of the role of the counselor, the most widely accepted conceptualization is the role description developed by the American Personnel and Guidance Association (APGA) and presented in figure 15.2 on the next page.[39]

The APGA policy statement on the role of the counselor is a comprehensive one which should be useful to any school administrator. Clearly outlining the many facets and scope of the counselor's job, it identifies the various individuals and groups with whom the counselor works. This statement should be studied by school administrators and shared with teachers, parents, students, and other relevant groups to develop their further understanding of the guidance program and the role of the counselor. The role description should also be utilized by the administrator in discussions with the guidance department members on the extent to which the proposed role of the counselor is actually being implemented in the school and the degree to which improvement is needed.[40] For administrators seeking direction on the role of the counselor in the school, the APGA policy statement should provide a valuable blueprint for identifying desired change.

Figure 15.2 The Role of the School Counselor.

A. The Counselor's Responsibility to the Student

1. Demonstrates respect for the worth, dignity, and quality of the student's human rights.
2. Shows concern for and assists in the planning of the student's educational, career, personal, and social development.
3. Aids the student in self-evaluation, self-understanding, and self-direction, enabling him to make decisions consistent with his immediate and long-range goals.
4. Assists the student in developing health habits and positive attitudes and values.
5. Encourages the student to participate in appropriate school activities with a view toward increasing his effectiveness in personal and social activities.
6. Participates in the planning and designing of research that may result in beneficial effects to the counselee.
7. Assists the student in the development of an awareness of the world of work and in the utilization of the school and community resources to that end.
8. Helps the student to acquire a better understanding of the world of work through the acquisition of skills and attitudes and/or participation in work-related programs.
9. Encourages the student to plan and utilize leisure time activities and to increase his personal satisfaction.
10. Clearly indicates the conditions under which counseling is provided with respect to privileged communication.
11. Assists in the student's adjustment to school and evaluates his academic progress.
12. Makes referral to appropriate resources whenever his professional or role limitations limit his assistance.
13. Assists the student in understanding his strengths, weaknesses, interests, values, potentialities, and limitations.

B. The Counselor's Relationship with the Teacher

1. Views the teacher as a member of the guidance team.
2. Serves as interpreter of the school's guidance program to teachers and familiarizes them with the guidance services available.
3. Shares appropriate individual student data with the teacher, with due regard for confidentiality, and assists the teacher in recognizing individual differences in students, as well as their needs in the classroom.
4. Assists the teacher in making referrals to other appropriate school personnel, such as the remedial reading teacher, the school nurse, the school's learning disabilities specialist.
5. Supports teachers of vocational and/or cooperative programs offering students on-site work experience.
6. Cooperates with efforts of the middle school/junior high school and senior high school teachers to articulate academic course work for the benefit of the student entering the senior high school.
7. Maintains an objective and impartial view in teacher-student relationships, endeavoring to understand the problems which may exist and to assist in their solution.
8. Assists in the planning of classroom guidance activities and acts as a resource person for obtaining appropriate up-to-date materials and information.

Figure 15.2 Continued

9. Makes current job information available to the teacher about the myriad of careers and job opportunities during and beyond school.
10. Involves the teacher in conferences with students and parents, promoting a better understanding of the student and his development.

C. The Counselor's Relationship with the Administration

1. Recognizes that the administrator is the major member of the guidance team whose outlook, leadership, and support create the atmosphere for success in his important school services.
2. Serves as interpreter of the guidance program to the administration, familiarizing it with the guidance services available.
3. Works closely with the administration in planning, implementing and participating in-service training and other programs designed to maintain and promote the professional competency of the entire staff in curriculum development, in adapting learning activities to pupil needs, and in effecting positive student behavior.
4. Serves as liaison between the guidance staff and the school administration by preparing pertinent information regarding student needs and abilities or other data related to the guidance program and curriculum development.

D. The Counselor's Responsibility to the Parent or Guardian

1. Provides the parent/guardian with accurate information about school policies and procedures, course offerings, educational and career opportunities, course or program requirements, and resources that will contribute to the continuing development of the counselee.
2. Makes discreet and professional use of information shared during conferences.
3. Assists the parent/guardian in forming realistic perceptions of the student's aptitudes, abilities, interests, and attitudes as related to educational and career planning, academic achievement, personal-social development, and total school progress.
4. Interprets the guidance program of the school to the parent/guardian and familiarizes him with the guidance services available.
5. Involves the parent/guardian in the guidance activities within the school.

E. The Counselor's Relationship with Significant Others

1. Maintains good communication with the office of the probate judge and with law enforcement agencies.
2. Retains a cooperative working relationship with community and social agencies.
3. Consults with students' previous counselors in order to utilize valuable knowledge and expertise of former counselors.
4. Maintains a close and cooperative relationship with the admission counselors of post-high school institutions.

Figure 15.3 Role of the Elementary School Counselor.

The Elementary School Counselor's Primary Functions

- Counsels individual students in order to facilitate their transition from home to school and to foster their self-understanding and self-reliance.
- Counsels groups of students for the purpose of offering individual students the opportunity to obtain greater self-understanding and confidence through interactions with their peers.
- Consults with teachers, other members of the faculty, and parents on child development and needs. In addition, the elementary counselor serves as a referral agent in regard to needed counseling and guidance resources outside of the school and home.
- Evaluates self and program effectiveness continuously for the purpose of identifying possible problems and needed improvements.

The Elementary School Counselor's Supportive Functions

- Consults with teachers, administrators and relevant others on the testing program, grouping and placement, pupil evaluation, curriculum development, articulation of guidance program with pupil data, pupil screening, and impact of the instructional program on children.
- Serves on curriculum planning committees.
- Provides in-service education when appropriate.
- Serves on special school and community committees dealing with topics such as drug education and family living.
- Consults with faculty, administration, and parents on career education.
- Interprets the functions of the counselor, and objectives and activities of the guidance program to students, teachers, parents and the general public.

Although the role of the counselor is basically the same, regardless of the educational level of the students, there are some differences. Those differences become clear when one compares the role description for the elementary school counselor presented in figure 15.3 with the role description in figure 15.2.[41]

As can be seen by a careful examination of the two role statements, the elementary counselor's role seems to focus much more than does that of the secondary school counselor on group counseling in regard to the personal development of the student, with an emphasis on consulting with different groups on the guidance needs of children. That elementary school counselors place a high priority on these particular aspects of their role can be concluded from a study by Julian Biggers, who asked elementary school counselors to indicate the amount of time they actually spent on various aspects of their job. Bigger's findings follow:[42]

Elementary Counselor's Activities	Percentage of Time Spent
Group counseling	20.6%
Consulting (with parents, teachers, principal)	18.2%
Individual counseling	17.2%
Testing (group and individual)	10.4%
Planning	7.7%
Case conferences	6.1%
Clerical/Nonguidance	4.9%
Classroom observation	4.7%
Home visitation	4.3%
In-Service	2.7%
Orientation	2.3%
Miscellaneous	1.6%

The elementary school counselor can make a major contribution to helping young children with their personal development and to helping teachers, parents, and others understand better the needs and potentialities of children. While there will undoubtedly be financial obstacles to establishing a counselor's position and a formal counseling and guidance program in elementary schools where none exits, every effort should be made to overcome those obstacles. In the final analysis, the money saved by deciding against establishing a position and program at the elementary level is spent many times over on secondary-level problems which either could have been avoided or reduced in their severity. To explore further concepts and guidelines for introducing a counseling and guidance program at the elementary level, consult the references at the end of the chapter.[43]

THE ADMINISTRATOR'S ROLE IN THE COUNSELING AND GUIDANCE PROGRAM

Although in many schools the position of guidance director has been created to accomplish certain administrative functions in relation to the counseling and guidance program, school administrators are still responsible for providing overall leadership and administration to the program at the building level.[44]

The leadership dimension of the administrator's role includes such responsibilities as:

1. Assisting counselors to remove obstacles to the effective performance of their jobs, and helping them to utilize their specialized talents for improving education in the school.
2. Working with counselors to increase their awareness of the guidance needs which have not been met for students, teachers, and parents; stimulating counselors to develop greater vision and creativity in planning how these needs might be met.
3. Developing on the part of students, teachers, and parents a better understanding of the guidance program and the role of the counselor and how these groups can best relate to that program and role.
4. Helping counselors to evaluate themselves and the guidance program on a regular basis to obtain information on effectiveness and to identify areas in need of improvement.[45]

Building administrators should share these leadership functions with the guidance director, if the latter position has been established. However, guidance directors are frequently counselors who may have little released time or professional training for carrying out the leadership function identified earlier. Therefore, in many cases school administrators may need to assume a leadership role relative to the counseling and guidance program, even if a guidance director is available.

Aside from the leadership dimension of the administrator's role in the counseling and guidance program, school administrators must assume administrative responsibilities for the program to be established and maintained at an appropriate level of effectiveness.[46] These responsibilities include providing (1) sufficient and appropriately located office space; (2) an adequate budget for supplies, occupational and educational information, testing, and professional activities; (3) sufficient secretarial assistance; and (4) a reasonable counselor-student ratio. Of course, the definitions of *sufficient, appropriate,* and *reasonable* depend on local needs and conditions. However, administrators should try to meet the standards covering these four areas of responsibility as recommended by authorities in the guidance field.

ISSUES AND PROBLEMS

The counseling and guidance program, similar to any other program in the school, is confronted periodically by issues and problems which can reduce its effectiveness if not resolved. The following three issues or problems are common to many schools' counseling and guidance programs.[47]

1. **The role of the counselor in resolving student discipline problems.** This issue periodically causes friction in many schools. Students who misbehave usually need help, and many administrators believe that the specialized skills of counselors should be utilized to help these students change their attitudes and behaviors.

Most counselors, on the other hand, believe that they should not be involved at all in working with discipline problems, at least not immediately after the student has engaged in misbehavior. Their position is that they are not disciplinarians and any association with a student who is a behavioral problem would tend to give them the image of administrator rather than of counselor, thereby making it more difficult to work with other students.

In many respects, it is unfortunate when the question of counselor involvement in helping to reduce student misbehavior becomes an issue or a problem in school. In the first place, counselors should never be given the responsibility of disciplining students. That involvement is inconsistent with the role of the counselor and is a function which should be performed by the administration of the school. Neither should teachers and administrators refer for counseling any students who have just engaged in misbehavior. Referrals to counselors at that point are inappropriate and make it unnecessarily difficult for them to work with the students later.

On the other hand, counselors can and should be expected to contribute their specialized expertise so that misbehaving students can better understand themselves and the consequences of their behavior. Through individual diagnosis, counseling, and other guidance techniques, students should also be able to develop more positive attitudes about themselves and others, and ultimately to become better school citizens.

The means by which counselors and students come together and the timing of their first conferences are key factors to the success of this approach. When counselors are to work with misbehaving students in the manner indicated, the counselors or the students should initiate the conference; it should not occur while students are still subject to disciplinary proceedings. If a teacher or an administrator refers a student to a counselor and the conference takes place while the student is being considered for disciplinary action by that same teacher or administrator, there is a real danger that, in the eyes of the student, the counselor could easily become implicated in the disciplinary proceeding. For counselors to work effectively with student misbehavior cases, their involvement needs to be separated as much as possible from the school's disciplinary measures.

Undoubtedly, counselors can play an important role in assisting students who have behavioral problems. Failure to utilize counselors to help these students means that a valuable resource would go untapped. Administrators need to recognize, however, that many counselors object to working with student behavior problems because of their counseling philosophy or due to negative experiences in the past. So unless administrators, in conjunction with the counselors in the school, develop sensible policies and procedures for counselor involvement in working with student behavioral problems, a major issue or conflict may occur.

2. **The role of teachers in the counseling and guidance program.** Before formal counseling and guidance programs were introduced, classroom teachers were expected to perform many guidance functions. Now, in most schools, the guidance role of the teacher is minimized and this responsibility is considered to be the province of the counselor and the guidance department. For example, a review of counseling and guidance journals suggests that many counselors appear to believe that teachers lack the specialized training and skills to play an important role in the counseling and guidance program. Seemingly supporting this contention are many teachers who believe that counseling and guidance is somehow separate from teaching, and that the school's formal counseling and guidance program obviates the need for them to become involved.

In spite of limited support for the guidance role of classroom teachers, they could make valuable contributions to the total counseling and guidance program. Their resources should be organized by the administrator in such a way that they can be utilized by the guidance department for the good of the students. Specifically, classroom teachers can and should be expected to perform the following counseling and guidance functions:

    a. Study individual students and become more aware of their needs, problems, and characteristics.

    b. Counsel with students on educational problems and, when sought out by students, on minor personal problems.

    c. Refer to counselors any students with social, personal, and vocational problems.

    d. Administer appropriate measurement instruments, such as standardized tests, to ascertain students' strengths and limitations.

e. Utilize data from the school's testing program, cumulative records, and suggestions from counselors in modifying the instructional and curricular program to meet the needs of students more adequately.

f. Interact on a regular basis with counselors for the purpose of pooling perceptions and knowledge about students and about how they might be helped to improve.[48]

In many schools, the question of the extent to which teachers should be involved in the counseling and guidance program has not been satisfactorily resolved. Obviously, teachers have other responsibilities; many teachers do not possess a great deal of time or inclination for performing guidance functions. However, teachers can make a valuable contribution to the guidance program, particularly in the area of helping special education students. School administrators are responsible for helping teachers better understand and accept their guidance role and for removing the obstacles to carrying out that role effectively.[49]

3. **The role of the administrator in the evaluation of the counseling and guidance program.** Evaluation of the performance of the school counselors and the effectiveness of the counseling and guidance program can present a problem. When administrators try to initiate evaluation procedures, they may encounter resistance. Counselors may infer that administrators feel dissatisfied with their work and become defensive. Or they may be opposed to any evaluation other than informal self-assessment.

Compounding these problems is the fact that much of the counselors' work is not conducive to evaluation. Counseling takes place privately and the nature of the conferences is usually kept confidential. Also, many of the outcomes of counseling and guidance, particularly in the area of vocational guidance, may not be realized until the students have graduated from school.

In spite of these problems, however, school administrators have a responsibility to evaluate all personnel and programs—including the counselors and the counseling and guidance program. To carry out this responsibility effectively, administrators need to be aware of the problems associated with evaluation of counselors and the guidance program; they need to move cautiously and cooperatively with the counselors in developing evaluation criteria and procedures.

Standards for evaluating a counseling and guidance program have been developed by Marguerite Carroll and approved for use by the governing board of the American School Counselors Association.[50] Although too detailed to be reproduced here, they represent useful criteria for purposes of program evaluation. Arlene Breckenridge reported a process for assessing counselor performance and Anita Mitchell and James Wiggins have developed criteria and methods for evaluating the effectiveness of counseling and guidance programs.[51] An approach referred to as results management or supervision by objectives merits investigation by administrators interested in counselor evaluation; it is described later in this chapter and in ERIC Report Ed–086–914, "Progress Report: Pupil Personnel Services."

After examining the organizational and individual dimensions of the counselor's position, Richard Podemski and John Childers identified five trends in counseling practice which may revitalize the school counselor's role. These include:

1. Moving from a philosophy of remediation to prevention.
2. Moving from direct service delivery to consultation and training.
3. Moving from individual work with clients to group work.
4. Moving from individuals or groups being the targets of counselor interventions to the organization or school.
5. Moving from a school-based philosophy to a school-community philosophy.[52]

These trends indicate the future direction of effective counseling programs.

PSYCHOLOGICAL, SOCIAL, AND HEALTH SERVICES

Although in many schools the counseling and guidance services may represent the total pupil services program, a comprehensive program also includes psychological, social, and health services.* These services are performed by school psychologists, school social workers, and school nurses respectively, all of whom can offer specialized assistance to students, teachers, parents, and the administration, beyond that contributed by the school counselors.

The assistance these members of the pupil services team can offer a school is potentially of great value (particularly in regard to the growing concern about the needs of special education students), but that potential is frequently not achieved. Part of the problem lies in a lack of understanding by administrators and teachers of the role of these pupil personnel specialists. A second important factor, though, is the way these services are organized and delivered. This section should develop a better understanding by school administrators of the role of the school psychologist, the school social worker, and the school nurse. Problems involved in the organization and delivery of their services are also discussed.

---

*There are other aspects of pupil personnel services in the schools, such as speech services. However, only those services most frequently offered at the building level are emphasized in this section.

THE SCHOOL PSYCHOLOGIST

Many school districts employ school psychologists. They typically work out of the district's central office and divide their time among several schools. They may or may not be assigned a permanent office in each school building, and their schedule usually varies from week to week, depending on the problems and needs of the schools with which they work. Their role may be specifically defined and understood by the groups who could utilize their services, but frequently in many schools their role is not well defined. And, it is certainly not well understood by school administrators. For example, Richard Hughes and Richard Shofer found in their study that only 9 percent of the psychologists had access to descriptions of their role and functions within their assigned schools.[53] This is inexcusable because there are excellent statements on the role of the school psychologist which, if studied and implemented by the school administrators and staff members, would help school psychologists to achieve more of their potential usefulness to the school.

While there is not total agreement on the role of the school psychologist and the role is somewhat in transition, one role description that merits review by the school administrator is presented in figure 15.4.[54]

As the role description in figure 15.4 indicates, school psychologists should be involved in a wide range of diagnostic, counseling, and program consulting activities. Their services should be utilized by students, teachers, parents, and administrators. One major problem, however, is that these groups are frequently not in agreement on the role the school psychologist should perform. When this problem occurs, it is usually based on a perception that school psychologists are too involved in testing and assessment, and insufficiently involved in consultation and program development.[55] In many respects, special education legislation has exacerbated this situation. Unfortunately, there is no easy answer to this problem.

Whether or not the proposed role outlined in figure 15.4 is actually implemented fully probably depends as much on a clear and complete understanding of that role by administrators as on any other factor. If administrators understand the role of their school psychologists and are committed to helping them fulfill that role, the potential for them making an important contribution to the school is more apt to be realized. On the other hand, when administrators possess an inadequate understanding of this role or are not committed to helping psychologists carry out their role, it is unlikely that they can operate effectively. In the final analysis, administrators hold an important key to psychologists' success within schools. (For further ideas on planning and evaluating school psychology services, see Charles Maker.[56])

Figure 15.4 Role of the School Psychologist.

1. Counsels with individual students who are self-referred or referred by teachers, administrators, or community agencies, to help them develop behavior patterns and attitudes which are appropriate to students' environmental and developmental stages.
2. Gathers sufficient information from previous records and through observation and assessment, to determine how a student can best be helped.
3. Assists the school staff to develop criteria and referral procedures for identifying students who need the services of the school psychologist.
4. Assists teachers, administrators, and parents to develop a greater understanding of student behavior, and to create a special climate in the school which maximizes learning and personal growth for the student.
5. Consults with teachers, curriculum specialists, and administrators on possible ways to improve conditions necessary for effective student learning.
6. Encourages teachers and other professional educators to accept responsibility/accountability for (and to help students accept responsibility for) growth toward predetermined goals.
7. Identifies and utilizes remedial/corrective resources available within the school or community.
8. Serves as a liaison between school and community.

THE SCHOOL SOCIAL WORKER

The school social worker's employment situation and work schedule are similar to that of the school psychologist in many respects. Social workers usually work out of the district central office, dividing their time among several schools. Their work schedules may vary from week to week, and they are viewed by many as a primary liaison between the school and the home. Their specific function is to provide assistance to "children who are having difficulties in using the resources of the school effectively."[57] The nature of their responsibility to the school can be conceived of as "a specialized service involving home and school case work with a minority of pupils whose school problems are primarily affected by family and neighborhood conditions."[58]

As with school psychologists, social workers' effectiveness has been hampered in many school systems by their poorly defined and poorly understood role. To partially remedy this problem, a proposed role for the school social worker is outlined in figure 15.5 for administrators' consideration.[59]

The proposed role described in figure 15.5. suggests that school social workers can perform a variety of useful services for students, teachers, parents, and administrators; in turn, these services help all groups understand and capitalize on the contributions that homes and schools can make together to educate students.[60] Again, whether these services are fully and properly utilized depends to a great degree on school administrators. Given school administrators who understand and are committed to implementing the role proposed in figure 15.5, the influence of school social workers should be significant.

HEALTH SERVICES

Addressing the need for comprehensive health education, Byron Nelson noted that

> In recent years health has become a major concern of the American public; and, as is the case with many other issues, education has been called upon to help solve the problem. Too often though, the problem has been addressed in a fragmented manner. Educators must be convinced that a comprehensive health education program is an essential part of the total school curriculum if it is to become a reality. They must truly believe that it will make a positive difference in the lives of boys and girls. Too often many ingredients found in a quality program are added randomly to existing or hurriedly developed programs.[61]

Generally, state laws require health education and, in the summer of 1977, Congress enacted Public Law 94–317 to improve the quality of health education and care for all children.[62] Nonetheless, the extent and quality of school health programs continue to vary considerably despite clear evidence of the growing health needs of students.[63]

Figure 15.5 Functions of the School Social Worker.

1. Counsels with parents and students on problems of student adjustment to school.
2. Utilizes community resources in the process of working with children and parents.
3. Consults with staff members concerning community factors which may be affecting problems of student adjustment in school.
4. Collaborates with teachers, administrators, and noninstructional personnel in gathering and sharing information about students, designed to modify or resolve student adjustment problems.
5. Acts as liaison between the school and community agencies.
6. Cooperates with community agencies by providing pertinent information about a student's school adjustment and achievement.

Figure 15.6 Role of the School Nurse.

1. Develops objectives and designs programs with the assistance of the school district (and public health agency) personnel and within school district philosophy and policy.
2. Assesses and evaluates the health and developmental status of students in order to identify those who should be referred for medical diagnosis or treatment.
3. Interprets the health and developmental status of the pupil to him, his parents, and school personnel.
4. Interprets the results of medical findings concerning the pupil to him, his parents, and school personnel.
5. Counsels the pupil, his parents, and school personnel regarding plans for eliminating, minimizing, or accepting a health problem that interferes with his effective learning.
6. Motivates and guides the persons responsible for pupil health to appropriate resources.
7. Recommends to the administration modifications in the educational program when indicated by the health or developmental status of the pupil.
8. Serves as health consultant and resource person in the health instruction curriculum by providing current scientific information from related fields.
9. Uses direct health services as a vehicle for health counseling.
10. Serves as liaison among the parents, school and community in health matters.
11. Serves as member of the placement committee for special education programs.
12. Evaluates program effectiveness and outcomes.

The primary function of school health services is to assess and diagnose the health status of students in the school and to work with teachers, parents, administrators, and others to promote better student health habits and practices.[64] The personnel for staffing a comprehensive school health services program should include a nurse, a physician, and a dental hygienist. (For an example of this staffing, see Godfrey Cronin and William Young.[65]) Whether these personnel are employed full time or part time depends on the size of the school or school district, availability of personnel, financial resources—and most important—the concept held by the educators of the district in regard to the role of each of these specialized workers.

Because school administrators are, in most situations, more likely to have contact with the nurse than with any of the other health personnel, an understanding of the nurse's role is essential. Figure 15.6 presents a proposed role for school nurses defining the nature of their services.[66]

Long perceived as deliverer of services such as examining students with health concerns, the role of the school nurse seems to be changing. The responsibilities of the nurse for acting as an advocate for the health rights of students and their families within the school setting and between the school and community, as well as a health educator for the students, faculty, administration, and the community seem to be assuming greater importance.[67] A major problem with this change in role emphasis, however, is that many people still do not understand what nurses do in a school, while others hold conflicting expectations for the role. For example, one study discovered that many students did not know what nurses did in the school, did not know when they were actually at the school, and perhaps most important, had a general aversion to seeking health care services.[68] Another study by Charles Tosi found that students and administrators did not believe it was necessary to emphasize the nurse's role as a health counselor and educator for health rather than deliverer of services; teachers, on the other hand, believed that the former role should be emphasized but they perceived the latter as actually occurring the most.[69] These studies suggest some of the problems to be addressed by administrators and school nurses if the potential contributions of school nurses are to be realized in school health programs.

The importance of providing health services in the schools has long been recognized in education, but the implementation of a program to that end has frequently been limited. Although the extent and quality of health services in the schools varies so widely throughout the country that generalization is difficult, the program in many school districts consists of no more than a part-time nurse whose time is divided among several schools, with perhaps only one and one-half days per week spent at each one. Until fairly recently, the majority of health services were provided through the physical education program.[70] This appears to be definitely inadequate for many schools, given the nature of the need for expanded preventative health programs and services. Ruth Rich noted that health education in schools has "evolved from a series of fragmented subject matter topics on principles of hygiene into a planned prevention-oriented curricular program with identifiable objectives and scope and sequence of health instruction for each grade level extending from pre-kindergarten through grade 12."[71]

In recent years, the health problems of students have increased dramatically. Drug involvement, venereal disease, AIDS, HIV infection, nutritional imbalance, obesity, adolescent pregnancy, dental decay, and other problems all strongly point to the need for a comprehensive health services program in the schools.[72] The program should probably emphasize referral rather than treatment, and it should help students experiencing health problems to secure proper medical assistance. Given the controversial nature of some of these problems, school administrators should involve students, parents, and community members on planning committees exploring the expansion of health education programs.[73]

Administrators need to recognize that the condition of students' health affects their educational motivation and performance in school. The school nurse and other health services personnel can and should play important roles in helping a school to ameliorate students' health problems. A useful description of a process for establishing the need for and introducing a more comprehensive school health program is provided by Floyd Boschee.[74]

ADMINISTRATOR RESPONSIBILITIES

Unlike the guidance counselor, other members of the pupil services team are typically part-time workers in a school. They divide their time among several schools, and their work schedules are sometimes unpredictable. The part-time nature of their assignment in any particular school frequently results in their not being considered as regular members of the school faculty. Therefore, when it comes to office space, secretarial help, and a budget for materials and supplies, the school psychologist, the social worker, and (to a lesser extent) the school nurse are likely to be left to shift for themselves. They may be able to rely on some secretarial help and budget assistance from the district office, but that support may not be sufficient to meet their needs.

At the minimum, school administrators are responsible for making sure that each of the pupil services specialists working in the building has an office, which may be shared with someone else but which should be available when the specialist needs it. It should be equipped with a file cabinet (which should not be shared), a desk, and sufficient side chairs so that the specialist may expeditiously proceed. The administrator should also make available to each of the pupil personnel specialists sufficient secretarial assistance to supplement the clerical support provided at the central office. Reports and much of the correspondence can more easily be prepared at the school than at the district office. In addition, provision should be made within the school budget for the purchase of those supplies and materials necessary for the psychologist, social worker, and nurse to operate effectively. Perhaps the best approach would be for the administrator to think of a total pupil services program and budget.

Although the psychological, social, and health services components of the pupil services program cannot succeed without administrators carrying out the tasks previously identified, the most important responsibility for the administrator is to provide leadership. Whether psychological, social, and health services are administered by someone at the central office or at the building level, the program cannot be successful without the leadership of building administrators. Specifically, their leadership responsibilities include the following:

1. Helping students, teachers, and parents to better understand the roles and functions of the school psychologist, social worker, and health workers. The functions and roles of these pupil services specialists are poorly understood in many schools. The building administrator who is willing to help develop an understanding on the part of others about these specialists' contributions to the school does much to increase the effectiveness of the pupil services program.
2. Working with pupil services specialists to increase their awareness of the unmet psychological, social, and health needs of students, and stimulating the development of greater vision about how these needs might be met.
3. Working with pupil services specialists, guidance counselors, and other faculty members to help these groups see how they can work together more cooperatively and productively.
4. Assisting pupil personnel specialists to evaluate their own effectiveness and the overall usefulness of the pupil services program.

ISSUES AND PROBLEMS

Administrators need to be aware of four major problems or issues associated with the delivery of psychological, social, and health services to the school. These are (1) inaccessibility, (2) underutilization, (3) inadequate coordination, and (4) difficulty of supervision.[75]

Inaccessibility

Because the psychologist, social worker, and nurse are usually part-time members of a school staff and have somewhat unpredictable work schedules, they are often not available to students, teachers, parents, or administrators when a problem arises. A person experiencing trouble frequently needs help immediately, or at least during the same day, and does not want to be told to wait until the next day or later in the week when the pupil services specialist is scheduled to arrive at the school. Although pupil services specialists might be called to schools in response to problems (if they can be located at another school or at their offices in the central administration building), such calls are not generally made unless an extreme emergency exists. Consequently, in the eyes of many students, teachers, and administrators, the limited accessibility of part-time pupil services workers poses a restriction severely hampering the effectiveness of the program.

The ideal solution to this problem would be the full-time assignment of a school psychologist, social worker, and nurse to each school. While an argument could be made that there is sufficient work for these specialists even in a small school, financial considerations and a limited vision of their potential contribution often rule out this possibility. Certain steps, though, should be taken by administrators to alleviate the inaccessibility problem.

1. Administrators should try to secure from each of the part-time pupil personnel specialists a commitment to an established work schedule at the school. In too many situations these specialists do not keep any scheduled office hours at a school and, as a result, others at the school do not know when their services are available. There may, of course, be times when a pupil services specialist is not able to keep office hours because of an emergency at another school. But generally it should be possible for all of the specialists to identify at the beginning of the year the hours when they will make their services available at each school.

2. Administrators should ascertain from each of the part-time specialists what their work schedules are when they are not at the school so that they can be reached if an emergency arises. This information may be difficult to obtain because the pupil services specialists may not have their work schedules well organized, or they may be apprehensive that the information may be used for monitoring their performance. In spite of any resistance administrators may receive when they seek this information, they have an obligation to find out where the pupil services specialists are most likely to be located when they are not in the school.

3. Administrators should communicate at the beginning of the year to students, parents, and teachers the work schedule of the part-time pupil services personnel at the school and indicate the procedures to follow to reach these specialists at other times. If people in the school are to utilize the services of the pupil personnel specialists, the schedule of their availability should be made common knowledge. And it is the administrators' responsibility to see that this information is communicated.

Underutilization

Judging from observation and comments by administrators and teachers, the services of psychologists, social workers, and perhaps nurses, are not being utilized to the extent that one might hope and expect. Many problems are not referred to these specialists simply because students, teachers, and administrators do not perceive that the specialists can be of any help, or because they are not sure how to work with them. In other cases, these specialists are loaded down with testing or routine tasks which do not capitalize on their creative contributions. Part of the problem lies in an inadequate understanding about the role of pupil services specialists and what services they can provide. Administrators can help ameliorate this problem by becoming better informed about the role of each of the pupil services specialists. But beyond that, they should take the initiative in helping the pupil services specialists to develop a better understanding of their roles.

Administrators probably also need to take a look at the school's referral procedures to these specialists. Referral procedures represent the main mechanism for utilizing the services of the pupil personnel specialists. So, if the referral procedures are inadequate or unclear, utilization of the pupil personnel specialists is limited. In essence, a school's referral procedures should include the following characteristics:

1. The types of problems which can be referred to either the psychologist, the social worker, or the nurse should be explicitly defined to the school staff.
2. Individuals who make referrals should be asked to state briefly the nature of the problems and their perceptions of the causes.
3. The faculty should know when the pupil services specialist will be at the school to receive the referral.
4. After the referral is received, there should be a preliminary conference between the individual submitting the referral and the pupil services specialist to determine the best plan of action for coordinating efforts.
5. An initial progress report by the pupil services specialist should be made within a week to the person who submitted the referral; a more complete report should be provided by the end of the semester during which the referral was initiated.

A referral form incorporating most of these characteristics is presented in figure 13.3.

Inadequate Coordination

Inadequate coordination of services is frequently a problem when two or more specialists are working with the same client. This problem is particularly prevalent in the pupil services program. All too often psychologists, social workers, nurses, and guidance counselors work independently, "doing their own thing," with little or no attempt to coordinate efforts in a unified approach.

Although pupil services specialists can make independent contributions to the school, their efforts would be significantly strengthened through a coordinated, collaborative approach to delivering pupil services.[76] Methods for developing such an approach could include organizing the various specialists into a pupil services team, appointing someone to coordinate the efforts of the team at the building level (perhaps the guidance director), establishing regular meetings of the team to focus on collaborative efforts and using the case conference procedure in working with students who have problems. This approach is especially appropriate for diagnosing and working with special education students.

The pupil services specialists may not be inclined or able to develop the team approach without administrative assistance. They may be used to working independently and may not see the need to work together in a collaborative effort. Therefore, administrators may need to take the initiative to organize the specialists into a pupil services team and appoint someone to lead that team.

Administrators would do well to involve the pupil services specialists in developing the concept of the team and how it should function, if they desire the specialists' cooperation. The idea of the team should not be imposed on its members. They may harbor mixed feelings about the team's merits, having previously been working independently. Those pupil services specialists who work out of the central office and spend only part time in a particular building may also resist the notion of someone at the building level heading their team. In this regard, administrators may define the main responsibility of the team leader as that of coordination rather than supervision. If the right team leaders are chosen, they should be able to exercise supervisory responsibilities informally.

Once the team concept has been accepted, the team organized, and a leader appointed, the scheduling of periodic meetings becomes important. Finding a time when everyone can be at the meetings is a difficult task for a team primarily composed of part-time specialists with different work schedules. Despite the problems involved, administrators should insist that teams meet at least monthly and more often as the need arises. A team cannot function effectively unless it meets often enough to develop a common frame of reference and cooperative efforts in problem solving. A good way for administrators to keep informed about the operation of teams is to request that the leaders send them copies of agendas and minutes for all team meetings. This procedure should result not only in administrators becoming better informed of the functioning of the pupil services team but may also cause team leaders to become better organized if they know that this information is expected.

An important team activity which administrators should try to promote on the part of the pupil services specialists is the case conference. The case conference is a meeting at which the various pupil services specialists, with relevant others, try to understand the problems of a particular student by examining the perceptions and data which each can contribute about the student. By utilizing and pooling the information and expertise of all appropriate parties, an insight into the student's problem and a possible resolution for it may be obtained—one perhaps not possible had a single specialist been working with the student independently.

Most pupil services specialists know about the case conference method, but because someone must take the initiative to organize the conference, it is not used often enough. To promote its use, administrators might assign their pupil services team leaders the responsibility for organizing such meetings and then request that team leaders report to them each semester about how many case conferences were held and with what success.

Tradition, current practice, and the varied work schedules of the pupil services specialists all mitigate against a coordinated, collaborative team approach; thus, it takes considerable vision, commitment, and human relations skills on the part of administrators to achieve this goal. There is little doubt, however, that such an approach is necessary for a totally effective pupil personnel program.

Supervision Difficulty

Perhaps the most perplexing problem for school administrators in regard to the pupil services specialists is how best to supervise them. The problem is threefold: First of all, each of the pupil services workers possesses specialized knowledge and skills which most administrators have not acquired and probably would have difficulty obtaining. The problems involved in trying to supervise personnel who perform tasks for which supervisors themselves are not proficient are readily apparent to all who have been in such a situation.

Second, the work performed by pupil services specialists is typically not visible to administrators because it is frequently carried out in privacy. This aspect of the problem is further compounded by the part-time nature of the specialists' work schedules.

Third, pupil services specialists probably perceive their superior in the district office as their only legitimate supervisor and may resist efforts by anyone at the building level to supervise them.

In many schools this set of problems has resulted in little or no building-level supervision of pupil services specialists. Of course, some supervision of these specialists is conducted by their superiors at the district level. But the latter individuals' concept of supervision may be limited, or they may be spread too thin by the considerable number of people they have to supervise. Therefore, it would appear that if pupil services specialists are to be supervised at the building level, school administrators have to design a system to accomplish the task.

Because administrators are not experts in pupil services and are involved with many other supervisory responsibilities, their best approach with the pupil services specialists may be to establish a system of supervision by objectives, or results management. This system of supervision includes the following steps:

1. Pupil services specialists would be asked at the beginning of every semester to identify the objectives they hope to achieve while working at the school. Proposed objectives might be requested for the areas of students, teachers, parents, and collaborative efforts. Objectives could be updated during the semester as a result of new developments.
2. At the end of each semester, all pupil services specialists would be requested to prepare and submit a short report indicating the progress which had been made in achieving the previously proposed objectives, the evidence for such progress, and the problems encountered in trying to achieve the objectives.
3. After the report is read by the administrator, each pupil services specialist would meet with the administrator to review the report's contents and discuss any possible need for improvement. The report could be a vehicle for initiating follow-up supervisory activities.

In light of the problems previously discussed, it is unlikely that administrators can or should engage in direct supervision of pupil services specialists. Even so, they should institute a system of supervision to help specialists evaluate their own performance and, at the same time, keep administrators better informed of that performance. The supervision by objectives results management approach to evaluation and supervision is such a system.

Review and Learning Activities

1. Define the primary purpose of the pupil personnel services program and the counseling and guidance program.
2. Identify the services that the counseling and guidance program can provide to groups associated with the school. What is the role of administrators in developing appropriate uses of those services?
3. Examine the special education program operating in your school and compare it with the program described in the text. How could the special education program in your school be improved?
4. How should school administrators make use of the counselor role description developed by the American Personnel and Guidance Association?
5. In which ways can administrators make a leadership and an administrative contribution to the counseling and guidance program?
6. Which three major issues or problems are frequently associated with the counseling and guidance program? How can administrators best prevent or ameliorate these problems?
7. In which ways can administrators make leadership and administrative contributions to improving the psychological, social, and health services of the school?
8. Describe the major issues and problems that frequently are associated with the psychological, social, and health services of the school. How can administrators best prevent or ameliorate these problems?

NOTES

1. See Daniel D. Sage and Leonard C. Burrello, *Policy and Management in Special Education* (Englewood Cliffs, N.J.: Prentice-Hall, 1986), chap. 1; and J. M. Kauffmann, *Characteristics of Behavior Disorders of Children and Youth,* 4th ed. (Columbus, Ohio: Merrill Publishing Company, 1989).

2. T. Page Johnson, *The Principal's Guide to the Educational Rights of Handicapped Students* (Reston, Va.: National Association of Secondary School Principals, 1986), chap. 1.

3. Education for All Handicapped Children Act, P.L. 94–142, United States Code, *20,* 1401 et seq.

4. Martha M. McCarthy, "Public Law 94–142 and Its Implications for Nonhandicapped Students," in M. A. McGhehey, ed., *Contemporary Legal Issues in Education* (Topeka, Kan.: National Organization on Legal Problems of Education, 1979), 138. For further discussion regarding the controversy surrounding 94–142, see Sage and Burrello, *Policy and Management in Special Education,* 55–56; and S. S. Goldberg, "The Failure of Legalization in Education: Alternative Dispute Resolution and the Education for All Handicapped Children Act of 1975," *Journal of Law and Education* (Summer 1989): 441–54.

5. "Education of Handicapped Children: Implementation of Part B of the Education of the Handicapped Act, Rules and Regulations," *Federal Register* (August 23, 1977), 474–518.

6. Education for All Handicapped Children Act, United States Code, *20,* sec. 4.

7. Education for All Handicapped Children Act, United States Code, *20,* sec. 1401 et seq.

8. Alice H. Hayden and Eugene Edgar, "Developing Individualized Education Programs for Young Handicapped Children," *Teaching Exceptional Children* (Spring 1978): 67–70.

9. LeRoy Aserlind and Ellen Browning, *Minds into the Mainstream* (Dubuque, Iowa: Kendall/Hunt Publishing Co., 1987), 53.

10. Jacqueline Reeves, "An In-Depth Study of the Mainstream Individual Education Plan in an Urban School District" (Ed.D. diss., University of Massachusetts, 1980). See also William McInerney and Stuart Swenson, "The Principal's Role in the Multi-Disciplinary Assessment Team," *NASSP Bulletin* (December 1988): 88–93.

11. *Federal Register* 41, no. 252 (December 30, 1976), 56986 and sec. 121 or 432, 56991.

12. Hayden and Edgar, "Developing Individualized Education Programs," 68.

13. Oversight Hearings, U.S. Senate Subcommittee on the Handicapped, July 1980 (Comments by Albert Shanker, A.F.T.). See also Sage and Burrello, *Policy and Management in Special Education,* 55–56.

14. Reported in *Education U.S.A.* (December 22, 1980), 137.

15. Reported in *Education U.S.A.* (May 1980), 285.

16. Ibid.

17. Lawrence Gaines, "Parental Satisfaction with Evaluation and Planning Team Conferences" (Ph.D. diss., University of California, 1981).

18. T. Page Johnson, "The Right to Due Process," *The Principal's Guide to the Educational Rights of Handicapped Students* (Reston, Va.: National Association of Secondary School Principals, 1986), chap. 4.

19. Research for Better Schools, *Exploring Issues in the Implementation of P.L. 94-142,* (Philadelphia: Research for Better Schools, 1979). Also see *P. L. 94-142, Section 504 and P. L. 99-457: Understanding What They Are and Are Not* (Reston, Va.: Council for Exceptional Children, 1987).

20. LeRoy Aserlind and Ellen R. Browning, *Minds into the Mainstream* (Dubuque, Iowa: Kendall/Hunt Publishing Co., 1987), 44–45.

21. Maynard Reynolds, ed., *Mainstreaming: Origins and Implications* (Reston, Va.: Council for Exceptional Education, 1976), 43.

22. Barry Guinagh, "The School Integration of Handicapped Children," *Kappan* (September 1980): 27–31. See also John O'Neil, "How 'Special' Should the Special Ed Curriculum Be?" *ASCD Update* (September 1988): 1–8.

23. Ganelda Sowers, *Observations of a Primary School Principal after Four Years of Experience with Mainstreaming* (ERIC Report Ed–153–342).

24. Marleen C. Pugach and Lawrence J. Johnson, "Peer Collaboration: Enhancing Teacher Problem-Solving Capabilities for Students at Risk." Paper presented at the annual meeting of the American Educational Research Association, New Orleans, 1988. See also Maynard C. Reynolds and Jack W. Birch, *Adaptive Mainstreaming: A Primer for Teachers and Principals,* 3d ed. (White Plains, N.Y.: Longman, 1988).

25. Maureen A. White et al., "Returning Students from Special to Regular Classes," *The Pointer* (Fall 1979): 97–104. See also David E. Greenburg, *A Special Educator's Perspective on Interfacing Special and General Education: A Review for Administrators* (Reston, Va.: Council for Exceptional Children, 1987).

26. John Salvia and Susan Munson, "Attitudes of Regular Education Teachers toward Mainstreaming Mildly Handicapped Students," in C. Julius Meisal, *Mainstreaming Handicapped Children: Outcomes, Controversies, and New Directions* (Hillsdale, N.J.: Lawrence Erlbaum Associates, 1986).

27. Barbara Larrivee and Linda Cook, "Mainstreaming: A Study of Variables Affecting Teacher Attitude," *The Journal of Special Education* (Fall 1979): 315–24. For a more recent discussion of teachers' attitudes, see Cheryll Duquette and Robert R. O'Reilly, "Perceived Attributes of Mainstreaming, Principal Change Strategy, and Teacher Attitudes toward Mainstreaming," *The Alberta Journal of Educational Research* (December 1988): 390–402.

28. Duquette and O'Reilly, "Perceived Attributes of Mainstreaming." 399.

29. Ibid.

30. Sage and Burrello, *Policy and Management in Special Education,* N.J.: 272–95.

31. Gary D. Borich and Deborah D. Nance, "Evaluating Special Education Programs: Shifting the Professional Mandate from Process to Outcome," *Remedial and Special Education* (May–June 1987):7–16.

32. Jeremy J. Lietz and Maxine Towle, "The Principal's Role in Special Education Services," *Educational Research Quarterly* (Fall 1980): 12–20.

33. Daniel P. Hallahan, James M. Kauffman, John Wills Lloyd, and James D. McKinney, *Introduction to the Series: Questions about the Regular Education Initiative* (January 1988): 3–5.

34. John O'Neil, "The 'Regular Education Initiative': Seeking Integration between Special, Regular Education," *ASCD Update* (September 1988): 4.

35. Leroy Aserlind and Ellen R. Browning, *Minds into the Mainstream* (Dubuque, Iowa: Kendall/Hunt Publishing, 1987); and Donald S. Marozas and Deborah C. May, *Issues and Practices in Special Education* (White Plains, N.Y.: Longman, 1988).

36. Gary M. Miller, "Counselor Functions in Excellent Schools: Elementary through Secondary," *The School Counselor* (November 1988): 88–93.

37. American School Counselor Association, *Proposed Statement of Policy for Secondary School Counselors* (Washington, D.C.: American School Counselor Assn., 1964), 4; also see Norman C. Gysbers and Patricia Handerson, *Developing and Managing Your School Guidance Program* (Alexandria, Va.: American Association for Counseling and Development, 1988); and S. Ehly and R. Dustin, *Individual and Group Counseling in Schools* (New York: Guilford Press, 1989).

38. Figure 15.1 was developed from an extraction and synthesis of statements contained in *Policy for Secondary School Counselors* (Washington, D.C.: American School Counselors Association, 1964); and Gysbers and Handerson, *Developing and Managing Your School Guidance Program.*

39. "The Role of the Secondary School Counselor," *School Counselor* (May 1974): 380–86.

40. Richard S. Podemski and John H. Childers, Jr., "The School Counselor's Role: Reexamination and Revitalization," *Planning and Changing* (Spring 1987): 17–22.

41. Figure 15.3 was adapted from the role description presented in "The Unique Role of the Elementary School Counselor," *Elementary School Guidance and Counseling* (March 1974): 221–23; and Carol Lynn Morse and Todd Russell, "How Elementary Counselors See Their Role: An Empirical Study," *Elementary School Guidance & Counseling* (October 1988): 54–62.

42. Julian Biggers, "The Elementary School Counselor in Texas: A Nine-Year Follow-Up," *Elementary School Guidance and Counseling* (October 1977): 15–19. These findings are consistent with those of more recent studies on elementary counselors' role perceptions. See Carol Lynn Morse and Todd Russell, "How Elementary Counselors See Their Role: An Empirical Study," *Elementary School Guidance & Counseling* (October 1988): 54–62; T. J. Russo and W. Kassera, "A Comprehensive Needs-Assessment Package for Secondary School Guidance Programs," *The School Counselor* (March 1989): 265–69; and W. W. Tennyson et al., "How They View Their Role: A Survey of Counselors in Different Secondary Schools," *Journal of Counseling and Development* (March 1989): 399–403.

43. Pamela J. Wilson, *School Counseling Programs: A Resource and Planning Guide* (Madison: Wisconsin Department of Public Instruction, 1986); and Charles L. Thompson and Linda B. Rudolph, *Counseling Children,* 2d ed. (Pacific Grove, Calif.: Brooks/Cole Publishing Co., 1988).

44. William R. Watts, "What Can One Expect from a School's Guidance Director?" *NASSP Bulletin* (October 1981): 34–37.

45. For an excellent monograph which describes the administrator's responsibilities in detail, see William A. Matthes and Robert Frank, *Strategies for Implementation of Guidance in the Elementary School* (ERIC Report Ed–048–602), 187–216.

46. Based on a number of interviews with professors of counseling and guidance.

47. Charles W. Humes and Thomas H. Hohenshil, "Elementary Counselors, School Psychologists, School Social Workers: Who Does What?" *Elementary School Guidance and Counseling* (October 1987): 37–45. Also see recent issues of *Elementary School Guidance and Counseling* and *School Counselor.*

48. Ruth S. Armstrong, *The Teacher as a Counselor* (ERIC Report Ed–187–663).

49. John R. Nattermann, "Teachers as Advisors: Complementing School Guidance Programs," *NASSP Bulletin* (September 1988): 121–24.

50. Marguerite R. Carroll, "Standards for Guidance and Counseling Programs," *The School Counselor* (November 1980): 81–86.

51. Arlene Breckenridge, "Performance Improvement Program Helps Administrators Assess Counselor Performance," *NASSP Bulletin* (May 1987); 23–28; Anita M. Mitchell, "Educational Excellence for All Students: Assessing the Adequacy of Your Counseling Program," *NASSP Bulletin* (December 1985): 23–27; and James Wiggins, "Six Steps toward Counseling Program Accountability," *NASSP Bulletin* (December 1985): 28–31.

52. Podemski and Childers, Jr., "The School Counselor's Role," 19.

53. Richard Hughes and Richard Shofer, "The Role of the School Psychologist: Revisited," *The School Psychology Digest* (Winter 1977): 22–29. For a more recent discussion, see Dorothy Pierson-Hubeny and Francis X. Archambault, "Role Stress and Perceived Intensity of Burnout among School Psychologists," *Psychology in the Schools* (July 1987): 244–53.

54. David H. Reilly, "School Psychology: The Continuing Search," *Psychology in the Schools* (January 1984): 66–70. Figure 15.4 is adapted from *Training Programs, Field Placements, and Credentialing Standards in School Psychology* (Washington, D.C.: National Association of School Psychologists, 1984), 27–34; and Noel LaCayo et al., "Daily Activities of School Psychologists: A National Survey," *Psychology in the Schools* (April 1981): 184–90.

55. Herbert H. Severson, Marianne Pickett, and Deborah J. Hetrick, "Comparing Preservice, Elementary, and Junior High Teachers' Perceptions of School Psychologists: Two Decades Later," *Psychology in the Schools* (April 1985): 179–86; and Douglas K. Smith and Mark A. Lyon, "Consultation in School Psychology: Changes from 1981 to 1984," *Psychology in the Schools* (October 1985): 404–9.

56. Charles A. Maker, "Guidelines for Planning and Evaluating School Psychology Services," *Journal of School Psychology* (Fall 1979): 203–12. See also Donald J. Dickinson and Sandy Adcox, "Program Evaluation of a School Consultation Program," *Psychology in the Schools* (July 1984): 336–42.

57. John C. Nebo, *Administration of School Social Work* (New York: National Association of Social Workers, 1960), 17.

58. Robert H. Mathewson, *Guidance Policies and Practice,* 3d ed. (New York: Harper & Row, 1962), 197.

59. Based largely on *NASW Standards for Social Work Services in Schools,* Policy Statement No. 7 (Washington, D.C.: National Association of Social Workers, 1978). For a related discussion see Isadore Hare, "School Social Work and Effective Schools," *Urban Education* (January 1988): 413–28.

60. Robert Constable and Herbert Walberg, "School Social Work: Facilitating Home, School, and Community Partnerships," *Urban Education* (January 1988): 429–43. And P. David Kurtz, "Social Work Services to Parents: Essential to Pupils at Risk," *Urban Education* (January 1988): 444–59.

61. Byron B. Nelson, Jr., "Principal's Commitment: A Key to Success," *Health Education* (October–November 1988): 6.

62. Georgia MacDonough, "School Health, 1977," *Journal of School Health* (September 1977): 425–27.

63. A. I. Rothman and N. Byre, "Health Education for Children and Adolescents," *Review of Educational Research* (Spring 1981): 85–100. See also David C. King, "Broad-Based Support Pushes Health Education beyond What the Coach Does between Seasons," *ASCD Curriculum Update* (June 1986): 1–8; and Joel D. Killen and Thomas N. Robinson, "School-Based Research on Health Behavior Change: The Stanford Adolescent Heart Health Program as a Model for Cardiovascular Disease Risk Reduction," in *Review of Research in Education,* ed. Ernst Z. Rothkopf (Washington, D.C.: American Educational Research Association, 1988): 171–200.

64. Charles C. Wilson, *School Health Services* (Washington, D.C.: National Education Association and American Medical Association, 1964).

65. Godfrey Cronin and William Young, *400 Navels: The Future of School Health in America* (Bloomington, Ind.: Phi Delta Kappa, 1980).

66. Based in large part on *Guidelines for the School Nurse in the School Health Program* (Kent, Ohio: American School Health Association, 1974). Also see Julia Muennich Cowell, "Health Services Utilization and Special Education: Development of a School Nurse Activity Tool," *Journal of School Health* (November 1988): 355–59.

67. Nancy Mathis, "School Nurses Seek Broader Role in Wake of New Health Concerns," *Education Week* (August 3, 1988): 11.

68. Michael Resnick et al., "Adolescent Perceptions of the School Nurse," *Journal of School Health* (December 1980): 551–54. See also Eva Miller and Joyce W. Hopp, "Perceptions of School Nursing by School Districts," *Journal of School Health* (May 1988): 197–99.

69. Char Tosi, "Role of the School Nurse as Perceived by Administrators, Teachers, and Students" (Research study, University of Wisconsin-Milwaukee, 1979).

70. Ruth Rich, "Scheduling and Staffing School-Based Health Education," *Health Education* (October–November 1988): 26–28.

71. Ibid., 26.

72. Floyd Boshee, "Comprehensive School Health Education: Directives for Development and Implementation," *Health Education* (October–November 1988): 36–38; Nathan L. Essex, Harold L. Bishop, and Lanny Gamble, "Five Critical Elements for School District AIDS Policies," *Record* (Fall 1989): 4–6; and *Drug Abuse* (Bloomington, Ind.: Phi Delta Kappa, 1987).

73. E. T. Lon Luty, "Controversial Topics in a Health Education Program," *Health Education* (October–November 1988): 39–43.

74. Boshee, "Comprehensive School Health Education."

75. These problems or issues were identified in a review of the literature and in a supplementary interview survey of principals, teachers, and pupil personnel service specialists.

76. For an example of this approach, see Jeffrey Zdrale, *Pupil Personnel Committee Meetings in Our Schools* (ERIC Report Ed–177–446).

16

• • • • •

Administration of the Student Activities Program

■

The student activities program, also referred to as the "extracurricular" or "cocurricular" program,* has been an accepted part of American education for many years.[1] Initially introduced in only a few schools to provide for the recreational and athletic interests and needs of students, it is now an integral component of the total educational program in the vast majority of schools in the United States.†

Even though the overall responsibility for administering the student activities program is sometimes delegated to a student activities director, in most schools the building administrator is assigned this responsibility directly and certainly is ultimately accountable. Therefore, school administrators must develop a comprehensive understanding of the various facets of the activities program so that they can operate it with efficiency and effectiveness. Included in this understanding should be knowledge about the objectives, scope, and organizational dimensions of the program, as well as its major problems. Administrators should also be knowledgeable about criteria and plans for evaluating the program because without regular assessment, improvement of the program is likely to be limited.

*We use the term *student activities* in this chapter rather than other terms because in practice it is the one authorities prefer.

†Although some people may believe that the student activities program is or should be confined to the secondary school, the program has been recommended for the elementary school for some time. See Harry C. McKown, *Activities in the Elementary School* (New York: McGraw-Hill Book Co., 1938).

PURPOSE, OBJECTIVES, AND SCOPE

The primary purpose of the student activities program has been and continues
to be that of meeting students' school-related interests and needs which are
not met—at least not to a sufficient degree—by the curricular program of the
school.[2] The objectives of the student activities program may vary somewhat
from school to school, depending on local conditions, but they should be logically related to the objectives of the overall educational program. Numerous
statements of student activities objectives have been proposed during the years;
an examination of these statements suggests the objectives of the program
should be to help *all* students to:

1. Learn how to use their leisure time more wisely.
2. Increase and use constructively whatever unique talents and skills
   they possess.
3. Develop new avocational and recreational interests and skills.
4. Develop a more positive attitude toward the value of avocational
   and recreational activities.
5. Increase their knowledge of and skill in functioning as a leader
   and/or as a member of a group.
6. Develop a more realistic and positive attitude toward themselves
   and others.
7. Develop a more positive attitude toward school, as a result of
   participation in the student activities program.[3]

The key word in the statements reviewed is the word *all*. The student
activities program should be for *all* students, not just the more active and
talented students; the objectives of the program should reflect this priority.
(In response to the public's criticism of academic standards, many schools
have considered imposing a no-pass no-play rule governing access to student
activities.)[4] While it may not be possible in some situations for all students to
participate in the activities program, total participation should remain the objective to which a school aspires. A school aiming at a higher objective than
may seem attainable is ultimately likely to accomplish more than the one with
more "practical" goals.[5]

The preceding objectives emphasize helping the students, not just providing an opportunity for them. A school should be responsible for more than
just providing an opportunity for students; it should be responsible for helping
students reach whatever objectives that opportunity is supposed to engender.
These objectives should include the development of certain student attitudes,
as well as knowledge and skills. Perhaps the most important objective of a

school's student activities program should be the development of a more positive attitude by students toward themselves, others, avocational and recreational activities, and toward school in general. These attitudinal objectives undoubtedly are difficult for schools to achieve but, if attained, are likely to show great carryover value into students' adult lives.

To achieve the knowledge, skill, and attitudinal objectives of the student activities program, the school should provide a comprehensive range of student activities including the offerings presented in figure 16.1.

The activities identified under each major category in figure 16.1 are illustrative of possible student activities.[6] Of course, different schools offer different activities, depending on the needs and interests of the students, as well as other conditions. In addition, the extent of the activities differs according to whether the school is elementary or secondary. However, two extremely important factors are the vision and commitment of the administration and staff to a comprehensive student activities program. Unless administrators and staff members of a school have the vision to develop comprehensive objectives for the total student activities program and the commitment to invest their own time and energy to achieve those objectives, the program will probably have a limited impact on the student body.

The main purpose of a student activities program should be to meet students' interests and needs. Without the vision and commitment of the administration and the staff, this purpose cannot be achieved; therefore, administrators are responsible for generating that vision and commitment on the part of the staff.

Figure 16.1 Major Activities Included in a Comprehensive Student Activities Program.*

Student Government and Publications	Performance Groups	Clubs and Organizations	Intramurals Boys' and Girls'	Athletics Boys' and Girls'
Student Council	Dramatics	Chess Club	Bowling	Basketball
Student Newspaper	Instrumental	Photography Club	Golf	Swimming
Student Yearbook	Vocal	Literary Club	Ping Pong	Tennis
Others	Debate	French Club	Others	Others
	Others	Others		

ORGANIZATIONAL DIMENSIONS

The emphasis thus far has been on the objectives and scope of the student activities program and on the vision and commitment of the administration and staff. However, if the program is to succeed, it must also be well organized. Good organization does not ensure the success of a program, but without it a program is likely to flounder.

In organizing the student activities program, administrators should consider the following principles:

1. **Each activity, as well as the total program, should have well-defined, written objectives.** The importance of establishing objectives for the total student activities program has already been noted. Administrators must work with teachers and students to define the objectives of each activity within the program. Activities without objectives lack direction and meaning and their effectiveness is difficult to evaluate.

In developing the objectives for each student activity in the program, the administrator should make sure that they are stated in the form of outcomes, that is, as increased knowledge, skill, attitude, or participation, rather than in the number of meetings of the activity.[7] The important thing is not how many meetings of an activity occur, but what the activity contributes in increased student participation, knowledge, skill, or attitude change.

2. **Each activity should be directed by a well-qualified, interested advisor.** This is easier said than achieved, and it may be an unattainable ideal for certain activities. However, obtaining well-qualified, interested advisors for the various components of the student activities program should be the objective to which administrators are committed. They should do everything within their power to achieve, or at least be working toward, that objective.[8]

To a large extent, the advisor of an activity is the key to its success. A competent, interested advisor can provide leadership and spark to a student activity; a poorly qualified, apathetic advisor can ruin it. Even a moderately qualified and interested advisor may not be able to provide the leadership necessary for an activity to blossom and grow.[9] The problem of securing competent, interested advisors is addressed later in the chapter.

3. **There should be a written role description for each advisor, as well as a developmental in-service program to upgrade competencies.** Each advisor to a student activity should have a written role description specifying the qualifications and responsibilities of the position, and the individuals and groups to whom the advisor reports.[10] Such a role description provides direction to advisors and can serve as a basis for evaluating the effectiveness of their work. In the absence of this role description, advisors have to create their own definition of their responsibilities, making an evaluation of their effectiveness by the administrator difficult.

A developmental in-service program to upgrade advisors' competencies is essential, particularly if the administrator has been less than completely successful in recruiting well-qualified advisors.[11] It seems peculiar that in-service education is provided for almost every other need, but apparently it is assumed that student activities advisors are all well-qualified and are never in need of updating their skills.

A developmental in-service program for student activities advisors should include learning opportunities for improving their skills in planning and organizing activities, decision making, communication, leadership, group dynamics, and program evaluation.[12] The in-service program should also regularly provide opportunities for all the advisors to discuss problems and ideas and to learn from each other.

Student activities advisors also can benefit from the experiences and recommendations of outside experts working in this field. Membership and participation in state and national associations of student activities advisors are probably the best ways of acquiring this assistance. Administrators should assume the responsibility for encouraging and stimulating this kind of professional growth.

4. **There should be written role descriptions for the student officers of each activity, and an in-service program should be offered to help them improve their competencies.** In many schools the student activities program seems to be based on the implicit assumption that the students elected or appointed to office are already familiar with all aspects of their jobs, and that they need no training to help them carry out their responsibilities effectively. Though there may be exceptions, in general this assumption is unwarranted.

Students are seldom familiar with the various responsibilities of the office to which they are elected or appointed and usually need on-the-job training. They should be provided with role descriptions identifying the qualifications and responsibilities of their positions, and with an in-service program to help them improve their leadership skills.* Specifically, they need help in improving their knowledge and ability in planning and organizing activities, decision making, communication, leadership, group dynamics, and program evaluation.[13] They also need to participate in state and national student activities associations; school administrators should see that the professional literature from these associations is accessible to the students.*

*An example of the type of role description needed for all student officers can be found in *Profiles of Student Council Officers* (Reston, Va.: National Association of Secondary School Principals).

*For example, the Division of Student Activities of the National Association of Secondary School Principals conducts workshops and publishes material for students involved in the student activities programs of their schools. School administrators should see to it that representative students have an opportunity to attend these workshops and to receive materials published by the NASSP Division of Student Activities.

5. **The various organizational meetings that are held as part of the student activities program should be well planned.** With the possible exception of performance groups, intramurals, and athletics, there are many organizational meetings held during the year by various student organizations. Because students and advisors are usually busy, these meetings are frequently not well planned.

If the meetings of an organization are to be successful, however, thought and time must be devoted to planning them. This includes a planning session between the advisor and the officers prior to the meeting, and a written agenda sent to the missing members of the organization before the meeting so that thought can be given to what will be discussed. Written minutes of the main points discussed and the actions taken during each meeting should also be sent to all missing members of the organization so that continuity between meetings is increased. The minutes maintain a public record during the year (and from year to year) on what the student organization is accomplishing. These basic management procedures may seem like red tape but, if constructively applied, they should increase the productivity of student organizations' meetings.

6. **A complete, written description of the total student activities program should be disseminated to students and other appropriate parties at the beginning of each school year.** The student activities program is for the students and, if they are to participate wisely, they need as much information as possible about the various aspects of the program. Perhaps the best approach for a school would be to publish a student activities handbook. Included in the handbook should be a description of each student group's purposes, objectives, types of activities, and the qualifications for membership and to hold office, as well as the advisor's name and who should be contacted about membership or for more information.[14]

This handbook could not only be very helpful to students in choosing their participation in the student activities program but could also provide a valuable source of information to the student advisors, the administration, and the rest of the professional staff. The handbook would need to be updated periodically to provide students with current information regarding all aspects of the student activities program.

7. **There should be a director of student activities and a student/teacher advisory council for the total program.** In too many schools the student activities program is composed of numerous groups and organizations, each seemingly going its separate way with very little overall program planning, coordination, or direction. As a result, there are conflicts in philosophy, use of facilities, membership criteria, and allocation of funds.

What is needed is a student activities director to take charge of the overall program, with an advisory group that can work with this individual in establishing policy for the total program and resolving significant disputes between student groups. The director should be an administrator or a teacher with released time, and at least one-third of the director's time should be devoted to carrying out leadership responsibilities.[15]

The activities director should chair the student activities advisory council and be responsible for calling meetings, stimulating discussion, and problem solving. The membership of the council should include representation from students, as well as from the activities advisors, and should function in an advisory capacity with the director. Through this organizational structure, better direction and coordination for the overall student activities program should result.

8. **The total student activities program and each of the component activities should be periodically evaluated to ascertain effectiveness and to identify areas in need of improvement.** According to Alyce Holland and Thomas Andre, appropriate measures for evaluation may include skills gained, changes in peer groups or models, exposure to different values, academic achievement, popularity, educational aspirations, educational accomplishments, and self-esteem.[16] The student activities program is like any other program offered by the school in that it needs periodic evaluation. Ideally, the program should be evaluated yearly, but this may not always be possible. James Sandfort noted that "many of the day-to-day problems in dealing with student activities (financing, staffing, and scheduling), and many of the calls for reform that affect student activities have come about because we have been less than effective in evaluating and revising our educational offerings."[17] It would appear that, at the very minimum, the program and each of its constituent parts should receive a thorough evaluation every two or three years. For, as Robert Frederick has observed, "It sometimes happens that particular activities are repeated year after year, not because of a genuine interest and need, but because we have always had them. The form lingers on after the spark of life has died."[18]

School administrators (or student activities directors) are responsible for making sure that student activities programs are evaluated periodically, although they may not be the ones who actually conduct the evaluations. In fact, wise administrators will, in the evaluation of a program, involve advisors and student leaders who participate in that program. While it might become appropriate to call on outside consultants in conducting the evaluation, school administrators are the ones who should initiate and bring to completion the periodic evaluation of the student activities program. If evaluation is neglected, administrators should be held accountable.

A number of excellent statements of recommended criteria are available to the administrator in evaluating a school's activities program.[19] Based on an examination of these statements, administrators should seek answers to the following questions in assessing the program:

a. Is the overall program and each specific activity meeting its objectives of improving student knowledge, skills, attitudes and/ or values? What is the evidence that objectives are being met?

b. What is the extent of student participation in the total program and in each activity? Are a majority of the students participating in the program? What is the evidence in regard to the degree of student participation?

c. Which kinds of students are participating in the program, and what is the nature of their participation? Do the non-college-bound students participate to the same degree as the college-bound students, and if not, why not? Do the girls participate to the same extent as the boys, and if not, why not? Do some students participate too much in the activities program?

d. Is the activities program well balanced and comprehensive, or do some activities dominate? Are any student interests and needs not adequately met by the program?

e. Is the total program and each of the activities well organized? (Specific aspects of organization were discussed previously.)

f. Are all aspects of the program supported sufficiently in terms of availability of facilities, funds, school time, personnel, and recognition? Or are some activities disproportionately supported?

These are questions that administrators should be asking periodically about the student activities program, and which they should be able to answer, if they are fully meeting their responsibilities for evaluating the program. The methods of evaluating the program vary from situation to situation but could include student questionnaires, interviews, analysis of participation data, and observation of organizational factors.[20] When administrators do not feel competent in evaluation methodology, they should seek outside help, but they should not use their own lack of competency to avoid evaluating the program.

9. **Each of the student groups in the student activities program should be required to prepare an end-of-the-year summary status report to be disseminated to all appropriate parties.** If the student activities program is to be administered properly, information is needed relative to the accomplishments of each student group. The general question that needs to be answered is, "What has happened to each student group during the year?" An end-of-the-year summary status report prepared by each student group would help answer that question.

The report need be only two to four pages and could be prepared co-operatively by the advisor to the group and the student officers. It should contain information on the progress, accomplishments, and major unresolved issues and problems evident at the end of the year. Copies of the report should go to the chief administrator of the school, the director of the activities program, and all members of the student group, for their information and reactions. Such a report would be valuable, not only in keeping people informed about the accomplishments and problems of each student group but also in pointing up the need for improvement or a new direction for a group to take. This report would also give administrators the information they need to administer the overall student program effectively.

MAJOR PROBLEMS OF THE STUDENT ACTIVITIES PROGRAM

It is difficult to generalize about the student activities program because of the variations among schools, but it is safe to say that in most districts the programs have not operated without problems.[21] Some of the problems have been associated with specific activities, while others have been rather pervasive throughout the program. In the latter category, the following three problems have persisted through the years: (1) difficulty in obtaining well-qualified, interested advisors; (2) apathy on the part of many students and/or over-involvement on the part of a few students; and (3) problems of financial support.

PROBLEMS IN THE RECRUITING OF ADVISORS

As pointed out earlier, the advisor is a significant key to the success of any student activity. A well-qualified, interested advisor can resuscitate a dying activity and can help a mediocre one to reach greater heights of achievement. A poorly qualified and barely interested advisor, on the other hand, is of little help to a student group and may cause it to deteriorate. Despite the fact that most, if not all administrators recognize the need for obtaining well-qualified, interested advisors, many administrators experience difficulty in securing them.[22] This is particularly true for nonathletic student activities. What seems to be the nature of the problem?

Part of the difficulty in obtaining well-qualified, interested advisors is a result of the recent expansion of girls' athletics and other related activities along with, paradoxically, a reduction of resources due to declining enrollments and/or inflation.[23] While this expansion of student activities was needed and, it could be argued, desirable, the result has been an even greater need for activity advisors with fewer potentially available. Complicating this situation is an apparently growing disinterest on the part of a number of teachers, particularly the more experienced ones, in supervising student activities. However, as Nathan Essex noted, the courts have agreed that school boards and administrators possess broad authority to assign teachers to service outside the regular academic setting even if it is not spelled out in school board policies. If the assignments are "reasonable, not demeaning in nature, and distributed in a fair and equitable manner. . . . Courts have consistently held that activities such as supervising school-sponsored clubs, programs, and activities are reasonably related to teachers' teaching duties even though the teacher's contract may not mention such extra duty assignments."[24] As a result of the courts' general support of teacher assignments to nonteaching duties, it is not surprising that there has been an increase in the number of collective bargaining agreements that limit an administrator's prerogatives in assigning the supervision of a student activity to a teacher.[25]

Another part of the problem is that in many schools certain advisors are paid for their sponsorship of student activities, while advisors of other activities in the same schools receive no reimbursement for their time and effort. For example, advisors to special interest clubs and organizations are frequently unpaid, while coaches of athletics and other performing teams, as well as advisors to publications, receive compensation. Although financial reimbursement should not be the sole motivating force in causing a capable individual to seek the advisorship of a student group, it is nevertheless an important factor that administrators should be realistic about. Potentially well-qualified individuals who might be interested in sponsoring a student club or organization are likely to think twice before volunteering their time and effort for little or no compensation when they see other advisors receiving appropriate remuneration for their contributions to activities.

Compounding the problem of compensation is the fact that in too many schools the salary differentiation among advisors seems to be based more on the status of an activity than on the extent of actual responsibilities. Coaches of athletic teams, for instance, are paid at a higher rate than advisors for intramural sports; advisors to public performance groups such as band or dramatics are paid more than advisors to nonpublic performing groups, such as debate.

Administrators could take additional steps to secure more qualified and interested advisors for the student activities program, such as providing better facilities, flexible scheduling, more funding, and recognition for some of the groups. However, removal of the inequities in the advisors' salary structure would represent the most important action toward improving the situation.

STUDENT APATHY VERSUS OVERINVOLVEMENT

A paradoxical situation that has plagued student activities programs over the years is the problem of student apathy versus overinvolvement. In many schools a large percentage of the student body does not participate in the student activities program. If one were to eliminate participation in athletics from the analysis, it might even be said that in most schools the majority of students do not participate in the activities program.

School administrators and student activities advisors usually attribute a lack of participation to student apathy, which may provide a label for the situation, but fails to explain the causes. The question that administrators and staff members need to investigate is, "Why is there student apathy?" or, "What is there about our program which fails to attract students in larger numbers?" Underlying reasons may include lack of information about the activities, poor scheduling, low status of certain activities, limited activities, restrictive admission requirements for membership in a group (e.g., a C average), and an inadequate understanding of the values to be obtained from participating in the student activities program.[26]

In investigating possible causes of student apathy or lack of participation, administrators need to concentrate on correctable causes rather than uncorrectable causes. Examples of the latter would be (1) outside interests such as television or video arcades, (2) after-school jobs, (3) disinterest in certain activities, and (4) apathetic students. All of these reasons have been given at one time or another as alleged causes of student nonparticipation in school activities. The problem is that these factors are, for the most part, uncorrectable because they are not under the direct influence of the school, or they represent symptoms and labels rather than causes. Instead of focusing on or emphasizing these explanations, administrators need to examine those causes which are correctable, such as (1) unawareness by students of a particular activity; (2) inability to see how an activity might be beneficial or interesting; (3) lack of awareness or inability to envision how they could play a role in a particular activity; (4) uncertainty about how students can get started participating in an activity; (5) conflicts caused by scheduling an activity at a certain time of the day; and (6) lackluster leadership by the activity's advisor.

Perhaps the place to begin in analyzing reasons for student apathy is with the nature of the activities program itself. Such an examination might reveal, as Grace Graham has observed, that "those young people who stand to benefit most from social experience in the activity program have the fewest opportunities to participate, whereas those students who have the least to learn from an activity program have the most opportunity to participate."[27] In some schools, the after-school scheduling of student activities disallows the participation of large numbers of students. Typical solutions to the after-school scheduling problem avoid taking students out during academic time; they include establishing an activity period, using rotating schedules, shortening class periods one day a week to gain time for an activity period, and replacing homerooms with activity periods.[28]

Although student apathy is a much greater problem than student overinvolvement, the latter should also be of concern to administrators. Overinvolvement manifests itself in two ways: (1) certain students get involved in too many activities, reducing the effectiveness of their participation; and (2) in some schools or during a particular period of time, a limited number of students may capture many of the top leadership offices in the activities program, thereby reducing opportunities for leadership growth by other students. Most administrators and student activities advisors seem to be aware of these problems and some have taken steps to remedy the situation by restricting the number of offices any one individual can hold.

However the problem of student overinvolvement in student activities is not an easy one to resolve.[29] Even the question of what constitutes "too much" participation is not readily determined. Obviously, the situation will vary, depending on students and their circumstances.

Part of the problem is that most schools do not even have a mechanism for monitoring the deleterious effect on the student of excessive participation in the activities program, with the possible exception of grade reports. Though grade reports might be useful as one indicator of the problem, grades can be affected by many variables. Perhaps the best steps a school can take are to keep better centralized records of the number of activities in which each student is participating and to ask advisors, counselors, and teachers to be especially observant of those students involved in several activities during a particular nine-week period.

PROBLEMS OF FINANCIAL SUPPORT

Although the public seems to feel that student activities are an important part of the total educational experience, the student activities program is often one of the first programs reduced when budget cuts need to be made.[30] One possible reason why this is true is that the student activities program is still perceived by many as an *extra*curricular program rather than an integral part of a student's education. Complicating the situation is the rising cost of student activities due to an expansion of girls' athletic opportunities and across-the-board inflation. Because of these factors, a number of school districts have had to eliminate certain activities and have increased student fees to support other activities.

The problem of financing student activities is not likely to go away, and it is not a problem for which there are easy solutions. However, a major step in the right direction would be for schools to do better jobs of demonstrating the value of student activities and keeping the public informed about the benefits. Although this step will not eliminate the problem of financing student activities, it will certainly help, and it needs to be begun before a financial crisis, not during one. George Burnett noted that, "In public education, a program's worth should not be judged on its ability to produce revenue, but on its educational value to the students it serves."[31] Recommended guidelines for administering a student activity budget are presented in chapter 6 on budget and plant management.

MAJOR PROBLEMS ASSOCIATED WITH SEVERAL SPECIFIC STUDENT ACTIVITY PROGRAMS

THE ATHLETIC PROGRAM

The athletic program has probably been the most successful of all the student activities, at least in the number of students participating and the degree of esteem awarded it by the school and the community. It has undoubtedly maintained some students in school who would have dropped out without this interest, and the program has made it possible for certain individuals to obtain scholarships to college and other kinds of recognition.[32] Athletics have also been a source of school spirit for many students and a means of entertainment for a large number of communities. However, the program has periodically been criticized and has had to face some serious problems.[33]

One problem that has continued to confront the athletic program is the matter of poor sportsmanship on the part of players and spectators. Poor sportsmanship by players usually manifests itself when they argue with the officials or become involved in fights with the opponents on the playing area. Poor sportsmanship on the part of spectators includes booing the officials, throwing articles onto the playing area, or fighting among the fans during or after a game. While the extent of the problem varies from school to school and sometimes from sport to sport, such behavior represents a serious problem that should be of concern to the administrator and the school staff.

The approach to unruly behavior on the part of athletes and the student body should not be dependent solely on greater control or more security, but should also include a planned program of developing better spectator and player sportsmanship.[34] The objectives of the program should be to teach good, sportsmanlike attitudes and behavior to athletes and to the rest of the student body. A beginning step for achieving this goal would be for a school to develop a sportsmanship code similar to the one presented in figure 16.2.[35]

The code in figure 16.2 and other aspects of the sportsmanship program should be implemented in physical education classes, assembly programs, after-school practices, and through the example of coaches and other adults in the school. School administrators can show the way through their own examples at games and by making clear to the coaches and the student body the importance attached to good sportsmanlike behavior. In the final analysis, administrators and the staff need to view the success of the athletic program not just in games won or lost, but in the amount of progress made by the athletes and the student body in learning better sportsmanship.[36]

Figure 16.2 Fundamentals of Sportsmanship.

1. *Show respect for the opponent at all times.*
   The opponent should be treated as a guest; greeted cordially on arriving; given the best accommodations; and accorded the tolerance, honesty, and generosity which all human beings deserve. Good sportsmanship is the Golden Rule in action.
2. *Show respect for the officials.*
   The officials should be recognized as impartial arbitrators who are trained to do their job and who can be expected to do it to the best of their ability. Good sportsmanship implies the willingness to accept and abide by the decisions of the officials.
3. *Know, understand, and appreciate the rules of the contest.*
   A familiarity with the current rules of the game and the recognition of their necessity for a fair contest are essential. Good sportsmanship suggests the importance of conforming to the spirit as well as the letter of the rules.
4. *Maintain self-control at all times.*
   A prerequisite of good sportsmanship requires one to understand his own bias or prejudice and to have the ability to recognize that rational behavior is more important than the desire to win. A proper perspective must be maintained if the potential educational values of athletic competition are to be realized. Good sportsmanship is concerned with the behavior of all involved in the game.
5. *Recognize and appreciate skill in performance regardless of affiliation.*
   Applause for an opponent's good performance is a demonstration of generosity and goodwill that should not be looked upon as treason. The ability to recognize quality in performance and the willingness to acknowledge it without regard to team membership is one of the most highly commendable gestures of good sportsmanship. With the fundamentals of sportsmanship as the points of departure, specific responsibilities and expected modes of behavior can be defined.

Used with permission of the American Association for Health, Physical Education and Recreation Publications.

A second major problem with which the athletics program has been confronted is the introduction of girls' sports. Historically, the athletic program has involved mainly boys, although girls have sometimes participated in certain sports, such as basketball and field hockey. Since the passage of Title IX of the USOE, however, girls' athletics have expanded greatly, putting tremendous pressure on school budgets and facilities. The challenge for school administrators is how to accommodate girls' as well as boys' athletics in existing physical facilities (which, in many localities, are already in short supply for boys' athletics and the intramural program), and yet keep within athletic budgets which have ballooned because of inflation and which are under attack by critics as being too large. This is not an unresolvable problem, and many schools have done a good job of accommodating girls' athletics through tighter scheduling and budgeting. Nevertheless, it is not an easy problem with which to grapple.

Most schools have probably done a good job in implementing Title IX, yet administrators should perform periodic audits to ascertain the extent to which the regulations are being met and to which improvement is still needed. (Useful nondiscrimination guidelines are provided at the end of the chapter.[37]) Examples of questions asked during such an audit are (1) How many teams are available for girls, as compared with the number of teams for boys? (2) What kinds of uniforms and equipment are girls' teams using, compared with boys' teams? (3) Do girls' teams receive equal and desirable time on the practice field and in the gym? and (4) Do girls' teams receive the same publicity as boys' teams?[38] The goal of administrative efforts in this area should be to make sure that the athletic needs of boys *and* girls are being *equally* met.

THE STUDENT COUNCIL

Most forward looking elementary and secondary schools provide an opportunity for students to participate in decisions about school affairs, usually through a group called the student council.[39] It generally comprises student representatives elected to their positions by the school's student population and an advisor usually appointed by the principal. The council may meet during the school day, but frequently tends to hold its meetings after school. Meetings may consist of hearing reports from various subcommittees, passing motions recommending certain actions to the administration, and raising problems or questions requiring discussion and possibly further investigation.

Although the specific objectives of the student council are not the same in all schools, the following are recommended:

1. To promote the general welfare of the school.
2. To foster, promote and develop democracy as a way of life.
3. To teach home, school, and community citizenship.
4. To provide school experiences closely related to life experiences.
5. To provide learning opportunities through the solution of problems of interest and concern to students.
6. To provide training and experience in representative democracy.
7. To contribute to the total educational growth of boys and girls.[40]

There is little doubt that a student council can become an important and valuable force in the school. For it to be successful, however, certain problems and crises must be averted or resolved. One of the major problems or issues which many student councils and administrators encounter is how much authority should be granted to the student council. That is to say, should the student council be an advisory group with authority only to make recommendations, or should it be given decision-making authority? This question has troubled schools for a number of years, but it became a fundamental issue with the advent of student activism in the late 1960s and still surfaces periodically in many schools.

Actually, there should be no confusion in an administrator's mind about the extent of the student council's authority. The building administrator is the one who is legally accountable to the school board for administering the school. Therefore, the student council can legitimately be given only the authority to offer recommendations in regard to how the school should be run. Administrators can delegate certain decision-making responsibilities to the student council, but final decision-making authority cannot be delegated to such a group unless the school board provides for this departure from normal procedure.[41]

An initial step that administrators should take to avert the authority issue from coming to a head is to develop an understanding by the entire student council and its advisor not only of the legal requirements and restrictions of an administrator's position but also the council's main function in light of these factors.[42] This should be done in a way that stresses the importance of the recommending role of the council while at the same time indicating that the council does not have a final decision-making role. Administrators should recognize, however, that regardless of the importance they attribute to the recommending role of the council, their reactions to its recommendations communicate more than any statements they may make about the council's usefulness.

If the student council is to believe it plays an important role in the school, administrators need to exercise extreme caution in rejecting its recommendations. Of course, this does not mean that recommendations which are clearly illegal or not in the best interest of the school must be accepted, although discerning which recommendations to accept and which to reject because of the latter criterion takes considerable administrative judgment and wisdom. Administrators should realize that they will probably have to compromise sometimes and, in certain instances, take risks in accepting recommendations which they believe to be impractical. At times, however, the only way students will appreciate the judgment of the administrator is if they are permitted to make their own mistakes.

The scope of many student council programs is another major problem. As set forth earlier, the student council has a rather broad mandate for taking action to improve the total environment of the school. However, if one looks at the actual activities of many student councils, the main thrust appears to be limited to fund-raising, organizing and promoting social affairs, and occasionally coalescing to promote some particular school issue, such as a new student lounge.[43] What seems to be lacking on the part of these student councils—and, perhaps, on the part of school administrators as well—is a deep understanding of the potential purposes and scope of the student council in a school and the kind of program that would accomplish these purposes.

Administrators should assume leadership responsibility for helping to resolve this problem. They should, in their own minds, be clear about the purposes of the student council, and they should make equally sure that the student council and its advisor are also clear about the purposes of the organization. Then they should work with the advisor, who in turn should work with the members of the council to develop a program each year that accomplishes those purposes.

Although some administrators may prefer a student council that confines its program to organizing social events, administrators truly interested in capitalizing on and encouraging the interests and skills of the students will help them to develop more far-reaching programs. Such a program should have as its main purpose the improvement of the educational and social environment of the school and the community.[44] Included in this program might be the following activities:

1. Conducting remedial classes in a disadvantaged neighborhood.
2. Refurbishing a community center for youth and adults.
3. Setting up a city-suburb exchange program.
4. Meeting with the principal to recommend new courses for the school's curriculum.

5. Arranging for an after-school series of school lectures on "Hot Topics."
6. Developing a form for evaluating class instruction.
7. Organizing a student-led seminar on contemporary issues to be offered in summer school, without grades or credits.
8. Setting up a corps of student tutors to help slow learners in the school.
9. Developing student-written individualized learning materials.
10. Meeting with community leaders to plan for more effective use of community resources.
11. Meeting with parents to explore school problems as parents perceive them.
12. Making a proposal to the school board for the hiring of teacher aides.

Participation in these and similar activities should help the student council to achieve its general purposes, to make a significant contribution to the school, and to ameliorate the two-pronged problem of student apathy and criticism of the council that "it never does anything worthwhile."[45] Such a program should attract student participation, provide valuable learning experiences for students, and greatly improve the image of the student council in the school. Given a full understanding of its purposes and the nature of its authority in the school, as well as continuous encouragement and assistance by the administration and the staff, the student council can become an important force for school and community improvement.

THE STUDENT NEWSPAPER

Every elementary and secondary school should sponsor a student newspaper as a part of its activities program. A student newspaper can provide valuable learning experiences for those students on its staff and can act as a source of information about student perceptions, student functions, and school and community activities and problems. The newspaper's basic purpose, in addition to providing journalistic learning experiences for students, is to inform the student body and other school personnel about school and community events of interest to students and to the professional staff.[46]

In spite of its potential and frequently realized worth, the student newspaper has been a source of considerable controversy in recent years.[47] Editorials attacking the administration and faculty and criticizing certain school practices and programs have appeared in some student newspapers. The use of obscene language and pictures of questionable taste in some student newspapers have also caused problems for school administrators and newspaper advisors.

Administrators have tended to react to these problems in several different ways: Some administrators have tried to ignore such problems in the hope that they would eventually disappear. Their success has been mixed. Some administrators have responded by initiating procedures designed to avoid in advance any undesirable (from the administrator's point of view) language, pictures, editorials, or articles.[48] These administrators have also tried to stop the distribution of student underground papers in school and, in some instances, away from the school grounds. Other administrators have developed policies and procedures to avoid or minimize problems.[49] The Student Press Law Center, in its Model Guidelines for Student Publications, encourages the adoption of guidelines: "Every school publication should consider specific and inclusive publication guidelines to aid students in deciding what material to publish. . . . Such guidelines, if properly drafted, can go a long way in preventing unnecessary confrontations between students and school officials."[50]

While it is difficult to assess the effectiveness of these efforts, it is worth noting that until recently students have generally achieved considerable success in their court challenges of unnecessary administrative censorship and restriction of their publications. Although the case law is still in somewhat of a flux, the courts have previously upheld students' rights to publish material, with the following exceptions:

1. *Libelous material* in articles causing defamation of character, such as statements which may unnecessarily expose individuals to hatred or contempt, or which could injure them professionally.
2. *Obscene and profane material.* Generally the courts have been more restrictive as to the language and pictorial representations from younger students than those from college students.
3. Material which would tend to *incite to disruption* the educational process of the school.
4. Material which would *clearly endanger the health and safety* of the students, teachers, and administrators.
5. Material which advocates destruction of school property.[51]

These standards were drawn in many respects from the landmark case, *Tinker* v. *Des Moines Independent Community School District,* in which the Supreme Court stated that neither students nor teachers "shed their constitutional rights to freedom of speech or expression at the schoolhouse gate."[52] The Court further stated that student expression is protected unless it "materially disrupts classwork or involves substantial disorder or invasion of the rights of others."[53] Other cases have found that material which is critical of school officials or discusses controversial issues generally may not be legally restricted unless it meets one or more of the five criteria previously listed.[54]

However, the Supreme Court set a new standard in the recent *Hazelwood* decision when it ruled that censorship of a high school newspaper produced as part of the school's journalism curriculum does not violate students' First Amendment right to freedom of expression.[55] The five-member majority of the Court, "while still leaving the burden of justifying censorship on school officials, gave Hazelwood [the school] much more authority to censor than had been available under the *Tinker* standard."[56]

Although the *Hazelwood* decision increases administrative authority, some educators predict that students will continue to seek ways to speak out that may not be socially acceptable and may be embarrassing to the school.* One avenue for expression may be a resurgence of interest in underground newspapers because school authorities do not have censorship rights over their content since they are not under the curricular control of the school and, thus, not subject to the standards established in the *Hazelwood* case.[57]

Any school requirement of administrative review of student material prior to actual publication and distribution must communicate in advance to students the specific and understandable criteria used in the review, must include a relatively short time period for the review, and must provide students with an opportunity to appeal an adverse decision.[58] While administrators can regulate the time, place, and manner of distribution of a student publication within the school, these regulations must be promulgated in advance of publication, must be clear as to their intent, and must be reasonable in their implementation.[59] Also, as Thomas Eveslage noted, school officials should be cautious in instances of prior review because "guidelines with prior restraint or prior review procedures get more intense judicial scrutiny when censorship of student publications occur."[60]

Some schools employ an approach which seems to be successful in resolving publication problems; they establish publications advisory committees.[61] Such committees are generally composed of the advisors for the newspaper and yearbook, the student editors of each of these publications, one or more representatives from the faculty and from the administration, and sometimes a representative from the local newspaper. The committee membership should be broadly based to capitalize on the capabilities and insights of a number of people who can contribute valuable ideas for the improvement of school publications.

---

*Administrators who are interested in keeping abreast of student thinking in this area should request to be placed on the mailing list of the Student Press Law Center, 1033 30th Street N.W., Washington, D.C. 20007.

The main purposes of the advisory committee are to develop policies and procedures concerning student publications in the school, to evaluate various aspects of the publications program, and to act as a hearing board for people who have complaints about school publications. The committee's actions are advisory to the principal of the school, who may or may not be a member of the committee. The primary advantage of such a committee is that it serves as a focal point for a continuous examination and upgrading of student publications, while providing a less emotional and more thorough process of resolving complaints and controversy surrounding student publications.

Although there is little doubt that guidelines and committees can help to promote good journalism in schools—and to avoid controversy—administrators should recognize that some controversy is not necessarily bad; in some instances it may represent a desirable learning experience for students. Perhaps this perspective has been best expressed by the Civil Liberties Union, which stated in its landmark pamphlet, *Academic Freedom in the Secondary School:*

> The student press should be considered a learning device. Its pages should not be looked upon as an official image of the school, always required to present a polished appearance to the extramural world. Learning effectively proceeds through trial and error, and as much or more may be sometimes gained from reactions to a poor article or a tasteless publication as from the traditional pieces, groomed carefully for external inspection.[62]

A FINAL PERSPECTIVE

The quality of a student activities program is primarily dependent on the vision and commitment of those people associated with the program. Any student activities program will, over a period of time, encounter certain problems. However, given proper leadership—particularly by the student officers, faculty advisors, and the principal of the school—these problems can be resolved, and the student activities program can make an important contribution to meeting school goals and student needs.

Review and Learning Activities

1. What are the purpose, objectives, and scope of the student activities program?
2. Which two characteristics of administrators and staff members are most important to the success of the student activities program? Why are these two aspects important?
3. Which principles should administrators follow in organizing or evaluating the student activities program?
4. Indicate the importance of continuous evaluation of the student activities program. Which questions should administrators be asking?
5. Define the major problems of the student activities program. Which factors seem to contribute to the problems, and how can administrators prevent or ameliorate the problems?
6. Discuss the major problems associated with the following student activities, the factors contributing to these problems, and ways that administrators can prevent or ameliorate them.
   a. The athletic program
   b. The student council
   c. The student newspaper

Notes

1. Ronald E. Gholson, "Student Achievement and Cocurricular Activity Participation," *NASSP Bulletin* (October 1985): 17–20.
2. Robert Frederick, *The Third Curriculum* (New York: Appleton-Century-Crofts, 1958), 58. For a more recent discussion of the student activities program, see Nancy A. Biernat and Edward J. Klesse, *The Third Curriculum: Student Activities* (Reston, Va.: National Association of Secondary School Principals, 1989).
3. For examples of other statements of objectives, see Sharon Wegner, *Extracurricular Activities Are an Essential Factor in the Student's Self-Concept, Socialization, and Future Success* (ERIC Report Ed–196–171). See also Alyce Holland and Thomas Andre, "Participation in Extracurricular Activities in Secondary School: What Is Known, What Needs to be Known?" *Review of Educational Research* (Winter 1987): 437–66.
4. Robert T. Tauber, "C-Average Rule: The Educational Psychology Behind It," *NASSP Bulletin* (April 1988): 42–45.
5. For an excellent and still relevant statement of the rationale supporting this position, see Ellsworth Thompkins, "Extra-Class Activities for All Pupils," *Federal Security Agency* (1950): 1–3.
6. See J. B. Grady, "Middle School Activities: More Meaningful with More," *NASSP Bulletin* (December 1979): 74–78; and Ward Sybouts and Wayne J. Krepel, *Student Activities in the Secondary Schools: A Handbook and Guide* (Westport, Conn.: Greenwood Press, 1984).
7. Holland and Andre, "Participation in Extracurricular Activities," 437–66.

8. For an example of how to do this, see Douglas D. Christensen, *Planning and Evaluating Student Activity Programs* (Reston, Va.: National Association of Secondary School Principals, 1978). See also Douglas D. Christensen, *Managing Student Activities* (Reston, Va.: National Association of Secondary School Principals, 1984); James A. Sandfort, "The Coming Assault on Student Activities: A Principal's Response," *NASSP Bulletin* (October 1985): 31; *Organizing Student Activities: The Book of Forms* (Reston, Va.: National Association of Secondary School Principals, 1988); and Jan Kurtz, *The ABCs of Advising Student Activities* (Reston, Va.: National Association of Secondary School Principals, 1988).

9. William Neal and Hack Hoggartt, "Congratulations! You're the Advisor!" *Business Education Forum* (May 1979): 3–4. This article contains useful suggestions for the new advisor to an activity.

10. *A Handbook for the Student Activity Adviser* (Reston, Va.: National Association for Secondary School Principals, 1979). See also *Ten Steps to Leadership* (Reston, Va.: National Association of Secondary School Principals, 1985).

11. James Vornberg, "In-Service Training for Student Activity Sponsors," *Catalyst for Change* (Spring 1979): 6–7. See also Sandfort, "The Coming Assault on Student Activities," 31.

12. John Gray and Angela Laird, *Skills for Leaders* (Reston, Va.: National Association of Secondary School Principals, 1987). In addition, the Division of Student Activities of the National Association of Secondary School Principals sponsors conferences throughout the year for all advisers interested in improving their leadership, motivational, and interpersonal skills.

13. June E. Thompson and Barbara Lacerenza, "Providing Leadership Education for the Future: A Curriculum Model," *NASSP Bulletin* (October 1985): 21–28; and, Judi Mackey, "Designing a Leadership Class," *Leadership* (October 1988): 28.

14. Sandfort, "The Coming Assault on Student Activities," 30.

15. Russell Stokes, Jr., "What Hat Do You Wear as an A.P.?" *Catalyst for Change* (Spring 1979): 8–12. See also Dennis De Neve, "A Study of the Status and Role of Activities Directors in California High Schools" (Ed.D. diss., University of Southern California, 1981).

16. Holland and Andre, "Participation in Extracurricular Activities," 453.

17. Sandfort, "The Coming Assault on Student Activities," 29–30.

18. Frederick, *The Third Curriculum,* 121.

19. See *Evaluative Criteria,* 6th ed. (Falls Church, Va.: National Study of School Evaluation, 1987); *Auditing the Student Activity Program* (Reston, Va.: National Association of Secondary School Principals, 1980); and Sybouts and Krepel, "Planning and Evaluating," *Student Activities in the Secondary Schools.*

20. For examples of various evaluating methods, see Christensen, *Planning and Evaluating Student Activity Programs.*

21. Ronald E. Gholson, "Research Notes," *Kappan* (September 1979): 67. See also Samuel Griffin, "Student Activities in the Middle School: What Do They Contribute?" *NASSP Bulletin* (April 1988): 87–92.

22. Ronald G. Joekel, "Student Activities and Academic Eligibility Requirements," *NASSP Bulletin* (October 1985): 7.

23. Vera J. Gordon, *Extra Curricular Programs—How to Survive in an Era of Austerity* (ERIC Report Ed–136–371).

24. Nathan L. Essex, "What Extra Duties Can, Should Teachers Be Expected to Perform?" *NASSP Bulletin* (October 1989): 101–2.

25. Ibid.

26. See Joekel, "Student Activities and Academic Eligibility," 3–8; and Tauber, "C-Average Rule."

27. Grace Graham, "Do School Activity Programs Build Better Intergroup Relations?" *School Activities* (February 1967): 6–7. Also, for an extensive review of various approaches for getting students involved, see *Models for Student Participation* (Reston, Va.: National Association of Secondary School Principals, 1977).

28. Joekel, "Student Activities and Academic Eligibility," 7–8.

29. For some still valid suggestions, see Neil F. Williams, "Encouraging and Limiting Participation in School Activities," *School Activities* (November 1964): 19–21.

30. Alec M. Gallup, "The 17th Annual Gallup Poll of the Public's Attitudes toward the Public Schools," *Kappan* (September 1985): 41.

31. George J. Burnett, "Interscholastic Athletics: Is the Tail Wagging the Dog?" *NASSP Bulletin* (November 1988): 114.

32. See Charles W. Peck, "Interscholastic Athletics and Delinquent Behavior: Appraisal or Applause," *Sociology of Education* (October 1979): 238–43. Also see Ronald E. Gholson, "Student Achievement and Cocurricular Activity Participation," *NASSP Bulletin* (October 1985): 17–20; and Tauber, "C-Average Rule."

33. See Delbert K. Clear and Martha Bagley, "Coaching Athletics: A Tort Just Waiting for a Judgment," *School Law Journal* (October 1982): 184–94; and Martha Bagley, "Athletics," in *Encyclopedia of School Administration and Supervision,* ed. R. A. Gorton, G. T. Schneider, and J. C. Fisher (Phoenix, Ariz.: Oryx Press, 1988), 37.

34. See Harold Meyer, *Crowd Control for High School Athletics* (Washington, D.C.: National Council of Secondary School Athletic Directors, 1970), 9–14; and Milwaukee Public Schools, *Milwaukee City Conference Code of Sportsmanship* and *Citywide Athletic Code of Conduct* (Milwaukee, Wisc.: Public School Documents, 1987).

35. Ibid.

36. Everett Abney and Judith Green, "Senior High Athletes—Winners or Losers?" *NASSP Bulletin* (November 1981): 93–96. Also see Glen Potter et al., "Making Interscholastic Athletics a Winner," *NASSP Bulletin* (September 1981): 50–55.

37. *Pupil Nondiscrimination Guidelines* (Madison, Wisc.: Wisconsin Department of Public Instruction, 1988).

38. Ibid., 44.

39. Nancy Webb, "Organizing a Student Council in the Elementary School," *Catalyst for Change* (Fall 1987): 4–5; and Samuel Griffin, "Student Activities in the Middle: What Do They Contribute?" *NASSP Bulletin* (April 1988): 87–92.

40. Based on a reading of Gerald M. Van Pool, *Improving Your Student Council* (Reston, Va.: National Association of Secondary School Principals, 1977). For an additional discussion of specific student council activities, see Robert D. Miller, "Student Growth through Student Activity Organizations," *NASSP Bulletin* (April 1987): 124–27.

41. James E. Ferguson, *Student Council Activity Resource Book* (Reston, Va.: National Association of Secondary School Principals, 1980).

42. Van Pool, *Improving Your Student Council,* 1–4.

43. Based on an examination of agendas of various student councils.

44. Lew Armistead, "Student Activities Can Generate Positive PR," *NASSP Bulletin* (October 1985): 33–36.

45. For information on additional Student Council projects, see James E. Ferguson, *Student Council Projects* (Reston, Va.: National Association of Secondary School Principals, 1982).

46. Any adminsitrator who wishes to develop a better understanding of the purposes and role of the student newspaper and its advisor should subscribe to the journal, *Quill and Scroll.*

47. Homer Hall, "Scholastic Journalism: What Is Its Future?" *NASSP Bulletin* (November 1988): 2–5.

48. Thomas Eveslage, "Publications Guidelines: A Way to Avoid Conflict and Courtrooms," *NASSP Bulletin* (November 1988): 21–26.

49. Ibid.

50. Student Press Law Center, *Law of the Student Press* (Iowa City, Iowa: Quill and Scroll Society, 1985), 56–57.

51. For a still relevant discussion of the court cases supporting these restrictions, see E. Edmond Reutter, "Student Discipline: Selected Substantive Issues," in Ralph D. Stern, ed., *The School Principal and the Law* (Topeka, Kans.: National Organization on Legal Problems of Education, 1978), 71–87.

52. *Tinker* v. *Des Moines Independent Community School District,* 393 U.S. 503 (1969).

53. Ibid.

54. *Sullivan* v. *Houston Independent School District,* 307 Supp. 1328 (S.D. Tex., 1969); and *Gambino* v. *Fairfax County School Board,* 429 F. Supp. 731 (E.D. VA, 1977).

55. *Hazelwood School District* v. *Kuhlmeier,* 108 S. Ct. 562 (1988). For a copy of the majority and dissenting opinions in *Hazelwood,* see "Text of the Ruling in *Hazelwood School District* v. *Kuhlmeier,*" *Education Week* (January 20, 1988): 20–22. (Additional articles which discuss the impact of the *Hazelwood* decision on students' freedom of expression include: E. M. Russo, "Prior Restraint and the High School 'Free Press': The Implications of *Hazelwood School District* v. *Kuhlmeier,*" *Journal of Law and Education* (Winter 1989): 1–22; and J. M. Abrams and S. M. Goodman, "End of an Era? The Decline of Student Press Rights in the Wake of *Hazelwood School District* v. *Kuhlmeier, Duke Law Journal 1988* 4: 706–32.

56. Mark Goodman, "Student Press Freedom: One View of the *Hazelwood* Decision," *NASSP Bulletin* (November 1988): 40–41. See also T. V. Dickson, "Attitudes of High School Principals about Press Freedom after *Hazelwood,*" *Journalism Quarterly* (Spring 1989): 169–73.

57. Mark Goodman, "Student Press Freedom: One View of the *Hazelwood* Decision," 44.

58. *Quarterman* v. *Byrd,* 453 F. 2nd 54 (4th Cir. 1971).

59. *Grayned* v. *City of Rockford,* 408 U.S. 104 (1972).

60. Thomas Eveslage, "Publications Guidelines," 25.

61. Molly J. Clemens, "When Will Principals Have No Need to Worry about Publications?" *NASSP Bulletin* (November 1988): 9–10.

62. American Civil Liberties Union, *Academic Freedom in the Secondary School* (New York: American Civil Liberties Union, 1968): 12.

PART

5

• • • • •

THE SCHOOL AND THE COMMUNITY

___

17

. . . . .

School-Community Relations:
Community Structure and Involvement

A school is not an independent or isolated entity; it operates in a social context, an important element of which is the local community.[1] The school draws its students from the community and depends on the community for much of its financial and social support. The community attempts to exercise its power over the school primarily through the school board, which has authority to establish policies and approve financial expenditures. The community also tries to exert its influence on the school informally through parent and special interest groups and individual contacts.[2] Because of these factors every administrator needs to develop a good understanding of, and competency in, building and maintaining effective school-community relations.

UNDERSTANDING THE COMMUNITY

THE SCHOOL ADMINISTRATOR'S COMMUNITY

The school community can be thought of as encompassing the total geographical area and population of a school district, or as comprising the more immediate area and population within an individual school's boundaries. While school administrators need to understand the total community, they need particularly to understand and develop good relationships with the local community that the school serves.[3] It is the local community that is sending its children to the school, and it is the people in this community with whom administrators are likely to have the greatest contact. Local residents are also the ones with whom administrators need to communicate the most because their opinions about the school are likely to be most influential. And although school busing has stretched the meaning of the term *local community* for many schools and made the task of understanding the community more difficult, the task is no less important because of this factor. As school districts extend their boundaries, not only are greater efforts by school administrators required but staff members also need to develop a good understanding of an expanded school community.

While many administrators may believe that they already possess a good understanding of the community, for the most part this understanding is based on irregular, random contacts with parents and other members of the public through occasional telephone calls, parents' meetings, open houses, and personal correspondence. Although these contacts are potentially valuable, all too often they tend to be casual, superficial, and not representative in nature. They do not in most cases lead to a good understanding of the many dimensions of the community.[4]

Also contributing to an insufficient understanding of the community by many administrators is their personal residency in a community other than the one served by their school. While we are not asserting that all administrators must necessarily live in the communities their schools service, such residence would make it easier to become more knowledgeable about the community, and it would certainly increase the administrators' accessibility. At the minimum, if administrators choose to live in another community than that served by their schools, they should have a systematic plan (such as the one described later) to gain knowledge about the community. This kind of a plan is recommended for all administrators, especially for those who do not live in the communities that their schools serve.

The most important step that administrators can take initially to develop good school-community relations is to study and better understand the school's local community.[5] A community is a very complex unit, but there are four elements to which administrators should pay close attention. Those elements are presented in figure 17.1.

In trying to develop a better understanding of the local community served by the school, administrators first need to study the kinds of people who reside in that community. Examples of questions which might guide their study include the following: What is the socioeconomic background of the people?

Figure 17.1 Major Community Elements.

Factor 1: People	Factor 2: Places Where People Meet	Factor 3: Methods of Communication People Use	Factor 4: Expectations and Attitudes

Examples
 	
A. *Individuals:*
Parents/nonparents
Professional/laboring
   class
Welfare clients
Working mothers/
   fathers
Informal leaders
B. *Groups:*
Parents' organizations
Social and fraternal
   groups
Informal groups
   (coffees, bowling
   teams)
	Examples
	
	Homes
	Churches
	Supermarkets
	Cocktail parties;
	   taverns
	Coffees
	Organizational
	   Meetings
		Examples
		
		Face-to-Face
		Telephone
		Letter
		Newsletter
		Radio
		TV
			Examples
			
			Attitudes about
			   children
			Expectations for the
			   school
			Attitudes towards
			   school effectiveness
			Interest in and
			   availability for
			   working with the
			   school

What percentage are professional, in contrast to blue-collar workers? How many are on welfare? Who are the informal leaders of the community? What percentage of the parents move each year? What percentage of the parents represent minority groups? What percentage of the people in the local community are parents/nonparents? In how many instances are both parents working outside the home? What percentage of families is headed by a single parent, and in how many of these situations is the parent employed?

Obtaining answers to the latter three questions is very important for developing a better understanding of the community. Evidence from the national scene indicates that the demographics of many local communities are changing.[6] For example, in many communities, the ratio of parents to nonparents has been significantly altered and the parents of students are in the minority.[7] This change suggests that schools must aim their community relations programs at nonparents as well as parents. The characteristics of the American family are also changing. While traditionally conceptualized as including two parents, one of whom was employed (usually the male), demographics now indicate that in most two-parent families, both parents have outside jobs. In addition, there has been a dramatic increase in one-parent families and usually this parent is employed.[8] Specifically, demographer Harold Hodgkinson noted that the school population has the following characteristics:

- 14 percent are illegitimate.
- 40 percent will have lived with a single parent by the time they reach age 18.
- 30 percent are latchkey children (returning to homes with no adult supervision after schooling).
- 20 percent live in poverty.
- 15 percent speak a native language other than English.
- 15 percent have physical or mental handicaps.
- 10 percent have poorly educated parents.[9]

Obviously, these changes pose challenges for school administrators as they attempt to involve parents in their children's education. Nonetheless, a study conducted by Joyce Epstein found that "single and married parents were equally interested in helping and willing to help their children on learning activities at home," and that "teachers who frequently used parent involvement in their teaching practice made *equal demands* on single and married parents to help at home, and rated single and married parents as *equally helpful* and responsible in completing learning activities."[10]

Although it is not inevitable or necessarily likely that these demographic changes will produce problems for schools, they do underscore the importance of administrators developing and periodically updating their understanding of the community through the use of a school census and supplementary school surveys. (We say more later in this chapter about responding to demographic changes.)

School administrators also need to become knowledgeable about the different groups and organizations to which the people in the local community belong. The particular groups and organizations about which administrators need specific information are those which have a special interest in education and in the school. These would be groups or organizations that discuss education from time to time in their meetings and who may even have a subcommittee for educational matters. (For an understanding of the power structure of a community, an excellent source is *The Structure of Community Power,* edited by Michael Aiken and Paul Mott, and published by Random House.) Figure 17.2 identifies groups and organizations about which administrators should be knowledgeable.

At the minimum, administrators should try to meet the leaders of the major groups and organizations in the local community the school serves and

Figure 17.2 Community Groups and Organizations with a Special Interest in Education.

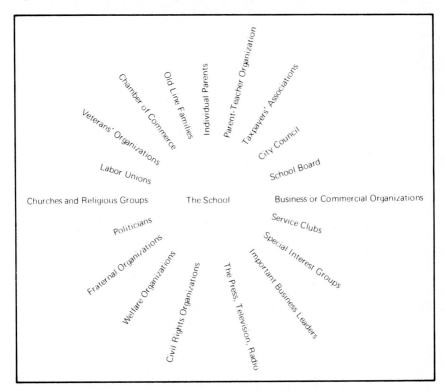

learn their points of view about education and about the school.[11] Administrators should be well acquainted with each group so that they can communicate easily with its leaders in a time of crisis and can utilize whatever expertise the members possess for improving the school program.

In addition to studying the individuals and the major organizations in the community which the school serves, administrators need to become more aware of the different places where people in the community meet and of the various methods of communication they use in discussing education and the school. These meeting places—whether they be churches, local stores, or social gatherings—are a part of the informal structure of the community. By familiarizing themselves with the informal structure of a community, administrators are in a better position to ascertain what people are thinking and saying about the school; they can also use the informal structure for communicating information about the school.[12]

The objective of administrators in regard to the ways people receive information about the school is to be aware of these channels so that they can capitalize on them when they communicate information about the school or need to find out what people are thinking. For example, if people in a community pay more attention to news about the school that they hear on radio or television than information they receive from the school newsletter or the city newspaper, administrators should be aware of this reality and take it into consideration in their communication practices. An understanding of the ways in which the people in a community receive information about the schools is essential for administrators who want to develop effective communication with the community.

Perhaps the most important element of the community about which school administrators need to become knowledgeable is the educational expectations and attitudes of its people. Most communities are not, of course, homogeneous entities, and administrators are unlikely to discover that everyone holds identical educational expectations and attitudes. Most communities are composed of diverse people and groups who are likely to hold somewhat different expectations and attitudes about education and the schools.

Regardless of this diversity, however, school administrators should try to understand the expectations and attitudes of the people in the community, for community expectations constitute the standards by which people evaluate the performance of the school. The current attitude of people in the community toward students and the schools reflects citizens' feelings about how effectively schools are meeting community expectations. Therefore, school administrators need to understand both the educational expectations and the attitudes of people in the community. As a result of such knowledge, they are in better positions to recognize the direction that the community would like to see education take in the schools as well as citizens' feelings about how successful the schools have been in meeting their expectations. (For a useful example of survey data focusing on teachers' and parents' expectations, see *The Metropolitan Life Survey of the American Teacher: Strengthening Links between Home and School.*)[13]

MAJOR PROBLEMS IN SCHOOL-COMMUNITY RELATIONS

Administrators should understand that school-community relations have never been completely trouble-free. From the very beginning of education in this country, there have been periodic differences and conflicts between the school and the community. In most communities, these differences and conflicts have usually not been severe, but in some periods school-community conflict has seemed to be rather widespread.

Although the basic causes of problems in school-community relations are complex and may vary according to the nature of a community and a school, two general factors are at work: professional challenges to community norms, and community challenges to professional norms. The first factor concerns those efforts by educators to change the educational program—efforts which in many instances have conflicted with community norms. Integration, sex education, and open education are only a few of the innovations that educators have tried to introduce which have, in one way or another, challenged the norm structure of many communities. When a community feels that its schools are going beyond or against community expectations and norms, it reacts negatively, thereby causing difficulties in school-community relations.

A second general factor which may cause problems in school-community relations is intensified efforts by many communities to ascertain and evaluate what is going on in the schools. These efforts challenge the professional norms of many educators, whose motto seems to be, "Trust us, we're the experts."

Increasing numbers of parents and other community citizens, however, have indicated that they no longer accept the word of educators that "everything is going to be all right." These community people want to see the results of the school's effectiveness; in many cases, they want to be personally involved in the decision-making processes of the schools. Administrators should not assume that all of the people of a community possess these attitudes, but they should recognize the growing national trend toward greater expectations for education.[14] Many citizens want to become involved in school decision making and to hold the school accountable for its educational effectiveness.*

These problems in school-community relations cannot be easily ameliorated. More effective communication between the school and the community, and greater community involvement, are necessary prerequisites. The remainder of this chapter focuses on ways in which school administrators might more effectively involve the members of the community in the school; the following chapter discusses school communication and the school's public relations program.

---

*A group organized for this purpose is the National Committee for Citizens in Education, which has its national headquarters in Columbia, Maryland, and local chapters in many communities. Another group is the Institute for Responsive Education, which has its national headquarters in Boston, Massachusetts.

COMMUNITY INVOLVEMENT

Many observers believe that the key to improving school-community relations is greater parental and public involvement in school affairs.* Oliver Moles, for example, has stated,

> Parent involvement in education is an idea whose time has come. Parent organizations, school officials, educators, and the U.S. Secretary of Education all endorse the concept. Teachers support it overwhelmingly. In a recent nationwide poll, over 90% of teachers at all grade levels wanted more home-school interaction. Each group is saying that schools cannot educate children alone and need the support, if not the active collaboration, of parents.[15]

While few educators would argue that parent and public involvement is unimportant, considerable confusion and uncertainty continues among school administrators about the concept of involvement and how to utilize it to improve school/community relations. The confusion and uncertainty seem to revolve around three basic questions: (1) What are the purposes of involvement? (2) What types of involvement are possible? and (3) What are the problems associated with parental and community involvement in the schools, and how can these problems be overcome? The following sections take up each of these questions, discussing and analyzing the ideas and issues concerned.

PURPOSES OF INVOLVEMENT

Many administrators have experienced difficulty in understanding the concept of involvement and in implementing a program of parental and community involvement in the schools, because they were not clear about the purposes which such involvement should achieve. Involvement has been presented so positively in the educational literature that it has frequently seemed to be the main objective of school-community relations rather than a means of improving education. Don Davies noted that the idea of increasing parent and citizen involvement is by no means new. In fact, he stated that "questions and

---

*Some authorities on school/community relations make a distinction between community involvement and participation, with the former stressing supportive activities while the latter emphasizes school decision making. (See Sandra Jowett and Mary Baginsky, "Parents and Education: A Survey of Their Involvement and a Discussion of Some Issues," *Education Research* [February 1988]: 36–45.) However, an analysis of the rationale behind this distinction suggests that the difference may be a matter of semantics more than anything else, and that the key factors are the form and substance that involvement takes rather than the existence of a separate concept called participation. In the following sections the terms *involvement* and *participation* are used synonymously.

conflict about parent and community relationships to schools began in this country when schools began. The debate changes in focus, vocabulary, and intensity according to the time, plan and political climate, but the underlying questions remain the same."[16] Some of the persisting questions Davies noted are

- What power should parents have over school policies and practices?
- What power should other citizens have?
- How should these powers be exercised?
- What should be the parents' role in the education of their own children?
- How can parents and citizens address their grievances and concerns about the schools?
- How much choice should parents have about what kinds of schools their children attend?
- How can public schools achieve legitimacy in the eyes of parents and the taxpaying public?[17]

Although involving parents and the public in the schools represents an important task, school administrators should understand that in the final analysis, involvement should be viewed primarily as a means rather than an end. Any involvement of others—regardless of the form it takes—should ultimately result in improving education, if the involvement is to be judged worthwhile.[18]

While the reasons for involving parents and other groups in school affairs vary somewhat depending on the nature of the involvement, advocates of involvement hope to achieve four main objectives:

1. Through involvement, parents and other citizens become more knowledgeable about school affairs, and as a result, they become
   a. better informed about what students are learning in school
   b. more understanding of the problems that the school faces
   c. more supportive of efforts by the school to improve the educational program
2. Through involvement with teachers and school administrators, parents become better equipped to provide learning activities at home, including developing students' social and personal skills, enhancing basic skills education, and contributing to advanced skills and enrichment education.
3. Through participation by parents and other citizens, the school receives ideas, expertise, and human resources, all of which improve school decision making and the educational program of the school.
4. Through involvement, parents and other citizens are in a much better position to evaluate the school fairly and effectively.

Perhaps Don Davies made the best summary statement of these objectives when he maintained that, "Meaningful citizen involvement can strengthen confidence in and commitment to the school, while making schools more responsible to citizens' diverse concerns."[19] As he later emphasized, "Parent involvement means more than cookie sales. It means helping to make the policies and carry them out."[20]

In each of the four objectives, several assumptions are made: First of all, it is assumed that parents and other citizens need to become more knowledgeable about school affairs, that involvement of some kind is the best means of their becoming more knowledgeable, and that greater knowledge results in more understanding and support on their part. (A Gallup poll has found that those individuals having some involvement with the school hold more favorable attitudes toward the school than those who have had no involvement.[21])

The second objective is based on research suggesting that parent involvement appears to improve student achievement. The major benefits of parent involvement include higher grades and test scores, better long-term academic achievement, positive attitudes and behavior, more successful programs and more effective schools.[22]

The third objective assumes that parents and other citizens possess ideas, expertise, or skills which would be helpful to the school, and that they are willing to make these contributions to the school. The fourth objective assumes that parents and other citizens need or want to evaluate the school, and that they will do a more accurate job of evaluating the school if they are in some way directly involved in what the school is doing. And finally, all of the objectives assume a reasonable degree of cooperation and commitment on the part of administrators, faculty members, and the community to the concept of involving parents and other citizens in the school.

The assumptions underlying the objectives of involvement may or may not be tenable, depending on the community and the school. Whether or not they are tenable, of course, has a bearing on the success of any program of community involvement in the school. To assist school administrators a number of professional organizations have developed publications and guidelines which are useful in organizing viable programs of parental involvement.[23]

BARRIERS

Unfortunately, in many situations there seems to be a large gap between the rhetoric of emphasizing community involvement and the reality of limited opportunity for parents and other members of the community to become meaningfully involved in school affairs. As Dorothy Rich has observed, "When parent involvement is discussed, it is as if the topic is too big, too discouraging, too hot, and too open for policymakers to tackle."[24]

Although the reasons for the large gap between the rhetoric and the reality of community involvement in the schools are complex, available evidence indicates that before citizen involvement increases in the schools and other aspects of school/community relations improve, certain barriers or obstacles may have to be overcome. For example, the faculty or particular segments of the school staff may resist a proposed program of increased community involvement in the schools. These faculty members may take the position that parents are better left alone, are not capable of making useful contributions to the schools, and might only interfere in areas best handled by school professionals. The motivation for such a stance against citizen involvement in schools is complicated, but, for many such teachers, citizen involvement represents an unconscious or direct threat to teachers' status as professionals, their job security, or their personal convenience.[25] In addition, as Moles pointed out, teachers may be burdened by their own home responsibilities, feel overwhelmed by the problems of their students and families, hold low expectations for parents' follow-up efforts, and may perceive a lack of parental support for academics.[26]

Of course, the resistance may be based primarily on a lack of understanding by the teachers about the purposes and advantages of increased citizen involvement. In any regard, administrators must work with their faculties to develop a better understanding of the objectives and values of increased community involvement prior to initiating any major community involvement activities in the school. Guidelines for accomplishing this are discussed by Oralie McAfee.[27]

A second major barrier or obstacle to increased community involvement and improved school/community relations may be the community itself. Changing community demographics may be causing a problem for the school in this regard. In most two-parent families both parents are employed, and in single-parent families the parent is likely to be employed or tied down with child care. As a result, parents are frequently no longer available for meetings during the school day and may be too tired to go to meetings in the evening. Some of these difficulties can be alleviated through more creative scheduling of meetings and by moving the location of the meetings from the school out into the community. However, involvement in school or community activities is not easy for many members of the community. Also, despite all the emphasis placed on increasing community involvement in the schools, administrators may encounter considerable disinterest on the part of parents and other members of the community in becoming more involved with the schools. Confronted with a perceived lack of interest, administrators who do not possess a deep commitment to involving the community could become easily discouraged and could give up on increasing community involvement, later rationalizing that parents and others really did not want to get involved. However, administrators who hold a strong commitment toward increased community involvement do not become easily discouraged but persist and, in most cases, eventually diagnose the causes of the disinterest and take steps to ameliorate the problem. (The problem of community disinterest and apathy is addressed more fully later in the chapter).

A lack of incentives and rewards is another barrier to increasing community involvement and improving other aspects of school/community relations.[28] In many situations few incentives or rewards are offered by the school district to principals who are favorably disposed toward increasing community involvement. Such individuals may not be discouraged from pursuing this objective, but they are not likely to receive much encouragement or recognition either. Perhaps even more important, no negative consequences are imposed by most districts' bureaucracies or school boards if principals exert little effort in improving school/community relations, provided that parent and citizen complaints to the district office do not significantly increase. In many school districts, as long as parents and citizens are quiet, community relations are taken for granted. It seems clear that unless school board and district administrators have an explicit policy emphasizing the importance of positive community relations and provide appropriate incentives and rewards to promote good school/community relations (as well as imposing negative sanctions for those administrators who drag their feet), a comprehensive program to improve school/community relations is unlikely to flourish.

Finally, it takes time, a high degree of competence, and commitment by an administrator to increase community involvement and improve other aspects of school/community relations. Although there is little doubt that the first two factors are important, the key seems to be *commitment*.[29] If administrators believe strongly enough in the value of community involvement in the schools and feel it is essential (not just desirable), in most cases they find the time and develop the capabilities to increase meaningful community involvement.

If, on the other hand, they lack a strong conviction about the importance of community involvement, they are likely to feel that its objectives are not necessary, possible, or worthwhile pursuing. The administrators' own attitudes are very significant factors.

TYPES OF COMMUNITY INVOLVEMENT

Up to this point, we have discussed the concept of involvement, without identifying various ways in which a school might involve parents and other local citizens. Although there are many ways to involve the community in a school, the six examples identified in figure 17.3 are illustrative of community involvement.

Figure 17.3 Types of Community Involvement.

1. Member of an organization such as PTA	2. Committee or council member to study problems, offer recommendations, or make decisions.	3. Parent education
4. Evaluation of some aspect of the school through responding to questionnaire or by observation	5. Resource person for classes; helper in media center, etc.	6. User of school facilities.

Each of the types of community involvement identified in figure 17.3 can potentially benefit both the school and the community. The school can gain from the contributions made by community members through their involvement; local citizens can derive satisfaction from their involvement. To help school administrators better understand the nature of the types of involvement listed in figure 17.3, an introductory description of each follows.

Parents' Organizations

Probably the most typical formal parental involvement is membership in a school-related parents' organization, the best known of which is the National PTA—the National Congress of Parents and Teachers. The PTA was organized in 1897 and now has local chapters in every state. Its overall objectives are to

(1) promote the welfare of children and youth in home, school, church, and community; (2) raise the standards of home life; (3) secure adequate laws for the care and protection of children and youth; (4) bring into closer relation the home and school, that parents and teachers may cooperate intelligently in the education of children and youth; and (5) develop between educators and the general public such united efforts as will secure for all children and youth the highest advantages in physical, mental, and spiritual education.[30]

For many years, the PTA was considered by a number of people to be little more than a coffee-and-cookies group that met several times a year to hear speeches and to discuss buying additional equipment for the school. As James Koerner observed, the PTA "is chiefly useful to the administrator for raising money for special projects and persuading parents who are interested enough to attend meetings that the local schools are in the front ranks of American education."[31]

This situation has changed to a large extent, however; many PTAs have become very active in trying to bring about improvement in the education of children. This change was exemplified, according to a recent president of the National Congress of Parents and Teachers,

> "when we dropped a section of our bylaws that stated that local PTA units should 'cooperate with the schools to support the improvement of education in ways that will not interfere with the administration of the schools, and shall not seek to control their problems,' and substituted, 'PTA shall work with the schools to provide quality education for all children and youth and shall seek to participate in the decision-making process establishing school policy, recognizing that the legal authority to make decisions has been delegated by the people to Boards of Education.' "[32]

The new statement makes clear that, while the PTA recognizes the legal right of the school board to make policy decisions, the members of the PTA expect to participate in the process leading up to such decisions. The new motto of a number of PTA units is "PTA—Parents Taking Action!"

The PTA has also broadened its membership base in recent years. While traditionally composed primarily of parents (couples) and teachers, it now seeks to include single parents, senior citizens, and particularly students.[33] Many groups have made a decided effort to include students, even changing their name to PTSA or Parent-Teacher-Student Association. In contrast, some parents have organized parent unions, which exclude administrators, teachers, students, and other nonparents, perhaps because of prior poor experiences.[34]

Whether a parents' group refers to itself as PTA, PTSA, or simply PA (Parents' Association), parental involvement in some type of an organization associated with the school is a desirable goal for school administrators. Through such involvement, parents can develop a better understanding of what goes on in the school and can make a useful contribution to improving education. While the performance record of parents' organizations is mixed, and they can be an irritant to school administrators if they overextend their authority, they can play a valuable role in helping the school and parents to improve educational opportunities for children.

The keys to successful parent organizations are principal's vision and commitment. As one principal emphasized, "The activities of the PTA are limited only by the principal's imagination and insight."[35] This observation was confirmed by a PTA president who noted, "The PTA in a school is just as good as the principal wants it to be."[36] Although both of these statements may somewhat oversimplify the task of initiating and sustaining a successful PTA, such a task is not likely to be accomplished without considerable vision and commitment by school principals.

Committee or Council Member

Initiation of a school committee or a school advisory council is another type of community involvement administrators should consider. For example, parents or other members of the community could be asked to serve on advisory committees to improve the homework policy, extracurricular activities, school-community communication, or the development of school goals. Many parents and other members of the community possess resources and expertise which could be of assistance to the school, and their utilization on advisory committees is a good way to capitalize on this source of expertise and resources.

The establishment of a parent advisory council for the school should also be considered. Parent or community councils at the individual school level have been mandated in several states and have been initiated on a voluntary basis in other localities.[37] The basic assumptions behind the introduction of these advisory councils seem to be that the councils would act to improve the channels of communication between the public and the schools, and that students would learn more as a result of increased parental interaction with the school. The council's main objectives seem to be

1. Facilitating school communication with parents and community.
2. Assisting in providing support to parents, teachers, students, and community members involved in school programs.
3. Participating in the decision-making process.
4. Informing and advising school staff regarding community conditions, aspirations, and goals.
5. Assisting with the development and monitoring of plans for school improvement.
6. Participating in the preparation of annual school assessment reports.[38]

Council activities seem to vary. One state study discovered that 8 percent of the councils participated in faculty selection and evaluation; 29 percent recommended changes in the curriculum and assisted in textbook selection; 34 percent assisted the school with desegregation, zoning, and the development of comprehensive plans; 34 percent helped identify budgeting needs and assisted in establishing spending priorities; 45 percent recommended ways of responding to student problems, such as vandalism; 60 percent advised the school in regard to community conditions, aspirations, and goals; and 73 percent of the councils participated in the development of the Annual Report of School Progress to parents. The latter activity involved the councils in conducting surveys to ascertain the attitudes of parents, students, and teachers toward different aspects of the school's program.[39]

While the potential of school advisory councils seems to be sizeable, their performance has been uneven. Several studies of the effectiveness of parent advisory councils revealed that many of the councils were not realizing their potential.[40] Although the reasons were typically complex and varied somewhat from one situation to another, major barriers to parent advisory councils' effectiveness usually revolve around issues of lack of ownership, incentives, authority, resources, representation, and organizational maintenance capabilities.[41]

The school principal appears to be a key factor in whether or not a parent advisory council is successful. A study by the Institute for Responsive Education found that all too frequently school principals directed and controlled the meetings and permitted committee members little meaningful impact on decision making.[42] In a related study, Susan Paddock observed that school principals attempted to control the purpose and flow of the meetings through one or more methods: (1) establishing the agenda and setting the priorities for the council; (2) providing information selectively to members of the council; and (3) pushing their own proposed solution to any problem or issue. Paddock concluded from her research that, "Parent involvement in decision making through participation in advisory councils is a myth."[43] This may in fact be due to discrepancies between administrators,' school board members,' and parents' perceptions regarding the role of parents in school-based decision making. Nancy Chavkin and David Williams found that administrators and school board members strongly supported traditional roles for parents (member of an audience, school program supporter, and home tutor), whereas parents indicated strong interest in shared decision-making roles (advocate, colearner, and decision maker) in addition to the traditional roles.[44] On the other hand, other research has documented the existence of effective parent advisory councils where parent involvement in decision making is high.[45] In these situations, as a result of leadership by the school principal, the "trust level was high and the interaction was open," and "on a substantial number of issues, the council had the authority to make the final decision or see that the final decision maker acted as directed."[46]

Parent advisory committees and councils are probably perceived by many administrators as a mixed blessing. Perceived problems, according to Richard Podemski, can include the following: (1) citizen committees or councils consume too much administrative time; (2) they often lack needed background and perspective for solving school problems and addressing issues; (3) they may not understand group dynamics or group decision-making procedures; (4) special interests of committee members may conflict with the need for the committee to reach consensus; and (5) citizen advisory committees and councils sometimes search for problems to justify their existence.[47]

Although administrators cannot eliminate all of the problems associated with citizen participation on school committees and councils, these problems can be either avoided or minimized if administrators adhere to the following guidelines:

1. Administrators should not establish an advisory committee or council unless they sincerely believe that parents and other community members have something important to contribute, and they are prepared to implement these recommendations not in violation of school board policy or state or federal law. (In situations where committees or councils are mandated by law, the first part of this guideline does not, of course, apply.) Unless administrators are willing to provide and facilitate meaningful citizen participation on important issues and problems, they are better off not establishing committees or councils, thereby avoiding citizens' and administrators' frustration and disillusionment.

2. If administrators establish citizen advisory committees or councils, they should clearly define and communicate to all members, in advance, the objectives, function, scope, and authority of the committee or council. If it is only an advisory committee to develop *recommendations* to submit to the administrator, then that function should be made clear to all participants.

3. Training should be provided to members of the committee or council on how to function effectively in a group. Many citizens have had little or no experience or training in this activity. Administrators should consider utilizing an outside consultant to provide the training.

4. All members of the committee or council should be kept well informed before, during, and between meetings, as to what is transpiring. Advance agendas and minutes of each meeting are minimum requirements.
5. The individual interests and talents of the members of the committee or council should be utilized to the greatest extent possible. There is little to be gained by either the school or the participants if the latter's potential contributions are not fully utilized.
6. Members of the committee or council should be rewarded for their individual and total contributions at every available opportunity. Committee and council work is frequently tedious, and periodic recognition of the value of the group's work by the administrator pays important dividends.

Citizen advisory committees and councils offer potentially major contributions to improving school-community relations and to assisting the school in improving the educational program. As Davies noted, "Advocates of parent involvement in decision making see such involvement as being based on democratic principles, linked to rebuilding the legitimacy of the schools, and providing support for efforts to change programs or policies.[48] Whether that potential can be realized or not depends as much on the attitude, vision, and leadership capabilities of the principal as on any other factor.

Parent Education

In recent years a number of schools and school districts have attempted to involve parents more directly in the learning of their children through programs of parent education. The basic assumption of such programs is that the school can teach parents how they can assist in the education of their children and, as a result, improve the motivation and achievement of students in school.[49] The main objectives of parent education programs usually include one or more of the following:[50]

1. To help parents acquire the understanding and skill to teach certain concepts and skills at home (e.g., reading readiness).
2. To help parents learn how to become educational managers of their children's work at home (e.g., monitoring homework).
3. To help parents become more effective in parenting (e.g., learning and practicing particular child rearing techniques).

The activities in a parent education program vary, depending on the objectives the school district is trying to accomplish. Examples of activities initiated by a number of school districts include special courses for parents on how to tutor their children, written materials and games to be used with children, in-home contact by school specialists to help parents with problem children, and facilitation of counseling or support groups for parents experiencing difficulty in rearing children. The Parents in Touch program in Indianapolis organizes workshops and seminars available to schools, ranging from curriculum questions and test procedures to self-development and effective parenting techniques.[51] And a rather comprehensive program developed by the Philadelphia School District consists of the following activities:[52]

- *Parent workshops.* Conducted throughout the school system twice a year; workshops help parents understand various aspects of child development and make use of learning materials in the home. Recent workshops have featured school discipline, testing, and other school-related topics.
- *Mini workshop series.* School administrators can request to have one of almost sixty workshops presented at their regular Home and School Association meetings.
- *Personalized reading and mathematical books.* On request, parents may receive graded materials in reading and math. Computer-generated booklets are also available to strengthen reading comprehension. These stories include references to the child and his or her friends.
- *Public awareness.* Parents of school-age children are informed of the variety of program activities through print and broadcast media.
- *Data Line.* A telephone resource center provides assistance and information to parents and pupils related to homework, program activities and school services. A Spanish language hotline is also available.

Another example of parent education by the school is this letter to the parents of students in one school.[53]

Dear Parents of Townsend,

Do your children make you feel guilty when you discipline them? How do you handle temper tantrums? Do you react to them or do you take action?

Mrs. Lucia Halyard, our guidance counselor, is planning a workshop for any interested parents. The purpose of the workshop is to help parents develop skills in conflict resolution and to discuss ways of assisting children in establishing good relationships at home and at school.

The first workshop is scheduled for Tuesday at 7:00 P.M. at Townsend Street School, Teacher's Lounge.

If you are interested in attending, please fill out and return the slip below.

Sincerely,
(Signed)

Robert T. Johnson,
Principal

The Home and School Institute based in Washington, D.C. has pioneered the development of home learning activities that "simultaneously reinforce practice in academic subjects, teach children useful daily life skills, and fit the time frames of today's working parents."[54] Useful structures that can facilitate parent participation in their children's learning include:

- Special interest groups for working parents, single parents, parent-to-parent issues, fathers.
- Parent-to-parent visitor programs that supply materials to families to use in helping children at home.
- Telephone hotlines that provide home learning activities.
- Newsletters that share tips from parents.
- Family learning libraries at local schools and libraries, containing learning materials assembled for families to use at home.
- After-school programs for students and families.
- Lounge areas in schools where families can meet to receive information and materials about child rearing and education.[55]

Although these ideas have existed for a number of years, their importance and potential impact are frequently minimized. The Family-School Partnership Act initiated by Senator Bill Bradley may turn the tide; it calls for a basic infrastructure of demonstration projects focusing on the role of the family as an educator and on teacher training to support the efforts of families.[56]

Despite the previously cited positive findings regarding parent involvement in student learning activities and the potentially positive benefits of parent education programs, school administrators need to be aware that initiating such a program may not be easy. The faculty may not accept the notion that parents can also be educators with something important to contribute to the total education process. Also, parents may not see themselves as educators and may believe that education is the job of the school. And financial support for a program of parent education may be difficult to obtain and sustain. While these potential problems could represent serious obstacles to initiating or continuing a program of parent education, they are by no means inevitable; for the most part, they can be overcome with appropriate leadership as described earlier in this chapter.

Evaluator

Although some administrators may recoil at the prospect of involving parents in the evaluation of their schools, in one way or another, parents evaluate schools all the time.[57] They may not evaluate schools in any scientific or formal sense, but parents do make evaluative judgments on the worth of different aspects of the school program. The real question, to which administrators need to address themselves, is whether it is better to allow parents to continue to make informal evaluative judgments (about which the school may not be aware and which in many instances are based on inadequate information and limited contact with the school), or to involve parents in some formal evaluation of the school's program. While the question is stated rhetorically and the answer is, hopefully, obvious, it is surprising how many administrators continue to behave as though the absence of a formal program of evaluation by parents means that parents are not evaluating the school.

Administrators and staff members need periodic, systematic, evaluative feedback from parents (and other members of the community) regarding their perceptions, feelings, and ideas as to the effectiveness of the school and how the school program could be improved. In this context, periodic evaluation means at least once a year, and systematic means that an attempt should be made to secure representative parents' viewpoints in the evaluation. School administrators need this kind of information if they are to keep themselves accurately informed on what parents are thinking and to correct any inaccurate perceptions. They can also find such information helpful in identifying aspects of the school program which may need improvement. Despite the fact that most parents are not professionally trained in education, they can nonetheless contribute valuable ideas for improving schools. Administrators should attempt to capitalize on this potential source of ideas.

Although many administrators try to involve parents in evaluating the school, these efforts are often informal or initiated only after the development of a serious problem in school-community relations. Informal contacts with parents and the community are necessary and desirable, but they cannot adequately substitute for a formally organized program of securing evaluative community feedback. In addition, the best time to obtain community input is *before* a problem reaches the crisis stage, not at the point of crisis. Periodic surveying of parental and community sentiment can alert a school administrator to a developing problem and may suggest a possible means of avoiding a crisis.

Before initiating a formal program of parental evaluation of the school, administrators should work with the staff. The faculty needs to understand the purpose and possible value of parents' evaluation of the school. The staff also needs to be reassured that the evaluation will not be directed at individual teachers. Although parent evaluation of teachers might have some value, it is such a potentially controversial area that administrators should steer the parent evaluation away from this topic—at least until their faculties better understand and accept the program.

Administrators should also attempt to work with parents on their role as evaluators of the school. Most parents have not been involved in formal programs of evaluation and need assistance if they are going to make constructive contributions.

After administrators have provided appropriate preparation for their staff and parents, they might consider various alternatives for involving parents in evaluating a school; two techniques particularly merit their attention. The first is the questionnaire method. Utilizing this approach, administrators (perhaps with consultant help) can design a questionnaire which asks for parents' reactions to or perceptions of the school program. The questionnaire can be long and comprehensive or short and specific, covering only a certain aspect of the school. An example of a short questionnaire is presented in figure 17.4 (An example of a longer questionnaire is the Metropolitan Life Survey of the American Teacher.[58])

A questionnaire can be sent to all parents or to only a random sample. In most cases, a questionnaire study provides schools with valuable information, although its usefulness depends as much on the care with which it is designed as on the cooperation of the parents.

A second good technique for involving parents in the evaluation of the school is the interview. An interview might be used as a follow-up to a questionnaire, or it may be used instead of the questionnaire, depending on the administrator's objectives. Usually it is not possible to interview all parents on a single matter, but through sampling procedures and in-depth interview techniques, the administrator should be able to secure representative views from parents. Interviews may be conducted either at the school, in the home, or by telephone. Provided with in-service training, teachers, counselors, administrators, and even parents should be able to conduct interviews and obtain valuable information for the school.

Figure 17.4 A Short Questionnaire for Parents.

Grade of your Child _____ School _____ Boy _____ Girl _____

      We would like your reactions to our new homework policy. Please indicate your feelings as to its good points and any areas needing improvement, and then mail this form back to the school.

Good Points

Areas Needing Improvement

(Please return by Monday. Thank you for your help.)

Regardless of the particular technique or approach used, administrators must recognize that securing parents' assessment of the school on a regular basis is essential. Parents will be evaluating the school whether or not administrators think it is desirable for them to do so. The task for administrators is to plan, design, and implement evaluative procedures for parents which aid in eliciting information and ideas for the improvement of the school program.

Resource Person, Volunteer

An excellent means by which schools can involve parents and the community at large is by encouraging them to serve as resource people or volunteers. Many people in most communities possess skills, knowledge, or ideas which might be made available to the school. Professional workers, craftspersons, individuals who have traveled, and those who have a particular area of expertise could serve as resource people and offer a great deal to supplement a school's curriculum. In addition, many housewives and older or retired people have time available and are willing to serve as helpers or aides to the school in the classroom, library, cafeteria, or guidance office. Usually, volunteers can be of assistance to school administrators and the school staff in five areas:

1. Informing the community about what the schools are doing.
2. Improving the perception of public education.
3. Encouraging students by recognizing achievement.
4. Increasing community involvement in the schools.
5. Providing additional resources to the schools.[59]

Generally a large number of people in every community possess resources of expertise, time, and energy, and are willing to volunteer their services to make major contributions to schools.

Schools which have initiated community volunteer programs have involved citizens in a wide variety of ways. Examples of citizen involvement include participating in a tutorial program to help students cope with the new pressures of competency testing; making daily calls to the homes of absent students; assisting teachers and office staff by typing, filing, collating, and performing other clerical duties; working in the library; operating audiovisual equipment; tutoring students in math; listening to students read; preparing instructional materials; reading stories to youngsters; and playing learning games with children. As one principal observed, "Just having another adult in the classroom who cares about a child is a marvelous asset. I wish we could have the senior volunteers five days a week."[60]

While utilizing community volunteers can potentially provide the school with additional resources and help, school administrators should approach the task of initiating a program carefully and thoughtfully. Perhaps the Fairfax County, Virginia, Pubic School's *Volunteer Handbook* put it best: "Volunteer programs should arise out of a clearly felt need for assistance in some area of the school program. A principal and a school staff must genuinely desire a program, and the community must be willing to serve and to accept orientation and training. And, however high the enthusiasm, experience in volunteer programs clearly indicates the wisdom in beginning with a limited, carefully run project, and expanding slowly."[61]

In all too many situations, the community is still a relatively untapped source of knowledge and assistance. School administrators have the responsibility of surveying the community to discover the different resource people and helpers who might be available. Then, through careful planning and appropriate training for staff members, as well as community volunteers, they should institute a program for capitalizing on these resources for the improvement of the school program. Materials on how to initiate and administer a school volunteer program can be obtained from the National Association of Partners in Education, 601 Wythe Street, Suite 200, Alexandria, Virginia 22314.

User of School Facilities

Possibly one of the best ways to gain parents' and other citizens' support for the school is to involve them in the use of school facilities. People who use the school building are usually more likely to support the school than those who have little or no opportunity to use the facilities maintained by their tax money.[62]

Imaginative administrators can find a variety of ways in which to involve parents and other members of the community in the use of school facilities. Probably the most widely known method is the "lighthouse school" approach.[63] In this approach, school buildings are kept open and lighted at night, and educational and recreational programs are offered by the school to members of the community. Participants may be charged a minimum fee, or the entire expense may be assumed by the school district as an investment in community goodwill and adult education. The objectives of this program are to provide

- An educational center where members of the community can study and learn.
- A neighborhood center for cultural and recreational activities.

- A center for social services.
- A center for utilizing school and community resources to help citizens solve neighborhood problems.[64]

Although such programs are usually administered by the district office, building administrators can help make them successful through cooperation and leadership. In addition, by periodically making themselves visible at the school while these programs are in process, administrators can extend their knowledge of and acquaintance with the community, and indicate their support of this community involvement.

In a more direct sense, administrators have an opportunity to involve community groups in the use of school facilities when they respond to their requests for the use of rooms in the building (at the end of the school day or on weekends). Many groups, such as scouts or local drama players, may request administrators' permission to use school facilities after school hours. The ultimate authority for granting this permission may be the central office, depending on school board policy. However, school administrators can act as either facilitators or impediments in securing permission for use of the facilities. Certainly, school administrators' attitudes and behaviors in these situations can evoke considerable good will or create ill will on the part of these community groups.

Another opportunity for community use of school facilities on which more administrators should capitalize, is that of inviting retired people to view student activities as the school's guests.[65] Retired people often have limited financial resources and social outlets so they may appreciate complimentary passes to watch athletic, dramatic, and music activities at the school. Some schools issue a "Golden Age School Activities Pass" to retired people in the community. This type of effort by a school can deliver dividends in increasing community good will; at the same time, it offers a service to the retired people of the community who have been supporting the schools for so many years with taxes.

Involving the community in the use of school facilities is not always an easy task for school administrators. Financial problems on the part of the district, lack of vision on the part of the school board and teachers, and inadequate cooperation from the custodial staff are three major obstacles which may have to be overcome by the school administrator. If administrators really believe that the schools are for all the people in the community, however, and if they are willing to exert their energy and time to resolve serious problems, a program of community use of school facilities should be possible and, in any event, remains desirable.

INVOLVING PARENTS: PROBLEMS

PARENTAL APATHY

Although community participation in the school has value, administrators should recognize that it is not without attendant problems. An initial barrier confronting school administrators who wish to involve parents in the schools is parental apathy. Ironically, despite the great recent emphasis on parental involvement, many administrators who have tried to involve parents report that they have encountered considerable apathy. For example, questionnaires sent to parents may not be returned, and meetings of parents' organizations are often poorly attended. A common complaint of many administrators is that parents are indifferent about school unless a controversial issue arises; otherwise, most parents seem to prefer to remain uninvolved in school affairs.

Realistically, schools cannot accommodate the active involvement of all parents and there will always be a number of them who simply do not care to participate in school affairs, regardless of how much effort the school expands in that direction. School administrators should also realize that many parents are occupied with full-time jobs; at the end of a long day, various leisure activities compete with the school for their available time. (For example, how many school administrators, if given a choice, would decide against spending a relaxing evening at home, watching television, reading, or engaging in another leisure time activity with the family, in favor of attending a meeting at the school?) Although most parents are interested in the school and many of them might be willing to become more active in working to improve it, administrators need to recognize that a number of alternative activities are competing for parents' available time.

School administrators faced with parental apathy need to approach these situations as they would any other problem: by attempting to define more precisely the nature of and reasons for the problem. A thorough diagnosis may reveal that parent apathy is only a symptom, rather than the problem itself.

The initial question administrators need to ask is, Why are parents apathetic? Until administrators attempt a systematic investigation of the reasons for parental apathy, they are unlikely to make much progress in ameliorating it, and any actions they take may be based on an incorrect diagnosis of the causes of the problem. An effective solution to a problem must be preceded by a correct diagnosis of the causes. Administrators, by trying to hypothesize as to the causes of parent apathy and then collecting data from parents on the hypotheses, are engaged in the process of diagnosis.[66] This process should provide direction for a possible solution to parent apathy.

Figure 17.5 Factors Which May Restrict Parental Involvement in the Schools.

	Parent's Response				
Reasons from Parent's Perception	Not Important	Of Some Importance	Fairly Important	Very Important	Extremely Important
1. Not enough time	_____	_____	_____	_____	_____
2. Not sure how to get involved	_____	_____	_____	_____	_____
3. Not sure the school really wants parents to get involved	_____	_____	_____	_____	_____
4. Not sure that I have the necessary skills and knowledge to get involved in school affairs	_____	_____	_____	_____	_____
5. No need to get involved; teachers and administrators already know what is best	_____	_____	_____	_____	_____
6. Have previously had poor or bad experience when I became involved in school decision making	_____	_____	_____	_____	_____
7. No one has ever encouraged me to become involved	_____	_____	_____	_____	_____
8. _____	_____	_____	_____	_____	_____
9. _____	_____	_____	_____	_____	_____

Figure 17.5 presents a questionnaire based on several analyses of parent apathy; administrators can use it to ascertain the reasons for parental apathy and the perceived importance of those reasons.[67]

As figure 17.5 suggests, the reasons behind parental apathy may be complex. Parental apathy should be viewed as a symptom of limited parental involvement in the schools, but not as its cause. Actually, parental apathy may be only a convenient label many administrators have used to affix blame on parents for not responding better to the school's attempts to involve them. Again, the basic question that the administrator needs to ask is, "*Why* are parents apathetic?"

A related question to be raised by school administrators as they investigate parental apathy should be, do the professional staff and administrators really want parents to become significantly involved in school affairs, and if we do, are we willing to work hard to secure that kind of involvement? Involving parents is a time-consuming, demanding, and at times frustrating task. Unless administrators and staff members are truly committed to parental involvement, it is not likely to be successful.

Many parents believe, rightly or wrongly, that the school wants them to be involved only in busywork or in providing support for the school, rather than in evaluating the effectiveness of the school or participating in school decision making. If administrators want to combat parental apathy, they probably need to provide more meaningful opportunities for parents to participate in school affairs. Most people are apathetic about taking part in a given activity unless they feel that they can make a significant contribution. (For further ideas on how to deal with the problem of parents' apathy, contact the National Committee for Citizens in Education, 10840 Little Patuxent Parkway, Columbia, Maryland 21044, and the Institute for Responsive Education, 605 Commonwealth Avenue, Boston, Massachusetts 02215.)

PARENTAL OVERINVOLVEMENT

Although parental apathy can be a troublesome problem for school administrators sincerely committed to parents' participation in the schools, an equally difficult (though opposite) problem for some administrators is parental overinvolvement.[68] The latter problem can take many forms, but it may be defined as parental involvement which tends to interfere with the operation and administration of the school by the professional staff and the administrator. Figure 17.6 presents some examples of parental overinvolvement, as perceived by many administrators.

Parental overinvolvement is a value judgment that is in the eyes of the beholder. What is considered to be overinvolvement by one administrator may be seen as appropriate or justifiable involvement by other observers. For example, community efforts to become involved in the textbook or library book selection process may be perceived as legitimate and reasonable by many parents, and yet may be regarded by school administrators and the faculty as overinvolvement on the part of citizens and interference with the management of the school district.

Figure 17.6 Types of Parental Overinvolvement.

1. Censorship of books or materials in the school by individual parents.

2. Efforts by individual parents or by groups of parents to become "excessively" involved in decision making about school policies and procedures.

3. Attempts to modify the school curriculum (e.g., ban on sex education) by pressure groups.

4. Regular or constant complaints by individual parents or parents' groups.

As problems of the schools have recently attracted increased attention from the media, parents have become more concerned about the quality of education and, as a consequence, many of them have tried to become actively involved in school affairs. Depending on the nature of that involvement and the concept of parental involvement held by school administrators and the professional staff, conflicts are possible.

Part of the problem is that active involvement by parents who have questioned the school's effectiveness or who have attempted to develop larger roles for themselves in school decision making represents a threat to many school administrators and their professional staffs who respond negatively. In some cases, much concern about parental overinvolvement is caused by administrators' own lack of willingness to be evaluated by parents and to share decision-making responsibilities with them. On the other hand, there is legitimate administrative concern in connection with certain parental involvement, such as attempts at censorship or the use of protest tactics by special interest groups.[69]

According to Frederick Wirt and Michael Kirst, the following factors are characteristic of special interest groups who use protest tactics against the school:

1. The use of protest indicates that regular channels for handling grievances and complaints are not functioning effectively for the special interest group.
2. The special interest that uses pressure tries to publicize their demands through communications media in hopes of attracting allies and supporters.
3. The special interest group that uses pressure tries to dramatize issues and problems rather than to present objective data.
4. Working with a special interest group that uses pressure can be a difficult and frustrating task for the school administrator.[70]

Despite the difficulties in working with special interest groups that use pressure tactics, administrators should not assume that the demands of the groups are without merit or that pressure by a group is necessarily bad. Historically in our society, necessary change has frequently been brought about only after the use of pressure. While not every method can be justified, pressure tactics may be needed in certain situations to bring about needed change. And, regardless of the methods used, the demands of a group should be considered on their own merits, separately from the tactics employed.

Administrators concerned about special interest groups who use pressure tactics or any other type of parental overinvolvement, should investigate the following possible causes of that overinvolvement:

- The regular channels for parental involvement and resolution of grievances and complaints are not functioning effectively.
- A misunderstanding. Perhaps the parents were not briefed clearly enough by the school as to the limits of their or the school's authority.
- An unrealistic or inappropriate notion of the value and concept of parental involvement on the part of either the parents or the administration, or both.
- An honest difference of opinion between the school administration and the parents on the role of parents in school affairs.

Parents' overinvolvement can create serious problems for the school. The school administrator's role in response to parental overinvolvement should be to investigate its possible causes and take whatever action seems appropriate and feasible in light of local circumstances.

A CLOSING PERSPECTIVE

Effective community involvement is not an easy objective to achieve. Frustrations and problems must be overcome, and little success is experienced without considerable hard work and persistence by the administrator. However, given administrators with strong commitments to a broad vision of the potential usefulness of community involvement, a successful program of community participation in the schools is attainable.

Review and Learning Activities

1. Why is it important that a school administrator maintain up-to-date knowledge about the community? Ascertain the extent to which your school has reliable and valid information about each of the factors in figures 17.1 and 17.2. How could this information be better utilized for instructional, curricular, and administrative purposes?

2. Why is it important for the school to involve parents and other citizens in school affairs? Ascertain the degree to which possible barriers to community involvement exist in your school situation. If you were the principal, how would you overcome these barriers, using the concepts presented in chapters 3 and 4?

3. If you were the principal of your school, to what extent would you introduce (or improve) each of the types of community involvement presented in the text? Which obstacles and/or problems would have to be overcome?

4. What are the two main problems that administrators might encounter in trying to involve parents? How can they best prevent or ameliorate these problems?

Notes

1. William O. Stanley et al., *Social Foundations of Education* (New York: Holt-Dryden Books, Henry Holt Co., 1955), 81.

2. See Frederick Wirt and Michael Kirst, *Schools in Conflict* (Berkeley, Calif.: McCutchan Publishing, 1982); and Joel Spring, *Conflicts of Interests: The Politics of American Education* (White Plains, N.Y.: Longman, 1988).

3. Eugene Litwak et al., *School, Family and Neighborhood: The Theory and Practice of School-Community Relations* (New York: Columbia University Press, 1974).

4. Barbara Kudlacek, "Special Interest Groups: Friends or Foes?" *NASSP Bulletin* (January 1989): 29–32.

5. Richard W. Saxe, *School-Community Interaction* (Berkeley, Calif.: McCutchan Publishing, 1975). See also Richard W. Saxe, "School-Community Relations," in *Encyclopedia of School Administration and Supervision,* ed. R. Gorton, G. Schneider, and J. Fisher, (Phoenix, Ariz.: Oryx Press, 1988), 230–31.

6. S. C. Ruffin, Jr., "Improving Urban Communities and Their Schools: A National Emergency," *NASSP Bulletin* (May 1989): 61–70.

7. Neal Nickerson and Amy Mook, "School Community Relations: Another Aspect of Instructional Leadership," *NASSP Bulletin* (October 1988): 44.

8. Joyce L. Epstein, "Parent Involvement: What Research Says to Administrators," *Education and Urban Society* (February 1987): 130.

9. Harold Hodgkinson, "What's Ahead for Education," *Principal* (January 1986): 6–11, cited in Milbrey Wallin McLaughlin and Patrick M. Shields, "Involving Low-Income Parents in the Schools: A Role for Policy?" *Kappan* (October 1987): 157.

10. Epstein, "Parent Involvement."

11. An excellent description of the objectives and influence of a number of these groups can be found in Roald Campbell, Luvern L. Cunningham, Raphael O. Nystrand, and Michael D. Usdan, *The Organization and Control of American Schools,* 3d. ed. (Columbus, Ohio: Merrill Publishing, 1985), chaps. 13, 14; and Frederick M. Wirt and Leslie Christovich, "Administrators' Perceptions of Policy Influence: Conflict Management Styles and Roles," *Educational Administration Quarterly* (February 1989): 5–35.

12. C. W. Leftwich and Yih Nan Lee, "School/Community Relations: A Building Approach," *Planning and Changing* (Summer 1986): 101–6.

13. Louis Harris, Michael Kagay, and Jane Ross, *The Metropolitan Life Survey of the American Teacher 1987: Strengthening Links between Home and School* (New York: Louis Harris and Associates, Inc., for Metropolitan Life Insurance Company, 1987).

14. "Can Parents Save Schools?" *Newsweek* (October 16, 1989): 74.

15. Oliver C. Moles, "Who Wants Parent Involvement? Interest, Skills, and Opportunities among Parents and Educators," *Education and Urban Society* (February 1987): 137.

16. Don Davies, "Parent Involvement in the Public Schools: Opportunities for Administrators," *Education and Urban Society* (February 1987): 147.

17. Ibid. See also William W. Wayson, Charles Achilles, Gay Su Pinnell, M. Nan Lintz, Lila N. Card, and Luvern Cunningham, *Handbook for Developing Public Confidence in Schools* (Bloomington, Ind.: Phi Delta Kappa Educational Foundation, 1988).

18. For a review of evidence which shows that parental involvement can, under the right circumstances, exert a positive influence on children's academic achievement, see Anne T. Henderson, "Parents Are a School's Best Friends," *Kappan* (October 1988): 148–53; and Beth Sattes, "Parental Involvement in Student Learning," *Education Digest* (January 1989): 37–39.

19. Don Davies, "The Emerging Third Force in Education," *Inequalities in Education* (November 1973): 5. For further information see *A Resource Guide on Parent and Citizen Participation in the Schools* available from the Institute for Responsive Education, Boston, Massachusetts.

20. Quoted by Patricia F. Store in "Parents Can Cause Change in Special Education," *Citizens in Action* (March 1979): 3.

21. George H. Gallup, "The Twentieth Annual Poll of the Public's Attitudes toward the Public Schools," *Kappan* (September 1988): 42.

22. Henderson, "Parents Are a School's Best Friends," 149. See also Julius Menacker, Emanuel Hurwitz, and Ward Weldon, "Parent-Teacher Cooperation in Schools Serving the Urban Poor," *Clearing House* (November 1988): 108–12.

23. See *Involving Parents in the Education of Their Children* (Eugene: Oregon School Study Council); *Teachers and Parents: An Adult-to-Adult Approach* (West Haven, Conn.: NEA Professional Library); *First Teachers: Parental Involvement in the Public Schools* (Alexandria, Va.: National School Boards Association); *Enhancing Parent Involvement in Schools: A Manual for Parents and Teachers* (New York: Teachers College Press); Melitta J. Cutright, *The National PTA Talks to Parents: How to Get the Best Education for Your Child* (New York: Doubleday, 1989).

24. Dorothy Rich, "Bridging the Parent Gap in Education Reform," *Education Horizons* (Winter 1988): 90.

25. See Henderson, "Parents Are a School's Best Friends," 149; and M. Laurie Leitch and Sandra S. Tangri, "Barriers to Home-School Collaboration," *Education Horizons* (Winter 1988): 70–74.

26. Moles, "Who Wants Parent Involvement?" 141.

27. Oralie McAfee, "Improving Home-School Relations: Implications for Staff Development," *Education and Urban Society* (February 1987): 185–99.

28. David Hollister, "School Bureaucratization as a Response to Parents' Demands," *Urban Education* (July 1979): 221–35.

29. McLaughlin and Shields, "Involving Low-Income Parents," 158. See also Dorothy S. Strickland and Eric J. Cooper, *Educating Black Children: America's Challenge* (Washington, D.C.: Howard University, Bureau of Educational Research, 1987), 70–104.

30. *PTA Magazine* (September 1971); also see Ann P. Kahn, "Parent Teacher Association, National (National Congress of Parents and Teachers)," in *Encyclopedia of School Administration and Supervision,* ed. R. Gorton, G. Schneider, and J. Fisher (Phoenix, Ariz.: Oryx Press, 1988), 189.

31. James Koerner, *Who Controls American Education?* (Boston: Beacon Press, 1968), 148.

32. Virginia Sparling, "PTA Involvement in the 80s: New Concepts, New Directions," *NASSP Bulletin* (January 1980): 25. See also "The PTA: Working 90 Years for Children, Families and Schools," *Redbook* (1987): 28–30.

33. Sparling, "PTA Involvement," 24.

34. Happy C. Ferandez, "Empowering Parents," *The Urban Review* (Summer 1979): 92–96.

35. James A. Sandfort, "The PTA—Is It the Forgotten Community Resource?" *NASSP Bulletin* (January 1980): 4.

36. "The Value of the PTA," *Today's Education* (May 1969): 30.

37. Ross Zerchykov, "Why School Councils?" *Equity and Choice* (Fall 1985): 37–38. See also Davies, "Parent Involvement in the Public Schools," 147–63.

38. See Nelson Price, "School Community Councils and Advisory Boards: A Notebook for Administrators, Why? Who? What? When? How?" (ERIC Report Ed–145–583); Davies, "Parent Involvement in the Public Schools," 151; and *School-Based Improvement: A Manual for Training School Councils* (Columbia, Md.: National Committee for Citizens in Education, 1989).

39. Gordon E. Greenwood et al., "Citizen Advisory Committees," *Theory into Practice* (February 1977): 12–16.

40. Marilyn Gittell, *Citizen Organizations: Citizen Participation in Educational Decisionmaking* (Boston: Institute for Responsive Education, 1980); and Owen Heleen and Frederick T. Miller, *Mobilizing Local Coalitions and Collaborations to Better Serve Children at Risk* (Boston: Institute for Responsive Education, 1988).

41. Jim Stanton and Ross Zerchykov, *Overcoming Barriers to School Council Effectiveness* (Boston: Institute for Responsive Education, 1979); and Don Davies, *Benefits of and Barriers to Parent Involvement* (Boston: Institute for Responsive Education, 1988.)

42. Donald Davies et al., *Sharing the Power? A Report on the Status of School Councils in the 1970s* (Boston: Institute for Responsive Education, 1978).

43. Susan C. Paddock, "The Myth of Parent Involvement through Advisory Councils" (Paper presented at the annual meeting of the American Educational Research Association, San Francisco, California, 1979).

44. Nancy Feyl Chavkin and David L. Williams, Jr., "Enhancing Parent Involvement: Guidelines for Access to and Important Resource for School Administrators," *Education and Urban Society* (February 1987): 164–84.

45. Miriam Clasby et al., "Improving Education in Florida: A Reassessment" (ERIC Report Ed–172–353).

46. A quotation by John Shadgett (who studied school-based advisory councils in Florida) which appeared in *Education USA* (March 10, 1980): 213; and Clasby et al., "Improving Education in Florida."

47. Richard S. Podemski, "Advisory Committees," in *Encyclopedia of School Administration and Supervision* ed. R Gorton, G. Schneider, and J. Fisher (Phoenix, Ariz.: Oryx Press, 1988), 28–29.

48. Davies, "Parent Involvement in Public Schools," 152.

49. Moles, "Who Wants Parent Involvement?" 142–44.

50. Ibid. See also Sandra Jowett and Mary Baginsky, "Parents and Education: A Survey of Their Involvement and a Discussion of Some Issues," *Education Research* (February 1988): 40–41.

51. Moles, "Who Wants Parent Involvement?", 143.

52. Oliver Moles and Carter Collins, "Home School Programs of Urban School Districts" (Paper presented at the annual meeting of American Educational Research Association, Los Angeles, California, April 1981). For additional ideas, see Roy Truby, "Home-School Projects That Work," *Education and Urban Society* (February 1987): 206–11; and Barbara L. Jackson and Bruce S. Cooper, "Parent Choice and Empowerment: New Roles for Parents," *Urban Education* (October 1989): 263–86.

53. Townsend Elementary School, Milwaukee Public School System, Milwaukee, Wisconsin.

54. Dorothy Rich, "Bridging the Parent Gap in Education Reform," *Education Horizons* (Winter 1988): 91.

55. Ibid.

56. The Honorable Bill Bradley, *The Family-School Partnership Act,* 100th Congress, 1st sess., 1987, S. 1157.

57. Jane C. Lindle, "What Do Parents Want from Principals and Teachers?" *Educational Leadership* (October 1989): 12–14.

58. Harris, Kagay, and Ross, *The Metropolitan Life Survey,* 103–17.

59. See Lew Armistead, "Building Greater Confidence in Education: Volunteers Are Important to our Public Relations," *NASSP NewsLeader* (November 1988): 5; and Lew Armistead, "Non-Parents Are Key Audience for School Support," *NASSP NewsLeader* (September 1989): 5.

60. Georgia Slack, "Volunteering Is In," *American Education* (April 1978): 6–10.

61. Quotation from William C. Parrish, "Volunteers in the Secondary Schools," *The Practitioner* (January 1981): 3. For further guidelines on planning and operating an effective volunteer program, see John W. Secor, "Launching a Volunteers Program," *Here's How* (National Association of Elementary School Principals April 1988).

62. Kenneth R. Stevenson and Terry Terril, "Avoid Dissension by Involving Citizens in Facilities Planning," *American School Board Journal* (November 1988): 30.

63. For the early roots of this approach, see Clarence A. Perry, *Wider Use of the School Plant* (New York: Russell Sage Foundation, 1910). For a more contemporary concept of this approach, see Jack D. Minzey and Clyde E. Le Tarte, *Community Education: From Program to Practice* (Midland, Mich.: Pendell Publishing, 1980).

64. John R. Hughes, ed., "The Community School and Its Concept" (ERIC Report Ed–073–531). See also H. Jurgens Combs, "You Can Improve School-Community Relations," *NASSP Bulletin* (April 1987): 126–29.

65. Nickerson and Mook, "School and Community Relations," 44–46.

66. This process is further described in chapters 3 and 12.

67. Ted R. Urich and Judith P. LaVorgna, "A Parent Involvement Program—Giving Opportunity a Chance," *NASSP Bulletin* (January 1980): 34–38. Also, James Smith, "The Relationship between Parents' Attitudes toward School and Their Involvement in School Decision Making." A Specialist Field Inquiry, University of Wisconsin-Milwaukee, 1973.

68. Roy R. Nasstrom, "Principals View Parents as Enemies," *Educational Communication* (July 1981): 35.

69. For an excellent book on the censorship problem, see Edward Jenkinson, *Censors in the Classroom: The Mind Benders* (Carbondale: Southern Illinois University Press, 1979). Also, for some helpful guidelines on how to deal with censorship protests, see Helen Lee, "Precautions Principals Can Take to Avert Censorship Protests," *NASSP Bulletin* (May 1988): 70–76.

70. Frederick M. Wirt and Michael W. Kirst, *The Political Web of American Schools* (Boston: Little, Brown and Company, 1972): 57–59. For a good discussion of the theoretical dimensions of special interest groups, see Wirt and Kirst, *Schools in Conflict.*

18

. . . . .

School-Community Relations:
Communication and Public Relations

Most administrators have long recognized the importance of effective school-community communication and the desirability of maintaining good public relations. Unfortunately, in too many situations, communication has been primarily from the school to the community with little attempt to secure feedback. The objective of the school's public relations activities has been to sell the school program.

School-community communication and public relations should be cooperative processes which are both honest and responsive. In the case of school-community communication, each party has something of value to communicate to the other and needs to seek feedback on whether its own message is being received and understood accurately. A school's public relations program must reflect honesty and integrity in all of its interfaces with the community to retain its credibility and the confidence and support of the community. In the following sections, different aspects of school-community communication and the school's public relations program are explored.

SCHOOL COMMUNICATION

TYPICAL PRACTICES

Traditionally the school has, for the most part, used two main methods for communication with its immediate community: the school newsletter, and the PTA or parents' meeting. (The telephone and individual conferences are two other means of communication used by the school on a limited basis to communicate with individual parents or other members of the community.)

The school newsletter has taken several forms, depending on the school and the school district.[1] It may be an informational bulletin developed and disseminated by the district office, describing noteworthy activities occurring in all the schools in the district; or, an individual school may publish its own newsletter, describing in more detail and to a greater extent than would be possible in a district newsletter, the major activities and school happenings that might be of interest to parents. The newsletter may be a semimonthly commercially printed news bulletin mailed to parents, or it may consist of an occasional, mimeographed information sheet sent home with the students. The school newsletter may be perceived by parents and the community as informative and worthwhile, or it may be perceived as containing little or nothing that is newsworthy or important.

The other major means by which schools try to communicate with parents and the community is through PTA or parents' meetings. At parents' meetings, information about some aspect of a school's program is usually disseminated, and there are opportunities for two-way communication between school personnel and parents. As Annette Conners observed, "Such two-way communications programs emphasize the importance of contact and communication with the public not only at the district level, but also by every attendance unit and by each individual teacher."[2] The meetings may be scheduled on a regular basis or they may be scheduled only irregularly. The meetings may be well attended by both teachers and parents, or by only a small percentage of parents and teachers. The programs at the parents' meetings may be informative to parents, or they may be perceived as presenting little or no real information about what is happening at school.

Regardless of the type of school newsletter and parents' meetings, it is clear that they reflect an attempt by the schools to communicate with the parents and community.* These questions need to be raised, however: to what extent are the school's communication practices with parents and the community effective? And, how could they be improved?

Despite a paucity of research data on the effectiveness of school communication practices with parents and the community, observation and analysis of available studies suggest that many schools are engaging in ineffective communications practices.[3] Criticisms have generally focused on the following aspects:

---

*There can be innumerable variations of the newsletter and parents' meetings described.

1. **Information disseminated by many schools has tended to be primarily self-promoting and not relevant to the immediate needs and concerns of the parents and the larger community.** This criticism is directed in part at the practice of communicating only the good news (e.g., National Merit Scholarships, the latest federal grant), while omitting the less desirable news (such as the truancy rate, or problems of vandalism or litter at the school).

A school should communicate to the home both favorable news and information about general problems. As John Wherry emphasizes, "Admitting a problem is not a weakness. It takes some courage, but it's seen as a strength. The public knows we are not perfect and is reassured to know that we are aware of our shortcomings as well."[4]

In most situations, news about problems reaches the home one way or another, regardless. Therefore, for purposes of increasing accuracy, and informing parents of steps being taken to alleviate troublesome conditions, the school should be as candid about its blemishes as possible. This would include factual information about the nature of a problem, what the school is trying to do about the problem, and what contributions parents and the community might make toward ameliorating the problem.

Criticism has also been directed at the tendency of schools to disseminate predominately that information school officials think parents and the public should receive, without securing feedback from these groups on what they actually want to receive. In a good school-community communication program, both types of information are disseminated.

2. **Communication from the school to the community is limited to those special instances when a school needs the community's support, such as in a bond referendum, a fund-raising event, or when a major crisis or problem occurs.** Otherwise, most schools' communication to parents and the community is sporadic. That the public would like to receive more information about the schools was indicated by a Gallup survey revealing that the majority of both public and nonpublic school parents were desirous of knowing more about the schools in their community. Specific areas included were (1) the curriculum, (2) qualifications of teachers, (3) current methods of teaching, (4) how the schools are administered, and (5) problems of discipline.[5]

3. **The schools' dissemination procedures are not reliable in many instances.** School newsletters not mailed directly to the home are frequently lost or destroyed by students whom the school uses as information carriers. Parents' meetings and parent-teacher conferences are often poorly attended and are an ineffective means of communicating with a large number of parents. Consequently, unless the information a school wishes to communicate to parents is actually mailed to them, in many cases it is unlikely to be received.

4. **The school has not sufficiently utilized means of communication in addition to the newsletter and parents' meeting for transmitting information to parents and the larger community.**[6] Other means of communication include radio, television, the newspaper, and regular parent and community visitations to the school. We say more about this later.

5. **The school has not tried hard enough to ascertain the extent to which its messages are being received, understood, and acted on by parents and the community as intended by the school.**[7] Conspicuously absent in many school situations is a plan for systematically and periodically seeking feedback from parents and community on how they are reacting to the information the school is communicating to them.

While poor communication practices are not characteristic of all schools, ineffective or inadequate messages and methods exist to a sufficient degree to cause concern among many parents, members of the community, and educators. Therefore, in the following section, ideas and recommendations are presented to help school administrators improve their communication effectiveness with parents and the community. (For an example of a comprehensive public information program, see Larry Ascough.[8])

IMPROVING COMMUNICATION

THE MESSAGE

One of the most important aspects of communication is the message. Potentially, school-community communication contains several types of messages. There is the message that the school wants to communicate, there is the one that the community wants to receive, and there is the actual message received by the community. Conversely, there is the message that the community wants to communicate to the school, there is the message the school wants to receive from the community, and there is the actual message received by the school. Complex? Perhaps, but school administrators should be aware of these six types of messages; they should recognize that to the extent to which the various messages within each set are congruent with each other communication may or may not be effective.

For example, a school may have a message that it would like to communicate to the community. However, the community may not be interested in that particular topic and may want the school to communicate with it on a different topic. When this happens, communication between the school and the community becomes impaired. Too often this situation exists because the school is not sending to parents and the larger community the types of information they would like to receive. (Of course, at times a school should send a particular message to the community regardless of whether the community wants to receive it, if the message is in the community's best interest.)

An important first consideration in improving school-community communication is for school administrators to find out which messages and information parents and the community wish to receive. They can begin developing a better understanding of the types of messages they should send by means of a study of community expectations for communication from the school. (A survey periodically administered to all or a sample of parents and other people in a school's immediate community would ascertain many of their communication needs.)

In conducting such an investigation, administrators should be aware of existing research studies on parental expectations for school communication. For example, in a study of fourteen schools, Anderson found that parents from the central city, city fringe-suburban, rural and urban areas all agreed that they wanted to receive "frequently" from the school eight different types of information. Listed in order of their importance to the parents, these categories were: (1) the grades and achievement of their child; (2) discipline problems involving their child; (3) the child's personal weaknesses or physical handicaps; (4) the child's talents and abilities; (5) a schedule of school events; (6) graduation requirements; (7) career information; and (8) information on the school's rules and regulations.[9] In addition, parents' responses pertaining to desiring information on "the needs and shortcomings of the school" tended toward "frequently." In a related study by James McGeever and Victor Wall, most parents indicated that they wanted more information from the school about school board decisions, possible careers for their children, the regular classroom, special education, student test scores, adult and community education, and class size. Those parents who reported receiving an adequate amount of accurate and reliable information also rated the quality of education highly and had a high degree of trust and confidence in public education.[10]

School administrators seeking insight into parents' expectations for information from their schools should find the results of Anderson's and McGeever's investigation helpful. Their research revealed the kinds of information that parents, regardless of population setting, want to receive from the school, as well as specific types of information particularly valued by parents in certain areas. However, their findings should be used only as a general guide to parental expectations for school communication, not as a substitute for the administrator's own specific investigation. School administrators interested in improving communication effectiveness should conduct their own studies of parents and other residents to ascertain their communication needs. This study should include an effort to discover any special language or cultural barriers that might make it difficult for some parents to understand the message the school is trying to send.[11]

THE MEDIUM

According to Marshall McLuhan, "The medium is the message." Even if McLuhan's observation was overstated, administrators who want to improve a school's communication effectiveness with parents and other citizens should examine the means by which the school is trying to send its message.

The best way to start would be to review the research on parents' preferences for how information about the school should be communicated to them. For example, when Gallup pollsters asked parents, "What are the sources of information you use to judge the quality of schools in your community; that is, where do you get your information about the schools?" 52 percent of the respondents identified the local newspaper, 36 percent identified students as a source, 33 percent indicated parents of students, 32 percent mentioned local television and/or radio programming, 28 percent identified other adults in the community, and 25 percent cited school board and/or faculty members as their source of information about the schools (figures add to more than 100 percent because of multiple answers).[12] In the study by McGeever and Wall, parents were asked to identify the single information source by which they would prefer to receive all their information about the schools. While there was no majority trend in the responses, those sources identified most frequently, in order of priority, were (1) school staff members, (2) newspapers, and (3) school publications.[13] And, Richard Bingham, Paul Haubrich, and Sammis White noted research suggesting that "parents get most of their information about school from their children and rely on phone calls or teacher conferences for additional information."[14]

While the findings from research studies should be not generalized as referring to all school settings, they can serve as a guide to parental preferences for certain channels of communication. (Parents' preferences—or lack of them)—for a particular medium of communication are partially dependent on the degree to which the school has utilized that method. If, for example, a school never used television for communicating school news, parents may not be aware of its potential.) However, as valuable as research might be, school administrators should still conduct their own investigation on parental preferences for school communication methods. This study might include ascertaining parents' preferences for the alternative channels of communication identified in research. The important question which administrators should try to answer is, by what methods would parents prefer that the school communicate to them?

In considering possible methods, administrators should investigate several innovative ways of communicating with parents and other members of the community. These recent developments include

1. The identification and utilization of key communicators who can help the school communicate important messages and reduce the incidence of rumors. Their use by one school has been described by Larry Litwin.[15]

2. Utilization of newspaper supplements to provide additional information about the school and to discuss school problems. Patrick McQuaid discusses the importance and power of newspaper supplements.[16]

3. Use of taped telephone messages which give parents information about homework, school activities, and services. The use of computerized phone systems have been reported in various school districts and indications are that their use will continue to increase.[17]

4. Utilization of radio talk shows to answer questions from the public and to act as a forum for discussing educational issues and problems.[18]

5. Use of cable television to present information to parents on school programs, activities, and services. Ted Klein and Fred Danzig provide an overview of public-access TV channels, cable-network programming, cable-TV advertisements, and videotext (two-way)/teletext (one-way) computer-to-television information-delivery systems.[19]

These alternative approaches for communicating with parents and other members of the public offer great potential for improving understanding of the school and what it is trying to accomplish.

As administrators examine various means by which schools communicate information to parents, they should also determine that the information is attractively packaged and the degree of reliability with which it reaches the intended recipients of the message. The printed word is one of the principal methods by which most schools try to communicate a message of general interest to parents. Frequently, the information to be communicated is mimeographed or dittoed, and copies are given to the students at the end of the day to be taken home to the parents. Parents complain that all too often the information does not reach them because it is lost or thrown away before the students reach home. Even in those cases in which the information arrives at the home, however, the format, typing, and quality of reproduction of the message may be unattractive, perhaps illegible, and not conducive to stimulating the parents to read the school's message.

While there are times when a school probably cannot avoid communicating printed information through a dittoed sheet or by the student carrier, administrators should try to limit their use. If the information the school would like to communicate to parents is important and represents something that parents definitely should read, the school should make every effort to communicate this information in an attractive, readable form. With the desktop publishing capabilities of microcomputers, administrators have found that high-quality graphic materials are now easy to prepare and produce. A publication administrators should find useful for improving the format and packaging of the information they send home to parents is *Putting Words and Pictures about Schools into Print.*[20]

A case can also be made that a school should make every effort to mail any important printed information it wishes to communicate to the home. Utilizing students as messengers to homes has not been a particularly successful practice in most school situations, for the reasons mentioned earlier. By mailing a message to the home, school administrators can be assured that the information will probably reach the parents. A bulk mailing permit is not an expensive item for a nonprofit organization such as the school, and the total cost of mailing information home from the school should not be an exorbitant expense. The main question administrators need to ask is, How important is it that the information the school is trying to communicate to the parents be received by them? If it is important, then administrators should strongly consider mailing the information to the home. (For further ideas on how to improve school communications, see the *School Community Workshop Kit.*[21]

FEEDBACK

School-community communication should be a two-way process. The school has something important to communicate to parents and other residents of the immediate community, and the school's professional personnel should recognize that the community and parents have something important to communicate to the school.

Among the kinds of information a school should seek from parents and other citizens on a regular basis is the following:

1. What are the expectations of parents and other citizens in regard to the types of educational programs the school should offer?
2. Which elements do parents and other citizens perceive as the strengths of the school?
3. Which aspects of the school program would parents and other citizens like to see changed?

4. To what extent are parents and other citizens receiving the types of information they desire from the school?
5. To what degree are parents and other citizens satisfied with the means by which the school communicates information?

Too often school administrators seem to be primarily interested in getting *their* message across, while giving little or no priority to ascertaining the message parents and other citizens want to receive or the message they would like to communicate to the school. For example, in a study by Richard Gorton and Paul Strobel, most principals gave lip service to the importance of seeking feedback from parents and other members of the community, but in practice their efforts were quite limited.[22] If schools are to improve their communication effectiveness with the community, administrators must give as much priority to developing a better understanding of the communication needs of the community as they do to transmitting what the school wants the community to know.

While administrators could employ numerous approaches to seek feedback, three methods in particular are recommended. (For ideas on additional methods of obtaining feedback, see Donovan Walling.[23])

One approach is to include space for feedback comments, suggestions, or questions in the printed information which the school disseminates. An example of this method is presented in figure 18.1.[24]

Administrators can tailor this approach to the kind of feedback they desire. If they want specific feedback on the content of a message, they are sending to the parents, they can design their questions accordingly. If, on the other hand, they are interested in more general or open-ended feedback, a portion of the newsletter can be designed with that purpose in mind. Using part of the school's information bulletin to seek feedback from parents and other interested parties is a relatively easy, low-cost means.

A second approach a number of schools have utilized to secure feedback from parents is the Parents' Invitation to Visit the School Program. This method differs from the traditional Parent-Teacher Conference Program or the Back-to-School-Night Program in that a smaller group of parents is involved, the discussion is less formal, and the meeting does not focus on the problems of specific children. The primary purpose of the Parents' Invitation to Visit the School Program is to provide an opportunity for a small group of parents to meet with the school administrator in an informal atmosphere to share ideas and perceptions. The meetings usually take place during school hours (or at night to accommodate working parents) on a biweekly basis; the school attempts to schedule as many of these meetings as possible during the year. An example from the elementary level of how such meetings are organized and

Figure 18.1 A Method for Obtaining Feedback.

How Come?

Do you ever wonder why certain things are done or are not done? Or why some things are done the way they are?? If so—and you have never had the time or opportunity to find out—use the form below and a reply will be mailed to you.

How Come: _____

_____

_____

_____

Name: _____

Address: _____

Mail to: School District No. 1
          8060 N. 60th Street

implemented is presented in figure 18.2.[25] (Jurgen Combs describes a variety of visitation and honors programs designed to develop positive parent and community support of schools.)[26]

Reports from schools and parents who have employed this approach are generally favorable. One thing, though, that administrators themselves should try to avoid during these meetings is dominating the discussion and concentrating too much on selling the school's program. The primary purpose of this meeting should be to provide an opportunity for parents to present their ideas, questions, and concerns—not just a forum for the administrator.

Although the previous two methods can provide useful feedback to schools, they do have shortcomings. The feedback portion of the newsletter allows only a limited amount of space for a response, and visits to the school are not convenient for all parents. This does not mean that administrators

Figure 18.2 Parents' Invitation to Visit the School.

Care to spend an hour or so at Dean School on a Thursday morning, sipping coffee and sharing your ideas and opinions with the principal? Want to offer a parent's perception of the school scene? Looking for answers to questions raised by some educational trend or practice or development?

Starting Thursday, February 24, and continuing through May, small groups of parents will be invited to Thursday morning coffees with the principal. These "sip and share" sessions will be held in the main lobby of the Dean School and will begin at 10:00 a.m. If you would be interested in attending one or more of these meetings, please indicate below and have your child return the slip to school. You will then be contacted by phone to arrange for a specific date convenient to you.

---

should reject these means of obtaining feedback. They should definitely be employed. However, administrators may need to utilize, in addition, a more comprehensive and systematic method of obtaining feedback from parents and the general public. If administrators really want to know what parents or other relevant groups in the community think about some aspect of education, an attempt should be made to survey them periodically through a formal questionnaire, followed by a sample of in-depth interviews. An abbreviated example of such a survey is presented in figure 18.3.[27]

The school survey is perhaps the most systematic and complete feedback approach. Designed for a variety of purposes, it can provide a great deal of useful information. Although probably the most costly of the feedback methods recommended in this chapter, its expense can be justified on the basis of the valuable information it generates. Administrators who would like assistance in designing a survey should see *How to Conduct Low-Cost Surveys* and *Policy and Survey Research*, both published by the National Public Relations Association in Arlington, Virginia.

RELATIONSHIP WITH THE NEWS MEDIA

The relationship between the school administrator and the news media has frequently been one of ambivalence and suspicion. As Gorton has noted, often the administrator perceives the reporter as a nuisance whose only interest is exposing the school's shortcomings.[28] On the other hand, the reporter may see the administrator as one who is secretive, defensive, and less than responsive to the public's right to be informed about what is happening in the schools.[29] While neither point of view is totally valid, there is enough truth in both perceptions to create grounds for a poor relationship. This is unfortunate because the news media does have a responsibility to obtain accurate information about

Figure 18.3 Jerstad-Agerhold Junior High School Survey.

Presurvey

Objective: To improve the present public relations and communications program between home and school.

Survey Data:
1. Person completing survey: Mother _____ Father _____ Guardian _____
2. In what grade level(s) are your children? 7 _____ 8 _____ 9 _____

- -

Instructions:
  Place a check (√) on the line indicating your preference with regard to the following questions and statements:

3. Have you received our November school newsletter? Yes _____ No _____
4. If "yes," how effective do you think it is in getting information about our school to our parents? (Check one.)

      1 _____   2 _____   3 _____   4 _____   5 _____
        very poor   poor   average   good   very good

5. When your child started junior high school, did you attend the orientation meeting for parents? Yes _____ No _____
6. If "yes," how useful do you think the orientation was for parents?

      1 _____   2 _____   3 _____   4 _____   5 _____
        very poor   poor   average   good   very good

7. Do you know about the Jerstad-Agerhold Junior High School Advisory Council of parents, teachers, and administrators? Yes _____ No _____
8. If "yes," please rate their effectiveness in getting information to our parents. (Check one.)

      1 _____   2 _____   3 _____   4 _____   5 _____
        very poor   poor   average   good   very good

---

the schools for the public, and administrators could more effectively utilize the news media to provide the public with information about various aspects of the educational enterprise.

The problem of a poor school-news media relationship does not lend itself to any simple solution; however, greater openness and candor by administrators would be helpful. Specifically, they should attempt to adhere to the following ten guidelines, which were extracted from an examination of several proposals for improving school-press relationships.[30]

Guidelines for Working with the News Media

  1. Don't wait for reporters to call you. Take the initiative and call the reporter first, especially when there is a crisis.

2. Regularly and systematically offer news and feature story ideas to the press. Don't be discouraged because your first half-dozen or dozen ideas are brushed off with no coverage or only a few lines. Keep trying. Not only is the law of averages on your side, but if you are alert, you will be sharpening your skills in identifying what makes a good story. Also, don't limit yourself to the newspaper. Initiate contact with radio and television news reporters as well.

3. Get to know the reporters and editors covering your school. If you don't have a speaking relationship with them, pick up the phone and introduce yourself. Let them know that you would be happy to discuss educational issues with them.

4. Find out the reporter's deadline requirements and try to cooperate. You need not drop everything for the press and, indeed, often you have more pressing responsibilities. But perhaps you can spare sixty seconds before a deadline or assign someone else to help or decide when you have time for the press before it's too late.

5. Be patient with reporters so that you know they have all the facts and understand them in the context of your interpretation.

6. If you don't know an answer, say so. If you know who does know, refer reporters to the source, but don't shuttle them just because you don't want the responsibility for the answers. If you don't know and don't know who does, agree to try to find out and call back, and do it.

7. Spend as much time as necessary explaining an idea or program to get it understood. A percentage of the people who feel they are misquoted are really people who didn't make clear what they were trying to say.

8. Be credible. Don't distort the facts even if they hurt. The media will usually believe what you say until you give them cause not to believe you.

9. Keep your head about errors. If a story has an error, decide whether the error invalidates the main idea of the story. If it doesn't invalidate the whole thing, you would probably still want to let the reporter know about it so the mistake won't recur on subsequent articles—but don't make a federal case out of it. A correction or a retraction on this level does more harm than good. If the mistake does serious harm (says the school play will be Friday when it is Thursday) or makes the whole story erroneous

(says the school board is thinking of closing down one of the high schools when they have decided not to do so), ask for a correction. You'll probably get it. When reporters do a good job on their stories, tell them.

10. Maintain your composure. Even though the reporter might call you during a crisis, be calm, cool, and collected. This type of image helps create credibility and a favorable impression of the administrator and the school.

These recommendations may not be easily implemented in all situations, but they are basically sound. Some administrators may believe that reporters are the ones who need to improve and not themselves, yet it seems clear that as administrators we need to put our own house in order before turning our attention to others.

FINAL COMMENT ON IMPROVING SCHOOL-COMMUNITY COMMUNICATION

Communication between the school and the community should be on a regular basis. Schools have frequently been criticized because their communication with local communities has been irregular, and then only at times of importance to the schools, for example, a bond referendum. Many administrators behave as though it is not too important for the school to communicate regularly with parents and the rest of the community. However, as Doyle Bortner has observed, "The community will acquaint itself with and express opinions about its school whether the school attempts to keep the people informed or not."[31] Regular and full communication between the school and the community is an important prerequisite for developing more accurate information on the part of both and, as a result, a more positive attitude toward each other.[32]

THE SCHOOL'S PUBLIC RELATIONS PROGRAM

PURPOSE AND OBJECTIVES

Most administrators would agree—it is essential that a school and school district maintain an effective program of public relations with the community. An initial problem, however, is that the term *public relations* in this context is subject to different interpretations, three of which follow:

1. The purpose of a public relations program is to *sell* the educational program to the people of the community, so that they

will take pride in and support their schools. (To do this, the public relations program should widely publicize the strengths of the existing school program.)

2. The purpose of a public relations program is to *interpret* to the people of the community the educational program that is in operation so that the people have a better understanding of what the schools are doing and support the school program. (To do this, the public relations program should explain purposes and procedures in reporting both the strengths and weaknesses of the existing school program.)

3. The purpose of a public relations program is to encourage community interest and *participation* in the school program. (To do this, the public relations program should solicit and utilize appropriate information, advice, and assistance of interested community groups and individuals in many aspects of school operations. It should also report and explain both the strengths and weaknesses of the existing school program.)[33]

Although few administrators would probably *openly* admit to subscribing only to the first concept of school public relations, the behavior of many administrators suggests that the other concepts have little appeal to them. Seldom does one find an administrator who reports to the community both strengths and weaknesses of the existing school program. While the concept of encouraging community interest and participation in the school program has received considerable attention in the educational literature and at conventions and conferences, the number of schools implementing the concept in full measure is less than overwhelming. The fact of the matter is that in practice most administrators have not accepted fully the concepts of public relations as defined in numbers 2 and 3.[34]

Perhaps the failure by most administrators to endorse and implement the latter two concepts can be attributed to a misunderstanding of how one gains support of the school by the public. If administrators are really interested in community pride in and support of the schools, the most effective way to achieve this objective is to be open and candid in reporting to the community on the effectiveness of various aspects of the school program and to encourage and utilize community participation whenever appropriate and feasible. Attempting to sell the educational program to the people of a community by publicizing only the strengths of the existing school program strains the believability of a school's communication and eventually seriously erodes its credibility. As Larry Hughes has perceptively observed, "To expect people to 'buy' simply because educators are selling is unrealistic. The terms buying and selling are used advisedly; it is recognized that any successful program will have to be the result of mutual planning, mutual understanding, and mutual trust."[35]

This does not mean, of course, that schools should not attempt to stress the positive. An example of a rather innovative way of stressing the positive was developed by the Piqua, Ohio, school district for its annual report to the community. In the report the school district indicated:

- 99.9 percent of the students were not suspended or expelled.
- 97.3 percent of the students were not tardy for class.
- 98.2 percent were not issued offenses or detentions for misbehavior in school.
- 98.1 percent did not cause trouble on the school buses.
- 93.4 percent were well behaved on the playground.
- 98.7 percent were not disciplined for fighting.
- 99.4 percent were respectful of the staff.
- 99.8 percent were not admonished for having drugs and/or alcohol on school premises.
- 99.6 percent were not involved in school vandalism.

(See William Wayson and his colleagues for other ideas on how to stress the positive.[36])

However, if a school continues to emphasize only the strengths of its program while covering up the weaknesses and isolating itself from community involvement, the risk increases that the public will begin to ignore, suspect, or fail to believe what the school says. As noted in the publication, *Ideas for Improving Public Confidence in Public Education,* "School officials must report successes and failures honestly and realistically. This must be an ongoing policy."[37] Administrators should keep in mind that an essential requirement for effective communication and public relations is credibility.

The best public relations program is based on an open dialogue with the public on the strengths, weaknesses, and problems of the school; it creates and maximizes opportunities for community groups and individuals to give information, advice, and assistance to the school. The specific objectives of such a program have been identified by Leslie Kindred:

1. To develop intelligent public understanding of the school in all aspects of its operation.
2. To determine how the public feels about the school and what it wishes the school to accomplish.
3. To secure adequate financial support for a sound educational program.

4. To help citizens feel a more direct responsibility for the quality of education that the school provides.
5. To earn the good will, respect, and confidence of the public for the professional personnel and services of the institution.
6. To bring about public realization of the need for change and what must be done to facilitate essential programs.
7. To involve citizens in the work of the school and the solving of educational problems.
8. To promote a genuine spirit of cooperation between the school and community in sharing leadership for the improvement of community life.[38]

ORGANIZATION OF THE PUBLIC RELATIONS PROGRAM

Public relations is not something that just happens. As Bortner has noted, "The school does have a choice: between unplanned and planned public relations, between disregarding or developing an organized public relations program designed to promote community understanding and support."[39]

To achieve the objectives of a planned public relations program, people and resources have to be organized. The final organizational design should clearly identify the various individuals and groups involved in the public relations program and the nature of their responsibilities.

While administrators in small school districts are primarily responsible for their school's public relations program, in many medium-to-large school districts a public relations or public information officer directs and coordinates the school district's public relations program.[40] The public relations role of school administrators in a district that has a public relations officer may be significant or quite limited, depending on how they and the public relations officer view school administrators as playing a potentially important role in public relations. Regrettably, there is also some tendency on the part of school administrators in larger districts to believe that public relations is something solely in the public information officer's province and that it should involve other administrators only if a problem develops at their schools.

Regardless of whether or not a district employs a public relations officer, building administrators should be key figures in the public relations program. The success or failure of the public relations program is likely to be determined at the building level, and the school administrator is a crucial variable influencing that determination.

Of the many different facets to their role in public relations, school administrators should perform the following tasks in cooperation with other members of the professional staff and representatives of the school community:

1. Develop or update the philosophy and objectives of the school's public relations program. Without clear specification and an understanding of the philosophy and objectives of the program on the part of everyone, it tends to flounder or go off in different directions.

2. Identify and define the public relations roles of the administrative team, the professional and certified staff, the students, and the community. Public relations should be the responsibility of all who are associated with the school. However, administrators need to define the precise nature of that responsibility, particularly for the personnel who work in the school.

3. Plan and implement a set of public relations activities to accomplish the goals of the program. The nature of these activities depends on the type of objectives adopted for the program, but a well-planned, comprehensive set of activities is needed. (For an excellent description of public relations activities which can be initiated at the building level, see William Wayson et al. and *Positive Public Relations for Principals—A Book of Lists.*)[41]

4. Concentrate your primary efforts in public relations on developing and sustaining the best possible educational program. A good educational program does more to improve public relations than any other factor. As Lew Armistead emphasizes, "If we are to build public confidence in education, certain things must take place. First and foremost, all educators must try to do the best job possible, for nothing replaces a good performance."[42]

5. Evaluate the school's current public relations program on a periodic basis to ascertain the need for adding, modifying, or eliminating public relations activities. The questions which the administrator should ask about the school's public relations program are "What are we now doing that we could be doing better? Which new activities are needed"? and "Which activities are unproductive"?

Figure 18.4 School-Related Factors Affecting the Public's Attitude Toward the School.

Classroom Factors	*General School Factors*	*School-Community Factors*

1. Teacher-student relationship
2. Homework policy
3. Grading policy and procedures
4. Classroom discipline
5. Friendliness and communicability of the teacher to the parents
	1. Type of educational program
	  a. program of studies
	  b. teaching staff
	  c. student activities program
	2. General school discipline
	3. General atmosphere in the school
	4. Appearance of the school building, inside and outside
		1. Receptivity and friendliness of school personnel to parents and visitors
		2. Effectiveness of the school in resolving school-community issues and problems
		3. The accuracy and completeness of information about the school as it is transmitted to parents
		4. The accuracy and completeness of information the school has about the community

In conceptualizing the type of public relations program most desirable for a school, administrators must recognize that many factors affect the public's attitude toward the school.[43] In a broad sense, almost everything that happens in or to a school can potentially affect the public's attitude. While administrators cannot always control or influence events or forces in the larger society that affect the public's attitude toward the school, they can at least try to do something about those conditions associated with the school that affect public relations. A number of school-related factors that can potentially influence the public's attitude toward the school are presented in figure 18.4.

An examination of figure 18.4 suggests almost everything that the school does may affect the public's attitude toward it. As W. W. Charters has noted, "Every aspect of the school, every remark by an employee of the school, every communication with the home, every subject taught, every service to the community, even the janitor's appearance is believed to affect public relations either favorably or unfavorably."[44]

Three factors particularly affecting a school's public relations image are the ways in which parent-teacher conferences are conducted, the manner in which the school responds to telephone calls, and the general receptivity of the school office to visitors, whether they be parents or other adults. A courteous, friendly, and helpful approach in these situations contributes greatly to a favorable public perception of the school; the expression (whether intended or not) of an impersonal, condescending, or disinterested attitude leads to a negative view of the school. It is the administrator's responsibility to impress on all school employees the importance of positive contacts with parents and the community.[45]

Even though the contribution of school employees to public relations can be significant, probably the single most important public relations agent for the school is the student.[46] Most of the factors identified in figure 18.4 affect students in some way; it is through the students that parents and the larger community gain many of their impressions about the school. Therefore, school administrators should give high priority to policies, procedures, and programs that result in the development of positive student attitudes and accurate student information about the school and its personnel.

EVALUATING THE SCHOOL'S PUBLIC RELATIONS PROGRAM

An important step administrators should take to improve their schools' public relations programs is to evaluate the current program's effectiveness because periodic evaluation of any program is required for continued improvement. To evaluate a school's public relations program, the administrator needs criteria and assessment procedures. Of the many attempts to design criteria for evaluating a school's public relations program, those developed by the National School Public Relations Association (NSPRA) are among the most useful for a school administrator.[47] Examples of criteria questions from the NSPRA's evaluation instrument follow:

- Does the district have a written, clear, and concise policy statement regarding its public relations program?
- Is the policy statement approved by the school board, published in its policy manual and reviewed annually?
- Does the policy statement express the purposes of the public relations program and provide for the delegation of such authority as necessary to achieve the purposes to an appropriate administrator?
- Is the policy statement included in the district personnel handbooks so that all staff members are aware of the purposes of the public relations program?
- Is the public relations program allocated sufficient human and financial resources to accomplish its goals?
- Does the public relations unit utilize feedback continuously to modify its activities to meet the information needs of its audiences?

- Does the public relations program include in-service training for other members of the school staff in the areas of school/community relations?
- Does the program encourage community involvement in the schools?
- Is there provision for continuous and systematic evaluation?

Whether administrators use a checklist such as the one by the National School Public Relations Association or another assessment procedure, they must recognize the need for periodic, systematic evaluations of their schools' public relations programs. In evaluating the programs, administrators should secure representative perceptions from every group associated with the school, including students, parents, teachers, and classified employees. If public relations is the responsibility of everyone in the school, and if the public is considered to include everyone in the community, then representatives of these individuals and groups should all be actively involved in assessing the effectiveness of the school's public relations program.

The leadership and impetus for evaluating schools' public relations programs must come from administrators. They must feel strongly about the need for periodic and systematic evaluation, or it probably will not occur. And, if a school's public relations program is not evaluated and upgraded, school administrators should be held accountable for the consequences of a negative or apathetic public attitude toward the school.

A FINAL NOTE

School-community public relations and communications are important tasks for school administrators. These activities should focus on giving an accurate, candid, and complete picture of the school's strengths and problems; they should also provide ways by which members of the community can communicate to the school their perceptions and needs. The goal of school administrators in performing these tasks should not be to manipulate public opinion, but to develop understanding, perspective, and commitment on the part of the community. Only the achievement of the latter goal can maintain school credibility and community support over the long run.

Review and Learning Activities

1. Review the situation in your own school in light of the criticisms presented in the text regarding communication practices with parents and the community. To what extent are the criticisms valid for your school? How would you improve matters?

2. Based on the concepts presented in the text, how would you improve the message aspect of school-community communications in your school? What problems and/or obstacles would need to be overcome?
3. Based on concepts presented in the text, how would you improve the medium aspect of school-community communications in your school? What problems and/or obstacles would you need to overcome?
4. How does your school or school district secure feedback from parents and the larger community? Draft a policy and a plan for improving feedback from parents and the larger community.
5. Evaluate the merits of each of the recommended guidelines for working with the news media. In what ways will your own attitude and behavior need to change so you can develop a good working relationship with the news media?
6. Ascertain the extent to which your school and/or district has a formal, written public relations program. Based on the concepts identified in the text, draft a comprehensive public relations program for your school.

Notes

1. As an example of meeting diverse community needs, South Division High School, Milwaukee Public Schools, in Milwaukee, Wisconsin prints its school newsletter in both English and Spanish.
2. Annette J. Conners, "Let's Hear about the Good Stuff!" *Clearing House* (May 1988): 399.
3. These criticisms come from reports and studies such as those published by the Institute for Responsive Education, Boston, Massachusetts, and the National Committee for Citizens in Education at Columbia, Maryland. Also see Philip T. West, *Educational Public Relations* (Beverly Hills, Calif.: Sage, 1985).
4. Donald Bagin and John H. Wherry, "Ten Ways to Improve Your Relationships with Your Public" (Paper presented at the annual convention of the American Association of School Administrators, 1982).
5. George Gallup, "Sixth Annual Gallup Poll of Public Attitudes toward Education," *Kappan* (September 1974): 25. See the September 1980 issue of the *Kappan* for a different (but not contrary) set of findings.
6. John H. Wherry, "A Public Relations Secret: Enlist Entire Staff for PR Effectiveness," *NASSP Bulletin* (December 1986): 3–13.
7. Dick Gorton and Paul Strobel, "Principals' Actions Fall Short of Stated Attitudes toward Community Relations," *Journal of Educational Communication* (July 1981): 35–36. See also Lew Armistead, "A Four-Step Process for School Public Relations," *NASSP Bulletin* (January 1989): 6–13.
8. Larry Ascough, "Managing the School PR Effort: Not an Impossible Task," *NASSP Bulletin* (December 1986): 14–18. See also Jane C. Lindle, "Market Analysis Identifies Community and School Education Goals," *NASSP Bulletin* (November 1989): 62–66.

9. Reviewed by Richard A. Gorton, "Comments on Research," *NASSP Bulletin* (February 1982): 98–101. For a more recent discussion, see Dorothy Rich, "What People Want from Schools," *Schools and Families: Issues and Actions* (Washington, D.C.: National Education Association, 1987): 18–25.

10. James M. McGeever and Victor Wall, "The Origin of Ohio Households' Opinions about Public Education" (Paper presented at the annual meeting of the American Education Research Association, Los Angeles, 1981).

11. Robert L. Marion, "Communicating with Parents of Culturally Diverse Exceptional Children," *Exceptional Children* (May 1980): 616–23.

12. Alec M. Gallup, "The Twentieth Annual Gallup Poll of the Public's Attitudes toward the Public Schools," *Kappan* (September 1988): 43.

13. McGeever and Wall, "Origin of Ohio Households' Opinions."

14. Richard D. Bingham, Paul A. Haubrich, and Sammis B. White, "Determinants of Parent Attitudes about Schools and the School System," *Urban Education* (January 1989): 350.

15. M. Larry Litwin, "Key Communicators—They Lock Out Rumors," *NASSP Bulletin* (January 1979): 17–22. For an additional discussion of the use of opinion leaders in public relations, see Patrick Jackson, "How to Build Public Relationships that Motivate Real Support," *NASSP Bulletin* (December 1986): 25–31.

16. E. Patrick McQuaid, "Kappan Special Report—A Story at Risk: The Rising Tide of Mediocre Education Coverage," *Kappan* (January 1989): K1–K8.

17. See "Phonemaster: Keeping in Touch with Parents," *NASSP Newsletter* (November 1987) and "Reach Out and Touch Your School," *Education Week* (December 9, 1987): 3; West, *Educational Public Relations,* 41–58.

18. For a good background discussion on the possible uses of radio, see Donovan R. Walling, "Radio Targets Selected Publics," *Complete Book of School Public Relations: An Administrator's Manual and Guide* (Englewood Cliffs, N.J.: Prentice-Hall, 1982), 171–87.

19. Ted Klein and Fred Danzig, *Publicity: How to Make the Media Work for You* (New York: Charles Scribner's Sons, 1985): 38–44.

20. *Putting Words and Pictures about School into Print* (Arlington, Va.: National Public Relations Association, 1982).

21. National School Public Relations Association, *School Community Workshop Kit* (Arlington, Va: NSPRA, 1987).

22. Gorton and Strobel, "Principals' Actions Fall Short."

23. Walling, *Complete Book of School Public Relations,* 85–93.

24. Edited from material employed by Brown Deer Public Schools, Brown Deer, Wisconsin. Used with permission.

25. Brown Deer Public Schools.

26. H. Jurgen Combs, "You Can Improve School-Community Relations," *NASSP Bulletin* (April 1987): 127–29.

27. Edited from material employed by Jerstad-Agehold Junior High School, Racine, Wisconsin. Used with permission.

28. Richard A. Gorton, "What Do Principals Think of News Media Coverage?" *NASSP Bulletin* (December 1979): 116–18. See also Richard Gorton and Maxine Newsome, "Reporters: Do Principals Trust Them?" *Record* (Spring 1985): 17–20.

29. Gene I. Maeroff, "The Media and the Schools," *The Reading Teacher* (October 1980): 7–11. See also Jack Hilton, *How to Meet the Press: A Survival Guide* (New York: Dodd, Mead & Co., 1987).

30. David Siegel, "No News Isn't Good News: Effective Media Relations," *NASSP Bulletin* (January 1989): 1–4; Jim Sellers, "When Newshounds Nip at Your Heels, Don't Kick: Co-opt Them with Kindness," *American School Board Journal* (April 1984): 41–42; *101 PR Ideas You Can Use Now . . . And More!* (Arlington, Va: National School Public Relations Association, 1985); *School Public Relations: The Complete Book* (Arlington, Va.: National School Public Relations Association, 1986); and Robert C. Shaw, "Do's and Don'ts for Dealing with the Press," *NASSP Bulletin* (December 1987): 99–102.

31. Doyle M. Bortner, "The High School: Responsibility for Public Relations," *NASSP Bulletin* (September 1960): 7.

32. Isobel L. Pfeiffer and Jane B. Dunlap, "Advertising Practices to Improve School-Community Relations," *NASSP Bulletin* (March 1988): 14–17.

33. First introduced in a study reported in *The Classroom Teacher and Public Relations* (Washington, D.C.: NEA Research Divison, 1959), 10. Observations would suggest that these three purposes are still current.

34. See Thomas F. Koerner, "This Month . . . from the Editor," *NASSP Bulletin* (January 1989): v; and Frederick I. Renihan and Patrick J. Renihan, "Institutional Image: The Concept and Implications for Administrative Action," *NASSP Bulletin* (March 1989): 81–90.

35. Larry W. Hughes, "Know Your Power Structure," *American School Board Journal* (May 1967): 33–35.

36. William W. Wayson, Charles Achilles, Gay Su Pinnell, M. Nan Lintz, Lila N. Carol, and Luvern Cunningham, *Handbook for Developing Public Confidence in Schools* (Bloomington, Ind.: Phi Delta Kappa Educational Foundation, 1988).

37. *Ideas for Improving Public Confidence in Public Education* (Arlington, Va.: National Public Relations Association, 1971).

38. Leslie W. Kindred, *School Public Relations* (Englewood Cliffs, N.J.: Prentice-Hall, 1956), 16–17; *The Basic School Public Relations Kit* (Arlington, Va.: National School Public Relations Association, 1980); and Walling, *Complete Book of School Public Relations,* 68–70.

39. Bortner, "High School: Responsibility for Public Relations."

40. See West, *Educational Public Relations,* 59–76.

41. Wayson et al., *Handbook for Developing Public Confidence in Schools.* Educational Communication Center, *Positive Public Relations for Principals—A Book of Lists* (Camp Hill, Pa.: Educational Communication Center, 1981).

42. Lew Armistead, "Getting the Education Team Organized to Speak Up for Schools," *NASSP Newsletter* (December 1980): 13; and James E. Lashley, "Attitude and Communication Build Public Relations," *NASSP Bulletin* (January 1989): 34–35.

43. For an early analysis of this point, see W. W. Charters, Jr., "In a Public Relations Program Facts Are Never Enough," *Nation's Schools.* (February 1954): 56–58.

44. W. W. Charters, Jr., "Public Relations," in Chester Harris, ed., *Encyclopedia of Educational Research* (New York: Macmillan Co., 1960), 1075.

45. Fred Splittgerber and N. A. Stirzaker, "What Your School's Front Office is Telling the Community about You," *Catalyst for Change.* (Fall 1988): 18–20.

46. Nickerson and Mook, "School and Community Relations: Another Aspect of Instructional Leadership," 45.

47. National School Public Relations Association, *Evaluation Instrument for Educational Public Relations Programs* (Arlington, Va.: National School Public Relations Association, 1978). See also Walling, *Complete Book of School Public Relations,* 85–99.

6

• • • • •

Career Considerations

19

• • • • •

Career Assessment

The pursuit of a successful career in school administration involves at least two major elements: (1) understanding and capitalizing on career and employment opportunities, and (2) possessing needed competencies and professional ethics. These aspects are discussed in this chapter, along with obtaining a position in school administration and planning for the first year.

CAREER AND EMPLOYMENT OPPORTUNITIES IN SCHOOL ADMINISTRATION

CAREER OPPORTUNITIES

When one considers career opportunities in school administration, principalship is usually the first and most frequently cited position. Although the principalship is perhaps the most important position in the administration of a school, a number of other positions include administrative or quasi-administrative responsibilities. Examples of these positions are identified in figure 19.1.

Most people seeking their first jobs in school administration do not begin as principals.[1] An exception would be the person who moves from a teaching position to an elementary school principalship or a secondary school principalship in a small school district. The more typical career pattern is for an individual to begin a career in administration by assuming one of the entry positions identified in figure 19.1, such as, administrative intern or assistant

Figure 19.1 Career Positions in School Administration.

		Entry Positions		
Assistant or Vice-Principal	Dean of Students Athletic Director	Administrative Intern	Administrative Assistant Grade Level Coordinator	Department Head or Unit Leader
		Advanced Position Principal		

principal. These positions can offer valuable experience and training for more advanced roles in school or district administration and can, in many instances, provide sufficient personal satisfaction and rewards so that they become permanent career positions.

The entry positions in administration represent important components of the administrative team of a school or school district, and the individuals occupying them should have opportunities to make useful contributions to the success of the school program. No one should consider an entry position as merely a stepping stone to a higher place in the administrative hierarchy. An entry position offers a potentially valid career in and of itself, rather than as a temporary stopping-off point before a move on to a more advanced position.

However, even if individuals decide that it is really the principalship or a position in district administration to which they aspire, it would be desirable for them to first obtain as much experience as possible in one or more of the entry positions in school administration. For example, a person who is now a teacher might seek the position of department head or unit leader in a school. Such a position, quasi-administrative in nature, could give one considerable experience in the administrative processes of goal setting, planning, organizing, and working with adult groups. It could also provide practice in supervising and evaluating teachers, if such responsibilities are associated with the job. All of these experiences constitute potentially valuable training in administration. Certainly, the experiences gained through being a department head or unit leader could be useful later when a person becomes a principal and interacts with the people occupying those positions.

Or an individual might prepare for the principalship by seeking on-the-job training as an administrative assistant, an assistant or vice-principal, or a dean of students.* Unlike the department head who generally teaches three or more classes, these other entry posts are usually full-time administrative

*See chapter 5, "The Administrative Team," for a description of these positions.

positions. Typically they differ in the responsibilities associated with each position, but they all offer potentially useful training for more advanced careers in administration. The problem is that none of these positions itself offers the kind of broad on-the-job training that a principal really needs.[2]

For example, although there are exceptions, the administrative assistant's role is frequently managerial in nature, concerned with budgeting, plant management, or student discipline, with little or no responsibility in the areas of instructional improvement and curriculum development. The primary duties of the assistant principal, vice-principal, and dean of students are usually confined to student discipline, attendance, scheduling, and transportation. Instructional improvement, curriculum, and budgeting are responsibilities seldom associated with these positions, although that situation is changing to some extent. It is true that in larger schools with two assistant or vice-principals, one of them may be assigned responsibilities for instructional improvement and curriculum development, but in such cases the individual occupying that position receives little experience in the other aspects of the principalship.

Perhaps the best on-the-job training for the principalship, at least in terms of breadth, is the administrative internship. The internship has existed in education for a long time, in one form or another.[3] But it was not until the early 1960s, when Lloyd Trump and others proposed the administrative internship as an important training vehicle for those interested in school leadership, that it assumed major stature. Since then, thousands of individuals have used this approach as on-the-job preparation for the school principalship; in some instances, school districts sponsor their own internship programs, often in cooperation with nearby universities. (Financial problems have caused many school districts to reduce or eliminate their administrative internship programs, thereby significantly limiting this type of preparation for administration. However, pressure is currently being placed on state legislatures to appropriate funds to finance internship programs.)[4]

Although the nature of experiences which interns receive may vary from district to district, the intent of most programs is to provide aspiring administrators with as much exposure to, and actual experience in, the various facets of the principal's job as possible. Therefore, anyone who plans to become a principal (or for that matter, to assume any of the full-time administrative positions in the school) should investigate the possibility of securing an administrative internship.

For further information on how to establish an administrative internship program and for a description of several examples of successful administrative internships, see the monograph, *The Administrative Internship*.[5]

EMPLOYMENT OPPORTUNITIES

Before deciding on a career in school administration, an individual should thoroughly investigate the employment opportunities. Generally, those entering the field of administration assume that if state certification can be obtained, there will be little or no problem in securing a job.* Many people, including those responsible for preparing administrators, believe that if administrative aspirants are willing to move to a new situation or wait until a vacancy occurs in their own districts, it is often just a matter of time before a job in administration can be secured. Many also implicitly believe that once a person acquires an entry position in administration, it will not be long before an opportunity to become a principal presents itself.

Any close relationship between these beliefs and reality is debatable. Unfortunately, there has been a paucity of data on employment opportunities; yet, demographic data suggest that nearly 60 percent of the school principalships will turnover during the 1990s as the present cohort of principals reach retirement age.[6] In addition, there is some indication that the turnover rate in the principalship is increasing as a result of the many problems and pressures that have become a part of a principal's job. Consequently, there may be more early retirements, resignations, and advancements to central office positions than was formerly the case. These projections provide a slightly optimistic forecast for aspiring administrators seeking positions in this decade; they may even indicate the onset of an administrator shortage. Such predictions are in marked contrast to the relatively stable administrative marketplace of the 1970s and 1980s when administrative openings were scarce and the number of certified individuals exceeded the number of positions available.[7] During the 1990s, rather than having administrative candidates competing for a scarce number of positions, districts may find themselves competing for a scarce number of able, qualified, and interested applicants.

While the available data suggest a relatively active employment picture in school administration, several factors should be kept in mind. First, observation would suggest that employment opportunities for prospective principals will continue to vary among states and regions of the United States as population trends shift and change; as a consequence, aspirants will have to do some investigating. Usually state departments of public instruction are a good source of general information on employment opportunities in school administration, and individual professors within a school of education may be especially good sources for such information.

---

*For certification requirements for administrators and supervisors in different states, check in a library for Elizabeth H. Woellner, *Requirements for Certification* (Chicago: University of Chicago Press, latest edition).

A second reason for investigating the local employment situation in school administration is that laws and court cases on sex and racial discrimination may provide greater job opportunities in school administration for women and members of minority groups. Although the evidence supporting these potential trends is fragmentary and contradictory, it is possible that continued attention to federal equal rights legislation and community attention to the importance of cultural diversity of school personnel may create more employment opportunities.

On the other hand, several studies have shown that the growth in employment of women and minority administrators, especially women, has been much less than one might have predicted after a period of civil rights legislation, regulations, and court decisions.[8] This situation could change significantly in the 1990s, however, as more and more people responsible for the hiring of administrators become familiar with the research which identifies the leadership strengths of these underrepresented groups and as individual women and members of minorities become more assertive in demanding that they be treated fairly in employment decisions. (For discussions regarding aspiring women in educational administration, see Gail Schneider and Sakre Edson; for an excellent book which describes the problems of becoming and being a woman administrator and offers suggestions for coping with those problems, see *Women in Educational Administration.*[9]

NEEDED COMPETENCIES AND PROFESSIONAL ETHICS FOR SCHOOL ADMINISTRATION

RECOMMENDED COMPETENCIES

One important theory concerning the competencies needed by administrators has been advanced by Robert Katz, who believes that the three basic skills needed by administrators are technical, human, and conceptual.[10] Technical skills are those which school administrators must possess to perform such tasks as budgeting, scheduling, staffing, and other similar administrative responsibilities. Human skills refer to interpersonal skills needed to work successfully with people in one-to-one or group settings. Conceptual skills are those which the school administrator needs to see the total picture and the relationships between and among its various parts. Katz believes that the relative importance of these basic skills depends on the level of administrative responsibility, with higher level administrators (e.g., superintendents) requiring more conceptual than technical skills, and lower level administrators (e.g., principals), needing more technical than conceptual skills.[11] Human skills, however, are important at all levels of administration.

John Daresh, in his study of the beginning principalship, found principals reported the need for additional technical expertise and interpersonal skills to help them do their jobs more effectively.[12] Specifically, the technical/procedural concerns of first-year principals included: how to read computer printouts from the central office, how to address various legal issues, how to budget time or material resources, and how to implement central office mandates. In terms of interpersonal skills, principals felt the need for better conflict management and community relations skills. They also reported feelings of isolation, expressing a need for more feedback from their teachers and from the central office regarding their performance.

In another context, Gorton has proposed five competencies essential for school administrators who want to function as leaders.[13] In question form, the five are

1. Does the administrator have the ability to identify accurately the problems which need to be corrected in the school?
2. Does the administrator possess vision as an educator? Does he or she recognize, understand, and see the implications of the various trends and social forces which are and will be affecting education and the larger society?
3. Does the administrator feel a strong need to be a leader? Does he or she have a strong drive to set and achieve new goals? Does he or she seek out opportunities to exercise leadership?
4. Is the administrator willing to assume a degree of risk in initiating leadership—and to face resistance, opposition, and personal or professional criticism?
5. Does the administrator possess good human relations skills, such as sensitivity to the needs of others?

In addition to the previous concepts, research on leadership and numerous personal reports from administrators are helpful in suggesting those competencies that a person should possess or acquire in pursuing a career in school administration.[14] Rather than reviewing all of these studies and reports, a self-assessment questionnaire has been developed based on a synthesis of this information and is presented in figure 19.2.

This self-assessment questionnaire is still in the process of being formally validated; therefore, it should not be used as the sole basis for making a decision about a career in school administration. The questionnaire is primarily intended to stimulate some serious thinking about potential for school administration, and to help identify possible areas in need of further improvement.

Figure 19.2 Self-Assessment Questionnaire for Prospective School Administrators.

	Some Improvement Needed	*Major Improvement Needed*	*Not Sure*
1. Are you objective about yourself and about others? Evidence?	_____	_____	_____
2. Do you possess ideas and convictions about improvements needed in education and the direction that education should take in the future? Evidence?	_____	_____	_____
3. Are you a hard worker, strong on perseverance and with a high energy level? Evidence?	_____	_____	_____
4. Do you possess a high tolerance for frustration, stress, challenges to self by others? Evidence?	_____	_____	_____
5. Do you possess considerable self-confidence? Evidence?	_____	_____	_____
6. Do you like responsibility? Evidence?	_____	_____	_____
7. Are you engaged in continuous self and professional improvement? Evidence?	_____	_____	_____
8. Do you have the ability to plan and organize a job? Evidence?	_____	_____	_____
9. Are you well organized in the use of your time? Evidence?	_____	_____	_____

Figure 19.2 Continued

	Usually	Some Improvement Needed	Major Improvement Needed	Not Sure
10. Do you have the inclination and the ability to solve or ameliorate difficult problems? Evidence?	_____	_____	_____	_____
11. Are you a good decision maker? Evidence?	_____	_____	_____	_____
12. Do you have the capacity to compromise and to be flexible? Evidence?	_____	_____	_____	_____
13. Do you possess the ability to know when to compromise and to be flexible? Evidence?	_____	_____	_____	_____
14. Are you able to influence others, to change their thinking? Evidence?	_____	_____	_____	_____
15. Do you have the ability to mediate conflict, to reconcile differences among others? Evidence?	_____	_____	_____	_____
16. Are you perceptive about the needs and problems of others, including those you don't like? Evidence?	_____	_____	_____	_____
17. Are you an articulate and effective speaker in front of a group, or as a member of a group, or as a leader of a group? Evidence?	_____	_____	_____	_____
18. Can you express yourself clearly, logically, and accurately in writing and speaking? Evidence?	_____	_____	_____	_____

Figure 19.2 Continued

	Usually	Some Improvement Needed	Major Improvement Needed	Not Sure
19. Are you knowledgeable about the concepts and principles presented in this text?	_____	_____	_____	_____
20. Do you possess a good capacity to learn, to "catch on"? Evidence?	_____	_____	_____	_____

In responding to the questions in figure 19.2, pay particularly close attention to the evidence used in determining the rating of the extent to which you possess each of the traits. It is usually difficult for anyone to be completely objective or knowledgeable about their own strengths and weaknesses. Therefore, before answering such a question as, "Are you well organized in the use of your time?" think about your experiences in situations which called for priority setting and efficient use of time, and perhaps even discuss performance and potential with others who may be more objective in their perceptions.

Prospective administrators are unlikely to possess all of the traits identified in figure 19.2. In fact, it is doubtful whether the vast majority of current school administrators possess all of these traits to a large degree. Nonetheless, each of the traits identified in the self-assessment questionnaire is an important characteristic for administrators to possess or acquire. Anyone lacking a majority of these traits is not likely to succeed in exercising school leadership. Therefore, make every attempt to conscientiously complete the Self-Assessment Questionnaire for Prospective School Administrators, and then seek improvement wherever needed.

In addition, explore the possibility of participating in one of the assessment programs sponsored by the national principals' associations and cooperating school districts; a review of administrator assessment centers is provided by Mike Milstein and Celia Fiedler.[15]

PROFESSIONAL ETHICS

The previous section emphasized that prospective school administrators should either possess or acquire certain basic competencies if they expect to pursue successful careers in school administration. However, competencies are only one prerequisite to success. To be successful in administration, a person also needs a set of ethical beliefs or standards for guidance or direction in the appropriate use of competencies. Without such beliefs, a person's competencies may be misused or misdirected; thus, the school may not receive the best kind of leadership. Therefore, every administrator should attempt to maintain high professional ethical standards to make a more positive contribution to the improvement of education in the school.

Prospective administrators might turn to various sources in an attempt to enhance their professional ethics. For example, the national administrators' associations have developed a set of recommended guidelines which have much to commend them. Developed with considerable involvement and input from school administrators throughout the nation, the standards represent the best thinking of practitioners on this important subject. They are presented in figure 19.3.[16]

The standards in figure 19.3 constitute a positive response to the need for ethical guidelines for school administrators. They should provide all administrators with a basis for directing their actions and also serve as evaluative criteria assisting administrators to determine whether or not they are acting ethically in professional matters. Prospective administrators are also encouraged to use the standards to consider not only how they might apply in individual situations but also the possible problems as well as advantages involved in acting ethically.

THE NEW ADMINISTRATOR

The person who possesses the competencies and professional ethics already identified should be able to pursue a career in school administration successfully. However, because of a lack of knowledge about how to proceed, some individuals may experience difficulty in obtaining a position in school administration; and some may encounter problems during the first year on the job because of inadequate planning and misplaced priorities. Guidelines for avoiding or, at least, ameliorating these problems are discussed in the following sections.*

OBTAINING A POSITION

The immediate objective of a person who has completed an administrator preparation program, obtained certification, and is ready to begin a career in administration, is to secure a position. Because employment opportunities in

---

*The ideas discussed in these sections may seem obvious or rather pragmatic in nature; however, contact with new administrators indicates that many need practical guidelines on how to obtain a position in administration and what to expect during the first year.

Figure 19.3 Statement of Ethics for School Administrators.

An educational administrator's professional behavior must conform to an ethical code. The code must be idealistic and at the same time practical, so that it can apply reasonably to all educational administrators. The administrator acknowledges that the schools belong to the public they serve for the purpose of providing educational opportunities to all. However, the administrator assumes responsibility for providing professional leadership in the school and community. This responsibility requires the administrator to maintain high standards of exemplary professional conduct. It must be recognized that the administrator's actions will be viewed and appraised by the community, professional associates, and students. To these ends, the administrator subscribes to the following statements of standards.

The educational administrator:

1. Makes the well-being of students the fundamental value in all decision making and actions.
2. Fulfills professional responsibilities with honesty and integrity.
3. Supports the principle of due process and protects the civil and human rights of all individuals.
4. Obeys local, state, and national laws and does not knowingly join or support organizations that advocate, directly or indirectly, the overthrow of the government.
5. Implements the governing board of education's policies and administrative rules and regulations.
6. Pursues appropriate measures to correct those laws, policies, and regulations that are not consistent with sound educational goals.
7. Avoids using positions for personal gain through political, social, religious, economic, or other influence.
8. Accepts academic degrees or professional certification only from duly accredited institutions.
9. Maintains the standards and seeks to improve the effectiveness of the profession through research and continuing professional development.
10. Honors all contracts until fulfillment or release.

This *Statement of Ethics* was developed by a task force representing The National Association of Secondary School Principals, National Association of Elementary School Principals, American Association of School Administrators, Association of School Business Officials, American Association of School Personnel Administrators, and National Council of Administrative Women in Education. Used with the permission of the National Association of Secondary School Principals.

educational administration may be limited in some states, obtaining a position may not be an easy objective for the prospective administrator to achieve. However, if one has performed well in a preparatory program, possesses the qualities necessary for success in school administration, and is persistent, that individual's chances of securing a position in administration should be greatly improved.

Figure 19.4 Placement Notices in Educational Administration.

---

1. High School Principal Vacancy in Large Urban School District
   Requirements
   a. Have three years' administrative experience.
   b. Possess effective interpersonal skills.
   c. Possess effective verbal and written communication skills.
   d. Able to document successful leadership experience working with multicultural populations.
   e. Able to document successful teaching and/or school administration experience in an urban setting.
   f. Have a proven record of generating and implementing instructional changes which have led to increased academic achievement of students.
   g. Have an effective record of working collaboratively with parents, teachers, and external agencies.
   Other qualifications include a Master's Degree, a current secondary principal's license or eligibility for such license. The salary range is $45,000 to $60,000.

2. Elementary Principal Vacancy in Medium-Size School District
   Requirements
   a. Collegial approach to staff, willing to work in a school-based management setting with active staff and parent involvement.
   b. Knowledgeable and experienced in whole language approaches to language learning.
   c. Experienced in providing bold leadership to educational endeavors.
   d. Knowledgeable of multicultural education as it relates to curriculum and instruction.
   e. Capable of integrating multidisciplinary approaches to teaching and learning.
   f. Experience in involving the school community and community agencies in the school program.
   Other qualifications include a Master's degree, a current elementary principal's license, and school administrative experience. The salary range is $37,000 to $45,000.

The initial step that individuals should take in seeking positions in educational administration is to register with their university placement offices. Usually any student attending a college or any graduate of a college can register with its placement office and utilize the placement services. Once registered with a placement office, vacancy notices such as those shown in figure 19.4 are available.

Seldom does a placement notice provide all the information about a position that one might desire. However, sufficient information is usually supplied so that applicants can make a decision on whether follow-up action should be taken regarding the notice. If the position is of interest, individuals should contact the placement office and request that a copy of their credentials be sent to the school district. Prospective administrators should also write to the school district expressing an interest in the vacancy, and advising that placement papers are being forwarded to the district's office. In the letter, applicants should state the reasons for their interest in the position together with a brief description of their qualifications with reference to any special factors of which the school district should be aware. If the district is interested, applicants are usually contacted within several weeks to schedule an interview.

Information on job vacancies in educational administration can also be obtained from state employment offices (which may have an educators' employment division); private employment agencies; city newspapers, which may carry vacancy notices; and also from the personnel office in the beginning administrator's own school district. Another potential source of information on administrative vacancies may be professors who served as the students' advisers in the university's administrator preparation program. Prospective administrators should take the initiative to explore and maintain contact with all possible sources of information on administrative openings. Rarely does a school district contact the prospective administrator first; aspiring administrators have to exert initiative and persistence to obtain positions.

An important factor which greatly influences the number and type of vacancies accessible is the prospective administrator's geographic mobility. Many vacancies for beginning administrators occur in small school districts and in districts located a distance from metropolitan areas. Individuals who are unable or unwilling to move to these districts, or who consider only vacancies in their own districts or in metropolitan areas, significantly restrict their opportunities for employment. The more mobile prospective administrators can be, the more likely they are to obtain positions.

Once prospective administrators have applied for vacancies and have been contacted by the school districts for interviews, applicants should take time to plan for the meetings.[17] Individuals who have been scheduled for interviews can usually assume that they are among several candidates being strongly considered for the vacancy. Generally, school districts give considerable weight to the results of these interviews in reaching decisions on candidate selection. It is therefore essential that candidates plan carefully for the interview.

Planning for an interview is really no different than planning for any important conference or meeting. First of all, candidates need information about the situation itself; in the case of a principalship, they need data about the school and the school district where the vacancy has occurred. Prior to the interview, a prospective administrator should attempt, if feasible, to visit the schools, talk with the administrator who is leaving, and try to become familiar with the school district and the community. The information and impressions that are gained will be invaluable in the planning for the interview.

Second, candidates should determine the objectives they want to achieve during their interviews, and then define the questions and comments which need to be offered to achieve those objectives. In addition to thinking about objectives and questions, time should be spent in trying to anticipate the kinds of questions which interviewers may ask. While it is impossible to anticipate every question that may be raised, the more questions that are anticipated and considered prior to the interview, the greater is the likelihood that the interview will be a success. For example, a study by Jerome Cook revealed that beginning administrators believed that interviewers were most interested in ascertaining the strengths of candidates in the areas of discipline, supervision and evaluation, and human relations.[18]

During the interview, prospective administrators should try to remain calm and poised. Individuals may experience some nervousness, which is perfectly natural and should not cause a problem as long as they do not overreact. Candidates should concentrate on listening carefully to the interviewer's comments and questions; if a question or comment is not understood, they should ask for clarification or elaboration. Candidates should not attempt to respond to a question or comment unless it is clearly understood.

In answering questions or making observations, prospective administrators should be perfectly candid. Rather than presenting what they think the interviewers would like to hear, candidates should provide their own views. This approach may cost an individual a particular job, but it is far better that applicants be candid at the outset, because discrepancies in philosophy or approach would probably surface later and cause difficulties. This does not mean that candidates should be dogmatic or argumentative during an interview; however, there should be a frank and full exchange of views.

At the conclusion of the interview, candidates usually are told that they will be contacted in the near future with regard to the school district's decision. Applicants who do not hear from a representative of the district within two or three weeks, should contact the district's office to inquire as to when a decision will be reached. During this interval, however, prospective administrators should be exploring alternative employment possibilities until an actual contract is received and an offer accepted. (For additional discussion on principal selection, see Frederick Wendel and Roger Breed and the *Principal Selection Guide* prepared by the U.S. Department of Education, Office of Research and Improvement.[19]

THE NEW SITUATION: ORIENTATION

Having accepted positions, new administrators need to become oriented further to their schools, school districts, and communities (unless, of course, the positions are in their own districts). New administrators may already have had opportunities to meet several associates and to visit the communities; but there probably remains considerable orientation to be acquired before school begins in the fall.

In this endeavor new administrators should secure and thoroughly read student and teacher handbooks as well as copies of the student newspaper. A careful examination should also be made of school board policies, the district office manual of procedures, and the district's master contract. All of this information should contribute to the process of familiarizing new administrators with current school and district problems, politics, and procedures.

Next, individual meetings should be scheduled with the superintendent, and relevant members of the central office staff. The new administrator's meetings with the superintendent and the central office staff should be for purposes of getting better acquainted and ascertaining how all parties can work together cooperatively. One topic for discussion might be the district's master contract.

Beginning administrators should also schedule individual meetings with the school's assistant principal, department heads and/or unit leaders, the cook, the head secretary, and the head custodian. It is particularly important that administrators pay attention to becoming acquainted with the latter three individuals; they can play a significant role in the administrators' success or lack of it, yet are frequently overlooked. And new administrators should see any student or parent leaders who are available and interested in conferring with them.

During these initial meetings, administrators should focus primarily on developing a good personal relationship with the people with whom they will be working at their schools, reviewing proposed activities and possible problems, and also indicating a receptivity to meeting with them again whenever the need arises. They should not attempt to cover too much in these first meetings. For example, unless the subject comes up naturally, administrators should wait until later to ascertain people's role expectations. It is more appropriate to discuss these topics after new administrators and the other school personnel have become better acquainted.

While becoming better informed about the school district and school personnel, new administrators should also try to become better oriented to the school community. Although they may have toured the community when interviewing for the vacancy, administrators' knowledge of the community at this point is probably rather superficial.

A good starting point for orientation to a community is a drive around the neighborhoods and commercial areas within a half-mile radius of the school. Such a drive should yield valuable impressions about the neighborhoods adjacent to the school, potential safety problems for students, extent and kinds of recreational opportunities for students, and possible student hangouts. The latter may include cafes, drugstores, video arcades, shopping centers, and similar places where students might congregate before or after school. Such places frequently represent the community from the student's point of view, and new administrators need to become more aware of that community.

Administrators should also try to become acquainted with the neighborhoods of those students who have to travel a long distance to the school. Because these students and their parents may feel isolated from the school, administrators should become more knowledgeable about their situations. If school is still in session in the spring when administrators are hired, riding a school bus might be considered to achieve this objective.

As administrators visit various neighborhoods of the community, they should capitalize on any opportunities to meet the residents, particularly parents. There probably will not be time to meet too many parents, but administrators should take advantage of those opportunities that present themselves in the situation.

Perhaps one of the better ways for new administrators to become informed about the culture, norms, problems, and personalities in a community is to read the back issues of the local newspaper, which are generally found in the local library. By browsing through the copies of the newspaper published during the preceding year, new administrators should become familiar with many important aspects of the community, including its significant groups and leaders, its problems and issues, and dates of special local events. Also generally found in the library is pertinent information about the community's governmental structure. Without question, local libraries are potentially very useful sources of material for orienting new administrators to their communities.

PLANNING FOR THE OPENING OF SCHOOL

In one sense, the orientation activities that have been described can be considered a part of planning for the opening of school. However, before mid-August, administrators should make some additional plans in regard to the start of the school year.[20] Although initial get-acquainted meetings should have been held with student, teacher, and parent leaders, administrators must meet with these individuals and groups again to plan activities to be held prior to the opening of school and during the first few weeks after school has started.

Administrators should also meet with their assistant principals and with department chairpersons or unit leaders to plan workshops which usually take place two or three days before school begins. Information should be solicited from these people about the workshops presented in the past at the school, and they should be encouraged to offer suggestions on how workshops could be improved. New administrators will certainly have their own ideas on what should be included in the workshops, and these ideas should be presented and reactions sought.

Topics for inclusion in workshops depend to a great extent on local circumstances. However, administrators should recognize that the total staff will be using this opportunity to size up the new administrator and will be listening carefully to what that individual has to say during the workshops. Although new administrators want to make good impressions, they should avoid raising people's expectations too much and refrain from the temptation to promise more than can be delivered.[21] Also, it would be preferable to postpone reviewing their own educational philosophy and expectations for the staff unless specific questions about them are raised. Until new administrators and their staffs become better acquainted, discussions about educational philosophy and expectations could be misinterpreted.

During the workshops, new administrators should be perceived as individuals who will try to work cooperatively with people to resolve problems; who are friendly, warm, and professional in interpersonal relationships; and who are well organized and hard workers.

In planning for the workshops, beginning administrators should take into consideration the needs of new teachers attending the meetings, and the needs of the total staff for enough time to do individual planning for the first day of school. They should also plan some activity providing an opportunity for the members of the staff (and perhaps their families) to socialize with each other. The preschool workshops should consist of more than just professional meetings.

In planning for the opening of school, meetings should also be scheduled with the school secretary; head custodian; chief cook; and student and parent leaders, such as the president of the student council, the editor of the student newspaper, and the president of the PTA. These meetings should be devoted to a review of proposed activities for the opening day and the first month of school (with a discussion of problems to be resolved), and steps which need to be taken prior to those activities. Careful planning before school opens can eliminate many problems that might otherwise arise later.

New administrators should also check on a number of important operational details at least several weeks prior to the beginning of school. These include ascertaining whether the items enumerated in figure 19.5 still require attention.

Figure 19.5 Checklist: Planning for the Opening of School.

---

1. **Development of the Master Schedule for the School.** Has it been completed? Does it need updating?
2. **Employment of Teachers.** Do additional teachers need to be hired?
3. **Allocation of Classroom Furniture and Textbooks.** Does each classroom have sufficient classroom furniture and textbooks to accommodate the number of students assigned to the room?
4. **Distribution of Teacher Supplies.** Has each teacher been allocated adequate supplies for the first week of school?
5. **Maintenance of the Building.** Have those aspects of the school which have been in need of repair been fixed? Has the school building itself been cleaned and floors waxed?
6. **Planning for the Cafeteria Program.** Have preparations been made to provide hot lunches on the first day of school?

Checking on some of these details may be delegated to the assistant principal. However, principals still retain the ultimate responsibility for making sure that everything operates smoothly on the first day of school. Even though new administrators may view themselves as instructional leaders, their staffs' initial judgments are based on their evaluations as to whether these newcomers are efficient administrators. The events of the first day of school greatly influence their evaluation.

PRIORITIES DURING THE FIRST YEAR

Regardless of whether or not administrators are new, they are expected to meet certain responsibilities. These include visiting classrooms; holding faculty meetings; conferring with individual students, teachers, and parents; developing a school budget; and many other tasks delineated in previous chapters.

The effectiveness with which these tasks are accomplished depends in part on the role that new administrators adopt. According to James Lipham, the administrator is "the individual who utilizes existing structures or procedures to achieve an organization goal or objective."[22] Lipham goes on to state that "The administrator is concerned primarily with maintaining, rather than changing established structures, procedures, or goals."[23] The leader, on the other hand, is defined by Lipham as "concerned with initiating changes in established structures, procedures, or goals; he is a disrupter of the existing state of affairs." Leadership, to Lipham, is "the initiation of a new structure or procedure for accomplishing organizational goals and objectives."[24]

A case can be made that, during the first year, new administrators should not function as leaders, as defined by Lipham, but should concentrate on administering the school. New administrators need to complete at least one year on the job becoming familiar with the school situation, before being in a good enough position to know which changes should be made and how they might best be accomplished. Also, new administrators should take the time to become competent in performing administrative tasks before beginning to initiate changes in existing procedures and policies.

Of course, new administrators may be forced to institute changes during the first year in response to problems whose solutions cannot or should not be delayed. However, as much as possible during the first year, administrators should avoid initiating major changes in established structures, procedures, or goals, or in any other way disrupting the existing order of affairs. To the extent feasible, such leadership activities should be postponed until new administrators become more knowledgeable about their school situations.

The priorities that new administrators should concentrate on during their first year are as follows:

1. *Obtaining a good understanding of all aspects of the educational program and the social context in which the school operates.* During the first year, new administrators need to become very familiar with what is going on in their schools, and why things are done the way they are. They also need to continue to learn about the school district's procedures and how the school relates to the total community.

2. *Developing a good interpersonal relationship with other people.* This includes students, parents, and central office personnel, as well as the teachers in the school. A new administrator's first year is a busy one with many tasks to accomplish, but time should be set aside to see students, teachers, parents, and other relevant people. These individuals determine the success of beginning administrators more than any other factor.

3. *Attaining a well-organized and smoothly operating school.* Most of the people with whom new administrators have contact will tend to view them as administrators, rather than leaders. If both roles can be performed effectively people will be pleased; but first of all, competency as an administrator must be shown. This can be achieved by running a well-organized, smoothly operating school. Having obtained this objective, new administrators can begin to function in the role of leaders if they possess the qualities needed for leadership.[25]

A CONCLUDING NOTE

For the individual interested in a new position in school administration, securing a job and planning and establishing priorities for the first year requires careful organization, persistence, and clear thinking. The administrator's first year undoubtedly is a useful learning experience but, at the same time, new administrators should realize that people expect effective performance regardless of whether or not individuals are new to the position. Two major factors that demonstrate the administrators' effectiveness are their response to problems associated with the school situation, and the efforts made by the administrators to pursue continuing professional development. The next chapter focuses on problems of school administration and the need for continuing professional growth.

Review and Learning Activities

1. Analyze the advantages and disadvantages of various entry positions in school administration.
2. What is the nature of employment opportunities in school administration in your state? What are the implications of this situation for the individual interested in pursuing a career in school administration?
3. What are the implications of the administrator competencies recommended by Katz and Gorton for your professional development and performance as an administrator?
4. Assess the extent to which you possess the traits identified in figure 19.2 and the ethical standards justified in figure 19.3. What are the implications of your assessment?
5. Which steps should individuals take and which factors should they be aware of in:
   a. Seeking a new administrative position?
   b. Becoming oriented to a new administrative situation?
   c. Planning for the opening of the school?
6. Why is it important for administrators to determine their priorities in a new situation? What would appear to be reasonable first year priorities for a new administrator?

Notes

1. Leonard O. Pellicer, Lorin W. Anderson, James W. Keefe, Edgar A. Kelley, and Lloyd E. McCleary, *High School Leaders and Their Schools* (Reston, Va.: National Association of Secondary School Principals, 1988); and James L. Doud, *The K–8 Principalship* (Alexandria, Va.: National Association of Elementary School Principals, 1988).

2. Karen S. Bennett, "What About Me? . . . Reflections from a First-Year Principal," *NASSP Bulletin* (September 1988): 132.

3. For an excellent review of the origins and various aspects of establishing and administering an internship program, see Don R. Davies, *The Internship in Educational Administration* (Washington, D.C.: Center for Applied Research in Education, 1962). Also see T. F. Flaherty, "Theory and Practice Yields Qualified Administrators," *Education* (November 1962): 128–29.

4. See National Commission on Excellence in Educational Administration, *Leaders for America's Schools* (Tempe, Ariz.: The University Council for Educational Administration, 1987), 10, 19–20.

5. Judith A. Adkison and Andrea Warren, eds., *The Administrative Internship* (Lawrence: University of Kansas, 1980). See also Kent D. Peterson, "Obstacles to Learning from Experience and Principal Training," *Urban Review* 17, no. 3 (1985): 189–200; and W. Eugene Werner, *The Internship* (Reston, Va.: National Association of Secondary School Principals, 1989).

6. Mark Anderson, *Inducting Principals: How School Districts Help Beginners Succeed* (Eugene: Oregon School Study Council, 1988).

7. Donald P. Mitchell, *Leadership in Public Education Study: A Look at the Overlooked* (Washington, D.C.: Academy for Educational Development, 1972).

8. Carol Shakeshaft, *Women in Educational Administration* (Newbury Park, Calif.: Sage Publications, 1987).

9. Gail Thierbach Schneider, "Career Paths of Women and Men in Educational Administration" (Paper presented at the annual meeting of the American Educational Research Association, San Francisco, 1986) and "Reaching for the Top—Are Women Interested? A Study of Career Aspirations of Women in Educational Administration" (Paper presented at the annual meeting of the American Educational Research Association, New Orleans, 1988). Sakre Kennington Edson, *Pushing the Limits: The Female Administrative Aspirant* (New York: University of New York Press, 1988); and Shakeshaft, *Women in Educational Administration.*

10. Robert L. Katz, "Skills of an Effective Administrator," *Harvard Business Review* 33, no. 1 (January–February 1955): 33–42.

11. Ibid., 42.

12. John C. Daresh, "The Beginning Principalship: Preservice and In-service Implications" (Paper presented at the annual meeting of the American Educational Research Association, Washington, D.C., 1987). See also Richard L. Spralding, "We Can Make Principal Induction Less Traumatic," *NASSP Bulletin* (November 1989): 68–74.

13. Richard A. Gorton, *School Leadership and Administration: Important Concepts, Case Studies, and Simulations* (Dubuque, Iowa: Wm. C. Brown Company Publishers, 1987), 77–84.

14. For example, James A. Lipham, *Effective Principal, Effective School* (Reston, Va.: National Association of Secondary School Principals, 1981); Arthur Blumberg and William Greenfield, *The Effective Principal: Perspectives on School Leadership,* 2d ed. (Boston: Allyn & Bacon, 1986); James M. Lipham, Robb E. Rankin, and James A. Hoeh, Jr., *The Principalship: Concepts, Competencies, and Cases* (New York: Longman, 1985); Richard Aieta, Roland Barth, and Steven O'Brien, "The Principal in the Year 2000: A Teacher's Wish," *Clearing House* (September 1988): 18–19; Donald M. Trider and Kenneth A. Leithwood, "Exploring the Influences on Principal Behavior," *Curriculum Inquiry* 18, no. 3

(1988): 289–311; William R. Snyder and William H. Drummond, "Florida Identifies Competencies for Principals, Urges Their Development," *NASSP Bulletin* (December 1988): 48–58; and John E. Walker, "The Skills of Exemplary Principals," *NASSP Bulletin* (March 1990): 48–55.

15. Mike Milstein and Celia Karen Fiedler, "The Status of and Potential for Administrator Assessment Centers in Education," *Urban Education* (January 1989): 361–76. See also Joseph J. Gomez and Robert S. Stephenson, "Validity of an Assessment Center for the Selection of School-Level Administrators," *Educational Evaluation and Policy Analysis* (Spring 1987): 1–7.

16. National Association of Secondary School Principals and National Association of Elementary School Principals, *Ethical Standards for School Administrators* (Washington, D.C.: NASSP and NAESP, 1973). For more recent discussions, see Kenneth A. Strike, Emil J. Haller, and Jonas F. Soltis, *The Ethics of School Administration* (New York: Teachers' College Press, 1988); Robert L. Crowson, "Managerial Ethics in Educational Administration," *Urban Education* (January 1989): 412–35; and Karl Hostetler, "Who Says Professional Ethics Is Dead? A Response to Myron Lieberman," *Kappan* (May 1989): 723–27.

17. See R. F. Viering, "How to Prepare for Your Job Interview," *NASSP Bulletin* (January 1988): 118–24; and Robert W. Eder and Gerald R. Ferris, *The Employment Interview: Theory, Research, and Practice* (Newbury Park, Calif.: Sage Publications, 1989).

18. Jerome Cook, "First Year Wisconsin Secondary School Principals: Their Opinions, Reflections, and Frustrations" (Specialist Paper, University of Wisconsin-Milwaukee, 1979). See also Stephen H. Davis, "Life in the Fishbowl: Revelations and Reflections of the First Year," *NASSP Bulletin* (December 1988): 74–83.

19. Frederick C. Wendel and Roger D. Breed, "Improving the Selection of Principals: An Analysis of the Approaches," *NASSP Bulletin* (May 1988): 35–38; and U.S. Department of Education, Office of Educational Research and Improvement, *Principal Selection Guide* (Washington, D.C.: U.S. Printing Office, 1987).

20. Some practical ideas on planning for the opening of school are given by Lawrence Roder and David Pearlman, "Starting on the Right Foot—A Blueprint for Incoming Principals," *NASSP Bulletin* (October 1989): 69–77; and Joe DiGeronimo, "Some Do's and Don'ts for New Principals," *NASSP Bulletin* (December 1985): 91–94.

21. Stephen H. Davis, "Life in the Fishbowl."

22. James A. Lipham, "Leadership and Administration," in *Behavioral Science and Educational Administration,* ed. Daniel Griffiths, 63rd Yearbook of the National Society for the Study of Education (Chicago: University of Chicago Press, 1964), 122.

23. Ibid.

24. Ibid.

25. For a discussion of approaches, constraints, and prerequisites to leadership, see Gorton, *School Leadership and Administration,* 71–94.

20

. . . . .

Need for Continuing Professional Development

This book has recommended a number of principles and concepts which, if appropriately utilized, should improve the administration of a school. The competencies that school administrators need to perform effectively have been suggested at various points and the many challenges confronting administrators have been stressed. Certainly it should be clear by now that the job of school administrators is not an easy one.

To demonstrate further the nature of the administrator's problem-filled job and the consequent need for continuous professional growth, the following two sections discuss the problems of new administrators and report on the types of problems faced by all administrators—new and experienced. The latter half of the chapter focuses on several approaches to continued professional development for school administrators.

NEW ADMINISTRATORS: FIRST YEAR PROBLEMS

Individuals who become school administrators are frequently not sufficiently aware of the scope of problems that can occur. As Arthur Blumberg and William Greenfield note,

> Whatever the reasons for wanting to become a school principal (some are more noble than others), most aspirants to the role have a vague understanding of how much it entails. The loneliness, the conflicts, the dullness of the routine, the "busy work," and the anguish that

accompany having to solve complex educational and organizational problems with extremely limited resources are usually not part of teachers' conceptions of the principalship.[1]

While Blumberg and Greenfield quite properly emphasize the problem nature of the principalship, these problems are not insurmountable and their impact can, with appropriate understanding and leadership, be largely minimized. The purpose of the following discussion is to develop a realistic understanding of the major problems that the beginning administrator may face during the first year, and to suggest appropriate perspectives and/or strategies for dealing with these problems.

It is difficult to generalize about the problems that beginning administrators may encounter because these problems vary with the administrator's background, training, personality, and school situation. However, discussions with and observations of new administrators suggest several problems that many of them faced during the first year. A majority of these same problems are also encountered to a certain degree by experienced administrators who move to a new situation.

THE ACCEPTANCE PROBLEM

Many beginning administrators are initially concerned about how students, parents, and particularly teachers will react to them. As beginning administrators in new situations, they naturally hope to gain acceptance by the groups with whom they will be working. But what type of acceptance should they be seeking? They want to be respected, but they wonder, "Is it important to be liked? And, if you seek the personal approval of the people with whom you work, will they still respect you?"

These are normal questions for any beginning administrator to ask. In fact, many experienced administrators who change jobs feel some concern about being accepted in a new environment. However, the beginning administrator usually is new, not only to the work environment, but to the job itself, so being concerned about other people's reactions is understandable. Whether a beginning administrator actually encounters difficulty in gaining the acceptance of others depends in large part on the acceptance that is sought.

When administrators decide that people must like them or must approve all decisions before action can be initiated, there are likely to be problems. One frequently may have to make decisions or take actions that result in a reduction of one's popularity, but it is better to do what seems right in a situation rather than what may be popular. Administrators who make decisions or initiate actions based primarily on their potential for generating favorable responses from those who will be affected by the decisions or actions soon learn that it is virtually impossible to please everyone. They also discover that decisions or actions which elicit immediate, favorable responses from those affected may not always lead to the best results in the long run.

On the other hand, administrators who never make any attempt to secure the approval or acceptance of a proposed decision by the persons whom it will affect cannot expect their continuing cooperation. While people may not need to like the administrator personally, or approve of all administrative actions, they generally must find the administrator or a majority of administrative acts acceptable if they are going to implement fully what that individual wants done in the school. Therefore, if people's feelings and reactions toward administrators and their decisions are not taken into consideration, a growing wave of discontent may emerge.

Probably the most appropriate response for beginning administrators in regard to the acceptance problem is to concentrate during the first year on administering well-organized, smoothly running schools. The achievement of this goal will favorably influence most people's acceptance of administrators, perhaps more than any other factor. Of course, they should also try to develop warm and helping relationships with the staff, students, and parents. In all likelihood, their judgment of an administrator depends primarily on whether the school is being administered effectively and is based only secondarily on personal considerations. Both factors may be influential but the former is the most important.

THE PROBLEM OF INSUFFICIENT TIME

During the first year, beginning administrators may frequently have the feeling that there is never enough time to do everything that needs to be accomplished. But the problem of lack of time is not limited to new administrators; it also frustrates experienced administrators, although perhaps to a lesser degree. For example, John Leary's study of elementary school principals found a significant relationship between perceived time management and administrative stress.[2] Also, research by James Doud on elementary school principals indicated that principals who spent more time on issues related to curriculum development and instructional leadership reported higher levels of satisfaction with their career choice than those who spent more time on discipline and student management.[3] And, Leonard Pellicer and his colleagues found that high school principals spent most of their time on meetings, frequently of an unscheduled nature, dealing with organizational maintenance tasks rather than instructional and curricular improvement activities.[4] These findings on principals' use of time contrasts with principals' reported preference for spending the most time on improving instruction and curriculum.[5]

The problem of having too little time can generally be attributed to four factors: (1) inexperience; (2) the absence of a system for organizing time; (3) the administrative job itself, which by its very nature is demanding and time-consuming; and (4) failure to delegate responsibility. Because there is little probability that the job of the administrator will become less demanding and most beginning administrators are initially employed in situations where the opportunity for delegating responsibility may be limited, we concentrate on analyzing the first two factors.

Due to inexperience, new administrators usually take longer to perform most administrative tasks. Irrespective of whether they have received excellent university training for their new role or have acquired previous experience as interns, administrators are performing many tasks for the first time. These duties take longer to accomplish until, with practice, shortcuts can be identified and errors eliminated. Therefore, until beginning administrators gain more experience, the time problem will not be significantly ameliorated.

However, as indicated earlier, inexperience is not the only cause of a fledgling administrator's problem of seemingly never having enough time. Another major factor is the absence of a system for organizing time. Unless administrators utilize such systems, they reach the end of many days and weeks, wondering why more was not achieved. Administrators may have been busy while at school, but at the end of the work period there may be little to show for their efforts.

One approach administrators might use to organize time more effectively is to keep time logs each day for a week or two, and then analyze how the time is being spent and how it might be utilized more efficiently. According to a study by Gilbert Weldy, administrators spend a certain portion of their time on activities which might be better organized or restructured, and a time log may be helpful in spotlighting possible problems.[6] In *Time: Notations on Time Use for School Administrators,* Robert Maidment makes a number of practical recommendations for improving administrators' use of time, including prioritizing activities, screening and stacking telephone calls, and planning work to save time.[7] (A second valuable source for ideas is *Time Management for Educators,* Fastback no. 175, published by Phi Delta Kappa, Bloomington, Indiana.)

Another approach which could be helpful to administrators trying to utilize time better is management by objectives (MBO).[8] Originating in the business sector, but now adopted by many school districts, management by objectives is a system by which administrators define objectives, establish priorities, plan a course of action for achieving the objectives, and evaluate success. By requiring beginning administrators to define what needs to be

Figure 20.1 Daily MBO Format.

Name _____ Date _____ School _____

Objectives for Today:

Plan of Action for Accomplishing Each Objective:

Evaluation Plan for Ascertaining Success:

---

achieved and to establish priorities, MBO can help to organize time more efficiently. And, by requiring administrators to evaluate whether or not objectives have been achieved, MBO can be helpful in ascertaining effectiveness and making changes where desirable and feasible.

Although MBO has more frequently been used in connection with semester or yearly objectives, it can also profitably be employed by beginning administrators to organize time on a daily and weekly basis. An example of a daily MBO format is presented in figure 20.1; this format can also be adopted for use on a weekly basis.

Until beginning administrators become proficient in using MBO, it may take more time rather than less.[9] However, the time spent in thinking and planning is an investment which should pay dividends in better decision making, even if it does not immediately save any time. In the final analysis, administrators may never entirely eliminate the feeling of having insufficient time to accomplish all the responsibilities, but MBO should be helpful in utilizing time more productively.

THE AUTHORITY PROBLEM

Many beginning administrators seem to experience difficulty in exercising authority during their first year. They either try to exert authority they do not possess, or fail to utilize the authority they do possess and should employ to resolve a problem successfully. The consequence of exercising authority that one does not possess can be resistance and even outright noncompliance; failure to exercise authority which the individual possesses and which circumstances require can result in a deteriorating situation and loss of respect or confidence in the individual who is supposed to exercise the authority. In either case, a general eroding of the perceived authority vested in an administrator's position can occur.

One reason why many beginning administrators encounter problems in the exercise of authority is that they have not examined carefully the nature and scope of their authority. Administrators should recognize that their basic authority is delegated to them by the school board and the superintendent of schools; therefore, they should understand clearly the policies and directives of the school board and the superintendent.

Unfortunately, in too many situations, the authority of administrators is not formally delegated or explicitly stated because it is believed to be inherent in the position or associated with the responsibilities assigned. Therefore, beginning administrators should attempt to secure as clear a reading as possible on the extent of authority actually possessed in the situation.

A second reason why many beginning administrators experience difficulty in exercising authority is that they do not seem to understand the limitations of authority or the conditions under which it is best employed.[10] Authority is not power. Administrators possess power if people can be *forced* to do what they don't want to do, even when the persons resist or refuse to accept administrative authority in a situation. Beginning administrators soon discover that they have very little power in most circumstances.

Authority, on the other hand, is based on people's acceptance of an administrators' initiatives because they believe the administrators have the right to direct them by virtue of their positions in the school organization and the authority vested in those positions by the school board and/or the superintendent of schools. While this authority, typically referred to as legitimate authority, has been severely eroded in recent years, it still exists in large measure if appropriately utilized.[11]

In exercising authority, beginning administrators should keep in mind the following guidelines, based on Chester Barnard's analysis of the authority problem in organizations:

1. In deciding on the need for an order and in its formulation, presentation, and execution, administrators should take into consideration how the order affects the recipients personally, recognizing that people are likely to question or resist orders which they feel are not in their best interest.
2. Administrators should take into consideration the strengths and limitations of those expected to implement an order, and should avoid, if possible, issuing orders for which people lack the necessary motivation, skill, or training to carry out.
3. Administrators should explain thoroughly the rationale behind each order and its relationship to the goals of the organization, and should not assume that people understand the reasons for an order or that they necessarily see the logic or value of an order.
4. Administrators should leave room for modifying the original order or its method of implementation. Flexibility and a willingness to compromise when appropriate are key factors in exercising administrative authority successfully.
5. Administrators should issue only those orders that will with relative surety be obeyed, or that can be enforced if they are resisted. Orders which cannot be enforced in one situation weaken administrators' authority for successfully issuing orders in other circumstances.[12]

By following these guidelines and working within the authority limitations of their positions, beginning administrators should be able to avoid most of the difficulties associated with the authority problem. In working with students, teachers, and other school-related groups, beginning administrators will probably find that the best approach is to utilize their expertise to influence or persuade people to take a particular course of action, rather than relying on their authority to direct them.[13]

THE EFFECTIVENESS PROBLEM

Understandably, beginning administrators may experience some concern about their effectiveness during the first year. After all, it is natural for administrators who are new to their jobs, and to the school situation itself, to wonder how effectively they are performing in their new roles. In spite of this concern, however, administrators may encounter difficulty in ascertaining that effectiveness.

In the first place, there may not be general agreement on the criteria to be used in evaluating administrators' effectiveness. Superiors may make the evaluation based on one set of criteria, teachers may use another set of criteria, students another, and parents still a different set. There may be a great deal of overlap in the criteria utilized by these groups, but the value they ascribe to each criterion may differ significantly. For example, both teachers and administrators' superiors might agree that maintaining good school-community relations should be considered in evaluating administrators' effectiveness but may differ greatly on their interpretations of and the importance they attach to this aspect.

A second difficulty that beginning administrators may encounter is that, although superiors and other groups with whom they interact may be constantly making evaluative conclusions, they may not explicitly communicate these conclusions or their bases to them. For example, in a study conducted by William Harrison and Kent Peterson, only 51 percent of the principals surveyed knew how superintendents accumulated the information on which they based their evaluations.[14] Specifically, one principal reported, "Last year I was never visited by the evaluator and I received all 'superior performance' ratings—not very effective or helpful to me."[15] In addition, unless administrators actively seek feedback from students, teachers, and parents, they also are unlikely to receive evaluations of their effectiveness. Most of these groups are in a subordinate role to administrators, and there is little if any tradition of subordinates' initiating an evaluation of their administrator (even though these groups are frequently making evaluative judgments of the administrator).

For these reasons then, many administrators receive little substantive feedback on their effectiveness. If administrators are in this kind of a situation, however, there are certain steps that should be considered. First of all, administrator evaluation criteria and approaches are being used in a number of school systems, and that information should be brought to the attention of the administrator's superiors. Dale Bolton, for example, discusses in his excellent book, *Evaluating Administrative Personnel in School Systems,* the purposes, roles, and methods of administrator evaluation.[16] Barbara Zakrajsek presents and analyzes fifteen discrete approaches to evaluating principals.[17] And the Educational Research Service periodically surveys the practices of school districts regarding administrator evaluation forms.[18] Thus, it seems clear that there is no shortage of ideas on administrator evaluation.[19] If administrators and superiors can agree on appropriate criteria and on an evaluation approach, then perhaps periodic assessment of the administrator by superiors can occur.

One method being utilized with increased frequency in administrator evaluation is the "evaluation by objectives" approach.[20] It typically involves several steps:

1. The identification of specific, expected responsibilities and competencies of an administrative position.
2. Joint assessment of the current performance of administrators performed by the occupants of the administrative position and their superiors.
3. The development and approval of a plan for improvement which includes objectives, activities, timetable, and standards and methods for determining progress or achievement of objectives.
4. Periodic meetings between the administrator and superior to review progress and problems.
5. Final assessment of progress or achievement.

An excerpt from one school district's administrator evaluation program is presented in figure 20.2 to illustrate a number of the concepts of the evaluation by objectives approach.

Evaluation of administrators by objectives, of course, does not lack critics.[21] It has been viewed by some as too time-consuming, anxiety-provoking, and subject to coercive manipulation by the administrator's superiors. An examination of these criticisms, however, suggests that, as with any method or technique, evaluation by objectives can be misused; nevertheless, the problems are not inevitable. Certainly, an essential prerequisite to the effective utilization of the evaluation by objectives approach is the presence of adequate trust and a supportive relationship between the administrator and the evaluator(s).[22] In addition, administrators being evaluated must believe that the evaluation criteria and methods being used are valid and reliable. If both of these prerequisites cannot be met, any evaluation system is unlikely to achieve its stated purposes. One useful way to meet these prerequisites is to provide administrators being evaluated with considerable input into the development of the evaluation system and with periodic opportunities to suggest improvements in the system.

Administrators should also consider initiating some type of effectiveness evaluation by peers, teachers, students, and parents.[23] Administrators interested in evaluative feedback from various reference groups might adopt the evaluation form used by superiors, or develop a new evaluation form to be used specifically by peers, teachers, students, and parents. Jerry Valentine and Michael Bowman developed the *Audit of Principal Effectiveness* to obtain appropriate feedback from teachers; such an audit provides principals with performance feedback they can translate into improvement strategies.[24] A less

Figure 20.2 Evaluation of Objectives Approach.

Intensive Evaluation Program
Target Setting Sheet

Administrator's Name _____

Standard No. _____

Indicators (Indicate by letter) _____

Date _____ Target no. _____

---

1. What is to be changed? (List characteristics of present situation.)

---

2. What desired change do you want to achieve? (Identify performance to be acquired)

---

3. How will you know when you have achieved the desired change? (List level of achievement to be reached.)

---

4. What will you do to achieve the desired change? (Specify conditions under which change is to be made.)

---

5. What resources do you need to achieve the desired change? (Consider such resources as time, materials, training, supervision, etc.)

---

6. When should the change be completed? (Specify date for target assessment conference).

Signatures:

Administrator _____ Supervisor _____

Figure 20.3 Reference Group Evaluation of Administrator's Effectiveness.

Date _____

Instructions: Please be as candid and complete as possible. I am very much interested in your perceptions of my effectiveness as an administrator, particularly your suggestions for improvement. You need not sign your name to this evaluation.

Strengths (please identify three characteristics, or actions that I have taken this year which you view as positive, and which you would like to see me continue).

Weaknesses (please identify three characteristics or actions that I have taken this year which you think I should work on in terms of self-improvement, or which you think I should eliminate).

complex, yet nonetheless effective feedback form which Gorton employed when he was a beginning administrator is presented in figure 20.3; an excerpt of a form which has been used in another situation for faculty evaluation of the principal is presented in figure 20.4.[25]

The evaluation form presented in figure 20.4 was developed by the principal of a school and five teacher-volunteers. The results of the evaluation were shared with the faculty by the principal, and attention was given to those items on which there was a significant discrepancy between responses to "What Is?" and "What Should Be?"[26] Obviously, such an evaluation system requires a secure principal who respects the judgments of the faculty.

Whether administrators use the evaluation forms presented in figures 20.3 and 20.4, or different ones, they should initiate some form of evaluation by students, teachers, and parents each school year. These are important groups to administrators, and their effectiveness perceptions can provide excellent feedback on performance, with suggestions for improvement.

Regardless of the evaluation system used, the key questions, according to Bolton, are the following:

1. Is the evaluation system helping administrators do their jobs better?
2. Is sufficient time being spent to implement the evaluation procedure?
3. Is the evaluation of administrators cyclical and self-correcting?
4. What results can be attributed directly to the administrator evaluation system?[27]

Figure 20.4 Principal Evaluation Survey.

The purposes of this survey are

1. To improve the school.
2. To provide information that will help the principal improve in effectiveness.

Instructions

1. This survey is intended to be anonymous.
2. Circle or check the appropriate response.
3. A response of "1" is lowest (never) and "5" is highest (always).
4. N/O means "I do not have enough information to form an opinion." (Note that N/O can be used in the "What Is" column. You can respond to the "What Should Be" column for every item.)

	What Is?	What Should Be?
A. Goal Setting		
1. The principal guides faculty toward setting personal goals.	1 2 3 4 5	1 2 3 4 5
2. The principal guides faculty toward setting building goals.		
a. Long-range	1 2 3 4 5	1 2 3 4 5
b. Short-range	1 2 3 4 5	1 2 3 4 5
3. The principal has personal goals.	1 2 3 4 5	1 2 3 4 5
4. The faculty is aware of those goals.	1 2 3 4 5	1 2 3 4 5
B. Taking Charge		
1. The principal guides development of school rules.	1 2 3 4 5	1 2 3 4 5
2. The principal supports enforcement of those rules (and personally enforces them).	1 2 3 4 5	1 2 3 4 5
3. The principal's disciplinary actions are fair and related to the rules.	1 2 3 4 5	1 2 3 4 5
4. The principal is not afraid to make a decision when necessary.	1 2 3 4 5	1 2 3 4 5
5. The principal takes command in "sticky situations."	1 2 3 4 5	1 2 3 4 5
6. The principal is viewed as an authority figure by the students.	1 2 3 4 5	1 2 3 4 5

(continued)

Figure 20.4 Continued

C. Communications		*What Is?*					*What Should Be?*			
1. The principal has time to listen to me and help me.	1	2	3	4	5	1	2	3	4	5
2. The principal tells people what is expected of them.	1	2	3	4	5	1	2	3	4	5
3. I feel free to talk to the principal about my concerns, successes, etc.	1	2	3	4	5	1	2	3	4	5
4. The principal is honest with me.	1	2	3	4	5	1	2	3	4	5
5. The principal communicates clearly.										
a. Written communications	1	2	3	4	5	1	2	3	4	5
b. Verbal	1	2	3	4	5	1	2	3	4	5
6. The principal communicates effectively with parents.	1	2	3	4	5	1	2	3	4	5
7. Parents feel free to approach the principal about a problem or concern.	1	2	3	4	5	1	2	3	4	5
8. The principal establishes and maintains favorable relationships with local community groups.	1	2	3	4	5	1	2	3	4	5

D. Teacher Supervision										
1. The principal discusses my teaching methods with me.	1	2	3	4	5	1	2	3	4	5
2. The principal allows my input in the supervision process.	1	2	3	4	5	1	2	3	4	5
3. The principal has adequate background information and input before he evaluates my work.	1	2	3	4	5	1	2	3	4	5
4. The principal considers my teaching as a whole.	1	2	3	4	5	1	2	3	4	5
5. The principal emphasizes specifics that are valuable to my growth.	1	2	3	4	5	1	2	3	4	5
6. I know how the principal feels about me, as a teacher.	1	2	3	4	5	1	2	3	4	5
7. The principal spends adequate time visiting my classroom to be a supervisory leader.	1	2	3	4	5	1	2	3	4	5

(continued)

Figure 20.4 Continued

E. Decision-Making	*What Is?*	*What Should Be?*
1. The principal is capable of making decisions.	1 2 3 4 5	1 2 3 4 5
2. The principal examines alternative solutions.	1 2 3 4 5	1 2 3 4 5
3. The principal seeks input before making important decisions.	1 2 3 4 5	1 2 3 4 5
4. The principal makes decisions and follows through promptly.	1 2 3 4 5	1 2 3 4 5
5. The principal permits shared decision-making in some areas.	1 2 3 4 5	1 2 3 4 5

Optional

1. If I were principal of this school, I would _____

_____

_____

2. I would like the principal to be more _____

_____

_____

3. I'd like the principal to be less _____

_____

_____

4. General comments _____

_____

_____

_____

THE SOCIALIZATION PROBLEM

Many, if not most beginning administrators finish their university course work and start their first job in administration with a certain degree of idealism. Once on the job, however, they are typically exposed to a socialization process which, in many cases, diminishes much of the idealism they may have acquired.[28]

Although this process starts on the day that administrators are employed, it is most clearly felt when they make their first effort to introduce change in the school. In many situations, the bureaucratic red tape that administrators must overcome before change can be introduced discourages them from implementing the improvements envisioned. They quickly discover that there are few incentives and sometimes considerable personal risks in trying to initiate school improvements. New administrators who attempt to introduce procedures that differ from those employed in other schools in the district may be viewed as mavericks by the central office and as loners by colleagues. Informal pressures by both may be brought to bear to make new administrators and their schools become "part of the district." The result may be a conflict between the educational needs of the administrators and the schools and the expectations of the school district or, even more likely, a compromise of the administrator's idealism.[29]

That the socialization process is important was demonstrated in a study by Edwin Bridges, who found that the longer administrators were exposed to the role expectations of the school district, the more their behavior was influenced by those expectations rather than by personal needs.[30]

In essence, the socialization process that beginning administrators are exposed to in a district is designed to encourage them to emphasize institutional expectations rather than personal needs. Regrettably, these expectations often do not leave much room for idealism or for different approaches to administering a school.

In spite of its potentially negative effects, the socialization process of the school district should not be completely rejected by beginning administrators. The process can be a positive one in acquainting them with the role expectations, norms, and sanctions of the district. (John Daresh and Harry Wolcott provide insightful discussions of the influence of role expectations, norms, and sanctions.[31]) Furthermore, several factors may minimize the possibly negative consequences of the socialization process.

First of all, simply recognizing that the process does exist should be helpful. Second, if beginning administrators follow an earlier recommendation to delay introducing change until they learn more about their jobs and their new situations, they probably will not be exposed to the negative aspects of the socialization process until they are more secure, and therefore in a better position to withstand certain pressures when they are ready to introduce change.

Finally, new administrators should not assume that there is no flexibility in the role expectations, norms, and sanctions operating in a school district. There may be room in the district for idealistic administrators who want to do things differently in their schools, if they know how to bend the role expectations, norms, and sanctions without breaking them. This will require knowledge, understanding, and, perhaps most important, risk taking to find out what is possible—but it can be done. And, if beginning administrators hope to retain the idealism that they possessed when they started in administration, that effort will indeed need to be made.

CONTINUING PROBLEMS OF MIDDLE MANAGEMENT

While the problems reported by one administrator may not be perceived as problems by another, attempts have been made to identify a common set of problems faced by most school administrators—both new and experienced.

For example, in Doud's study of elementary principals for the National Association of Elementary School Principals, a representative national sample of elementary school principals was asked about the extent to which each of thirty-six possible problem areas was currently or potentially (within the next year) troublesome.[32] Only four were rated as being major problem areas. Ranked from high to low, they were:

1. Providing programs for underachievers.
2. Coping with state regulations and initiatives.
3. Effectively meshing instruction with special academic programs.
4. Increasing parent involvement.

The major responses for urban principals were substantially higher for seven of the problem areas than for principals from other communities. These were level of parent involvement, managing student behavior, pupil absenteeism, dismissing incompetent staff, changing composition of the student body, declining test scores, and crises management.

In general, an examination of the problems identified by elementary school principals reveals three main categories of concern: (1) restructuring and improving the effectiveness of schools in their districts; (2) evaluating and relating to the professional staff; and (3) diagnosing and responding effectively to student misbehavior.[33] These areas of concern are treated extensively elsewhere in this text. The subjects of teacher supervision and evaluation and personnel problems are discussed in chapters 8, 9, 10 and 11; student misbehavior problems are examined in chapters 13 and 14.

Elementary school principals, of course, are not the only administrators who experience problems in their jobs. In a study for the National Association of Secondary School Principals a team of researchers found that a majority of the respondents in a national sample of high school principals ranked the following problems in order of importance:

1. Time taken up by administrative detail
2. Lack of time
3. Inability to obtain funds
4. Apathetic or irresponsible parents
5. New state guidelines and requirements
6. Time to administer/supervise student activities
7. Variations in the ability of teachers
8. Inability to provide teachers time for professional development
9. Insufficient space and physical facilities
10. Resistance to change by staff
11. Problem students
12. Defective communications among administrative levels
13. Long-standing traditions[34]

The problems identified by the high school principals appear to be different from those reported by the elementary school principals; these differences probably reflect dissimilar methods of questioning the two groups of principals. Certainly, there is adequate evidence that elementary principals also experience time problems, although the problem of apathetic or irresponsible parents may be more serious on the secondary than on the elementary level. In any case, this text has offered a number of suggestions for responding to these problems.

ADMINISTRATOR STRESS AND BURNOUT

One problem common to both elementary and secondary school principals is administrator stress, sometimes resulting in burnout.[35] According to Edward Iwanicki, stress is believed to emanate from three major sources: societal, organizational, and role related, while burnout has been defined as emotional exhaustion, depersonalization, and reduced personal accomplishment.[36] Although most elementary and secondary school principals do not experience high levels of continued stress or become burned out, the problem of administrative stress and burnout is perceived to be a serious one for an increasing number of administrators. For example, research suggests that more individuals are leaving the principalship at an earlier age than would be expected.[37] In trying to ascertain the reasons for premature retirement from the principalship, the major sources of dissatisfaction were the job itself and relations with superiors. In addition, respondents noted that the following sources contributed to their dissatisfaction: policy and administration, lack of achievement, sacrifices in personal life, a lack of growth opportunities, lack of recognition and too little responsibility, and relations with subordinates.[38]

Studies have shown that excessive time demands and heavy work loads are some of the possible causes of stress. Gorton found in his investigation of factors associated with administrative stress that the following six conditions contributed the most stress to high school principals:

- Feeling that I [the principal] have too heavy a work load, that I cannot possibly finish during the normal work day
- Imposing excessively high expectations on myself
- Feeling that I have to participate in work activities outside of the normal working hours at the expense of my personal time
- Having to make decisions that affect the lives of individual people that I know (colleagues, staff members, students, etc.)
- Complying with state, federal, and organizational rules and policies
- Trying to resolve parent-school conflicts[39]

In a related part of his study, Gorton attempted to ascertain those factors that contributed to the stress of elementary school principals. The five most important factors identified by the respondents were:

- Complying with state, federal, and organizational rules and regulations
- Trying to resolve parent/school conflicts
- Imposing excessively high expectations on myself
- Feeling that meetings take up too much time
- Trying to complete reports and other paperwork on time.[40]

An examination of the two sets of factors that contributed to the stress of principals reveals that at least half the factors are common to both elementary and secondary school principals. (Factors not in one list but in another were rated as contributing at least moderate stress.) Examining the various factors reveals that stress is caused by both internally and externally generated pressures. For example, "Imposing excessively high expectations on myself" is a type of internally generated stress, while "Complying with state, federal, and organizational rules and policies" is a response to external pressure. And stress from "Feeling I have to participate in school activities outside of the normal working hours at the expense of my personal time" may be caused by a combination of internal and external pressures. Psychologists have long recognized that to some extent (and for some individuals to a large extent) people generate their own stress in addition to that which the external environment itself may be contributing.[41]

On the other hand, evidence suggests that the school principalship itself has perhaps become more difficult. Blumberg and Greenfield conclude from their study of effective principals who have stayed in their roles that

> the principalship need not be a "grinding-down" type of work. A job is a job. However, we think it is quite possible that, when the individual involved wishes to change things, to move a faculty, quite the opposite will develop. That is, the same hassles, interruptions, and routine will become debilitating. Recall the comments "It was the continuous hassle, the sameness of the hassle, the predictability of the hassle" and "I wonder sometimes when I leave at the end of a day just what it is that I have done." Perhaps this last point is the key. The principals about whom we've written have needs to do something and what some of them, at least, said is that the very nature of the demands put on them stood in the way of their doing. Their sense of achievement became limited and this was ultimately frustrating for them.[42]

These two researchers found an important message in their findings for school policymakers. "Put simply, they will need to start attending to the general welfare, growth, and development of their best principals—as they will likely lose them, if not in body, then in spirit. They will have to provide thinking time for them and resting time, as well."[43]

Another study of school principals reported by Frances Roberson and Kenneth Matthews found that the most frequent sources of stress for principals were related to having work loads they considered unreasonable. These included feeling that meetings take too much time, trying to complete reports and other paperwork on time, feeling that their work load is too heavy to finish during the normal work day, and feeling that they have to participate in school activities outside normal working hours.[44]

Whether the school principalship today is more difficult than it has been in the past can be debated.[45] Certainly, the problems of the late 60s and early 70s, such as student and parent activism, teacher militancy, racial strife, and drug abuse seem to be as serious as today's problems of low student achievement levels, high student dropout rates, drug and alcohol abuse, and increased state and federal mandates focusing on school accountability measures. However, even if today's principalship is not more difficult than in past years, the perception that it is contributes to the reality for many principals and observers. Fortunately for administrators experiencing stress, there is no shortage of recommended programs and materials for understanding and ameliorating the causes of stress.[46] Nevertheless, they should keep in mind that stress is inevitable in most jobs of an administrative nature and that a stress-free job is probably not only unlikely but also may not even be desirable for maximum productivity. Most people need at least some pressure to motivate them to aspire to a higher level of performance. The fact that administrators face many problems need not discourage those considering careers in school administration. Despite these problems, research shows that a large majority of elementary and secondary principals' morale or satisfaction is high.[47] Although any position has problems associated with it, if a person can become an effective problem-solver, administration can represent a rewarding and successful career.

ADMINISTRATIVE TRANSFERS AND REDUCTION IN STAFF

Shifting student enrollments, persistent inflation, and taxpayer revolts have caused many school boards to transfer some of their school administrators to other schools or other assignments within the district. In addition, recent attention on site-based management has led to a reduction in central office personnel and subsequent reassignment of school administrators. While these school board actions do not appear to be on the same scale as those taken with teachers, the impact on individual administrators affected can be the same. Administrators who have been elementary school principals but are reassigned to junior high schools as assistant principals because of the closing of elementary schools experience major changes in their professional careers, which probably require considerable adjustment. Nevertheless, at least in these situations, administrators still have administrative positions in their school districts. In other situations, it may become necessary for school boards to reduce the size of the administrative staff and actually lay off some administrators and reassign others to administer more than one school. Administrative reduction in staff raises all of the problems and issues discussed in chapter 8, "Special Personnel Problems."

Administrative transfers and reductions in administrative staff may be inevitable in a growing number of school districts. In such situations a policy and plan should be developed by the school board with considerable involvement and input of the building administrators and supervisors, the two groups likely to be most affected by transfers and layoffs. Such a policy and plan should make clear the criteria determining the need for transfers and layoffs, as well as determining who should be transferred or laid off. Appropriate due process safeguards also need to be defined adequately.

CONTINUING PROFESSIONAL DEVELOPMENT

After individuals have completed a preparation program, obtained state certification, and secured positions as assistant principals or principals, they have a natural tendency to feel that they have arrived. At this point, administrators have probably invested considerable time and effort in preparation for school administration, and now that they have jobs, continued professional development may be one of the least attractive objectives to contemplate. Administrators may realize that there are still a few remaining deficiencies in their backgrounds and may acknowledge the need to keep up to date on new approaches in education. But administrators think, "*More* education or professional development? Never! At least, not for the moment. There are too many things going on in school and there just isn't time to engage in further professional development."

Fortunately most school administrators eventually recognize and accept the fact that they must engage in continuing professional development to remain effective in their schools, and they find ways to organize their time better so that they can pursue such activities. Finding enough time will always be a problem for practitioners. But individuals who feel strongly about the need for self-improvement somehow find time for it, while those without such strong convictions never seem to have the time for continued professional growth; eventually the latter experience professional stagnation or regression.

For administrators who are sincerely interested in continuing professional development, a variety of opportunities exist. According to John Daresh, these include traditional courses offered through colleges or universities; institutes, workshops, or seminars; competency-based training programs; in-service academies where structured learning experiences are provided on an ongoing basis; and networks of formal and informal associations of individuals in different schools or districts.[48] Too often professional development has been perceived as representing only more course work. Although additional courses can make a contribution toward the further professional growth of administrators, other activities are equally valuable. These can range from membership on committees of state and national professional associations to a planned program of reading certain professional journals and books published during the year.

In the following sections we discuss briefly a number of professional growth activities, including additional course work.

PARTICIPATION IN PROFESSIONAL ORGANIZATIONS

Every school administrator should belong to and participate in local, state, and national professional administrator organizations.* These organizations can offer many opportunities for professional growth and development, and the administrator can benefit greatly from active participation.

*At the national level, the professional association to which most elementary school administrators belong is the National Association of Elementary School Principals; most secondary school administrators belong to the National Association of Secondary School Principals.

At the district level, a forward-looking local school administrators' association will organize in-service meetings for its members, sponsor trips and visitations to schools where innovative programs are being implemented, and involve its members extensively in making recommendations for the improvement of education in the district. All of these activities can contribute to the continuing professional development of administrators.

If, for some reason, an administrator's local professional association does not have a professional improvement program similar to the one described, the administrator can exercise leadership in the interest of initiating such a program. Professional improvement activities should not be left solely to universities or to the state or national administrators' associations. There should be an ongoing program of professional development for administrators within every district, and the local administrators' association should play a large role in planning for and implementing this program.

At the state and national association levels, administrators find a wide variety of opportunities for professional growth. While beginning administrators may either not feel ready or possess enough available time to become an officer of a state or national association, there is no reason why individuals should not be able at least to participate in one or more of the committee activities of the professional associations.

Most school administrators' state and national associations have standing committees in the areas of curriculum, student personnel, and research, among others; frequently they are anxious to involve members of the association in these activities. By participating on a committee, administrators have an opportunity to develop leadership skills and to exchange ideas with colleagues. From such involvement, administrators should be able to broaden their perspectives beyond their local situations, and at the same time make useful contributions to the professional associations.

In addition to office-holding and committee work, state and national professional associations offer potentially significant opportunities for the professional development and improvement of any administrator through annual conventions. At each convention there are presentations and discussions about problems, issues, and new approaches in education, and there is considerable time for school administrators to interact informally. Certainly the chance to get away from it all and to recharge one's emotional and professional batteries before facing the trials and tribulations of the job again is a legitimate part of the need to attend a convention.

Whether attendance at state or national conventions results in the further professional development of administrators depends primarily on the extent to which they actively pursue available opportunities. Administrators who spend most of the time socializing may enjoy the convention, but probably will not derive much professional growth. This is not to say that there should be no socializing at a convention or that such activities are without value. Quite the contrary.

However, if administrators are to benefit fully from conventions, they need to plan and organize time judiciously so that it is possible to attend and participate in meetings covering a wide range of professional topics, as well as to examine the various convention hall exhibits of new materials or technology which could be utilized in their schools. A state or national convention represents a tremendous opportunity for additional professional development and improvement if administrators capitalize on it.

As a supplement to their annual conventions, the national associations and many state administrators' associations have recently initiated a series of professional development seminars or institutes which offer considerable opportunity for the continuing education of administrators. At the state level, these seminars or institutes frequently take the form of workshops scheduled for two consecutive weekends and may be cosponsored by the state association and a cooperating university. Participants are usually able to obtain university credit for their work; the topics explored at the meetings are typically very timely and relevant. Because practitioners do not have to spread such activities over an entire semester, as is generally the case in university courses, they are better able to arrange their schedules to participate in the programs sponsored by the administrators' associations.

The format and advantages of the institutes offered by the national associations are similar in many respects to the state associations' programs. The main differences lie in the greater variety of topics explored, greater availability of nationally renowned speakers and resource people, and more numerous options in regard to the time schedule of the institutes. Figure 20.5 shows examples of the topics that have been explored in institutes sponsored by the national administrators' associations.[49]

As figure 20.5 shows, the national institutes and conferences represent a significant opportunity for the continuing professional development of administrators. The topics are relevant and cover a wide range of professional issues and new approaches. The meetings are scheduled so that administrators are seldom away from their jobs for too long a time. Without a doubt, the national institutes and conferences offer school administrators a tremendous opportunity to continue professional development with a minimum of disruption to the everyday work schedule.

Figure 20.5 Professional Development Programs.

ASCD Professional Development Opportunities

Organizing a Successful Peer Coaching Program
In-Depth Instructional Supervision
Cooperative Learning Strategies
Integrating Reading, Writing, and Oral Language across the Curriculum
Designing a Study Skills Curriculum
Curriculum Alignment
Planning an Accountability-Based Curriculum
Learning and Teaching Styles
Developing High-Performance Work Systems in Schools
Managing Student Behavior
Restructuring for Site-Based Management
Planning Staff Development for Effective Teaching

NAESP Principals Academy

Leadership Behavior and Group Processes
Performance and Evaluation
Workshop on the Administration of Early Childhood Programs
plus,
   National Fellows Program
      One week summer programs on current issues
      College campus setting
      Maximum principal-to-principal interaction and fellowship
      Continuing Education Units awarded
   Scholars Seminar
      Two-and-a-half day summer program
      Focus on research into practice
      Presentations by scholars
      Small group interaction sessions
      Latest educational research
      Continuing Education Units awarded

NASSP Summer Institutes

Critical Thinking Skills
Understanding and Improving Intercultural Relations
Educational Leadership for the 1990s: Focus on Learning
Leadership: Effecting Change and Improving School Climate
Building Self-Esteem in Students
How to Get More Done through Delegation and Team Building

SCHOOL DISTRICT PROFESSIONAL DEVELOPMENT PROGRAMS

There is no hard, comprehensive evidence on the extent and quality of professional development programs for administrators sponsored by local school districts. The evidence that exists suggests that most professional development programs offered by school districts for their administrators suffer from the same defects and problems associated with teacher in-service programs, a topic addressed in chapter 11.[50] Such defects and problems typically include the lack of a formal policy and plan for the continuing professional development of school administrators, insufficient involvement by administrators in the development of in-service programs, inadequate incentives for participating in continuing professional development, a superficial evaluation of what was learned during the in-service programs.

Inadequate and ineffective professional development for administrators at the local school district level is not inevitable. Good professional development programs at the local school district level are in operation. For example, Administrator Training Academies, such as one developed between Kansas State University and the Topeka School District, have been established by school districts, frequently with the assistance of university professors.[51] Joseph Murphy and Philip Hallinger provide a thorough description of eleven staff development programs which may represent the current era of administrative training. Among these are Maryland's Professional Development Academy, the North Carolina Leadership Institute for Principals, the Institute of Educational Administration (in Australia), the American Association of School Administrators' Model for Preparing School Administrators, the Center for Advancing Principalship Excellence, the Far West Laboratory Peer Assisted Leadership Program, the Harvard Principals' Center, Lewis and Clark College's Summer Institute for Beginning School Administrators, and the I/D/E/A/ Collegial Support Group Model.[52] In addition, the U.S. Department of Education has developed and funded the Leadership in Educational Administration Development (LEAD) program which has centers to address the needs for school leadership development in each of the fifty states, the District of Columbia, and six Caribbean and Pacific territories. It seems clear that there are sufficient ideas and examples of good programs for any administrator who would like to bring about improvement in a school district's professional development program.[53]

PROFESSIONAL READING

Most school administrators usually work ten- to twelve-hour days, and many of their evenings are occupied with various school-related meetings. School administration is a demanding job and seldom is an evening when administrators do not arrive home weary and fatigued. Therefore, when administrators finally get an evening or weekend free from the demands of their positions, professional reading may be the last activity that they would like to pursue. Even though administrators realize the benefits of professional reading, they have neither the energy nor the motivation to do so, and other less-demanding alternatives may seem more attractive.

While it is not easy for school administrators to engage in a program of professional reading, they must make the effort to keep informed and avoid falling into a professional rut. Although administrators may find the summer months more convenient for reading, particularly books, they should also set aside three or four hours a week during the regular school year—perhaps on weekends—for reading professional journals. A planned program and regular schedule of reading professional journals during the school year and summer months is a must for administrators serious about maintaining professional growth and development.

In addition to professional journals, each year administrators should try to read several books concerned with education or related matters. A book can provide a deeper understanding of a subject than a journal article and frequently contains data and information that one could not easily derive from an article.

The problem for administrators who contemplate reading books is that the task may require an extended period of concentration and time that is not normally available during the regular school year. However, the winter and spring holidays and the summer months should be convenient times for administrators to delve into several books. By setting a goal of reading one book during each holiday period and at least one each month during the summer, administrators could maintain a program of reading five to six books a year. Although such a program cannot be represented as extensive, it is at least a beginning on which administrators can expand, depending on available time and developing interest.

The types of books administrators should read will vary, of course, depending on their interests and needs. Insofar as possible, an attempt should be made to read broadly, rather than only books on education. Any administrators unsure about which books to select for reading, can consult the book review section of the *Kappan* for books on education and the book review section of the *New York Times* for those dealing with various aspects of our society. The important factor, though, is not how administrators make the selection, but that they do become committed to scheduling some time during the school vacation periods and summer months for reading books that provide professional and personal benefits.

RESEARCH

Many administrators shudder at the sound or sight of the word *research*. They may have gone through a preparatory program in which they were required to read research articles or to undertake research studies. In pursuing these activities, administrators have sometimes had research experiences which were not pleasant. As a result, many administrators are gun-shy about research and often do not perceive it as a means of furthering their professional growth and development.

This is regrettable because research is only a systematic method for seeking an answer to a question or a possible cause of a problem. Although some methods are more complex and sometimes more difficult to understand than others, research—reduced to its essential elements—is simply a means of investigating something about which one would like to learn more. Using research procedures forces administrators to become more systematic and objective in investigating a question or problem; the primary advantage of using research methods is that the information ultimately obtained is likely to be more valid and trustworthy than if such methods were not used.

At this point, prospective administrators may be wondering, "What kind of research could I do in my school?" Actually, the school setting does not lend itself to conducting all types of research studies, and the administrator's main job is not that of researcher. However, the following four examples illustrate the kinds of research studies usually possible in a school; administrators might consider initiating or becoming involved in similar studies at some stage:

Follow-up Studies. Combination questionnaire-personal interview studies to gather information from graduates on their career and further training patterns and their recommendations for improving the school program.

Feedback Studies. Combination questionnaire-personal interview studies to obtain information from students, teachers, and/or parents on their perceptions of the effectiveness of some aspect of the school program, such as the curriculum, and their recommendations for improvement.

Current Status Studies. Standardized testing and/or questionnaire studies to obtain current information; for example, on student achievement and ability, the dropout rate, or the percentage of students participating in student activities.

Diagnostic Studies.   Studies designed to shed light on why, for instance, some students underachieve and are truant; why some teachers are not as effective as they should be; or why certain curricular programs are not working the way they should be. The research methodology would depend on the area being investigated, the availability of instruments, and the flexibility of the school district in permitting such research to be conducted.

Each of these studies can generally be conducted within a school setting and should provide administrators and others with useful information for improving the educational program of the school. These inquiry-based, research studies may be necessary if the school program is to be improved in any substantial sense. As a result of participating in research studies, administrators not only make contributions toward improving their school programs, but also become more knowledgeable about their schools and ways to improve them, thereby increasing their own professional growth and development.

PROFESSIONAL WRITING AND PUBLIC SPEAKING

Most textbooks that discuss continuing education recommend professional writing and public speaking as a means of professional development. However, the observable evidence shows that relatively few administrators engage in these activities.

There is little doubt that administrators can further develop professionally through writing and public speaking. The self-discipline, concentration, planning, and organizing required for professional writing and public speaking are valuable for school administrators. Many administrators lack not only time to engage in writing and speaking but also the confidence or skill for performing these tasks. Neither their undergraduate nor graduate training has prepared them for professional writing or public speaking. Therefore, although they may recognize the need to do more professional writing and public speaking and may even feel remiss, many administrators simply choose to avoid these tasks when opportunities present themselves.

In light of the problems previously discussed, it may not be realistic to recommend that administrators engage in professional writing and public speaking as a means of further professional development. Still, these are useful activities if administrators are willing to invest the extra time and effort necessary for accomplishing them. Administrators who lack confidence or skill in public speaking should consider joining a Toastmasters group or taking a speech course. The way for administrators to start professional writing may be by describing an aspect of their school programs which would be of interest to other administrators in the state and could be included in a state publication.

Later, as skill and confidence develop, administrators can try to write articles for national publications. (Kenneth Henson has written a useful book on how to write for professional publication.)[54]

Writing and speaking well are difficult tasks for most people, not just for administrators. But as an administrator has ideas and convictions—in other words, something to say—an attempt should be made to communicate those thoughts to people through professional writing and public speaking.

ADVANCED COURSE WORK

Most administrators quickly discover after they take their jobs that their initial administrator preparation program did not prepare them for every aspect of school administration. The preservice preparation program is usually designed to meet state certification requirements for administrators (which are minimum standards) and to provide a foundation of knowledge and skills on which they can continue to develop building blocks of competency. Some of these building blocks can be achieved through on-the-job experience and others as a result of pursuing the activities already discussed in this section on continuing professional development.

One important way in which a person can continue to develop professionally is by taking additional courses. By this means administrators can fill in gaps in their preparation programs and become better informed about some of the newer approaches and ideas in education.

If administrators would like to develop further professionally by taking additional course work at a university, the first step might be to write or call the chairperson of a department of educational administration for an appointment. Before conferring with the chairperson, however, administrators should spend some time analyzing their particular strengths and limitations, and the challenges currently confronting the school. As a result of this analysis, administrators are better able to identify and define their special needs for further professional development, and the university department chairperson or an assigned adviser is in a much better position to help plan an appropriate program of course work and related learning experiences.

Administrators might also give some consideration to whether or not the course work is to lead to an advanced degree or certificate. For many administrators, the main reason for seeking additional university course work seems to be to obtain an advanced degree. Actually, there is no evidence that possession of a doctorate or specialist's certificate makes it any easier to obtain, hold, or succeed in a job in school administration. Although some school districts prefer that applicants possess a doctorate or specialist's degree, the final decision on candidates is usually based on factors other than their degrees, as long as they have been certified by the state. Many, if not most school districts, include provision for an increase in salary for those who obtain a specialist's certificate or doctorate, but the increase is usually slight and hardly justifies the time, effort, and money invested by the individual.

The only truly legitimate reason for administrators to take advanced course work is that they want to increase professional knowledge and skills. If this is the main motivation, it is perfectly reasonable to plan a program in such a way that it leads to an advanced degree. The primary goal of administrators, though, should be to increase their learning so that more effective leadership contributions can be made toward improving their school programs.

A FINAL NOTE

Throughout the book and particularly in this chapter the problem dimensions of school administration have been emphasized. School administrators who are not able to anticipate and prevent or resolve problems successfully are not likely to perform effectively as administrators nor to provide the leadership needed to improve educational opportunities. If individuals possess or can acquire and maintain through continuous professional development the personal qualities and competencies discussed in this book, they should be able to respond effectively to present and future challenges and opportunities for leadership.

Review and Learning Activities

1. Define the nature of each of the five typical problems which many new administrators face during their first year. Describe how each of the problems might be avoided or resolved.
2. Analyze the similarities and differences between the problems of the elementary school principal and the problems of the secondary school principal. What are the implications of these problems for the school administrator?
3. Identify and define the possible obstacles that an individual may encounter in the contemplation of a need for continuing professional development.

4. Describe the possible professional growth opportunities by participating in the following activities and indicate what the administrator needs to do to capitalize on these opportunities:
    a. Membership in professional organization; school district professional development programs
    b. Professional reading
    c. Research
    d. Professional writing and public speaking
    e. Advanced course work

Notes

1. Arthur Blumberg and William Greenfield, *The Effective Principal* (Boston: Allyn & Bacon, 1980), 9–10. A follow-up on the professional careers of the principals highlighted in the first edition is provided in the second edition of *The Effective Principal* (1986).

2. John Francis Leary, "Stress, Time Management, and Selected Demographic Factors of Elementary School Principals" (Ph.D. diss., University of Connecticut, 1987).

3. James L. Doud, *The K–8 Principal in 1988* (Alexandria, Va.: National Association of Elementary School Principals, 1989), 88–93.

4. Leonard O. Pellicer, Lorin W. Anderson, James W. Keefe, Edgar A. Kelly, and Lloyd E. McCleary, *High School Leaders and Their Schools Volume I: A National Profile* (Reston, Va.: National Association of Secondary School Principals, 1988).

5. Ibid., 67.

6. Gilbert R. Weldy, *Time: A Resource for the School Administrator* (Reston, Va.: National Association of Secondary School Principals, 1974).

7. Robert Maidment, *Time: Notations on Time Use for School Administrators* (Reston, Va.: National Association of Secondary School Administrators, 1989).

8. The credit for the origination of the concept of MBO is usually given to Peter F. Drucker, *The Practice of Management* (New York: Harper & Row, 1954).

9. For a concise review of the concepts of MBO and their practical application, see Walter G. Hack, "Management by Objectives," in *Encyclopedia of School Administration and Supervision,* eds. R. A. Gorton, G. T. Schneider, and J. C. Fisher (Phoenix, Ariz.: Oryx Press, 1988), 162–63.

10. For an extensive discussion of the ideas in this section, see Richard A. Gorton, *School Leadership and Supervision: Important Concepts, Case Studies, and Simulations* (Dubuque, Iowa: Wm. C. Brown Company Publishers, 1987), chap. 3.

11. Ibid., 52–63.

12. See Chester Barnard, *The Function of the Executive* (Cambridge, Mass.: Harvard University Press, 1948), 165.

13. For a further discussion of this type of influence, see Gorton, *School Administration and Supervision,* 67–68.

14. William C. Harrison and Kent D. Peterson, "Evaluation of Principals: The Process Can Be Improved," *NASSP Bulletin* (May 1988): 1–4.

15. Ibid., 3.

16. Dale L. Bolton, *Evaluating Administrative Personnel in School Systems* (New York: Teachers College Press, 1980).

17. Barbara Zakrajsek, "Evaluation Systems: A Critical Look," *NASSP Bulletin* (January 1979): 100–110.

18. Educational Research Service, Washington, D.C.

19. See Kenneth A. Leithwood, "Using *The Principal Profile* to Assess Performance," *Educational Leadership* (September 1987): 63–66; William C. Thomas, "A Faculty-Based Needs Assessment Process for School Administrators," *NASSP Bulletin* (December 1987): 5–10; Jerry W. Valentine and Michael L. Bowman, "Audit of Principal Effectiveness: A Method for Self-Improvement," *NASSP Bulletin* (May 1988): 18–26; Jerry J. Herman, "Evaluating Administrators—Assessing the Competencies," *NASSP Bulletin* (May 1988): 5–10; and Harrison and Peterson, "Evaluation of Principals."

20. For further reading on this approach, see Jerry W. Valentine, "Performance/Outcome Based Principal Evaluation" (Paper presented at the annual meeting of the American Association of School Administrators, February 1987, ERIC Report Ed–281–317).

21. Jan Muczyk, "Dynamics and Hazards of MBO Application," *The Personnel Administrator* (May 1979): 51–62.

22. James M. Lipham, Robb E. Rankin, and James A. Hoeh, Jr. *The Principalship: Concepts, Competencies, and Cases* (New York: Longman, 1985): 298–302.

23. See Bruce G. Barnett, "Using Peer Observation and Feedback to Reduce Principals' Isolation," *Journal of Educational Administration* 27 (1989): 46–56; and Allan S. Vann, "When Teachers Grade the Principal," *Principal* (March 1989): 46–48.

24. Valentine and Bowman, "Audit of Principal Effectiveness."

25. Developed and used by principal Curtis Kittleson at Manitou Springs Elementary School, Manitou Springs, Colorado.

26. Personal correspondence from Mr. Kittleson.

27. Bolton, *Evaluating Administrative Personnel in School Systems,* 123–24.

28. Daniel L. Duke, "Why Principals Consider Quitting," *Kappan* (December 1988): 308–12.

29. Jacob W. Getzel, "Conflict in Role Behavior in the Educational Setting," in W. W. Charters, Jr. and N. L. Gage, eds, *Readings in the Social Psychology of Education* (Boston: Allyn & Bacon, 1963). See also William Greenfield, "Moral Imagination and Interpersonal Competence," *Instructional Leadership: Concepts, Issues, and Controversies* (Boston: Allyn & Bacon, 1987), 56–74.

30. Edwin M. Bridges, "Bureaucratic Role and Socialization: The Influence of Experience on the Elementary Principal," *Educational Administration Quarterly* (Spring 1965): 19–29.

31. John C. Daresh, "The High Hurdles for the First Year Principal." (Paper presented at the annual meeting of the American Educational Research Association, Washington, D.C., April 1987, ERIC Report Ed–280–236); and Harry F. Wolcott, *The Man in the Principal's Office: An Ethnography* (New York: Rinehart and Winston, 1973).

32. Doud, *The K–8 Principal in 1988,* 130–33.

33. Doud, *The K–8 Principal in 1988.*

34. Pellicer, et al., *High School Leaders and Their Schools,* 19. See also Robert J. Vadella and Donald J. Willower, "High School Principals Discuss Their Work," *NASSP Bulletin* (April 1990): 108–11.

35. Walter Gmelch, "Administrative Stress," in *Encyclopedia of School Administration and Supervision,* eds. R. A. Gorton, G. T. Schneider, and J. C. Fisher (Phoenix, Ariz.: Oryx Press, 1988), 13–14.

36. Edward R. Iwanicki, "Teacher Stress and Burnout," in *Encyclopedia of School Administration and Supervision,* Gorton et al., 284; and C. Maslach and S. Jackson, *Maslach Burnout Inventory Manual* (Research ed.) (Palo Alto, Calif.: Consulting Psychological Press, 1981).

37. Duke, "Why Principals Consider Quitting," 308.

38. Ibid., 309. See also Fred C. Feitler and Edward B. Tokar, "School Administrators and Organizational Stress: Matching Theory, Hunches and Data," *The Journal of Educational Administration* (Summer 1986): 254–71.

39. Richard A. Gorton, "Administrator Stress: Some Surprising Research Findings," *Planning and Changing* (Winter 1982): 358–59. See also Paul Bisher and Ken Young, "Leadership Styles and Job Stress," *Record* (Fall 1989): 15–17.

40. Richard A. Gorton, "Elementary Principals and Stress" (1981 paper).

41. Meyer Friedman and Ray Rosenman, *Type A. Behavior and Your Heart* (New York: Alfred A. Knopf, 1974).

42. Blumberg and Greenfield, *The Effective Principal* 2d ed., 201.

43. Ibid.

44. Frances R. Roberson and Kenneth M. Matthews, "Stress among Principals—Reports of Two Studies Discuss Causes and Prevention Strategies," *NASSP Bulletin* (September 1988): 79–85.

45. See Mike Milstein and J. Farkas, "The Over-Stated Case of Educator Stress," *Journal of Educational Administration* (July 1988): 232–49; and Thomas Wiggins, "Stress and Administrative Role in Educational Organizations," *Journal of Educational Research* (November–December 1988): 120–25.

46. For examples of strategies for coping with stress, see Roberson and Matthews, "Stress among Principals"; Larry W. Cooper, "Stress Coping Preferences of Principals," *NASSP Bulletin* (September 1988): 85–87; James E. Lyons, "Managing Stress in the Principalship," *NASSP Bulletin* (February 1990): 44–47; and Thomas Monteiro, "Stress and the Administrator—A Look at Theory and Reality," *NASSP Bulletin* (April 1990): 80–85.

47. Doud, *The K–8 Principal in 1988,* 21–27; and Pellicer, et al., *High School Leaders and Their Schools,* 22–24.

48. John C. Daresh, "Administrator In-Service: A Route to Continuous Learning and Growing," in W. Greenfield, Jr., *Instructional Leadership: Concepts, Issues, and Controversies,* 328–40.

49. Examples taken from summer program listings of the Association for Supervision and Curriculum Development, the National Association of Elementary School Principals, and the National Association of Secondary School Principals, 1989.

50. John C. Daresh, "Status of Research on Administrator In-Service," *National Forum of Educational Administration and Supervision* (Fall 1985): 23–31.

51. "Leadership Academies: Elixir for Common School Ills," *The School Administrator* (February 1989): 23–24.

52. See Joseph Murphy and Philip Hallinger, "Some Encouraging Signs in Staff Development for School Administrators," *Journal of Staff Development* (Fall 1986): 13–27; and Joseph Murphy and Philip Hallinger, eds., *Approaches to Administrative Training* (Albany: State University Press of New York, 1987).

53. Bruce Barnett, "Incorporating Peer Observation in Administration In-Service and Preservice Training Programs," *Planning and Changing* (Winter 1988): 224–36; L. J. Spence, *Mentorship Programs for Aspiring and New School Administrators* (Eugene: Oregon School Study Council, 1989); John C. Daresh, "Collegial Support: A Lifeline for the Beginning Principal," *NASSP Bulletin* (November 1988): 84–87.

54. Kenneth T. Henson, *Writing for Professional Publication,* Fastback No. 262 (Bloomington, Ind.: Phi Delta Kappa). See also Philip T. West, "Writing: Part I—To Communicate," *National Forum of Applied Educational Research Journal* 1 (1988–89): 10–13.

Index